THE POLITICAL ECONOMY OF TRANSITION

The *annus mirabilis* in the eastern part of Europe inaugurated an unprecedented movement toward society-wide changes throughout the communist world. These were partly based on widely held ambitions for pluralistic democracy and market-based resource allocation. This book addresses the most salient policy questions around the challenge of transforming these economies from their planned, administrative past to vibrant market-based entities.

Initially, the broad range of analysts, and policy makers advocated a predominantly neoclassical approach. They viewed the task of transformation as consisting primarily of stabilization, privatization, and liberalization rather than of the construction of markets supported by all of the institutions required for them to function well in a society-wide context. By disregarding the "initial conditions" or the legacies of over forty years of state-socialist policies throughout society, their critical importance for path-dependent transformation was largely ignored.

Van Brabant considers in turn the wider set of challenges facing these economies – stabilization, privatization, liberalization, institution building, and developing and maintaining the sociopolitical consensus – before examining the evolving role of the state. Finally, he discusses options for integration into the world economy and whether the transformation is sustainable.

Using concrete examples from the eastern European countries, this work systematically examines the initial conditions of transformation, the challenges of transformation, the results achieved to date, the policy tasks ahead, and the manner in which policies have been pursued before drawing useful lessons for policy makers in other countries.

Jozef M. van Brabant is currently Principal Economic Affairs Officer at the Secretariat of the United Nations in New York. His major academic interest is in the economics of the planned and now the transition economies and, recently, in the economic aspects of remaking Europe.

ROUTLEDGE STUDIES OF SOCIETIES IN TRANSITION

THE POLITICAL ECONOMY OF TRANSITION

Coming to grips with history
and methodology

Jozef M. van Brabant

London and New York

First published 1998
by Routledge
11 New Fetter Lane, London EC4P 4EE

Simultaneously published in the USA and Canada
by Routledge
29 West 35th Street, New York, NY 10001

© 1998 Jozef M. van Brabant

Typeset in Baskerville by Keystroke, Jacaranda Lodge, Wolverhampton
Printed and bound in Great Britain by TJ International Ltd, Padstow, Cornwall

British Library Cataloguing in Publication Data
A catalogue record for this book is available from the British Library

Library of Congress Cataloging in Publication Data
A catalogue record for this book has been requested

ISBN 0–415–16946–1

TO MIYUKI: MANY THANKS, AGAIN!

CONTENTS

CONTENTS

CONTENTS

CONTENTS

TABLES

ACRONYMS

ALMP	active labor-market policy
BFTA	Baltic Free Trade Agreement
BTPA	bilateral trade and payment agreement
CAP	common agricultural policy
CEFTA	Central European Free Trade Agreement
CIS	Commonwealth of Independent States
CMEA	Council for Mutual Economic Assistance
EBRD	European Bank for Reconstruction and Development
EC	European Communities
ECE	Economic Commission for Europe
EEC	European Economic Community
EFTA	European Free Trade Association
EIB	European Investment Bank
ESOP	employee share-ownership program
EU	European Union
Euratom	European Atomic Energy Community
FDI	foreign direct investment
FTO	foreign-trade organization
GATT	General Agreement on Tariffs and Trade
GDP	gross domestic product
GDR	German Democratic Republic
GSP	General System of Preferences
G-7	Group of Seven
G-24	Group of Twenty-four
IBEC	International Bank for Economic Cooperation
IBRD	International Bank for Reconstruction and Development, *see* World Bank
IEO	international economic organization
IIB	International Investment Bank
IMF	International Monetary Fund
MFA	Multi-fibre Arrangement
MFN	most-favored nation

MFT monopoly of foreign trade and payments
NGO nongovernmental organization
NIE newly industrializing economy
NPO not-for-profit organization
NTB nontariff barrier
ODA official development assistance
OECD Organisation for Economic Co-operation and Development
PAYG pay as you go
PCA Partnership and Cooperation Agreement
PHARE *Pologne/Hongrie – assistance à la restructuration économique*
QR quantitative restriction
R&D research and development
SME small and medium-size enterprise
SNA system of national accounts
SOE state-owned enterprise
TACIS Technical Assistance to the CIS
TNC transnational corporation
UNO United Nations Organization
USSR Union of Soviet Socialist Republics
World Bank International Bank for Reconstruction and Development
WTO World Trade Organization

PREFACE

The transformation of the economies in transition was from the outset bound to be complicated and divisive – a very long-term policy task. Turning the previous state-socialist economies and polities into societies firmly anchored by stable pluralistic democracy and a functioning market economy could never have been a mean feat. The sheer scale of the undertaking and the scope of the societal reengineering to be forged in one way or another would have been sufficiently daunting. In the absence of a reasonable minimal consensus on how best to proceed in and among the social sciences; in the assistance organs; and in the transition economies themselves, the assignment became even more cumbersome. No theory of the main regularities of the transition process was at hand. In many respects, though several treatises on transition matters are now available, a consensus on what must be done and how is still lacking. But progress is being booked.

For many social scientists, including the economics' profession, the "events" of 1989–1991 in the eastern part of Europe opened up a nearly completely unanticipated research agenda of vast scope and with a cornucopia of challenges in need of urgent policy innovation. The transition issues since 1989 have, of course, been heavily influenced by specific time and space parameters. Seen in a more detached perspective, they have been of acute interest also in broader international debates. The range of the, at times intractable and perplexing, tasks cropping up has since been continuously enriched. By its sheer magnitude and complexity, transition has spawned a nearly indigestible mass of materials on the most diverse aspects of these research and policy agendas. It is not only the sheer bulk, but the variety of research and commentaries tabled to date, let alone the policies embraced since 1989, that simply prohibit an exhaustive treatment of the subject in the literature. It also complicates sifting the chaff from the corn. Yet, distilling an appropriately balanced "view" on transition has become an urgent matter for students, scholars, policy makers, and the broader community interested in challenging international affairs. This monograph does not pretend to provide a critical survey of this rich literature; at least not an exhaustive one. Nor does it intentionally rehearse well-trodden fields. Instead, it provides the nonspecialist with an impartial, yet fairly comprehensive, hopefully intelligent, overview of the issues that matter in booking progress with the transformation of the state-socialist economies over the longer haul.

Putting it simply, the pivotal tasks all revolve around "managing the economy and society more generally." That consists of mobilizing the capacities in place and acquiring new ones as a matter of top priority with the goal of compressing the costs of the transformation and accelerating the realization of the transition's core aspirations, hopefully in a consensual manner. Only thus can stability, transparency, and progress be achieved in a reasonably equitable fashion. Unless that core of the transformation is adequately understood, analysts are bound to zero in on the wrong target. My view may not be completely novel to the specialist – now frequently referred to under the moniker "transitologist." Nevertheless, by focusing on the critical role of policy management in several dimensions I hope to goad even the specialist into taking yet another reflexive look at received wisdom.

An integral part of transforming the structures of the transition economies is merging these societies into the concert of democratic nations and into the expanding global economy. Those have been the twin ambitions of many, but by far not all, transition economies since the start of the so-called *annus mirabilis* in 1989. The road to gratification of these aspirations has since been rather bumpy, however one prefers to rationalize the experiments conducted in the interim. A better understanding of this, for some unanticipated, outcome to date; of why one should have reckoned with it from the very outset; and of what could have been undertaken to ensure a more persuasive, less costly turn of events, one that can prospectively still be targeted, provides the central objective of this study. By proceeding in this manner, insights emerge for modulating policies in the years ahead, for how best to reorder the agenda in the more wayward transition economies, and for deriving instructive lessons for other economies that may soon have to commit themselves to such wholesale restructuring.

Clarifying these issues is warranted for several reasons. One is that there is nobody who can honestly claim to be fully abreast of the entire *problématique* of the transition. Only slowly have useful monographs taking a holistic perspective (Lavigne 1995; World Bank 1996) been coming to the fore. Second, very few of those committed to studying the transition as a systemic issue or assisting it as a scholar or adviser, let alone as policy maker, have done so with a solid background in the "history" of these countries; of course, not just some rationalization of the time sequence of high politics, wars, and revolutions. Without a solid understanding of the broad culture, ethnicity, religions, politics, and so on of these countries individually and in their group context, it is well-nigh impossible to gain a solid grip on the autonomous features of the mutations under way. I stand by this maxim no matter how confident one may be of one's own recipe and regardless of how much influence one may covet, or be able to exert over decision makers in these countries: Only when one comprehends why these countries were different from each other and from the rest of the world does it become clear that the straightforward application of experiments set up in ivory towers or the transplantation of those tested in other settings can at best be problematic; more often than not, this proposition entails avoidable policy errors. Third, I consider the "remaking of Europe" in particular a truly historical event. I have deliberately tried to eschew (western) eurocentrism in this analysis. Nonetheless, the reconstruction of the "old continent" has ramifications for a wide array of activities intrinsically of interest to the broader community of economists and others challenged by international economic events. Fourth, I am convinced that moving away from state socialism is not necessarily a unique event, determined by concrete circumstances of time and place – the "1989 events." Instead, instructive guidelines for designing the transformations in these countries could have been drawn from other experiences. Likewise, highly useful, indeed sobering, lessons can be derived from the unique experiments conducted in these countries in order to enhance prospective policy making elsewhere.

In preparing this overview of the transformational *problématique*, I have benefited from numerous contacts with colleagues, friends, and acquaintances in Europe and the United States. Occasionally they took the form of a casual chat, phone call, e-mail message, or letter. More often, these feedbacks crystallized at more structured meetings and conferences. I trust that those whose sage advice I have internalized will find it reflected here. To those whose counsel I have ignored in part or in whole, I can only counter: Try again and harder next time!

As with most of my work over the past two decades plus, this book too was written in my own time. The views reflected here are mine and are not necessarily shared by my employer, the Secretariat of the United Nations Organization (UNO) in New York.

Finally, I am delighted to acknowledge the generosity and patience with which my family has tolerated, once again, my wandering off into yet another book-writing adventure, in spite of earlier resolutions to abandon any further professional ambition of the kind. But the challenge of clarifying the uniqueness of the transformations under way in the eastern part of Europe, and elsewhere, at a time of wildly varying menus advocated and ambitions coveted by many commentators on those issues, proved too alluring. My heartfelt gratitude for the forbearance and for so much more . . .

Ossining, NY, 7 July 1997

INTRODUCTION

The *annus mirabilis* with its drawn-out aftermath has ushered into the social sciences in general and economics in particular a nearly completely new set of research topics and opportunities for investigating them with some urgency, given the diverse needs of policy makers. Radical economic, political, and social transformations of defunct one-party regimes present in many ways a unique *problématique.* This is so in part because the state-socialist support base of the political systems had already earlier collapsed or it had been under severe strain for some time. We are now nearly a decade down this transformation road. In many ways, the experiences have been without precedent in peacetime. They have been unique, baffling at times, and exhilarating in disproving sturdy expectations or in sharpening widely held precepts. One might therefore at first glance argue that the "events" in transition economies offer lessons only for other, similarly destabilized societies embarking on remaking themselves wholesale. Apart from its intrinsic merits as history, such a peripatetic inquiry would not be very illuminating, if only because the number of one-party, administratively planned regimes extant has rapidly dwindled, arguably to Cuba and North Korea. But change has not invariably been in the direction of democracy and market building!

The experience of the economies in transition has not been all that singular, however. Nor has movement been uniformly in the "desired" directions. For one thing, the design of the transformation agenda could have reflected more closely the realities deriving essentially from the legacies of state-socialist planning. Also, the adversities encountered when these societies were turned into "planned" economies could usefully have been recalled. Moreover, a good dose of common sense would have helped to fashion imaginative, yet less disruptive shifts in societal relations (Cairncross 1985) than what has occurred since 1989. That has frequently been lacking because of ideology or purely technocratic appreciations responding at times to a warped view of a highly convoluted reality. I emphasize too that the stage of the transition to date is not particularly comforting. Indeed, not all so-called transition economies have been progressing with forging a coalition in favor of democracy and market-based resource allocation. Also, the gains recently scored by some countries do not warrant complacency: I certainly

1

do not perceive them without serious qualification as reassuring harbingers of sustainable catch-up growth. Nor do I view this achievement soon to be within reach of the laggard countries.

Placed in the above perspective, many lessons can be derived. One could, for example, take stock of the inconclusive, in many ways ill-defined, debate about the major components of the transition agenda and their various parameters as propounded by adherents of the dominant Manichean dichotomy between "good" and "evil" paths to societal transformation. The former are ascribed to the shock-therapy mode while the latter are imputed to more gradual approaches to socioeconomic transformation. Alternatively, one could investigate concrete, country-specific policy measures for which a more rational problem-solving approach might have been contemplated. The latter is manifestly not the path that I take here, as I clarify below. A third way would inquire into why the transitions in a number of countries have been derailed for all practical purposes and what might conceivably be undertaken to put the engine back on track. In discharging this objective, I rely on the lessons taught by successful transitions but also by the failures sustained elsewhere.

Section 1: The essence of the transition and economic transformation

The essence of the transition at its inception was twofold. One component revolved around the construction of pluralistic democracy. The other focused on erecting a viable, and hopefully vibrant, market economy anchored to the fundamental right to private property, which should in time become the dominant ownership format. In what follows I am not really concerned with the construction of pluralistic democracy, a topic adequately dealt with by political scientists and others better versed in such matters than I am. However, political democracy cannot be rigidly divorced from the functioning of a market economy; it certainly cannot be detached from constructing a market economy on the ruins of state socialism without losing touch with reality. For one thing, policy makers, including in economic matters, must heed the new polity in flux. Likewise, one can only hope that political democracy will in due course spawn a thick societal cushion composed of all kinds of agents of civil society. These not-for-profit organizations (NPOs) encompass more than the conventional nongovernmental organizations (NGOs): All organizations involved in societal matters, except individual households, whose activity is not really scrutinized in the marketplace. They have a critical role to play in advancing toward and in the proper functioning of a fairly advanced market economy. They are indeed essential in moving steadily forward with modernization. But they are also crucial in reaching a consensus on a feasible transformation agenda. When not available, such NPOs need to be erected swiftly to help formulate, implement, monitor, assess, and fine-tune transformation policies.

Similarly, constructing a market economy cannot be a simple technocratic exercise; nor can management of that economy once in place. Incipient political democracy requires a voice in its elaboration. Those managing the transition have multiple options to choose from in an environment characterized by pervasive uncertainty. Not only that, because most choices are not particularly conducive to strengthening the sociopolitical fabric in the short run, managers need to coopt all the support they can conceivably muster. A minimal socio-political consensus on forging ahead with the fairly rapid mutation of the remnants of state socialism into a functioning market economy is required. Without it, the paradigmatic market that these countries aspired to in the early phases of their transition is unlikely ever to be relevant. Furthermore, the kind of economy needed for these countries to play a constructive role in, and profit from, integrating into the framework of the European Union (EU) will be long in crystallizing.

Embarking on market-oriented reform has, at least conceptually, two angles. One is the mutation process itself, during which the new environment is shaped. This requires putting in place new policies, institutions, and policy instruments. An integral component thereof is the formulation of an economic policy aimed at a modicum of stability. How to avoid imbalances and the pressures they bring to bear on prices and other incentive systems, or if they occur how best to address them, forms one important element of macroeconomic policy making. The other is how best to operate within the market economy once established. Here a new philosophy of macroeconomic policy to maintain steady economic growth at some desired rate should act as beacon for economic policy.

In this volume, I do not deal with this second dimension, except for reference purposes and to punctuate what these economies are hoping eventually to construct. In other words, my principal purpose is helping to understand the *process* of shifting from disintegrating, or already collapsed, administrative planning under a monoparty system to laying sound foundations of a viable market economy, one that in a reasonable period of time can function construc-tively within the context of a Europe being remade. By this I do not mean to suggest that all transition economies could conceivably become EU members (Brabant 1996). But all do need to work out a constructive relationship with the EU, for which various governance capabilities are mandatory.

Key is that broad-based market-oriented reform cannot be transplanted in a vacuum. Its takeoff evolves necessarily in the presence of at least two legacies of state socialism. One is the coexistence of features of bureaucratic adminis-tration with indirect coordination mechanisms, the latter in principle gaining ascendancy as quickly as circumstances permit; but it poses serious obstacles to microeconomic restructuring in particular. The other is the absence of firm macroeconomic policies, institutions, and policy instruments other than those inherited from the most recent variant of state socialism. Of particular importance are the peculiar role of money, prices, wages, exchange and interest rates, and other indirect coordination instruments in the inherited economic model. Their instrumentality was debilitated by pervasive subsidies, payments in

3

kind, material balancing, and other nonmarket instruments that cannot be expunged all at once without inflicting utter chaos upon society. Furthermore, there is little autonomy in consumption, saving, and investment behavior of individual economic agents on the transition's eve. And few had been more than perfunctorily exposed to foreign competition. Domestic markets had been segmented in several ways. These buffers need to be removed soonest, entailing adjustments that, in the end, are likely to exacerbate inflation, unemployment, income dispersion, and wealth differentiation, among other variables that matter in securing and sustaining a minimal sociopolitical consensus.

Section 2: Principal purposes of this monograph

There are three but with very unequal weights. One is to explain the nature of the *process* of the transition toward political democracy and a market economy, given the starting conditions in the various countries. I shall be especially concerned with the formulation, implementation, and modulation of the economics of the transformation agenda. The second purpose is to inquire into the sustainability of the gains registered to date by examining the policies and institutions required to climb onto that platform and stay on it for an extended period of time. Finally, I draw lessons for policy makers of countries that prospectively have to embrace incisive structural change under unusual circumstances, including transition economies that have failed to deliver on their original ambitions or whose principal goals have remained locked into a variant of the state-socialist mind-set.

In appraising the consistency and potential of moving meaningfully toward the desired state of economic transformation, it is essential to gain a proper perspective on how economic agents view the tasks of coordination, how these perceptions evolve, and the degree to which governance of society is capable of eliciting measures to correct outcomes at variance with the intentions and ambitions of policy makers. This may require frequent fine-tuning of policies, institutions, and instruments in response to assessments of performance with a view to reinvigorating the impetus to transformation. In the first instance, this clarification is a matter of technical economics. Whether the costs of transformation are acceptable and the remedial measures feasible are issues that derive importantly from the robustness of the sociopolitical consensus. That includes sentiments on how best to eject from degenerative (or already degenerated) administrative planning and move toward market-based resource allocation, set primarily within the framework of pluralistic political democracy. Unlike many other commentators, I place the critical issues at stake in solidifying the sociopolitical consensus supportive of incisive transformation at the core of the investigation.

Though the various actors involved in debating transformation strategies have voiced a diverse range of "opinions," there are essentially two stylized strands. One approach – "shock therapy" – emphasizes the importance of wholehearted commitment to the liberal economic-policy agenda constructed around the so-called "Washington Consensus." This encompasses primarily rapid stabilization, liberalization, and privatization at the start of the transition and the introduction of many other elements of the transformation agenda as early as feasible once the process gets under way. The other – "gradualism" – stresses the importance of proceeding in a more evolutionary fashion, given that the success of constructing markets depends importantly on putting in place the latter's core "institutions" and making them work reasonably well.

Adherents of these convictions have after some time of intemperate exchanges, largely in the mode of parallel monologues, agreed broadly on the main components of a coherent transformation strategy. Yet, they differ significantly, among others, in terms of sequencing, timing, sectoralism, intensity, and speed of the measures to be promulgated, particularly during the early years of the transition. True, adherents of the more liberal kind of policies won out in most transition economies that have embarked on meaningful changes in part because they postulate a deceptively easy, almost self-evident agenda for action that easily ambushed any attempt to table a persuasive case for a more evolutionary approach. But also because the latter concurred with the precepts, and hence gained the full endorsement, of the major western assistance providers, notably the International Monetary Fund (IMF or Fund) and the World Bank Group. The evolutionary view has also lost because it hinges on agreeing more comprehensively on how "market institutions" mature and markets function. The long-term horizon for the completion of transformation under this approach distracts attention from what others see as the more immediate tasks at hand, as if path dependency were not something to be concerned about. And indeed gradualism has all too often been confounded with the absence of, or endless vacillation with, transition policies in countries where the ideological-political debate on the principal features of what needs to be undertaken has not yet been settled; or where this occurred only after a wrenching and protracted economic depression sustained in a thoroughly polarized sociopolitical situation. The latter manifestly do *not* form part and parcel of desirable transformation in how I perceive these matters.

Ironically, once the transitional depression takes hold, it becomes clear that many of the vital elements involving incisive structural change can by their nature be realized only gradually. Putting it another way, even if markets functioned reasonably well and the destruction of assets and jobs could be contained to what needs to be shed, the magnitude of "creative destruction" required throughout the economy is so large that no government could survive the upheaval engendered by setting all forces loose at once as per the precepts of "shock-therapists." That case is *a fortiori* more compelling when markets are not present or when they function asymmetrically or simply badly. Under those circumstances, managers of the transition cannot afford to rely upon "markets" to elicit the required transformations. Managing the scarce government funds earmarked to tide over those economic agents that in time must adjust or disappear therefore forms an important ingredient of "gradualism." It is one that deserves to be better understood.

Under the circumstances, the core question then becomes primarily how to sustain credibility of transformation policies, while moving further ahead with the envisaged agenda. The choice between "gradualism" and "shock therapy" as a result becomes moot. Working back from that point, the choice between the evolutionary and the rapid approaches at the start of the transition depends largely on the starting conditions – the opportunities afforded by the period of "extraordinary politics" (Balcerowicz and Gelb 1994). But the logical, technically coherent case for the evolutionary approach still deserves to be affirmed if only to clarify the distinction between what should ideally be done and what can realistically be undertaken, given the legacies of state socialism and the opportunities for boldly forging ahead. Indeed, market-oriented coordination can succeed only when economic agents have confidence in the framework within which they can pursue their own interest.

Section 3: Ideology and economic analysis

It is probably impossible to write a relevant book on the transformation from a wholly positivist point of view; after all, economic policy and politics are necessarily endogenous (Cairncross 1985; Krueger 1997). But I endeavor to clarify as much as possible the policy choices available to managers of the transitions. Positive economics purports to explain economic processes free of ideology by proposing some assumptions regarding human behavior under constrained supply circumstances, whence properties of feasible and efficient resource allocation are derived. This branch of economics has been most fruitful in depicting a world that has no real counterpart: The ability to conduct controlled laboratory experiences, as in the "hard" sciences, with a view to formulating propositions that are held to be generally valid until proven wrong. Positive economics has generally little to say about real-life policy making; but some strands do aim at approximating their propositions as closely as possible to prevailing realities. While useful insights have thus been gained in a variety of economic situations, the analysis of transition economics has suffered from two serious infractions of applying the above methodology in charting policy. One has been the blind faith in propositions, often of an ivory-tower or heuristic-textbook variety, developed for fairly mature market economies to the situation of a degenerated planned economy under transformation. The other has been, in Henri Bergson's memorable phrase, "the illusion of retrospective determinism" (Garton Ash 1996, p. 18), which posits that what actually occurred in the various transformations *had* to happen.

Both approaches are generally hard to resist. The first because it enables those not schooled in the *differentia specifica* of state socialism, and indeed in the broader history and culture of the affected societies, to pretend to deliver solid advice to managers of the transitions or to comment "with insight," often laced with an autocratic and arrogant self-confidence, on what should and could be done. In a number of cases they have dished out a lethal brew given that so much of this policy attention has been supported by bi- and multilateral organizations with initially virtually no "institutional knowledge" of the specifics of the transition economies. The ability to be able to intervene with a ready-made handbook on transformation has apparently been comforting to them. This all the more in view of the confirmatory support for such a self-confident assertion elicited by the legion of western consultants, easily swayed eastern consultants, the new political élites in the transition economies, and economic analysts more generally.

The second approach has been utilized with the intent of persuading the unbelievers and the weakly committed as an *ex post* justification of the errors committed in the methodological reductivism underlying the behavior just sketched. There is indeed a thin line between the privilege of erring and revising one's stance under the weight of circumstances, on the one hand, and the illusion of retrospective determinism, on the other. Even worse is when the latter is invoked for self-justification in the mode of *post hoc ergo propter hoc*. Without intending a caricature, the stylized explanation runs as follows (World Bank 1996). At the beginning of the transformation naïve optimism prevailed that the combination of macroeconomic stabilization, of internal and external liberalization, and of privatization, preferably pursued in "shock-therapy mode," would in and of itself poise the country swallowing this medicine for recovery and sustained growth after a short interval with a contained contraction of output and welfare. Had "we" known about the actual contraction and the "impurities" of the recommended adjustments, we would have contained the harm. But since the contraction had to happen anyway, one should look forward rather than backward. *Magnum miraculum est homo!*

I do not find it particularly helpful, or even illuminating, to engage in the predominant triumphalism suggesting, almost by sleight of hand, that state socialism was not only a complete waste from cultural, economic, intellectual, moral, ideological, political, strategic – in short, from all – points of view. The lodged claim that the collapse of the eastern economies "was the final spectacular demonstration of a phenomenon that was already indisputably clear" (Boeninger 1992, p. 269), if such a statement has any meaning at all, also leaves the painful impression that economic agents in transition economies have not at all built for themselves expectations of the postcommunist society in which they desire to live and function; or that they would willingly submit to imposed extraneous "volitions" (Lindblom 1977, 1990). At the same time, these encompassing pronouncements suggest that the intellectual ferment about socialism elsewhere has been a complete failure *ab ovo* (Birnbaum 1996; Moene and Wallerstein 1993; Temkin 1996a, b). These arguments not only refer to the past, but also strongly intimate that, precisely because of the utter bankruptcy of state socialism (though the difference is rarely drawn), there is an imperative need to move immediately away from this failed recipe for organizing society and promoting economic development toward a "proven menu," which is presumed to exist. Even a mediocre chef simply shudders at such a culinary travesty! It is furthermore maintained that this switch can be accomplished quickly. By embracing such an exceedingly narrow gauge for channeling the daunting complexity of the required transformation, ready-made strategies formulated in that spirit can lead to abject failure only when the outcomes are placed within the context of society as a whole (Pickel 1992).

This discouraging outcome is preordained not necessarily by wrong analyses or malicious intent on the part of the advisers. At the very least, it derives from a convoluted sequence of unanticipated consequences of a lasting nature that at some point with increasing certainty derail whatever grand *ex ante* strategy policy makers may take as their case for action. This is particularly ominous if these undesired emanations tending to subvert the basic goals of the transformation cannot be reversed. That has threatened most transition economies. It has befallen some. For the same reason, calls for first agreeing upon a constitutional framework and then letting the transition run its course, with newly empowered agents doing what is "right for them" (Rausser and Johnson 1993), although perhaps logically possible, are simply naïvely misguided unless some benevolent autocrat were simply to impose such a new constitution.

This harsh judgment is admittedly a caricature, although only a mild simplification, of much of the "new" writing about the transition economies. Yet, my rendition captures some of the underlying biases and salient features of much wishful thinking about what these economies hope to, and realistically can, prospectively accomplish. In many ways, this approach completely ignores these countries' societal preferences and their ongoing rapid transformation (Csontos, Kornai, and Tóth 1997). The hope initially placed in their being able to emulate the west's experience quickly and without too much pain has been bitterly dashed. It is now painfully evident that no single blueprint, if ever available, can be transposed to these societies. Could it have been anything but gross naïveté, or sheer arrogant self-confidence, to aim at compressing two centuries of capitalist failures and triumphs into a few years through the kind of regressive "social engineering" witnessed these past few years?

Of course, there is plenty of historical precedent, positive as well as negative, on how basic precepts that enjoy social support in the transition economies can be emulated, however incompletely, from successful experiences elsewhere. Certainly, the institutions, policies, and policy instruments associated with some of these precepts have been widely tested in market economies. Their advantages and disadvantages can thus be clarified to those in charge of transformation policies; some can undoubtedly do so for themselves. But these lessons are, on the whole, likely to be relevant only in terms of the final phase of the transition. That, however, is hardly pertinent to the problems at hand, particularly in reaching informed decisions about how to transit toward this end phase.

How best to pick and choose and transplant from the west's experiences what seems worthwhile to the transition economies is a task for economists and policy makers (Kornai 1992; Laski 1992), not just politicians. Economists should be in a position to offer a realistic appraisal of the probability with which such a graft, even if tempered, may work out, given the circumstances and aspirations of the transition economies. It is, however, arrogant for advisers to pretend that they can offer – indeed that they are proposing – smooth, professional solutions awaiting simple enactment lock, stock, and barrel. Such pretension is at best a poor substitute for the "narcotic effects of the Communist mystique of historical necessity" (Michnik 1993, p. 19) from which vast layers of the populations of the transition economies need to be weaned. Neither is it realistic to expect these societies to formulate swift transformations that will forestall social and political discontent or that can be implemented without hammering out and preserving, in spite of inevitable adversities, a minimal sociopolitical consensus. The risk of setting off sizable inflation and unemployment, and provoking a rapid widening of income and wealth dispersion, thus rending social cohesion, is simply too large to stumble blindly along with "easy" policy advice. At the very least, a clear distinction should be drawn between a state and a process, and for each between the transition itself and its desired ultimate outcome. Equally important, the legacies of over four decades of state socialism for transformation must be clear before endorsing rapacious anarchy as a viable policy option.

This book therefore offers more nuanced positions. At first sight they may impart the appearance of deliberateness rather than being of the action-oriented kind – the real requirement of transition management. If so, I beg the reader to sit back for a moment, reread the cursed passage, and rethink matters holistically.

Section 4: Terminological conventions

Because so many policy makers and commentators are so very touchy about nomenclature, I deem it instructive to justify some of my terminological choices. Using the designation "economies in transition" or "transition economies" interchangeably chiefly for all the countries in Europe that used to be managed through some form of mandatory central planning, within the context of a single communist party as sociopolitical arbiter, arouses opposition. Many do not want to be lumped together either under the above designation or under the post-Yalta "Eastern Europe," even if the latter is used purely for geographical tagging (Terry 1994). Similarly for other notions that have been coined in the literature (see Brabant 1992a, pp. 6–9). I am fully aware of these sensibilities. Referring to these countries individually or to the twenty-seven as the economies of central and eastern Europe, the Baltic States, and the Commonwealth of Independent States (CIS) is simply too clumsy. For one thing, one would then have to explain what precisely is behind the labels of central Europe or east-central Europe, invoking the region's western Christian background as opposed to the Orthodox Christianity of the rest of the group. That certainly poses problems for countries such as Armenia and Georgia, which also have a western Christian background. Moreover, the terms east-central and central Europe bear a heavy historical load, which I wish neither to invoke nor to explain away.

There is no easy solution. Two features are incontrovertible: These countries are by and large geographically located in the eastern part of Europe and they are without exception still continuing with their transformation from state socialism to pluralist democracy and market-based resource allocation. Claims that some are no longer in transition are spurious at best. I therefore insist upon using the designation "economies in transition" or "transition economies" interchangeably, depending on euphony, to refer chiefly to the cited twenty-seven countries in societal transition. Occasionally I use the notion "eastern part of Europe" as an alternative designation. I have no other motivation in lumping them into one group. I refer intermittently to events in some of the Asian countries formerly with state socialism, and now in their distinct kind of economic transition, simply to clarify matters.

In this context, eastern Europe is utilized as distinct from the former Soviet Union or Union of Soviet Socialist Republics (USSR). Unless I specify it differently, it encompasses Albania, Bosnia and Herzegovina, Bulgaria, Croatia, the Czech Republic, Hungary, Macedonia, Poland, Romania, Slovakia, Slovenia, and Yugoslavia; when reference is to the period when Czechoslovakia and the former Yugoslavia were still intact, I do, of course, mean those countries rather than the successor States; I then include the German Democratic Republic (GDR) among the group. The designation CIS is here utilized solely as the post-Soviet Union without the three Baltic States (Estonia, Latvia, and Lithuania); in this, I disregard the shifts in the composition of the CIS, whether formal or not, since it was first constituted in late 1991. When there is no room for misunderstanding, eastern Europe since late 1991 includes the three Baltic States. Otherwise I mention these three countries separately.

Second, the notions "communism," "socialism," and "central planning" are not very appropriate to refer to the decades of experience with "building communism" in these countries. Since they neither reached communism nor did they really practice socialism as commonly understood, I prefer the designation "state socialism" as a shorthand to refer to the entire period of single Party control with some form of centralized economic administration. The latter was by no means coterminous with "central planning" as in the orthodox economic model of state socialism. With the incisive administrative reforms, many facets of central planning were replaced by central administration or even by bureaucratic bargaining.

Third, it is not easy to characterize the events since 1989. In some sense, even though they were nonviolent, with some exceptions (such as Romania), they were revolutionary. This certainly applied to some countries; at least to the first phase of the transition. As Vilfredo Pareto (1935) posited it, revolution is above all a matter of élite change, whether or not brought about through violence, civil war, or similar upheavals. Given the changes in government and the shift toward pluralist democratic politics beginning with 1989, there was a revolution in this sense (Gabanyi 1997). But this characterization is not appropriate for all countries. Nor can it usefully be invoked to infer that the present situation in many transition economies has surfaced from revolution. Even limiting our discourse to movement toward pluralistic politics, there has been severe back-tracking in several countries. There is no certainty at this stage that these setbacks will be reversed any time soon. If only for those reasons, in what follows, I tend to avoid the term "revolution," preferring instead the more neutral, although admittedly less eye catching, "1989 events" and their immediate aftermath.

I realize, fourth, that the just proposed convention conflicts with the first one. That is to say, not all transition economies as commonly categorized are in transition in the sense in which I propose it should meaningfully be defined. All are in transition from various variants of state socialism to some other state, but not necessarily toward greater political pluralism with democratic institutions and market-based resource allocation. Some engage only in the latter, as in several Asian countries. But the latter and indeed several of the conventional Balkan countries are far from yielding highly centralized control over the political mind and the economic interests of their citizens. Caution therefore needs to be exercised when generalizing findings or propositions.

Fifth, the focus of the volume is undoubtedly on the transition economies. But I cannot possibly ignore actual and potential relations between these countries and the western European structures. In order to avoid confusion, throughout the volume I shall designate the western European integration movement, other than the European Free Trade Association (EFTA), as the EU, regardless of the appropriate organizational format over time. I shall deviate from this only when reference is to a concrete historical phase, and then cite the European Economic Community (EEC) and European Communities (EC). I do likewise for the executive organ of the EU. This is presently known either as the European Commission or, more officially, as the Commission of the European Communities, and before the merger of the three Communities (the EC, European Atomic Energy Community or Euratom, and the European Coal and Steel Community) in 1967 as the Commission of the European Economic Community. I am aware of the finely hewn message that is intended thereby to be conveyed (Brabant 1996, pp. 5–6). Just the same, unless there is room for misunderstanding or misrepresentation, I shall utilize only the designation European Commission or Commission.

Sixth, for better or worse the transition economies on the whole aspire to emulating levels of living, productivity, income, and wealth in western Europe, and by extension in members of the Organisation for Economic Co-operation and Development (OECD). This is awkward as membership of the OECD has been expanded to countries, such as Mexico, that can hardly be taken as exemplars of what the transition economies are aspiring to; it includes Turkey, which the transition economies certainly do not seek to emulate. Likewise, three transition economies (Czech Republic, Hungary, and Poland) have in the mean-time become OECD members. Just like Mexico, these countries have not joined the ranks of the "western rich" because they have suddenly become economically prosperous. Rather, they have enacted certain codes that the OECD cherishes and it was thought that membership would enhance the credibility of further transformation policies, thus alleviating one instance of pervasive uncertainty. Unless stated explicitly otherwise, OECD here refers to the "traditional" twenty-four member countries.

Finally, I draw in this volume a fairly sharp distinction between transition and transformation. Inasmuch as transformation policies intimate incisive actions over a fairly protracted period of time, I much prefer this term over "transition policies," which suggests temporizing and a fairly short-term horizon. I use "transition policies" to designate the process of moving away from the remnants of communism and administrative planning toward some variant of political democracy and market building. In contrast, I invoke the notion "transformation policies" guardedly to refer to a strategy for embarking on incisive, far-reaching structural mutations at a pace that takes advantage of, and when necessary can maintain, a sociopolitical consensus on the costs inflicted by the transitions in a bold way, with or without external assistance. The overarching objectives are essentially jettisoning the one-party political system with a largely degenerated administratively planned economy. I exclude from this purview transition economies that still lack a basic consensus on transformation or whose aims differ fundamentally from those specified here.

Section 5: Measurement problems during the transition

In assessing success and failure with just about any aspect of transition policies daunting measurement and conceptual problems need to be addressed. Even more so, the myriad of observers cannot reasonably agree on the appropriate indicators, whether or not they can be specified and quantified. The origin of this calamity is complex. But four reasons may suffice for now. First, inasmuch as the pretransition phase was characterized by pervasive economic imbalances with measured prices not even approximately reflecting true scarcities and quantum adjustments taking the relief, the true pre-1989 levels of production, consumption, and welfare are simply not known. Queuing and its costs as well as the marked differences in official and second-economy prices are typical examples; similarly for the appearance of many new goods of different quality and, I should add, the disappearance of low-price goods that were demanded by some layers of the population (such as soap or grains without fancy packaging and merchandising). These distortions of economic magnitudes, which may well be completely undeliberate, complicate comparisons over time and across countries. Another set of problems pertains to trade statistics owing to the impossibility of adding up the part of trade measured in transferable rubles and that expressed in convertible currency evaluated at quasi-meaningless exchange rates. No single rate could bridge the enormous differences in relative prices.

Second, the statistical apparatus inherited from state socialism is all but completely unsuited to monitoring trends in an emerging market economy.

Reporting on firms was essentially based on inventorying the socialized, particularly the state, sector; that is, just about the entire economy. Such comprehensive assessments can now no longer be undertaken, and not only because of financial constraints. The emergence of literally thousands of small firms, for example, makes it all but impossible to count their activities in any complete sense. Sampling and stratification must be resorted to as alternatives. But experiences to enact such methods are frequently lacking. In addition, with transformation a number of new economic, political, and social phenomena emerge on which accurate and timely information, and its dissemination, is vital. Examples are unemployment, poverty, and crime. Not only that, the statistical categories (such as the system of national accounts [SNA] as contrasted with material-product accounting) that international agencies insist upon being introduced in these economies are oftentimes quite alien to practitioners or challenge computational capacities.

Third, a particular problem arises in intertemporal and cross-country comparisons because much of the statistical information collected under state socialism was either not disclosed or only in a misleading or truncated format. This can be remedied comparatively quickly. Another large array of information was compiled according to methodologies and organizing criteria that were difficult to reconcile with internationally agreed-upon concepts and formats or practices commonly accepted in international trade and finance. For most countries, renorming those data will require more time and effort. Even with international assistance, success can be assured only if the potential recipients fully support these endeavors through staffing policies, building the requisite minimum institutional infrastructure, and displaying an unwavering commitment to implement agreed-upon programs. Unfortunately, the transition evolves with a compression of state activities by design or as a byproduct of austerity measures in the public service, including in statistical reporting and analysis. The near collapse of the Hungarian statistical office presents one case in point (Hardtkamp 1997). It is all the more serious since Hungary under state socialism, and indeed before that, had an excellent reputation comparable to that held by all but the most sophisticated services in industrial countries.

Finally, most new economic agents have little or no interest in reporting their economic activity, including for fiscal reasons. The magnitude of the second economy probably rose significantly in all countries, at least early on. Nobody knows its exact extent. But the size of the second economy prior to the transition was certainly not zero anywhere. Again, nobody knows even approximately its proper size, then or now. Estimates as a result vary widely (Kaufmann and Kaliberda 1996).

In short, statistics of transition economies leave a lot to be desired. Constructing appropriate deflators is only one instance of serious problems given the rapidly changing mix of goods and services in the economy, and the fact that observed prices now reflect more closely true scarcity whereas under state socialism this was rarely the case; just like in foreign trade, distortions could not be captured by a scalar. By virtue of the magnitude and depth of the structural change under way, the transition presents a number of awesome index-number problems. Ignoring them creates confusion, to say the least. If only because of their evident incompleteness, the statistics being produced have been utilized by both advocates and detractors of the transformation to document their preconceptions. In many cases they have furnished ammunition for waging political battles. The detached economist can only look with dismay at the way in which the available quantitative information is being abused, sometimes out of ignorance but more often out of an urge to prove a contestable point by citing selective, or purported, evidence or interpreting prevailing data with a known bias one's own way. A typical point made, particularly by the multilateral agencies, is: "Under planning, the output of state enterprises was often exaggerated, whereas during the transition, output of the private sector has tended to be underreported, sometimes by large margins" (Melo, Denizer, and Gelb 1996, p. 399). One or the two apply for some magnitudes at some point in time for some countries. But was not one of the problems of state-socialist statistics that firms sought a "soft plan," hence had an interest in hiding reserves of various kinds, not just inputs? Even so, the partial finding does not suffice to infer that aggregate output now is underreported while it was previously overstated, thus making the *real* negative impacts of transition policies smaller than reported and understating the positive achievements.

Some economists and sometimes the international economic organizations (IEOs) construct their own magnitudes. These are not necessarily superior to the officially reported data or amplifications thereof. I cite two examples, without attributing them to individuals. In the absence of a more or less reliable measure of inflation in one CIS State, the resident representative of a core IEO went diligently once a week around the large food markets in the capital and recorded prices there for some twenty staples. To these numbers were added impressionistic data on the evolving prices of services and manufactured goods, the latter chiefly as posted in state retail outlets. The individual preferred to utilize this measure suitably aggregated, rather than the official magnitude, as an indicator of the country's inflation in arguing for or against delivering the IEO's assistance. There is, of course, no way of telling whether this measure was superior to the one officially reported.

A second example is the case of "growth" in Estonia in 1994. One IEO insisted that statistical problems in Estonia were so large that an own estimate was in order. This was appropriately placed within a range of supposedly plausible outcomes – from 1 to 6 percent. Needless to say, these numbers varied widely from those disclosed by Estonia's central bank or statistical office. In the end, the IEO opted for the upper end of its own estimated range, thus insisting on 6 percent growth, whereas the other institutions reported only negative growth of various magnitudes. Only after two years was one of the latter data accepted, and so growth in 1994 for Estonia is now reported at around −3 percent (compare EBRD 1995, p. 194 with EBRD 1996, p. 192). But other international agencies, such as the World Bank (1996, p. 173), still cling to the 6 percent!

For these and many other reasons, I utilize statistics rather sparingly and then mostly for illustrative purposes, and invariably with a solid nugget of salt. For virtually all, one or more of the above caveats (and undoubtedly other defects) should be borne in mind. But I can cite only the most egregious measurement errors, particularly those utilized for propaganda purposes by observers on either side of the fence. The reader should exert caution in utilizing numbers, and I can only flag up potentially debilitating traps.

Section 6: A road map

The volume is divided into three parts. Part I paints the backdrop of the transition. Chapter 1 sketches the broad setting for the policies, institutions, and instruments under state socialism, the focus being on the core generic features of the orthodox economic model and the industrialization strategy embraced by the vanguard of state socialism. Chapter 2 carries that analysis forward from the most important reform experiments of the 1960s to the transition's eve, whence the legacies of state socialism for transitions can be extracted. Chapter 3 sets forth the broad contours of the transformation strategy as well as the key parameters to be heeded in applying such an agenda to any individual transition economy.

Part II clarifies in detail the core components of the transformation agenda and their various qualifiers, the emphasis being on the choices confronting policy makers. Chapter 4 is devoted to stabilization in three senses: stock and flow stabilization as well as pursuing stable macroeconomic policies. Chapter 5 deals with the myriad issues of internal and external liberalization. The entire gamut of privatization, not just divestment, issues occupies us in Chapter 6. The focus of Chapter 7 is erecting the "institutions of the market," encompassing broadly the infrastructure of institutions, laws, the attitudes of economic agents, and all the other elements that identify any one "market economy." Although the sociopolitical sphere does not form an intrinsic part of the economist's trans-formation remit, it is not very helpful to set forth the problems the transition economies face without reference to knitting and mending society's fabric. That I do in Chapter 8. One of the unique institutions to be thoroughly overhauled in the transition economies is the state. By virtue of the history of these countries and its legacies, as well as the coercive powers available to the state, it is a very special institution that warrants special treatment. Chapter 9 is devoted to the most important issues at stake.

Part III deals with topics that can be grouped under three themes. One is the merger of these economies into the global framework. Though foreign-sector liberalization, including for production factors especially to attract foreign direct investment (FDI), forms an integral part of the transformation agenda, merging these economies fully into the global financial, monetary, and trading regimes in place, and into the EU in particular, does not. Yet, both are of critical impor-tance, as I underline in Chapter 10, especially in view of the area's experience with policies and institutions associated with the Council for Mutual Economic

Assistance (CMEA). Chapter 11 considers the new political economy for global activism sparked by the transitions in the eastern part of Europe. Chapter 12 ponders the sustainability of the recovery observed in some transition economies, and gaining a similar platform elsewhere, into catch-up growth over a protracted period of time.

The Conclusion highlights a few of the salient elements discussed, but placed within the broader perspective of the lessons that can be extracted from the experiences of the transition economies. I do so primarily for other countries that may have to launch incisive structural transformations of their societies, but also for transition economies that have not so far resolved core ingredients of their own transformation strategy or that did at one point and then backtracked for whatever reason. Some critical implications for regional and global governance are drawn as well.

Part I

HISTORY, STARTING CONDITIONS, AND TRANSFORMATION TASKS

Except at the creation or in the laboratory, the remit of policy making is rarely the quintessential *tabula rasa* permitting virtually any option to be carried out upon simple choice. The Olympian heights of economic theory are far removed from the world in which economic agents *must* make decisions, are compelled to reveal their options and preferences fairly quickly, and normally have to justify their choices and actions. When democratic circumstances do not prevail but policy makers aim precisely at eliciting the emergence of such a pluralistic polity, a window for "extraordinary politics," as Leszek Balcerowicz (1993, 1994), the architect of the Polish shock therapy, termed it, may open. By its very nature this has a rather confined time dimension, perhaps up to twelve months.

This window of opportunity certainly applies to the transition economies that form the main subject of this inquiry. It is also valid *mutatis mutandis* for the economies that have thus far eschewed political transformations paralleling those experienced in the eastern part of Europe. Variations across countries and over time, as a rule, derive from the *differentia specifica* of these societies. That is to say, some of the "national" features are more deeply rooted in the history (to be defined) of each of these countries. Inasmuch as managing the transition can realistically be envisaged only in a concrete setting, it is important to be clear about the main starting conditions for effectuating the envisioned societal turnaround. Some will be short-lived, and they should be of concern only if they could inhibit transformation managers from holding on to their precepts on what needs to be done. Very often, such concrete circumstances prevent even the implementation of the "optimal course" of transformation designed by the best economic and legal brains. Others are much more deeply engrained, and so there will not only be hysteresis in the true sense of that term in physics, but also a lingering effect of the past in shaping the future. Path dependency is unavoidable.

It would be an impossible task to characterize the starting conditions for individual transition economies one at a time. But this degree of detail is not really required to gain a solid perspective on the generic starting conditions. I shall do so primarily by tying in three different components of the past: (1) where these economies come from and what that implies for the present and future, (2) the circumstances prevailing on the transition's eve, and (3) the broad tasks of a coherent transformation agenda. This sets the stage for a comprehensive discussion of the individual components of a coherent transformation strategy in Part II and its implementation. I also illustrate some of the specific circumstances to watch out for when examining any one economy's transition features. In the latter case, I proceed by way of, admittedly highly selective, examples. Judicious choice should impart a flavor of the complexity of the issues at stake.

There are various ways in which one can legitimately proceed. I prefer to look at matters from four angles: the "institutions" in place, the ideology that is being overthrown with the transition, the legacy of the policies pursued chiefly in the recent past with their objectives spelled out, and an evaluation of the extent to which these objectives had been realized. To do so cogently, it is important to be clear about the antecedents of these starting conditions, as discussed in the opening two chapters.

1

HISTORICAL BACKDROP

A cogent overview of the recent "history" of the transition economies prior to the "1989 events" is important. I confine myself largely to the period of state socialism. But a few references to the state of affairs, or perceptions thereof by the then ruling élites, that contributed to the inauguration of state-socialist economic policies provide useful pointers to the objectives of those advocating the communist alternative. My basic reference here is what communist adherents thought could and should be done about the degree of industrial underdevelopment with low-productivity in agriculture and substantial rural overpopulation. Whether these objectives failed to be accomplished, or were realized not quite to the degree their advocates had originally hoped for, is a different question. But it needs to be addressed too.

In tackling these issues with some economy, I prefer to look at six topics: (1) the broad backdrop to recent history and communist ideology, (2) the doctrine of communist economic development, (3) the economic strategy and its evolvement, (4) the institutions innovated to serve both the ideology and the strategic aims of development, (5) the policies adopted with the institutions in place to realize the strategic ambitions, and (6) the major signposts in policy making aimed at imparting a new impetus to economic growth without fundamentally changing the strategic aims of state-socialist economic development. The first five topics form the heart of this chapter. Because the reform discussions are rather complex and are directly related to the starting conditions of transition, I defer that treatment to Chapter 2. Given the nature of this volume, however, I can at best hope to set forth some important pointers to the "past" that formed the stepping stone toward "1989" and beyond. If this highly condensed rendition whets the reader's appetite for a more rounded review of the complex issues at stake, it will have accomplished its purposes.

After a brief examination of history and ideology in communist doctrine, I detail core precepts of economic development therein. Next I clarify the communist strategy of industrial development. Then I examine the orthodox economic model, with a detailed discussion of the policies and its institutional infrastructure in the two last sections. I conclude with pointers to the economic dilemmas that emerged from orthodox central planning because they set the stage for the reform episodes and ultimately the collapse of state socialism.

Section 1: History and ideology

Without a fundamental grasp of the historical backdrop to the transition, it is very difficult to conceptualize operationally how best to mold the transformation agenda. I have in mind here real-life policy options. Ideally, this package should reflect the full menu with the advantages and disadvantages of each choice laid out so that managers of the transition are properly informed before choosing a policy course. Several caveats on this proposition are in order (see Chapter 3).

One could well argue that a good grasp of the history of these countries, not just the communist past, is helpful in appreciating the dimensions of the policy and institutional shifts embarked upon since 1989. I shall attempt to do so here only by recalling briefly two of their aspects. One is the evolution of communism as a doctrine from its Marxist roots to how it evolved first in the Soviet Union and later in the other countries that constituted the "socialist camp." Strictly speaking that encompassed Albania, Bulgaria, China, Cuba, Czechoslovakia, the GDR, Hungary, (north) Korea, Mongolia, Poland, Romania, the Soviet Union, Vietnam, and Yugoslavia; though some add to that group Cambodia (as Kampuchea) and Laos when these countries dabbled with communism. The other is that the doctrine of communism was not home-grown in the vast majority of these countries. The same applies to many of the facets of how communism was implemented. Notably in the eastern part of Europe, it was widely perceived to have been imposed from the outside, that is, by the Soviet Union, as one consequence of World War II. Since it had not evolved domestically, and with few exceptions doctrinal refinements of the original theses did not occur, the depth to which communism was anchored in people's minds, especially beliefs in its chiliastic-salvationist origins, was rather shallow. Just the same, some of its traits lingered in people's minds as acquired rights or dogmas, particularly during the first transition years.

There are many ways to encapsulate the communist ideology. The lack of professional consensus about the quintessential features, particularly the dynamics, of communist regimes (Janos 1996) has been one important rationale for the diverse explanations current in the literature. I consider communism at its origin to have been a reconstructionist paradigm, that is, an ideology based on a set of "laws" designed to reorganize the world from the bottom up. Its essential ambition is to provide a better – at some stage portrayed as *the* ideal – alternative to capitalism and all of its nefarious emanations. Several other paradigms of communism in vogue can be subsumed under this fundamental objective or the ultimate ends of this purposeful movement. Thus totalitarianism, charismatic salvationism, forced modernization, being the vanguard of the party for change, and the bureaucratic paradigm of communist organization can all to a large extent be brought home under the reconstructionist paradigm rather than treated as separate ways of capturing the essence of communist ideology. They can indeed be interpreted as instrumental emanations of the way in which communist ideology sought to redesign the world order or gradually evolved in a manner that, in retrospect, can hardly be reconciled with its origins, except by agreeing upon how best to capture the essence of its dynamics.

Section 2: The ideology of communism and core precepts of economic development

Placed within the cited framework, communist aspirations in Russia, and later communism in the Soviet Union, were the outcome of a long historical struggle between various intellectual factions on the best way for Russia to overcome its backwardness. This was certainly true for its level of economic development and wealth-generating capacity from manufacturing activities. But Russia was backward also in several other dimensions. As far as its economic underpinnings are concerned, the country was widely perceived to embody at best a limited capacity for catching up with countries that had gone through a successful industrial revolution, and thus transforming itself to reach par with the stronger states they underpinned, mainly in the western part of Europe. In simple terms, the "socialist" wings of the intellectual and political debates, which eventually won out, insisted upon having an autocratic state as the driving force for modernization from above. But conceptual approaches to how this could be accomplished varied considerably among the several left-wing factions.

In a reductionist fashion, one might contrast the position of the Mensheviks with that of the Bolsheviks. The former insisted upon forming a modern (nineteenth-century) bourgeois democratic state as the motor of industrialization. It would eventually crystallize from an internal design for reform and development. In contrast, the Bolsheviks advocated political revolution independent of the particular stage of socioeconomic development attained. Both visions appealed to the claims made by Marx and his orthodox epigones, based on historical destiny, although orthodox Marxism had not considered Imperial Russia ripe for a "socialist revolution." In the more traditional approach, in contrast to options rooted in the left-wing extremes of Bolshevism, socialism would emerge organically from the internal contradictions of capitalism. It would also intrinsically lead up to the communist welfare state. That is to say, capitalism should already have been firmly entrenched in society and sprouted its internal contradictions before the "vanguard" of society could be anticipated to set off the communist revolution without running the risk of "revolutionary infantilism." Rather than adhering to this immanence of capitalism, the Bolshevik faction advocated an externally oriented strategy for reconstructing the existing world order by means of revolutionary violence as a viable – perhaps the sole – option for modernizing Russia through homogenization. By liberating in this manner in particular Europe, Vladimir I. Lenin hoped that the proletariat of the more advanced countries would assist Russia in its efforts to emerge from economic backwardness.

That Bolshevik position was most seriously underpinned on a "scientific basis" by appealing to the core presumptions of classical Marxism. The latter make sense for countries that seek to enter "the modern world late, and [have] to achieve political and economic modernization simultaneously and quickly" (Dahrendorf 1990, p. 48). But the Bolsheviks transformed Marxism in accordance with the economic and political realities of Russia, entailing the rise of a class to hegemony that had nothing but the Party to support it. But it did set in motion a slow, and ultimately ineffectual, in some respects even destructive, process of industrialization. Classical Marxism suitably transformed through a remarkable *sui generis* reading provided the Bolsheviks with the methodology for discerning historically correct political positions. Out of this the Party became the twentieth-century counterpart of a traditional religious movement, its ideology being the functional equivalent of the doctrine of divine right. That is to say, as Andrew C. Janos (1996, p. 5) puts it: "for the first time in modern history a movement of the radical left could claim to have the key to absolute wisdom in overriding the principles of popular government." Not only was this cast in chiliastic-salvationist terms. By its very essence, the Bolshevik appeal to essential traits of Marxism rested on the idea of terrestrial perfection in harmony, humanity now being free from material deprivation as well as boredom and frustration generated by the industrial division of labor and the production process.

This, I submit, provided the logical foundations for the political and economic structure of the Leninist state. Variations thereof emerged with successive Soviet leaders and, to some degree, in the countries to which the ideology was exported, notably in Albania, China, Vietnam, and Yugoslavia. It is the rationale of total, single-minded devotion rather than mechanical obedience on the part of the chosen few constituting the vanguard of society. It is also the explanation of the intuitive irreverence of rebels ready to storm the bastions of traditionalism, capitalism, religion, philistinism, and so on at least of the early Bolshevik regime. These two cultures – total subservience justified by the idea of salvation and non-conformism – were soon to become at serious odds with each other, and in time one was bound to perish. However, these internal contradictions of the chiliastic-salvationist foundations of early communism did not come to the fore until the rivalries among Lev D. Trotskiy with his advocacy of the permanent revolution, Nikolay I. Bukharin with his emphasis on abandoning revolution in favor of socialist development, and Josef V. Stalin with his stress on forced industrialization through rapid resource mobilization, if necessary in a Draconian fashion, were eventually settled in the latter's favor.

It is out of this ideological battle that in time the details of the design of the communist state emerged through the filter of étatism. Stalin accordingly adopted whatever element of classical Marxism and Leninism was congruous with his perception of the requirements for a strong state. By the same token, whatever might have undermined the authority of building up and maintaining such an all-powerful state was ruthlessly eliminated. That determined the tactics utilized to bring about the communist politico-economic system of centrally administered planning. This included forced and rapid collectivization of agriculture, stifling labor discipline, forced labor reallocation to enhance the planners' economic flexibility, planning from above, and nearly complete subordination of economic organization and policies to the supreme goal of rapid industrialization by force-fully developing a broad base of heavy industry eventually to support a militaristic stronghold. It also explains public ownership of the means of production to provide the state with flexibility in mobilizing and allocating resources. And it even helps to rationalize the emphasis on public education and on spreading literacy, the attention devoted to making available to the masses certain aspects of high culture and the desire to improve the system of medical and more general health-care services. These were designed as objectives worth pursuing to ensure healthy and literate Party recruits and workers for executing the priorities of the state-directed development program. Finally, it provided the origins of the system of terror and the purge as quintessential instruments of state policy. These *modi operandi* were embraced not just for the state's self-preservation. An essential motivation for this choice was strengthening the state and its capacities to rule and conquer.

When the use of mass terror and sweeping purges at strategically chosen intervals as tools of policy in the very visible hands of the state were markedly eased after Stalin, "rank" in all of its formats became entrenched. Instead of enduring the hard realities of Soviet life and the intractabilities of human nature and social existence as a price worth paying in serving the strengthening of the state, the communist vanguard now began to explore modifications and numerous avenues for more immediate gratification. Hiding their experiences behind fulsome praise for the salvationist design, the agents of the Soviet state, those hardened in the trenches of economic mobilization as well as in the rural class struggle, resigned themselves to human folly and the inevitable imper-fections of any social construct. In the process, they arrogated for their own purposes whatever the regime's needs for administration and management permitted. State-socialist incrementalism rather than the rigidities of the police state became an act of faith. By resigning themselves to incrementalist social engineering based on the legitimacy wrestled through the more mundane arts of administration and management, the leaders found it very difficult to sustain their earlier ability to exact total commitment from their subordinates. They also had qualms about blithely disregarding rules and regulations issued to ensure the efficient functioning of the political system.

With the new rhetorical commitment to rules and socialist – later real-socialist – development, arrogating personal or group advantages became the depressing features of daily life in the Soviet-type society. These took various forms, including bickering about the meaning of central commands (political as well as other), feigning compliance with them through various subterfuges, or implicitly threatening to subvert the leaders' intentions through mere foot dragging and lack of enthusiasm. Those in command from the highest echelons down to managers and political commissars eventually grabbed whatever they could and circumstances permitted, thus adding overt domestic social inequalities to the sources of dissatisfaction created by the vision of material superiority of the capitalist world. This inegalitarianism was not as a rule expressed in terms of monetary-income and material-wealth differentiation. Instead, it took the form of all kinds of privileges, reaching from material gratification *in natura* to positions of power and influence, with very few checks and balances. This diversion of resources from what would have prevailed under a more pluralistically organized society was to some degree neutralized by the steady flow of benefits – admittedly small increments over time – to the population at large. It was also condoned because, with the weaning of terror and political mobilization, the people at large began to reclaim a small private domain for breathing and speaking more freely in the circle of friends and family. That included operating in the unofficial economy. Note that this does not necessarily mean being engaged in criminal or corrupt activities as per socialist legality.

This development of Soviet society in the post-Stalin era had its counterpart in the greater diversity of communisms in the dependent or clientelistic states, particularly the eastern European ones and Mongolia (the other Asian states and Cuba then being preoccupied with altogether other priorities). Those that remained solidary with the Soviet Union (notably Bulgaria, Czechoslovakia with the exception of the brief 1968 spring, the GDR, and Mongolia) clung most closely to endorsing the purpose of the state as one of promoting proletarian internationalism and operational codes, reflected in both public policy and the cultural norms fostered by the party leadership. The other members of the European socialist camp became liberal or reformist in their developmental goals and instruments (Hungary, Poland, and Yugoslavia), radical developmental (Romania), or neorevolutionary (Albania).

Unfortunately for the sustainability of these regimes, in all of this diversity the leadership invariably failed to identify sources for motivating agents and thus to generate sustainable gains in labor productivity, to encourage innovation and risk taking, to diffuse available technology, and to sustain catch-up with best-performance in the global economy. These developments had economic but also broader sociopolitical angles. All would have been required to underpin "intensive" development, as opposed to the "extensive" development precepts of Stalinist-type economic development based on the mobilization of resources, be it the mopping up of idle or underutilized resources; the reallocation of primary production factors; or the injection of new capital. Even if the goal had not been putting together an economic regime capable of generating long-term popular welfare on a fairly predictable basis, the reformist leadership failed miserably even to sustain shorter-term coercive potential and military prowess.

Seen over the long haul, the diversity that emerged in eastern Europe did not quite put these regimes on fundamentally different trajectories from that of the Soviet Union. Nonetheless, the circumstances of the state-socialist collapse and the patterns of transitions away from orthodox communism (hence the legacies of their own postwar experiences), were significantly shaped by their own political variants of the incrementalist changeover from Stalinism (except Albania and Romania for political life) and the cultures they attempted to spawn. For one thing, in few of these regimes had communism been pursued on a wide scale as a political or ideological creed prior to the postwar events. As a result, the orthodox ideology of the Stalinist perversion was not especially deeply entrenched. This was in part the consequence of the fact that many of the first-generation leaders had been witness to the clash of two cultures in the 1930s mentioned earlier, and many of them became victim of the last wave of Stalinist-type purges. They were replaced by yes-men of a sort who fortunately, with rare exceptions, proved to have but a short political life span.

Thus the roots of the switch in the developmental states, notably in Hungary, Poland, and Yugoslavia, can be found in the failure of the respective regimes to deliver the consumer society on which they had staked their legitimacy since the 1960s. The failure of the solidary regimes emanated from external events, specifically Mikhail S. Gorbachev's abandonment of internationalism, the global struggle, and the safeguarding of socialist hegemony. This was noticeably enhanced by the blatant corruption in regimes such as Bulgaria's. Had it not been for the corruption and the reprehensible excesses of grandeur of leaders in Albania and Romania, these regimes might well have held out for longer than they did. In fact, their successor regimes, after a modest interval of extraordinary politics, and economics as well, were backtracking toward that stage prevailing before the all too evident corruption doomed their communist predecessors; whether the political renaissance initiated in 1997 in these countries can improve on the dire situation remains to be seen.

Section 3: The communist strategy of industrial development

Many of the aberrations of state-socialist economics as concerns effective resource allocation stem from the underlying communist ideology. This holds in particular for the strategic vision of economic development, given the primacy of the dynamic strengthening of the state, held by the vanguard of society. But it holds also for the economic model of the socialist economy. True, initially the static allocation of resources tends to be subordinated to the dynamics of development – or growth for the sake of industrialization *per se*. Nevertheless, once state-socialist incrementalism takes root, the ideology of sustaining state power in an evolutionary manner pervades precepts on economic organization. Frequent tinkering with this or that aspect of the structures inherited from classical communist construction (see Chapter 2) are a clear emanation thereof.

A growth strategy is a complex of interrelated measures designed to mobilize and allocate economic resources with a view toward attaining one or more long-term developmental objectives with the assistance of proper policy instruments, institutions, and behavioral rules; the latter constitute the economic model (see Section 4). By manipulating the policy instruments and by setting specific behavioral rules for all economic agents through new institutional arrangements, the managers of the state-socialist economy envisage deploying resources in such a way that backward, agrarian countries or economies too dependent on "calico industries" will mature rapidly into industrial strongholds. Communist doctrine distinguishes here among agrarian, industrial-agrarian or agrarian-industrial, and industrial countries. After World War II, the first group included Albania, Bulgaria, Romania, and Yugoslavia, as well as the Asian countries; Hungary, Poland, and the Soviet Union, as well as Cuba, belonged to the second group (with Hungary as industrial-agrarian); while Czechoslovakia and the GDR were the only industrial ones. Irrespective of development potential or industrial maturity, each country is impelled to install a standard socialist industrial base anchored to a strong metallurgical sector as the pace maker of rapid growth elsewhere in the economy. This base is largely patterned after the Soviet industrialization experiences of the 1930s as resumed after World War II. Through force of circumstance, the Soviet experience of the 1930s was revered as the archetype to which all socialist societies should conform.

It is difficult to understand this inflexibility in policy making without reference to the two cultures touched upon in Section 2. Soviet industrialization had been pursued as a result of political expediency and ideological transformations on the end justifying the means. True, the Bolshevik political victory in Russia sought to give the Marxian doctrine a dominant, or even monopolistic, position also in the formulation of economic policy. Nevertheless, the eclectic economic doctrine officially espoused was of little practical help in modeling economic priorities or putting in place the policies and instruments through which these priorities could be pursued. Indeed the economics of the "communist society" was something that Soviet decision makers invented on the go if only because the "scientific socialists" had shied away from detailing their precepts on communist construction informed by their basic philosophy.

The Soviet development doctrines upheld as verities for all other "fraternal" regimes were thus essentially based on practical experience, in spite of doctrinal rationalizations in theoretical discourses. Just the same, the relentless fostering of industrialization under central guidance in the Soviet Union was inspired by certain broad concepts and suggestions of the Marxian classics, whose analyses were congenial to the way of thinking in the first socialist state. The origin and key components of Soviet growth doctrine are usually expounded in terms of "development laws" to be respected and adhered to by all socialist societies. Before explaining them, it is worth our while to digress briefly and clarify the general nature of an economic law in socialist thinking.

The formulation and meaning of an economic law need to be understood in the context of the framework developed by the preceptors of communism, or borrowed by them from other thinkers, especially nineteenth-century positivism and Hegelian philosophy of history (Brabant 1980, pp. 61ff.). According to their method of analysis, a law as a cognitive concept signals a general, internal, essential, and necessary relationship between two or more phenomena of nature, the human mind, the economy, society, and so on. This nexus is presumed to be stable in the sense that it will be reproduced under identical circumstances.

26

Unlike legal principles (with their normative laws) or objective findings (as in physics), an economic law can exist only through human activity. Whereas the laws of production, for instance, are evidently everywhere the same, at least in the longer run, by themselves they are not at all laws of nature. Some are steeped in technological requirements while others depend on limitations of human capacity and psychology; or they are conditioned by the prevailing institutional, political, and ideological environment. The essential feature of Soviet development doctrine is that state socialism can dispense with the negative aspects of some laws of capitalism (such as exploitation and imperialism) and that people can and should master these phenomena of human nature in full awareness of their own behavior, which they can thus better understand, and role in historical development.

On the basis of historical materialism, Marxists regard history and all human society as inherently determined by laws that, like physical laws, cannot be altered by human interference. But the economic laws of socialism are not deterministic: Historical development, while independent of human preferences, occurs only through human activity and humans can, that is, they are free to, act according to or against these laws. Seen in an historical dimension, people will reflect these laws and benefit from knowing them by recognizing and mastering them, and acting accordingly. This is the meaning of the "freedom to understand historical necessity." Through the knowledge and recognition of these laws humans will be able to transcend isolated and in some ways superficial appearances. This is the crucial step toward comprehending the inner essence of their own behavior.

Perhaps most important is that these socialist prescriptions are considered universally applicable, regardless of palpable differences in knowledge, resource endowments, production capacities, and the like at any moment of time and over time. The latter are supposedly subsidiary, if not altogether irrelevant, to the formulation of concrete measures in observance of the basic laws of development. Acting according to these laws depends upon a recognition and understanding of historical necessity. But application of these principles to speed up historical development is quite another matter: Molding economic activity in compliance with these laws and guiding it depend crucially on the understanding, or interpretation, by the *primus inter pares* – the Soviet paragon.

The intellectual foundations of the socialist development strategy can be outlined by way of three basic Marxist-Leninist propositions on economic development: (1) the eschatological goal of historical development, (2) the material-technical foundations of this development, and (3) the means by which these foundations can be gradually solidified. A brief restatement of these antecedents may help to understand the ideological constraints under which the leaders of state socialism conceived their country's development path.

The distant, yet ultimate, objective of socialist growth is the realization of the so-called *communist welfare state*, a society in which people are rewarded according to their needs and contribute according to their abilities. Human behavior there is unconstrained by having to fend for one's own material needs or predilections. To

27

attain this stage of human evolution, even if only in a remote future, state-socialist policies must aim at as high a growth rate as possible, particularly by elaborating and extending the material and technical prerequisites of communism. The economy must therefore produce as large and as diverse a selection of products as feasible so as to meet present and future needs to the greatest extent. In the immediate postwar years, this task was understood to imply that each state-socialist economy should aim at a *relatively* self-sufficient economy. The doctrine on socialist economic development, as well as the policies designed to bring this about with targeted institutions, has as its prime objective the elaboration of a more or less autarkic economic complex. One must be clear on the concept of relative autarky.

Autarky is not synonymous with complete severance of all foreign contacts, although at one time a narrowly defined self-sufficiency was certainly immanent in the socialist concept of how best to allocate scarce resources. This was perhaps most pronounced in the Soviet Union prior to World War II. Its economic relations with the nonsocialist world after World War II, particularly at the height of the Cold War, were also highly confined. But trade among the socialist countries took off rapidly after postwar reconstruction. Nevertheless, the pivotal focus of socialist economic policy is the creation of a well-balanced, diversified industrial economy that can function relatively independently of business fluctuations and other disturbances propagated from abroad, particularly from the "capitalist world economy." Such an ambitious development goal is predicated on establishing the prototype economic complex borrowed from the Soviet Union. Using the laws of socialist development as inspiration, or rationalization after the fact, the key goal of this strategy is central steering toward balanced growth, primarily in extending industrialization in breadth, to complete in record time the material-technical foundations of socialist society.

To embark on this growth trajectory, the law of *planned proportional development* must be respected. The communist welfare state as ultimate objective will eventually be achieved, accordingly, by centrally planning, guiding, and controlling all-around growth in an orderly manner. Recall here the earlier view on the role of state power in communist ideology and how it got corrupted over time. The qualification proportional needs some clarification. The doctrine of proportional development essentially aims at attaining a high rate of growth by overcoming inherited imbalances; indeed by correcting consciously and unconsciously induced disequilibria. The mobilization of resources to unclog such new bottlenecks serves to sustain the next growth phase until the welfare state will have been achieved.

One important instance in which socialist policy makers looked to Marx for support of empirically built-up principles is the third law on *comparative growth magnitudes among various economic sectors*. Without going into the details, this third Marxist-Leninist proposition rests on the belief that the expanding economy depends critically on a characteristic increase in the "organic composition of capital," or the proportion between capital and labor in the production process.

28

It means that created factors of production play an ever-growing role in sustaining steady growth. The law holds that the first department in the Marxian reproduction scheme should grow faster than the second. The first department in this analytical approach to growth propulsion consists of the production of the means of production or investment goods. The second department refers to the production of the means of consumption or consumer goods. This third law furthermore requires that growth of the production of investment goods to augment the capacity for producing these goods should at least equal growth of the second department. Although the law does not specify it explicitly, economic policy during the first years of communist construction also ensured that consumption financed by the public sector would grow faster than private consumption. This follows from the ideological stress placed on bolstering the provisioning of public goods to the citizenry, thus strengthening their capacity to enhance the power of the socialist state. In other words, the approach at first adopted held down household consumption; in principle, it could not increase by as much as gains in average labor productivity might have warranted. Indeed, at the start of socialist construction, average consumption levels could even decline for a few years. But this proved to be acceptable only for a comparatively brief period of time and even then it could be enforced only under rigid state controls.

In focusing on the strategic precepts of growth propulsion, Marx's scheme of long-term growth articulates the Soviet stand on rapid industrialization in breadth well. Translated into more familiar terminology, the socialist growth doctrine focuses primarily on the acceleration of a few crucial economic sectors especially by injecting capital goods acquired through involuntary savings. Indeed, the socialist growth strategy reserves a central place for amassing production factors in priority sectors and appropriating most of the current "surplus value" (which is the Marxist notion for the contribution of labor to value added that is not directly compensated for) not for present consumption but for the financing of the expansion of selected production sectors, at the expense of agriculture and services in particular. Accordingly, the growth efforts of state socialism were directed especially at steadily enlarging the various sectors of heavy industry producing energy, metals, chemical products, construction materials, and machines. In this, the engineering sector received particular attention as the backbone of socialist modernization. This was pursued most rigidly during the forced industrialization drive of the 1930s in the Soviet Union and later on throughout the European planned economies.

These development principles suggest some momentous implications for actual economic policies, with repercussions for the state of affairs on the transition's eve. First, the growth strategy focuses on the most important links in the process of developing backward economies. Managers of the state-socialist economy generally opt for a dual technology. Sophisticated production methods with a relatively high capital-to-labor ratio are preferred in the locomotive sectors of the moment, while other activities receive much less attention or are operated on the basis of existing, obsolete technologies with a low capital-to-labor ratio. Priority development in selected sectors also calls for establishing large enterprises to capture economies of scale and the advantages of mechanization and automation, particularly as they appear to policy makers when major investment decisions are called for. Moreover, available equipment must be operated continuously, whenever feasible, until beyond repair as by far the larger share of disposable investment funds is earmarked for extending industry in breadth, not in depth. This strategic choice entails a predominantly *extensive* course of economic development: Growth is sought primarily from new ventures to attain eventually a "well-balanced" industrial economy. Efficiency considerations as such are not important in the determination of the structure of the state-socialist economy. This is reinforced by the chosen economic model, until the latter runs into severe obstacles and the search for more *intensive* development gets under way.

Note that the tradeoff between extensive and intensive development policies is intrinsically different for each economy. It also varies over time as economic progress is made at different speeds. That point is reached when the net return in terms of marginal value added for the last unit of expenditure in extensive activity equals the net return in terms of marginal value added from intensive activity. Because these tradeoffs vary across countries and over time, differentiated development policies would have been in order. The cost of each country simply emulating the Soviet experience in the end turns out to be forbidding.

Another implication of the strategy is the gradual improvement in the quality of human capital. The lack of an educated and solid, technically trained labor force was a severe bottleneck in the period between the two wars in the Soviet Union and later elsewhere. This can be surmounted either through formal education or by attracting unskilled labor to the factory and investing in massive training on the job. Because socialism calls for rapid development *per se* with full employment, the first alternative was initially not viable. Instead, industry absorbed labor indiscriminately, partly to lessen the capital constraint, but also because the factor was not considered scarce. This behavior admittedly entailed a wasteful utilization of labor resources. But it also enabled policy makers, especially in the more agrarian economies, to reap substantial social benefits from large-scale and diverse practical experience. Their growth could be sustained by injecting capital and labor simultaneously, thereby shifting the production locus and deferring the decelerating growth prospects likely to occur when operating under diminishing returns from factor substitution.

Arguably the most important implication, particularly for the smaller economies, is the following: The possibilities offered by foreign economic cooperation are at best poorly exploited. Although the pursuit of autarkic development, in some cases buttressed by strident nationalism, yielded rapid and historically very significant industrial expansion, it could not avoid serious contradictions and tensions. Because these were never adequately resolved, the vacillation thus occasioned cast a pall over many well-meant endeavors and impressive achievements, and hindered the full exploitation of the development potential of these countries. The lack of coordination of national growth efforts and the particular policy bias pursued emerged to a large extent from a myopic application of Marxist-Leninist precepts.

Section 4: The orthodox economic model

A growth strategy must be buttressed by an appropriate economic model. The latter comprises institutions in the narrow sense, micro- and macroeconomic policies, behavioral rules, and policy instruments that policy makers feel they require to formulate the strategy more concretely and to implement it. In other words, it encompasses all means to shape the near-term components of the strategy; to implement the strategy; to assess more or less continually achievements against targets; and when necessary to initiate expeditious revisions in current goals. Defined in such an inclusive manner, an almost limitless set of features could be highlighted to capture the model. I shall refer here only to the essential ones, especially those that bear on the starting conditions of transition and their legacies for path dependency during transformation.

When first introduced in the Soviet Union, and later in other planned economies, particularly in Europe and Mongolia, but to a lesser extent elsewhere, the economic model of state socialism exhibits the following principal features: (1) central planning in physical detail of nearly all economic decisions and restrictive regulation of the decision-making role of economic agents at a high level of centralization; (2) nearly exhaustive nationalization of capital, natural resources, and, in most cases, land; (3) collectivization of agriculture in combination with state agricultural firms, though this aim is not always a policy beacon; (4) strict regulation of labor allocation, but outright conscription remains the exception; (5) a pronounced disregard of indirect coordination instruments and associated policies and institutions for steering resource allocation whenever feasible; (6) managerial autonomy highly circumscribed by central planning and by the controls exerted by local Party and, in most countries, also trade-union interest groups; (7) channeling most economic decisions through a complex administrative hierarchy, which tends to handle matters rather bureaucratically; (8) in spite of central regulation and administration, a minimum of personal initiative must be condoned – and to some degree accommodated within the planning framework – in order to implement, let alone to fulfill, plan instructions at all levels of production and consumption; and (9) rather rigid separation of the domestic economy from foreign economic influences, regardless of partner and type of transaction.

Some of these characteristics need to be clarified briefly. For expository purposes, I shall discuss the policy sides of the model next, leaving the more institutional aspects for Section 6. This is admittedly a somewhat artificial distinction as some "institutions" of the state-socialist model embody "policies" and vice versa. Central planning as the all-embracing feature of the model amply illustrates this conundrum. Nevertheless, this way of proceeding will prove helpful when detailing the starting conditions for transition (in Chapter 2), when discussing what needs to be done in order to move swiftly toward the desired market economy (in Chapter 3), and in order better to grasp the detailed components of the transformation agenda later on, particularly the institutions of the market (in Chapter 7) and the role of the state (in Chapter 9).

Before highlighting the salient features of the orthodox economic model of state socialism I want to advance one proposition: If the model has to support crucial components of the targeted growth strategy, it is incumbent upon the leadership to adapt it as economic development alters the size and structure of the economy, thus the conditions for future expansion. It is especially important to enact timely changes in one or more of the institutions, policy instruments, or behavioral rules when key components of the growth strategy are reinterpreted by the communist vanguard. There may, then, be various reasons for reconsidering the model. These range from changes in the strategic outlook, to poor results obtained with the model in place, and to accommodate interim changes in socioeconomic or political circumstances. That provides in Chapter 2 the backdrop to the specification of the starting conditions.

Section 5: Economic policies of state socialism

In a sense, the alpha and omega of economic policies under classical communism is central planning in physical detail, and it is therefore artificial to separate its policy from its institutional bearings. In what follows, I shall nevertheless segment the two and zero in here on central planning as the overriding policy designed to implement the state-socialist modernization strategy. Whereas one could well discuss many policy aspects of central planning, I prefer to disentangle from this notion eight types that central planning as an instrument could have served in alternative modes. I shall also say something about adjustment policy, even though in principle that falls fully within the compass of sequential central planning, for it prepares the ground for the discussions of reforms with their legacies in Chapter 2.

5.1 – Centralization policy

A good part of the interrelationship between the institutional aspects and the policies of the state-socialist economy derives from the fact that, by definition, both are dominated by a hierarchical system of planning and administrative management. Central decision-making authority is vested at the apex of national political power (not necessarily the central government) to ensure a close interdependence notably between the political and economic aspects of its conception of governance, and indeed to protect social obligations if only to strengthen state power (see Section 2). But there is more to this social commitment than the end simply justifying the means of amassing power. Within that framework largely normative behavioral prescriptions are issued for all economic agents and sanctioned as such.

Centralization policy embodies a number of features, including on nonprivate ownership of virtually all the means of production (except labor, of course); on the hierarchical organization of the economy (including on the collectivization of agriculture) at a high level of centralization; on the authority to issue and channel instructions; on setting priorities and preempting many instances of producer and consumer sovereignty; and on the place of the national economy in the regional and international division of labor. Recall that centralized ownership initially takes the form of state ownership at the central, provincial or regional, or local levels. In some countries, notably Yugoslavia, this is soon replaced by notions of "collective ownership," rendering the "community" the legal owner of most means of production in contrast to having the state as owner on behalf of society. Ownership at that early stage refers to all attributes of property (see Chapter 7).

As the core of the traditional model, planning policy means selecting development targets and allocating resources to fulfill those aims to the fullest extent. The enterprise under state socialism is therefore more an engineering outfit whose entrepreneurial decisions are preempted (see Section 6). Even if management displays creative innovation, a flair for risk taking, and leadership initiative, these take at best second rank to the planning instruments and objectives set by a select circle of Party members, especially the Politburo, on behalf of the Communist Party as society's vanguard. Resources are essentially allocated by central fiat, but not necessarily by one central administration. Nor are they prescribed for all goods and services at all stages of production and distribution. Not only is this inherently impossible in such a vast country as the USSR, but also it would have been organizational nonsense to plan, for example, the production and distribution of local produce solely by the center. Nonetheless, the fiat system does indicate that all *gosplan* offices at lower rungs of the planning hierarchy depend on the central planning administration and cannot in principle autonomously resolve allocative matters.

Policy makers endeavor to formulate instructions to be translated into concrete plans so that they leave no alternative to their execution, while safeguarding a close linkage among economic, political, and social goals. For that reason, the plan assigns producers mandatory targets on inputs and their origin, outputs and their destination, pricing, wages, capital allocation, profit norms, and many other aspects of what would in any market environment as a rule be within the compass of entrepreneurial discretion. In other words, managerial behavior concerning what is to be produced, how production is to be organized, what inputs are to be used, and so on is, in principle, settled by the norms specified in the plan, not by the foresight, risk taking, and creative ability of an entrepreneurial élite. The latter's initiative and leadership, if present, are not to impinge on the priority of fulfilling physical yardsticks.

The Soviet theory of central planning, hence the leading thought behind the economic policies and organization throughout the socialist camp, crystallized as

33

one resting on quantity calculations. Ideological precepts may have contributed to spurning value planning. However, three crucial circumstances advocating the primacy of the former over the latter may have been prevalent, particularly in the Soviet case. First, centralized control and guidance of the economy are embraced to support the forcible transformation of an agrarian economy into a diversified industrial society. If growth *per se* is the objective, it does not matter much which particular sectors are selected to propel economic expansion. The pursuit of a fleshed-out, preconceived development strategy may merit the suspension or significant modification of market signals, though not necessarily without considering the cost implications of such a choice. Second, the state-socialist strategy and economic model do not take due account of a country's specific factors of time and place. Real scarcity indicators would therefore generally fail to further the central objectives. Instruments of indirect economic coordination to ensure static efficiency are too inflexible to facilitate the drastic changes necessary to bridge the gap between the presocialist and the industrial society. Static efficiency is in any case overwhelmingly subordinated to the goal of producing dynamic mutations through modernization. This is at first to result from the core heavy-industry sectors that planners and their political bosses believe to provide the foundation for solid economic expansion more or less independent of fluctuations in levels of economic activity or prices abroad. Finally, the introduction of central planning follows closely on radical transitions in political and economic power. Given the severe shortage of entrepreneurial talent in backward economies with economic responsibilities often reverting to agents who are hardly familiar with the complexity of economic administration, it may be desirable to allot only the narrowest degree of freedom to individual production units.

Needless to say, the real world of production and consumption differs substantially from this paradigm. For one thing, conscious human activity cannot be reduced to the simple act of pulling a lever. Some scope for local decision making needs to be reserved for agents because the planning center cannot possibly steer the economy in full detail. Indeed, the coordination function of the plan, while crucial, has its distinct limits. This circumstance should be recognized and reflected in planning policy. The omniscience required to formulate the ideal central plan is already unrealistic at the outset of socialist planning. It is even more so when the reality of implementation is contrasted with inflexible plan prescriptions. It is important to be clear that the limits of planning have a "time" as well as a "space" dimension. To overcome "time inconsistency," planning needs to be done on an instantaneously revolving basis. To overcome "space inconsistency," those entrusted with planning need to have at their disposal instantaneously all information required to reconcile divergent claims on limited resources. All this is clearly impossible.

Indeed, the appropriate functioning of an increasingly complex economy on the basis of coordinated directives and regulations demands that marked modifications be introduced in essential assumptions underlying the presumption that the plan can be all encompassing. In fact, the compelling logic that planners and their political mentors *must* be conscious of the limits to central planning as a rule emerges very early on in state socialism. Arguably one of its most compelling causes is that the leadership gets quickly confronted with various levels of uncertainty in economic decisions and that it is not self-evident how best to come to grips with them. This arises from the existing or rapidly growing complexity of steering an economy. It also emanates from the fact that planning is intrinsically a stochastic process, if only because activities such as international trade and agriculture depend on events that are largely beyond the scope of the information at the disposal of central planners and, moreover, beyond their control. Such uncertainty has to be mitigated either through more flexible planning or by *ad hoc* solutions formulated by microeconomic agents. Because the lower tiers of the planning hierarchy normally harbor preferences that do not fully coincide with those of central policy makers, their decisions mesh with the center's only by fluke. The plan must therefore eventually be supplemented with proper criteria for guiding the choices of economic agents according to a limited set of central preferences.

A brief focus on agricultural policy as part of the centralization aims is in order. Two broad objectives determine the organization of socialist agriculture (see Section 6). One is to do away with the traditional independence of farmers. This is not an easy matter in countries with a deeply rooted sentiment for such autonomy or where agrarian reform was introduced only shortly before the advent of state socialism or is as yet to be undertaken. Planners are keen on securing comparative independence of food supplies by ensuring that domestic capabilities meet mandated domestic needs, and in some cases generate surpluses for export to procure the foreign exchange required to import the means for implementing the industrialization strategy.

An equally essential component of the initial phases of the socialist growth strategy is the mobilization of agricultural resources in support of industrial progress. The more left-wing Soviet policy makers in the 1920s argued that the startup of socialist growth could be financially facilitated by confiscating the agricultural surplus ("primitive accumulation") as tribute to industrialization. Whether this actually financed industrialization is still a controversial topic. Beyond doubt, however, is that the sector played a crucial role in releasing labor for industrial activities during the first phase of modernization. Its salience in stepping up its net marketed output for local consumption to feed the industrial labor force and for earning foreign exchange, which in turn permitted capital imports in support of industrialization, is similarly beyond dispute. Industry financed from the budget, on the other hand, provided the means by which agriculture could be modernized and intensified; hence the controversy of the "net contribution" of agriculture. When all is said and done with state socialism's demise, the net contribution of agriculture may well turn out to have been negative. There can be no doubt, however, that its supporting role was critical during the early industrialization drive.

An integral part of centralization policy is the role of the Party at all levels of the planning hierarchy in economic, political, and social affairs. In the economy, local and regional Party administrators play a crucial role in channeling information, including on enterprises and consumers within their area of responsibility, up and down the ladder. The instrumentality of these Party levels in formulating, implementing, and streamlining centralization policy should be beyond dispute. This is true as much at the policy as at the organizational level, and I return to this salient component of state socialism in Section 6.

5.2 – Monetary policy

In a market economy, monetary policy has distinct tasks. They include currency and price stability, managing reserves, possibly issuing prudential regulations and supervising financial institutions, in most countries functioning as lender of last resort, creating a framework for appropriate credit policies and managing interest rates, and possibly financing the central budget (but not necessarily by printing money). Oftentimes, some of these functions are entrusted to the central bank (such as acting as treasury of the government, ensuring price and exchange-rate stability, providing lender-of-last-resort functions, enacting and implementing prudential regulations, and supervising financial institutions). Note that since the early 1990s in particular a trend has emerged to strengthen the independence of the central bank and have it act primarily as the custodian of currency and price stability. Bank supervision and prudential regulation, for example, can be delegated to specialized institutions. However organized, it would be a mistake to argue that such institutional independence is absolute, that is, altogether divorced from the political process, even in the country with the staunchest defense of the independence of the central bank, as in Germany. After all, the central bank *must* be involved in, and indeed support, the government's socioeconomic policies for otherwise the bank itself would be without supervision, possibly altogether beyond democratic control. This could create dysfunctional confusion in policy making.

All this is very different under state socialism. The core of economic decisions there revolves around central planning as just described. As a result, macro-economic policies typical of the market economy are rather passive or altogether absent. Monetary policy is particularly passive as the entire aim is to control transactions through the planning administration. As a matter of policy, but also organizational convenience, the economy is segmented into two monetary circuits that are only tenuously connected. One involves households, who have little monetized wealth and whose current monetary revenues consist largely of wages paid in cash and few transfers from the government. This revenue is either consumed or saved. Savings are either held in a state financial institution or, through the grey market, exchanged for foreign currency. The other flow circuit is essentially between the state and state-owned enterprises (SOEs) in the broad sense, that is, including all agents other than households and the central, regional, and local state administrations. Direct transactions among SOEs tend to emerge only with the crystallization of administrative reforms. The state uses the banking network not only as its treasury but also to enforce prompt settlement of mutual payments among SOEs and to finance mandated investments or regular production tasks, chiefly as stipulated in the physical plan. If the state's revenue falls short of its expenditure, it "borrows" from banks or authorizes money emission.

That is to say, intermediation under state socialism is based on signals rooted in administrative planning that reflect the planners' or the Party's preferences, rather than those emitted through the collective behavior of economic agents bent on pursuing their own interest. The only moderately active monetary policy is directed at ensuring that transactions between households and the rest of the economy are kept simple. This is steered through price and income policies, and indeed the center's predilections as regards assets that households can accumulate. Also, monetary control is fairly easy since the domestic economy is all but insulated from abroad. The only link in principle is through a highly centralized account for price equalization (see below) and to finance (sterilize) larger-than-planned external deficits (surpluses). First and foremost it requires political discipline. A more active monetary policy to equate household revenue plus the net change in private savings with the value of the consumer goods earmarked for distribution during the plan period is sporadically instituted to counter open or repressed inflation. This usually takes the form of a confiscatory type of monetary or currency reform.

Possessing money in such an economy does not necessarily guarantee access to goods and services – the quintessence of poor internal commodity and financial convertibility. Without appropriate provisions in the central plan and bureaucratic accommodation, enterprises cannot obtain resources or dispose of their output, or trade their assets for that matter. Households earn income largely from labor services. They are offered a limited range of goods and services in official retail outlets as per the plan with some access to "free peasant markets" and own production; later on, the second economy can be accessed as well. The range of real and financial assets is extremely confined. In short, consumer sovereignty under state socialism is severely dammed in by central policy as well as by prevailing institutions and instruments.

5.3 – Fiscal policy

In a market economy, this serves several objectives, including: (1) financing mandated government expenditures; (2) ensuring some degree of income redistribution according to the prevailing sociopolitical consensus; (3) constraining wealth differentiation such as across generations; (4) enforcing some social objectives, including discouraging consumption that is deemed socially harmful (such as drugs) and promoting socially appropriate behavior (such as low-cost child care); and (5) protecting society to some degree against foreign competition.

All this is configured quite differently under state socialism. Fiscal policies are subordinated to the general aims of the plan and social precepts on income differentiation, profits, and price regulations. In some sense, the economy is run like one giant corporation – say, CPE Inc. – with the board of directors made up essentially by a select group of Party members, usually the Politburo. As a result, most revenues and expenditures of all agents subordinated to this CPE Inc. are funneled through the central budget. Direct control is ensured, thereby obviating the need for an active fiscal policy. It is only with the expenditures and revenues of households in their transactions with CPE Inc., and indeed in their reciprocal transactions for the few permitted types of exchange, that possibly another policy with fiscal overtones is required. Since the vast bulk of household revenue consists of wages earned in the socialized sector, and independent contestation of wage norms set by CPE Inc. is rare (see income and welfare policies below), even in those relations there is not much room for fiscal policy. Only in two areas can it apply: in relations abroad (not necessarily for protectionist purposes) and in regulating socially desirable and undesirable consumption via indirect taxes and fees. The primary preoccupation of fiscal policy is with indirect taxation mainly to ensure some equilibrium between demand and supply of consumer goods and the orderly fulfillment of plan instructions by SOEs and socialized farms.

Of course, the moment CPE Inc. begins to authorize agents to pursue their "own" policies, with each having an "own" budget financed in part from its own performance evaluated by some criterion other than plan-target fulfillment, the role of fiscal policy perceptibly expands. Net enterprise revenue has now to be distributed between the budget and the enterprise, capital expenditure has to be jointly financed and hence amortized, the room for wage flexibility rises, and so on. This is better dealt with under the discussion of reforms in Chapter 2, however.

5.4 – Financial and credit policy

Credit policy is overwhelmingly geared toward facilitating the implementation of investment targets chosen by the center, regardless of how these decisions are arrived at. Capital investments are overwhelmingly financed from the budget, rather than via retained profits or funds raised in capital markets. Appropriated investment funds are allocated with minimal regard for macroeconomic efficiency. No scarcity levies are applied. Credit is issued also for interenterprise transactions, but largely on a "revolving" basis. There is little if any consumer credit.

The passivity of monetary policy is reflected in the adherence in practice, if not necessarily in theory, to basic tenets of the real bills' theory of credit. This posits that credit should reflect real flows, in which sense it becomes "productive," hence conducive to monetary equilibrium and to low inflation. Accordingly, loans are extended for well-specified purposes, granted for fixed periods of time, secured by real assets, repayable in a sense, and centrally regulated or even administered on a planned basis. In the production sphere, funds are simply made available to facilitate the allocation of resources previously earmarked in the plan. Financial assets of firms are as a rule limited to bank deposits. Financial assets of households are generally limited to cash, lottery tickets, saving deposits, and occasionally government or enterprise bonds. Especially government bonds are often floated with minimal regard for consumer sovereignty. Saving for investment purposes by households is not actively promoted. During periods of administrative reform, wealth can be formed also by purchasing housing and perhaps even small service firms; but most capital assets are withheld from households. Similarly in the case of enterprises: They are not encouraged to raise their net asset value as the budget finances investments and the plan mandates resource allocation according to precepts of central decision makers.

5.5 – Price policy

Price policies provide a case in point of the subordination of value criteria to physical targets under state socialism. Prices are not utilized for allocative purposes, except to a limited extent in relations between CPE Inc. and households, and among the latter. They are largely bookkeeping units, traditionally calculated by the center on the basis of average sectoral costs measured over some period of time without making due allowance for capital, land, and resource scarcities. They are generally held unchanged for long periods of time. This is not necessarily because the price theory derived from Marx's labor theory of value, on which core components of price policy are predicated, calls for such stability (Brabant 1987b, pp. 34–62).

There are other reasons for this state of affairs. The center disposes of inadequate information to set correct product-specific prices for all goods and services, thus complicating the process of revising prices. Also, the price stability cherished by planners to facilitate plan implementation and to guide consumer behavior by definition deters a more active price policy. Furthermore, socio-political considerations frequently conflict with the need of prices to impart timely information to producers and users. Very often such contradictions have to be resolved in an *ad hoc* fashion, including by tolerating queues or contriving "new product" prices that refer to only nominally different goods (for example, adding a button to a garment). Finally, ignoring actual and potential feedback from production and consumption too leads to the ossification of prices at their "historical" level; essentially when first introduced or upon very infrequent comprehensive revisions.

It is against the backdrop of the overriding policy priority of accelerating industrialization in breadth by means of highly centralized planning, and the control functions it permits to be discharged, that features of state-socialist pricing need to be rationalized. First, a relatively autonomous three-tier system of producer (or wholesale), agricultural procurement, and consumer (or retail) prices emerges. State socialism has, of course, other prices, such as for handicraft products and in free peasant markets, as well as related scarcity indicators, such as interest and exchange rates. I lump all of these elements together under the price label because none ever adequately reflected prevailing scarcities. Second, each price regime is steered separately through the cited policy choices and institutions (see Section 6). The disparity between producer and consumer prices is as a rule very considerable, but it can be positive or negative. This derives not only from commercial margins (such as normal insurance, handling, and transportation fees) and the government's fiscal needs. Also the room for negotiating the actual price effect of product quality and modernity further compounds the precarious relationship between retail and wholesale prices. Each price system is in fact managed largely independently according to criteria deemed suitable to reach specific objectives in the social sphere or in the sphere of plan formulation, implementation, and control. In the worst case, there is no longer any readily discernible parametric relationship between the two price levels and their dynamics. Finally, as noted, domestic price processes are to a large extent insulated from external trade, making it difficult to define the notions tariffs and protectionism under state socialism.

As a matter of policy, prices of consumer goods are normally fixed in such a way that a reasonable balance is struck between supply and demand; feedback from prices has, therefore, invariably been left at the discretion and ingenuity of production managers. Once set, price overhauls occur only at long intervals – at best the medium-term plan period – and even then they normally do not affect all individual prices. Even on the free market, particularly in peasant outlets, prices can only marginally influence production although they fluctuate due to seasonal variations and state supply policies. Consumer-price stability is a solid constant of the credo of socialist policy makers and their ideological exhortations, at least until the later phase of state socialism. Furthermore, low prices for essentials and high prices for all but a few key manufactured goods can be upheld only because of the government's subsidy-and-retail tax policies. As a result, consumers are very reluctant to tolerate any retail price change. This changed in some countries only during the later phases of administrative reforms (see Chapter 2).

5.6 – Foreign-trade policy

The foreign trade and payment regime is passive in the selection and implementation of the development strategy. An integral element of orthodox planning is the more or less complete disjunction of the domestic economy from external influences, especially in the microeconomic sphere, by means of special instruments and institutions (see Section 6). At some point, this choice may have been inspired by the fact that an ambitious growth path must be trodden without taking into account all relevant internal and external market conditions; policy makers do not make use of sophisticated plan techniques and instruments to

40

guide and control plan execution by indirect means; and growth targets are not selected on the basis of real opportunities. Interaction with other economies is compressed to the minimum still compatible with the overall development goals centered on rapid industrialization. However, for economies that cannot be autarkic because of size or resource endowment, severing domestic decision making from world-market criteria and pursuing a foreign-exchange policy that is not really a policy but a denial of access to this resource for anyone not identified in the plan or by political preferences, and even then only at a rate with a tenuous link at best to the cost of earning foreign exchange that egregiously distorts allocation, have ominous consequences.

Foreign-trade policy is also designed to ward off the transmission of un-expected influences (that is, unplanned changes) from abroad even for economic activities for which autarky cannot be pursued. This imparts a very special flavor to embedding adjustment policies in the planned economies. Familiar instruments of the transmission mechanism in a market environment – prices, terms of trade, exchange rates, tariffs, quotas, preferential arrangements, and so on – simply do not operate under state socialism in even an approximately similar fashion (see subsection 5.9).

A crucial implication of this setup is that most decision makers are unaware of or poorly informed about the real economic cost of their import-substitution policies. From the planner's point of view, this does not matter much so long as autarky reigns supreme, domestic price autonomy is adhered to, and allocative losses are borne for the sake of modernization. Once external processes are consciously exploited to improve allocation, however, it is not quite clear how best to dovetail trade opportunities with domestic centralization. This conundrum assumes particular importance once the potential for extracting the surplus from the traditional sector nears exhaustion and policy options under state socialism come to parallel those typical of market economies. But that ushers a dilemma into the debate of state-socialist control and improving resource allocation (see Chapter 2).

5.7 – Income policy

This is rather simple, designed largely to ensure that households obtain the revenue necessary to procure the goods and services that the state funnels into official retail outlets, supplemented on the margin with outlays in peasant and handicraft markets; as income control weakens, a part of income is obtained and spent in the second economy. Incomes in sectors other than agriculture, handicrafts, and some services are essentially limited to wages and bonuses, with little variation among workers or correlation with effective productivity levels. Wage rates are not, of course, identical throughout the economy. But the differentiation is rather narrow, particularly within given sectors; "scale creep" becomes a typical feature, particularly once the rule of terror eases, however. In cooperative agriculture, incomes depend on nominal profits derived from

41

assigned output and sales at fiat procurement prices. Additional revenues are obtained through sales on free peasant markets and the initially highly confined second economy. Both are regulated indirectly by the center in the sense that informal rules confine the range for tolerable price divergence, no matter the agent's resourcefulness.

5.8 – Welfare policy

It is useful to distinguish here among three goals of socialist welfare policies. One derives from the overpowering, paternalistic role of the state over the individual. Another can be traced back to the desire of the political leadership to strengthen state power, hence encourage a healthy, educated, and reasonably satisfied population for the state's interest. Finally, policy makers also harbor a genuine desire to overcome the inequities of the societies they inherit. But it is not easy to disentangle the three motives. Take health policy. A healthy population provides able-bodied workers, and may thus serve state ambitions. At the same time, socialism strives for the communist welfare state and is therefore supportive of providing basic health benefits. Centralized delivery of such services in physical terms ensures that the state reaches its goals. Similar considerations can be applied to other components of welfare policy, including education, the arts, child and elderly services, and health care more generally.

The upshot of the above is that the ratio of social-welfare entitlements to over-all income, or relative to earned wages and associated pecuniary emoluments, under state socialism is very high. Compressing these benefits, except perhaps early on in "building communism," becomes unacceptable to the population at large. Citizens in due course treat such transfers as entitlements, that is, debts of the state or political leadership to society at large. This sentiment becomes particularly entrenched when such provisions are perceived to be a tradeoff for limited political freedom (Kornai 1996a, b).

5.9 – Adjustment policy

In a market economy, such a policy is required for reasons that can be grouped under two headings: shocks from abroad and domestic disturbances. Shocks from abroad may be due to unexpected price changes or foreign-exchange crises. Domestic perturbations may stem from fiscal imbalances that are not properly financed, monetary policy that is not in line with the state of the economy, drastic shifts in household preferences, unexpected calamities, and so on.

Under state socialism, however, disturbances occur either by design or by planning error. But they are as a rule fully taken care of through the planning instruments and institutions in place. The considerable control over domestic price formation and the allocation of resources exerted by central policy makers affords the latter the tools to segment markets. Domestic markets are steered separately from the economy's involvement abroad. Foreign economic operations are broken up into those with "fraternal countries," developed market economies or the "capitalist" world, and developing countries, the latter often chosen on a preferential basis in function of ideological commitments or foreign-policy goals of state socialism. Domestic markets consist of producer and consumer sectors. Furthermore, financial aspects of relations in each of these markets are as a rule dealt with separately from real flows. Whereas communication among these various layers is not fully proscribed, the intermeshing occurs largely through other than market signals.

In principle, planners can adjust the level of domestic consumption and investment as well as the pattern of production in response to unanticipated changes in exports and imports. The foreign trade multiplier and similar foreign-trade adjustment mechanisms observed in the market context therefore either do not exist under state socialism or they operate in a very muted form. The real impact of deviations between planned and realized magnitudes manifests itself at least at the macroeconomic level. Because the budget acquires windfall gains and has to offset losses incurred in foreign trade, the price-equalization account accumulates or loses financial resources. Unplanned inflows to the budget should be neutralized. Unplanned losses may inhibit the implementation of some planned targets. The reason is simple. The presumed independence of the domestic economy from foreign influences in the monetary sphere does not mean that feasible trade decisions can be made in violation of the familiar requirements of foreign-exchange balance. Usually, planners set their export targets according to what they perceive to be the imports implied by the selected output targets (see Section 6). Any inconsistency among these variables *ex ante* requires further iterations until a feasible combination of output, investment, trade, and consumption levels obtains. A deviation from the *ex ante* targets may disturb the balance of payments. Although this can be counteracted in several ways, in principle planners try to avoid unhinging the delicate balancing involved in putting together and implementing a feasible domestic plan.

Section 6: The institutional infrastructure of the state-socialist economy

One can dissertate at length on the essential institutions and policy instruments of orthodox state socialism and on their functioning over time in the various countries. Even greater controversy exists over their ultimate importance in the overall scheme of things in the emergence, apex, and foundering of state socialism; hence their legacies for the transition. I consider here only those that are most critical in order to come to grips with the essence of the orthodox state-socialist economy and what went wrong with it, seen against the requirements for ensuring steady growth over the long haul.

6.1 – Comprehensive central planning

Given the ambition of state socialism to control economic activity in great detail, the central planning administration forms the most critical component of the traditional model. Organized in the form of a huge and regimented bureaucracy, it provides the framework for the allocation of resources by central fiat. The plan is as a rule drawn up through a limited number of iterations between the center and economic agents in the socialized sectors, possibly via ministerial or regional-planning intermediaries. Integral to this process are "informed guesses" about consumption preferences, the weather, and foreign-trade activity, especially trade that is not circumscribed by bilateral trade and payment agreements (BTPAs) or similar planning instruments. The center as a rule starts the process by setting key priorities such as on the desirable rate of growth, investment volume, total military requirements, and increases in social expenditures. These targets are distributed across the sectoral ministries, and possibly the regional planning administrations, and then coordinated with the needs and possibilities of individual economic units, possibly via lower-level planning organs.

Putting it simply, the central planning administration (patterned quintessentially after Soviet *gosplan*) or its regional variant draws up a number of material balances. A material balance is essentially a ledger sheet with input and output sides defined for a specific period of time. "Output distribution" to households, the public sector, other enterprises, inventory formation, and exports is on one side. The "input requirements" of labor, capital, energy and other raw materials, intermediate inputs, and so on (including from abroad) are on the other side. Most balances refer to the calendar year. But for some key products (especially fuels and raw materials) material balances are drawn up for the medium and long term as parts of strategic planning. This is especially important for the five-year plan, whose framework for expediting modernization assumes the power of a fetish (the so-called *pyatiletki* or five-year mentality). For some goods (for example, coal, iron, steel, oil, and gas) these balances can be kept in quantity terms. For most goods and services, however, and indeed the economy as a whole, these balances are by necessity kept in value terms.

As such, the material balance resembles a row and a column of a large, if primitive, input-output table, but without offering the latter's desirable properties for generating a coherent approach to resolving inconsistencies. For example, when an exogenously set vector of final demands cannot be reconciled with resource availabilities and intersectoral requirements, the input-output approach leaves no doubt about the infeasibility of that bill of goods. At least some of its components must be revised since technological coefficients and factor resources are presumably immutable. This is much harder to track with material balances, even if constructed meticulously for many goods. Without an algorithm for resolving inconsistencies it becomes cumbersome to reconcile material balances, and so iterations must for all practical purposes be limited to a few rounds. The final outcome is unlikely to be a coherent plan from the outset.

There are, then, three important features of the instrumentality of planning as a coordinating instrument: (1) ensuring that the planners possess the right information about resource availabilities and production capacities throughout the economy, and to some extent in comparison with world markets, even if interaction with the latter is spurned for political or ideological reasons; (2) the effective processing of that information into a coherent overall plan that is relevant for those entrusted with its execution; and (3) ensuring that inconsistencies in the original plan or those stemming from unforeseen circumstances are effectively resolved during implementation with minimal disruptive effects elsewhere in the economy; this requires informal resourcefulness. These three fundamental technical requirements, quite apart from the politics and ideology underlying state socialism, present insoluble problems to technicians and policy makers alike.

The Communist Party with its regional and local cells forms an integral component of central planning and tends to parallel the institutions of government. Local Party cells are a sort of watchdog, a caretaker of local interests, but also an expediter when plan instructions are contradictory or cannot be implemented for other reasons. The local Party "boss" can very often be relied upon to ensure that materials are moved on time because his standing depends on how economic agents in his ward perform. The Party's tentacles therefore form an important "transmission belt" not only in ideological, political, and social matters. Indeed the Party plays a crucial role also in ensuring the smooth conveying of information and when necessary in supplementing it with its own pull and push over resources.

6.2 – Enterprise decision making

Production and distribution of critical goods and services are planned in physical detail, thus severely circumscribing other economic transactions. The plan endeavors to formulate instructions so that they leave no alternative to their execution. Managerial initiative and leadership, if present, are not to impinge on the priority of meeting physical yardsticks. The same applies even more to the entrepreneurial questions pertaining to the startup of new firms or the expansion of existing ones. Such decisions are entirely a matter for planning and budget financing, even if accommodated through nominal banks in the later stages of socialist administration, as examined below.

An SOE is not really like an enterprise in the market context. Instead, it is institutionally treated as an executing unit of the planning administration. It receives its instructions from above and adheres to those instructions preferably according to the letter of the enterprise plan, provided the latter is transparent for management. The central allocation of resources through mandatory plan instructions insulates the producer sector against any disturbance that the planner chooses to neutralize. Such a plan can be fully transparent only if all the information at the disposal of enterprise managers (usually the director, chief engineer, and chief bookkeeper) is fully and accurately disclosed to the planning center and the latter reads this information accordingly. The center's prescribed allocation of primary and intermediate inputs determines by and large to what extent the SOE can hope to attain set output targets. Some degree of flexibility is built into the plan because the center is well aware that it cannot prescribe all parameters required by microeconomic agents, plan instructions are sometimes faulty, or they are outdated by implementation time. By and large, however, there is only very limited room for exploring adjustment in economic structures according to indirect economic indicators.

Passing on appropriate information about resource availabilities and production capacities from the lowest levels of planning to enable the center to draft and reconcile plans to maximum effect has been problematical from the earliest stages of planning. Political control by Party agents still imbued with ideological fervor and the threat of terror initially ensure docility and compliance with plan instructions on the part of SOE managers. But with the waning of terror and the incrementalist compromises corrupting Party discipline, managers (and indeed in many cases the local Party and trade-union cells) became more and more motivated by their own concerns.

6.3 – Efficiency indicators and resource allocation

Whatever its origin or justification, state socialism takes it as axiomatic that it must exert effective control of the economy, in particular of productive resources, in pursuit of its socioeconomic and political objectives through appropriate policy instruments and associated institutions. The accepted premise, perhaps implicitly, is that tools of indirect regulation are not dependable, in part because they elude central control. Resource allocation under state socialism therefore proceeds largely through other signals, some of which may be concealed as a result of the discretionary authority of the political leadership in the selection of priority targets, the allocation of cheap but rationed credit and critical primary inputs, and the regional allocation of resources.

Technical rules on static economic efficiency under state socialism are rather primitive, and moreover passive. The theory of planning, and its application under concrete circumstances, focuses on quantity calculations, as distinct from value planning. Ideological precepts and historical circumstances as well as economic backwardness, exiguous entrepreneurial talent, and the strong preference for extensive industrialization as *the* economic strategy (see Section 2) all contribute to this choice. In consequence, the dynamic results of economic expansion are considered far more important than securing static efficiency.

6.4 – Indirect coordination instruments and institutions – the emasculated role of prices

Market-type instruments and institutions under central planning are rather primitive and passive, thus reflecting the passivity of the underlying policies. This holds for goods and services, and even more for the allocation of production factors. Many features typical of a market economy are simply usurped by central planning. The deliberate choice to underplay value planning through the price mechanism carries over to nearly all familiar market-type instruments and institutions. In fact, the organization of the economy and economic policy are simply to enhance the realization of priority goals expressed mostly in physical terms. Other policy instruments are not to interfere with the plan's execution, although they do to some extent. Because of the critical importance of pricing in resource allocation, I focus on this here.

Socialist price policies provide a case in point of the subordination of value criteria to physical targets. Industrial wholesale prices are traditionally calculated by the center on the basis of average sectoral costs. Because average branch production costs constitute the core of all price computations, the procedure for assessing them is a crucial determinant of how "informative" the resulting administered prices can be. The basic approach is to distribute overall branch costs of live and embodied labor (that is, the administered cost of labor, capital, and intermediate products, plus some standard markups) for some past period of time over total branch output. These reference costs are at times justified with reference to "socially necessary labor expenditures." Recall that this concept in Marxist theory implies that marginal producers vacate the sector and others expand their scale of operations until in equilibrium averaging leaves nobody at a big loss or extraordinary gain. In the ideal planning environment, this structural adjustment process is controlled by plan iterations designed to yield an efficient solution. State socialism only rarely honors this dynamic requirement, however. As pure Marxian value prices, they should generate overall surplus value sufficient to fund the aggregate reproduction process. But this is not necessarily the sole preoccupation of planners. Note that in these "historical" calculations the scarcity of capital, of nonreproducible natural resources, and of land is rarely duly reflected. Initially spurned for doctrinaire reasons, increasingly bureaucratic inertia and the primacy of quantitative planning inhibit the construction of more appropriate prices. This misconception of the economic dimension of costs leads in particular to a significant downward bias in the whole-sale price of commodities with very little transformation relative to that for processed goods, especially manufactures with a small natural-resource content. Furthermore, the true cost of imports and real export opportunities are poorly reflected in administered prices. True trade results cannot be assessed because of pervasive price-equalization behavior, on which more below.

Consumer prices are, as a rule, divorced from wholesale prices by a complex network of subsidies and taxes reflecting in part government preferences. The wholesale price of consumer goods is normally set after the imposition of the turnover tax or the deduction of the subsidy from the producer price. The latter is the aggregate of the average branch cost of capital and labor as well as a profit markup. The industry price is derived from the sum of the producer price and any applicable tax or subsidy. The wholesale price is the industry price augmented with the wholesale margin, including a profit markup. Finally, the retail price equals the wholesale price plus a retail margin, including a profit markup.

Agricultural procurement prices, and indeed foodstuff prices in official retail outlets, are set differently. The strategy pursued depends on the organization of agriculture, the specific goals the government seeks to reach through its procurement, and the planning center's influence over peasant markets. The latter enjoy considerable freedom within self-policed rules on what is acceptable in the context of state socialism. There are, of course, other prices, such as for handicraft products, but these matters should not detain us here. In addition to these major dichotomies, prices are generally kept unchanged for long periods of time for rather eclectic ideological reasons, but also to facilitate plan implementation and guide consumer behavior, as discussed in Section 5.

Because average production costs are inferior to marginal costs with an upward sloping supply curve for the branch as a whole, the above pricing rule suggests that there are always firms that lose money and others that gain. This occurs not simply as a transitional phenomenon. Rather, it is a process immanent in the logic of the traditional pricing procedures. Unless firms are abandoned and new ones created to compete, this calls for the continual redistribution of value added in each sector and also across sectors. This cross subsidization is accommodated via government budgets. The actual transfer may be arranged at the central or local levels. But ultimately it is the fiscal redistribution at the central level that financially extricates loss-making firms from their predicament and ensures that profit-making firms funnel their profits to the central budget. Note that such enterprise results are manifestly *not* as a rule indicative of the underlying net worth or profitability of the enterprise in *economic*, as distinct from administrative (socialist accounting), terms. Cross subsidization may be perfectly rational in the planning context. Yet, price equalization across firms is not a convincing justification for the widespread redistribution of value added among sectors so typical under state socialism. Neither can it explain the need to manipulate price levels and relative prices with a view to generating adequate means to finance accumulation.

6.5 – Monetary instruments and institutions

Because of the preeminence of central planning, the role of monetary policy is confined, as discussed earlier, and so is the need for monetary-policy instruments. Since planners mandate the financing of development with financial intermediaries restrained to bookkeeping functions, the institutional structure of financial markets, and therefore their nature, is vastly simpler than in a typical market economy. There is as a rule a monobank, although it may oversee several subordinated agencies dealing with specific tasks. Monetary flows in the latter economy are split into two poorly linked flow circuits, as noted. One involves households, who have little monetized wealth and whose current monetary incomes consist largely of wages paid in cash and some transfers from the government (though most of the latter are made available, in whole or in part, *in natura*). This monetary revenue, possibly augmented with the monetized part of physical revenues when, in fact, transferred to other agents at a price, is either consumed or put aside. Savings are either deposited in a state financial institution or, through the grey market, exchanged for foreign currency. The other flow circuit is essentially between the state and SOEs, direct transactions among SOEs being confined to exceptional circumstances until the era of administrative reforms. The state uses the banking network not only as its treasury but also to ensure that mutual payments among SOEs are promptly settled and that mandated investments or regular production tasks, chiefly as stipulated in the physical plan, can be "financed."

That is to say, intermediation under state socialism is based on signals rooted in administrative planning that reflect "planners' preferences," rather than in the preferences revealed through the collective behavior of economic agents bent on pursuing their own interest. Because there are no independent domestic or foreign commercial banks, planners need not concern themselves with the control of their lending behavior such as through reserve or liquidity ratios or interest rates. Because credit is usually made available through the monobank in order to implement the plan, there is no secondary credit expansion in response to changes in the monetary base. Likewise, interenterprise transactions are as a rule recorded at the monobank, or its specialized agencies, with minimal credit issued except for investment purposes. That is fully covered through the central budget or by issuing "high-power money."

Another feature of monetary instruments is that there is as a rule no direct link between domestic and external transactions, whether on current or capital account. Transactions with nonresidents are centralized in the foreign trade bank, if such a branch exists, and otherwise in the external department of the monobank. Furthermore, there is no need to control the operations of international banks and transnational corporations (TNCs) because SOEs cannot independently borrow abroad, except perhaps in a strictly legal sense (such as Polish firms in the 1970s in order to circumvent US bank regulations).

6.6 – Financial instruments and institutions

I treat here financial and capital markets on a par. Capital markets as in a market economy do not exist. Surely, there are state-owned insurance companies and banks under state socialism, state bonds are issued, some limited real-estate transactions take place, and so on. But there is no stock or bond or real-estate market in the proper sense. Capital is earmarked mostly from the "surplus value" generated in the socialized economy and by mobilizing household savings. These can be voluntary or compulsory, *ex ante* and thus planned or *ex post* and thus manifested in some form of monetary overhang (see Chapter 4). As a result, planners need not worry about the prices and yields of financial assets, interest rates, their effects on expenditures, or open-market operations, or about the entire infrastructure to accommodate and guide such transactions.

The planned economy, after some years of working only with a monobank, as a rule spins off a number of branches of the monobank into one or more so-called commercial banks. State socialism may in time have a construction, investment, foreign trade, or agricultural bank as specialized agencies of the monobank that deal with particular sectoral economic tasks. In addition, there is a state-owned savings bank with a very wide network throughout the country to collect household savings. Because they fulfill a very different role from their counterparts in the market environment, they are not really banks in the proper sense.

6.7 – Fiscal instruments

Because of the planned economy's fiscal policy (see Section 5), its fiscal instrumentarium is highly confined. Income taxes are virtually nonexistent as wages and incomes are regulated by other means (see pp. 41–2). Excise taxes and subsidies are widespread particularly for consumer goods. Taxes and subsidies are also applied to trade, but mainly in order to preserve domestic pricing autonomy rather than from explicit protectionist stances. In principle, the net surplus of SOEs accrues to the government budget. This should not be confounded with a corporate income tax, however.

6.8 – Income and welfare instruments

Incomes in sectors other than agriculture, services, and handicrafts are essentially limited to wages and bonuses, with little variation among workers or correlation with actual productivity levels. In cooperative agriculture, incomes depend on nominal profits derived from assigned output and sales at administratively decreed procurement prices. Additional revenues are obtained through sales on free peasant markets and the initially highly confined second economy. Both are regulated indirectly by the center, including through moral suasion and voluntary restraints on the part of agents. Because the center, in principle, controls wages and monetary transfers, which are the primary sources of disposable incomes of households, it is a matter of indifference whether these incomes are regulated through direct income taxes or through the prescription of wage rates. In the orthodox socialist economy, essentially the latter method is favored.

6.9 – Consumer behavior

An important segment of economic activity cannot be planned to the degree the socialized sector is. Households, and consumers more generally, react to market-like signals in at least two ways. As providers of labor services they are guided by central wage controls, albeit imperfectly. Workers really cannot freely choose not to work without adverse sanctions. But they can change occupation rather freely because of "scale creep" (except during the early years of communist regimentation), decide to hold more than one job, volunteer for overtime, and determine the pace of work to some degree. But the response to incentives on the part of labor is certainly not a unique function of the labor rewards offered, as often posited in simplistic macroeconometric models.

Similarly, though planners are in principle equipped with a fully malleable wage system, their degree of freedom is rather confined by sociopolitical imperatives. Nonetheless, there is undoubtedly some flexibility that permits practical decisions based on indirect coordination instruments separately from norms set by the plan. Such incentives are not really adjusted to attract more labor when required to fulfill the plan or to ease the effective supply of labor when plan priorities call for moderating the pace of expansion. Planners set in principle the wage system autonomously. But job security and socialist egalitarianism ensure downward inflexibility of the money wage, limited room for wage differentiation, and strict bounds on the erosion of nominal wages through price changes.

On the other hand, consumers can decide with considerable sovereignty how to spend their income. Although such decisions are made chiefly in reaction to market-like signals (such as prices of goods and services and interest rates on savings), the latter are only infrequently adjusted to ensure balance in partial consumer markets. The plan aims at overall equilibrium in consumer markets, *ex ante* surpluses in some partial markets being offset by deficits in others, and households are expected to substitute accordingly. Consumers may, however, decide not to spend because they cannot find adequate substitutes at a reasonable search cost, perhaps not even in the second economy (whether officially condoned or not) or they may voluntarily save for some future purchase, possibly because of earmarked savings accounts. Their principal choice in either case is simply between cash holdings (possibly in foreign currency acquired surreptitiously) or savings in the monobank system at comparatively modest interest rates that are inadequate for proper intertemporal intermediation.

6.10 – Foreign trade and payments

The institutions and mechanisms for conducting trade under state socialism result from two experiences. One is the Soviet-type industrialization path of the 1930s as resumed after the war. The other crystallizes around the deliberate choice to shun the postwar IEOs, notably on trade (Brabant 1991b); and the failure of these countries among themselves to adopt a comprehensive, internally consistent regional economic policy in the late 1940s (Brabant 1989, pp. 25ff.) in the CMEA context. By compressing the interaction with other economies to the minimum still compatible with rapid industrialization, each country sought to isolate itself from the world economy, including its fraternal partners, in search of protection against foreign events. The dominant traits, in addition to the above, are bilateralism, currency and commodity inconvertibility, the monopoly of foreign trade and payments (MFT), and special foreign-trade organizations (FTOs) that buffer domestic economic activity against interactions with foreign sectors.

External economic relations do not form a coherent component of the planned economy. Organizationally, there is virtually complete disjunction of the domestic economy from activities abroad. This is accomplished by the nationalization of the foreign trade and exchange systems. The former resorts under the Ministry of Foreign Trade, which is in principle in charge of the MFT. This is expressly instituted to neutralize all influences from abroad, whether positive or disruptive, including with respect to "fraternal" partners, and thus to further domestic policy autonomy. It usually delegates the authority to trade to a few tailor-made FTOs entrusted with transactions by broad economic sector, by trade direction, and possibly by type of settlement currency. These purchase domestic products for export and sell imports at domestically prevailing prices. Differences between fiat domestic and foreign prices expressed in domestic currency via the official or commercial exchange rate(s) are offset through the so-called price-equalization account, which is a component of the central budget. In some cases, import levies are applied, but they play no allocative role. They are just another tax (see p. 50).

To the extent that trade cannot be forgone, in the real sphere domestic processes are insulated from direct interaction with agents abroad, the FTOs acting as buffers. If direct influences are barred whenever possible, indirect influences are minimized as well. Actual trade events can impact on the domestic economy, but usually not through price pressures because domestic prices are set autonomously. But there are possibly macroeconomic impacts of trade developments, particularly in financial magnitudes as the real economy is shielded as much as possible until matters can be reversed during the next planning period (see Section 5). BTPAs with *ex post* flexibility and autonomous pricing facilitate this state of affairs.

Price instruments constitute an integral part of the foreign trade regime to safeguard domestic priorities. The ability of planners to control their foreign trade prices is highly confined. For one thing, the strategy (see Section 2) compresses trade to the necessary minimum for ideological, political, and planning reasons. Also, these economies possess few commodities for which they command a lead position in global markets. Even in the case of the Soviet Union suppliers tend to be price takers especially in western markets. In trade among state-socialist economies, however, planners adopt an own set of price-formation principles, based on a mixture of ideology, planning needs, political considerations, economics, and others. The mechanics thereof should not detain us (see Brabant 1987b). Suffice it to note that intra-CMEA prices differ markedly from global prices as well as from domestic prices in trading partners, that they tend to be low for unprocessed or semiprocessed goods and high for manufactures, that they remain comparatively stable over long periods of time (until the end phase of the CMEA), and that they are as a rule fixed bilaterally in intergovernmental negotiations in which a whole range of considerations other than comparative advantage play a role.

Price equalization is the central instrument through which the microeconomic effects of differences between domestic and trade prices are neutralized. The size and composition of these subsidies and taxes may or may not have been planned. Divergences from planned magnitudes cannot remain without effect on the economy, however. That is to say, disturbances incurred in foreign relations, whether of foreign origin or because of domestic inability to meet planned export and/or import targets, are propagated into the domestic economy primarily through quantum variations. But these are precisely to be avoided whenever possible by offsetting actions resulting from *ex ante* or *ex post* macroeconomic decisions. In that case, the real adjustment is deferred to the next planning period (see Section 5).

The planning of the level and composition of trade, as of other economic activities, is largely intermeshed with the overall system of material balances. Whether to import or to produce domestically is usually resolved by considering domestic availability and the need to pay for imports. In any case, the central planner exhibits only a marginal interest in reaping the potential benefits of export-led growth or in minimizing the real economic cost of the preferred import substitution, even if those magnitudes could have been accurately assessed with the information and instruments on hand. Material balancing is hardly conducive to the exploitation of trade opportunities, however. Planning the geographical distribution of earmarked trade is largely a function of the home economy's need for noncompeting imports and their availability in alternative markets, export commitments and pressures, and BTPA commitments embedded in material balances. Comparisons of prevailing prices as basic inputs into trade decision making are rarely made as the price-equalization mechanism siphons off trade profits and offsets losses. Such differences are inconsequential for subsequent allocative decisions. This near-irrelevance of prices applies also to the official exchange rate.

To mitigate uncertainty in trade, managers of state socialism try to forecast trade flows as accurately as possible. Born out of necessity in the immediate postwar setting (Brabant 1973), detailed *ex ante* BTPAs at relatively stable, if artificial, prices suited the administrative planning system fairly well. It also facilitated the implementation of one or another country's political aspirations, whose realization would have been much more chancy if agreements had been concluded in a multilateral fashion or if these countries had adhered to multilateral trade, monetary, and financial regimes (Brabant 1991b).

Finally, a brief word about the CMEA as an institution and planning instrument for the underlying regional policies, if extant at all, reflect essentially the smallest common denominator of national policies on planning and foreign relations, but especially the USSR's. Over time planners develop special trade, pricing, payment, and settlement regimes for CMEA relations that differ markedly from those observed in market economies (Brabant 1987a, b). For one

53

thing, trade is conducted largely in the context of BTPAs, with bilateralism becoming reinforced over time rather than relaxed as in market economies. The terms at which such trade is conducted result from intergovernmental negotiations with product prices rarely reflecting scarcities prevailing in the CMEA countries or in the global context, and with a degree of bilateralism and structural bilateralism that permits at best small payment imbalances (Brabant 1973).

If required, credit is provided for in the BTPAs and recorded in transferable rubles within the accounting system operated by the International Bank for Economic Cooperation (IBEC). If imbalances occur *ex post*, credits are granted by the IBEC but in fact incurred by the partner that on balance fails to receive the contracted goods corresponding to that imbalance. Only in exceptional cases are transactions settled in convertible currency. The same applies to regional credits for longer-term purposes related to jointly financed investment projects ostensibly coordinated through the International Investment Bank (IIB). Both banks maintain correspondent relations with non-CMEA agents, overwhelmingly in convertible currency. Like domestic commercial banks under state socialism, however, they are not really banks. Their "planning" varies with the degree of harmony among the national plans and cooperation among governments and Parties.

6.11 – Enterprise and social organization

Unlike in a market economy, the enterprise (including related microeconomic units other than households) under state socialism has a quintessential social function. It is also selected to deliver on political mobilization. Both functions expand over time, but on balance more so for the former than the latter. In the social realm, the enterprise's obligations include facilitating work through child and nursery care, particularly to bolster female participation in the labor force. In time, however, the tasks reach further and the SOE becomes a repository of society's organization and commitment to deliver welfare, whatever the latter's motivation (see p. 42). In addition to child care, the socialist enterprise is a repository of abilities to arrange for some health care, access to holiday and resort centers, facilitation of other leisure activities, education (especially vocational training and technical schools), in-house training, housing, canteens with access to goods otherwise in short supply, and so on. The large SOEs in some countries provide in addition power and heating stations, cultural centers, stadiums, sport clubs, clinics, and so on (Dąbrowski 1996). Taken together, the cost of these provisions amounts to a marked share of the nominal take-home wage of workers. Even as recently as the mid-1990s, with depressed provisioning, the social expenditures of large SOEs in Russia accounted for one fifth of the wage bill (Freinkman and Starodubrovskaya 1996).

Undoubtedly the most important among the perquisites unrelated to actual job performance, but not the actual job, delivered by the SOE is low-cost housing. This hinders voluntary labor mobility beyond the already confining limits imposed by state socialism to a fairly small commuting distance at given transportation facilities. Workers bent on moving not only have to find a new job, but also a package of nonpecuniary benefits associated with the new workplace. In addition, the enumerated nonwage social and other benefits facilitate "organized" labor mobility. Migration abroad is either strictly forbidden or fully controlled through interstate agreements. SOE housing locks in employment. Not only does this inhibit the emergence of a real-estate market. In spite of planning, there is a chronic undersupply of housing, certainly in urbanized areas with large SOEs.

Although it may at first sight appear idiosyncratic for a firm to discharge social-welfare functions, this delegation of the state's obligation is not altogether odd. For one thing, the SOE is a "collective organization" in a triple sense. It is a basic instrument of planning owned by the state (or collectively). It is also meant to be a "collective" rather than an organ where workers simply trade their labor services for wage remuneration. Not the least, as distinct from private organizations where still permitted, it is the expression of the leadership's political preferences in a dual sense. It is a unit under state and Party control. As such it is also meant to be a vanguard for the political education and ideological maturation of a large segment of the active population, and thus designed as a recruiting ground for the Party and its magnanimous distribution of benefits not accessible to the population at large. The result is considerable social regimentation, at least outwardly.

A rationale for this policy can be found in various features of administrative planning. Organizationally, the delivery of social-welfare provisions promised by the state is thus strongly decentralized; beneficiaries can be reached directly with minimal transaction costs, which is especially important in large and less-developed countries with poor infrastructure. But it remains this only for as long as the system can be safeguarded against the eventually staggering costs of rent seeking and, in some cases, outright corruption. Furthermore, because socialist development policies appropriate resources largely on the basis of instruments other than those typical of market allocation, this employment system in principle ensures the physical distribution of many goods and services in accordance with societal precepts rather than individual preferences.

6.12 – Agricultural organization

With the exception of post-1956 Poland and Yugoslavia after the initial centralization fervor waned by the late 1940s, all state-socialist economies amalgamate land into one type or another of agricultural collective. Once restructured into this format, agriculture is exploited as an important contributor to the financing of the first stage of industrialization. It is important to be clear about the nature of agricultural cooperatives (the quintessential *kolkhoz*, though other variants emerge at various points in time). These involve nominally independent cooperative ownership of the means of production under close state scrutiny to exact the agricultural tribute. In some cases, large land holdings are first expro-priated ("dekulakization") and redistributed to the smallholder, though soon enough these lands and related resources are fused into collective exploitations, but only for a short while in Poland and Yugoslavia. In spite of the drive toward cooperatives, the longer-term aim of state-socialist organization is to transform agriculture too into the industrial-organization mode by creating equivalents to the SOE. But this drive is not enforced to its logical extent in any economy. The state-agricultural firm (the quintessential *sovkhoz*, though other variants appear) is essentially conceived like an SOE with workers earning a wage and obtaining access to perks similar to those available in manufacturing. This is in sharp contrast to the benefits accruing to the cooperants in *kolkhozy*, whose remuneration essentially depends on their own production and indeed the procurement policy pursued by the state, especially the determination of ex-farm prices. Over time, however, even in the *kolkhoz* SOE- type remuneration becomes the norm in many countries.

Regardless of whether one focuses on the state or the cooperative farm, in all economies they tend to be very large undertakings in terms of arable land, size of herds, many by the degree of mechanization, or membership. As a rule the state farms are even larger and more mechanized than the cooperatives, thus mirroring the penchant for gigantism in industry. These exploitations are essentially the main deliverers of bulk agricultural goods for export and to the domestic food-processing industry. The agricultural niche markets are increasingly serviced through the free peasant plots and the corresponding rural retail markets, including second-economy transactions. The latter's importance rises as central controls and police terror wane, and indeed as the authorities reconcile them-selves to the fact that such markets are instrumental in meeting elementary consumer needs and even private aspirations. In several eastern European countries, agricultural collectives are eventually, especially during administrative reforms (see Chapter 2), permitted to engage in other activities, usually related to food processing.

6.13 – Motivation and incentives

As examined, the central plan cannot provide the sole framework for mobilizing economic activity in a reasonably efficient manner, including by eliciting on a timely basis proprietary information held by microeconomic agents. Aside from the myriad of technical problems arising in constructing a consistent plan, two crucial variables must be mentioned. One is the exploitation of economic units other than households as automatons (sort of the ideal production technology of neoclassical economics). The other is that households as providers of labor and consumers of goods and services cannot have their behavior completely prescribed without ill effects on productivity even under the most regimented labor-procurement norms or distribution system. That is to say, individuals need to be motivated as producers as well as consumers.

Such motivation can result from various positive and negative incentives. Ideological convictions, Party discipline, or police terror may spur on some individuals to deliver maximum effort for some period of time. Prestige and power may motivate others. For most citizens as producers more is needed to coax maximum effort out of them, however. Pecuniary remuneration and emoluments, such as wages and bonuses, are undoubtedly important. But there are other incentives that can mobilize individuals to deliver their level best, such as remuneration *in natura*, recognition of a job well done by way of citation or medal, obtaining special privileges (such as shopping at the enterprise or a privileged vacation), and ultimately disguised forms of wage and income differentiation. The latter benefits are as a rule reserved for top-level management and the Party *priviligentsia* (see Section 1). It is in the nature of things that human behavior eventually perceives those benefits not directly related to work effort as an acquired right rather than an incentive to work.

6.14 – The emergence and importance of the second economy

An operational definition of the second economy is by no means easy. In essence it encompasses economic activity occurring outside the official economy. But that is not very accurate, even if the notion refers only to monetized transactions. For it would include criminal activities for which economic resources are contracted in monetary transactions. Second-economy activity encompasses such production and consumption acts that, if legally permitted and not onerously taxed, would be conducted in the open economy. But that too is not really an operational definition. These are indeed not-quite-legal activities, such as the resourcefulness of SOE managers in plugging holes in their plans, that may or may not be monetized, but almost certainly are not "taxed" in any meaningful sense. The important thing to recognize is that the unofficial economy in non-criminal activities crystallizes chiefly from two sources. One is lax control over state assets, thus permitting some individuals to appropriate resources from the state on a "small" scale. True, in and of itself that would be a criminal activity according to prevailing legal prescriptions. But it is rarely legally enforced. Likewise for activity undertaken without theft that is by definition prohibited by the state or subjected to onerous costs otherwise. This point is critical for assessing the second economy during transition, which I do in Chapter 5. The other is that such resources are utilized to produce goods and services that the official economy does not provide or not in sufficient quantities.

However defined, over time the relaxation of enforcement of state property rights, usually in the form of user rights but increasingly also usufruct rights and in some cases outright appropriation, increases and the perceived inability of the official production and distribution units to deliver the goods and services desired by consumers decreases. All this, of course, in relative terms. As a percentage of measured gross domestic product (GDP), the share of the noncriminal second economy by the end of state socialism in some countries amounted to nearly a quarter. Elsewhere it was less, perhaps 10 percent. But in no economy that experimented with reforms was the second economy a negligible proportion of overall productive economic activity. This is not at all trivial when assessing the early results of transformation policies (see Part II), including the size of the depression and the entrepreneurial ability of "postsocialist man."

Conclusions

The dilemmas of the state-socialist economy emerge very early on in attempting to reach the broader societal goals pursued under the communist banner. The centralized model as the handmaiden of state-socialist industrialization is instrumental in promoting a consistent, rapid, and radical transformation of a relatively backward agrarian economy into an industrial society. It does so largely by removing various bottlenecks to steady growth. Induced economic disequilibria and shrewd empiricism, combined with autocratic or even dictatorial control of society, may successfully stimulate structural change and rapid growth in underdeveloped countries, basically by mobilizing idle or underutilized resources as well as enforced savings. It may even help to accomplish this structural change in spite of an unstable regional or global economic environment, initially domestic strife over sociopolitical organization, inexperienced management, a labor force unaccustomed to the industrial production mode, a burdensome agrarian overpopulation, and other impediments. As the economy progresses and becomes more complex and diverse, however, the informal pursuit of disequilibria as channels for identifying the next "growth locomotive" becomes a costly and inappropriate approach to steering sustainable high growth. In the more developed countries, the outcome measured in terms of sustaining the hoped-for significant pace of expansion over time was quite disappointing.

Dissatisfaction on the part of central decision makers, of the managerial élites and their immediate supporters, and indeed of households as providers of labor and as consumers with at best slowly rising, egalitarian levels of living sets the stage for seeking economic reform. The leadership of state socialism soon finds itself saddled with several dilemmas: limits on the absolute volume of available resources, distributional conflicts between consumption and investment and in intersectoral allocation, unrealistic goals, organizational mismanagement, and difficulties of coordinating decisions for a more complex economy with the institutions and instruments at hand. Competent managers and élites too become quickly disenchanted with state socialism, if only because the "system" holds them responsible for "their" failures but as a rule does not really reward them properly materially or otherwise; it certainly allows them little room to display their capabilities, perhaps even out of ideological commitment. Finally, households as consumers and workers are unhappy with the lack of choice in consumer markets and the harsh conditions of work that do not generally reward labor according to its real contribution to output. Many instances of well-being evident in western Europe remain far beyond the reach of the eastern consumer. The outcome is paradoxical: The benefits that state socialism imparts to society at large are increasingly being taken for granted and gratification of economic ability is sensed to lag well behind the minimum incentive required. As this paradox is increasingly brought into the open with the waning of state terror and censorship, the social conflicts over adequate provisioning and distribution gain momentum.

The culmination of these dilemmas, and gradually of more open conflicts, finds its reflection at first in internal soul searching: Reforming the state-socialist system to preserve it becomes the motto certainly of political leaders and their sycophantic supporters. Growing acquiescence on the part of the other partners identified in giving the regime yet another chance at proving its worth provides a temporary breathing space for political and organizational maneuvering. The treadmill of administrative reforms becomes engaged, but with divided and mixed enthusiasm, and even apprehension, on the part of nearly all concerned.

2

REFORM TINKERING AND THE STARTING CONDITIONS OF TRANSITION

The essential features of the state-socialist economy and its ideological back-drop underwent various modifications over time, right up to the transition's eve. I discuss the most important generic administrative reforms. Once that is accomplished, I draw a summary of the starting conditions for transition and the difficulties ahead with swift economic transformation. Of course, the outcome of transformation in any economy is conditioned by much more than the economic and political environment. Indeed the behavior of the individual economic agent when suddenly entrusted with more encompassing responsibilities than under state socialism must be taken into account. But I cannot provide a philosophical or sociological discourse on these societies.

There are various ways in which one can legitimately proceed. I first look at the reforms pursued over nearly thirty years in most state-socialist economies in an attempt to improve efficiency. From that discussion, as well as the prevailing features of policies mainly during the second half of the 1980s, I draw next the economic-policy dilemmas and macroeconomic imbalances on the transition's eve. These form an essential backdrop to grasping the starting conditions of the transition inaugurated in one country after another, beginning with mid-1989, as well as to the formulation, adoption, implementation, assessment, and fine-tuning of the transformation agenda. Thereafter I engage in a brief discourse on the reasons for the collapse of state socialism. This is followed with an examination of four dimensions of the transition's starting conditions: the "institutions" in place; the ideology that is being expunged, but in some countries only perfunc-torily; the legacy of the policies recently pursued with their objectives spelled out; and an evaluation of the realization of these projections. In the course of this exploration I emphasize the specific circumstances analysts should watch out for when identifying the conditions prevailing in any one economy about to embark on sweeping restructuring. Country detail I can of course provide only by way of examples that impart a flavor of the complexity of the most relevant features of systemic transformation policies.

Section 1: The treadmill of administrative and organizational reforms

In view of the peculiar organization and of the deeply rooted Marxist-Leninist ideology, reform of orthodox state socialism is a complex adventure. Even if inaugurated as a strictly technocratic economic change, thoroughly justified within the context of the prevailing ideology, once under way the reform movement affects virtually all dimensions of society, including its ideological base, its political framework, and indeed society's dynamics, unless all too prematurely aborted. It also tends to spill over into the fraternal countries. Even its principal features are rarely restricted to economics, if only because modifications sought in economic behavior, such as through price and wage stimuli, are bound to affect social attitudes and the more general comportment of economic agents. Likewise, whether successful or not, reform experiments leave dire legacies for the transition's leadership. But here I address chiefly the economic tangents of evolving state socialism.

It is important to be conversant with the salient differences between the economic environment envisioned in reforms and that presently targeted by transformation policies. But it is also instructive to bear in mind what went wrong with the reform experiments. All too often the state-socialist economy is said to be inherently unreformable if sustainable growth is to be regained. Otherwise, it is asserted, state socialism cannot adhere to its broad ideological commitments, as distinct from clinging to political power. I disagree with this sweeping assessment. But I cannot detail the full argument (Brabant 1980, 1987a, 1989, 1990) as I am here chiefly concerned with the key ingredients of the generic economic reforms pursued with various degrees of intensity since the early 1960s in order to contrast them with the generic transformation agenda.

1.1 – The reform setting

Economic reform under state socialism aims at enhancing the way in which resources are allocated with the goal of satisfying present and future, private as well as social, needs better than heretofore. It is usually triggered by the emergence of palpable macroeconomic imbalances and the ensuing ideological, political, and technical soul searching. As a rule, a marked slowdown in the pace of economic performance over some period of time, perhaps even a recession, in combination with one or more severe macroeconomic imbalances, provides the backdrop to reform tinkering.

A reform's salient features may range from the philosophy of development policies to revamping, or upgrading, economic institutions and technical guidelines for economic behavior, notably in the microeconomic sphere. Its envisioned compass may extend from changing human psychology all the way to reengineering the nuts-and-bolts of the planning institutions and instruments designed to ensure macroeconomic coordination. Basically some variant of

61

central planning with a widespread bureaucratic administration is maintained. But supplementary policies and instruments are wielded to improve economic coordination and restore economic balances. This entails some modifications in the perception and assessment of economic rationality and efficiency under state socialism. Note that economic rationality typical of a market economy is not necessarily congruent with that held by the political leadership of state socialism. Notions such as profit, real scarcity, cost, market, and material reward in a market environment cannot be transposed to the state-socialist economy, however reformed, without major qualifications.

At various stages of the economic reforms, also the notion "economic mechanism" surfaced. That too encompasses changes in the orthodox economic model, but of much greater depth and breadth. As a rule it aims to establish new institutions and policy instruments, and transform their application, either to replace or to complement the existing policy environment. It also normally targets more active monetary, financial, fiscal, trade, price, and income policies. It furthermore reserves a more prominent place for indirect coordination instruments and institutions, but still within the overall context of state-socialist administration. Even so, the detailed nature of the central plan and the over-whelming hierarchical structure of the "planning mechanism" undergo incisive modifications. This holds especially in the links – organizationally but also in the real sphere – of the domestic economy with economic processes abroad, especially with market economies.

Virtually every single reform launched prior to 1990 is sought in response to acute social and political concerns and altered societal precepts. These issues as well as economic preoccupations should therefore best be tackled holistically. Unfortunately, once the dominant ideology of state socialism was firmly implanted, few leaders were ever prepared to look at society as an organic whole and tailor reform programs accordingly (see Chapter 1). As a result, reform blueprints never address society's ills in a single, coherent approach. Even those conceived in a fairly comprehensive technical economic and organizational framework are never fully carried out either in spirit or according to the legally sanctioned formulation. This applies to the industrialization strategy and especially the unavoidable repercussions of model tinkering for the strategy as such. Thus although some changes in the development strategy away from rapid industrialization in heavy industry are embraced in the process, piecemeal changes in the administrative-organizational aspects of the centralized model constitute the alpha and omega of the first wave of reforms in eastern Europe. Strategic shifts occur also but primarily in response to circumstances rather than as a well-thought-out approach.

1.2 – The timing of reform

The process of change was stretched over some thirty years, albeit with varying degrees of intensity and with many setbacks. Alternative ways of improving economic performance, notably as a means of moving from "extensive" to "intensive" growth, are explored. Some start soon after the centralized economic model was installed in eastern Europe, already in the late 1950s, and the extensive growth strategy (that is, generating sustainable growth largely from net additions to factor inputs) runs into severe bottlenecks. These are not just failures to meet growth expectations. Also consumer needs as officially prescribed (or promised by the political leadership) or, in some cases, as demanded by the population at large, cannot be met. At the latest by the early 1960s, or the end of the second industrialization wave in eastern Europe proper, reform experiments begin to be launched. By then it is clear that the centralized model is not particularly well suited to bolstering gains in factor productivity as distinct from raising output primarily by augmenting factors of production.

As a result of this evolution over such a protracted period of time, all state-socialist economies, except perhaps the Asian ones and to some degree Albania's, get somehow modified. The decision to tinker in major ways with the economic model in particular signals the start of a process that eventually lets administrative planning degenerate into bureaucratic behavior. More often than not the outcome is most conspicuous in the instrumental relationship between the leadership and economic agents, rather than in regaining growth or in imparting a stimulus to improve resource allocation along economic (that is, real scarcity) criteria. Pervasive bureaucratic bargaining between SOE management and their ministerial planners, and in some cases laterally among large SOEs or their associations, rather than strict control from the top down, becomes the dominant organizational trait in most countries.

It is important to be aware of the concrete setting for reform and its time dimension, even under the best of circumstances (say, minor macroeconomic imbalances, widespread sociopolitical support, and a comprehensive blueprint to which the leadership is committed). Because changes in the economic model must start from the policy instruments and institutions in place, an economic reform is by definition an evolving process. Gradual maturation is required to formulate and anchor the necessary laws and regulations. A certain degree of experimentation and fine-tuning is almost inevitable. Time is also needed to elicit even minimal attitudinal changes in economic agents. Exhortation may work in some cases. But workers and consumers change their behavior largely in response to more tangible incentives. Similarly, incentives must be innovated to ensure that the behavior of economic agents can suitably be coordinated at the macroeconomic level. That requires, among others, an appropriate monetary policy, perhaps assisted with a real fiscal policy; shifts in the financial infrastructure so that effective intermediation can emerge in support of enterprise decentralization; a reorientation of trade by commodities and trading partners to capitalize on prevailing comparative advantages and indeed to identify new, dynamic ones; and modulating the behavior of managers, workers, and households through material and other incentives.

Any reform discussion has to heed the environment in which state-socialist planning arose and evolved (see Chapter 1). The orthodox model was in place in the USSR from the late 1920s to the early 1940s and then once again, as well as in eastern Europe, from roughly the postwar reconstruction phase in the late 1940s at least until after Stalin's death. Following a brief interlude in the eastern part of Europe and a temporary easing in the Soviet Union, the second industrialization wave inaugurated after the 1956 events within the context of the orthodox model lasted well into the first half of the 1960s. Various attempts at recentralization and forced industrialization, this time through imports and foreign borrowing, were launched in the 1970s too. They had, however, dire consequences for macroeconomic balances and the ability of the political leadership to deliver on their overt or tacit social commitments.

1.3 – Types of reform

The state-socialist model has been the subject of nearly continuous modifications of major or minor dimensions. Minor modifications are introduced in order to fine tune certain production, distribution, consumption, income, or trade norms and regulators without changing substantively the basic features of the model in place. Major changes signal economic reform. But in practice there is no neat distinction between the two. In fact, they may occur simultaneously. Even when reform can be unambiguously identified, it is a considerable simplification to speak of the first or second or third wave of economic reforms, or to associate a reform with any particular date without making it crystal clear what precisely is meant. Three generic types may suffice to set the stage for a discussion of the variants of the orthodox model: (1) the selectively decentralized model aimed at in the 1960s, though there were striking differences among the blueprints and even more among the changes actually wrought; (2) the modified centralized model that came about after the reversal or interruption of the reform attempts of the 1960s; and (3) the decentralized planning model envisaged in several eastern European countries and partially implemented in some during the 1980s.

Though reform experiments focus in particular on modifications in the organizational model, in some respects they also affect the development strategy, once the bottlenecks with highly centralized economic administration become all too glaring. Various substitute models are proposed and many different experiments enacted. None succeeds in the end. Of course, none ever harbors the ambition of the transformation presently under way. Perhaps most important is that virtually all reform concepts acted upon without exception failed to address the core of economic decision making and coordination. Instead of pursuing the embedded logic of economic decentralization and providing appropriate incentives, these countries invariably retain the major features of central administration of the day-to-day affairs in macro- as well as microeconomic spheres; in some cases only a part of this centralization is replaced by the cited variants of bureaucratic bargaining. Genuine decentralization steered through dovetailed macroeconomic policies, with their supporting instruments and institutions, is never targeted. Apprehensions rooted in ideological convictions about the ability of market-oriented decision making to yield the desired output profile may furnish one argument. Also pervasive lack of confidence on the part of the leadership in its own ability to guide spontaneous forces within a coherent macroeconomic framework of its design and under its overall control can be held responsible. This provides one critical legacy for the transition (see Section 4).

It is important to be aware of the distinction between reforms in eastern Europe (except perhaps Albania) as contrasted with those of the Soviet Union and of Yugoslavia since the early 1950s. Furthermore, within eastern Europe, it bears to distinguish between the vanguard reformers (notably Hungary and Poland) and others, where experimentation remained confined (such as in Bulgaria, the GDR, and Romania) or ambitious reform was nipped in the bud through outside policy intervention (as in Czechoslovakia). Finally, even in the most tepid reform in eastern Europe (again excepting Albania), unlike in the USSR until the first debates about *perestroyka*, efforts to improve the systems are most conspicuous in external links. Reforms in other countries with state socialism are better treated in Part II.

1.4 – The selectively decentralized model

Selective decentralization is the objective of the reforms launched especially in the 1960s. The prime goal is to modify managerial behavior as well as the structure and extent of incentives in view of the growing complexity of detailed physical planning for a fast-maturing economy and considerable shifts in the external commercial and political environments. These reforms encompass in some respects fundamental transformations in the organization, the infra-structure for decision making, the habitual policy instruments, and some of the supporting institutions of the centralized model.

Although by no means quite uniform, the selectively decentralized models exhibit common transformations in policy instruments and some of the support-ing institutions of the centralized model. They focus nearly exclusively on engineering a more pragmatic division of administrative and economic duties between the center and local planning tiers, including SOEs. Almost without exception, firms are absorbed in or brought under the authority of much larger economic associations. Devolution emerges in the sense that ministries or central administrators no longer vie to determine unilaterally enterprise policy. The associations are invested with the responsibility of guarding the "social interest" of the firm. But the separate units obtain greater latitude in the formulation of an appropriate enterprise policy as well, by facilitating local decision making on the basis of cost-benefit analyses and in recognition of market preferences, especially with regard to foreign economic interactions. Selective decentralization aims at elevating foreign trade to a crucial activity in propping up domestic growth, which itself is guided by and harmonized with domestic decision making.

To face up to the multiple opportunities in domestic and trade sectors, various ways to stimulate more efficient trade relations are explored without, however, completely abandoning policy autonomy.

Foreign-trade reforms as a rule affect four areas: (1) price formation, price levels, and relative prices, possibly including a more effective link between domestic and external markets by setting surrogate exchange rates; (2) the central regulation of trade largely on a macroeconomic basis; (3) the specific operation of the MFT, which finds itself being strengthened and weakened at the same time; and (4) the promulgation of links with foreign firms through some variant of industrial cooperation, including joint ventures. Although the various measures resorting under these four headings are loosely connected in partial reforms, innovations in the trade sector are intended to be harmonized with each other and with internal changes in countries coveting more comprehensive streamlining.

In spite of these ambitions and the measures actually enacted, the basic philosophical precepts on central regulation of the economy are kept intact. This holds for the broad goals of extensive growth and the domestic core of the traditional model. In other words, the selectively decentralized model retains central planning and its administrative machinery and aims largely at administrative streamlining. SOEs can now influence to various degrees the formulation and/or the implementation of the central plan. Associations are called upon not only to embrace measures that facilitate attainment of centrally prescribed targets, but also to set and modify some of the norms previously dictated by central fiat. The number of directive plan indicators is generally significantly reduced. Material balancing is confined to essential products. Gross output measures are replaced by other control levers such as sales, net output, profits, net export revenues, and so on. Material incentives are attached to other plan targets. In some cases, they are formally associated with actual values of the aforementioned success indicators through norms on the permitted level of incentives. These are in principle set annually for each type of economic agent through a complex administrative decision process, basically for lack of a sufficiently flexible price system.

The logical outcome of the most ambitious reform, had it been carried to fruition, would have enabled central planning to guide and control microeconomic decisions by indirect means, leaving detailed choices as regards how much of what the SOE should produce with given resources up to genuine firm decisions guided by qualitative and quantitative macroeconomic policies. The latter should have enabled the center to ensure that the gap between the precepts underlying the central plan and the motivation of agents entrusted with day-to-day local planning and decision making would not grow into an abyss. There might have been some continuing need for the associations but their role in formulating SOE policy and appraising performance would by necessity shrink ultimately to the purely administrative intermediation between the center and autonomous economic agents. At the same time, by disengaging itself from some of the detailed chores of instructing production units, the center should have formulated strategic decisions on the basis of longer-term planning for structural change and productivity gains. Within that framework, selective indirect co-ordination instruments should have guided shorter-term enterprise activity.

In the process, SOEs obtain more authority, though by no means the exclusive right, to determine premiums, basic salary scales, the hiring and firing of personnel, and so on to foster productivity. They begin to be entitled to influence costs directly through a more careful selection of inputs and suppliers, by producing according to market demand, and even by using their authority over price formation. Profit is slated to become a more meaningful category, especially to determine premiums and social benefits to workers, to generate internal finance, and to guide entrepreneurial behavior. Exclusive authority cannot be delegated to enterprise managers because the objective of full employment and the broader social aims of state socialism remain vital ingredients of overall policies. Instead of many detailed prescriptions with regard to employment and wages, there is a tendency to confine controls to a few norms and indirect regulators. But this is not a linear, unidirectional process for it is interfered with and, after some experimentation, prematurely abrogated.

When economic decisions are no longer the exclusive prerogative of the central planner, and the compass of involvement in foreign trade and finance is widened, the task of coordination becomes more urgent and complicated in comparison to simply dovetailing physical yardsticks. Other coordination policies, institutions, and instruments must therefore be developed. Among this arsenal, typical commercial-policy instruments such as customs duties, more active exchange-rate policies, explicit quantitative restrictions, more realistic pricing, and so on are eventually to be addressed. Arguably the most pivotal of the coordination instruments and policies in urgent need of improvement is relative prices in the broad sense, including by linking the various domestic price tiers and the latter with trade prices. Establishing wholesale and retail prices that are indicative of relative scarcities prevailing in the economy, relative to both domestic and external indicators, may act as the fulcrum for reforming the entire economic mechanism. But loosening the stickiness of the price regime, improving the information content of prices, and forging a better link between domestic and trade prices should not be equated with freely fluctuating prices.

Liberalization of the price regime means that early on in the reform prices are reset roughly in line with prevailing production costs, if only to reduce subsidies and attain the desired level of profitability for different branches of the economy. However, comprehensive price revision by itself can move prices closer to under-lying costs only with a more appropriate computation of average production costs. Even if the latter are properly assessed, planners need to maintain prices in line with real or perceived scarcities on a timely basis, at least intermittently. Nonetheless, greater flexibility in administrative price formation, either by central recalibration or by delegating some authority over price formation to the lower planning tiers, but with considerable ideological and political shackles, is aimed at so that prices continue to convey meaningful information to the plan executors.

With respect to the information content of prices, all countries gradually feel compelled to make room for a more active role of prices, even if set by central fiat, in regulating production and distribution. Although prices never fully reflect true scarcities, they undoubtedly are moved closer to actual production and import costs. In some cases they even react to changes in supply and demand. Elsewhere most prices continue primarily to be parameters that transmit orders from the center to the lower planning units and are utilized for accounting and control purposes. This, of course, begs the core question: To what extent can such prices act as guidelines for enterprise decisions? It may well be the case that firms have no direct control over price formation, although they are expected to react to the parameters issued by the pricing authority. These may or may not reflect somewhat better the true scarcities of capital, land, natural resources, and foreign currency at the time of their introduction. In a few countries, prices provide feedback on the state of product markets to central policy makers and firms or their associations dispose of some authority to revise prices from time to time in response to cost changes.

Even in countries where price adjustments become a nearly continuous process, such movements are permitted only within preset margins that are fairly rigidly controlled through administrative channels. Three generic price types come to the fore: administratively set prices as under classical state socialism, market-determined prices (but subject to a vast array of informal controls), and prices whose flexibility is bounded from below or above, or both. The countries that allow such partial flexibility, in the first place Hungary, normally commit themselves to broaden the scope for periodic price adjustments. The category of centrally controlled prices should shrink in favor of the "from-to" group and, to a lesser extent, of freely fluctuating prices. But this planned evolution is only rarely adhered to for practical reasons. Retail prices are also modified in principle to ensure approximate balance in consumer markets and to hold inflationary pressures in check. The process is not entirely devoid of administrative arbitrariness, however, as resource allocation does not generally proceed according to true scarcity values. The subsidization of prices for most essential goods and services, as per the countries' preferences, becomes more and more onerous over time.

Prices are by no means the only coordination instrument to be overhauled. Extensive use of selective fiscal, credit, and income policies aimed at inducing firms and households to act in accordance with overall plan objectives is fostered too; but largely as a supplement to, not a substitute for, direct control over key economic processes. Note that even in the most market-minded economy the envisaged selectively decentralized model typically entails significant, if perhaps concealed, elements of nonprice resource allocation. Most might have been intended for the short run. But subsequent events, and efforts launched to combat the perceived adverse consequences of reform, tend to inhibit their anticipated removal. Even if the latter occurs, preferences of the ruling political and administrative élites continue to enjoy a disproportionate weight. The link between imbalances and price movements in most reforming countries becomes somewhat more transparent, but more so when prices can move within overall boundaries. External imbalances as a rule cannot be transmitted to the domestic price mechanism because of the continuing focal role of the MFT and price equalization, even though that is now practiced with greater circumspection. However, in the trade-dependent countries policy attention is focused on the degree to, and the speed with, which real trade costs are reflected in domestic prices. For that purpose pseudo exchange rates are adopted and trade results factored more completely into price recomputations. Very few, however, allow trade results to influence domestic prices directly, even if economic agents in the process obtain latitude in generating individual product prices.

A sharp distinction should be drawn between using trade results in domestic resource allocation and in profit calculations. The former is introduced in an attempt to motivate producers or traders to promote the streamlining of selected types of trade contracts. But SOEs are not necessarily entitled to pass on real costs. So their decisions on matters not covered by the plan are perforce reached on the basis of what appears to be profitable from their point of view. Naturally, this coincides with socially profitable decisions only by fluke. Although trade prices undeniably exert a growing influence on domestic prices, the price system in most economies, on the whole, remains relatively inflexible until the very end; but more so for consumer than for producer prices. For the former, various subsidies and taxes buffer domestic prices against socially undesirable changes in the cost of living. Though ensuring a high degree of stability, the rigidity inherent in setting administrative prices comes into sharp conflict with the desire of planners to utilize prices as one of the key allocation levers at all levels of decision making.

A greater role is accorded to money and finance. Budget financing of investments in existing SOEs, except for major expansion, is as a rule replaced by retained profits and bank loans for which the borrowing SOE is in principle responsible; also some consumer loans for durables begin to be issued. Central authorities closely supervise bank financing, however. But they do utilize interest rates as a means of allocating funds with somewhat greater rationality than under the orthodox model. Key investment decisions, such as financing new factories, remain the exclusive prerogative of central authorities so that they can foster the development strategy, however. In some countries, more flexible use of interest rates, credit, and fiscal levers is enforced through greater differentiation. Furthermore, retail and wholesale trade networks are improved to service consumers and to facilitate the transmission of some of their preferences to producers. But retail-price flexibility and enterprise autonomy fall well short of the minimum required to ensure timely adjustments between demand and supply in individual markets. None of the reforms envisions the creation of autonomous financial or capital markets in which local or foreign agents can mobilize voluntary savings.

Note that the above reforms are conceived and pursued largely independently of each other. Not only that, the intellectual ferment around these reforms is poorly linked to the policy debates at the CMEA level. This is facilitated in part by the measurable increase in the room for east–west trade and cooperation, beginning in the mid-1960s. Given the paramount role of trade considerations in the panoply of reform measures, raising trade dependence and rationalizing trade by partners and commodity groups are usually high on the policy agenda. One may therefore surmise that the reforming economy becomes less protective, certainly after some hesitation. But it is hard to verify this conjecture by simply examining differences between domestic and trade prices, either in comparisons over time or across economies. There can be little doubt, however, that even the most reform-minded economy continues to demonstrate a substantial proclivity for protection.

1.5 – The modified centralized economic model

The modified centralized model emerges in response to the abrupt halt of selective decentralization in all economies, except Hungary, at the latest by the early 1970s; even Hungary's reform pace slows down markedly, and is reversed for a while, with key components of its envisioned "mechanism" remaining on the drawing board for close to a decade. Some of these derailments are due to sociopolitical concerns. Others because the hoped-for stimulus to factor productivity fails to materialize. The initial attempt to rectify the situation is by way of reverting to central resource allocation, reducing the autonomy of firms, curbing the flexibility of decision-making instruments, and sanctioning other retreats from selective decentralization. The resultant modified centralized models retain essential features of the MFT's transformation; in some respects, these efforts are strengthened in marked contrast to the abrogation of the more domestic reform components.

There is, however, no return to strict central planning. For one thing, the original motives for streamlining economic organization do not evaporate with the abandonment, downsizing, or curbing of selective decentralization. Particularly important in this regard are the challenges emanating from the felt need to boost factor productivity, to provide sufficient resources for consumption, and to finance economic modernization. Those explain why major and minor aspects of this modified centralized model are revised rather frequently, chiefly to combat actual and emerging imbalances. In searching for an appropriate positive adjustment strategy, especially payment problems with market economies play an instrumental role.

The modified centralized economy explores other means than indirect coordination to attain its goals. Two are important. First, many policy makers view the crystallization of east–west détente as a signal to import technology, if necessary by borrowing in capital markets. The second path taken by some countries consists of resolving in an *ad hoc* manner the question of how best to reconcile output maximization with certain rules and regulations on input minimization when the coordination mechanism is exceedingly incomplete. This applies to experiments in bureaucratic decentralization in virtually all countries that earlier had made intermediate economic units responsible for their own decisions. The control hierarchy of the recentralized model, though reshaped, is essentially kept in place. The only exceptions occur in Czechoslovakia in 1967–8 and in Hungary since 1968.

In some countries, this central control proceeds with changes in coordination mechanisms and institutions, including the administrative regulation of price changes. Though still under political control, frequent price revisions and changes in enterprise profit tax rates are enacted to reflect modifications in macroeconomic policy and the gradual moving closer toward genuine micro-economic decentralization. On the whole, however, partial recentralization is replete with hedges because no country passes the experimental stage or policy makers resume the on-off partial reform cycle pursued earlier. As already indicated, this modified centralized model tends to be unstable. Major and minor aspects are revised rather frequently in response to domestic and external economic events. Emerging imbalances in domestic service sectors, in supplies of raw materials and fuels procured from CMEA partners, and in the external-payment situation of several countries in relations with market economies, play an important role in launching a search for an appropriate positive adjustment strategy.

This is especially pronounced in foreign sectors, for which many SOEs retain the right to engage in trade directly and the link between domestic and trade prices is not entirely severed. It is strengthened through the creation of surrogates for exchange rates that influence at least the accounting of firms engaged in foreign transactions. At the policy level, this stance is affected by two seminal events. On the one hand, efforts to bolster socialist integration and regional inter-action are explored with determination. Renewed interest in regional integration surfaces at first from the forceful abrogation of the first reform wave through political (Soviet) intervention and resentment about the failed earlier search for laying a firmer foundation for genuine regional integration. Regional economic cooperation is to be strengthened also because trade and economic cooperation abroad, in spite of partial recentralization, are expected to impart a rejuvenated impulse to growth and factor-productivity gains. Against the latter backdrop of aspirations, an all-out drive is launched to upgrade production facilities by importing complete technologies especially from the industrial economies with financing made possible through the oil-surplus recycling by large commercial banks.

Though the period is directly related to the difficulties encountered with the effective interlinking of the member economies, the results remain meager. Indeed the loose integration-policy blueprint endorsed in the early 1970s with its convoluted, certainly ill-defined, strategy for forging ahead focused neither the minds of policy makers nor economic activity. Even modifications in this integration approach, taken largely in response to tightening supply constraints in the region and also in east–west relations beginning with the late 1970s, fail to change matters. Ultimately, what materializes at the CMEA level, at least until about 1985, reflects very much the rather conservative reform attitude of Soviet policy makers as well as, by the late 1970s, the growing concern in virtually all CMEA members on how best to overcome a variety of unanticipated domestic and external constraints on short-term policy flexibility.

1.6 – The decentralized economic mechanism

Finally, effective decentralization and coordination of decisions including through indirect policy instruments and institutions, in contrast to the simple devolution of administrative authority typical of earlier reforms, is resorted to by few economies. The selectively decentralized economic mechanism in Hungary is the culmination of a protracted effort with many vacillations. In Poland, it emerges hesitantly after the drawn-out societal crisis, following the rise of *Solidarność*. In some other countries blueprints are drawn up. Some are haphazard, however, and others simply fail to take off. Their emergence is as a rule associated with other, more or less radical societal mutations, especially *perestroyka* in the Soviet Union; but these I do not consider here.

Economic decentralization aims at curbing administrative guidance in determining output, resource allocation, and the distribution of incomes; eventually it should be abolished. Medium-level control agencies are either suppressed or transformed into the central management of nationwide SOEs. The remaining firms are formally released from their administrative subordination to the state administration. Strict plan targets and physical norms are replaced by general requirements to satisfy domestic demand, to meet obligations contracted abroad by the state or firms, and to achieve satisfactory export performance in world markets. Centralized resource allocation in some respects is to be complemented, but not generally replaced, by market-type transactions in the means of production. But the latter remain highly monopolized and strongly controlled by the state. Though SOEs are still under political control, frequent price revisions and changes in enterprise profit-tax rates are enacted to reflect modifications in macroeconomic-policy stances and the gradual movement toward genuine microeconomic decentralization.

Entrepreneurial activity is coordinated through market-type economic links rather than through vertical chains of administrative commands. Supply and demand can influence more flexibly domestic prices that are related to world prices. They can thus guide input-output decisions. Profits are intended to become the appropriate measure of a firm's contribution to the economy as a whole and the basis for rewarding staff. The "nonmaterial" sphere and infrastructure by necessity remain the responsibility of central authorities. Central planning of the material sphere focuses more and more on structural decisions and on economic strategies for the longer run. But a coherent macroeconomic policy needs to emerge to regulate income distribution, saving and investment behavior, monetary policy, fiscal behavior, wage and price movements, and so on.

Among the instruments of the decentralized economic mechanism, the following are the most critical. First, rather than losing in importance, the role of planning for strategic structural decisions is reinforced, as discussed. Second, the material-technical supply system is decentralized, economic agents obtaining the responsibility to settle some of their input and output decisions themselves; lateral negotiations especially among SOEs are now encouraged. Third, economic agents are expected to react to changes in indirect economic parameters rather than to bureaucratic instructions. These include prices, exchange and interest rates, and larger differentials in wage schedules. Fourth, enterprise behavior is evaluated largely on the basis of net performance indicators with profit acting as the paramount success criterion. Subsidies for wholesale and retail prices or for ailing SOEs are to be compressed and gradually abolished. Firms that cannot be turned around need to be discontinued, and this requires a government policy on bankruptcy. Finally, the decentralized mechanism necessitates changes in and additions to the economic institutions of state socialism. The transformation in the planning sphere is, of course, associated with the downsizing of the role of economic ministries and planning associations in the day-to-day affairs of economic agents under their jurisdiction. Also, a credible monetary policy requires that the monobank becomes a bank of issue and lender of last resort in charge of monetary policy. At the same time, its former "accounting" (so-called commercial) tasks are to be entrusted to a network of financial institutions that cater in principle on a competitive basis to the financing requirements of economic agents, possibly including consumers. But progress is slow even in the most radical reform. Thus, in Hungary the banking reform is not enacted formally until 1987. Budget financing continues, however.

In the foreign-trade sphere, FTOs are transformed into effective self-accounting trading firms or their tasks are assigned to individual producers. The decentralized economic mechanism may change the character of cooperative organizations, including in agriculture. It invariably imparts some important role to small-scale private or cooperative firms, particularly in service sectors. Finally, new forms of ownership are promoted not only within the domestic sphere, such as through the encouragement of small-scale private enterprise, but also by attracting capital from abroad through joint ventures or the establishment of special economic zones.

Because of the concerns about increasing factor productivity, economic reforms particularly in the smaller, trade-dependent economies seek to give high priority to trade expansion. Precisely because of dependence on intragroup markets, a more trade-intensive growth strategy can mature only if CMEA partners accommodate such shifts or if economic agents cannot explore outside channels much more intensively. Because the latter course is not considered advantageous, owing to the resumption of the Cold War and Soviet predilections regarding regional cohesion, a somewhat more positive attitude toward regional economic cooperation comes to the fore, affecting both trade strategy and model. But that stance on CMEA integration fluctuates a good deal over time. Substantive differences in the positions defended by the various members at any moment of time are evident until the CMEA's demise (Brabant 1989, 1990, 1991a).

Section 2: Policy dilemmas and macroeconomic imbalances in the 1980s

As just underlined, three decades of tinkering with the state-socialist economy failed to produce a measurable fillip to factor productivity. Though results were not altogether negative, in many respects these experiments worsened the environment for generating sustainable growth. Some observers perceive its overall rationale as quintessentially immanent in socialism, that is, in collective ownership of the means of production and a policy commitment to confining the dispersion of income and wealth under strong state tutelage. I do not share such a pat explanation. There must be a more genuine rationale to explain the failure of state socialism in a cogent manner. In one way or another, that essentially derives from its peculiar *sui generis* features. Much of this had nothing to do with socialism *per se*. Or the latter provided at best a veneer for other pursuits, such as seeking, and preserving in a fossilized state, nearly unchallenged state power for its own sake and clinging to an outmoded ideology.

Without attempting a complete explanation of the failure to reinvigorate the framework for bolstering productivity growth, I propose to examine here eight policy dilemmas construed around salient economic, political, and social imbalances. These prevailed in particular at the eve of the transition, though with quite different degrees of intensity in the various countries. One could undoubtedly identify others. Those I select are critical in grasping why state socialism imploded in the eastern part of Europe. They also help to understand the core nature of the legacies for transition in general and for the formulation, implementation, and fine-tuning of transformation in particular.

2.1 – Coordination

Even though the reform formats embraced for some three decades did not alter the basic precepts of central planning, they vexatiously complicated reaching macroeconomic control and maintaining microeconomic incentives. Such devolution was essentially sought to enhance central decision making by mobilizing the information about the real economic opportunities available to subordinate economic units. At the same time, entrusting them with wider responsibilities called for another layer to coordinate decisions, thus ensuring that all would enhance the center's policy objectives. In appraising the consistency and potential of moving meaningfully toward economic decentralization, it is

74

essential to gain a proper perspective on the evolution of how economic agents view the tasks of coordination and of the degree to which measures are taken to correct outcomes at variance with the reform's intentions. This may require frequent fine-tuning of policies, institutions, and instruments to guide the reform back on track. In the first instance, this clarification of the inevitable disruptions and adjustment costs implied in introducing reform, and of what can or should be done about them, is a matter of technical economics. Whether these costs are acceptable and the remedial measures feasible are adjudicated chiefly at the sociopolitical platform.

In moving toward genuine decentralization, firms need greater latitude in setting input and output mixes and prices, in determining individual wages and bonuses in proportion to actual profits and related performance yardsticks, in borrowing from banks at realistic interest rates, and in taking greater risks in the expectation of gaining rewards in particular from technological progress. Since the state (or its subordinate agencies) remains the ultimate owner, this increased responsibility for decentralized decision making must be steered through appropriate incentives and control mechanisms to safeguard the center's property rights. Microeconomic autonomy and responsibility can be combined effectively only if the proper signals are emitted to economic agents. Without this, lower-level organs invested with broader decision-making rights pursue their own interests. Allowing this divergence between private and social interests to fester without appropriate safeguards offers one ingredient for grasping the implosion of state socialism.

One basic objective of any economic reform anchored to administrative decentralization is to link enterprise autonomy with economic accountability, that is, self-financing and profitability. But the two need not coincide. In virtually all reform attempts, decoupling occurs shortly after the reform's start. The reason is simple: The Party leadership, government authorities, and in a number of cases enterprise managers, for lack of appropriate incentives, react through traditional peremptory actions to imbalances that the reforms are intended to address as well as to those unavoidably unleashed in the process. Policy makers attempt to improve such coordination through the heuristic methods of central administration. Invariably, this vacillation between decentralization and recentralization involves a good deal of bureaucratic maneuvering. Without clear-cut oversight mechanisms either coordination founders or recentralization repeats the problems of centralized decision making.

Because of the distortions in the evaluation criteria typical of the state-socialist economy, enterprise accountability as a rule is attainable only after a protracted, often socially and politically bruising, transition. From society's point of view, given distorted wholesale prices, it is counterproductive to expect economic agents to formulate decisions on the basis of wrong signals. It is equally unproductive to hold them accountable for disappointing results, however "rational" the underlying decisions taken within the given microeconomic context. Because prevailing institutions, rules, regulations, and behavioral patterns cannot be altered overnight, enforcement of "wrong" behavior is almost inevitable. Perhaps most important is that without competition, determined efforts to foster an effective entry-and-exit policy in the microeconomic sphere, and indeed to promote enterprise-led restructuring, it is a veritable challenge to infuse some modicum of rationality into economic behavior that has been so thoroughly dominated by administrative and political logic.

Decentralization should be pursued without necessarily depending fully on the vagaries of day-to-day market signals. For example, even though interest and wage rates are far from market clearing, firms can be held accountable for managing capital and labor resources more responsibly than under strict central planning. In the same vein, they can be asked to shoulder the burden of excessive inventories; at any rate, for hoarding material and capital resources that could be productively employed elsewhere. With some appropriate signals, firms can also be expected to show greater concern for proper pricing, inventory control, catering to user or final demand, and so on. True, these partial ways of entrusting economic agents with greater responsibility fall well short of genuine decentralization. But they *may* provide a useful first step in launching a meaningful transition toward that stage provided policy makers allow for some flexibility in structural adjustment.

One can, then, distinguish among three layers of instability with the type of decentralization enacted when adequate coordination cannot be ensured. One is the devolution of central planning authority in favor of regional or ministerial planning and budgetary centers, which may give rise to regionalism. Another layer links these levels with the ultimate producers. The risk here of bureaucratic interference in, and circumscription of, enterprise affairs is always present. Perhaps graver problems of coordination are ushered into economic management with the devolution of enterprise decision making and the weakening of the strict administrative allocation of resources in favor of horizontal relations among SOEs.

Throughout the reform experiments the principal constraint on the output of firms remains differential resource availability that cannot be rebalanced through other means than the centrally imposed mechanisms. Moreover, whatever resources planners make available to economic agents can be modified somewhat through nonvalue indicators, such as informal negotiations about obtaining more inputs or subsidies, a reduction in tax rates, easier access to bank credits, greater subsidies, and lower input or higher administered output prices. As a result, profitability fails to act as a signal for exit and entry of firms, thus motivating SOE managers into exploring other channels for mobilizing resources.

Because assignment of comprehensive plan targets in some form remains intact, the economic rationale for decentralization is rarely clear-cut. Oftentimes, firms have to procure inputs, including of labor, through other means than centrally prescribed norms. Lax credit control, monetary authorities simply continuing to finance SOEs in accordance with the central or regional plan regardless of economic justification, exacerbates imbalances. In more than one respect, these result in stockpiling of unsaleable goods. Because central rewards for output fulfillment remain more potent than those for attaining profit, however configured, and workers pressure for distributing retained earnings, enterprise management has an incentive to circumvent wage scales or inflate bonuses. In other words, enterprises and lower-level planning organs become more and more independent in ensuring their own viability in the short to medium run, but never fully within clearly set guidelines on managerial behavior for the economy as a whole. Protecting society's interest by maximizing long-run asset values does not figure highly in fine-tuning decentralization. With lax central control and essential bureaucratic coordination of decisions within firms, among firms, and between firms and planning offices, the outcome is predictable: Local decisions rarely agree with society's interest; any central crackdown only exacerbates the problems of administrative coordination.

This stop-go attitude toward decentralization, or fundamental reluctance even to consider genuine decentralization as a complement of central planning for structural decisions, stems intrinsically from the profound conservatism of the political leadership throughout the state-socialist countries. This is in marked contrast with the leadership's vision and enthusiasm during the early years of revolutionary fervor, and even the forward-looking vanguard role of communism and ideological commitments. This paradox has multifaceted origins in human behavior in general and in the corruption engendered by absolute power in particular – a subject embedded in the incrementalist engineering cited in Chapter 1. But its full analysis is well beyond the ambition of this volume.

2.2 – The dilemma of price reform and rectifying domestic imbalances

Coordinating decentralized decisions mainly through the price mechanism (for goods, services, and factors of production, including the signals connecting the domestic with foreign markets) is in practice extraordinarily difficult. If planning cannot encompass all economic activities, as it surely could not by the late 1980s, marked progress should have been made with other coordination instruments, especially prices. This logic fails to persuade core policy makers with ominous consequences for the transition. However, this disagreement provided only the outer veneer of the reality that price reform is one of the most complex and politically most sensitive policy tasks. One reason is the ideological-political credo of state socialism. Another is that technical problems encourage the leadership to cling to considerable price inflexibility and segmentation. Because of its practical obstacles, introducing meaningful changes in price levels and pricing policies slows down the pace of reform, no matter the degree of political support. Popular resistance to upward price adjustments even for quasi-public and public goods remains formidable. The promise that this should improve factor productivity, wages, goods' availability, and levels of well-being is widely pooh-poohed. Price reform is therefore strongly resisted by the population at large, by core firms dependent on hidden subsidies, and by entrenched Party and trade-union interest groups.

Yet, throughout the reforms, but particularly during the 1980s, policy makers find it increasingly counterproductive, as well as financially taxing, to maintain prevailing distortions through large price subsidies, even for basic goods and services. Consensus emerges also that, for technical reasons, it is not wise to avoid passing on basic changes in trade prices, especially those incurred in relations with market economies but increasingly also in CMEA relations. The authorities in time also become persuaded that it is not very productive to command production and consumption decisions mainly through physical appropriations. In other words, circumstances compel nearly all state-socialist economies to reevaluate their pronounced preference for stable prices. As a result, instead of the erstwhile predictable landscape of constant retail and inflexible wholesale prices with changes introduced only after long intervals, from the late 1970s at the latest the situation becomes increasingly differentiated. A decade later, price stability prevails in no economy. But it does more in some (such as Czechoslovakia, the GDR, and the Soviet Union) than in others (notably Hungary and Poland). In no country is price adaptability reinforced to elicit greater harmony between demand and supply over the plan period. Predictably, where large consumer price subsidies are maintained and the pressure emerges to contain the aggregate volume of subsidies if the budget is not to become unhinged, informal and formal quantity rationing of available goods and services is imposed. Surreptitious price increases, such as by substituting nominally different products, becomes the norm. In some countries, formal consumer rationing and chronic queuing become endemic. Because they do not affect households equally, popular resentment against the *priviligentsia* mounts.

In spite of the gradual shift in policy sentiment, a palpable multiplicity of approaches to pricing remains firmly entrenched until the very end of state socialism. This not only holds for the level and structure of domestic prices, but also pertains to the relationship between the various domestic and external price tiers. Even if some of those (such as wholesale prices with trade prices observed with market economies) are connected at one point of time, this link is rarely maintained when the required price adjustment conflicts with one or another element of the prevailing ideology or, more often, political conditions in the country. Price adaptation need not have been instantaneous, of course. Even so, intricate questions arise regarding the desired speed of price adjustment because core sociopolitical facets of a state-socialist economy may be affected by the particular choices made.

Finally, the comprehensiveness of the price reform and at what levels it should be carried out need to be configured and intermittently reevaluated. But policy makers very soon become weary of its implications, especially the redistribution of incomes usually in favor of the better-to-do layers of society resulting from the compression of consumer taxes for luxuries and durable consumer goods in combination with the augmentation of prices for essentials. True, this effect could have been offset by compensating households through income transfers from, say, income taxes. This presupposes a well developed fiscal policy, which is not typically a feature of even the most market-minded state-socialist economy.

Central government control over domestic price policies under the reform variants introduced continues to be either absolute or it takes on a modified form until the very end of state socialism. Absolute control prevails in economies that adhere to orthodox price formation and stability, perhaps the only change being the more frequent resetting of fiat prices. This worsens imbalances as other-than-price mechanisms have to bridge the gap. In the consumer sphere, this results in involuntary savings, resort to transactions beyond the control of central government, rationing, queuing, product substitution, and other emanations of repressed inflation. In some instances, the second economy also interacts with the producer sectors, which yields imbalances in interenterprise transactions and complicates macroeconomic control. The more central authorities accommodate these imbalances through the issuance of money without "commodity coverage," the greater the pressure that builds up.

2.3 – Intermediation

The success of decentralization depends importantly on the degree to which state socialism accommodates intermediation, financial and otherwise. Wholesale trade, interenterprise contacts, and bank financing are essential "institutions" to permit enterprises to improve their perception of economic efficiency. No single country with state socialism proves capable of making adequate arrangements for these essential institutions or other forms of intermediation for that matter.

Perhaps the most glaring failure of state socialism in search of reform is the absence of even minimal financial intermediation. True enough, the monobank gets decentralized in several countries prior to the transition's eve, with Hungary the furthest advanced. Its central bank is transformed, but only in 1987, into chiefly a bank of issue and domestic lender of last resort entrusted with controlling the money supply and overseeing the financial and monetary systems more generally. The more practical day-to-day aspects of "commercial banking" are increasingly left to specialized banks, to be sure in state ownership, where economic agents obtain loans that in principle are rationed by economic means, but fully within macroeconomic guidelines on monetary policy, including the financing of the central plan. Most of these institutions are set up to serve particular purposes, including regular banking business, investment, foreign trade, agriculture, industry, construction, and other activities. In some, multiple banks compete for business. Similar objectives are coveted in other countries (notably Bulgaria, China, and Vietnam) and contemplated for policy action in Mongolia, Poland, and the Soviet Union. But little is actually accomplished on the transition's eve; in China and Vietnam progress arrives in go-stop-go mode.

Financial reforms never come to grips with two critical issues. One is the stock of assets and liabilities of the newly created banks. Invariably the portfolio of the monobank is simply disaggregated into sector-specific assets and liabilities without any attempt at all to assess their real worth. These loans had chiefly accommodated central-plan implementation. In consequence, not only do the various so-called commercial banks start from very unequal conditions, but also their portfolios are of unequal quality, leaving most banks weakly capitalized and with a large portfolio of "bad debts" to be worked off. That should have been done prior to establishing these banks so that they could conceivably have engaged in commercial banking of a sort.

The second critical issue is how best to allocate funds among borrowers and whether the center allows real positive interest rates to ration loans even if that were to lead to bankruptcies and a temporary slowdown in the sustainable pace of economic activity. Proper interest-rate policies to enforce capital scarcity and to motivate agents to save for productive purposes are a *sine qua non* for banks to be viable autonomous entities. In most countries, ideological inhibitions allow only for a narrow range of interest-rate differentiation. Rarely is any serious effort made to control the money supply by technical-economic means, as distinct from rather crude policy- or ideology-driven *obiter dicta*. The banking system's paramount task is to control the monetary flows necessary to facilitate plan execution, thus keep credit within planned boundaries. Under those circumstances, its contribution to containing imbalances remains minimal.

Effective decentralization without permitting direct negotiations among firms is in practice inconceivable. Given the backdrop of central and administrative planning, this restructuring is difficult principally because economic agents have so few parameters at their disposal to devise effective wholesale-trade contacts and ensure that contract enforcement is legally protected. But areas of convergence occur. Economic agents are undoubtedly interested in endeavors for which it is in any case difficult to set a true scarcity cost without allowing for uncertainty. The larger the maneuvering room and the more exploratory the venture, the greater scope there should have been, "institutions" permitting, for interfirm cooperation.

Matters are of yet another order of complexity in organizing contacts in production and marketing. But some areas of cooperation can in principle be allowed, such as trading excess resources in one firm either intertemporally or among themselves at a mutually satisfactory price. This is not likely to clear all imbalances because there is a price imputable to the uncertainty of acquiring the resources when they eventually become needed. Even with absolutely fixed fiat prices well removed from true scarcities, direct enterprise contracts can help to boost efficiency. But the room for socially counterproductive microeconomic decisions is extended beyond what would have otherwise prevailed. Against that backdrop there is never any doubt about the travails required to realize genuine wholesale trade. In most countries, it remains an empty slogan, reflecting at best a rather poor understanding of the requirements and behavioral conditions of true markets. The repercussions are evident not only in domestic trade, but also in the various haphazard attempts to establish joint ventures with western firms;

those with fraternal countries called for in the terminal wave of CMEA reforms never really take off, in part because of inherent contradictions with the "CMEA cooperation mechanism."

2.4 – Poorly conceived macroeconomic policies

In coordinating decentralized decisions, just as important as the effective intro-duction of indirect coordination instruments and their associated institutions are appropriate macroeconomic policies. The latter must prop up and fine-tune the policy instruments and institutions for indirect coordination, and indeed induce economic agents into raising factor productivity. Another task of macroeconomic policy, and here lies the central role of statewide planning, is accommodating orderly structural change and revamping of growth strategies, including through large-scale investment projects, regional policies, and indeed appropriate industrial policy (Brabant 1993a). Finally, there is a need to maintain control over all quintessentially socialistic activities, including education, medical care, the arts, and basic infrastructure.

To enable effective bank intermediation, prudential regulations and super-visory activities have to be put in train. Monetary policy needs to be activated and extended to many new economic activities to ensure stability at the macro-economic level, to let the central bank act as the effective lender of last resort for decentralized financial institutions, and to regulate absorption in line with available domestic and borrowed resources. Measures need to be taken to provide greater diversity of assets to households. The latter can be created without necessarily encroaching on the socialist ideology regarding property (see Adaman and Devine 1996; Nuti 1987, 1992a, b). Very little of all this is in place by 1989. It is not always clear whether these halfway measures act as a stimulus or provide a further impediment to decentralization.

Greater parametrization of the economic environment of state socialism can be advocated only while addressing the need to transform domestic and regional institutions. Medium- to long-term policy issues, including on income distri-bution, aggregate savings and investment, the nonmaterial sphere, productive infrastructure, and especially the evolving situation of the economy, should have become the primary concern of central planning. Most other decisions could have been reached under macroeconomic guidance. It would also have been crucial to foster greater competition among CMEA members and, where possible, also with other firms in global markets. Trade guidance could have been provided indirectly, including through an effective tariff policy, the abolition of nonparametric subsidies and taxes buffering domestic from foreign prices, and an active exchange-rate policy.

To mobilize the proprietary "information" of economic agents for improving resource allocation, the leadership needs to recognize that reform is a protracted process rather than a once-and-for-all switch based on a single blueprint. Only with determination could the most important levers for decentralization (such as wholesale prices anchored to trade prices, effective exchange and interest rates, wage compensation according to performance, much more active consumer prices, greater coordination of the economy as a whole according to clear parameters set in line with social-profitability criteria, and more active credit policies) have been activated. Decentralized agents need a predictable and reliable, and when possible a transparent and stable, framework of rules and regulations applicable to all. This presupposes that there is room for lower-level decisions and that the interests of economic agents are reflected in the criteria by which decisions can be reached. Such model modifications could have been engineered if the leadership had made a determined effort to separate the basic premises of state socialism from its more incidental features. At the very least policy makers should have wedded themselves to fostering flexibility in resource allocation, including on personnel policies and exit and entry of firms. Policy should have placed greater priority on regulating income and wealth than on prescribing in detail what and how to produce.

As examined in Section 1, few of the above requirements for effective decentralization were met even though in some countries many had been contemplated at one point or another. Some had actually been introduced on an experimental basis, especially in Hungary. But with the emergence of the first sociopolitical difficulties associated with perceived imbalances and lagging growth performance the leadership preferred to revert to central intervention rather than to forge ahead with determination in laying solid foundations for more effective coordination of decentralized decisions.

One important macroeconomic dilemma emerged in the 1980s. Policy makers in state socialism had always been careful about maintaining conservative budget control, save perhaps with the revolutionary introduction of "socialist methods" in the early 1920s in the USSR and the late 1940s in eastern Europe; similar loosening occurred in China and Vietnam at their revolutionary stages. By the second half of the 1980s, however, budgetary control had gradually begun to slip in several countries, most glaringly in the end in the Soviet Union (see Section 4).

2.5 – Anemic productivity growth

In spite of the many reform attempts, growth in the reforming countries rarely recovers to the pace envisioned by the leadership in comparison with either the "golden" years of the 1950s and early 1960s or planned magnitudes. One need not laboriously recompute the national accounts of planned economies according to internationally accepted standards (say, SNA) to buttress this proposition. Particularly in the 1980s, following the gradual feeding through of world fuel prices into transferable-ruble prices, the debt crisis in several of the smaller countries, inability to reform the CMEA from within, and failure to participate in the virtuous circle of growth provided by active competition for intra-industry trade, the growth record of most countries remains dismal. Even with the switch in resource allocation to protect consumption and cut investment, particularly in previously favored activities, productivity gains remain at best paltry. Two reasons may suffice by way of explanation. Until the very end, the mainstream methods of economic administration fail to encourage better use of resources, including by emulating best-practice technologies. Even turnkey imported technology fails to bolster productivity largely because workers have lost faith in promises of future rewards for extra effort now. Inability or reluctance on the part of managers to join forces with foreign capital, and thus jump into the virtuous growth circle of intra-industry trade, in a form suitable to state-socialist conditions only exacerbated matters.

2.6 – External imbalances: debt, poor export performance, and current-account deficits

In addition to encumbering the coordination process, reforms also usher greater complexity into the foreign-trade sector. Although external imbalances cannot influence domestic prices directly, their scale swells so much that sizable macroeconomic repercussions ensue and must be worked off largely through interventionist methods. Certainly, some of the causes for these external imbalances are rooted in mechanisms that remain largely beyond the control of planners, in spite of the CMEA's protective environment. The consequences are very serious, though: An above-plan expansion in exports to contain external-payment pressures tends to aggravate domestic consumer imbalances; shifting the composition of imports in favor of intermediate products strains consumer markets and exacerbates demand pressures. These impact indirectly the domestic price level and relative prices. That is to say, sudden external shocks create disturbances that challenge policy makers of state socialism into remedial adjust-ment. But here the disequilibria immanent in the inflexibilities of direct control under state socialism form a stumbling block. That is not to belittle the sizable external terms-of-trade and interest-rate shocks that some of these countries must weather. But I attach more importance to built-in domestic rigidities. These not only lead to disturbances, but also make it very difficult to respond quickly and properly to external shocks.

The CMEA enmeshment provides a special dilemma. With roughly half to three fourths of overall trade conducted with clearing-currency partners, the reforming country in isolation, such as Hungary, has little choice beyond buffering domestic pricing and decision making against CMEA operations that are at variance with the reform's objectives. By the late 1980s, when the USSR surfaces in the van of reform thinking, the chances of revamping the special CMEA trade, pricing, clearing, and payment regimes improve considerably. But experiments pointing in the direction of realistic prices, direct links between firms across borders, currency convertibility, and so on prove to be too little too late to stave off the collapse of CMEA trade once the transition gets under way and political precepts gain the upper hand.

The dilemma of split trade with considerable domestic price autonomy holds until the very end. Most reforming economies at best aim at replacing the multiplicity of prevailing exchange rates by narrowing the differentiation of each group of commercial and noncommercial coefficients in the two or three major clearing zones (transferable ruble, convertible currency, and clearing), to harmonize these commercial and noncommercial rates per currency zone, and eventually to reach a uniform exchange rate subject to overall foreign-exchange policy, perhaps even current-transaction convertibility. But moves in that direction too come far too late. In fact, several countries move against the current by expanding the already bewildering diversity of exchange rates and segmenting further already unintegrated markets at home and abroad.

As indicated earlier, economies encountering volume constraints on imported inputs from the CMEA or experiencing sharp adverse terms-of-trade effects borrow funds in western markets. Some do so on top of the capital inflows engineered for the "economic maneuver," following the abrogation of earlier reform attempts. But a substantial component of these loans is earmarked somehow to support domestic consumption. Rather than taking these signals of temporary difficulties as a cue to adjust economic structures and raise participation in global markets, the decision to finance has ominous consequences for a number of countries (excepting Czechoslovakia, whose favored treatment by the Soviet Union is perhaps compensation for the enforced "normalization" after the 1968 events, and the GDR, which benefits from resource transfers from western Germany). Debt-servicing obligations become onerous. Countries either continue doggedly to service their debt (as in Hungary), resort to a Draconian compression of domestic absorption to repay the debt ahead of time (as in Romania), or they are eventually forced to default (as Bulgaria and Poland) or reschedule (as in several countries).

Whatever the method embraced, it confines the room for policy choice even for a leadership keen on effectuating structural change. Lackluster policy commitment to the latter in addition further exacerbates an already dismal export performance for any but the most basic goods. These countries steadily lose market share in non-CMEA trade to the more dynamic newly industrializing economies (NIEs). To make matters worse, by the late 1980s some are actually running sizable surpluses with CMEA partners basically because the Soviet Union is unable to put in place an effective strategy to address its then severe losses in terms of trade and raise output of fuels and raw materials to keep supplying its CMEA partners.

2.7 – Social crisis

One of the "grand bargains" between the political leadership and the population at large made sometime in the late 1960s or early 1970s trades off tacit support for the regime in place against the leadership's promise to deliver to the population at large a steadily rising level of living. In some countries, Poland in particular, this commitment is made in full awareness that domestic resources as utilized cannot suffice to buttress such a strategy and, at the same time, permit capital accumulation for "intensive growth." The ominous decision to borrow in western capital markets, including via direct government-to-government or government-guaranteed loans, as explained, had fateful consequences. These funds are partly utilized in support of the social compact, including imports of consumer goods. But also for investments, via turnkey plants, that simply do not pan out. Either the new products produced are soaked up at home or they cannot be sold abroad at anything near the hoped-for profit; nor can inputs from domestic origin supplant the continuing dependence on hard-currency imports.

To counter this ominous cycle of ever-increasing debt, with rising terms-of-trade and procurement pressures from within the CMEA, without cutting all too much into sustainable consumption, investments are scaled back. Without a purposeful exploitation of the breathing space thus gained, these cutbacks are bound eventually to undermine efforts to regain growth. Yet, consumer gains fall short of the promises made by core policy makers. They certainly fail to impress households to work harder or to shift their tradeoff between leisure (and second-economy activities) and work at a remuneration that is poorly linked to performance. Rising state-socialist incrementalism only steels households into expecting at least small increases in annual per capita incomes. When this becomes no longer feasible, much of the legitimacy arrogated by the political and bureaucratic leadership loses its support from below.

2.8 – Crisis in CMEA relations

The CMEA as the key "market" for all state-socialist economies until its very end crimps the room for policy maneuver by any one country in isolation. It is more an obstacle than a boon to reform, however conceived, in the member countries. This holds especially for trade sectors. Given the conservative Soviet preferences for the "socialist world market" almost to the CMEA's demise, in spite of solemn political commitments to enact meaningful transformation in regional-integration endeavors (Brabant 1990, 1991a), these relations are hardly supportive of shifts in economic policies envisioned by the bolder reformers. By 1989 it looks as if, at long last, a significant improvement in the "integration mechanism" can be agreed upon. But that comes far too late and in any case it offers far too little for the more adventurous members. With the eruption of the transitions, the vanguard calls essentially for moving to "world market conditions" at the earliest opportunity. This code word of sorts masks the underlying antipathy toward the CMEA, especially the Soviet Union. The central European leadership in particular is firmly bent on turning toward the west with a possible medium-term accommodation of Soviet trade provided the latter continues to subsidize its exports for the duration. That obviously conflicts with fundamental Soviet interests, given the multidimensional economic, political, and social crisis unleashed by *perestroyka*.

The precipitate move toward enforcing "world market conditions" renders the rapid collapse of CMEA exchanges and economic collaboration unavoidable. This is largely an endogenous shock (except for the developing-country members – Cuba, Mongolia, and Vietnam). As a result, some of the blame for the ensuing chaos must squarely rest on the shoulders of the central European transition leaders and their advisers.

Section 3: The multifaceted origin of state socialism's collapse

Why state socialism imploded so spectacularly is a question that will keep legions of researchers arguing for years to come. I do not pretend to have a patent explanation. I can only hope to clarify some of the more economic developments that may have hastened the abrupt demise of state socialism. Very often socialism *per se* is blamed for all the ills faced by transition economies. But without specifying what kind of socialism one is castigating, it simply becomes hopeless to isolate cause from effect, let alone to reject socialism peremptorily without running the risk of ridicule or being blamed for apostatic blasphemy.

These themes dominate much of the current commentary and provide ill-founded justifications formulated as all-embracing judgments. Most are at best misleading; they may even be slanderous. Much of the presumed pervasive failure of socialism as an encompassing counterpart doctrine to capitalism, under the circumstances, is nothing but ideological grandstanding (Abouchar 1991; Nolan 1992). In many cases, it is ironically an interpretation that largely amounts to procommunist logic (Butenko 1992, p. 1069) in the worst socialist-realist distortion of common concepts: What must be will be! The nostrums about the bankruptcy of socialism, and thus capitalism's singular triumph, which has been a *non sequitur* of sorts in itself, are not warranted on scholarly grounds. Nor does such an approach help much in formulating a proper transition strategy or the best tactics for implementing, monitoring, assessing, and fine-tuning it. Admittedly, for better or worse, it may win the hearts of those for now called upon to steer the transition. For all of these reasons I confine myself to explaining some of the economic events that contributed to the fall of communism to the extent they clarify the transition's starting conditions.

First, the "dynamics" of state socialism (see Chapter 1) eventually rendered ideology and communist convictions into empty props. The erosion of the original revolutionary fervor backed up with terror and abject submission to Party discipline led to the emergence of a peculiar kind of nonideological bureaucratization. That is to say, the gloss of state socialism, which is a *sui generis* variant of "socialism," gradually faded, leaving the building blocks of these societies without a reasonably coherent internal structure. If badly shaken it can be sustained only with a major evolution not just via reform tinkering, but also in ideological commitment.

Second, the tacit social consensus forged between the reform leadership and the population at large – acquiescence on the part of broad layers of society in the Party's political primacy in exchange for easing control over the individual's mind and life and, moreover, while providing steady gains in per capita income – had come unraveled by the lack of dynamic adjustment of state socialism alluded to above. By the late 1980s there was considerable apathy on the part of the population at large. The social crisis with its dilemmas (see Section 2) presents only one side of this calamity.

Third, by the late 1980s the political leadership of many countries had lost control over basic macroeconomic aggregates. As far as budgets are concerned, consumer price subsidies and financing the "social component" of people's levels of living, meager as they generally were, had assumed proportions that with slow growth at best could be characterized only as an intolerable burden. This was further aggravated by the priorities accorded to maintaining a sizable military, and in a number of countries a large police state. The authorities of several countries lost control also over external balances, the earlier financing of imported equipment not having paid off in terms of new output and export revenues. This left very little room for policy flexibility. Neither suasion nor police tactics were suited to cajoling the population at large once again into trading off present well-being for elusive future promises.

Fourth, for all the inefficiencies of state socialism, arguably none was as glaring as the system's built-in inability to adapt itself in line with its own productive potential and, even more, in line with competitive forces in international markets. Its salience came fully to the fore with the inability to transit to "intensive growth." It surfaced even more conspicuously with the growing external constraints especially in the fuel-importing countries once CMEA prices began to move in tandem with world prices, albeit with a lag, and secure supplies of fuels and raw materials from the CMEA could no longer be relied upon. The many attempts at "reform" launched either aggravated matters or failed to improve the productive environment, whose foundations became increasingly obsolete in terms of best-practice technology in world markets.

A long array of reasons contributed to the fossilization of economic structures. A good part of the explanation rests with the growing gap in levels of technological sophistication brought about in part by deliberate policy choice. The segmentation of civilian from military sectors of the economy further inhibited the transfer of technological knowledge to productive exploitation for civilian purposes. Furthermore, segregation in foreign links to accommodate various formats of CMEA collaboration (albeit in some instances by circumstances rather than policy choice) was not at all helpful in fostering best-practice production technologies, let alone heeding comparative advantages. The inward-orientation of especially the smaller countries sustained a wide panoply of domestic production at great intrinsic cost. Moreover, the thoroughly conservative disposition of the leadership when it came to accommodating the more buoyant types of technological innovation, particularly in electronics and computerization, figured prominently in raising the disproportions in technological sophistication compared to best-practice global standards.

Finally, by the late 1980s, the vast majority of thinking citizens in these countries had developed a pervasive distaste for the state (Kornai 1990a). The spark that promised relief from the latter's overbearing weight in societal affairs, the wasteful allocation of scarce resources during decades, the opprobrium of communism, the excesses of the Brezhnev era, the economic bumbling of the spasmodic Gorbachev reign, and so on bunched into a broadly based, if shallow, vote for the alternative of political democracy supported by a market economy anchored to private property. These generated almost instantaneous popular support for the period of extraordinary politics.

Section 4: On the starting conditions of economic transformation

There are various ways to characterize them, but only in rare cases are they defined in strictly economic terms. Thus, the situation in China in the late 1970s (following the devastation wrought by the Cultural Revolution) and in Vietnam in the mid- to late 1980s (in the aftermath of the country's calamitous unification based on the north's experiences and institutions) was mainly conditioned by severe economic setbacks, political-ideological divisions between the two parts of Vietnam, and intra-Party debates in China. But there never was any overt sign of serious ideological opposition or political discontent among the masses. It was mainly the string of failures in economic affairs, including notably inability to ensure basic food supplies, that propelled the search for reform in these countries. By contrast, in the eastern part of Europe the process was without exception multifaceted. One must therefore factor into the transition equation country-specific as well as systemic economic, political, and social starting conditions. I shall touch upon the latter two mainly for their reciprocal interaction with economic circumstances, rather than in an attempt at painting a rounded sociopolitical overview.

The other crucial general consideration is that the starting conditions can rarely be termed unambiguously positive or negative for the pursuit of genuine trans-formation. Some developments seemingly favoring one component or another of the transformation may, in fact, be an obstacle when considered from another angle. Workers' self-management provides a case in point. But many other conflicting factors are best taken into account. Among the adverse circumstances in the eastern part of Europe were differential impacts of various adverse external shocks, the sanction regimes imposed by the global community, war and civil unrest, natural calamities, and the size and extent of western assistance. Finally, different starting and/or implementation conditions may or may not warrant going "fast and deep." But they surely exert an impact on the outcome of the transition, given its path dependence (Hausner, Jessop, and Nielsen 1995), if only because of the differential economic, political, and social costs thereby imposed.

4.1 – Political conditions

Perhaps the overriding feature of the transitions' starting conditions was the state of crisis present when the transition erupted or brought about by the transformation agenda chosen in the country or in main partners. This state of crisis by necessity has sociopolitical overtones. But it is useful to differentiate its ideological-political from its more economic aspects. Whereas the economic circumstances were *mutatis mutandis* similar in all countries (see subsection 4.3), the ideological and political preconditions for transition were not, particularly when the Asian and European experiences are compared.

Throughout the eastern part of Europe, communism as an inspiring ideology based on a fundamental chiliastic-salvationist creed, during some periods enforced through state terror and a great deal of authoritarian control, had all but completely dissipated by the late 1980s. This disenchantment had come to the fore not only for the vast mass of Party members. It was even more the case among the upper echelons of Party and government. There were some exceptions, of course. But few leaders by the late 1980s had maintained their ambition, except perhaps for hortatory or public-relations purposes, to construct the communist welfare state in any foreseeable future and improve their societies according to a preset agenda. Attempts to recast perceptions by the Brezhnev doctrine on "really existing socialism" – "a pretty pure form of what it pretends to have overcome" (Dahrendorf 1990, p. 21) – foundered. However, state socialism had endowed its citizens with several "assets" whose relevance to the shaping of the transformation deserves to be fully appreciated: broad-based welfare policies that households had gradually come to accept as an entitlement; channeled thought processes, largely in a paternalistic mode; lack of entrepreneurship, a good deal of dysfunctional experience in the second economy, and poor mobility of workers and management; considerable security in respect of health, education, medical care, pensions, jobs, and civil protection; and economic structures poorly geared to the consumer and intermediation.

The extent to which communist fervor had fibrillated into lackluster ideological commitment, condoned paying ever greater lip service to "communist" ideals, and fostered incrementalist social engineering in combination, then, contributed to forging a special sociopolitical environment for transition. By the time the latter erupted, demands for change by existing lobbies (such as the evangelical church in the GDR or trade unions in Poland), the underground opposition among the intelligentsia (as in Czechoslovakia and Hungary), or *ad hoc* oppositional groups (as in Czechoslovakia) left no choice but rapidly to replace the political forces in place – in the first instance the communist political *nomenklatura*, but in some cases also their social and economic rent seekers.

The degree to which these groups were able to ensure the transfer of power and to galvanize their own ability to govern depended importantly on two factors. One was the way in which these new forces could persuade the population at large of the desirability of moving toward political pluralism as an arbiter of political rivalry, a claim that was often vocally and financially supported from abroad. The other was the degree to which the various interest and oppositional groups in place had benefited from the level of political liberalization, and perhaps even the degree of democratization, permitted before state socialism's collapse. This could be an advantage as well as a disadvantage. Thus *Solidarność*, which had benefited from the long struggle for sociopolitical and economic emancipation in Poland, negotiated a transfer of power on a rather precarious compromise. By contrast, the velvet revolution in Czechoslovakia managed to arouse widespread popular support for a more inclusive negotiated transfer of power, although overt anticommunism was not broadly based or even particularly pronounced prior to the velvet revolution; but that new political power went to individuals with little experience in politics. In Hungary, the transfer occurred largely from within the existing Party structures. In Bulgaria and Romania the counterforce came about in a much more *ad hoc*, fragmented mode, setting in fact the stage for a return of former apparatchiks to power. Their professed claims to building democracy and the market economy not only sounded hollow more often than not; they were just that.

In several federations, anticommunism combined with independence claims by various political groups, in some cases even factions in the Party. Such sentiments determined the outcome of the transition's inceptions in several Baltic, Caucasian, and Central Asian States; it also played a major role in inciting the Yugoslav conflagration. Although much milder, resentments against the perceived Czech overlordship over the Slovaks contributed to the latter's leaders raising their demand for either huge economic concessions or the breakup of the republic, an option that the Czech counterpart was only too eager to honor with dissolution. The above political circumstances have at least one factor in common: Proindependence sentiments determine the extent and urgency of the need to build a new nation, hence the degree to which the political leadership can focus primarily on the demands of economic transformation. This depends to a large extent on the prior experience with "regional" administration. In that sense the successor crisis in the Czech and Slovak republics as well as in Croatia and Slovenia was less acute and less disorderly than in other new independent states.

Certainly in the new independent states, but also in other transition economies, an important factor in pursuing transformation is the quality of state administration and the degree to which the legal system had been transformed during the search for decentralization. Thus, Hungary had a pronounced advantage over, say, Czechoslovakia, let alone the Balkan States. Of course, the absence of a legal infrastructure and of a well-honed civil service in many of the CIS States, as distinct from Czechoslovakia and Yugoslavia where a federal structure had applied for some years, proved to be a severe obstacle in formulating and, even more, in implementing transformation policies.

Finally, the degree to which the pretransition regimes had felt committed to buttressing a strong military, and perhaps even an adventurous foreign military policy, varied enormously among the countries. The motivations at their origin do not matter for this inquiry. Suffice it to observe that this degree of military commitment had a number of consequences, including in the economic arena. Among the latter, the implications for budget financing and indeed for henceforth drastically curtailing the production of military goods and services no longer valued with transition are most salient.

4.2 – Social conditions

No transition can realistically be envisaged in the absence of minimal socio-political support for the various hardships and uncertainties engendered (Melich 1997). Many factors influence the thickness and robustness of the cushion for experimental transformation policies. But I limit myself to eight. First, countries enjoying a great degree of ethnic homogeneity are not likely to have to deal with rival claims by various ethnically based interest groups. This has been an important factor, albeit with different intensity across the various states and over time, in the successor States of the USSR. It also played a major role in the Yugoslav conflagration. Ethnic differentiation presents particularly acute problems in countries where the erstwhile ruling ethnic group suddenly finds itself in a minority position, and is being eased out, however gently. This may have implications for preferred economic links or modes of operation to be emulated in the new country. It may also affect the foreign policy, including economic affairs, of the country with which this spurned ethnic minority identifies itself.

Second, the presence of militant trade unions, as in Poland, that operate as a dissident group under another name may help to negotiate an orderly transfer of political power. At the same time, as noted, it also saddles the new regime with a dire legacy from such a settlement. Not only that, the radical trade union, just like the *ad hoc* political opposition groups, as in Czechoslovakia, presents an ostensible united front more by its opposition to the regime in place than by a common understanding of what should and could prospectively be undertaken. Once the transition gets under way this front is likely to rend quickly if only because some subgroups oppose some of the "desirable" transformation policies for their own economic interests. Yielding on acquired workers' rights, as in Poland, entails either political rivalry and fragmentation or a special kind of buyout.

Third, much the same comment can be invoked for other interest groups. In countries with some tradition of managerialism fueled by a strong degree of enterprise independence, as in Hungary, it proves very difficult to dislodge managers. Since their past and present benefits stem to a large degree not from profit making or maximizing the value of assets, but from bureaucratic rent seeking, asset stripping, or profit diversion, it is not always crystal clear how best to neutralize this group. It will surrender its privileges only at some "price," whether monetary or not. Its ability to perform under the new circumstances is unknown. The most strongly entrenched managers may well have functioned constructively under state socialism, and may be genuinely concerned for the "well-being of their workers' brigade," but their talents may well fall short of minimal requirements to perform quickly the entrepreneurial activities typical of a successful firm in emerging markets.

Fourth, whatever the merits of the social-welfare policy pursued, especially after the first wave of administrative reforms in the eastern part of Europe, the population at large and workers in particular harbor expectations that most, if perhaps not all, of those services *should* be continued at little to no direct monetary cost. This is particularly important for groups having future claims on the state (such as the young for education, the elderly for pensions and medical care, and the handicapped for basic support) as a counterpart of their earlier forced savings. Pension claims are here the outstanding example; but there are evidently others. In societies with an aging population and with already a large layer of retirees, this group may well oppose parts or all of the transformation policies envisaged. Note that the socialist welfare state in the Asian economies was never as developed as in the eastern part of Europe, thus facilitating the absorption of the impact of the transformation on government budgets.

In this connection, the special constraints arising for households as providers of labor services and as consumers need to be recognized. Having been exposed for so many years to relatively low and stable prices for a wide array of basic goods and services, households tend to be reluctant to part with implicit subsidies. This places formidable restrictions on the room for maneuver for policy makers bent on revamping the government budget. Because income differentiation had been frowned upon for so long, it is not likely to be tolerated quickly by the population at large. Finally, households may be reluctant to give up full employment and other social-welfare and security guarantees.

Fifth, the demand and supply pressures that potentially disrupt market balances under state socialism are deeply embedded in the behavior of economic agents and cannot be rectified overnight. For one, the entrepreneurial élite was by and large appointed through bureaucratic and political connections, rather than for their demonstrated managerial aptitude. Moreover, the "animal spirits" of capitalist entrepreneurship are simply not present as the orthodox planning model fails to encourage the kind of decision making required in a market environment. Time is needed to inculcate the new spirit into existing and new managers, and policy makers need to nurture along this transformation process too.

Sixth, though educational attainments under state socialism were closely supervised, indeed geared to some extent by the needs of the state, the situation in the various countries was far from uniform. True, on average the level of education attained was high. But in the more developed countries literacy rates and educational accomplishments were far superior to what they were else-where. In some countries, notably in Hungary and Poland, the better educated (not just the *priviligentsia*) had benefited in addition from some foreign education, including in the west, and exposure to western academic communities. In countries such as Czechoslovakia, where contacts with the west were contained, domestic intellectual sophistication was sufficiently advanced to permit a reasonably flourishing underground culture to contribute to the educational sophistication of the élites-to-be. In some instances, the cynicism meandering through the Party élites had that benefit.

Seventh, fiscal revenues must urgently be consolidated by minimizing distortions in microeconomic decisions. This is especially so because these societies place a strong value on limited income differentiation, nearly free education and health services, fostering the arts for the wider public, and related social services. That fairness may distort economic efficiency needs to be factored into the macroeconomic policy setting. To improve levels of living, it is necessary to use resources efficiently and for this purpose to reward persons unequally. To control income disparity, measures can be taken that minimize resource misallocation. The extent of income inequality and the means of keeping it within acceptable bounds are decisions that deserve priority attention to release creative ability, stimulate entrepreneurship, and exploit prevailing and emerging opportunities with the goal of attaining a higher, yet sustainable, rate of growth.

Two problems arise here. One is that the state's tax administration is simply not set up to cope with taxation under a market environment; much less has it the capabilities to transform itself. At the same time, with the emergence of market forces and the toning down of activities in SOEs, fiscal revenues come under severe pressure. Economic agents are extremely reluctant to report their revenues in an environment where the state does not possess much credibility, where tax rates are onerous, or where broad layers of society are formally or otherwise exempted from the fiscal levy. This is admittedly normal psychology. But it takes on a special dimension in the case of the countries under review, given their over forty years of experience with statism and the desire to catch up quickly in an environment characterized by rags-to-riches opportunities.

Finally, demographic pressures enter from a different angle. In societies with a young population and a recent elevated birth rate, the large cohorts entering the labor force in the first years of the transformation may find it particularly cumbersome to obtain jobs. They may already earlier have found it more difficult to afford schooling the way their preceding generations were supported by the state's educational policies. Whether they will quickly adapt, join dysfunctional groups, or remain at the selvedge of society is offhand unclear.

4.3 – Economic conditions

I find it useful to distinguish among the countries utilizing three criteria: (1) existing economic structures, (2) experiences with administrative reform, and (3) the prevalence of crises and the intensity of the dilemmas referred to in Section 2.

4.3.1 – Inherited economic structures

It is instructive to look at least at the sectoral makeup of these economies, their level of economic development, the degree to which private enterprise (possibly in the form of the second economy) had developed and been tolerated under state socialism, and the degree of openness of these economies. Clearly, in largely rural-based agrarian economies, such as in Asia, reform authorities do not have to come to grips with an overdeveloped industrial sector resting on markedly distorted choice criteria. In Vietnam, as distinct from China, socialist industry was essentially of the light variety, making it easier to redeploy assets. Countries with much too large an industrial sector usually also exhibit a higher level of economic development. But that need not be the case, such as in comparing, say, the former Soviet Union with Hungary or Poland. The explanation is simply that the industrial distortions were much more deleterious in the former than in the latter, possibly because state socialism matured in and existed far longer in the Soviet Union and the latter's aspiration to military superiority was unique.

Although the overall economic structure of state socialism is not very well adapted to economic survival under open competitive conditions, this is especially the case for overdeveloped heavy industry. The transitions start with a misallocated portfolio of assets that cannot easily be rearranged. Not only that, industry is made up of gigantic SOEs that tend toward self-sufficiency. Furthermore, the modernity of this infrastructure, particularly in the "older" sectors of heavy industry because they received the brunt of attention in the earlier industrialization phases, left a lot to be desired. Moreover, these firms' output mix was largely geared toward plan-and-agreement-driven domestic and CMEA demands, rather than by their competitive position even if its management had been bent on pursuing such a course for its own interest. This was particularly so when it came to presentation, service provisioning, lightness and compactness, technological sophistication, and other features than simply "raw product availability" that warrant a value-added markup in the international economy.

Countries whose reforms had tolerated private enterprise, such as in agriculture, handicrafts, and small trading shops, find it easier to transfer similar activities from the state and to encourage economic agents to save and invest their means in similar activities. That is not to say that by 1989 there was a substantial degree of private property, except in agriculture in Poland and Yugoslavia. Very often private activities were associated with the transfer, usually on a partial or surreptitious basis, of user rights to state assets (such as off-hours' use of plant and equipment by workers in Hungary in the late 1980s).

Finally, countries that had followed a more open regime, particularly with respect to western Europe's markets, as a rule find it easier to come to grips with the requirements of moving toward a liberal market economy. That includes notably ability to market, to adopt and use a more meaningful exchange rate, to link domestic with foreign prices, to encourage FDI inflows, and to take effective advantage of the various assistance facilities provided by the international community (see Chapter 11).

Nowhere did state socialism accommodate economic intermediation (such as banking and a legal infrastructure for protecting contracts or property rights) or the provisioning of all kinds of services typical of the market economy. Such would have been very difficult without reasonably flexible and scarcity-related prices to funnel useful information and guidance to economic agents. This remark is independent of the character of price reform – intermittently (as in most countries with state socialism) or almost on a revolving basis (as in Hungary by the 1980s and Vietnam by 1989) – that managers are willing to consider and act upon. True, managers of several other countries (Bulgaria, China, Poland, and the USSR) were by the late 1980s contemplating price adaptability on a revolving basis. But they never in fact went over to that stage. And so, the absence of effective intermediation and services quickly proves to be a severe handicap, but more so in the more developed countries than in the more agrarian, rural-based economies.

Fostering market-driven intermediating services as a distinct alternative to the bureaucratic approach practiced especially during the later phases of state socialism is by no means an easy task. Even if tackled promptly and with deter-mination, bridging the gap that separates the inherited structure from having in place the essential ingredients of a market-based system of resource allocation is bound to take time, frequent assessments, and fine-tuning. Overcoming handicaps as they become more visible is a distinct task for transition managers and assistance deliverers. This is especially important since the prime task must be the identification of a new, sustainable growth path in spite of the adversities of transformation policies (see Chapter 12).

In a market setting there is a correlation between the demand for services and the level of economic development. The strategy and model of state socialism, however, deliberately placed overwhelming emphasis on *productive* economic activity. In the Marxist context, this means essentially physical output, notably of agriculture, construction, and industry, as well as services directly required in the production process, such as transportation of material inputs or final products. Services to consumers and households, ranging from education all the way to passenger transport, were considered *nonproductive*, and perhaps for that reason glaringly underemphasized in the assortment of outputs that the state placed at the disposal of households. Examples thereof are laundromats, consumer lending, and retail banking. But the range is very wide indeed and in some cases, such as telecommunications, they were underemphasized even in the production sphere. However, some services typical for a market economy were superfluous with good central planning or bureaucratic coordination. Recall as examples the intermediating activities that ensure that production takes place and that the distribution of the products is organized reasonably efficiently.

Without services such as transport, banking, telecommunications, computer software in all of its formats, design, publicity, financial and accounting services, legal assistance, and so on a reasonably modern industry in a market environment cannot survive. The services inherited from state socialism were rudimentary at best, and even so not particularly well suited to assisting especially the emerging private sector under market conditions. Distribution, for example, was under-capitalized and understaffed. Insurance was poorly developed. Accounting, legal, and travel agencies were primitive or nonexistent. Telecommunication services (such as telephone, fax, telex, and satellite hookups) were notoriously poor and unreliable, and frequently unavailable to the vast majority of the population. The entire retail, hotel, restaurant, and café infrastructure was scarce and of poor quality. Public transportation was often unreliable. Private transportation was rudimentary.

With a grossly underdeveloped service sector in depth as well as in breadth, demand for services during the early stages of transition was bound to be very intense. A first impetus arises from filling the gaps of state socialism (such as laundromats, restaurants, consumer banking, accounting services, and cafés), even in a poor economic environment. Any return to growth requires the development of all kinds of services typical of the market economy. These can be reliably provided only with a substantial role for government intervention via regulatory regimes, prudential regulation, supervision, and setting other institutional and legal rules of the market framework on a priority basis to ensure a reasonable level playing field for all actors in the economy (see Chapter 7).

4.3.2 – Reform experiences

Whatever one may think of the reforms since the 1960s (see Section 2), they generated positive as well as negative elements for the formulation and implementation of transformation policies. Positive aspects are no doubt a better understanding of what is needed for effective decentralization by many economic agents. Especially in the smaller countries, a better grasp of the instrumental and institutional requirements of the market economy crystallized. How policies to bolster incentives and sound macroeconomic policies can be formulated and implemented, and indeed assessed and fine-tuned, under real-life circumstances – with primitive institutions at best – is a different matter, however. Negative influences are the poor economic coordination on the transition's eve, the emergence of the second economy, skepticism with respect to the role of the state in the economy, and deep-seated distrust as regards the ability of the powers-in-place to discharge those functions. On balance, however, the knowledge gained from the most consequential reform must be counted as a bonus in forging ahead with transformation, certainly in comparison with nearly unchanged state socialism on the transition's eve.

4.3.3 – Various economic crises and policy dilemmas

Without rehearsing the discussion of Section 2, it is necessary to underline the divergence in the prevailing economic crises and policy dilemmas in the various countries. Arguably the greatest economic crisis was the inability of the political leaders to live up to their ambitions; at least to deliver the steady gains in per capita income, albeit at a modest pace, they had promised by way of stabilizing their hold on power. Neither domestic reforms, nor borrowing money and technology from abroad, nor shifting resources away from cherished industrial priorities, had spawned the structural change required to become a more competitive economy. The economic landscape on the transition's eve consisted of a vast infrastructure of state-owned assets allocated to the production of goods and limited services most of which cannot stand the test of international competition. But that does not mean that with restructuring most of these activities cannot survive at all.

State socialism had opted for many investments with a view to catering to domestic needs, and to a limited extent to respond to demand from within the CMEA area. With the latter's collapse, the disintegration of several federations, and the dramatic shift in aggregate domestic demand away from supporting the military and heavy industry, and in some cases much of domestic output, in the very short run many capital assets would have had to be liquidated. The changes to CMEA and former union demands could be more easily accommodated by countries with fuels and other natural resources, in part because of the opportunity to shift their "trade" to world markets. Whereas there never was any doubt about the scale of restructuring needed, many SOEs allowed some restructuring phase would have been able to survive. New incentives provide a critical impetus to changing behavior. Time for adjusting structures in place can accomplish the rest.

By the late 1980s, the room for policy flexibility had become very confined indeed. Domestic as well as external forces were at work here. Domestic control over money aggregates had in some countries (Poland, the Soviet Union, and Yugoslavia) been lost. The chief culprit was the lax control over the budget in contrast to the earlier fiscal rectitude because the leadership felt impelled to live up to some of its social promises, and was thus reluctant to adjust prices of essential goods and services without having the means to deliver in a "clean" manner. But the budget had also come under pressure because of external-debt service and in many countries indeed substantial losses in terms of trade. I return to the foreign-sector dilemmas below.

4.3.4 – Prior experience with the second economy

Confining the attention here to those activities that in a market environment are not criminally illegal (though not necessarily coming under the prevailing fiscal regime), but were forbidden or barely tolerated under state socialism, the experiences in the second economy provide a double-edged sword as regards the entrepreneurial lessons learned by economic agents. Much of the second economy under state socialism was based on shady access to resources; in a number of cases outright theft. Some agents under transition could probably capitalize on this experience and become "honest entrepreneurs." Cut off from such sources of supply, most might not be able or willing to begin dealing in the "legal" economy (see Chapter 5).

In some countries, however, an "open" second economy had been tolerated, however grudgingly. Agents with experiences gathered there, as in Poland and the former Yugoslavia, can be expected to join the burgeoning private sector with a head start. One can think here of the Hungarian experiences with manufacturing in nominal collective farms or the access some agents in manufacturing had to the capital resources of their firm at a nominal fee to work during off-hours for their own benefit. Note, however, inasmuch as most of these activities also comprised a hidden subsidy component, it is not self-evident that second-economy operators are invariably better placed to "make" it legally in the emerging market environment.

The shadier sides of the second economy fostered widespread corruption, deep-seated furtiveness, and general dishonesty not limited to pilfering and theft as much as it sought to cater to the needs created by the poor coordination of state socialism. Though the second economy on the whole provided the lubricant that made the inefficient administration of state socialism function, it also etched an enduring legacy for the behavior of economic agents. This has placed them largely beyond sociopolitical controls, epitomized by the *bespredel'* phenomenon rampant in the CIS States. This damage can hardly be undone and reversed overnight.

4.3.5 – External links

The foreign sector remained arguably the weakest link of state socialism. This was noticeably more important for the smaller countries. But even for the Soviet Union, the foreign sector in spite of spectacular terms-of-trade gains and massive increases in exports of fuels in the 1970s and early 1980s constituted its Achilles' heel, especially when fuel prices collapsed by the mid-1980s and the output and export stream could not be maintained. Differential exposure to trade, especially manufactures, with western countries constituted a considerable advantage for some countries, in spite of external imbalances and foreign debt, which stemmed primarily from domestic imbalances and failures to undertake genuine structural adjustment.

On the whole, the foreign sector remained weak in at least three respects. One was the perennial problem of how best to bridge the gaps between the almost unchanged CMEA regimes and world exchanges, and indeed how to ensure that the CMEA would grow into a more constructive organism supportive of economic reforms. Less reliance on the CMEA and more on market economies, particularly under decentralized trading, was therefore an advantage. The other was the weak export performance of these economies in world markets. For all practical purposes, their main convertible-currency earnings stemmed from raw materials, fuels, and labor-intensive manufactures. Some of them had run into very sizable external debts on at least one occasion. Finally, the foreign sector's linkup with domestic economic magnitudes until the very end remained exceedingly weak in some countries and not particularly robust in any of them. This was perhaps nowhere more so than in accommodating foreign capital inflow. True some variant of joint ventures had been tried, and in some countries a range of foreign firms had established a foothold. But on the whole state socialism remained outside the burgeoning flows of FDI. Even in portfolio relations, the flows were essentially restricted to borrowing in international capital markets via syndicated, government-guaranteed, or government-to-government loans.

4.4 – On the balance of the starting conditions

It is not easy to classify which countries had clearly "better" starting conditions. Some inherited fewer macroeconomic imbalances from the period of communism (Czechoslovakia, the GDR, and to some extent Hungary but not for the external side); fewer structural distortions (Hungary, Poland, and Slovenia); and a partially decentralized, somewhat liberalized economy with some vestiges of the institutions and policy instruments of a market economy (Hungary, Poland, and the former Yugoslavia). There may have been remnants of the experiences with democratic traditions (as in Czechoslovakia) and the market economy (the Baltic States and several eastern European countries). But the latter should not be overemphasized. After all, even in the country with the most recent democratic tradition, by 1989 over fifty years had passed since more or less "normal" conditions conceivably prevailed. The same applies, though perhaps a bit less strongly, for the remembrance of market conditions. Certainly in the countries where postwar nationalization was less drastic and swift, a class of older people remained with experiences in operating, say, small shops, market-type trading in its original content, and negotiating contracts. But just the same, conditions of the 1990s differ markedly from those of the late 1940s.

Conclusions

The treadmill of administrative and organizational reforms on which state socialism evolved from about the early 1960s to its demise failed to give rise to the desired "maneuver" toward intensive growth. A boost to factor productivity in all too many cases remained elusive in spite of very substantial resource commitments. Surely some of these investments had been ill-advised in retrospect either because of deliberate political preferences or the massive distortions in resource allocation. Perhaps even more important, incentives for workers and managers to raise their performance to best practice elsewhere remained highly inadequate. Augmented with the "social consensus" tradeoff of sorts, the burdens imposed on government budgets kept rising. Even temporary borrowing did not impart a breathing spell for more productive economic reforms, giving indeed rise to further imbalances and starker policy dilemmas. As a result of state-socialist incrementalism, policy makers in the end clung too rigidly to their own positions of power and privilege. But there are evidently other origins of the regime's demise.

If one looks at the desirable transformation agenda as a compromise between what ideally should be done and the means available to accomplish it, this chapter provides the latter and part of the former. The situation with state socialism on the transition's eve was such that many policies, institutions, and instruments had to be reconceived almost from the ground up. The task would be cumbersome, in part because of the complications introduced during the reform era. But the latter, in spite of its many failures, had some positive traits for forging ahead with economic restructuring as well. Toward which goal this effort should be undertaken will become clear only after the next chapter, and indeed Part II, dealing with the transformation agenda.

3

THE MARKET ECONOMY AND
THE TRANSFORMATION
AGENDA

Since the transition economies must manage transformation under concrete circumstances of time and place, politics in reality may well not leave enough leeway to chart an "optimal" agenda and pursue carefully each of its elements as part of a coherent whole. But as a firm beacon, the significance of such a consistent agenda should not be ignored. "Optimal" under the circumstances presumably means completing the economic transformation as rapidly as possible so that sustainable economic growth can begin to pay off while minimizing the socioeconomic cost and the duration of the transformation process. The latter could conceivably be condensed into an aggregate "discounted cost" to be weighed off against the discounted benefits of democracy and a market economy. Whose discount factor and cost-benefit assessment should apply here are offhand unclear. Nor is the determination of the takeoff point for sustainable growth in practice straightforward. Textbook optimal trajectories are just that!

In polarized societies as in the transition economies on the eve of the switch, it is imperative that something bold be undertaken rather quickly if only to jolt economic agents out of their lethargy. Eschewing this opportunity to embark on meaningful change may well set back the transformation process in time and exacerbate its eventual costs, given the dilemmas these countries faced in the 1980s and the starting conditions for the transition (see Chapter 2). Even so, much of the apprehension about transformation and many of the errors committed to date could have been avoided or minimized if those under fire had better understood what was at stake and formulated their concrete strategy accordingly. Not only that, wielding the economic ax to settle intrinsically ideological and political battles is not usually the most fruitful option. Alas, economists are not good at configuring the tradeoff, except in the spirit of Henri Bergson's "illusion of retrospective determinism" (Garton Ash 1996, p. 18).

This chapter addresses the issue of the basic contours of an "ideal" transformation agenda for a generic transition economy. I use the qualifier judiciously. The fairly comprehensive agenda that I explain here in the generic mode, and elaborate on at length in Part II, allows for realistic policy choices over a long period of time. It can still provide the backdrop for the formulation and implementation of concrete policies. I am well aware that, given the window of political opportunity with the transition's eruption, no single manager could have scrutinized the entire package to assemble a fully deliberated, tailor-made program. But at least the subsequent modulations and refinements in many countries could have been conceived, and evaluated, within the coherent whole of the agenda presented here.

First, I introduce the misplaced juxtaposition between "shock therapy" and "gradualism." Then I elaborate key notions of the establishment of a market. Next I discuss the broad building blocks of the transformation agenda. Thereafter I examine two critical issues: how to erect markets while transforming the entire society and the salience of ensuring appropriate coordination. I then explain the basic qualifiers of this transformation agenda and briefly summarize the major instances of uncertainty. Before concluding I raise two questions. One concerns "our" prior knowledge about what could be undertaken, and how, in terms of bridging the gaps between the broken-down state-socialist and the desired market-type economies. The other focuses on assessing success and failure of transformation policies.

Section 1: Shock therapy versus gradualism – a pointless debate?

I earlier distinguished between transition and transformation policies in a broad frame of reference. More narrowly conceived, transition policies are frequently identified with "gradualism" while transformation policies tend to be equated with "shock therapy." This is not very useful in tackling holistically the complexities at hand (Islam 1993, pp. 186–9; UNECE 1993, pp. 6–10). The same applies to the notion "big bang," which is usually seen as a very abrupt and marked shock. In addition to these three terms, the legion of peripatetic experts on the transition economies have ushered into the debate on how best to address transition challenges a broader, emotive vocabulary. Examples are cold turkey, jump start, and the primacy of adhering to the neoliberal agenda. These notions have at times been utilized with colorful aphorisms, such as "you don't pull teeth slowly"or "amputate a leg bit by bit," and "you cannot cross a chasm in two jumps." This terminology is hardly germane to the tasks at hand. It is therefore better avoided in a dispassionate discourse of what needs to be done to move from the broken-down planning system to functioning markets. I illustrate this point here by a brief discourse on the nearly senseless juxtaposition of "shock therapy" and "gradualism," with at the end a parenthetical note on "big bang."

The phrase "shock therapy" is technical terminology usually applied by psychiatry departments in hospitals and mental institutions as a last resort to treat patients suffering from certain types of severe mental depression and catatonic schizophrenia. It literally means nonsurgical treatment of physical or mental disorders. The electrical shock propelling current through the body, and thus stimulating nerve cells, notably in the brain, with a view to resuming more normal functions, is designed as a *therapy*. The essence is altering the chemistry of the brain by exciting nerve cells with the aim of relieving the enumerated *symptoms* by applying the electroconvulsive shock. The curing agent is not the application of the electrical shock, but the relief, if it occurs, brought on by the convulsion. Furthermore, following the convulsion, this hoped-for benefit is likely to become evident, if at all, only gradually, usually over a protracted period of time. In some patients, it can be attained only after administering further shocks, literally in the sense of *electroconvulsive therapy*, in yet another attempt to induce relief and possibly a cure for the diagnosed disease over a long stretch of time. But it may well fail to produce that result.

Shock therapy is in the first place a *therapy*. The notion *shock* can be utilized also in other senses, such as in the case of a violent collision, concussion, or impact (say, the cavalry charging into the masses) or a body of workers selected for some especially arduous task (say, Stakhanovite shock troops). It can also connote a sudden and disturbing physical or mental impression, such as the debilitating impact of learning about somebody's untimely passing. In the latter case, it could not possibly be associated with therapy, as the shock is the registered act of some interaction between persons or on the part of one or more persons reacting to a certain disturbing event. It is ironically this latter sense of "shock" that has become associated with economic policies in the "shock therapy" mode. Indeed, their purpose is not to administer the shock to treat the symptoms of the underlying disease, but to apply a curative therapy that unfortunately involves a shock. In other words, in contrast to the well-established medical use of the term, economic shock is the (unintended?) consequence of the therapy, possibly because of misdiagnosis of the disease that "shockers" may have earnestly felt they were attempting to cure.

Not only is the notion shock therapy not very appropriate in clarifying the policies pursued in some transition economies, but also the discussion has been needlessly obfuscated because of failure to specify clearly the kinds of policies coming within the compass of shock treatment. The metaphor as used by economists implies a short, sharp shock with immediate effects. In that sense, it should not be too far removed from the textbook's neoclassical abstraction of instantaneous and costless adjustment to a new equilibrium. Though "instantaneous" should be handled elastically in this case, one must wonder whether a three-to-five year economic depression can still meaningfully qualify as a shock, let alone a therapy. I find it also quite illogical to argue in the mode of *post hoc ergo propter hoc* that because the convulsion provoked in some countries, notably Russia in 1992, failed to elicit stabilization shock therapy was not applied (Åslund and Layard 1993; Economist 1993, p. 96). The language of the shockers, however inappropriate from a clinical perspective, promises unambiguously a more rapid adjustment than is possible in practice. As a result, shockers must bear some responsibility for the bouts of disappointment, fatigue, and disillusionment, bordering in some cases on sheer despair, observed in a range of transition economies.

If the metaphor of shock therapy is taken literally, namely as the application of scientific wisdom to provide quick and lasting relief from a severe disorder, two observations are in order. One is that, even if one suffuses one's linguistic discomfort, the notion itself is simply inapplicable to systemic transformation. It is a paradox of sorts that such a strategy in reality *cannot* be implemented. As I argue below, certain necessary and desirable changes *can* be introduced quickly; other modifications *must* be done quickly, perhaps in the form of a shock as *one* intrinsic element of a more encompassing package of measures; and there is a range of mutation tasks that simply *cannot* be accomplished rapidly. For the market economy to function properly, there is a need for near-simultaneous *completion* rather than for simultaneous *start* of the various components of the transformation agenda (see Section 3). Second, it should not, then, come as a surprise that the record of the alleged shock therapies pursued has not been very distinguished. But also this is a topic that has been vigorously argued about by advocates and detractors of shock therapy alike. Neither selective memory and statistical manipulation nor elastic use of the notion "success" has been very helpful in conducting a cogent, dispassionate discussion (see Section 9).

Shock therapy in contrast to presumed gradualism typically implies the simultaneous and rapid deployment on all fronts of all relevant categories associated with the transition. This encompasses comprehensiveness, sequencing, speed, intensity, and sectoralism as possible qualifiers for at least four broad ranges of policy actions: (1) macroeconomic stabilization in both the stock and the flow senses; (2) liberalization of domestic and foreign markets, including fostering a rapidly expanding private sector based largely on savings; (3) privatization of state-owned assets, including other forms than sheer divestment through outright sales or giveaways, notably commercialization and corporatization, and possibly restructuring, of the assets controlled by the state and by its various interlocking interest groups; and (4) institution building or erecting the framework within which market-based economic decisions, including by new private economic agents, can be taken and political choices voiced in a transparent, predictable, reliable, and comparatively inexpensive manner.

By contrast, gradualism connotes an approach involving a good deal of attention to appropriate sequencing of the various components and subcomponents of the cited policy package. Sequencing and sectoralism inevitably affect other attributes of the policy program, including the ability to correct in a timely fashion for unanticipated events (setbacks as well as newly arisen opportunities), unless one were to postulate an omniscient sage capable of conceptualizing the entire range of issues pertaining to the transformation of a degenerated or rapidly crumbling state-socialist economy. Because of the time dimension of gradualism, a fifth block of policy concerns, namely establishing and maintaining a sociopolitical consensus, is at least tacitly postulated.

Note that gradualism is sometimes confusingly applied to designate policy choices made by default in countries, such as in most of the CIS States at least until recently, that have not really embraced incisive transformation policies.

Although perhaps useful as a rhetorical device, designating such a transition as "gradualism" is not a meaningful comparison with policies conceived in the "shock therapy" mode. It certainly does not present a fair picture of the options available to policy makers. That really imparts doubts about the credibility, or the intentions, of those drawing the comparison. The same applies to the favored portrayal of gradualists by shockers as aiming at restoring the *status quo ante*, that is, a return to collectivism with a good deal of bureaucratic planning. That is manifestly *not* a genuine transformation option. Needless to say, the truth is virtually always much more nuanced than either doing nothing or aiming at the restoration of state socialism.

As a point of convenience, countries such as Bulgaria in 1991, the former Czechoslovakia in 1991, the GDR in 1990, Mongolia in 1992, Poland in 1990, Romania in 1991, Russia in early 1992, and the former Yugoslavia in early 1990 are considered to have adopted shock therapy, though the time dimension is not always handled with minimal care. Some succeeded in bridging the induced recession and returned to growth after a considerable period of time. Others faltered and may have tried a second round of shock therapy. Most other transition economies, including those that adopted shock therapy at first and failed, are reckoned to have embraced gradualism, when not completely temporizing, in tackling the issues at hand. These include notably regaining a modicum of economic stability and forging ahead with the long process of pursuing the intricate and multiple mutations in economic, political, and social structures that, when all is said and done, determine whether or not these countries will succeed in locating, and advancing along, a new growth path (see Chapter 12).

Observers of the drawn-out debates on "shock therapy" versus "gradualism" as referring to transition economies can, I trust, in retrospect only be struck by the all but pointless controversy thereby engendered. We now even have a claim to have proved that when shock therapy fails gradualism can succeed (Dehejia 1997)! At least the latter realizes the fallacy of invoking Mussa's (1986) theorem for transition economies. That states that when one rigidity prevents market adjustment it is best to remove it swiftly; when there are many such rigidities that cannot be removed all at once, the "theorem" simply does not hold. Particularly distressing was the way in which the virtues of shock therapy continued to be upheld, not in spite but *because* of (Åslund 1992; FT 1993; Sachs 1993) the rut into which policies conducted in the "shock therapy" mode in most transition economies stumbled. Failure to stabilize was often equated with failure to adopt "shock therapy" (Economist 1993, p. 96)! I do not, of course, want to dispute that there is a substantive bone of contention for "shockers" and "gradualists" alike to chew on. But the core of the debate is not really about the comprehensiveness of remaking the eastern part of Europe. Similar incredulity is aroused by argument to the effect that there is still a better than even chance that one could find a sufficiently large number of people in fundamental disagreement with the notion that many aspects of their societies must be thoroughly overhauled. The massive disdain for the old regimes and a strong will for more pluralistic decision making and reaching a more vibrant market economy demonstrated in successive political quasi-revolutions suggest otherwise.

In more than one case shock therapy has been advocated (Åslund 1995a, b; Åslund, Boone, and Johnson 1996; Åslund and Layard 1993; Boycko, Shleifer, and Vishny 1995, 1996a, b) to fight political battles with economic instruments. One must wonder whether this is appropriate. I explicitly exclude from my purview the pursuit of shock therapy as a cudgel to rid the transition economy of the most obdurate political and administrative legacies of state socialism. Of course, there was an urgent need to overcome the latter's legacies, including the abuses of power, as soon as possible to break irreversibly the back of the old regime. At least the bureaucracy, lethargic managers of SOEs, the political intelligentsia, the inflationary expectations of consumers, the syndrome of chronic shortage, and so on need to be restructured or abolished. Could these more political purposes not primarily have been accomplished through the political process? Eliminating this "political capitalism" (Staniszkis 1991) is easier said than done, given the problems endemic in moving toward a democratic culture from the entrenched positions (Mokrzycki 1991; Staniszkis 1991, 1992). Not only that, the new governments in these countries tend to be rather weak and are not fully supported by the existing civil services.

Even so, the argument made by "shockers" that economic instruments, notably property rights to state assets, be utilized *en masse* to forge an irreversible coalition for transformation and improved resource allocation rings hollow. The "market" in these countries was at least as weak as the "state." As a result, in numerous cases "political capitalism" transformed itself into the shriller disparities of primitive capitalism. Never in peacetime have so few acquired so much from so many in such a brief period of time. Perhaps a dose of carefully chosen authoritarian shock was useful. All this has proved once again that one of the hardest lessons to learn in a world where publicity-seeking politicians or their advisers propose dramatic near-instantaneous solutions for every conceivable problem is that positive change usually comes about slowly, that it requires a sustained commitment to a goal whose achievement is far from guaranteed, and that nonergodic path-dependent behavior cannot be avoided. But that much should have been clear from any appropriate reading of shock therapy.

In sum, the argument between shockers and gradualists has tended to divert attention from the paramount issues of formulating, implementing, assessing, and fine-tuning transformation policies. In that sense, it has wasted valuable time, including for policy makers in transition economies. The latter could have allocated their highly constrained skills better to pondering two crucial matters: to establish a credible transformation strategy and to create and maintain popular support for its implementation. This includes rapidly correcting for any adversities rather than letting them fracture an already fragile sociopolitical support base.

Notwithstanding this skepticism about shock therapy, the first task of governing the transition is to stabilize the economic situation, thus removing one vital dimension of uncertainty in these already labile economies. By that I do not simply mean macroeconomic stabilization, or the removal of imbalances in internal and external sectors through Draconian policies. Under some conditions, this may well be the first order of business, notably when the transition erupts in an environment with runaway inflation, a loss of confidence in macroeconomic policies, a government lacking popular support, a loss of control over basic monetary aggregates, and/or inability to stabilize the fiscal regime. This was roughly the case with Polish and Yugoslav stabilization policies in 1990. These were from the outset designed to break the back of a near-hyperinflationary situation rooted in pervasive and largely adverse economic, political, and social expectations. Some of the CIS States (notably Belarus, Russia, and Ukraine) and rump Yugoslavia at some point of the early 1990s fit this generic category rather closely too.

It would be wrong, however, to apply this blanket label to all transition economies. Indeed, in most the initial conditions for a meaningful transformation were not at all as bleak as some observers have tended to depict them. True, the underlying current of the socioeconomic reality in virtually all transition economies had earlier been on a downward, corrosive path leading to a severe malaise in some countries (see Chapter 2). But the really dramatic slide occurred *with* the implementation of transformation policies. The reason is simple: A genuine stabilization program, preferably one tied in with a blueprint on how best to enact fundamental structural change, cannot avoid temporarily depressing sustainable levels of economic activity. One could theoretically argue, provided market adjustments occur flexibly, and indeed find evidence in real-life experiences (such as Israel in 1985 and Hungary in 1995–6), that transformation of a transition economy via rapid stabilization policies need not imply a contraction of output. However, to generalize this into a principle for all transition economies (as in Nuti and Portes 1993, p. 11) is not a useful proposition. The vast bulk of these economies at the eve of transformation policies exhibited deeply rooted inflexibilities and had no markets. Yet the need to engineer massive economic restructuring is great. In practice, then, there is bound to be a lag between demand-management measures and supply responses, resulting in some output erosion. The latter's dimension is directly related to the starting conditions as well as the implementation circumstances (see Chapter 2). As experience has shown, a minimum of two to three years seems required before growth resumes; but much longer before strong, sustainable expansion can be counted on.

If substantial imbalances characterize the starting environment, as noted, the first order of business should be coming to grips with the prevailing economic situation as a prelude to setting the real sequence of transformation measures once a firm grasp over the socioeconomic situation has been gained. The most egregious imbalances must be eliminated through monetary and fiscal instruments, as well as through a more than trivial measure of price and trade liberalization. But these are not all-or-nothing options, as Michael Bruno (1992) cogently argues; in fact, either-or choices for policy makers occur fairly rarely.

Even if needed such policies cannot stand apart from other mutations that need to be conceptualized; molded into a coherent transition strategy; implemented under adverse conditions with pervasive uncertainty; and monitored, assessed, and fine-tuned as circumstances permit. If they are, policy reversal is almost preordained.

Policy credibility matters. It is indeed constructive to have credible policies in place and hold on to them. However, adhering at all cost to policies that are not working or that are inhibiting the realization of other transformation components for the sake of ephemeral credibility is not conducive to proper governance (see Chapter 7). Central on the agenda should be sound macro-economic management, including in fiscal and monetary policies as well as with respect to external liberalization, and a vision of the broad direction into which structural change should preferably evolve, while defusing any suspicion that the current transformation process may be retracted. It is hard to envisage how this could be accomplished without an activist government, obviously one markedly differing from the remnants of state socialism, in areas where it possesses an intrinsic comparative advantage or can build it up fairly quickly.

Before moving to the essence of what is at hand, a succinct word on "big bang." I am aware that the notion means different things to different people. To some it is synonymous with shock therapy. Perhaps for that very reason it has virtually disappeared from the debate around transition policies. As in the case of shock therapy in its original connotation, a big bang has its origin outside economics. It is borrowed from the epistemology of cosmology, more particularly astrophysics. In that context, it designates the act by which the universe was created, perhaps through a big interstellar collision or some other force that radically transformed matter into the universe as we know it. Whereas a big bang ought to imply the simultaneous and speedy implementation of all dimensions of the transformation strategy, most adherents differentiate their advice on speed, sequencing, sectoralism, intensity, and comprehensiveness of transformation measures. Note that three of these qualifiers have a time dimension. By that very act, it usurps whatever meaning creating something suddenly out of the nebulae of prime matter might otherwise have in economics.

Section 2: The market as social institution

Before looking at the essential role of markets in Section 4, it must be made clear what one means by "*the* market." As Jan A. Kregel (1990, p. 45) put it, "most economists have mistaken the force of competition for the man-made institution called a market" when they argue the virtues of the free-market mechanism that is supposed to coordinate self-interested individual actions. Indeed, as Lionel Robbins (1952, p. 56) observed, "the pursuit of self-interest unrestrained by suitable institutions, carries no guarantee of anything except chaos." A market is essentially a set of institutions set up by humans rather than an immutable part of the natural environment. For that very reason, there are various market

108

configurations with specific institutions for letting the forces of competition unfold. The latter provide a constraint on self-interested behavior of individual agents, channeling it into a confined range of mutually compatible outcomes. Those that do not enjoy this attribute as per the evaluation of participants induce some agents to advocate changes in the institutions that form the market before allowing the forces of competition to resume operating. This action will be initiated by those benefiting from or harmed by the outcomes that do not conform to the established market institutions; or by the state as market guardian and protector.

Not only that, most advocates of free markets have also tended to assume that, as an organizational and coordinating mechanism, markets are cost-free and that private transaction costs are zero or negligible. This is simply not so. Even to create and sustain reasonably functioning markets, some burdens must be borne by society at large over a considerable stretch of time. These include in the first instance the creation of a legal framework for the identification, protection, and enforcement of contracts regarding all kinds of market-based transactions. At times, as in societies that have a particular proclivity for litigation, reliance on explicitly detailed contracts with spelled-out pecuniary costs and benefits leads to increased dependence on laws, lawyers, litigation, and codified procedures (C. Johnson 1987, p. 159) for ostensibly market-based contracts that in other societies are handled with a greater degree of trust in partnerships. It also involves the creation of an entire industry that insures against risk. Both are costly indeed.

The stylized "facts" of neoclassical economics, or "the tyranny of this impeccably 'objective' paradigm," in Alice Amsden's (1993a) words, posit that, when available, properly functioning markets for production factors (capital, labor, land, and other natural resources) as well as for all kinds of goods and related services must aim at efficient resource allocation, that is, the maximization of the sum of the discounted values of consumer and producer surpluses (Hay 1993, p. 2). This outcome is almost trivial. The key operands of this circular statement are "properly" and "when available." One or more markets may not be available or function only poorly because either no equilibrium exists or economic agents do not behave competitively, thus leading to market failure. This may be deliberate through bounded rationality or opportunistic behavior. If so, one must investigate how quickly functioning markets can be erected and what could conceivably be done in the interim to mitigate market failure.

In what follows, then, the notion "market" means a particular set of institutions in which chiefly competition guides self-interested behavior of economic agents in such a way as to produce a limited set of acceptable outcomes, which are thus classified as coherent or mutually compatible (Kregel 1990, p. 47). This all but excludes the possibility of adhering to the basic tenets of the neoclassical approach in formulating policy options appropriate for systemic transformation. It would indeed otherwise presume that the market produces order out of chaos at no cost by providing perfect information about self-interested actions on the part of economic agents. This would at best be of trivial interest. The real world is riddled with imperfect and asymmetric information as endowments over which agents have property rights. Furthermore, the specifics of marketing and production technologies are hardly such that atomistic competition among economic agents solely bent on maximizing their profit or utility can be presumed to prevail, let alone to emerge, in an entirely orderly manner. Moreover, gathering and processing this information is costly. As a result, cases in which the neoclassical paradigm might even approximately hold are at best rare. Furthermore, there are scale economies and externalities that, when not corrected, distort market outcomes. Also monopolies and oligopolies exist, mostly but not all "network industries." Others are subject to corrective action. But both need to be regulated through other than pure market channels (Willig 1993). Questions may even arise with respect to the tradeoffs between efficiency and equity that the market, left to itself, would at best inadequately address. This is certainly so given the precepts that linger on in the transition economies in the presence of poorly functioning markets. The real world is indeed characterized by externalities and less than competitive behavior. Under some conditions, notably when the cost of government failure is inferior to that of the market failure it is trying to correct, intervention of some kind might be warranted to ensure an outcome that approximates the benefits of competitive markets. This may even extend to individuals engaging in subverting the organized market, a sort of "counter market" that in time may lead to useful adaptations and improvements in the way behavior in society is coordinated.

The prospects for a steady transition to genuine market-oriented systems in the eastern part of Europe are at this juncture quite promising. Even so, their crystallization cannot reasonably be expected within a brief time span. Indeed, an existing market, however congruent with the neoclassical paradigm, cannot be transplanted lock, stock, and barrel in record time without causing severe dislocations, leading to the endogenization of "the market"; in some cases, the transplant may be rejected altogether. In approaching the core issues, technical economic affairs should be separated from sociopolitical precepts on wealth and income distribution, unless the latter are still the basic elements of ongoing, unsettled political rivalry, as in most Balkan and CIS States. One of the main purposes of such a new environment is to improve the efficiency of resource allocation and, at the same time, fulfill tasks that the market will normally not, or only inadequately, take care of. In view of the considerable constraints on perfect competition, asymmetries of information, restrictions on the ability to contract, limits to designing comprehensive incentive rules, and other real-life features (Stiglitz 1994; 1997a, b), many markets simply do not function properly. If only for that reason, one may seek relief through nonmarket intervention, provided the latter is not itself subject to failure whose cost exceeds the dimension of the market distortion to begin with.

Section 3: A taxonomic framework

The paramount issues of formulating, implementing, monitoring, assessing, and fine-tuning transformation policies revolve around establishing a credible agenda and eliciting and maintaining popular support for its implementation. Given the four interlocking economic components (stabilization, liberalization, privatization, and institution building) of the transformation strategy with their five qualifiers (speed, sequencing, comprehensiveness, sectoralism, and intensity), one could specify a four-by-five matrix in which the various options available to policy makers are laid out. Table 3.1 provides a summary of crucial entries of such an agenda, with **S** designating that quick measures are in order, **G** that time is required, and **C** that policy choice on moving forward faster or more slowly with the relevant measure prevails. Note that I have simply identified some, but by far not all, of the generic policy choices. In any case, either-or choices in the case of transformation are rarely the appropriate approach to the tasks at hand (see Part II). A preferred combination would have to specify carefully the initial conditions, the legacies of the past, the opportunities for moving ahead with the agenda in the light of prevailing resources, and the resilience of the sociopolitical consensus as regards the magnitude, timing, and distribution of the inevitable adjustment burdens.

It is important to treat cells in this matrix realistically. By necessity some have only one option and others are all but empty apart from timing. Thus, stabilization in the stock sense – coming to grips with the excessive money emissions of the past, if applicable – must be pursued quickly, with great intensity, without much sequencing, with perhaps minor sectoralism, and a good deal of comprehensiveness. But even in this domain there is choice, such as between enacting a monetary reform, inflating away the monetary overhang, or saturating domestic markets with goods and assets (see Chapter 4). Of course, if the leadership prior to "1989" observed macroeconomic rectitude through sensible policies, there is no need for stabilization in the stock sense; the cell is thus empty. By contrast, stabilization in the flow sense – ensuring that current monetary and fiscal policies generate macroeconomic balance, perhaps after a "soft landing" – might be pursued through regular policy measures after monetary reform or inflation has eroded the monetary overhang or stabilization in the stock sense.

Note that there is a substantial difference between pursuing stable macroeconomic policies and stabilization in the flow sense. The latter can be required only if the transition itself sets off imbalances that cannot be contained quickly, possibly as a result of attempts to come to grips with inherited imbalances. Thus, price liberalization may ignite or exacerbate underlying inflation, thus worsening inflationary expectations. That needs to be contained by credible disinflationary macroeconomic policies. The required policy maneuver cannot be confined solely to tight monetary policy, of course. Current stabilization must tackle the fiscal side as well. Whereas policy makers may commit to a marked reduction in expenditures and/or a sharp rise in fiscal revenues in order to reach budget

Table 3.1 Selected principal components of a coherent transformation strategy

Qualifier	Main transformation component				
	Comprehensiveness	*Speed*	*Sequencing*	*Sectoralism*	*Intensity*
Stabilization					
Stock sense					
monetary reform	S	S	S	C	S
combat inflation	C	C	C	C	C
Flow sense					
fiscal control	G	G	G	G	G
monetary control	S	S	S	C	S
Liberalization					
Domestic					
prices	C	C	C	C	C
interest rates	C	C	C	C	C
property	G	C	G	G	C
business	C	C	C	C	C
External					
devaluation	C	C	C	C	C
cut trade monopoly	C	S	C	C	C
currency access	C	S	C	C	C
Privatization					
Restitution	G	G	C	C	G
Petty	C	C	C	C	C
Large	G	G	G	C	G
Market institutions					
Legal codes	G	G	G	G	G
Legal institutions	G	G	G	G	G
Financial agents	G	C	G	G	C
Property rights	C	C	G	C	C

Source: Based on Brabant 1993c, p. 80.
Note: See text for meaning of S, C, G.

balance relatively quickly, realities are likely to quickly defeat any attempt to adhere to any such stance. The implication then is to pursue stabilization in the flow sense by following a coherent adjustment program formulated against a sensible horizon. Also other policies, such as on credit and bankruptcy, may be needed to anchor the disinflationary stance.

Note that concrete parameters for each option in each cell must be specified. For most there is usually policy choice, albeit perhaps within narrow limits. For example, it is not indifferent whether the currency is devalued by 20 or 100 percent. True, there may be a real need for a quick and huge devaluation to arrive at a realistic exchange rate as an important parameter for guiding microeconomic choices. Even so, there is not much point in engineering a huge overdevaluation that is bound to trigger inflation, provide greater protection than desired for domestic producers, and erode people's savings in domestic currency while favoring those who managed to save in hard currency, whatever the official regulations in place. Corrective inflation is one thing. Setting off an inflationary spiral is altogether different. It is essentially to the type of policy choice in generic transformations that Part II is devoted.

There are also policies that could be introduced quickly but might be ushered in over a more protracted period of time. This includes price and foreign-exchange liberalization. The argument frequently invoked by those advocating shock therapy that, for example, trade and price liberalization cannot be introduced gradually is simply not true as the experience of all transition economies has demonstrated, albeit to greatly varying extents. Even a casual reading of postwar history of developed countries (both those in Asia and Europe) quickly underlines the lack of rigor of the argument. The really important point that those favoring the "all-or-nothing" approach perhaps intend to suggest is that, in their view, these postwar policies could and should have been introduced more rapidly than policy makers felt they had a sustainable mandate for. Policy makers do not like to move into *terra incognita*, meaning big departures from experience (Tobin 1993, p. 94). That is to say, the truly important requirement of such policies is not so much that they be gradual but that they be credible. And advocates of such a position should then spell out precisely what policy makers after World War II might have undertaken to shore up credibility, thus forestalling or defusing potential social unrest or dysfunctional political discontent.

Credibility is not simply a matter of providing information or making propaganda about the ultimate benefits of the transformation. What is needed is a coherent program with a sequencing of measures that policy makers and the population at large can support, if only tacitly, not because it is *the* preferred technocratic approach (Funke 1993). But there is no magic, let alone simple, formula according to which government can best secure that goal. Policies are credible when most actors are confident that the government's course is feasible and will be adhered to, barring untoward circumstances. In functioning democracies, the verdict of the ballot box as well as of social peace between elections will have to be heeded. Of course, in other environments, policy makers may avail themselves of more encompassing "extraordinary politics." Once the policy is firmly put in train, confidence will be associated with quickly emerging signals for changing economic behavior, including in resource allocation.

Finally, there are transformations that *cannot* be accomplished quickly. Examples are privatization, restructuring the SOEs, or laying the institutional foundations for market-based decision making without intolerably straining the sociopolitical fabric. In this, I explicitly include reform of the broader public sector, encouraging the establishment of a dense network of agents of civil society related to economic transformation and sustaining the consensus, condensing but strengthening the role of the state in economic affairs more generally, and forming functioning political parties attuned to the art of compromise in democratic parliaments (see Chapter 9). But even in these domains some tasks, such as small-scale privatization, can be carried out much faster than others, such as divestment of large SOEs. Most advocates of shock therapy appear to believe that a radical transformation in attitudes, expectations, and behavior in economic agents can conceivably be aroused in a comparatively brief period of time. Neither logic nor history supports this!

The above suggests that, in practice, the distinction among the policy tasks that can be carried out quickly, those that must be accomplished rapidly, and those that cannot be attained at record speed is, at best, fluid, if perhaps not altogether artificial. For example, calling for restructuring government revenues and expenditures as part of stabilization policies in practice is not at all easy. Raising revenue depends on reforming the fiscal infrastructure. On the expenditure side, the entire range of contingent commitments, such as interenterprise debts, and how best to rearrange and finance the sociocultural functions of SOEs need to be rethought. All this in part depends on privatization, SOE restructuring, the social safety net, and the stimulus provided for the emergence of new small and medium-size enterprises (SMEs). The latter hold the key to successful transformation as they, and perhaps FDI, are the real carriers of change (see Chapter 12). There is, however, much less of a consensus about the speed and intensity with which an orderly sequenced transformation strategy can realistically be implemented. The same applies with respect to the precise meaning of the construction of political pluralism and a market economy. Experience has demonstrated the potential for political backlash in a weakly anchored democracy under impact of the intolerable burdens that shock therapy may impose.

When the sociopolitical debate on even the broad aims of the transition remains divisive, such a retrenchment may well occur. Whether politics in such an environment differs substantially from the disappointing results obtained in some transition economies remains to be seen. I am not a partisan of a transition whose leadership is not committed to popular support, hence to some form of pluralistic decision making. A leadership consisting chiefly of a narrow oligarchy similar to – let alone identical with – the erstwhile Politburo and Central Committee in more than one way, with vast resources amassed through the less than legal acquisition of instant fortunes, is manifestly not what the aspirations of "1989" were all about. A state that has not in deeds forsworn state socialism, that acts without accountability to society, and that shackles media is *not* what the more thoughtful proponents of radical change prior to the transition had been striving to bring about.

Section 4: Intermediation, markets, and transformation

One of the more daunting complexities of a country's transformation agenda is to ensure effective intermediation in contemporaneous and intertemporal resource allocation. The selection is a vital ingredient of the process whereby functioning markets (for goods, services, labor, and capital) may eventually take root with minimal failures. To reach that stage various regulatory or even interventionist regimes as a rule need to be contemplated.

In this context, it is useful to recall that the heart of the market economy toward which the transition economies aspire is the exchange of goods or services for money or vice versa at a realistic transaction cost, whose dimension needs to be reduced to ensure progress through effective intermediation. Exchange means, in essence, the transfer of property rights associated with the object of the exchange from one economic agent (the agent bent on selling part or all of his/her property) to another (the agent bent on acquiring part or all of the property attributes) under various contractual arrangements, ranging from simple use (the *ius utendi* in Roman law); through access to the usufruct (the *ius fruendi*, which is generally combined with the first); to the final disposition (the *ius abutendi*, which includes as a rule the two other characteristics of property rights) of the object in question. Exchange does not, of course, take place for its own sake. It does so because the net residual benefits accruing to the purchaser are expected to exceed the net residual benefits that the seller perceives he is yielding in return for the acquisition of a good with larger net expected residual benefits. Transaction costs must, then, be smaller than the difference in residual gains, depending on who bears the transaction costs. Progress results when the proportion of the transaction cost relative to the difference in residual gains declines over time. The three critical issues at stake – securing property rights in law, transferring property rights at an affordable cost through effective inter-mediation, and improving the utilization of the transferred property rights – involve issues of law, of market intermediation, and of the microeconomics of exerting property rights. These issues are critical for the economy in question to regain an adequate growth path that can be sustained for some years. Only once this is secured can transition managers count on continued sociopolitical support for transformation. That depends importantly also on orderly blotting up the unavoidable burdens inflicted on society.

One paramount task of the transition is to remove ambiguity about the nature, assignment, and protection of all property rights in law and jurisprudence (see Chapter 7). Without it, property rights cannot be fairly contested in market transactions with enforceable contract-like properties. It is also doubtful that new assets by accumulating "real" property can be safeguarded. Of course, settling these legal matters does not guarantee that transactions will take place, let alone in the volume and intensity desired to forge ahead with modernization. Such exchange must in practice be facilitated by measures to compress the "transaction costs" for most operations as earlier indicated. Another salient task is to facilitate such exchange of property rights in order to render more and more complex transactions commercially viable with steady modernization. Once its various legal angles are secured, the key problem is how best to attain the minimum degree of intermediation, in terms of both instruments and agents, to arrive at affordable transaction costs and reduce their real level steadily in the process of moving toward the completion of the transformation process. Using money as standard for comparisons requires that those holding money for transaction or precautionary motives believe that this "liquid asset" can be mobilized to acquire other goods or services on demand with some degree of predictability. Once the economy becomes monetized with a fairly credible currency, effective intermediation follows the division of labor according to "assignment rules." Accomplishing all this is easier said than done, as those managing the transition have been discovering the hard way.

Assignment as a rule proceeds through the vestiges of an incipient capital market. These are normally provided by the foundations of commercial banks in their most elementary form: arranging payments; collecting savings, even if only short term; financing credible longer-term investment projects; and gradually marketing new financial instruments, including to finance government deficits, as well as assisting with the exchange of existing assets. Once the latter materializes in some orderly fashion, the essential vestiges of an emerging secondary financial market are being moored, leading eventually to the elaboration of a fully fledged capital market, whose intensity and breadth depend on the nature and volume of (largely monetized) transactions to be intermediated. Only in this way can the institutions that buttress a modernizing market economy be truly completed.

The above suggests that a market is about contracts. These are usually implicit. Even when explicit it is all but impossible to specify all parameters of the object of exchange. Purchasing vegetables and fruits in the literal market is fairly straightforward and easy, and few agents would wish to write an explicit contract for such transactions; but some do. On the other hand, acquiring a residence is a much more complex undertaking. Few agents do so without an explicit contract, even though it is impossible to specify all of the residence's property rights. Contracts must therefore be enforceable, even when not explicitly spelled out. For that to hold institutions (literally as well as figuratively) must be in place to assure the contracting parties that their agreement can be arbitrated on its merits by a neutral party (see Chapter 7).

As the cited examples suggest, there are various "categories" in a functioning market economy. This holds for the objects of exchange. Markets for goods and services differ markedly from markets for labor and capital. Furthermore, there are not only individuals who exchange such goods and services. Societal preferences in such an economy must be regulated through appropriate "market institutions" and macroeconomic policies in support of the realization of societal preferences. Resource allocation in such an environment can be aimed at maximizing output only if *all* enumerated markets operate properly. Furthermore, markets function more or less smoothly only when there is an adequate institutional and legal framework for economic activity, ownership, enterprise formation, intermediation, and so on. These rules and regulations, and their institutional infrastructure, need not be overly complex. In fact, simplicity and clarity are beneficial features of the legal and institutional frameworks to enhance

resource allocation. Finally, activities of microeconomic agents need to be coordinated. If the market fails to do so according to society's consensual preferences,
they need to be accommodated through other governance mechanisms, including
the state's.

To grasp the essential differences in the various markets for goods, services,
capital, and labor, it is important to remind ourselves of the "institutions"
required to ensure smooth resource allocation according to some maximand.
Competition is key. It may be rather straightforward to arrange for reasonably
functioning markets in ordinary goods and services. Liberalizing market access
to foreign competitors is one avenue. Competition can also be enhanced by
encouraging the creation of new SMEs, for which at least a rudimentary banking
system that effectively intermediates must be in place. Also the separation of
economic from other functions of SOEs and deconcentration of economic
activity, especially in huge conglomerates, can help foster competition. That
serious obstacles inhibit funneling adequate information to individuals to bolster
the growth of SMEs is rarely fully appreciated by commentators bent on leap-
frogging the "natural evolution" of economic forces.

Foodstuffs and informal domestic services are typical examples of objects of
exchange for which flourishing markets can be created almost overnight with
minimal regulation. Note that some are required to protect the environment,
people's health, citizens' safety, and so on. For more complex goods, such as
durable consumer goods, and indeed for many services, such as real-estate transactions, markets function properly only once a host of pertinent institutions are
in place. In the case of durable consumer goods, those include the manufacturer's
reputation, consumer financing, after-sale service, showroom facilities, and
formal warranty. For housing rentals, the explicit or implicit lease must be
enforceable via a reliable arbitrating organ such as a court (see Chapter 7).

Yet a different order of complexity surfaces when one considers labor and
capital markets. Efficient resource allocation for capital assets can take place only
when the tradeoff between present and future consumption is properly intermediated. For that a flexible capital market, including for land and real estate,
is indispensable. Clearly, this requires a financial infrastructure in the form of
a competitive network of intermediating financial institutions of domestic and
foreign origin, again placed in a well-defined and economically sensible legal
framework. In the first instance, this should consist of a competitive network of
commercial, and later investment and merchant, banks. There should also be
room for pension funds and for the management of their assets, and insurance
companies covering a wide variety of risk. In time it also requires a stock
and bond market that enhances the intertemporal allocation of resources and
regulates the acquisition and disposal of wealth in all its forms.

Given the starting conditions and the recent "history" of transition economies,
it would be foolhardy to expect a fully integrated financial infrastructure to be
in place within a short period of time. In most countries, in fact, one may well
question whether policy makers should aim at erecting a broad capital market at

home in record tempo. Some of its components are absolutely indispensable to smooth resource allocation. This certainly applies to nurturing a competitive network of commercial banks and insurance companies of various degrees of specialization. Banks and investment houses may initially take care of issuing bonds and shares in companies without there being a fully operational stock market. To be reasonably effective, however, a host of regulations and effective surveillance are required (Fischer 1996, 1997). I return to this question in Chapter 7.

Recall from the preceding chapters that labor markets under state socialism were rather simple. Workers could on the whole decide where to work with relatively mild interferences once past the early efforts at regimentation in some countries. Some also confined mobility of labor by imposing controls, such as access to large cities. The Soviet *propiska*, which legally prohibited individuals from moving away from their residence and seeking a job beyond a given radius, was typical in this respect, and remained in force until well into the transition. The freedom of workers to choose their job was, however, circumscribed to a large extent by the nonwage component of labor rewards, especially housing. Likewise, on the supply side labor markets essentially guaranteed a centrally prescribed wage scale (but scale creep with frequent movement between SOEs was endemic), some standard nonwage benefits, and a lifetime job.

In other words, labor markets in the beginning of transition are rather inflexible. Moreover, many of the supporting institutions in developed countries, such as labor exchanges and unemployment provisions, are simply not available, largely because they had no place under state socialism. Given the scope and magnitude of required restructuring, a large segment of the labor force must be remobilized. Otherwise sizable structural unemployment or labor redundancies in firms become chronic. The first taxes the central budget while the latter inhibits enterprise restructuring. Room must be made to negotiate labor contracts, whether individually, by firm, or by sector. This includes more flexible choice between work and leisure, and a much wider wage scale tied to productivity, than under state socialism. For that to obtain, expectations of workers as regards lifetime-job guarantees and labor rewards poorly tailored to work effort must be radically revised. Until these labor-market institutions emerge, market failure is endemic.

The real challenge for managers of the transition, then, is not that some markets function poorly. Rather, because the entire infrastructure for market-based decision making is *in statu nascendi* over a protracted period of time, decision making can for now be efficient only in a restricted sense. Furthermore, it remains highly uncertain how quickly functioning markets can realistically be innovated. Moreover, some become operational sooner than others. And some will continue to transgress on the conditions for best-practice allocation; this holds in particular for factor markets. Yet, managers must forge ahead expeditiously with trans-formation. Other coordination mechanisms with transitory institutions, policies, and instruments can be imagined either as a substitute for or as a complement to absent or poorly functioning markets. Provided governance capabilities are available, some should be embraced because some market failures can be rectified to some degree. Given that markets crystallize over time and asymmetrically, dynamic governance in tune with pragmatic subsidiarity is called for (Brabant 1993a, pp. 125–7). That is to say, the realistic choice of policy package in the four dimensions with respect to the five attributes invoked earlier depends critically on the nature and strength of a country's economic, political, and legal institutions; on its social cohesiveness and traditions; and on the conditions prevailing at the start of the transformation process. These factors obviously differ among countries and thus determine the speed at which economic behavior and institutions can realistically be transformed.

Note that credibility in the sense invoked signals not solely policies that are credible, but policies that can also be implemented and sustained in a credible way. In other words, a good deal of the feasibility of transformation processes depends on the imagination, and indeed cunning, of the political leadership, not only to project confidence in their economic programs, but also "to create and sustain a popular consensus behind a positive vision of the society at which they are aiming" (UNECE 1993, p. 7). While it may not be very politic to propose up front an estimate of the magnitude, duration, and the distribution of transformation costs, policy makers cannot avoid preparing measures for attenuating their impact on the more vulnerable segments of the population. Moreover, since the costs of the transformation become tangible much more quickly than the benefits, the degree of social support, with given safety nets, determines the scale of the shock that can be sustained without derailing the entire transformation program or setting it back for years.

From these broad observations it follows that "*the* market economy" is an abstract notion. Aiming at the "mythical country of laissez-faire capitalism, orthodox monetary policies, and free trade" (Pettis 1996, p. 6) is similarly unreal. Whatever real-life variant may be envisioned, it can in reality be introduced only gradually, its speed depending on the prevailing disarray and on the acceptable cost of adjustment, including in correcting errors. Moreover, unanticipated developments may call for fine-tuning the transformation strategy or perhaps even temporarily for reversing the order of policy priorities as per the original blueprint for tactical reasons. Whereas the construction of a market economy and its proper management cannot be altogether devoid of politics, the ambition to establish a functioning pluralistic, market-based economy sets an agenda for transformation that encompasses modifications in basic institutions in the broad sense, in socioeconomic policies, and in a large variety of policy instruments. The transition economies must re-create markets almost from the ground up, in the process remilling their most essential nuts and bolts. In contrast to the diversity in the pace of transformation, much greater uniformity prevails for the particular coordination mechanism to be aimed at as the outcome of the transformation. Indeed, these economies must set property rights; create a solid financial infrastructure, perhaps even stock exchanges and other securities markets; establish private enterprises and commercialize SOEs, and eventually divest most of them; erect the constitutional infrastructure for property rights and for how best to legally protect them; establish the rule of law and enforce it; embrace the principle of profit-oriented activities; motivate human behavior into accepting income and wealth differentiation; promote the agents of civil society; and so on.

Section 5: Coordination failures

The stylized "facts" of neoclassical economics posit that, when available, properly functioning markets as defined must aim at efficient resource allocation. The unrestricted entry and exit of economic agents is held to stimulate a continuous search for more cost-effective ways of producing goods and services, including new ones, that can be marketed at home and abroad. Moreover, information about these competitive pressures is most reliably transmitted through flexible prices. Market-based incentives are most effective at the local level. Even assuming that the search process is solely the responsibility of local firms, maintaining best-practice performance still depends on well-functioning markets. Obstacles to price flexibility in the form of monopolies or regulations slow down the search process by reducing the speed with which individual firms can take new initiatives and factors of production move to activities with higher returns. Where both physical and human assets are specific to a particular activity, as is still the case with much industrial production, even the threat of opportunistic behavior and rising transaction costs can restrict the effectiveness of market relations. Some markets exhibit chronic failure (Ledyard 1987; Stern 1989; Stiglitz 1989b, 1997b); this may be deliberate through bounded rationality or opportunistic behavior (Dunning 1992a, p. 21).

5.1 – Market failure

This is not the proper place to rehearse in great detail the well-known instances of market failure or the lesser known ones of government failure. Any textbook provides the details. But a perspective with a particular focus on transition economies, given their unique market and government failures, is warranted. It is useful to distinguish among three layers of market failures. One is familiar from developed market economies: Efficient resource allocation may not emerge for lack of adequate competition, externalities, public goods, increasing returns, sunk costs, and so on. A second group can be extracted from the development literature: The prevalence of poorly integrated markets, the need to foster rapid catch-up, increasing returns, and the size of the gap between social and private costs and benefits are examples. But there is a third group that stems from the absence of markets or from poorly functioning components of the markets in place. These problems are particularly endemic in countries that seek to bridge the chasm between a broken-down state-socialist system and a functioning market economy. Certainly the latter instance of market failure should be addressed, if only because the construction of functioning markets is arguably the highest priority in economic transformation once basic stabilization regained. Where possible and when capabilities are available, the other two classes of failures can be investigated as well. The most important buttress for this proposition is that the transformation in general, and the pursuit of markets in particular, is afflicted by nonergodic path dependence (Pickel 1992). It is therefore important to do the right thing as early as possible in the mutation process.

The most important task for managers of the transformation is to assist in the creation of markets through *market-conforming* measures. The real challenge is not that some markets function poorly. Rather, because the entire infrastructure for market-based decision making is *in statu nascendi* over an extended period of time, decisions can for now be efficient only in a restricted sense. What emerges in the interim exhibits various shortcomings. Note that market failures are only a necessary, by no means a sufficient, condition for public policy. Indeed, the pathology of market shortcomings provides only limited help in prescribing therapies for government success (Wolf 1990, p. 17). This makes it even more essential to compare market failures with the potential shortcomings of non-market efforts before administering remedies. Yet market failures provide the most convincing rationale for attempts by government or the "nonmarket" to remedy them. In any case, the position that nearly all public goods and services can be perfectly provided through private enterprise cannot be maintained. But this is more the case for financing such production than for actually producing these goods and services. As a result, there is by necessity an important economic role for the state in some transactions.

5.2 – Government failure

The starting point for distinguishing between the market and the nonmarket is that agents of the former derive their principal revenues from prices charged for output sold to purchasers who can choose whether to buy, what to buy, and from whom on the basis of their disposable resources. Nonmarket organizations, whether close to the state or not, derive their revenues chiefly from taxes, fees, donations, or other contributions that are generally not directly linked to services rendered. Public policies designed to compensate for market shortcomings generally take the form of legislative or administrative assignment of particular functions to one or another nonmarket agent in order to produce the specified outputs that are expected to redress the market's shortcomings. Such outputs can be regulatory services, pure public goods (such as defense), quasi-public goods (such as education and health), and administering transfer payments (such as welfare programs).

Unlike private-sector NPOs, government and its agencies derive most of their revenue from mandatory taxes or user fees. These are provided simply by virtue of the fact that membership in that polity, to a large extent, is universal and compulsory (Stiglitz 1989a, p. 21), certainly when contrasted with the implications of voluntary membership in most NPOs. Because of these coercive powers, government has a distinct role to play also in managing and steering economic development. Yet, evidence shows that governments are far from omniscient, selfless, or social guardians and that mistakes incurred are not corrected without substantial costs.

Government failures of omission and commission (Krueger 1990; Stiglitz 1997a, b; Wolf 1990; World Bank 1983a, b; 1987; 1988; 1991; 1992) are the public-sector analogues of market failures. They stem from the absence of non-market mechanisms for reconciling calculations by decision makers of their private-sector costs and benefits with the corresponding societal ones. As public-choice theory emphasizes, the self-interest of politicians and bureaucrats is an important factor in understanding nonmarket processes. But the latter should not be restricted to the government sector for there are many other activities that are not properly monitored for their profit dimension in the marketplace. Because these NPOs play a vital role in ensuring the coordination that is so salient for proper governance (see Chapter 9), their behavior needs to be better understood and integrated into the analytical framework as well. That motivation simply cannot be reduced to the way in which organs producing goods and services for competitive markets are adjudicated. What is more, to the extent that bureaucratic control in large organizations exists also in private firms whose overall results are monitored in the marketplace, the defects imputed by public-choice theory cannot be limited to government (Wolf 1990, pp. 5–6). A rounded theory of nonmarket behavior therefore requires more than what strict public-choice theory by itself can provide (Brett 1988).

It is critical to be clear about the compass of nonmarket activities. Aside from various national and lower-level governments, they extend to a host of institutions: foundations, universities, NGOs more generally, nonproprietary health-care institutions, and many others. In economic affairs, they encompass a range of institutions such as industrial associations, trade unions, marketing boards, and consumer-interest groups. All of these provide services that facilitate the operations of decentralized economic activities. Their decision-making sphere cannot be confined to the provisioning of private goods, however. That is to say, all organizations whose suitable performance record cannot be reduced to a singular optimization function (such as profit making) to which they can be held accountable in the marketplace tend to conform more to the features of the nonmarket than to those of the market. They are hence more prone to the associated types of failures, including those typically invoked with respect to social choice (Weitzman 1993; Wolf 1990, p. 6).

Government failures can encompass a wide array (Killick 1990, pp. 12ff.; Stern 1989, 1991; Stiglitz 1997a, b; Wolf 1990), but I can look here only at their more egregious emanations. First of all, the information available to government may be seriously deficient and its perception and understanding of the consequences of any action it may take flawed. Government might then simply aggravate the error it is trying to correct. Second, governments do not have full control over their activities, although their authority is evidently more extensive than what is available to private agents. This is perhaps more the case in an emerging democracy than in either a firmly embedded autocracy or a mature democracy with well-defined channels for decision making. Third, there are intrinsic problems in improving the accountability and control of bureaucracies because it is here in particular that there is no real "bottom line" to accounting or quasi-automatic termination mechanisms. But it should be remembered that it is inherently difficult to define surrogate metrics for "performance" in the public sector (Wolf 1990, pp. 51ff.). Substitutes that have been proposed in the political debate are elusive and arguable. That most "production" in the public sector is by definition single-source output encourages decision making on other grounds than efficiency or quality. It also divorces those processes from advances in technology that could be easily adapted. Thus, the absence of sustained competition contributes to the difficulty of evaluating the quality of nonmarket outputs. Undesirable results of this kind are often exacerbated by corruption, nepotism, and other malpractices issuing from special-interest groups. Finally, government has to finance its activities through fiscal levies that are compulsory. In the absence of lump-sum transfers, such levies inevitably distort resource allocation because effective relative prices are skewed relative to what they would be without the specific tax.

5.3 – A complementary coordination mechanism?

The private sector can take care of many allocation tasks. But it has various shortcomings in dealing with public goods; strong externalities; natural monopolies and other monopolies that are difficult, risky, and expensive to contest because of sunk costs (Fine 1991); shortages of entrepreneurs and managerial talent (Alan Rufus Walters 1987, p. 41); large inequalities in the distribution of incomes, achievements, and freedoms (Sen 1991, p. 421); and others. Such market failures may under some conditions justify state intervention, supervision, or regulation.

Obstacles to market flexibility provide a rationale for launching market-conforming measures by the government that can either improve the flow of information to economic agents or enhance their capacity to render its use more effective. In some instances, governments need to take decisive, positive, and coordinated actions to help economic actors grasp the nature of markets and improve their functioning (Dunning 1992a, p. 4). In lesser developed economies, this may call for a strong developmental state (Deyo 1987, p. 12) to put in place a corset of controls that remain elastic and can be jettisoned when the desired "shape," once reached, can be regulated by other means. Publicly spirited people may be called upon to steer and guide the modernization process not only to guard against market power and to elicit greater "self-regulation" (Chick 1990, p. 5). That in turn requires a clear definition of the public interest and how it inherently changes over time.

Market-conforming policies recognize the effectiveness of markets where they work. Obstacles to price flexibility in the form of monopolies or regulations or considerable uncertainty and intransparency slow down the search process by increasing informational costs, by reducing the speed with which individual firms can take new initiatives, and by braking the pace of factor reallocation to activities with higher returns. Where both physical and human assets are specific to a particular activity, even the threat of opportunistic behavior and rising trans-action costs can restrict the effectiveness of market relations in part by raising the option value of waiting. These obstacles to market flexibility provide a rationale for launching measures that can either improve the flow of information to firms or enhance their capacity to make more effective use of it.

Market-conforming measures aim at removing regulations and controls in product and factor markets and at improving flexibility, such as by strengthening the discipline of exit and entry at early stages of competition. Antitrust policies, the privatization of state assets, and more consistent fiscal policies are examples of measures that seek to diminish the politically motivated allocation of resources and the associated opportunities for rent seeking. Such market-enhancing measures may be part of a broader, explicit industrial policy fully embedded in the transformation agenda. Furthermore, measures that reduce transaction costs have an important place on the core agenda of transformation because they enhance the search potential of firms striving for more cost-effective ways of producing higher-quality products. The government has therefore an additional role in reducing or meeting these costs, including by acquiring information about relative prices and technological achievements in alternative markets, and to shore up investment decisions. Corresponding policy measures include the provision of public goods in such fields as education, transportation, and communication; training to stimulate general competence in science and technology; fostering research and development (R&D); and furnishing nonprice information (such as about currently available and prospective technologies, product standards, and market conditions abroad) that firms find it difficult to collect themselves.

Such market-conforming measures exhibit two crucial features. They avoid discriminatory action favoring resource flows to chosen sectors or firms within a particular sector. In other words, it is an "industrial policy" that manifestly does *not* seek to "pick winners." Such measures can also be rapidly introduced and their effects quickly felt. However, in the context of evolving economic structures as in transition economies, entry and exit pressures might not provide the desired direction (R. R. Nelson 1986). A wide array of financial, technical, managerial, and exporting capabilities are frequently lacking. In their absence, the speed with which price incentives can take root at the firm and industry level is often at the expense of the desired direction. In particular, such incentives can encourage short-term decision making to the benefit of luxury consumers and rent seekers rather than productive investment. If interest groups have the capacity to distort state actions, there is no reason to assume *a priori* that they are less effective in distorting free markets until effective competition materializes.

124

This does not amount to a case against ongoing liberalization. Carefully managed measures in favor of actions consistent with the broad objective of upgrading economic activity cannot always be reconciled with the priority of liberalization. The latter is likely to be effective under two very different circumstances. One is in mature industries with well-established search facilities and familiarity with a chosen product, when an established industrial base with functioning markets and property rights exists; where market integration extends across national boundaries; major process technologies are well-established and familiar; and the required knowledge base is not set to change in the foreseeable future. Under those conditions, changes in the product mix are incremental, and relatively easy to predict. Also, liberalization measures can act as a powerful corrosive agent against sclerotic forces, particularly where an overly politicized or overburdened state has extended its economic responsibilities well beyond its own competence or where credible policy initiatives have been seriously eroded by domestic and external shocks.

Also *market-augmenting* and *-correcting* policies may have a role to play. It is important to ensure that markets are *integrated* to benefit from competition among all economic agents, domestic as well as foreign. To carry out many of these tasks an activist state may be required, particularly during the earlier phases of the transformation. This holds certainly for expeditiously erecting the key institutions of the market, ensuring that the "institutional" legacies of state socialism are eradicated soonest, and evaluating the desirability of establishing some protective measures during the transformation to avoid the legacies of state socialism encroaching on the emerging market economy or nipping it in the bud.

Once the possibility of differences among firms and industries is recognized in terms of their technological capabilities; trading potential; and access to finance, the idea of an equilibrium position around which identical agents gravitate no longer holds much relevance for policy makers. If the search process of decentralized production and consumption units, either in contemporaneous or intertemporal decisions, does not spontaneously generate the desired outcomes in response to price signals, policy itself may be targeted at altering an inherited pattern of economic activity. If entry and exit problems are deeply rooted in the history of the specific structures in place, and learning and scale economies as well as externalities are pervasive, the state may consider the merit of providing specific supports to investment and technology policies (Grossman 1990). Where a large initial fixed "sunk cost" is a prerequisite for reaching a competitive scale of production, this may involve R&D outlays or investment in establishing a reputation that the private sector may not be able to effectively contest. Specific policy interventions in these areas seek to reverse market failures (Wade 1990).

Catch-up for latecomers with poor "social capabilities" (Abramovitz 1986) needs to target the acquisition of such capabilities. Market-correcting policies may be effective for particular industries and under certain conditions. Just as sequencing is central to liberalization, so is targeting. This is less likely to be effective when a mature market economy prevails because of its interlocking complexity, firms become more diversified, and economic agents in place are in a stronger position to identify profitable opportunities outside their traditional national base. Effective catch-up is contingent on inaugurating a far more coordinated approach to creating an environment conducive to rendering new activities viable. Technology, investment, and training cannot proceed independently of each other. They must be supported by a mutually consistent goal around the core of economic modernization, which reaches well beyond the horizon of individual firms (see Chapter 12).

5.4 – Other failures

As revealed through the political process, society may hold strong feelings about noneconomic attributes of resource allocation, such as income distribution, poverty and deprivation, other basic rights, and equality of opportunity of the citizenry (Dasgupta 1986; Kay 1986). Indeed, it has become more and more accepted that NPOs and government should play a symbiotic role in ensuring that the present citizenry does not overexploit resources, thus denying future generations access to them. Concerns about forestalling global warming, conserving the rain forests, and protecting endangered animal and plant species fall in this category. But there are evidently many other societal interactions that have become widely, though not unanimously, accepted as legitimate tasks of government intervention (Stiglitz 1997a, b).

Section 6: Comprehensiveness, speed, and sequencing

Whereas "sequencing" was the fashionable subject for economic debate on transition in 1990 and early 1991, it was soon thereafter rejected as superfluous by those adhering to economic mechanics in favor of speed and comprehensiveness (Blanchard *et al.* 1991; Calvo and Frenkel 1991a, b; Dornbusch 1991a, b; Fischer 1991; Guitián 1991; Klaus 1991a, b; Lipton and Sachs 1990a, b; Sachs 1991a, b, c, 1992). In the wake of the economic calamity and the daunting problems of transformation, others stressed the need for sequencing (Bruno 1992; Carlin and Mayer 1992; Newbery 1991; Nuti 1991, 1992b; Nuti and Portes 1993; Portes 1991) as an essential element of the transformation. The international organizations continue to advocate *ad nauseam* that speedy and comprehensive action pays off (World Bank 1996). But it is not mentioned that the recovery and growth attained in the early starters have not yet led to a marked improvement in average output and wealth prevailing before the transformation. Poland is an exception. But even in 1996 it only marginally exceeded 1978 output levels!

In response to the pervasive economic contraction associated with transition, the issue of sequencing resurfaced fairly soon. It continues to be paramount in designing, implementing, monitoring, assessing, and fine-tuning transformation policies; in some that revolves around second-generation programs. It is incumbent upon policy makers to minimize the duration and depth of the economic slump, and to foster moving onto a new, sustainable growth trajectory. They must also be wary of the magnitude of the changes in policies as well as concerned about the order in which they are introduced. In any case, mutations in economic structures and behavior can materialize only over time. There simply is no alternative to some sequencing in order to infuse a certain order when implementing the various transformation components. Only then can the unavoidable adjustment costs be contained to a workable minimum, spread over wide layers of society and time, and sanctioned through consensual decision making.

The argument over whether reform should be rapid or gradual is sometimes obscured by the mixing up of macro- and microeconomic considerations, on the one hand, and of long-run structural changes with macroeconomic stabilization issues, on the other. Once a transformation program gains credibility, the question of gradualism versus shock therapy becomes secondary. Structural transformation in countries with runaway inflation is inherently difficult because of the uncertainty with marked inflationary expectations. Further, stabilization in such economies has to reckon with obdurate supply-side problems that can be tackled only over years.

Probably one of the most important determinants of successful transformation is whether the government is able to create and maintain credibility in its program. Stabilization based on devaluation and liberalization generates political resistance, perhaps after an interval of "extraordinary politics," because the population sees the immediate costs of extensive, interrelated changes more clearly than the long-run benefits. Moreover, this resistance cannot be mollified through the established political process for the mechanisms available to smooth the rougher edges of dissent are rather primitive. Not only that, the lingering mistrust of and suspicion about government on the part of broad layers of the population must be overcome. Appropriate sequencing to gain and sustain a minimal sociopolitical consensus is therefore unavoidable if anarchy and chaos are to be averted.

As I underline in Part II, my preferred order of proceeding encompasses measures that should be done quickly and rather comprehensively. I include here, but not necessarily in this order, macroeconomic stabilization, price liberalization, anchoring property rights, entry and exit, corporatization and enterprise restructuring, the creation of a viable commercial-banking infrastructure, setting up a minimal social safety net, labor-market restructuring, and trade and foreign-exchange liberalization. A second tier of measures encompasses desirable speedy actions. I include here ensuring effective competition, putting in place the legal infrastructure of markets, divestment of state assets, current-account convertibility, and encouraging foreign investments, preferably FDI. These actions all have a time dimension that cannot be compressed to just a few months or even years. A final tier comprises longer-term actions. These include the creation of an adequate regulatory environment; starting "large privatiza-tion" through the outright sale of SOEs; creating some components of capital markets beyond commercial banking; ensuring reliable statistics; streamlining the flow of dependable economic, political, and social information more generally; setting up an independent pension system; and instituting new accounting rules. I advance the above rough order of steps to be set rather gingerly. Indeed, the actual transformation *must* be tailored to the tasks at hand, to the starting conditions of each individual transition economy, to available governance capabilities, and to the experiences gained during implementation.

Section 7: Critical instances of uncertainty

In contemplating the order of priorities in moving forward with the transition, the various categories of pervasive uncertainty, particularly those prevailing during the early phases of the transition, should be heeded. Generically they can be detailed under seven rubrics. First there is *cost uncertainty*. Early on during the transition, prices are on the ascent. The precise dimensions of this inflationary path are unknown. But it is clear that the incidence will be more severe in some transition economies than in others. It may actually emanate in several bursts, beginning with nearly complete liberalization for goods and some services. This stems partly from the inherited imbalances. But also the transition agenda actually adopted plays a crucial role in determining the duration and height of inflation. Without monetary control and disinflation discipline, price drift may well run amok, thereby creating a situation that is thoroughly averse to productive invest-ment and indeed the proper functioning of emerging markets.

Second, there is broad *demand uncertainty*. Macroeconomic policy and market-driven transformation policies make any reasonable forecast of domestic demand impossible; any prediction has been far off the mark. Not only is there deeply embedded uncertainty about future income streams and their distribution, consumers are likely to change their demand patterns very quickly, given that the environment within which they henceforth have to formulate decisions on their life-cycle choices is changing dramatically. Not only are the options mutating very quickly. Also the economic environment is extremely fragmented and does not yet offer the hedging instruments that may eventually emerge. This uncertainty tends to be exacerbated, in a number of cases quite uselessly (Laski 1996), by monetary and fiscal stances that are oblivious of their cumulative implications for incomes and effective demand. Domestic demand uncertainty can be exacerbated only by policies that aim to sever all inherited foreign economic ties and restructure them with a view to knitting close ties with comparatively new partners.

Third, *monetary uncertainty* affects virtually all nominal magnitudes or titles. The reason is simple. With the breakup of federations the old national "currency" loses its character. A new currency, possibly an interim one without legal tender, is not likely to be credible unless drastic steps are taken to earn this qualifier soonest (see Chapter 4). Also, monetary policies so discredit the currency in many countries that, once policy makers do wed themselves to a solid transformation agenda and make its implementation stick, they might just as well adopt a new currency. Various options to reach such a platform are available. Even without contemplating a new currency, confidence in money holding or in the security of nominal instruments is likely to remain fragile for some time to come under impulse of the kind of macroeconomic policies adopted. By virtue of insisting on monetary orthodoxy, interest rates are raised substantially to real positive levels. Conservative monetary policies raise these rates further in an attempt to anchor credibility; that in the end may well turn out to be elusive. Confidence in money holding or in the security of nominal instruments (including wages, pensions, stipends, and pecuniary social transfers) is likely to be undermined until economic actors can be won over again. That too will have an impact on the room for the scope and horizon of contracts even when the legal environment is in place.

Fourth, there is still very substantial *legal uncertainty*. Property rights early on are ill-defined (see Chapter 7). The legal environment of the firm (including contract, labor, and bankruptcy laws) must emerge from legislation to be codified and tested. Effective divestment is tantamount to unseating a wide range of managers and workers. Privatization policies are on an exceedingly uncertain path, even in the legal sense for assets pilfered from the state in one form or another, including those acquired for a price that society deems to be iniquitous. The neofeudal way in which a substantial volume of property rights have recently been arrogated through outright or near-outright theft by the intrepid may yet become the stuff of civil strife in a wider context as broad sociopolitical consensus on validating those acquisitions remains tenuous. For society at large, this is most nefarious when it comes to residence for those living in urban areas and the land, as well as buildings and equipment, for the rural segment.

Fifth, *political uncertainty* gives rise to considerable doubt about whether the early reform leadership will remain at the helm for sufficiently long to make the transformation irreversible. And it is by far not clear who is likely to take their place and what platform will then be favored. These successor governments are not necessarily going to be more stable until the democratic party structure solidifies and parliamentary compromise becomes the acceptable instrument for settling sociopolitical disputes (Comisso 1997). This has implications for the reliability of commitments made by previous and present governments that earlier constituted dependable assets in people's wealth portfolio. The course of events even in the more stable countries, including in central Europe, is not particularly comforting in this respect.

Sixth, there is what may be termed *structural uncertainty*. Because of the highly monopolized nature of economic activities in transition economies, there is an overwhelming need for a procompetitive, efficiency-oriented restructuring of the entire economy. How to foster this is unclear, particularly when countries emerge from ruptured federations or jettison collaborative groupings in a dysfunctional manner. Many adjustments need to be undertaken to accommodate new flows of goods, services, and production factors. This makes it highly uncertain in what form present companies can survive physically, in part under impact of domestic and external competition. True, a measured pace of privatization could help in clarifying these structures. But the process is bound to be protracted, painful, costly, and very messy. Breaking up existing conglomerates and encouraging new actors to enter the economy, including from abroad, should enhance competition.

Finally, for want of a better term there is likely to be *personal uncertainty*. This stems partly from the transition: job insecurity, unemployment, loss in real incomes and of liquid wealth, erosion of expectational incomes and social services, and so on. But personal insecurity also derives from the disintegration of state authority. This frequently is a direct consequence of state agents privatizing themselves. Issues such as corruption, extorsion, assault, theft, and other criminal activities exacerbate personal uncertainty, particularly when compared with what prevailed under state socialism.

In other words, for some time into the transformation decisions must be made in a very uncertain environment. Its depth and breadth depend on the inherited weaknesses, the boldness of the transformation programs put in place, and the "luck" and "pluck" of transition managers, including in obtaining relief from abroad. Pervasive (black) noise, meaning random fluctuations that exhibit no pattern at all, complicate the preparation of informed decisions because contingencies cannot really be assessed. This has important repercussions on the order in which markets can emerge and their transitional, and perhaps other, failures rectified.

Section 8: Knowledge and information in formulating transformation policies

One of the most banal, and distressing, platitudes of the rapidly expanding inventory of discourses on transformation has been that economists, and other interested observers, know how a market, a centrally planned, or an administered economy functions, and how the transition from a market to a planned economy was accomplished; but they know next to nothing about undoing the planning environment and coming to grips with the wide-ranging legacies of the earlier dominance of the monoparty in societal affairs. The euphemisms embraced to describe this vexing state of affairs, ranging from turning omelets into eggs and *bouillabaisse* or its variants back into fish, though perhaps amusing, have been neither appetizing nor very illuminating. The arguments appear to be largely "a cry of despair against the second law of thermodynamics" (UNECE 1993, pp. 7–8). A moment's reflection in all objectivity quickly demonstrates that these and related metaphors fail to connect with the transformation's reality, and are therefore unable to illuminate it.

It is, of course, true that there are no hard-and-fast transformation rules, inasmuch as thus far no single transition economy has succeeded in overcoming the multiple legacies of state socialism. But this is not quite the same as asserting complete ignorance of what economic transformation entails. First of all, it is sheer rhetoric, if not outright arrogance, to maintain that "we" really know how to transform a market into a command economy; all the more so when at the same time these experiences are flagrantly ignored. At the very least a thorough knowledge of the hindrances encountered in introducing state socialism should have made it clear that no recipe exists for justifying either omelet or *bouillabaisse* metaphors. Virtually all countries passed through "disastrous attempts [at] building . . . new institutions from scratch and radical changes in the forms of ownership" (Hussain and Stern 1993, p. 64).

Furthermore, "we" have knowledge of the dimensions of systemwide changes in a variety of settings. Since World War II, several economies have moved from a deeply engrained war-economy footing with heavy government regulation and administration to a civilian, market-oriented mode of production with various degrees of success. Likewise, numerous market economies have made attempts to divest themselves of the most odious kinds of state intervention and rigidities in societal structures. Also a number of developing countries characterized by weakly integrated markets and a limited resource base have experience with mutating from variously regulated development and managerial models to one grafted onto major elements of a market economy. Certainly, most of these changes, as in postwar western Europe, were enacted in environments in which the basic market framework was still in place. Whether this makes a huge difference for most components of the transformation is offhand not clear (see Chapter 7).

Moreover, the key components of a functioning market economy are known. These assume that various actions are taken both in building institutions and in changing attitudes of all economic agents – management, workers, administrators, and households. Similarly, the ongoing policy agenda, as discussed, is fairly clear. What is not so far known with any certainty is the best sequencing of the various elements of the transformation, given the complexity of the macroeconomic agenda and its fragile sociopolitical setting in transition economies.

Even as concerns the re-creation of market economies pleading complete ignorance is neither helpful nor strictly true. Certainly, there are no hard-and-fast rules about the nature, composition, and speed of real-life transformations. In spite of successful progress in some countries, a full-fledged market economy with robust democracy remains an aim. Many caveats by way of exceptions for privatization, changes in economic structures, tailoring the social safety net to what can be financed and to sound supports, and enterprise transformation, for example, need to be progressively overcome. Admitting this is not quite the same as baldly asserting complete darkness in the toolbox of what needs to be done during transformation; what could be done and how it could best be accomplished; how the various components could most usefully be sequenced; and at what speed they could be introduced, monitored, assessed, and fine-tuned.

Note that my approach differs in major respects ·from those drawing on the methodological aberrations discussed in the Introduction. I also disagree with the otherwise interesting case in logical semantics that Leszek Balcerowicz (1993, 1994, 1995a, b) has recently presented, on which more in the next section. I shall refrain from identifying how difficult the problems seemed to be at the outset, but it would clearly be useful and fair, as Balcerowicz argues, to compare the options chosen at the transition's inception with those that were realistically available when the choice was made and their counterfactual outcomes, to the extent this can be reliably assessed. I also agree with his emphasis on the need for rapid movement toward liberalization and monetary control in case of near-hyperinflation or worse. But it is patently wrong to generalize this to all transition economies or to seek confirmatory statistical and other arguments in support of own policies on the ground that everybody else has been reading the results wrongly, for whatever self-serving motive.

At least "we" *do* know that the transition economies manifestly do not possess markets, competition, an adequate regulatory framework, suitable corporate governance, or the predictable and well-molded macroeconomic and legal arenas within which agents can pursue their own interests in an orderly manner. We also *do* know that to allocate resources reasonably efficiently, functioning markets are required for all kinds of intermediate and final products and services. Such markets can accomplish set tasks more or less smoothly only when there is an adequate institutional and legal framework for economic activity, a diverse range of property rights that can be protected, a solid financial infrastructure, un-complicated entry-and-exit rules, entrepreneurial decision making, corporatized and commercialized SOEs until most state assets can be divested, incentives to motivate human attitudes toward income and wealth differentiation, and other essential features of reasonably mature market-based economies. Finally, activities of microeconomic agents need to be coordinated through macroeconomic policies that in part mirror the consensual preferences held by society's subjects. All these and a myriad of other "market institutions" need to be in place in a fairly coherent fashion for the market economy to operate properly.

But concern should not be mainly about maximizing static resource allocation and ensuring an adequate pace of reproduction. The primordial economic task of transition once basic stability is regained should be the identification of a more dynamic growth path and the application of policies within established institu-tions and instruments that are likely to facilitate accessing this growth path and advancing along it. At that stage, purely allocative decisions can be left to the market for as long as society is willing to tolerate even egregious market failures. However, maintaining dynamism in economic development is not something that can be accomplished by a once-and-for-all change in economic structure (Brabant 1993a, pp. 175ff.). It must be a fairly continuous process of identifying and exploiting temporary advantages or conditions that promise to yield such advantages, provided the proper preliminary measures to seize the opportunity are put in place.

We also know that at the transition's inception these countries inherit policies, institutions, and policy instruments that have no place in a market economy; they may actually be inimical to the orderly emergence of markets and must therefore be eradicated. Policies, such as price liberalization, can be reformulated relatively easily. But to do so, and to carry them out, with the institutions and instruments at hand is inviting avoidable uncertainty and may even exacerbate the risk of failure. Some legacies of state socialism can be stamped out rapidly. But jettisoning all instruments, institutions, and policy aspects of planning without having in place a robust alternative coordination mechanism can be a risky course to pursue.

Moreover, markets in transition economies will remain incomplete for a long time to come. Even once the transformation will have been completed, policy makers must attempt to come to grips with market imperfections, and prevent government failures from aggravating them or from providing the wrong responses to the sociopolitical consensus on precisely what the state should endeavor to accomplish. Furthermore, all transition economies must undergo soonest measurable changes in the sectoral composition of output and, within each broad type of activity, in the range of SOEs that can with some degree of assurance reasonably be expected to survive under competitive conditions. This can be accomplished in a number of distinct ways. The cleanest may arguably be through the trial-and-error triage of emerging markets. The cost of proceeding in this fashion may be frightfully high, however.

Section 9: Success and failure with transformation policies

Another of the more distressing aspects of the by now ubiquitous commentaries on transition economies is the simple lack of agreement on what constitutes success or failure of particular policies or even about when the transformation will have been completed. On the first issue, the diverse commentary stems in part from differing views on what the policies chosen were designed to accomplish, on the options that were realistically available to policy makers when they embarked on the measures being adjudicated, and on a selective reading of statistics combined with an elastic interpretation of positive and negative evidence. Thus, can a stabilization episode leading to chronic budget deficits, sizable unemploy-ment with downward real-wage pressure, and high inflation be termed a success, even though at the same time the program eliminates shortages in domestic markets and turns the current account into a healthy surplus by bolstering exports for some period of time?

I really do not know *the* answer. But a more nuanced interpretation than either outright "success," as advocates of shock therapy claim, or "failure," as promoters of gradualism propose, seems warranted. One of the more graphic ways of evaluating macroeconomic policies used to be through the definition of the misery index, that is, the simple addition of poverty, unemployment, and inflation minus growth; or only of some of these variables, the last two in particular. One may squabble over quantifying these rates. There are good reasons for error, as indicated in the Introduction. However measured (see Table 3.2, which lists official data for growth, inflation, and unemployment), there can be no doubt that the misery index has been rather poor since 1989, in spite of improvements, especially in growth and inflation. As noted earlier, an upturn, however welcome, is not necessarily indicative of successful transformation.

Measured growth probably understates actual performance on several counts, owing to the penchant for tax dodging and the weak tax administration in these economies. This is exacerbated by the fact that the second economy for now remains on an expansionary trajectory within that twilight zone. The incentives to join the formal open economy are not yet apparent to many agents (see Chapter 5). Likewise, consumer's life has improved in the sense that queues are gone and the quality of goods and services has improved, both elements being as a rule only poorly reflected in measured performance. There are fundamental index-number problems, but also sheer physical measurement difficulties. Statistical offices in transition economies need to change their systems and habits inculcated under administrative planning. But one should not overstate this. For one thing, there was a sizable second economy prior to the transition. Similarly, queuing was not invariably a loss of resources as those with a very low shadow cost of time did earn some revenue by standing in line on behalf of relatives and friends – perhaps an odd, yet productive kind of intermediation! And indeed, the disappearance of so-called "low-quality" goods, often badly presented and poorly packaged goods whose intrinsic quality was not really contested (think of the ubiquitous soap of real-existing socialism), has not invariably been a boon to the consumer who was perfectly satisfied with having the "shoddy" good available at a low price. Many of these goods have disappeared not because of competition or subsidies, but precisely because of oligopolistic markets.

Likewise, when unemployment rates are low, as in Russia, they are considerably understated because workers continue to draw a basic salary or avail themselves of free or nearly free services that are intrinsically unrelated to work performance in many SOEs (see Chapter 2), or they stay on the enterprise roll without drawing a salary just in case of free distribution of shares with divestment. High unemployment rates may exaggerate simply because the social safety net captures not only the genuine unemployed, but also those skillful enough to avail themselves of the benefits even though they have no intention of joining the labor force if offered a job or work in the second economy. On the other hand, when real transaction costs of registering as unemployed rise, when the real value of benefits is small relative to what can be earned in the informal sector, or when unemployment benefits are exhausted or not available (as for school leavers), measured unemployment may substantially understate total unemployment (UNWES 1994, pp. 187–98).

Measuring inflation is also tricky as it is beset by numerous index-number problems, particularly at a time of rapid structural change in production, consumption, income, and wealth. In countries where the index is suspiciously low, one must look for any grievous bias in weights. A typical example is where

Table 3.2 Growth, inflation, unemployment, and misery index, 1991–6 (compound and average annual growth rates)

	Growth GDP/NMP				Inflation (Dec/Dec)			Unemployment			Misery index		
	1991–5	1994	1995	1996	1994	1995	1996	1994	1995	1996	1994	1995	1996
Albania	-2.5	9.4	8.6	n.a.	15.0	6.0	n.a.	18.0	13.1	12.3	23.6	10.5	n.a.
Armenia	-16.2	5.4	6.9	4.0	1762.7	32.0	5.6	6.0	8.1	9.7	1763.3	33.2	11.3
Azerbaijan	-17.5	-19.7	-12.0	1.0	1786.8	84.5	6.8	0.9	1.1	1.1	1807.4	97.6	6.9
Belarus	-9.6	-12.6	-10.0	3.0	1957.3	244.2	39.1	2.1	2.7	4.0	1972.0	256.9	40.1
Bosnia and Herzegovina	n.a.	n.a.	n.a.	n.a.	94.7	-34.2	3.2	n.a.	n.a.	n.a.	n.a.	n.a.	n.a.
Bulgaria	-3.4	1.8	2.1	-10.0	122.0	33.0	311.1	12.8	11.1	12.5	133.0	42.0	333.6
Croatia	-7.3	0.6	1.7	4.4	-3.0	3.7	3.5	17.3	17.6	15.9	13.7	19.6	15.0
Czech Republic	-3.0	2.6	4.8	4.4	10.3	8.0	8.7	3.2	2.9	3.5	10.9	6.1	7.8
Estonia	-6.7	-2.7	2.9	3.5	41.8	28.8	14.9	5.1	5.0	5.6	49.6	30.9	17.0
Georgia	-27.0	-30.0	2.4	11.0	9197.5	57.4	13.7	3.8	3.4	3.2	9231.3	58.4	5.9
Hungary	-2.3	2.9	1.5	0.5	21.3	28.5	19.9	10.4	10.4	10.5	28.8	37.4	29.9
Kazakhstan	-14.6	-18.8	-8.9	0.5	1156.8	60.4	28.6	1.0	2.1	4.1	1176.6	71.4	32.2
Kyrgyzstan	-12.8	-20.1	-5.4	6.0	87.2	31.9	35.0	0.8	3.0	4.5	108.1	40.3	33.5
Latvia	-13.4	0.6	-1.6	2.5	26.1	23.3	13.2	6.5	6.6	7.2	32.0	31.5	17.9
Lithuania	-17.6	1.0	3.0	4.0	45.0	35.5	13.1	4.5	7.3	6.2	48.5	39.8	15.3
Macedonia	-10.0	-7.2	-2.9	1.6	55.1	11.2	0.3	33.2	37.2	39.8	95.5	51.3	38.5
Moldova	-17.4	-31.2	-3.0	-8.0	104.6	23.8	15.1	1.0	1.4	1.5	136.8	28.2	24.6
Poland	2.2	5.2	7.0	6.0	29.4	22.0	18.7	16.0	14.9	13.6	40.2	29.9	26.3
Romania	-2.2	3.9	7.1	4.1	61.9	27.7	56.8	10.9	9.5	6.3	68.9	30.1	59.0
Russia	-9.0	-12.7	-4.2	-6.0	214.8	131.4	21.8	7.1	8.2	9.3	234.6	143.8	37.1
Slovakia	-3.0	4.9	6.8	6.9	11.8	7.4	5.5	14.8	13.1	12.8	21.7	13.7	11.4
Slovenia	-0.6	5.3	3.9	3.5	18.3	8.6	8.9	14.2	14.5	14.4	27.2	19.2	19.8
Tajikistan	-16.8	-12.7	-12.4	-17.0	1.1	2338.4	40.6	1.8	1.8	2.4	15.6	2352.6	60.0
Turkmenistan	1.5	-18.0	-16.0	n.a	n.a.	n.a.	n.a.	n.a.	n.a.	n.a.	n.a.	n.a.	n.a.
Ukraine	-15.0	-22.9	-11.8	-10.0	401.1	181.7	39.7	0.3	0.6	1.5	424.3	194.1	51.2
Uzbekistan	-3.8	-5.2	-1.2	2.0	1281.4	144.1	n.a.	0.3	0.3	0.4	1286.9	145.6	n.a.
Yugoslavia	-16.8	2.5	6.0	4.3	8E09	110.7	60.3	23.9	24.7	26.1	8E09	129.4	82.1

Source: UNECE 1996a, 1997

Notes: GDP = gross domestic product

NMP = net material product

Misery index is the sum of inflation and unemployment minus growth

135

the consumer price index is slanted in the direction of goods and services whose prices have not yet been liberalized; services of all kinds with their controlled and subsidized prices are typical during the first years of transition. A large weight for rents, transportation, and basic utilities, for example, contributes to low measured inflation. Also, large inflation can overstate the price drift as inadequate account is taken of the improvement in quality and assortment of goods.

When all is said and done, however, there can be little comfort in the level of the misery index or its evolution since 1989. In many transition economies, inflation, however measured, remains stubbornly high (the only exceptions are Croatia, the Czech Republic, Slovakia, and Slovenia). I find it hard to attribute this, after years of transformation, to the virulence of inflation prior to the adoption of stabilization policies, as Leszek Balcerowicz (1993, p. 20) contends in the case of Poland. Likewise, unemployment rates have tended to abate only recently in the smaller economies, while they continue to rise in some of the larger CIS States. Finally, though growth is now positive at a fairly healthy rate on average and in most of the smaller economies, and is expected to become positive in most of the transition economies by 1998, the pace continues to be quite uneven, tepid, and volatile as compared to what should be possible, given the catch-up to be accomplished in these economies, and what many observers had expected at the outset of the transition.

Leszek Balcerowicz (1993, 1994) has made an impassioned argument on how best to view the transition choices and their results. His argument is of more than trivial interest for at least two reasons, quite aside from the fact that as former Deputy Prime Minister and Minister of Finance he was the architect of the Polish "shock therapy," and thus responsible for some of its implications. Though he opines with insider information, he is also motivated by the need for self-justification. Even so, I want to stress the usefulness of his analyses of both the theory and practice of transformation policies. I highlight two of them. One tries to move the focus of the transformation debate away from logical fallacies by pointing out that the proper comparison in evaluating success and failure should be between the actual course pursued and what could have been accomplished had another choice been made among the options realistically available at the outset of the transformation policies, with particular reference to Poland. Second, he points out the importance of evaluating policies in terms not only of the drift of the overall stance, such as monetary stringency, but also of the concrete elements of each policy package. This may be very difficult indeed under hyperinflationary conditions when, because of the political-regime change, there is suddenly an opportunity for "extraordinary politics" – wielding the economic weapon for political purposes – to launch a radical transformation (see Section 1). But his very analysis underlines the yeoman tasks that derive from any earnest attempt to keep everything in a proper perspective. Thus, should stringent monetary policy imply the fairly quick imposition of real positive interest rates well above zero? Should high nominal rates be maintained when real rates begin to rise because of a drop in underlying, measured inflation, for any length of time so as to stamp out inflationary expectations perhaps twice over, as it were?

I have little to disagree with his overall theoretical and policy approach to what is desirable under hyperinflationary conditions, such as he claims existed in Poland, in the former Yugoslavia in late 1989, or Vietnam in early 1989. One can nicely debate whether at least the Polish situation was truly hyperinflationary in late 1989. Were expectations of economic agents such that without countervailing savage policy intervention hyperinflation would have fed on itself for some time or did the measured inflation largely reflect administrative price adjustments, such as administered in mid-1989? But this syndrome cannot be generalized for all countries, even if with transition an opportune political window for temporary radicalism is opened. Second, Balcerowicz's reading of some of the "data," poor as several statistical measures undoubtedly are, is also suspect. If one wants to make a lot of the elusive second economy during transition, for example, then one should manifestly *not* overlook its existence under administrative planning, such as prevailed in Poland for many years. Furthermore, the argument that people in 1990–1 spent their savings on durables previously not readily available is not saying much about the income gains that he intimates the population at large actually earned almost from the transition's inception; it also ignores consumer reaction to dramatic changes in relative prices. Additional analytical and statistical defects should be noted (see Brabant 1995a, pp. 384–6).

Before concluding this excursion, a brief word on when the transformation will be over. Here too commentators and policy makers have been rather lackadaisical in claiming that "their" country, as contrasted with another, of course, has completed the transformation and is now a "normal" market economy. This may be useful public relations and it undoubtedly wins some kudos in political and journalistic skirmishing. But it simply is not so. A normal market economy is one that functions well, that is not beset by rampant bank failures, where enterprises are largely privately owned and work for their own profit, where governance of economic organizations is effective, where taxes are not onerous, the social safety net is tailored to what is sound social policy and fiscally affordable, where government and external imbalances are not too large and soundly financed, and so on. Without all this, effective transformation has yet some way to go. The second reason is perhaps a bit more complex. The transformation will really be over only when the economy has embarked on a self-sustainable growth path permitting catch-up with levels of income, wealth, and productivity prevailing in western Europe. Despite resumption of growth in many transition economies, there can be no room for complacency (see Chapter 12). The evidence that these countries are presently on a self-sustainable growth trajectory is not particularly compelling.

Conclusions

I trust the above has underlined the complexity of coming to grips in a dispassionate manner with the tasks at hand when countries commit themselves to abandon the broken-down realities of state socialism and begin their search for pluralistic democracy and market-based decision making. This should be evident from the transformation agenda as sketched in broad brush strokes here. There are many other items to be borne in mind as I discuss in Part II. Virtually none of these market features was present in any country on the transition's eve. In many respects, little progress has since been made with a number of the critical features, particularly in capital and labor markets, but also in some services. "Little" is, of course, a relative concept. When one looks at how far these countries have successfully removed the core threats of and inequities engendered by state socialism, the achievements recorded since mid-1989 are truly astounding. But when compared with the tasks set for these societies to function as "normal" democracies with a solid market foundation, the progress made to date has been disappointing, in some cases quite meager, as I underline in Part II. In a number of transition economies substantial retrogression has occurred after the first momentous changes promised a more rewarding outcome. The more subtle and qualitative transition tasks ahead therefore remain utterly daunting.

Part II

COMPONENTS OF THE
TRANSFORMATION
AGENDA

The following chapters examine in detail the five components with their five qualifiers of the coherent strategy for economic transformation proposed in Chapter 3. Two remarks are necessary to justify the choice of six chapters. From among the "institutions of the market" I single out the state as a topic for special attention for two reasons. One is that the economic role of the state in the transition, as argued in Chapter 9, is by necessity *sui generis*. Also, the proper role of the state in more general policy making, such as in the posttransition period, is almost always far more encompassing and complex than most economists, particularly the champions of liberalism, have been willing to concede. While it is true that professional economists cannot foreclose political choice with its various responsibilities, they should be in a position to proffer professionally sound options, with their various advantages and drawbacks spelled out under alternative scenarios, for policy makers to choose from. Also, as justified in Chapter 3, I consider the establishment and maintenance of a social safety net to constitute an integral part of good governance during the transformation, not just something that may be politically desirable to avert sociopolitical flak being projected onto the application of "professionally smooth" strategies. Policy making during the transition is by necessity rather messy. How else could one engineer societal transformations in the real world?

It is admittedly a bit awkward to treat the various components of a coherent transformation agenda in separate chapters. For one thing, many of the topics included in one chapter are intricately interrelated with others discussed elsewhere. For example, stabilization in practice cannot be pursued without liberalization. But confounding the two is not the most useful approach. I decided to treat them separately, with appropriate cross references, even at the risk of some repetition and redundancy. I can conceive of no other way in which the qualifiers on sequencing, sectoralism, intensity, comprehensiveness, and speed can be handled systematically in anything like a comprehensive overview.

Finally, as already emphasized, one must choose between a conceptually satisfactory treatise and one that details the transformation in one or perhaps a few countries. I prefer to place the accent on the former objective. Examples of the various components of the transformation agenda with their particular qualifiers referring to individual country experiences I provide essentially by way of illustrating the conceptual approach. For more detailed analyses of any one economy's experiences since 1989 the reader is referred to the specialized country literature.

4

STABILIZATION AS AN EARLY
POLICY TASK

The first group of major policy topics to be addressed in any transformation agenda comprises stabilization (see Chapter 3). As summarized in Table 3.1 (p. 112), this can logically be separated into stock and flow stabilization. Determined policies aimed at regaining macroeconomic stability should logically be considered separately from pursuing prudent macroeconomic policies to ensure that basic aggregate balances are not perturbed, thus possibly generating situations that are unsustainable or that exert deleterious effects on economic activity.

I first explain why brisk stabilization may be required and why the pursuit of prudent macroeconomic policies must be a priority for policy makers in general and for those managing the transformation in particular, once basic stabilization is achieved. Next I examine the initial approaches chosen by most transition economies. I take stabilization to mean here essentially ensuring that the foundations for a stable currency are in place, although this was by no means self-evident for many of the successor States, as I discuss next. Some have opted eventually for a currency board, which I briefly clarify thereafter. Then I look at the broad meaning and purposes of stabilization programs, with particular reference to the challenges of transformation. In the following two sections, I detail monetary and fiscal policies, and their institutions and instruments, during the transition. I conclude with a few notes on desirable tightness in macro-economic stances.

Section 1: The need for stabilization and
macroeconomic prudence

Macroeconomics in any functioning market economy is all about policies that through appropriate institutions and instruments aim at coordinating the interests of economic agents with a view to maximizing society's welfare. The means utilized to proceed in a transition economy and the objectives to be served under a more democratic environment differ in principle from those targeted under state socialism or a mature market economy. As assessed through pluralistic means, society's preferences may be very complex, not necessarily a monotonic function of the availability of goods and services. There are furthermore competing claims on how best to reconcile individual preferences at any point in time and over time, in spite of possibly aberrant fluctuations until the political environment settles on new *modi operandi* for governing society. To accomplish that task an adequate and sustainable social compact is required. This should validate the macroeconomic stance and its realization in the most cost-effective way feasible. Perhaps most important are monetary and fiscal policies, possibly supported through price, income, and wealth policies. I can only brush over the complicated topics of general stabilization and ensuring a stable macroeconomic environment. Any standard textbook (such as Stevenson, Muscatelli, and Gregory 1988) provides the details.

A stable macroeconomic environment is characterized at least by a monetary policy suited to the degree of vibrancy in the economy and by a fiscal regime that does not overtax, yet enables the government to finance its mandated current expenditures, including servicing the public debt. The most visible symbols of such an environment are low fiscal deficits, low inflation, a sustainable current-account, and so on. Which magnitudes of these variables are deemed "stable" is a question that has been answered variously. Thus in the EU a presumption prevails that if the fiscal and government debt exceed 3 and 60 percent of GDP, respectively, inflationary pressure is considered to be too large and government debt unsustainable without some restructuring in the near term if stability is to be maintained (Brabant 1996, pp. 103–8).

Why is stability so important? As outlined in Chapter 3, the macroeconomic environment constitutes the framework within which economic agents operate on their own account. With transition, that room vastly expands. Macroeconomic stability now becomes a quintessential intermediate public good whose provision cannot be contracted out to the private sector. One reason is that it is entirely nonrival, meaning that the enjoyment of its benefits by one household or firm proceeds without impinging upon its availability to another. It is furthermore nonexcludable, meaning that it is impossible to deny households and firms the benefits of macroeconomic stability. Financing such an environment forms the natural province of the state (see Chapter 9). Seeing to the creation of such an environment and to its maintenance ranks among the inescapable responsibilities of those "governing" society.

Providing a stable environment is important if only because it removes one important instance of uncertainty. Inflation as one emanation of macroeconomic imbalance impairs or distorts economic performance; but more so for some economic operations than for others. It contributes significantly to the uncertainty that economic agents face. This applies to firms as well as households, and indeed to various levels of government and NPOs. It pervades microeconomic activity. Macroeconomic instability can be confined to national policy making for various failures in the monetary, financial, or fiscal policy. The short and the long is that national and international economic agents are no longer willing to absorb monetary or nonmonetary debt in quantities sufficient to finance the government's budget deficit in a noninflationary manner and without unduly raising real borrowing costs. But national instability may arise also from an unsustainable rise in externally financed private-sector spending leading to a foreign-exchange crisis with large private-sector losses. Eventually this entails a larger-than-anticipated budget deficit, possibly because of an actual or anticipated bail-out. Or it may stem primarily from regional or global systemic failings to prop up the framework (see Chapter 10).

The technical costs of achieving and maintaining macroeconomic stability are not very high. All it requires is a confined noncorrupt staff in the central bank and treasury in charge of designing and implementing macroeconomic policy; provided, of course, that the latter seeks stability. When instability arises, the technical costs of rectifying the situation are also quite low. However, the political costs of eliminating the real resources appropriated through high inflation and nontransparent budgetary and quasi-budgetary procedures represent the real obstacles to change. True, the volume of real resources appropriable via the "inflation tax" (meaning the decline in the real value of base money that economic agents are prepared to hold) is limited for economic agents will shift toward holding foreign currency for their transaction needs or to other, more stable, assets for their accumulation needs. It is basically up to the policy makers in place to bite the bullet: Either compress expenditures, which may be socially unacceptable, or raise fiscal revenues, which may be hard to implement in a weak environment. This is not an easy political task for different layers of society are variously affected by the inflation tax; likewise for the impact of stabilization measures.

Why is macroeconomic stability important for producers? This can be deduced from the preeminent task of the firm: Assemble capital, labor, and inter-mediate inputs to produce goods and services to be marketed at a profit. The more complex the production and marketing "technology" and the longer the time that elapses between the firm's expenditure and its revenue stream, the riskier even otherwise sound entrepreneurial decisions become. This is arguably largest for complicated investment decisions, which by definition involve the commitment of resources today in anticipation of uncertain returns at some point in the future. One can argue that on balance the impact of high inflation on investment is likely to be negative. This stems largely from the fact that there may be a positive option value to waiting. When "sunk costs" (that is, the difference between the investment outlay and the value of the assets once committed) are considerable, it may pay to delay private investment until there is sufficient commitment to the reform process and credible stabilization steps are set. Financing such investments may also be adversely affected by high inflation. Private markets tend to fully index short-term interest rates but not the capital value of outstanding long-term debt (Buiter, Largo, and Stern 1996, p. 21). Putting it another way, with macroeconomic instability the "transaction cost" of engaging in entrepreneurial activity rises because negotiating the various contracts, and indeed monitoring and enforcing them, rises, thus affecting enter-prise performance. It is not material to the discussion whether these contracts are explicit or implicit, market-mediated or administratively determined, repeated or one-off, or with insiders or outsiders.

These costs for firms are the larger when inflation is not fully anticipated. That prevails when information is imperfect or held asymmetrically. High inflation tends to be associated with price variability and uncertainty, thereby complicating entrepreneurial decision making. In the absence of complete contingent markets, which are a theoretical abstraction, management is exposed to false and confusing signals emitted by unanticipated high inflation. It is unclear in particular whether the price change is temporary or durable. Likewise, the price change may require an allocative response if the structure of prices is being altered, but not if the change in the end stems from a rise in the general price level. The disproportionate rise in the "noise" impairs the allocative efficiency otherwise promoted by appropriate price signals.

That "noise" may be exacerbated by the effect of movements in the exchange rate, when macroeconomic managers or politicians decide to forgo exacerbating inflation through emission of base money for borrowing abroad that exerts upward pressure on the exchange rate. Of course, this can be only a temporary solution. But very often its short-term nature is ignored, and thus a foreign-exchange crisis is eventually set off. Many enterprise decisions will, then, have been based on price signals and rules of the macroeconomic framework in effect before the crisis. Indeed, investment and production processes set up on their basis may no longer be financially viable after the crunch. Writeoffs of such investments impose heavy deadweight losses on society.

Note that high inflation itself derives generally from the whole range of contracting arrangements among economic agents, notably from the nature of wage- and price-setting mechanisms. But high inflation is generally nothing but a monetary symptom of underlying disagreements about sociopolitical priorities or conflicts, usually over public spending in the broad sense. The latter's resolution is a precondition for coming to grips with inflation in a durable manner. That is to say, credible and sustainable macroeconomic responses, rather than the stop-go cycle of embracing stabilization measures only to abandon them when social conflicts erupt, are necessary. These affect entrepreneurial decision making in an uncertain manner, depending on which monetary and fiscal levers are activated once the political decision to rectify the situation is taken. Their effects may be direct (such as interest rates for investment decisions or after-tax profitability). But they may also be indirect (such as an induced recession shrinking the market for the firm's product).

A stable macroeconomic environment is also important to households as consumers, savers, and suppliers of labor services. Various channels can be distinguished through which inflation as the manifestation of macroeconomic instability affects households. Very high inflation, even if anticipated, can divert significant resources from socially productive activities to privately rational but socially unproductive activities such as hyperactive financial manipulations that divert attention from production and marketing tasks. Rent seeking is another example. Inflation affects decisions regarding consumption and the accumulation of wealth, as well as the latter's composition. It is also a critical variable in determining the likelihood and duration of unemployment, regardless of contingent-benefit systems. There are, of course, other determinants of unemployment that are largely idiosyncratic or specific to the individual. But there is a common component reflecting the macroeconomic state of affairs, against which no insurance can be bought.

A brief digression on involuntary unemployment is warranted. Unlike the new classical economists, I subscribe to the notion that not all fluctuations in output and employment represent desirable (Pareto-efficient) shifts in the "natural" rate of unemployment. Aggregate demand and supply shocks can generate deviations of the actual unemployment rate from the "natural" rate and of actual from capacity output. Furthermore, these deviations may be persistent rather than transitory. A well-designed stabilization policy does not amplify such fluctuations through inappropriate monetary and fiscal policies. A monetary policy that ignores predictable endogenous fluctuations in velocity or that does not carefully examine and interpret monetary indicators does not qualify for that category. Moreover, it should try to buffer and offset shocks producing deviations of the actual from the natural rate originating in the domestic private sector and abroad, at least through the automatic fiscal stabilizers.

Imperfect indexation in public and private sectors means that high and uncertain inflation is accompanied by major redistributions of resources from creditors holding debt in domestic currency to their corresponding debtors. More generally it entails a redistribution from the economically weak, unsophisticated, and dispersed agents to the economically agile and well-connected. The inflation tax is oftentimes regressive. The reason is simple: It becomes a wage tax in countries where the financial wealth of workers depends almost exclusively on their cash holdings. This is true in most developing and transition economies. The better-heeled in such societies are able to hold their financial wealth in assets yielding high real interest rates and various sheltering opportunities.

Similar comments can be formulated for the state agencies and NPOs more generally. The effects of macroeconomic instability can be debilitating when inflation is not fully anticipated. The real value of tax collection erodes, especially as tax payers have a self-interest in delaying the transfer of their dues. Also expenditures escalate, some in unpredictable ways and others because of built-in indexation. The ability of state agencies to borrow shrinks. Confidence in government suffers in consequence. Proper budgeting becomes well-nigh impossible, thus aggravating uncertainty. The ability of NPOs to discharge their mandated tasks gets eroded as the real value of committed funds shrinks and previously expected, perhaps contracted, disbursement commitments cannot be honored.

Section 2: The initial approach chosen in transition economies

All transition economies inherit macroeconomic imbalances of some sort. It is therefore important to anchor firm stabilization policies to eradicate, certainly not aggravate, them. That must involve a reduction of budget deficits, a rise in interest rates, the pursuit of anti-inflation policies (perhaps through a tax-based income policy), holding wages in check even though inflation is eroding real incomes and wealth, and strengthening foreign competition through trade liberalization. These policies must be addressed to all economic agents by enforcing hard budget constraints.

In the initial approach to stabilization in the transition economies it was thought useful to stamp out inflation, that is, reduce it in record tempo to the "low" levels of western Europe. As the cost of such a policy approach (such as output losses, unemployment, losses in income and wealth, insecurity, and pauperization) kept rising, a creeping target of "acceptable" inflation during the phases of transformation has been set by those most interested in stabilizing these economies. This holds in the first instance for the IMF, but also for other multi-lateral agencies. Many of the latter's officers believe that "large" inflation makes it impossible for the market to function as prices are distorted, interest rates become negative and thus discourage savings, investment decisions are impossible to make because the trajectory of the economy in the years ahead becomes unpredictable, many economic agents seek to alienate themselves from the formal economy, and so on.

The precise magnitude of "acceptable levels" during the transformation has shifted markedly, however, in part because the debate on the nexus between growth and low to moderate inflation is far from over; the evidence mustered to date is not particularly persuasive (Stanners 1993, 1996). The point is that economists really do not know at what level of inflation the economy deteriorates. Large inflation is corruptive, destroying not only the economy but also rending the sociopolitical fabric. The recent experience of Yugoslavia illustrates this well (Lyon 1996). At the other extreme, there is also considerable evidence that pursuing near-zero inflation is deflationary in the sense that monetary policy has to be kept so tight that interest rates are too high to permit most investments. But a vast range of inflation targets lie between zero and perhaps 40–50 percent per year, and we really do not know at which point economic agents are no longer determined to produce and invest in anything but simple intermediation, shady operations, and economic crime.

It would in any case be useful to distinguish for transition economies the inflation that is largely statistical, in the sense that with liberalization prices adjust to real scarcities, from the inflation that is set off by deficit spending, indexation, excessive devaluation, and so on. This is not just the distinction between stocks and flows for no transition economy was able to liberalize all prices at once for reasons I clarify below. Prudence is also warranted because with the transition, and for some period during the transformation, the behavioral characteristics of economic agents cannot be known; those gleaned from the evolving situation are unlikely to be stable, hence useful for economic policy.

2.1 – Stabilization in the stock sense

To come to grips with the instability in the stock sense, epitomized by the "monetary overhang" (an elusive, but important category as explained in the next subsection), part of money in circulation, comprising currency and deposits of various maturities, needs to be sterilized. There are essentially two ways of doing so: (1) confiscation *de jure* through monetary reform (possibly with a staggered release of the funds in whole or in part as the supply situation improves) or *de facto* through inflation, and (2) the sale of goods under state control to augment domestic supply of real and financial assets.

Redressing past imbalances involves not only tackling excess money but also the distortions in economic behavior through "forced substitution." Part of the money supply must be sterilized perhaps through outright confiscation. But other means are available. These include raising the price level by accelerating inflation, freezing bank deposits, selling imports at prices that reflect the market exchange rate, divesting state assets, creating new financial assets bearing real positive interest rates, and fostering private capital formation. Except confiscation and inflation, the introduction of all elements of this stabilization package depends on the creation of new, market-oriented "institutions" and frequently the enactment of various laws for which time is needed. For example, sale of state assets requires firm property rights. Creating new financial instruments depends on having in place an appropriate financial infrastructure with all of the physical institutions and legal regulations associated therewith. None of these "institutions" can be set up quickly even under the most favorable circumstances. All this underlines the need for a certain measure of structural reform even to achieve the bare fundamentals of correcting past policy errors; it requires certainly far more than a clumsy confiscation of bills in circulation such as was carried out in the USSR in January 1991. Otherwise, price liberalization and devolution of decision making cannot but aggravate the instability that policy makers set out to correct.

2.2 – The monetary overhang

An inherited sizable monetary overhang must be eliminated on a priority basis. What precisely the monetary overhang is, and how best to come to grips with it, has been the subject of considerable controversy. How to tackle it I discussed in the preceding subsection. Its nature is something else. Some western observers deny the existence of the monetary overhang as a notion that "violates the most basic of economic principles" (Cochrane and Ickes 1991, p. 101), in this case that the shadow value of money is zero. This argument is not compelling, considering that households under state socialism keep money for purposes that do not exist in a market environment. One might call this savings for the eventuality that low-priced goods and services in official retail outlets will appear. Otherwise it would indeed make no sense to expect households to keep money instead of spending it on goods from alternative, grey and black markets. Its shadow value need therefore not be zero prior to the transition. But this evaluation changes almost immediately with modification in the supply of goods and services and in their relative prices. The point is that when the market economy is allowed to emerge and shortages disappear with the clearing of markets, the behavior of economic agents mutates.

Many analysts have adopted a rather bizarre definition of monetary over-hang. A typical "easy" approach is that recently reported by World Bank staff. In their study, Martha de Melo, Cevdet Denizer, and Alan Gelb (1996, p. 400) define monetary overhang as "the percentage change in real wages minus the percentage change in real GDP over 1987–1989." Quite apart from the problems of measuring real wages and GDP levels, including in their study, the notion obtained clearly cannot represent the monetary overhang that matters to stock stabilization. Conceptually, the monetary overhang in a state-socialist economy without alternatives to official markets consists of the accumulation of financial assets, usually in the form of cash or savings, that households and firms would have spent if the goods and services they wanted to procure, even as second best, had been available in a market-clearing sense either on the quantity or the price side of the equation, or in a suitable combination. Such assets should not be confounded with voluntary or imposed savings (in the sense explained in Part I). The "monetary overhang" is held by economic agents in anticipation of brighter market conditions. Presumably with liberalization this mass of money will chiefly be spent, thus influencing the level and pattern of aggregate demand early on in the transition.

But stock stabilization entails far more than simply blotting up the apparent monetary overhang. That must be concerned with the level and pattern of demand early on in the transition consists of all the funds reallocated with market liberalization. As such it comprises the "hot money" of the monetary overhang in the strict sense that households and firms had been keeping on hand prior to the transition's eruption, but also a considerable proportion of "forced substitu-tion" spending, be it in official or other markets. This reallocation affects not only the structure of relative prices but also the absolute level, given that price liberalization will be completed only over time and that some prices move farther and faster than others in response to imbalances between demand and supply in partial markets. Once prices are freed and most shortages eliminated, spending patterns may change drastically as compared to the quantity-rationed patterns of state socialism.

The currency overhang in the narrow sense can be soaked up in various ways, as indicated. One is through currency reform: At a certain date the currency in circulation is replaced by a new currency and the exchange is enacted on a less than one-to-one instantaneous basis. This may involve destruction of part of the old currency, such as that accumulated from actually or presumptively less-than-legal economic activities. It may also involve the more gradual exchange of current cash holdings, possibly with full interest compensation over time. All it accomplishes is that part of the money in circulation is temporarily sterilized until local markets can be better supplied. Barring some clumsy efforts at withdrawing bills from circulation at the end of *perestroyka* in the Soviet Union, no transition economy has overtly opted for currency reform at the transformation's inception.

An alternative way of coming to grips with the "monetary overhang" is to sell assets held by the state to private agents, thus blotting up their involuntary savings (and indeed attracting other savings as well). Few transition economies have considered this path too. The core problem has been, even in countries committed to rapid privatization, that establishing property rights and organizing asset sales, even in the case of petty privatization, takes time. Coming to grips with the monetary overhang is an urgent matter. Any postponement is likely to encourage some economic agents in the twilight between administrative coordination and market-based allocation to take advantage of the situation and enrich themselves not because of their ability to take risk, but primarily because of their position (such as during the so-called *nomenklatura* privatization). By the time asset sales can be organized, the transition economies have already opted for a third path to tackling the monetary overhang.

Reaching a "good" national currency can also be envisaged by Draconian stabilization policies that, in fact, erode the real value of the currency in circulation. The latter has invariably been the path chosen in the transition economies to date (see Table 3.2, p. 135), some through an early abrupt price liberalization and others after some temporizing, ostensibly because a more overt confiscatory monetary reform, if the authorities could have mustered the requisite administrative capabilities and the vision to do so, would have been "highly unfair." While I am sympathetic to the argument questioning the administrative capabilities and strategic vision of governments in transition economies, I am much less inclined to accept the excuse for labeling the currency-reform option more confiscatory and less equitable than the inflation tax. Both destroy, indeed *must* at least temporarily neutralize, a good part of the monetary mass in circulation when the reform is launched. Inflation does so across the board for holders of local-currency assets. It works more against the small saver than the savvy grey-area operator. As a result it may be even less equitable than outright monetary reform with staggered conversion. Of course, there will be political fallout for the "shock" once the electorate recovers.

2.3 – Flow stabilization

This encompasses the second sequence of measures to ensure that the national currency can fulfill its intended tasks. It essentially means that current macro-economic stances are formulated and applied so as to preserve or (gradually) restore basic balances; the two are not identical, however. In most realistic cases, it implies that monetary circulation is placed under some largely independent monetary authority, such as the Central Bank (see Chapter 7). The latter is, then, the guardian of the currency's stability and for that purpose regulates other institutions involved in financial transactions, including notably the banks but other agents in emerging financial and capital markets as well. An essential ingredient is that the Central Bank does *not* act as the government's financier. Rather, the government has to finance its mandated tasks through appropriate fiscal levies. This requires first and foremost that fiscal reform be pursued with determination and that any deficit incurred be financed through recourse to the financial system rather than the printing press.

Gaining stability in the flow sense is a function of monetary and fiscal policies conducive to managing money supply and the balanced financing of mandated expenditures. Apart from the latter, measures must be embraced to control the growth of the money supply. Initially, such fiscal and monetary policies are best kept at a rather elementary level, if only because the appropriate institutions and policies are lacking (Melo and Denizer 1997). But the objective of the switch should be to ensure a tight macroeconomic stance to avoid an inflationary spiral or a premature rupture of the social consensus. There may also be a need to enact price and income policies, if only to hold wage increases in check and provide for a minimal social safety net. Stabilization in the flow sense, then, simply cannot be attained by mutating economic institutions, policies, policy instruments, and perhaps other features of the framework in place for managing the economy. Structural reform and stabilization policies can therefore be kept separate only in an analytical context, not in responsibly managing transition.

The fiscal contribution to stabilization could be regarded as a simple matter of reducing the budget deficit in combination with policies for credibly financing any remaining budget deficit in a noninflationary manner. However, the shift to the market economy requires far more fundamental changes in the role of government (see Chapter 9). At its core stands the fact that with transition the government loses its power to control the economy directly. It will henceforth have to work primarily through indirect tools for influencing economic behavior. Fiscal consolidation is therefore likely to be predicated on substantial structural change in both revenues and expenditures. For one thing, subsidies in one form or another to firms and households must be compressed sharply. Where redistribution is mandated through the social consensus, it should primarily be done through transfer payments rather than by subsidizing selected goods and services, though some "specific egalitarianism commitments" (Stiglitz 1997b) may prevail. Also, more and more of the budgetary revenues have to be generated through the introduction of income, expenditure, and corporate taxes comparable to those typical of market economies. The latter implies in particular that the targeted fiscal system needs to be fair, not too complicated, and nonconfiscatory with a tax administration capable of enacting those principles without corruption or other abuses of power. This is much easier blueprinted than acted upon, given the labile environment in most transition economies. Simplicity and fairness with comparative ease of collecting taxes may therefore well call for an intermediate phase (Schweikert and Wiebelt 1996) of fiscal reforms (see Section 7).

The shift to a market environment also forces radical changes in the role of money and credit as compared to what prevailed under state socialism (see Part I). For one thing, money now has to perform a more active role in guiding resource allocation, and thus appropriate governance capabilities must be acquired. An effective monetary policy constitutes a key policy tool in ensuring an adequate supply of money and credit, in obtaining a "good currency" soon after the transition's start, in maintaining the stability of the exchange rate, and in helping to move toward sustainable currency convertibility (Begg 1996). I do not consider the latter an urgent task of transformation policies under most circumstances (see Chapter 5).

Monetary control can be exerted through various channels. In an ideal economic setting, monetary and fiscal policies are perfectly coordinated and chosen, and there is thus no need for an independent central bank (Fischer 1996, p. 35). Alas, no country possesses an environment with perfect information utilized in a genuinely altruistic manner with a view to optimizing economic decisions. A coordinating agent is thus required. One way that has worked well is by delegating authority over money supply to a relatively independent organ. This will generally be a central bank endowed with a considerable degree of autonomy within a well-specified constitution; it does not, however, necessarily mandate independence on the part of the central bank. In countries where such a state cannot be quickly reached, largely because policy makers cannot agree on monetary priorities, other means of monetary discipline can be explored. Indeed, several countries have resorted to a currency board (see Section 4), which furnishes a rather simple rule for monetary policy; but that is unlikely to be helpful for very long in most of the larger economies. A genuine central bank is eventually required. It is therefore instructive to bear in mind the desirable role of the central bank in managing monetary stability and in sustaining a balanced macroeconomy.

Proper monetary control can be attained in several ways, but the results obtained depend on putting in place a functioning two-tier banking system. The creation of a genuine central bank to manage monetary policy, to act as lender of last resort, and to regulate the commercial banking sector (and later on other components of financial, risk, and capital markets) so as to hold lending within prudent bounds is eventually indispensable. Policy tools such as reserve requirements, discount rates possibly diversified across various kinds of assets, and ceilings on loanable funds need to be put in place quickly and adjusted in the light of economic developments, including the rate of credit growth and exchange-rate pressures. The central bank inherited from state socialism should cease to be, and act as, the government's treasury. Public deficits, instead of being accommodated, should be financed through financial markets, however primitive; if really nonexisting, close budget balance should be strived for. At

151

best, central-bank lending should be limited to extraordinary circumstances. In this one must realize that sophistication in financial markets during transformation will have to be acquired gradually.

At the same time, commercial-banking activities should be devolved to an emerging banking sector. Actual financial intermediation between savers and investors can be discharged by a network of competing commercial, merchant, and investment banks, possibly departments of a universal-bank system as in Germany and Japan. Also other financial institutions, such as insurance companies and pension funds, will come to play an important role in due course. In this connection, the foreign-exchange regime needs to be firmly anchored. Making the currency of the transition economy eventually fully convertible is a key item on the policy agenda of open economies aiming at integrating themselves into the global economy. These two issues can be treated separately, although they are closely related (see Chapter 5). Likewise, the construction of deep financial and capital markets is a task that needs to be properly sequenced with priority attention allotted to ensuring that comparatively primitive, but functioning commercial banking prevails (see Chapter 7).

Just as the central bank should not act as the government's treasurer, commercial banks should finance endeavors at their own risk. Commercial banks, whatever their origin or ownership, should not subsidize borrowers and ration credit according to the inherited rules of the game. Instead, they should adjudicate on a fair basis loan requests lodged by any credible borrower. For that constraint to bite with the establishment of independent commercial banks, it is necessary to clean out the loan portfolio of the monobank and/or its subordinated commercial-bank affiliates and capitalize new and recapitalize existing commercial banks in a way that will not inhibit these institutions from quickly performing their intermediating functions on a strictly commercial basis. But special technical assistance may be required to promote a banking culture (see Chapter 7). However, not all loans contracted prior to the establishment of commercial banks are uncollectible. Much depends on how SOEs are structured, and indeed on the overall health of the economy (see Chapter 7).

2.4 – Pursuing a stable macroeconomic environment

As argued in Section 1, a stable macroeconomic environment is a public good that benefits all economic agents. The uncertainties and deterrents to investment and sound decision making associated with macroeconomic mismanagement, as well as the deadweight losses of prior decisions based on *ex post* wrong signals, constitute the quintessential "public bads." Since the transition economies face so many, and in some so large, imbalances at the start of transformation policies, a key question is how quickly they should try, and can be expected, to provide the public good of a stable macroeconomic environment. Many commentators have stressed the benefit of forging ahead quickly in order to reap the benefits of stabilization soonest, almost regardless of the cost entailed. I find this not the proper way to proceed with disinflation in a thoroughly uncertain environment, when some managerial capabilities are available or they can soon be acquired from abroad. Neither do I find their other contention terribly persuasive: The long-term costs of moving more slowly exceed those incurred by applying some form of "shock therapy." Clearly, there must be a tradeoff between the costs incurred in bringing about a sound economic environment and the benefits supposedly gained in terms of setting the stage for a resumption of substantial growth for some period of time.

Section 3: Money as an instrument and weapon

The history of money in modern societies has by no means been linear. Mature economies have learned to appreciate the salience of money and of preserving its purchasing power if it is to fulfill its intermediating functions efficiently. The benefits in general, and even those accruing to policy makers with a shorter-term horizon, exceed the temporary advantages that might be gained from debasing the national currency through the inflation tax when all factors are duly taken into account. This was not unknown at various historical periods. Such a motivation has also been present in several transition economies. Officials in a number of countries, particularly those emerging from defunct federations, had little knowledge about how best to conduct macroeconomic policy or forge ahead with the formulation and implementation of a transformation agenda. Very often these policy makers were torn between the broken-down systems and the absence of a credible alternative to their eyes, a rather perverse approach toward gradualism (see Chapter 3).

Mainly academic economists have devoted much attention to specifying explicitly the underlying conditions for shoring up a currency's purchasing power. But people's confidence or lack thereof, which is the driving force behind the comportment of economic agents and decision makers, has always been at the root of the credibility and stability of a currency. Any policy undermining the trust that agents have in, or are potentially willing to show for, a currency is bound to be counterproductive, in the sense that there will be flight out of the currency, perhaps after some lag, into another currency or into real assets. Of course, for a while a currency may be debauched, thus exercising a positive influence on the net worth of those who manage to avoid being misled by money illusion, without immediately provoking such an open flight. At some point, however, even those currently subject to money illusion will rationalize their real-balance behavior, including on holding liquid assets for whatever purpose.

In other words, the quality of a currency is critically conditioned by the psychology of those utilizing it. Once confidence becomes dissipated, it is not easy to regain it; as a rule it exacts a stiff price. This cost revolves essentially around the requirements that induce economic agents to hold balances of the targeted national currency, in preference to a more readily recognized currency, for transaction and precautionary, rather than chiefly speculative, motives in the expectation of being able to utilize it ultimately to pay for real transactions. Maintaining confidence can by no means be taken for granted. Nor can it be restored following a simple recipe. Rather, those entrusted with safeguarding the currency, and with monetary policy more generally, have to respect the instrumental value of money when it is responsibly managed. Debauching the latter should be warded off under most circumstances – war and revolution are one thing; economic reconstruction for sustainable growth is something quite different. It may yield short-term "gains." But it is bound to complicate coordination, and indeed maintaining macroeconomic stability, in a longer-term perspective. Money is a serious matter that deserves careful attention. Over the past several years this feature has not quite obtained in several transition economies. As such, the absence of an instrument that can legitimately be called money enormously complicates revamping the financial system and putting in place the vestiges of a functioning capital market.

The role money plays in a market environment, or in an economic system that is moving toward an environment in which indirect economic coordination is becoming essential, differs substantially from what it was under state socialism or its legacies lingering at this juncture (see Chapter 2). Fostering appropriate inter-mediation for a rapidly evolving environment from administrative planning to a market-based system of resource allocation is a distinct task for those managing the transitions. This is all the more important when regaining and sustaining some positive growth path constitutes a core priority among the requirements for securing continued sociopolitical support for the transformation agenda. The latter is needed to absorb in an orderly fashion the unavoidable burdens that incisive structural change inflict upon society at large, in spite of sincere or pious policy intentions. This is a very real constraint that does not seem to impress most professional economists and officials from assistance-providing international organizations (UNECE 1994, pp. 1–2).

Before one can meaningfully inquire into the stages of building a functioning market economy to coordinate decentralized decisions, it is important to remind ourselves that to function properly economic agents must have access to a national currency. Such a currency must at the same time be a "good" standard of value, unit of exchange, and store of value. It should also be exchangeable for other currencies, at least to permit some transactions, and to possess this quality at a fairly predictable, if not necessarily immutable, exchange rate. The transactions for which such convertibility of the national currency can be envisaged are various. At the very least this quality of the national currency should extend to the acquisition of foreign currency by residents engaged in authorized transactions abroad, such as licensed traders. This is the so-called internal convertibility achieved by several transition economies early on in their mutation.

In principle, a transition economy could adopt another country's currency, thus subjugating its emission, and ultimately its monetary, policy to that of the reserve currency. In the process it would forgo most of the benefits of seigniorage and of the inflation tax accruing from having an own currency that economic agents are prepared to hold. A similar purpose, but without these drawbacks, can be served by enacting a currency board (see Section 4). Base-money emission would then depend on foreign-currency assets with the country's monetary policy largely geared by that pursued in the reference currency's economy. I focus here on the issues revolving around creating and managing an own currency, because that is the main task of policy making in transition economies, regardless of objections by academic commentators.

To merit convertible-currency status in the sense of "convertibility" as per article VIII of the Articles of Agreement of the IMF, a national currency must be available for exchange for "current transactions" (meaning transactions on current account and a few others, including for the "reasonable servicing" of external debt and for unrequited transfers for some specific purposes) with minimal interference. The path toward gaining such a degree of currency convertibility is subject to policy choice and depends on concrete circumstances, including the ability of policy makers to manage the foreign-exchange market. Under some conditions, it may be preferable to move toward a greater degree of currency convertibility not by suddenly freeing up the foreign-exchange market but by organizing gradually a much more generalized access to foreign exchange for authorized traders. Currency auctions for a comparatively brief period of time (months rather than years, of course) may be instrumental in realigning expectations of economic agents. They may also help to locate the approximate "equilibrium exchange rate" at which foreign-exchange policies could usefully be directed. The transition's duration depends on how quickly a reasonable interbank foreign-exchange market can be erected. The latter must be able to funnel appropriate information in a transparent manner to all authorized agents, and soon to all desirous of acquiring foreign exchange.

Before a national currency can aspire to convertibility status, in whatever sense, it must fulfill distinct functions in domestic transactions, such as the three cited earlier. For better or worse, a national currency gears economic trans-actions among most domestic economic agents, particularly once it gains legal tender; the authorities are concerned about appropriating seigniorage; and agents have minimal confidence in the currency for transaction, and hopefully also precautionary, purposes. It is therefore important to pause briefly with the requirements for realizing the conditions in the case of one transition economy's "new currency." I choose here the experience with the *karbovanets* – the interim currency of Ukraine, which has since been replaced by the *hryvnya* as a full-fledged national currency – because this enables me to cover most of what I want to underline in connection with establishing a national currency in a transition economy.

Although it was first introduced in June 1992 on a par with the ruble to supplement the physical shortage of ruble notes supplied by Russia's *Gosbank*, I am concerned with the later phase, when the *karbovanets* was adopted in November 1992 as the interim national currency between moving away from the Soviet (and later Russian) ruble and creating an own legal currency, the *hryvnya*.

Pending the latter's creation and once the Russian ruble had been spurned, the *karbovanets* became a surrogate national currency. There can be little doubt, though, that the *karbovanets* poorly fulfilled the cited money functions. Although it was in principle freely transferable to acquire goods and to turn goods into currency in Ukraine's market, the *karbovanets* remained a poor standard of value, given the inflationary environment. Indeed, a currency's value is essentially determined by what can be bought with it, or what economic agents expect to be able to obtain for it once the currency is used for intertemporal intermediation; this in the end depends on contemporaneous and intertemporal demand and supply conditions. The *karbovanets* was also an inadequate medium of exchange because holders of money balances on the whole preferred other liquid assets than the *karbovanets*, even for transaction purposes, with some exceptions. It was certainly not a good store of value for accumulation purposes, given the rapidity with which the *karbovanets* depreciated between November 1992 and early 1995, when the still ongoing stabilization efforts were firmly introduced. It depreciated markedly even against the Russian ruble before the latter was approximately stabilized!

In correcting this situation, a currency fulfilling the three cited qualities need not necessarily be a legal currency or be backed through reserves. Indeed, real money needs takers, not backers, because takers count on others accepting it from them and those accepting it in turn count on their being able to acquire a reasonably predictable bundle of goods and services of their choice. A currency backed legally with gold or other convertible currencies is desired not primarily because it would be exchangeable into gold or convertible currencies *per se*, but rather because of the credibility this inspires: It provides confidence that currency can be used to acquire a certain bundle of goods and services at home or, by recourse to exchange markets, in foreign markets. By its very nature and actual functions, then, the *karbovanets* never complied with this weighty condition until stabilization efforts were credibly put in place, and adhered to in spite of adversities, in the course of 1995 and with periodic hiccups since then.

Finding takers for the currency required more than simply redenominating the *karbovanets* into the *hryvnya*, at whatever exchange rate. To move from a "bad" (the *karbovanets*) to a "good" (the *hryvnya*) currency, some kind of monetary reform in Ukraine was required. It was pursued through monetary control over more than a year, until the *hryvnya* was introduced in September 1996. But problems of controlling inflation, delayed progress with creating markets, and negative experiences with the Soviet and Russian ruble as well as with the *karbovanets* have made agents wary about placing much faith in the new currency. As a result, the *hryvnya* has been depreciating since its introduction and is now subject to a currency corridor (see Chapter 5).

Section 4: Main features of a currency board

Money has been utilized as a weapon in a number of transition economies. In many of the newer states the formulation, implementation, monitoring, assessment, and fine-tuning of macroeconomic policies in general, and monetary policies in particular, have remained rudimentary at best. The experience of Bulgaria in early 1997 illustrates that even in established countries conducting a responsible monetary policy has not been easy. Precisely for these reasons, renewed attention has been called to the virtues of establishing a currency board in conjunction with embracing a rather passive monetary policy as an alternative to an active monetary policy conducted by a central bank. Before going into the latter in the next section, it is useful to be aware of the role of a currency board in the context of transformation policies directed at regaining sustainable growth at the smallest cost. The latter will as a rule be impossible without a minimal degree of monetary stability. Otherwise incentives for economic agents remain difficult to grasp, few are interested in channeling savings into long-term investment, economic activity disappears into the underground, savings are parked abroad, resources are not allocated well, and so on.

Monetary stability can be regained via alternative paths. A currency board offers but one. Since I am here not interested in theory, I explore the currency-board mechanism only because some advocates (B. Gray 1993; Hanke 1994, 1997; Hanke, Jonung, and Schuler 1993; Nash 1995) have recommended it as a quasi-magical solution for regaining monetary control while ensuring a direct link with the world economy on the least distorted terms for a diverse range of countries, including transition economies. In that sense, the currency board sounds too good to be true. Nonetheless, if properly installed and operated under the right circumstances (IMF 1997a), a currency board *may* provide a useful vehicle during the *early* phases of the transformation process, when governance capabilities are weak and establishing policy credibility is of the utmost importance; as Bulgaria's experience underlines, this point may well come after years of stop-go transition measures.

4.1 – The nature of a currency board

Before evaluating whether the currency board is a superior scheme for transition economies than a firm central-bank policy, one must be clear about what a currency board is and what it can accomplish. Quite simply, it is a monetary arrangement that establishes a direct, credible link between the base of the domestic currency and a country's foreign-exchange reserves with two-way convertibility guaranteed at a fixed exchange rate. It was first introduced in the mid-nineteenth century by Great Britain in its overseas territories as a device to save on transaction costs in transferring sterling balances to the far-flung reaches of the empire. To do so the colonial administrations were encouraged to emit their own paper and coin fully convertible on demand into sterling, which was held in the City. As a result, Britain's seigniorage did not decline. Furthermore, the metropolitan country's interest rate and price level continued to percolate through the empire. Note that most commercial banks in the colonies were in any case branches of mainstream City financial institutions. Whenever in difficulty, they could call upon their home base for liquidity. The latter in turn could rely on the lender-of-last-resort function of the Bank of England.

These benefits do not quite prevail when a sovereign country emits its own paper and coins with the backing of its foreign-currency reserves. It is the emitting country that derives seigniorage from issuing "its currency" and depositing part or all of its foreign-exchange reserves in fairly secure and liquid interest-bearing foreign securities; it derives that benefit also from the erosion of its currency (because of loss or destruction). It may also make a gross profit from the spread between the buying and selling price of foreign exchange. Its costs, of course, add up to the expenditures of printing and coinage, and of running the exchange. Finally, the link between the price and interest levels in the country with a currency board and its reference economy can at best be tentative until the former gains real credibility through deeds rather than through a mere institutional arrangement.

Not all currency boards are identical. Some restrict agents or the purposes of convertibility. Others circumscribe the nature of the link, whether for 100 percent or less, or the way in which currency reserves are to be maintained (in the board's vaults or partly in negotiable interest-bearing instruments of considerable liquidity and security). Still others establish the currency board in lieu of a central bank with its anchor enshrined in a clear law. In some countries, the exchange-rate anchor is fixed but, at least in theory, adjustable according to preset regulations. In Estonia, for example, the currency board is subject to a law that requires parliamentary approval for modifying the fixed link of 8 *kroon* to the German mark with margins of 3 percent (Bennett 1993; Buch 1993a; Hansen and Sorsa 1994; Hansson 1993; Kallas 1993; Lainela and Sutela 1994). Though the board cannot alter the exchange rate, nothing prevents parliament from modifying the law or exchange rate when it judges it to be in the country's (or the policy makers') interest. Very similar arrangements apply to Lithuania, with the exchange rate of 4 *litas* fixed to the US dollar; but the Lithuanian board's convertibility is far more restrictive than Estonia's, essentially limited to authorized traders on current account, and is now slated to be gradually phased out (*The Economist*, 3 May 1997, p. 69). Bulgaria too adopted a currency board as of July 1997 under pressure of the IMF.

An orthodox currency board, such as utilized in the former British colonies, is one in which "monetary policy is extremely rule-bound" (Hanke and Schuler 1994a, p. 13). In fact, the currency board takes the place of the central bank and is designed explicitly to remove all discretion, all opportunities for exerting political pressure on monetary policy, at least as far as base money is concerned. It is merely an office that engages in exchanging "its local" against foreign currency and vice versa. It does not have the power to sterilize flows in the balance of payments, impose exchange controls, affect interest rates, act as lender of last resort, or set reserve requirements for commercial banks. An orthodox currency board does not take responsibility for ensuring that bank deposits are convertible into its notes or coin (Hanke and Schuler 1992, p. 15). Furthermore, by its very nature it implies full convertibility on both current and capital accounts. That is to say, an orthodox currency board is extremely passive: "It simply exchanges its notes and coins for reserve currency, or the reverse, in such quantities as market participants demand" (Hanke and Schuler 1994b, p. 4). It has no power to modify the supply of base money independently of the wishes of market participants and their preference for holding local rather than foreign currency. Conversion may be mandatory, though this is not so in an orthodox currency board.

Most existing currency boards, including those of transition economies, are modified. This means that countries have a central bank or a similar institution entrusted with some or all of the cited powers denied to an orthodox currency board. For example, Estonia backs not only currency but also bank reserves (Villanueva 1993). The chief promoters of orthodox currency boards dislike and counsel against establishing modified currency boards because "their rule-bound and discretionary elements are contradictory" (Hanke and Schuler 1994a, p. 13), allegedly rendering them rather unstable. On the other hand, they are supportive of orthodox currency boards as "the only way republics of the former Soviet Union can ensure stable currencies and their sovereignty" (Hanke 1994, p. 10). Steve H. Hanke, who has been the most enthusiastic proponent of the mechanism, would probably extend this idea to the successor States of Yugoslavia as well; Boyden Gray (1993) even transmits it to all transition economies and Nathaniel Nash (1995) waxes confidently about it as the solution for inflation in developing countries in the next century! If so, why has the idea made only slow progress, including in transition economies? There must be more to the argument than its promoters like to air.

At least three conditions must be met (Hanke, Jonung, and Schuler 1993). First, the country establishing a currency board must secure a sufficient amount of foreign reserves to ensure an adequate supply of base money. Second, it must set an exchange rate (say, domestic per reserve currency unit) that is realistic for if it is set too high (low) foreign exchange accrues (vanishes) from the export (import) surplus and capital inflow (outflow). Finally, it must issue notes and coins equal to the initial foreign reserves and make them legal tender. It is important to stress the difference between money supply and base money; the two should certainly not be confounded. In any economy with commercial banks money supply is not rigidly related to foreign-exchange reserves (Alan Walters 1987). Nor is it true that inflation and interest rates converge toward the levels of the reserve-currency country. Hong Kong, which has one of the most orthodox currency boards, has experienced substantial inflation, even quite recently (Peebles 1994, p. 1060; Alan Walters 1992, pp. 5–6).

4.2 – On the advantages of a currency board

The full advantages, as well as disadvantages, of a currency board depend on the concrete situation of any one country at a particular point in time. Clearly, the greatest advantage is credibility in the sense that political authorities cannot force the monetary authority to lend it money, and so policy makers either go to market for their borrowing or have to bring the budget under control. That is to say, a currency board depoliticizes the monetary system and insulates the public purse against those bent on debauching the currency (Alan Walters 1987, p. 742). This does not mean, however, that with a currency board the government's budget must necessarily be in equilibrium by reducing expenses or raising taxes, or a combination of the two, as some contend (Buch 1993a; Nash 1995). The latter holds only if the government is unable to borrow at all – an unlikely event under most realistic circumstances.

Second, it is fairly straightforward to administer an orthodox currency board since it only exchanges reserves against base currency. It is easy to understand for the public at large right down to the last little man holding notes in front of the exchange window. This is something worth considering particularly for countries whose domestic agents have been accustomed to quite different conditions for so long with inflation being altogether a daunting, almost inexplicable phenomenon. This consideration might be quite important for transition economies, particularly those without central administrative experience or durable and reliable policy makers. One may legitimately voice skepticism, however: Is it not rather odd to assume or to believe that a currency board is credible and instills confidence because of its institutional format? Could it not be the case that the properties presumed to derive from the institution of the currency board – stability, transparency, and confidence – derive from prior conditions for their emergence? If everything is in place and all the preconditions are met, one may well ask tongue-in-cheek what purpose a currency board could serve and why a stronger commitment on the exchange rate would be required.

Third, a currency board compels a government to adopt responsible fiscal policy. Since it cannot bully the central bank, it will have to tap private markets for financing any deficit. One might object to this by invoking the chicken-and-egg problem: If a government can be presumed to be sufficiently determined to introduce a credible currency board, it should also be capable of balancing the budget or of financing deficits by going to market. There is perhaps a time-inconsistency dimension to this in the sense that a government determined to set up a currency board in a credible manner may be thrown out of office and replaced by a government that would otherwise have been less determined to balance the budget, reluctant as it is to undermine the currency board's credibility. This is by no means trivial in some transition economies.

Finally, a credible currency board *can* lower the risk premium and therefore exert a moderating impact on domestic interest rates (Hansson 1993, 1994).

4.3 – Systemic disadvantages

As already noted, the broadest systemic disadvantage is the loss of flexibility as a tradeoff for credibility. The basic problem is the following: How can one adjust to policy shocks (such as differential price movements, productivity gains, and speculative capital inflows) requiring a change in the real exchange rate when that policy tool has been removed? With a credible currency board, domestic wages, prices, and interest rates rather than the nominal exchange rate have to bear the burden of adjusting the real exchange rate. Wages and prices might be sticky downward and interest rates may be tied too closely to interest-rate policies abroad (Lainela and Sutela 1994, pp. 42ff.). If so, a recession might be required to reach a real exchange rate compatible with a sustainable current-account deficit. Clearly, a currency board does not preclude an exchange-rate adjustment (Osband and Villanueva 1993; Villanueva 1993). But its touted advantages are likely to suffer if the exchange rate were to be adjusted after policy makers' insistence that such would be precluded under their currency board. Both Estonia and Lithuania, given the large discrepancy between domestic inflation, even if mainly on account of price adjustments of nontradables or differential gains in productivity, and the pace of price changes in their trade markets, have periodically been subject to destabilizing devaluation rumors. In fact, Lithuania has now set a program for gradually replacing its currency board with a central bank; this is expected to entail a devaluation of the *litas*.

Second, there are risks associated with a fixed link to a foreign currency, particularly when the latter is not representative of the country's mix of expected foreign-exchange earnings, primarily from exports. This applies to both Estonia and Lithuania. Openness with a stable international economy playing the role of a monetary anchor is extremely important. It is also risky when the reserve currency is subject to undesirable fluctuations, whatever the reason.

Third, particularly in an orthodox currency board deposits of the domestic banking system are not convertible or subject to the rules of the currency board. Banks take deposits completely at their own risk and must ensure adequate reserves to honor depositors' claims. This makes domestic banks vulnerable to runs – for purported solvability and liquidity reasons (Buch 1993a) – since, by definition, there is no lender of last resort. Unless one has a small commercial-banking sector or most banking operations are entrusted to affiliates of large foreign banks, control over the banking sector even under a modified currency board is quite limited.

Fourth, raising domestic interest rates is not a particularly effective instrument. Speculative capital inflows might be unleashed while domestic debtors are punished and investors discouraged. It may work for a while because some people want to speculate. But eventually its impact is very negative from a fiscal point of view. History tends to buttress the proposition that currency boards work well when capital inflows are positive; but a problem emerges quite quickly when speculative capital flows reverse themselves (Calvo 1992, p. 23).

Fifth, one may well question the advantages of a currency board beyond those stemming from having a fixed exchange rate and reaching the fiscal and financial preconditions for its appropriate functioning. Given the prevailing uncertainty and magnitude of necessary adjustments in transition economies (including in government budgets, foreign-exchange imbalances, enterprise indebtedness, and the weak banking sectors), considerable costs tend to be associated with a strong commitment to a fixed exchange rate; also difficulties arise in ensuring that the preconditions for the proper functioning of the currency board will be realized.

Sixth, the argument that interest rates and the pace of inflation will trend down toward those observed in the reserve-currency country holds only under rather restrictive conditions on full credibility of the currency board and there being only base money. The latter implies no commercial banking beyond taking deposits with near 100 percent coverage and no capital transactions. But this would already contradict the very basis of the currency-board mechanism!

Seventh, one may well argue that if a country's politicians are bent on abusing the currency there is no guarantee that the fixed rate will be kept or that the currency board will not altogether be replaced by a central-banking system. Particularly when a country has very little banking expertise, it would seem preposterous to confine policy making to a currency board and hold credibly onto it for lack of banking skills. Neither would it seem useful to impede the latter's emergence through some modified form of a currency board with a confined central bank, one that exerts monetary control by restricting bank operations essentially to facilitating reciprocal payments (Rostowski 1994a). If the authorities can commit to reform, why would they require so drastic a remedy and if they remain inclined to inflate, why would they agree to a currency board (Lainela and Sutela 1994, p. 52)?

Finally, currency boards may give rise to alternating deflationary and inflationary pressures. Particularly when the domestic deposit base is limited, a currency board suffers from a deflationary bias. Money supply is rigidly tied to the availability of foreign exchange, whose supply can normally be augmented only by generating an export surplus – the wrong kind of resource flow for a country bent on switching growth paths and renovating its infrastructure – or long-term productive capital inflows in an environment that is more likely to encourage speculative capital. If foreign investment cannot be mobilized on a credible longer-term basis, the currency board may be inflationary and incoming funds must be sterilized. The country's ability to do so may be very limited for institutional reasons. It may also be quite costly relative to the real, not the touted, benefits obtained (Eatwell *et al.* 1995, pp. 179–81). If translated into productive investments that generate an export surplus later on, the built-in deflationary bias is postponed.

4.4 – The proper time for a currency board and when to abandon it

I find it irresponsible counsel to sketch solely in the abstract the advantages of a currency board as a prelude to recommending for or against such an institutional arrangement for any one country (B. Gray 1993; Hanke 1994, 1997; Nash 1995). This smacks of unprofessionalism when presented without reservations as a distinctly better alternative to the policy advice hitherto propounded by the IMF (Hanke 1997). Such policy advice makes sense only when it heeds concrete circumstances: governance issues, credibility of the policy commitment and stability of the decision-making levels, the monetary base, foreign-exchange reserves, a functioning commercial-banking system, degree of openness of the country and its size, the ability to select an exchange rate and hit it right from the first try, and so on.

A pure currency board would seem to be most useful when all, or nearly all, of the following characteristics prevail: The deposit base of the banking system is small; policy makers are mainly interested in securing the note issue of a highly open, but financially unsophisticated economy; and the government in power lacks fundamental governance capabilities or is inhibited from exerting them, given the battles for control among contending factions that are only beginning to crystallize into normal political parties (Liviatan 1992). For that very reason, such institutions have worked very well in entrepôt economies. Elsewhere, countries will have to decide on how to handle the other central-banking functions denied to a currency board: lender of last resort, bank supervisor, and trustee of monetary policies. Simply forgetting about these tasks entails too much vulnerability.

The above observations suggest that a currency board is possibly warranted when a country's administrative or political circumstances demand that a minimum of monetary stability be restored soonest even though, for the time being, the authorities cannot persuasively enforce minimal good governance, including in monetary affairs. This is likely to be more so in a small open economy with a narrow monetary base (Eatwell *et al.* 1995, p. 181) than in a big, fairly closed economy with at least a rudimentary commercial-banking infrastructure, particularly if the country's output is below potential for circumstances partly beyond its abilities and the monetary base is very small. It may also help to bolster the credibility and the clarity of the transformation program. But there are costs, including forgone seigniorage and inflation tax (Eatwell *et al.* 1995, p. 180). A currency board is essentially a primitive arrangement, quite similar to the absolute gold standard (Fischer 1996, p. 34). It rests on the obsolete notion that equates money with banknotes, paradoxically as under state socialism (see Part I). At the same time, one should be aware of the limitations inherent in the currency-board mechanism and try to devise ways to cushion the blow of future shocks without generating a costly crisis (Calvo 1992, p. 24) when the ax falls (Hansen and Sorsa 1994), as inevitably it will.

To believe that policy makers can just hit on the right nominal exchange rate in a transition economy, given the prevailing uncertainty, borders on the miraculous. Most transition economies have opted for a wildly undervalued exchange rate (see Chapter 5). This ironically cushions against foreign competition but pushes vulnerable domestic activities dependent on imported inputs out of business. However, eventually the economy will tend toward an equilibrium real exchange rate. It will do so through inflation. In other words, one should be aware of the fact that by implementing a currency board, or maintaining a fixed-rate system otherwise, in an environment with pervasive uncertainty, policy makers necessarily fix beforehand an initial period of inflation. This should not be considered a failure of transformation policies; it should simply be recognized and acknowledged. A real appreciation of the exchange rate is likely to exert palpable pressure on export earnings and renders speculative capital inflows attractive.

Because of the strictures, and real disadvantages, of a currency board when monetary policy is to be utilized as an integral ingredient of the policy package designed to guide the economy onto its transformation path, the device may no longer be the more desirable way of arranging monetary control over the money supply once the initial phase of the transition has been successfully weathered. Even if a currency board may be a proper policy step to reach credibility early into the transformation agenda for a small, open, and financially rather unsophisticated economy, the institution itself should evolve into something more stable. At the very least, measures will have to be taken to exercise some control on preventing a run on the banks from being so sudden and large that there is not even time for central policy makers to react. This is likely to be particularly pronounced when serious efforts are directed at regaining a sustainable growth path, which implies jumping hurdles to overcome the minimal catch-up. In that sense, the currency board will eventually need to evolve toward a central-banking system within a full monetary constitution (Honohan 1997), as Lithuania is now trying to engineer (*The Economist*, 3 May 1997, p. 69).

Much of the argument advocating a role for a currency board during the phase of incipient transition centers on generating credibility. This the currency board can possibly achieve. It cannot, however, guarantee flexibility, something that will eventually be required to generate sustainable growth with comparatively rapid catch-up. Not only that, given the uncertainty during transition and the firm hand needed on the tiller to identify a new growth path, and even more to walk along it, credibility of the currency board cannot be ensured forever in any case. That is to say, the currency board is eventually bound to lose its very justification, except perhaps in countries with very strong links to the monetary institutions and instruments of the currency to which they peg, as in the Commonwealth.

If the currency board must eventually be replaced by central-banking arrangements and a proper monetary policy, three issues arise: (1) What type of central-banking arrangements will be appropriate, given the concrete circumstances of transition economies? (2) When should the transfer to central-banking arrangements be best entertained? and (3) How should it be accomplished in order to minimize adverse credibility effects? I return briefly to the first question toward the end of this elaboration. The third question is particularly acute when the transfer entails a *de facto* exchange-rate realignment. The loss in credibility is perhaps more acute in the case of devaluation. I invoke this circumstance because the point chosen for moving toward a new monetary arrangement is unlikely to coincide with the theoretically optimal one, that is, when adverse credibility effects can in principle be minimized. In all likelihood the transfer will coincide with a crisis in adhering to the fixed exchange rate of the currency board, even though in theory there is nothing in the currency-board mechanism that prevents a change in its statute, be it by parliamentary act or otherwise.

As regards the second question, it would be more useful to engineer the shift to a proper central-banking system once minimum governance capabilities for formulating the main responsibilities of central-bank control – managing the money supply, conducting a responsible exchange-rate policy, acting as lender of last resort, issuing and modifying prudential regulations, and supervising banks and other financial institutions – will have been mastered. This could be ensured by actively launching efforts to acquire such capabilities almost from the moment the currency board is put in place. Of course, if preparations for the transition are introduced too openly the credibility of the currency board may from its inception be less robust than it could have been. On the other hand, if the acquisition of these skills is deferred until the pressure on the currency board becomes untenable, the transition to central-banking arrangements may be enforced under less than desirable circumstances.

In other words, there is a clear tradeoff between up-front credibility and ability to steer firmly the transition process. The major criterion for choice is infusing credibility not so much into maintaining a constant nominal exchange rate with full convertibility than well in persuading domestic and international economic actors of the earnest intentions, demonstrated and firmed up through deeds, to conduct appropriate monetary and exchange-rate policies within the context of responsible overall transformation policies, including with respect to monetary management. To enhance this credibility, it may be wise to coordinate the efforts directed at moving toward central-banking arrangements with the assistance of multilateral financial agencies, the Fund in particular, as Lithuania has been doing. Not only can such collaboration furnish at low cost essential buttresses of central-banking governance and of the required institutional arrangements (see Chapter 10). It can also strengthen credibility and facilitate staving off adverse pressures once it becomes clear that the transition to central-banking policies is under way. This will be quite acute when the switch occurs under circumstances that suggest that the fixed exchange rate of the currency board is unlikely to be maintained under the emerging central-banking system.

Of course, one of the most critical issues is likely to be the determination of the actual functions to be discharged under the central-banking arrangements, given the stage of the transformation of any one country with a currency board. This has been one important policy issue in transition economies that have eschewed currency boards, however primitive the central-banking institution's infrastructure and governance capabilities have remained. I return to this issue in Section 6, after briefly touching upon formally agreed programs to regain stability.

Section 5: Stabilization programs

A stabilization program is essentially a plan embodying a coherent framework in which a wide range of policy issues are addressed with a view to closing certain internal and/or external imbalances that are unsustainable in the medium to long run. Its origin may be actual or anticipated inflationary and exchange-rate pressures. It provides a framework for disinflation or stabilization in the flow sense, although there may initially have been a motivation to come to terms with a "monetary overhang." That is to say, stabilization programs are normally embraced, possibly at the urging of a multilateral financial agency, to come to terms with structural imbalances in domestic budgets and/or the external sector. The two are as a rule related though not in a one-to-one fashion. Transitory imbalances in either domestic or external sectors are in principle best addressed through temporary borrowing in domestic or foreign markets.

Fundamental problems of financing government budgets or the current account need to be corrected through a host of domestic policy measures, usually in combination with foreign-sector reforms, over a comparatively brief period of time. The aim is to encourage a reallocation of the country's resources toward more productive economic activities, the compression of domestic absorption, and bolstering exports over some period of time. It is preferable to aim at reaching such higher efficiency and competitiveness in foreign markets by reducing and switching expenditures fairly quickly, if external financial resources can be accessed to close the imbalances in the short run. In the absence of private financing, a country may seek an agreed program with a multilateral agency to force through rather rapidly the changes required to restore balance in its domestic and/or external accounts. But speed of adjustment cannot be the sole criterion. Stabilization programs routinely generate possibly sizable social and political costs that may be more destabilizing than the economic imbalance(s) that the program is intended to correct in the first place. There is, then, a trade-off between the effectiveness of the stabilization program in terms of its results and undertaking meaningful structural economic adjustment.

The policy measures included in a stabilization package can be quite diverse and tend to vary from program to program. They usually entail an exchange-rate devaluation to discourage imports and stimulate exports, and upward adjustments in domestic real interest rates to foster savings and guide investments to more productive endeavors. At the same time, pricing policies are to be geared increasingly to reflect real scarcity, for instance, by eliminating retail-price subsidies, industrial-policy supports, and market rigidities especially for labor. Loosening up

166

domestic regulations that inhibit flexibility in resource allocation or that interfere with the incentives for economic agents are also envisioned both in domestic and external sectors. Liberalizing the trade and payment regimes by moving closer to currency convertibility at a more realistic exchange rate forms part of the program. Removal of regulatory strictures on exit and entry, on obtaining access to financing, on being able to compete abroad, on premature welfare advantages, and so on are also included.

Stabilization programs usually are deflationary, though that need not hold in fact or even in theory, provided flexibility in resource allocation and institutions is present, or external resources can be temporarily tapped. But that is precisely the crux of the matter as in most cases imbalances arise because of imperfect flexibility rooted in structural or institutional aspects of the economy in question and external lenders, and perhaps domestic agents as well, have lost faith in the country's economic management. Imbalances as a rule arise because of excessive absorption in private and/or public sectors. That excess demand for domestically produced and imported goods and services will have to be curbed in an orderly fashion. The compression is typically achieved by reducing public outlays through fiscal policy and by restricting credit through monetary policy aimed at compressing real private investment and consumption in some suitable combination. In addition to those actions on the demand side, contemporary stabilization programs also target purposeful changes on the supply side. The latter will be especially important in economies with built-in rigidities on resource reallocation. The transition economies qualify for this status.

Stabilization and adjustment policies are bound to depress levels of economic activity if the imbalances addressed originated in the first place from output levels that exceed long-run capacity. Nevertheless, with few exceptions, a macro-economic adjustment program entails a contraction of economic activity, which may in fact inhibit the improvement in economic efficiency that it was designed to elicit. As recent experiences in many developing and transition economies have amply underlined, austerity usually has a disproportionate impact on investment, which by lowering the growth of capital reduces the capacity to produce over time, and thus may entail contraction over a protracted period of time. This conflict between economic efficiency and the need to improve the current account may stem from a variety of sources. The most important are: (1) "overkill" or excessive adjustment measures causing a contraction in economic activity; (2) optimistic assumptions of domestic-market flexibility, thus overstating the speed and benefit of expenditure switching; (3) import cuts affecting not only final consumption but also demand for intermediate and capital goods for which no substitutes from domestic production are available in the short run, thus crimping capacity utilization; and (4) the compression of domestic absorption falling disproportionately on investments, thereby weakening future production capacity.

Demand management can take on various forms. The primary objective is to reduce expenditures by cutting purchasing power through controlling nominal flows to various actors in the economy. In the household sector, for example, nominal wage levels can be more strictly controlled, thereby possibly reducing household income and expenditure. In the enterprise sector, the reduction in aggregate credit supply from the banking sector curtails investment outlays and urges firms to reconsider their inventory policies. Government expenditures need to be compressed while net indirect taxes are normally raised by cutting or eliminating government subsidies. This direct reduction of government demand alleviates pressures on credit and money markets. Furthermore, the government normally curbs the rate of growth of money supply. Expenditure switching is aimed at bolstering export supply and discouraging import demand. A substantial devaluation raises the domestic price of imports and, in many cases, of exports, and thus can be expected, after dissipation of the factors behind the familiar J-curve effect (by which, upon devaluation, the current account worsens in the short run), to reduce domestic demand and divert it to domestically produced import substitutes. Domestic suppliers on balance tend to divert goods from the domestic market to exports.

Supply measures of the adjustment package can take on various forms as well. They mostly consist of enhancing resource allocation by direct and indirect policy means. Direct instruments are in the sphere of tariffs, exchange rates, interest charges, and, in many cases, key product prices. Indirect instruments are contingent on changes in the underlying institutions, such as the liberalization of the trade and payment regimes, or the imposition of controls over nominal variables. Better management of aggregate credit and money supply also improves the setting of financial markets and thus indirectly affects aggregate investment and inflation.

Orthodox stabilization programs are generally conceived within the framework of the Washington consensus with the accent on liberalization. In several transition economies, however, as well as in some developing countries, so-called heterodox stabilization programs have been formulated and applied with some "success" (see Chapter 3). The latter's emphasis is also on liberalization but with important levers being "anchored" not to flexibility but at some target level. Various anchors have been used. Most common has been a reference fixed exchange rate for some time, followed by a crawling peg. Others have preferred controls on nominal wages by levying special wage taxes. Several countries embraced these two anchors and in addition made some commitment on reining in money supply. Clearly, with several anchors problems of internal consistency of the anchors and aggregate macroeconomic policy are bound to arise. However, these problems generally remained unresolved in stabilization-policy stances in the transition economies, with considerable consequences for the sustainability of the effort.

Section 6: Monetary policy and instruments during transformation

In contrast to the substantially passive stance of monetary policy under state socialism, with the transition and the movement toward decentralization money comes to perform an active role in guiding resource allocation. An effective monetary policy constitutes a key tool in ensuring an adequate supply of money and credit, pursuing domestic price stability, maintaining reasonable stability of the exchange rate, and helping to move toward sustainable currency convertibility. As indicated earlier, these tasks when restricted to their elementary level, certainly early in the transition, are comparatively easy to perform by a small staff at the central bank, provided the political will to enable that staff to discharge its professional responsibilities is present.

Various systems of monetary control could conceivably be envisaged. But the delegation of control of the money supply to a relatively independent agent seems to work well in mature market economies. At the very least, the banking system inherited from state socialism needs to be reorganized, as noted. Provided the authorities do not opt for a rigid monetary rule such as a currency board (see Section 4), a central bank is as a rule entrusted with several tasks. Given the confined room for governance capabilities, it tends to be endowed with wide powers over monetary control; but at the same time with fewer instruments than would be normal in a mature market economy (Begg 1996; Melo and Denizer 1997). Its tasks include managing the money supply with a view to currency and price stability, ensuring an appropriate exchange-rate policy, acting as lender of last resort, and enforcing prudential regulation, and bank supervision. The latter in particular can at some point be hived off to another central institution. But for quite some time going into the transformation, setting the rules of the game for financial institutions comes within the competence of the central bank.

Some advocates of monetary conservatism have called for endowing the central bank essentially with a constitutional statute like that of the *Bundesbank* – pursuing primarily price stability within its fairly independent status. This is unlikely to be the foremost task of the central bank early on in a transition economy. The reason is fairly simple: Until deep financial and capital markets begin to firm up, the central bank will by necessity have to take on roles that other institutions will eventually take over. Price stability can be only one beacon of the central bank's work program. Furthermore, independence must be seen as a relative concept, even in the case of Germany. While it may be admirable to constrain central-bank behavior principally to ensuring price stability, arguing this case for countries that still have to jump many hurdles in order to catch up with the western European economies, notably in terms of firming up financial and capital markets, seems to me not particularly compelling. Even in a country like Germany – recall only the way the unification was engineered! – the central bank's policy is subordinated to the broader goals of making economic policy. There can be no room, not even at the EU level, for a truly independent central bank, for who would then monitor it and ensure that it play a constructive role in economic policy?

At the very least, the central bank must be in charge of monetary policy. As the key institution in formulating and implementing macroeconomic policies, a revamped central bank needs to be entrusted with steering monetary policy, including in support of stabilization and regulation of commercial banks, with a view to maintaining as much buoyancy in the economy as can be afforded under the peculiar circumstances of the transition, as noted earlier. Correcting large inherited imbalances is a *sine qua non* for imparting credibility to the transformation agenda. Instruments to control money supply need to be adopted. This could include monitoring levels or rates of growth of money supply, setting a ceiling on loanable funds, modulating interest rates and reserve ratios, engaging in rediscounting activities, and managing the exchange rate. It is particularly important to recognize that little can be accomplished by way of economic devolution in a latent or actual inflationary situation. Key, then, is arriving at reasonable economic stability. But that does not necessarily mandate disinflationary policies aiming at rooting out inflation to zero and stamping out inflationary expectations in the short run.

Monetary policy must at least focus on managing money supply, that is, ensuring that it stays within certain parameters, including the state of the real economy. The central bank can do so through direct or indirect means (Alexander, Baliño, and Enoch 1996). Direct means refer to the central bank's use of its regulatory powers. This contrasts with indirect means, where it uses its influence on money markets as the issuer of reserve currency (meaning currency in circulation and bank deposit balances with the central bank). The latter instruments act through the market by adjusting in the first instance the underlying demand for, and supply of, bank reserves, utilizing market-based incentives (including open market operations, reserve requirements, and central bank lending facilities). Direct instruments operate by setting or limiting either interest rates or the amounts of credit outstanding through regulations, such as credit ceilings and directed lending (meaning at the behest of authorities rather than for commercial reasons).

Initially the central bank in a transition economy can at best try to influence money supply by direct means, even though direct controls of credit and interest rates entail some inefficiency and resource misallocation, thus provoking some measure of disintermediation. One reason is that in the absence of, or with poorly functioning, financial and other markets, efforts to influence money supply, credit demand, and interest rates indirectly through changes in the liquidity conditions of commercial banks and other financial institutions are unlikely to be very effective. In an environment characterized by rudimentary and noncompetitive financial systems, direct controls may be the only policy option until the maturation of the institutional supports for applying indirect instruments.

Direct methods of monetary control are appealing for several other reasons. For one thing, they are perceived to be reliable in controlling credit aggregates, and perhaps even their distribution and costs, at least in the early phases of moving toward market-based monetary control. They are also easy to implement and explain. Furthermore, their operating costs are comparatively low. And they are attractive to managers of the transition bent on channeling credit to meet specific objectives. In time, however, a switch to more active measures tailored within the context of market conformity should be engineered. There is indeed a tradeoff between the cited advantages and the costs of inefficient resource allocation and ineffectiveness arising from the evasion and inequity that direct instruments entail. These are perhaps more deleterious in inhibiting the development of more sophisticated, market-based competition in financial transactions, a precondition for switching to catch-up growth and swift modernization (see Chapter 12). The expeditious movement toward indirect instruments of control should be entertained *pari passu* with market incentives becoming more and more effective, liberalization of domestic and foreign market access through currency convertibility, and freeing up trade from administrative constraints (Wong 1992). There will then be room in the transition economy to prepare itself "gradually" for indirect monetary control.

This raises not only the issue of "gradualism" but also of "sequencing" of monetary reform (Alexander, Baliño, and Enoch 1996; Begg 1996; Melo and Denizer 1997; Wong 1992). Formulating satisfactory solutions depends very much on circumstances. In a transition economy, these include the overall state of the economy, the maturity of market-based decision making, and the availability of competent financial institutions operating within functioning prudential regulations and bank-supervision structures. One sequence of measures has worked particularly well in many Asian countries (Wong 1992, pp. 16ff.). This encompasses first the introduction of market-based monetary instruments through reforms of monetary-control procedures. Only in this manner can the central bank anticipate reserve developments and modify bank liquidity at its own initiative and with the required degree of flexibility. Early steps might include the introduction of new monetary instruments, such as treasury bills, auctioning procedures for such instruments, and changes in the modalities through which banks obtain access to the financing facilities at the central bank's disposal.

Almost equally urgent, given the sorry state of the commercial-banking infrastructure in transition economies (see Chapter 7), is reform or creation of prudential regulations and supervision. This includes loan classification and provisioning, capital-adequacy requirements, and limits on loan concentration. Weak financial institutions must be recapitalized, restructured, or liquidated in an orderly manner. The development of financial markets beyond effective commercial banking could be envisaged at a later stage even though the maturity of available financial markets remains an important determinant of the effectiveness of indirect monetary control. But as soon as the first two steps (market-based monetary instruments and prudential regulations and supervision) are reasonably completed, market-based instruments of monetary control can be applied to commercial banks. This should parallel the gradual removal of direct control instruments. As market-based decision making matures in a more and more transparent and open environment, interest and exchange rates become gradually more important parameters. Indeed, they increasingly become the instruments through which monetary policy is transmitted to the real economy. It is therefore important that monetary policy be dovetailed with fiscal and external policies to avoid inconsistencies between targeted demand and supply in financial markets, undesired interest rates, and volatility in exchange rates.

Commercial banks should be closely monitored for their efficiency in intermediating between savers and investors, in ensuring effective and timely reciprocal settlements among all (but perhaps initially only commercial) agents, and in marketing a limited range of new financial instruments, including to finance government deficits. Once the banking sector is reasonably robust, the central bank needs to provide regulatory support to market participants, including by disseminating information, if only to enhance the scope and effectiveness of competition in at first a limited range of financial services.

Given the state of affairs under transition, it would be utopian to expect a fully functioning central bank to be in place early on during the transition. Operating procedures of central banks are bound to vary from country to country, reflecting different stages of economic and financial development as well as different preferences regarding the foreign-exchange regime, among other factors. However, efforts should be made soonest to put in train basic procedures for achieving monetary and credit targets. These encompass the setting of the desired path for the demand for reserve money, basing it on an intermediate-target variable (such as broad money) that is consistent with overall policy goals. The next estimate is a desired path for the operating target variable (such as net domestic assets of the central bank) based on the desired path of reserve money. On the basis of forecasts for the major elements of the central bank's balance sheet, the projected path for the operating-target variable is assessed, assuming that there are no net sales of government securities and no change in other policy instruments. Finally, the policy response to the deviation between the desired and the projected path of the operating-target variable needs to be decided.

There should be no doubt, however, that for the transition economies to achieve catch-up and sustainable growth, and indeed to participate effectively in EU integration, "deep" financial and capital markets will eventually have to be set up with a fairly sophisticated central bank and related regulatory and supervisory agencies. Erecting such a deep market is a complex process that requires competitive financial institutions, substantial infrastructure, and a sophisticated legal and regulatory framework. Even though the absence of such a deep market inhibits efficient intermediation, this cost should be preferable to having in place a "weak" financial infrastructure that may look "deep" in legal and organizational terms, but in fact fails to support the real economy where it is urgently needed. Again, gradualism and sequencing are on the order of the agenda for promoting the emergence of a deep financial market.

Section 7: Fiscal policy and instruments during transformation

As seen in Part I, fiscal policy under state socialism was chiefly concerned with indirect taxation. In countries, such as Hungary, that had genuinely tried to decentralize economic decision making to the enterprise level, some kind of income-tax policy for SOEs had been instituted. But otherwise, SOE profit was essentially siphoned off as revenue to the budget, after withholding for various kinds of mandated enterprise funds (such as for social purposes, for capital renewal, and for comparatively small new capital expenditures), particularly with administrative reforms. With the movement toward an economy based on private property and market coordination, this needs to change drastically in order to ensure that mandated expenditures can be financed from adequate fiscal revenues raised in the least distortionary manner.

It is important to bear in mind that, as with so many variables, fiscal policy during the transition takes on special features from what it is in a mature market economy or its shape once the transformation nears completion. At the same time, one should bear in mind that the transition economies initially possess weak tax administration and customs machinery, including the technical infrastructure to handle the increased number of taxpayers (C. W. Gray 1991); lack experience with mass taxes based on voluntary compliance; do not possess appropriate accounting systems or a legal framework within which firms, and taxation authorities, can readily operate; and need to encourage domestic saving and foreign investment to finance restructuring and moving toward a new sustainable growth trajectory.

To balance the government's budget, fiscal reforms are needed. These can be fleshed out only over time but the first steps in that direction must be set soonest to avoid large budget deficits relative to GDP. Moving toward a market setting erodes the state's erstwhile absolute authority to treat net revenues of firms as its own. Furthermore, there is an urgent need to adopt an income-based tax policy for both corporate and private sectors. A reasonable fiscal approach consistent with creating a market environment encompasses a combination of direct taxes on firms, on natural resources, on wealth, and on personal incomes. These may have to be supplemented with a value-added tax system, which is preferable to other indirect taxes, but in some cases excise taxes on specific commodities, possibly a sales tax, and tariffs may be required; whenever the cost incurred by government can be directly imputed to specific users or activities explicit user fees need to be set as equitably as circumstances allow. The paramount task is to create a system of revenue generation and outlays that allows the government to discharge its functions, as mandated through the sociopolitical process, while maintaining macroeconomic balance, promoting economic efficiency, ensuring an acceptable dispersion of incomes, and minimizing distortionary fiscal levies or subsidies.

Fiscal reform also comprises shifts in centrally mandated expenditures. The broad use of pricing policies for redistributive purposes must be severely curtailed

173

in favor of income transfers. It is very important to eliminate subsidies for failing firms by expeditiously enforcing bankruptcy or restructuring procedures; given the institutional lacunae in those domains, however, it may be useful for transition managers to seek a few showcases for restructuring or bankruptcy rather than to immobilize broad swaths of the economy, pending due process. Rather than remaining the main instrument for the redistribution of funds as under state socialism, the financial policy of the state must now become more limited in some sense, chiefly in support of regaining stable growth and sheer governance for mandated functions.

Ideally, in a democratic environment, fiscal policy should be the outcome of the consensus-building process. On the one hand, fiscal revenue has to be secured by taxing economic agents, including private actors. On the other hand, fiscal expenditures are designed to raise welfare in society by making some citizens better off without harming any one. There are then three levels of discourse: (1) the ability to raise tax revenues and the tax base, (2) the level of the budget and the financing of any gap between expenditures and revenues, and (3) the level and composition of expenditures deemed necessary to secure and stabilize the sociopolitical consensus and to act in conceptualizing expenditures according to social preferences.

At the start of the transformation, fiscal reform was envisaged as a fairly straightforward matter of instituting a more broadly defined income tax, of replacing the more onerous indirect tax levies with a value-added tax, of levying various user taxes, of conceiving a cascade-like network of import duties, and putting in place an appropriate excise tax regime. Some even thought that they could import the fiscal systems of western Europe with minor modifications. Two developments were taken as axiomatic. One was that the economic downturn would be shallow and short-lived so that most SOE profit would continue to accrue to the budget, pending privatization at which point corporate tax would take the relief. It was also taken for granted that the newly emerging private sector, including through the divestment of state assets, would belong to the official economy once the restrictions on entry and exit lifted.

These assumptions were invalidated fairly quickly, but not until after the budgets of the transition economies initially benefited via a marked gain in SOE profits deriving chiefly from the one-off revaluation of assets in consequence of the very substantial revision of transaction prices. Many SOEs in the first year of transformation gained markedly from their large stocks of inputs and semi-processed products acquired at the "low," administered prices of state socialism that could now be utilized in finishing manufactures and sold at the new price at home or, after devaluation of the national currency, abroad at a sizable profit. That these firms were not properly concerned about their long-term asset valuation only exacerbated this shift toward short-term survival strategies. In some cases, this was a real windfall: Inventories under market conditions need not be as extensive as those prompted by shortages and ill-coordination of state socialism.

174

Soon into the transition, however, fiscal balances come under strain for three reasons. One is the collapse in output, and in levels of economic activity more generally. This cuts deeply into the profitability of operations, hence taxable revenues. Second, the tax base itself shrinks markedly with the transfer of assets from state to private property, the latter operators being extremely averse to joining the legal economy and paying taxes. Also, many prefer to consume their capital in the short run, thus compressing reported net profitability. Revenues from other activities are either beyond the reach of the taxing authorities, notably in the second economy, or prove to be too complicated to be actually levied for lack of an adequate taxing administration or infrastructure. Furthermore, some part of the formal economy benefits for some time, particularly in the case of FDI, from various tax holidays. Finally, upward pressures on expenditures appear fairly quickly in spite of the quite rapid elimination of the vast bulk of enterprise and price subsidies. Expenditure requirements surge in particular because of commitments undertaken earlier under state socialism (such as for pensions, health care, and education) and those that the deteriorating environment imposes upon the managers of the transition (such as for poverty alleviation, unemployment benefits, other social-welfare provisions, and for funding larger pension claims than had originally been accommodated, as detailed in Chapter 8). But other upward pressures on expenditure categories and downward ones on revenues arise because of the loss of control even over SOEs during transition and the dysfunctional hiving off of tasks somehow to be accomplished to the government (such as servicing the bad bank debt). One could put it as follows: The fiscal crisis in most transition economies arises in the short run from a shortfall in revenues; but its longer-term instability hinges critically on reaching a new arrangement on the appropriate level and distribution of taxation, which may or may not stem from "overspending" (Mizsei and Rostowski 1994, p. 1). These prove to be easier to work out once solid recovery gets under way. The need for a broader agenda for fiscal reform, consisting of far more than simply applying a few other taxes, is then felt.

Perhaps the greatest calamity, certainly in the CIS States, arises because taxing authorities are simply unable to collect even from firms or persons willing and able to pay. The entire infrastructure of tax administration inherited from state socialism is simply not suited to applying a modern tax code in a fair and equitable manner. Of course, the calamity with the civil service, the rampant corruption among tax inspectors and collectors in some countries, and the sheer criminal behavior of some private-sector actors exacerbate the calamity. Note that under the circumstances the old state sector continues to act as the main provider of fiscal revenues with exorbitant levies that constrain these firms and inhibit them from undertaking urgently needed restructuring even when management in place is up to that task. Taxing away all the flexibility in these firms simply to obtain some revenue for the budget is not the most desirable instrument to prop up a fair and equitable market economy.

175

Conclusions

The above considerations suggest that it would be desirable to reach "stabilization" quickly and then sustain it as an important public good. In practice, however, few countries are in a position to adhere to such a stance for very long. While monetary stringency can be tightened, provided the political will to do so prevails, on the fiscal side rectitude is not generally possible until fiscal reforms can be put in place and the nose dive engineered by the transformation comes to an end. It is not just a question of political will to be "prudent." Very important is that several policy stances coming under this label depend on the availability of institutions and policy instruments that can be put in place only over time (see Chapter 7). Prudent macroeconomic policies will then almost certainly call for engineering a "soft landing" rather than forging ahead with "shock therapy." The latter can be most useful only under rather restrictive conditions, such as hyperinflation with a broadly based loss of confidence in the political leadership and in the future of the local economy and currency. A soft landing does not require a sophisticated fiscal system as some claim (Mizsei 1994). Rather than putting this in place on paper or as per the legal code (McDermott and Wescott 1996), it might be more constructive to move more gingerly toward emulating the fiscal systems of mature economies, and focus first on collecting the required taxes in the most effective way possible (Schweikert and Wiebelt 1996). That will almost certainly involve greater differentiation and modulation on the side of indirect taxes than on the side of income taxes, even though such a taxing infrastructure may fail to be equitable and fair, given its inherently regressive nature.

5

INTERNAL AND EXTERNAL
LIBERALIZATION

The second major component of the transformation agenda comprises "liberal-ization." In the domestic economy, this refers in particular to widening and deepening the decision space accessible to all economic agents, the policy parameters for guiding their behavior, and the institutions for facilitating coordi-nation. Among the instruments prices figure prominently. When appropriate I shall differentiate among prices for goods and related services, wages, interest rates, and other parameters of the alternatives offered in the emerging market setting. Price adaptations are expected to be actively encouraged by macro-economic policy makers to modulate the behavior of microeconomic agents. Internal liberalization also refers to facilitating exit and entry of firms. This is particularly crucial in environments that prior to the transition were regimented by central decision making. For the same reason, I stress explicitly liberalizing property transactions, including real estate. But contract sanctity and its legal enforcement are also critical (see Chapter 7). Perhaps most important, a market economy without adequate competition and without properly structured incen-tives to foster it is unlikely to be very efficient. That competitive environment must in the first instance emerge from within these economies. But also traded goods and foreign actors appearing in domestic markets are essential. Note that incentives need not necessarily be material or pecuniary; they could be entirely of a moral dimension. What matters is that they be properly tailored. They should be individually appropriable and directly associated with the effort made.

Arguably an equally important component of this agenda item concerns external liberalization. Several actions are required, including managing the exchange rate as a quasi-price for clearing foreign-exchange markets; the abolition of the MFT to permit external competition and the direct linkup between internal and external prices; devolution of access to foreign exchange for all legitimate economic agents; and regulating trade through conventional trade-policy instruments, such as tariffs, rather than through the myriad of implicit protection instruments inherited from state socialism. In addition to embracing domestic administrative and economic measures regarding external behavior, the transition economy can also avail itself of the benefits of multilateral (regional as well as global) regimes. That merger too forms part and parcel of integrating these countries into the global economy. But these more institutional aspects I defer to Chapter 10.

Before focusing on internal and external liberalization, I explain coordination as the central task of markets. Then I examine four elements of domestic liberalization: prices of goods and services, interest rates, other instruments of monetary and fiscal control, and wages. The salience of fostering competition, including by integrating the second economy, is underlined thereafter. The next sequence revolves around measures in the foreign-trade sectors, including the abolition of the MFT and price equalization, instituting commercial-policy instruments, managing the exchange rate, financial-market liberalization, and easing access to foreign exchange. The last section provides a brief overview of trade reorientation. In conclusion, I highlight the interconnectedness of liberalization with the other components of the transformation agenda introduced in Chapter 3.

Section 1: Coordination in a market environment

One major contributing factor to the seemingly irreparable decay of planning under state socialism was the cumbersomeness of coordinating the economic activities of the various state, collective, cooperative, and private agents with the instruments at hand (see Part I). Whereas moving to the market economy is predicated on introducing an entire array of liberalization measures that have little direct bearing on coordination *per se*, the success that can thus be booked depends nonetheless on the degree to which the various activities of economic agents thus elicited can somehow be harmonized. In the context of the transition economy, given the asymmetric emergence of markets on the ruins of the state-socialist economy, coordinating the socioeconomic system in considerable flux during the transformation differs from what is required in a functioning market economy.

The market economy tautologically encompasses decentralized economic behavior of a great variety of private, public, and intermediate agents pursuing diverse interests. Interactions among individual agents are in the first instance geared by the price mechanism. These various decisions are dovetailed either by individuals acting and reacting within the set framework of macroeconomic policy and its associated institutions and instruments. In addition, coordination may be codetermined through the intervention of policy makers in a regulatory mode to ensure compliance at the microeconomic level. These are basic preoccupations. One critical policy decision in transition economies must, therefore, be the establishment of open and competitive markets by fostering market-based price flexibility for virtually all goods and services.

Recall that I view prices as summarizing the terms at which alternative products, services, or production factors in whole or in their user or usufruct modes are traded. The concept therefore includes domestic wholesale and retail prices, wage rates and labor-related emoluments, interest rates, and also the exchange rate (that is, the price of, in my approach, domestic currency expressed per unit of the reference foreign currency). How these critical terms for trans-actional exchanges are set and within which parameters economic agents are induced or permitted to pursue their own interests are major determinants of feasible allocative outcomes.

Given the wide distortions in relative and absolute prices under state socialism (see Part I), price liberalization is fundamental to progressing toward the market environment. There is little disagreement among transition managers that price liberalization should be enacted early on and be fairly comprehensive. There is much less of a consensus, however, on whether liberalization should be decreed all at once or be phased in more gradually, and in the latter case with which kind of sequencing. One favored sequence in early discussions about transformation was to free up wholesale prices and interest rates first, next consumer prices, then trade prices and the exchange rate, and finally nominal wage rates. But this was always a controversial political and technical issue. No single transition economy has pursued it to its full logic.

Price liberalization of goods and services was politically controversial from the start because it could not but exert a palpable impact on the purchasing power of nominal variables in domestic currency. That effect would be spread unevenly among the various layers of the population in a predictably regressive form. Thus those who had been able to hold their savings in hard currency were bound to reap a considerable windfall from the local currency's devaluation. Many services heavily subsidized under state socialism would prospectively fall beyond the reach of many households. For example, housing rents were at derisory levels under state socialism. Bringing them up to market level immediately, even if such markets could have been conjured up, would have occasioned a huge redistri-bution of access to residential services, with potentially devastating social, as well as political, consequences.

But there are also technical problems. For one thing, the behavior of prices once liberalized in an environment that is anything but competitive, and more-over characterized by uncertain reactions on the part of economic agents, cannot be reliably predicted. Another concern is that price liberalization may trigger inflation, not just a correction for price distortions inherited from state socialism. The risk of igniting such a process is very real, given the rigidities and downward inflexibilities in prices (notably wages) anticipated at the outset of the transition. A key question raised in this connection is whether price liberalization should be enacted before or after putting in place a minimum battery of measures designed to enhance domestic competition. Furthermore, there can be no certainty about the degree of competition that can be fostered primarily by opening up markets to foreign goods and services. Should greater stress be placed on encouraging the emergence of new, thus differently motivated, domestic agents through private capital formation, demonopolization, the breaking up of conglomerates, and other measures?

Especially the adherents of liberalization at nearly any cost propose to move first to free up trade and foreign exchange. Multiple purposes would thus be served. It fosters trade, hence props up domestic demand and provisioning. At the same time it bolsters competition in domestic markets, thus whittling the rent seeking that domestic monopolies otherwise engage in upon the freeing up of domestic prices. Furthermore, it shakes up domestic producers and exposes consumers to what the world market has to offer. Moreover, it imports an adequate bundle of prices for traded goods that, through factor-price adjustment, in time exert an impact on prices of nontraded goods as well. Whether the latter can be accomplished in an orderly fashion depends to a large extent on the initial gap between absolute domestic and foreign prices, the comparative distortions in relative domestic and foreign prices, the "normal" trade intensity of the country (particularly for manufactured goods), and the level of economic activity that can be shored up during the mutation.

If domestic prices are pervasively distorted, if the country has a natural proclivity for relative autarky, if devaluation is very marked, and if the transition-induced recession is substantial, moving toward scarcity pricing in the above fashion may be very costly. Especially in countries that had not moved very far down the decentralization ladder under state socialism (see Chapter 2), the distortions prevailing on the transition's eve are very considerable. The adjustment cost in terms of inflation, unemployment, bankruptcies, erosion of wealth held in domestic currency, poverty, destruction of capital in place, and other impacts on the socioeconomic framework likely to ensue from plunging into the new price system without safeguards can therefore be anticipated to be very large. It may even fail to induce the most important change coveted by the transition economy: Revising production structures in a comprehensive manner. In other words, trade liberalization is a necessary but by no means a sufficient condition to foster greater competition.

Section 2: Prices of goods and services

Because prices prevailing at the start of the transformation do not reflect scarcities and there are perceived to be limitations to how quickly prices can be freed up gradually, the "shock-therapy" approach places much emphasis on freeing up most prices almost all at once soonest to foster more efficient resource allocation. The exceptions are as a rule housing rents, transportation, health care, utilities, wages, and very often various types of fuels and electrical energy. Wage controls in particular are viewed as critical in generating quick stabilization. Note that it is also hotly contested by those who have to bear the brunt of the adjustment burden, if not with the transition's inauguration because of its "stunning effect," then after a short interval. Even so, an important prerequisite is corrective adjustment of the terms at which alternative products, services, and production factors are traded among clearly defined owners of property rights. Thus, relative prices of necessities in terms of luxury goods, of foodstuffs against manufactures, often of nontraded against traded goods, of most services in terms of goods, and of primary products in terms of finished goods must rise; the real return to capital must be raised to foster savings; the level and dispersion of labor remuneration need to be synchronized more closely to reflect shifts in average labor productivity; the cost of foreign exchange must be set "accurately" through a sizable devaluation; and so on. Is it desirable to leave these adjustments up to as yet primitive markets? Or could central policy makers usefully impart basic directions for and rough magnitudes of adjustments to be worked off?

The approach chosen by all transition economies has been gradualism of a sort. Most countries adopted a major liberalization of prices for most goods and services early on, usually once basic terms of the political economy of transition had been set; in some cases price liberalization was used as an instrument to dislodge opposition to societal restructuring. Typically excluded from this policy were basic user fees for state-owned housing, transportation, medical services, and utilities. Oddly enough, in several countries appropriate adjustment in energy prices in the broad sense was excluded as well; the "odd" refers to the crucial percolating role of these costs throughout the economy. More gradual adjustments of energy prices have as a rule been opted for. Also excluded for a considerable period of time was liberalization of wages and, in some countries, of the price of loanable funds.

The danger of setting off a wage-price spiral in this manner was very real as workers and trade unions could be anticipated to seek compensation, perhaps after a brief truce, for the erosion of their real wages as a result of the "corrective inflation" induced by price liberalization. To forestall that, several countries embraced some kind of tax-based income policy. That essentially meant restricting wage liberalization. This was enacted at least in the socialized sector; but in some cases for all too long erroneously also in the private sector. Increases above a norm, which itself was chosen as a fraction of the changes in consumer prices, became subject to a punitive wage tax levied on the infringing firm (the notorious *popiwek* in Poland is perhaps the best known example). This was applied across the board without consideration at all for differential changes in labor productivity – an odd stance given the ostensibly liberal bent of policy makers in 1990. As already noted, applying this rule to workers outside the socialized sectors made no sense at all, and the rule was therefore reversed after some months. Admittedly, tax-based wage policies are effective in dampening domestic absorption and the pace of inflation, given the large share of the wage bill in overall value added. However, the resulting compression of real wages may push the lower-paid layers of society, and the households used to all kinds of transfers under state socialism, into poverty. In these circumstances, the construction of a social safety net becomes even more urgent (see Chapter 8).

If policy makers choose to liberalize the trade and foreign-exchange regimes in part to import a set of relative prices, a phased introduction of prices for traded goods is not possible. External-sector liberalization even complicates the gradual phasing in of scarcity prices into domestic transactions of nontraded goods. But other policy options to cushion the impact are available. Thus managers of the transition can provide "guidance" to simultaneous domestic price and trade liberalization, especially when either or both are enacted incompletely, as has been the case in all transition economies. They can first reset domestic relative prices of key commodities, such as fuels and basic ores; with minimal delays emerging markets can thereafter determine the prices of other goods and subsequently fine-tune even prices of basic goods. But this option has generally been rejected as something smacking too much of planning and government interference.

Price liberalization in domestic markets cannot be limited to goods and related services. Whereas policy on the pricing of labor has been heavily interventionist in many countries, it has been the obverse in the pricing of capital and foreign exchange. Especially in view of the need to steer monetary (as well as fiscal) policy in a direction that soon yields a stable macroeconomy, ceilings on interest rates for all kinds of financial transactions need to be lifted too. Under state socialism, real interest rates tended to be substantially negative in countries with open inflation and they appeared to be so in countries with repressed inflation. Point measurement was never easy, as is the case for real rates even in a market environment. The movement toward positive real interest rates during the transition is something overdue as compared to earlier rates. But note that this does not warrant raising interest rates on outstanding loans. Not only is this equivalent to imposing an inefficacious tax on loans, but also it is unfair and perhaps illegal. Retroactive interest-rate rises were disastrous notably in halting the supply response of farmers in several transition economies early on, including Bulgaria and Poland.

Whereas the decision to lift ceilings on interest rates is up to policy makers, ensuring that the resulting rates clear markets is a different matter. Financial markets, even if well developed, are notoriously prone to failures (see Chapter 3). When they are only in *statu nascendi*, they are unlikely to yield proper interest rates. In any case, even the central bank's monetary policy cannot immediately set "accurate" interest rates because the behavior of economic agents under transition is by definition in flux and can be known only through trial and error over some period of time. Even so, the advice under the circumstances has been to aim at positive real interest rates as quickly as possible. Since real interest rates are ideally defined as nominal interest rates minus the *expected* pace of inflation for the rate's relevant time dimension, they cannot be known. The makeshift arrangement has been to aim at a nominal interest rate at least exceeding the pace of actual (usually wholesale) price inflation or its extrapolation into the future. This is not a proper approach on theoretical grounds. Whether it is appropriate in the prevailing political economy of the transformation has been the subject of fierce debates in the literature (Fry and Nuti 1992; Nuti 1996). I can impart only some of its flavor here.

Fiat interest rates in general impede efficient financial intermediation. When they are set too low, yielding negative real interest rates, they encourage demand for loans without fostering an efficient utilization of savings. They also discourage savings, whether from domestic or foreign sources. Conversely when they are set too high they encourage savings and an inflow of speculative funds from abroad, but discourage investment. Positive real interest rates are a prerequisite for improving the efficiency of investment, hence for raising the rate of economic growth, even without increasing the level of investment. That is to say, if financial intermediaries allocate loanable funds more efficiently than other allocative mechanisms, greater financial depth caused by higher real deposit rates itself improves the quality of the capital-allocation process.

Sustainable real interest rates should ideally be geared to the expected real rate of return obtainable on productive investment. This is easier argued as a theoretical proposition than implemented, certainly in as convoluted an environment as that of transition; this is even more so in the context of transformation. Many transition economies prefer to set positive rates with a sizable margin over observed inflation in a determined effort to ration demand for loans and stamp out inflationary expectations. Doing so for too long becomes self-defeating, however. For one thing, too large a margin between prevailing rates and what can reasonably be posited as the marginal productivity of capital truncates the time span for which loans are allocated. It almost becomes impossible to obtain loans for the longer term, particularly in countries with sizable inflation and interest rates. This discourages investment, thus aggravating the depth and duration of economic depression early on in the transition.

In a trade- and exchange-liberalized economy, there must be some relationship between the level and structure of domestic interest rates and those prevailing in international capital markets, taking into account the differential price inflation, which must exert an impact on movements in the exchange rate. In many transition economies, interest-rate differentials have been higher than necessary to offset expected currency depreciation and indeed often differential inflation rates. This initially reflects lack of credibility of exchange-rate policies (Nuti 1996). Over time, however, with continuous real, and occasionally nominal, revaluation of domestic currencies and the slowdown in inflation, interest-rate differentials make foreign and national investment in domestic financial assets attractive.

This discussion suggests that initially high real interest rates may be required to counter the burst of inflation due to price liberalization and currency devaluation unleashed early on. When inflation decelerates, as it does fairly quickly once monetary austerity takes hold, maintaining sizable interest-rate differentials and currency devaluation can actually generate or exacerbate inflationary expectations, thus setting off an undesirable spiral. Once built into wage negotiations and pricing behavior, these inflationary expectations can be self-fulfilling. Under certain conditions it may then become desirable to compress the interest-rate differentials and the pace of crawling devaluation.

I discuss details on the desirable exchange regime, which is part and parcel of price liberalization, under foreign-sector reform (Section 4 and beyond). Suffice it to note two things. One is that the multiplicity of exchange rates under state socialism needs to be replaced by a unified rate, perhaps after some transition, if only because lingering transactions denominated in transferable rubles cannot be translated into convertible currency without serious reservations and trade behavior during the transformation is uncertain. Arriving at a uniform exchange rate differs, however, from permitting much more generalized access to foreign exchange in a market-simulated fashion, from setting the exchange rate in such a setting, from moving toward current-account and capital-account convertibility, and indeed from relying on the exchange rate as an anchor for domestic stabilization. I return to these topics in Section 6 and beyond.

Section 3: Fostering competition

Markets can be extremely useful conveyors of knowledge and information. They also provide a low-cost framework for coordinating competitive transactions by economic agents acting on their own account (see Chapter 3). To reach that stage of market functionality, the transition economy must foster competition with great determination. That initially requires coming soonest to grips with several legacies of state socialism (see Chapter 2). These include overcoming the drawbacks of the thoroughly monopolistic and concentrated economic structures with special bureaucratic ties, the highly circumscribed nature of property rights, the long-standing injunction against individuals holding most kinds of real assets, and vast protection against foreign competition. Regarding natural monopolies, the transition economy must innovate soon a sufficient, yet flexible, regulatory infrastructure to forestall potentially predatory behavior. Also some externalities may have to be taken care of through government action (see Chapter 9).

As concerns conglomerates and most monopolies, if feasible at all, the authorities should carefully evaluate to what extent they can be functionally broken up without losing the advantages of scale accruing from vertical or horizontal integration. But some of the functionally diverse conglomerates can probably be disaggregated into viable smaller units with a more homogeneous and focused business goal. Judicious combination of such action with competition from abroad and from within, notably from new SMEs, should provide the first avenue to seeking remedial action. In most cases, promoting effective competition at home, including through imports, quickly creates a critical minimum stratum of competitive markets for traded goods and related services upon which further progress can be vigorously pursued.

3.1 – Fostering new firms

Creating a thick layer of new firms is of particular importance. SMEs, especially new ones, can be expected to play a critical role not only in charting a sustainable growth path (as shown in Chapter 12), but also in the short to medium run in contributing to stabilization and recovery. With reference to the latter objectives, new small firms form one of the crucial "institutions" of incipient markets (Borish and Noël 1996; EBRD 1995), and their emergence and growth may need to be fostered via state-sponsored, but nondiscriminatory, loans at favorable interest rates. The size of a "small" firm is not well defined. Conventionally in the usage of OECD countries, an SME is taken to be a firm with up to 500 employees and a small one perhaps with up to 100 employees. In many transition economies, however, the new small firm is likely to be smaller than that, perhaps fewer than 50 employees and a microfirm fewer than 10 employees (EBRD 1995). The critical question is the small firm's growth path to the status of SME as defined and eventually to a large firm that fits properly into a mature market economy fully embedded in the global framework (see Chapter 10).

The expansion of new small firms has been vigorous during the transitions in countries where room for their emergence has been made or at least where the political process has been too weak to inhibit their flowering. This deserves to be explicitly recognized. The major reason is that all transition economies in the early stages of transformation had a substantial, if varying, gap in trade and service sectors. These were generally activities forcibly suppressed or held in check under state socialism, or they were simply not needed at the time. With domestic liberalization the demand for many of these, largely nontraded, activities soars. That can be met at the outset generally with little capital investment. If a functioning commercial-banking sector were to be in place quickly, financing new firms would, of course, further expedite matters. Without an effective payment system for businesses, transaction costs are likely to remain high. Poor infrastructure (including telecommunications, transportation, and other support services) too does not help. But financial intermediation at the outset of the transition is not really the key obstacle, as the path taken by the vibrancy of new small firms in economies that have not prevented their emergence has clearly underlined (Mickiewicz 1996a, b; A. Richter and Schaffer 1996). Nonetheless, for as long as economic, as well as political and social, uncertainty remains high, the new small firm's range of activities is likely to extend to easily exploitable niches, usually of an uncomplicated nature and with a short-term horizon. Emerging from the economic depression can therefore provide an important impetus to expanding the breadth and depth of activities in which these new small firms engage.

In some transition economies, political uncertainty continues to be quite high, is hence not particularly conducive to the dynamism of smaller firms, except in the above-cited niche markets. It is not the threat of a return to state socialism that matters; that is probably quite small at this stage. Rather, it is the danger of political chaos with as yet weak democracy that might be usurped by a turn toward authoritarianism of the right and *dirigiste* economic policies that inhibit a market-inspired renaissance. The legislative processes of the structural transformations, including notably on property rights, restitution, compensation, privatization, and ultimate divestment, are far from complete.

Small firms face substantial obstacles early on in the transition, when markets are not yet functioning for a variety of reasons. Yet these firms thrive on relatively flexible markets. Without the availability of commercial real estate or proper zoning that can be rented on a predictable contractual basis with a minimum of hassle, the startup costs may be forbidding. That the legal prescriptions on intellectual property rights and discretionary technology are not well defined in many of these countries does not help either. The absence of functioning markets for now raises the transaction costs that private agents have to contend with in gearing up their ventures. The more innovative firms could benefit from better linkages among industry, academia, and government-supported research (see Chapter 8). Stretching the economic horizon for these ventures may well be something within the ambit of governmental action (see Chapter 9), particularly when markets are not yet functioning well. The authorities have done comparatively little to encourage such private capital formation, yet it could have bolstered competition, solidified the middle class, and anchored democracy through public initiative and safeguards.

At the same time, experience in several transition economies (Haggard, McMillan, and Woodruff 1996) has shown that even with limping markets new small firms are created at a prodigious pace. Some thrive and others disappear at a rate that as a rule surpasses that of a "normal" market economy. Those that excel do so in spite of the weak legal system. Firms operating in the absence of laws of contract and reliable enforcement mechanisms may nonetheless possess a variety of informal mechanisms for contract enforcement. Some are initially in the second economy, mainly for fiscal reasons (see subsection 3.3). Those that prosper do so largely because they innovate their own "regulatory regime." This includes trust at pain of severing a relationship and losing a reputation held up by sharing information, often on an informal basis. In and of itself such an informal regulatory regime may encourage emergence from the underground economy into the open. Because the new firms provide competition with SOEs and fill voids often appreciated by SOEs, they force productivity improvements even in existing SOEs. Of course, their emergence reduces the power of bureaucratic control over the economy. And by stimulating factor-productivity gains and growth, these firms *may* create space for deep macroeconomic and structural reforms to take off without debilitating societal interaction.

However, one needs to recognize that emerging capitalists in transition economies find the climate for business rather stifling, riddled as it is with all kinds of bureaucratic and institutional impediments and a limping financial infrastructure. This is particularly so for moving beyond the intermediation phase and the provisioning of other simple services. This is holding back the expeditious reabsorption of the unemployed, who now constitute a drag on fiscal resources and jeopardize sociopolitical stability in most transition economies (see Chapter 8). Although benefits of new firms in a formally unregulated environment may be palpable during the early stages of the transition, these entities eventually need vigorous market and social institutions that facilitate the exchange and dissemination of information in order for them to succeed and expand (see Chapter 7). The reason is simple: Transaction costs of informal organization are high and tend to skyrocket with the complexity of the object of informal exchange.

In order to take advantage of the potential stimulus to growth and employment from fostering SMEs, two broad issues arise. One is creating the enabling environment for SMEs legally to emerge. Domestic liberalization with free exit and entry is a necessary condition. But it is by far not a sufficient one. Bureaucratic obstacles (hindering access, for example, to real estate, communications, trading licenses, and foreign exchange, in addition to onerous fiscal regimes and various wage taxes) tend to be the real obstacle to the emergence of legal firms. And those moving in the second economy (not the criminal one, of course) have essentially restricted their own fields of operation to intermediating in comparatively simple trade or to providing services. This poses an important question in its own right: How can the vibrancy of the second economy be coopted? I address this in subsection 3.3.

The other set of questions revolves more around the sustainability of the transformation: How can the newer ventures, particularly in servicing and inter-mediation, grow to medium-size firms and beyond? In particular, how can they move into manufacturing, still largely dominated by SOEs or their nominally privatized successors, on which sustainable development is presumably pre-dicated? I deal here with the first question if only to emphasize that new private firms constitute one of the most critical institutions of transformation. The role that these new firms will hopefully play in the years ahead contrasts in several dimensions with the gigantomania of state-socialist SOEs, the remaining SOEs, the privatized large firms that have not yet linked up with foreign capital, and even the privatized smaller firms (Mickiewicz 1996b, p. 405). Whether a strong case can be made for Tomasz Mickiewicz's (1996a, p. 1200) contention that all but the *de novo* firms "suffer from being influenced by the socialist heritage" depends, of course, on the room for maneuver allowed in firms and the enabling environment for undertaking structural change. Clearly, new small firms can enter the transition economy in swashbuckling style. But their "owners" too may have been infected with the state-socialist virus, such as the negative factors inherited from the second economy or, as in Poland, from having been allowed, albeit rather grudgingly, to operate in the open under adverse conditions of the years of stagnation and socioeconomic conflict. Once again, this underlines the importance of the enabling environment rather than of privatization, divestment, and ownership as such.

There are several reasons why I attach such importance to SMEs. For one thing, direct ownership and control, which is possible in the small and perhaps even the medium-size firm, is substantially more attractive than share ownership to most savers in transition economies, if only because retained profits constitute the major funnel for business expansion. Moreover, small firms embody the spirit of independence from government that has been a yearning for the more entre-preneurial layers of these societies for decades. Of course, that entrepreneurial spirit is by no means limited to industrial operations. It is by letting it pervade the allocation of the trade and service streams potentially embedded in existing assets that a solid middle class can be (re)constituted, and this matters for the emergence and anchoring of civil society (see Chapter 7). It also provides the key ingredient of effective competition in many markets supplemented by liberalization of trade and foreign-exchange regimes. Also, because of immediate and clear ownership control, small firms in particular are likely to provide a faster response to urgent consumer needs in these countries. The same applies even more to reviving entrepreneurship after the many decades of suppression under state socialism. Finally, SMEs can stimulate regional economies and create local jobs particularly in areas where unemployment has been taking its toll on the sociopolitical support for the transition. Provided macroeconomic policy adjusts and thus creates the necessary room for initiative, the early drift forcing operations away from regional markets will by its nature be contained.

3.2 – Encouraging existing firms to become more competitive

Within existing firms too actions can be taken. In these emerging markets, managers must be chosen not for their political standing, whether measured by old or new precepts of political probity, but primarily for their professional acumen to maximize net asset values on behalf of the ultimate owners in exchange for well-defined rewards. To attain this, the monopoly power of large specialized firms and their associations must be sharply curtailed by physically breaking them up or putting in place a sufficient regulatory framework, including on antitrust and market access. Above all, it necessitates breaking the nexus between the center of political and macroeconomic decision making and SOEs as regards managerial controls, incentives, and budget dependence. That is one of the reasons for the encompassing notion of privatization I advocate in Chapter 6.

One way of ensuring independence of SOEs from central tutelage is by rapidly selling them off. But there are evidently many other ways of achieving autonomy (Pannier 1996; Sood 1990). The elimination of the "petty tutelage" exercised by ministerial and planning bureaucracies should not necessarily dissipate state ownership, certainly not simply for its own sake. In the smaller transition economies, even after breaking up existing monopolies, in the short run competition is likely to remain weak. Liberalization of trade and exchange regimes can usher in competitive pressures on the performance of core domestic firms. So will the vigorous promotion of private SMEs.

Particularly in the case of SOEs, government policy initially should seek to emulate as much as possible incentive schemes that have proved their usefulness for corporate management in market economies (Pannier and Schiavo-Campo 1996; Stiglitz 1997a, b). Of course, SOEs should finance themselves through the incipient commercial-banking sector at realistic, largely market-determined interest rates to the extent they can be "set," given the convoluted situation in transition economies. For that to work well, basic accounting reforms are required and bankruptcy proceedings must be instituted. Only then can the profitability of SOEs, hence the contribution of management to raising asset value, be ascertained. Under these conditions, it becomes easier to terminate fiscal and regulatory haggling between SOEs and government, which is a basic prerequisite for fiscal reform (Tanzi 1991). Unless a determined move is made to cut off virtually all enterprise-specific subsidies, the credibility of gradualism in the transformation process is in jeopardy. Perhaps a package of measures can be designed with a set target date for the complete phasing out of such subsidies. In the interim, subsidies should be made available chiefly in a form that provides a strong incentive for management to prepare for the "market" over a fairly short period of time.

Managerial incentives need to be enforced quickly, even though there is little hope of changing entrepreneurial attitudes immediately or replacing old-style management all at once. There is simply no army of well-trained, market-oriented managers standing in the wings ready to take over. In any case, progress with transition, and indeed with transformation, policies will necessarily have to be booked with the bulk of the resources inherited from state socialism. That is, gradualism will be required to nurse along changes in managerial behavior itself.

A particular set of incentives is associated with flexible exit and entry. The establishment of new economic ventures and the restructuring or liquidation of existing ones under state socialism was the prerogative of central administrators and those high up in the Party hierarchy. Economic scarcity as such rarely played a role therein. Naturally, one of the first acts in the transition is to open up access to resources at home and abroad on a fair basis. Entry is easy to arrange once the bureaucratic obstacles are overcome. As I have indicated for new small firms, these are by no means confined to registration and related acts. Rather, it is getting access to resources, from the most picayune to the most difficult, that complicates entry and spinoffs from existing conglomerates and multiproduct firms. Entry should not, of course, be restricted to domestic agents. Indeed entry of foreign goods, services, and production factors (mostly capital) deserves to be promoted, given the obstacles that the transformation has to grapple with. But foreign-sector liberalization is based on the more general case benefiting from competition and specialization.

3.3 – The second economy and its role in liberalization

Defining the second economy is not an easy matter as the activities subsumed thereunder range from the simple dodging of tax and social-security obligations all the way to blatant criminal activities. Whereas the latter can be brought under control only through effective law enforcement with a newly regained strength of the state (see Chapter 9), some of the activities at the other end of the range can be thought of as being entirely transitory, many deriving simply from the rational decision to escape the taxes and regulations applicable to the formal sector generally made possible by a poorly functioning state (Rose-Ackerman 1997).

In-between is a broad range of second-economy activities that bear kinship to corruption (see Chapter 8).

Seen in its extreme stylized format, escaping from the formal economy has advantages and disadvantages, most of which can be expressed in monetary terms. The former can be labeled "net profits after paying current expenditures" and the latter as "potential costs" of not being in the formal sector. Neither the former nor the latter are carved in granite. As the transformation takes hold one or the other, and possibly both, are gradually affected, thus changing the decision rule on whether to stay in the informal sector or move into the formal one. The advantages of being in the informal sector consist essentially of not having to incur the costs of being in the formal sector. Those consist of an entry cost, which may be considerable in an emerging market economy, as well as the cost of staying formal. Entry costs vary but they can be captured by the price a would-be entrepreneur has to pay in order to set up a firm other than the costs incurred in terms of assets that directly contribute to executing the envisioned economic activity. The cost of staying formal consists essentially of the price the owner incurs to continue operating, aside from the direct cost of producing the envisioned activity. These may range from profit taxes, to levies on wages, to administrative expenses (such as keeping books), all the way to payoffs to protection rackets (see Chapter 8).

Being not formal has also distinctive costs and more general disadvantages (Loayza 1997). To the extent that state agencies vigorously police economic activity, the penalty of being found out in the informal sector may be very stiff. For some time, bribes may do the trick. But eventually the full formal penalty must be paid, and this may mean not just money but forfeiture of assets and indeed prison terms for the principals involved. Weak state authority, very lax enforcement, and easily bribable policing officers form a recipe for rendering this cost rather derisory; but it is not zero in the expectational sense. Furthermore, by definition the informal sector is deprived of the public services that can be accessed only by being in the formal sector. This is perhaps most onerous for the unenforceability of property rights and the difficulties of engaging in formal contracts with the emergent intermediating agents. Informal agents cannot avail themselves, for example, of police protection and legal security of their property. They cannot engage in contracts that are justiciable, and this matters, for example, in obtaining loans, insurance, and the protection of incorporation. And those operating in the informal sector, including workers, cannot benefit from other public services such as social welfare, pensions, unemployment compensation, training, government-sponsored credit schemes, and so on. This latter drawback may be more onerous for workers than for owners.

Given the cost and benefit structure of operating in the informal sector, as the cost of informality rises, the incentive for economic agents to become legal strengthens. But this curbs the informal sector only if the cost of joining and staying in the formal sector, at given expected benefits, do not outpace that rising levy. Onerous costs of joining and operating in the formal sector discourage entry. Likewise, raising the cost of being informal may nip in the bud an entire range of activities that are socially, as well as privately, beneficial, and may in fact provide stepping stones toward joining the formal sector.

Clearly, operators in the informal sector will fairly quickly run into formidable constraints, confining their ability to expand as the economic environment improves. One can as a result reckon with positive path dependence: Successful transformation in all of its aspects is likely to reduce the magnitude of the informal sector; economically because of the need for expansion and security of property rights, politically as the state's role in governing society strengthens, and socially as more and more individuals perceive the benefits of accessing public services. One of the most critical variables is stamping out corruption of state-agency officials and acquiring governance capabilities to ensure that informality is held in check (see Chapter 8).

There clearly is a tradeoff between encouraging economic activity, even if in the second economy, hence beyond taxing authorities, and ensuring that the burden of societal transformation is levied fairly. *A priori* the informal economy should not be suppressed at all cost. It would be counterproductive for the authorities to clamp down so harshly on these activities that they simply vanish. Societal costs and benefits should be carefully assessed in the light of the need and ability to govern society. Once state authority is reestablished, it might be useful to grant some amnesty to the second economy provided its operations are legalized as of a certain date. This may not be an equitable treatment of economic agents as inevitably some of the illegally earned wealth will thus be whitewashed. This is alas unavoidable. Given the social benefits of the small firms, not to mention the seeming inevitability of a sizable second economy early on in the transition (Kaufmann and Kaliberda 1996), there may well be a solid case for pursuing that route.

Section 4: Abolition of the MFT and its implications

Integration of the transition economies into the world economy as an integral ambition of transformation policies requires basically four interrelated steps. One is to open up the domestic economy by replacing the MFT with more conventional commercial-policy instruments and institutions. Another is to obliterate quickly all vestiges of CMEA integration. But this does not necessarily mandate severing nearly all CMEA commercial ties, come what may. Third, integration into the world economy was from the beginning associated with full participation in global economic regimes, including quick membership for those that did not already belong in the IEOs or fully subscribing to their regimes otherwise. Finally, from early on most transition economies have coveted quick membership in the EU and in the interim to forge strong ties with it; I can discuss this moving toward EU integration only insofar as it bears on the main theme (but see Brabant 1995a, 1996). None wanted to be sucked into any new regional arrangement regardless of economic logic or western support for such a scheme

191

(see Brabant 1990, 1991a, 1995a). I defer discussion of the broader institutional aspects of merging into the world economy to Part III.

How best to transform the trade and payment systems of the transition economies in a credible manner has been one of the most widely debated questions in designing a comprehensive, speedy, sectorally attuned with appropriate intensity, and properly sequenced transition. Since policy makers covet opening up their economies, the measures taken are evidently critical in determining the character of domestic economic transformation, in spurring on the integration of these economies into the world economy, and indeed in preparing these countries for effective membership in multilateral economic organizations. Which steps to take, with which instruments, with which intensity and determination, and in which order are altogether different matters. The answers have been based on orthodox trade theory as well as on political precepts, including quick merger into the EU (on which more in Chapter 10). Much attention has been reserved for opening up these economies to global competition in as many dimensions as feasible without worrying too much about its manifold economic, political, and social ramifications. Paradoxically, after the initial burst of liberalization enthusiasm, policy makers of transition economies have by design sought to come to grips with most of these "most urgent" and "chronic" issues of a "proper" transformation strategy far more slowly and partially (Köves 1994) than the sense of urgency and drama that the original advisory whirlwind imparted; in many cases, serious reversals have been sustained since then.

The case for trade and capital-flow liberalization has been based on incontestable, if highly theoretical, credentials. The discussions have at times given the impression that a liberal trade regime can engineer economic wonders, even though its record is, at best, debatable (Dornbusch 1992; Krugman 1995). The theoretical case on which these imputed benefits are predicated is well known. Without going into details, trade liberalization is expected to improve resource allocation in line with social marginal costs and benefits; to facilitate access to more advanced or better-suited technology, inputs, and intermediate goods; to enable an economy better to take advantage of economies of scale and scope; to bolster competition in domestic markets; and to provide progrowth externalities, including by shaking up established transformation activities, thereby creating a favorable "Schumpeterian environment especially conducive to growth" (Dornbusch 1992, p. 74). Arguably even more beneficial than these static benefits can be the growth-promoting, hence dynamic, effects of trade liberalization, which should help to carve out a new growth path. Actively eliciting inflows of foreign investment, particularly FDI, including through privatization, is a critical focus of the latter's compass.

Whereas these claimed advantages have impeccable credentials in standard economic theory, their practical realization is not self-evident at least until the economy being opened up gains an environment conducive to comparatively flexible adjustments to the new demand and supply schedules; that is, a fairly coherent market orientation. Otherwise foreign competition may eliminate domestic production, perhaps inadvertently and inordinately through shifts in demand for "new" goods, without the freed-up resources being mobilized for growth-promoting activities. The outcome may then be a potentially sharp cutback in aggregate economic activity, which cannot but compress sustainable levels of absorption or welfare. Whether this occurs right away after trade liberalization, apart from flexibility on the supply side, depends on the availability of foreign exchange.

In advocating a rapid, decisive turn away from state socialism commentators agree that the MFT must be abolished quickly because the comparative autarky it afforded had been detrimental to growth and wealth creation under state socialism. That institutional arrangement therefore has to be abolished early on during the transition. Only in this way can managers of the transition anchor a more effective relative price system and strengthen competition in domestic markets. Economic agents must be enabled to engage directly in foreign-economic activity within established rules and regulations, including on commercial and foreign-exchange policies. In most transition economies, any registered economic agent is now entitled to engage in trade within the set framework. Because of weakening state authority, indeed its disintegration in some cases, many unregistered agents have come to utilize trade channels to provision the second economy and engage in illegal activities.

But there is another reason for concurrence on foreign-sector reform: The interest of virtually all transition economies in integrating themselves quickly and fully into the international economy. That too requires that transition managers pay special attention to foreign sectors. In the first place that entails fostering exports. Domestic price liberalization and a more realistic exchange rate, through their impacts on competition and price information funneled in from world markets, have been contributing to export promotion. But it also encompasses promoting financial inflows, joining or activating membership in IEOs and their underlying policy regimes, and taking a more active interest in how the global economy functions with a view to identifying where precisely the transition economy might belong, including in the "return to Europe" context.

It bears to recall in this connection that rapid integration into the world economy, the EU in the first place, has been predicated on destroying inherited ties in the CMEA framework irrespective of the latter's economic foundations. There probably is not much sense in investigating the entire drama of the CMEA's destruction all over again. Suffice it to recall that the eradication of CMEA interdependence was accomplished radically and far more extensively than emerging competition on the basis of incipient market forces would have wrought. Proceeding in this manner was never appropriate on economic grounds. I return to this question in Chapter 10 because trading on the basis of solid economic foundations has implications for present and future commercial policies, including in the context of forging a more constructive relationship with the EU, but also in reviving mutual trade and diversifying markets more generally.

Section 5: Instruments of trade policy

Fairly soon after the "1989 events," many transition economies began to replace their bewildering variety of unorthodox nontariff barriers (NTBs) with more conventional protectionist instruments. Policy makers in most transition economies and their advisers have generally agreed on the urgent need for erecting a quite liberal trade regime applicable to all authorized agents with few, if any, NTBs and low, preferably uniform, tariffs (Krueger 1997). The argument has been based on mainstream economic theory (see Section 4). Opening up a previously closed economy, particularly when it adopts a fairly liberal regime and it is "small," to international competition augments the choice in consumption, production, technology, and siting, and thus lifts levels of living and wealth. The well-known theoretical result that the latter's optimal trade policy is one with zero tariffs has been invoked for many transition economies. Whether this is an appropriate maxim in real life is offhand unclear. Several factors explain the gap between anticipations and results.

Key is that many of the expected benefits materialize only once integrated, well-functioning markets exist that are in equilibrium prior to the opening up and can reasonably smoothly revert to equilibrium soon thereafter; that is, there is near-instantaneous adjustment not just in product but also in factor markets (see Chapter 3). The theory also assumes implicitly that the liberalizing economy is at a satisfactory stage of maturity, hence not bent on catching up with more productive partners except through normal production and trading channels. This suggests that the anticipated advantages of liberalization tend to crystallize only once there exists an environment that permits comparatively flexible adjustments to new demand and supply schedules; in other words, *after* erecting a functioning market economy and a reasonable case can be made for the convergence, with "minor" exceptions, of private and social marginal costs and benefits in resource allocation. Early during the transition, foreign competition may eliminate an inordinate share of domestic production without the freed-up resources being mobilized for export-led growth. Aggregate economic activity may plunge, reducing levels of living, especially when foreign exchange is scarce and domestic supply is rather inelastic.

It is in any case wrong, for reasons of both theory and policy making, to presume that economic interdependence prior to "opening up" must be rapidly destroyed (Fischer 1992). As a matter of trade theory, it *may* be desirable to maintain in the short run commerce that must be displaced in the course of transition as the commodity composition and the geographical direction of trade are modified. But there is no reason to believe that the optimal restructuring of trade is synonymous with annihilating all ties forged in the past. As a matter of political economy, moreover, a very rapid, forced compression of trade, hence production, may stop a reform process in its tracks. Experience in transition economies suggests that trade-related shocks in moving away from state socialism can cause output to contract too quickly, thereby undermining for many actors the credibility of transformation policies.

The nature of protection through trade policy has been much debated, given the startling gaps between relative domestic and world prices that the transition economy needs to overcome soonest. Nobody has doubted the need to transform soonest nearly all NTBs under planning into explicit *ad valorem* tariffs, unlike their height and dispersion. The opposing sides have focused either on forestalling the collapse of large segments of economic activity early in the transition or on the beneficial effects of market penetration from abroad on domestic competition and price formation. If only for the latter reasons, it would be counterproductive to erect formidable trade barriers or to maintain the inherited protective measures in a different guise. From the point of view of enhancing competition and fostering export-led growth, commercial policy should be liberal and simple. It should be uniformly applicable to all, perhaps subject to certain explicit social preferences. Foreign competition could be a major guarantor of market orientation. Putting in place high tariffs as a substitute for the past separation of domestic and foreign economic agents simply to protect uncompetitive industries would be highly unwise. Once the transition has been bridged, fears that foreign competition destabilizes the still fragile domestic market economy should dissipate. The orderly adjustment to world competition *could* be part of a realistic industrial policy and good economic governance, provided capabilities are available or they can be quickly acquired, including through targeted foreign assistance (Brabant 1993a), as underlined in Part III.

A special question arises with respect to the determination of the degree, the extent, and the administration of protection (Winters 1994, 1995). Many transition economies initially sought to switch rapidly to a very liberal regime. Since then several have had to reverse this stance largely under pressure from domestic interest groups and the disarray among those administering the trade regime in the process of implementing the transformation agenda. That too should be part of good economic governance because turf battles inevitably end up in greater protectionism.

Some commentators, notably Ronald I. McKinnon (1991a, b) and John Williamson (1990, 1991), have suggested that very early on in the transition all nontariff protection be converted into explicit *ad valorem* tariffs structured into perhaps half a dozen cascading categories. Moreover, such protection should remain rather high, possibly by maintaining for now the level implicit in the bewildering variety of trade-inhibiting institutions and instruments of state socialism. And the transition economy should commit itself according to a precise time schedule to reduce the level of these tariffs and eventually narrow their dispersion. The objective of such an exercise would be to forestall the collapse of large segments of industry (especially the so-called "value-subtracting" or "negative value-added" enterprises) early in the transition.

Those arguing for high tariffs to be reduced over some precommitted time period are primarily concerned about the need for an adjustment phase to permit domestic producers to withstand foreign competition (and perhaps to provide fiscal revenues, given the unraveling of the fiscal regime inherited from central planning). The drawback of this policy choice is, of course, precisely that it obviates the kind of preferred environment for fostering competition by weakening domestic monopolists and funneling scarcity pricing into the transition economy rather quickly. I tend to favor the latter position, provided fiscal revenues can realistically be raised otherwise and some orderly income transfers can be arranged in a credible precommitment format so that the structural changes to the economy can be enacted in some orderly fashion. Once again, the latter could be part of a realistic industrial policy and good economic governance (see Chapter 9), provided minimal capabilities can be mobilized (see Chapter 7).

Whereas some protection of existing economic structures could usefully be entertained under precisely defined conditions, it would be counterproductive to erect formidable trade barriers for the transition economy. Certainly, it would permit policy makers to alter economic structures gradually, hence avoid sudden dislocations with all attendant consequences. But it would also hamper competition and the transfer of an effective system of relative prices for traded goods. Furthermore, in view of the weak central actors in the transition economies, credibility for the phasing-out of customs duties, even if a waiver under the General Agreement on Tariffs and Trade (GATT), now the World Trade Organization (WTO), could be secured, would be rather low. Moreover, it is probably an insuperable task to make explicit the degree of protection widely enjoyed under state socialism.

Rather than aggravate price distortions and introduce levies that may be hard to repeal, the transition economy could resort to temporary income transfers. This would permit sectors potentially threatened by bankruptcy to operate below real cost, yet the government would not have to support full unemployment claims. Such a policy choice could also enable valuable assets to survive the rigors of the transition and become profitable by normal market norms. There is, of course, little hope that policy makers of the transition can neatly separate the potentially profitable firms most deserving of subsidies from others that in any case have to be fundamentally restructured or eliminated. But some guidance can be taken from firms able to cover variable costs.

Section 6: Managing the exchange rate

The orthodox case for trade liberalization in the transition economies has been predicated on relatively low protection with an exchange rate that should help to maintain equilibrium in the current account over the medium run. Because the gap between pretransition and world relative prices is considerable, no single devaluation can avert palpable adjustments in demand and supply well beyond those normally ensuing from the terms-of-trade effect of an exchange-rate movement. Because export schedules are unknown it is by no means obvious by how much the home currency should be devalued to enable policy makers to sustain external balances and whether a stable nominal exchange rate should thereafter function as a key anchor for the design of transition policies.

The advisory proffered by the most market-oriented adherents has been unambiguous: Choose the nominal exchange rate as anchor once the home currency has been sufficiently devalued to compensate for unknown, but anticipated "corrective inflation," preferably erring on the side of caution by undervaluing the domestic currency, and then hold it stable for a sufficiently long period of time to impart confidence and credibility to transition policies. Ironically, the devaluation may be excessive if, as in western Europe after World War II, the structural adjustment is such that targeted policies are likely to improve matters in a comparatively brief period of time. Given those conditions, a sizable devaluation debilitates economic activities that, under the normal conditions of the market being aimed at, would have been able to survive on their own. In addition, most observers have not given adequate attention to the potentially destabilizing effects of a fluctuating real exchange rate as a result of domestic inflation, which is bound to quickly hollow out the temporary comparative advantage afforded by a marked devaluation. Yet, an unstable real exchange rate cannot but add to the hazards of economic restructuring via an export-led strategy (Fry and Nuti 1992), primarily toward the EU. This is particularly so since the transition economies, given lost CMEA markets and geopolitical realities, are bent on redirecting trade to western markets. Of course, the psychological effect of an unstable nominal exchange rate is considerable for households regardless of the real effect. Moreover, because of so many price dichotomies and adjustments in relative and absolute prices that are not fully synchronized average indicators may not be relevant for particular classes of economic agents; they are so for individual agents only by fluke. That is to say, there is once again a tradeoff. But I deem it desirable to move nominal and real exchange rates in tandem, without full synchronization (Halpern and Wyplosz 1996). A managed nominal exchange rate is preferable to a heavily undervalued fixed rate. In any case, there is a need to be careful about "nominal" versus "real" exchange-rate targeting (Schweikert 1994, 1995).

As a concomitant of a liberal trade regime, most commentators have advocated liberal access to foreign exchange within a proper exchange-rate regime. There can be no doubt that the perplexing multiplicity of exchange rates under planning must be replaced with a single one or at best two (one for duly authorized commercial transactions and the other for private trading). Note that even a dual exchange rate does not obviate the need to bridge the considerable gap between pretransition domestic and world relative prices. Sizable adjustments in demand and supply will ensue. Given that future export and import schedules, or the type and volume of foreign investment that may materialize, are unknown, it is not obvious by how much the home currency should be devalued and how stable the exchange rate should be thereafter to sustain external balance at near-full employment. The extent of the devaluation and the management of the nominal exchange rate should therefore figure prominently in the transition debate.

Whether the key commercial rate should be fixed or flexible (and how it is to be linked to any other rate) is one of those "either-or" choices that many theoretical economists and inexperienced policy makers are fond of. In practice, given the instability and uncertainty of the transition, a one-off solution is not feasible. The policy question is more about what kind of crawling peg or managed float should be entertained and at what intervals the exchange rate should be adjusted to avoid imparting adverse credibility effects into currency trading and, by extension, into transition policies. The issues at stake are paramount to book progress toward meeting the conditions for current-account convertibility. Only under those circumstances is there a realistic chance of attracting the kind and volume of FDI that most countries are coveting.

One key item on the agenda for transition is whether the exchange rate should be undervalued to foster exports and discourage imports or devalued by just enough to anticipate the "corrective inflation" likely to ensue from price liberalization. Should it instead be set closer to purchasing power to avoid a sharp cut in the real value of wages and incomes? Unfortunately, there are no unambiguous answers to these questions (Ghosh *et al.* 1996). Fact is that most transition economies have chosen an undervalued exchange rate, erring on the side of caution, as compared to the rate that would maintain balance in the market for foreign exchange, at least for merchandise and related transactions. This choice has been suggested more by concern about infusing some anchored certainty into an exceedingly volatile socioeconomic and political situation (Camdessus 1995a, b) than by invoking solid economic arguments. On the latter ground, the choice is probably wrong. But it may be wise political economy provided it does not become a fetish, as was the case in Poland from January 1990 until May 1991 (Fry and Nuti 1992). In any case, there are at least two other critical aspects of the design of such a liberal trade regime that bear careful scrutiny. One is convertibility of the currency. The other is the phasing in of the new regime as part of the transformation strategy.

Soon after the start of the transition, monetary matters in many successor States were complicated by the breakdown of the federal monetary regime. In some cases, notably the CIS States, this had been kept intact for far longer than was desirable from any economic, and even political, point of view (Brabant 1992b). In others, makeshift pseudo currencies were introduced. In yet a third group, usually after some spectacular inflation and loss of currency value, the option was for a currency board (see Chapter 4). Some transition economies have fared well with fixed exchange rates. Others have done so with floating ones. Yet another group has managed to sustain stability with an adjustable peg or a "currency corridor." Experience indicates that there is no one superior regime, although one would tend to lean toward fixed, but adjustable, exchange rates. The main reason is that it dampens inflationary expectations on the part of broad layers of the society. If credible, it also infuses the transformation with greater certainty and reliability, and thus removes some of the pervasive uncertainty besetting the policy environment (Ghosh *et al.* 1996).

198

Section 7: Financial-market liberalization and capital-account convertibility

At least a brief word is needed separately about the capital account, both its liberalization and the currency's convertibility for those transactions. Theory tends to treat international capital movements as an extrapolation of conventional open macroeconomics. This takes it for granted that external financial liberalization is desirable because it enhances efficiency in resource allocation even if at the loss of policy autonomy – the ability of governments to achieve national objectives by using the policy instruments at their disposal. It is widely recognized that this proposition holds only if other imbalances, such as budget deficits, inflation, and imperfections in goods and factor markets, are eliminated. Since these obstacles cannot be removed overnight, sequencing of external liberalization is generally accepted. Many observers argue that domestic financial markets and the current account should be liberalized before the capital account and, with greater controversy, that fiscal balance and monetary stability should be attained before external liberalization.

This position raises three broad questions: The nature of the benefits claimed from domestic and external liberalization, what constitutes a sufficient resolution of domestic problems, and when can one best proceed with domestic financial liberalization under imbalances (Akyüz 1993b, pp. 144–8) as a precondition for moving toward external financial liberalization? It may be useful to bear in mind that the latter policy stance can logically be disaggregated into: (1) the ability of residents to borrow freely in international markets and nonresidents to lend freely in domestic markets for other reasons than financing trade, (2) allowing residents to transfer capital and hold financial assets abroad and nonresidents to issue liabilities in domestic financial markets, and (3) permitting debtor–creditor relations among residents in foreign currencies. To the extent that (1) is primarily motivated by the need of firms to finance investments in productive capacity, FDI is more desirable than other types of foreign investment, comprising bonds, commercial loans, and equity investment.

The benefits claimed for external financial liberalization are generally based on the belief that the internationalization of finance, like domestic liberalization, allows savings to be pooled and allocated globally through capital movements in response to productive-investment opportunities. By thus equalizing rates of return on investment, adjusted for risk differentials, global resource allocation is ameliorated. In capital-short countries, net inflows lower domestic real interest rates, bringing them closer to world level. Likewise in the case of domestic liberalization: By removing restraints on interest rates or credit allocation the real rate of interest climbs, thereby encouraging savings and production for exports. Note, however, that this also raises the cost of debt, including for domestic firms. Oligopolistic firms find it easier to offset it through price increases in the non-traded sector in contrast to firms confronting stiff foreign competition. The latter can mainly agitate on real wages, lest their ability to preserve real profit, hence retention for investment purposes, be undermined (Akyüz 1993b, pp. 146–8).

I have used the word "belief" in the above summary without intending to cast aspersions. Yet, the position taken on external liberalization rests on the features of the model posited: Views about how the global economy operates that are hardly realistic. Judged by the degree to which differences in the rates of return on capital have been reduced, even in major industrial countries, capital movements as such do not invariably improve the international allocation of savings; nor has the link between savings and investment in individual countries been removed (Akyüz 1993a, pp. 51–2). The assumption that capital movements occur in search of real returns on investment does not generally hold. Most flows are propelled by portfolio decision makers in search of short-term capital gains (Akyüz 1993b). These more speculative capital movements exert pressures on exchange and interest rates as well as on asset prices that have little to do with underlying fundamentals. In other words, financial openness as defined may create economy-wide problems regardless of the order of liberalization and the sequential removal of distortions. The exposure to short-term, speculative portfolio decisions for countries that are not in fundamental equilibrium is much greater – the very nature of the instability providing opportunities for quick windfall profits – because policy makers can influence the size and direction of flows through monetary policy only to a limited extent.

Those limitations reside in the ability of countries to attain the domestic liberalization that provides sufficient protection against speculative capital movements. For as long as fundamental domestic balance is not realized, the real question for transition economies is manifestly not liberalization as such, but rather what kind of a network of controls can conceivably be put in place to encourage capital inflows into production, as distinct from speculative flows during the transition. Part of the latter are capital-market policies to orderly scrap obsolete human and physical capital, to encourage rapid technological upgrading and modernization, and to secure the conditions for moving toward and maintaining a considerable degree of stability not only in economic, but also in political and social affairs. Under those conditions, domestic and external finance should serve the modernization objectives rather than the other way around (see Chapter 12).

Section 8: Access to foreign exchange

One may be skeptical about the desirability of reaching too fast for convertibility, especially on the capital account, by the transition leadership, but there should be no qualms about policy measures that promote fast and far-reaching access to foreign exchange. The distinction between the latter and currency convertibility is not always appreciated. Convertibility is actually the polar case of liberalization of access to foreign exchange. Once the foreign-exchange market functions well and encompasses virtually all of foreign exchange available for current-account transactions, for example, the authorities might just as well declare convertibility, such as in the IMF's sense, via a regime with (managed?) flexible exchange rates for duly authorized agents (capital flight still being forestalled to the extent concrete circumstances permit). However, the experience with flexible exchange rates in recent decades has not been very positive. Frequent over-shooting has imparted into the economic environment greater uncertainty than is generally desirable. Some measure of foreign-exchange control rather than free floating may therefore be warranted.

The reason why there may be room for intermediate regimes here too is that foreign-exchange markets cannot be expected to function reasonably well from the outset. Exchange is scarce, there is asymmetric access to information on "markets" that determine the supply and demand for foreign exchange, capital flight should be averted, all available exchange should be mobilized such as through mandatory surrender for some period of time, authorities need to differentiate between authorized and other economic agents, and a case may exist for ensuring availability of certain goods (such as fuels, foodstuffs, and medication) without them becoming prohibitively expensive. Any such interference may call forth a secondary market in foreign exchange available at a premium. Arbitrage between the two may yield sizable benefits to insiders. Even so, with minimal governance capabilities, one could argue the case for running this risk rather than the much larger one attendant on imposing suddenly a single price on an economy with literally thousands of implicit exchange rates. One can, then, imagine circumstances that may make it advisable to pursue the generalization of access to foreign exchange over some period of time (months rather than years, of course), provided governance capabilities are available. This can be organized via open auctions for increasing amounts of available foreign exchange accessible to all duly-authorized agents (such as licensed traders), if only to minimize the danger of capital flight. Critical in advocating such auctions is the flexibility of the nominal exchange rate for liberalized transactions. More controlled access to foreign exchange for the procurement of the cited essentials may be vital. By engaging in such "monitored" auctions, transition managers can soon obtain a better grasp of the equilibrium exchange rate. That in turn would make the move toward genuine current-account convertibility less hazardous, hence raise the probability of its sustainability.

These considerations should apply with full force to the transition economies too and strengthen the case for some measure of foreign-exchange control until two conditions can be met. One is that policy makers must confidently be able to set a reasonable exchange rate and, barring untoward events, maintain it over some period of time (perhaps a minimum of six months) without being pressured to change the rate on account of differential price movements. The other is that the authorities must have in place the institutions and policy instruments to manage the foreign-exchange regime, preferably according to a crawling peg. This calls for adequate foreign-exchange reserves. The theoretical argument for freeing up the capital account early on during the transition is not particularly compelling, as already argued. Perhaps more important, currency convertibility makes sense only once the economy regains basic overall balance, with positive growth and an appropriate assortment of competitive exportables so that balance-of-payments equilibrium can be maintained over the medium run. But I recognize that many commentators have argued the reverse: liberalization as a means toward sustainable export-led growth (Schweikert 1995). The merits of this advocacy even for small, trade-dependent economies in disarray are debatable (see Chapter 12).

Section 9: Reorientation of foreign economic activity

Whereas many components of the transformation agenda have been introduced much more gradually than rhetoric and early naïve enthusiasm had advocated (Köves 1994), this has oddly enough not been quite so especially for the geographical gravity pole of external economic relations.

9.1 – Collapse of the CMEA and economic unions

Perhaps most spectacular, and costly, has been the abrupt crash of economic relations within the context of both the CMEA and the now disbanded federations (to some extent Czechoslovakia, but especially the USSR and Yugoslavia). On economic and political grounds, some of this trade undoubtedly merited to be phased out expeditiously, given that it had hardly been nurtured on the basis of scarcity indicators. But there has been a degree of dysfunctional overshooting stemming in part from the textbook assumptions about trade, thereby ignoring the necessary institutions, among other factors. There is no point in rehashing once again the CMEA's collapse (Brabant 1990, 1991a) or why the earlier federations could not be held together (Brabant 1992b) with the policies embraced. But just a few notes by way of implications of CMEA involvement for the subsequent problems of the transition need to be clear. Their nature, if perhaps not quite their full extent, was entirely foreseeable, given the CMEA's peculiar trade, pricing, settlement, and payment regimes.

Recall that the CMEA's essence was fourfold: (1) market separation through the MFT adhered to by each member but administered according to its own rules; (2) artificial trading prices; (3) rather rigid equalization of trading with domestic prices to preserve autonomy for trade and other economic decisions for each country's policy makers; and (4) comprehensive interstate BTPAs arranged around some odd rules, notably regarding pricing, payment, and settlement. All of these features were maintained separately from the links these countries maintained with the outside world. Only a small proportion of trade chiefly with the industrial countries was based on almost normal trading conditions; the almost referring to several instances of discrimination maintained against "state-trading countries" by the principal actors in global relations.

The resulting patterns of trade were on the whole in support of maintaining economies that were by design without competition from within and sheltered against external competition; that engaged in widespread redistribution of incomes throughout their own economy, but were reluctant to do likewise on a regional level, even among like-minded CMEA partners; and that had their economic priorities selected by the political and bureaucratic powers in place, rather than through a preset framework within which economic agents formulate their own strategies in pursuit of their own profit motive.

Part of the calamity into which the transition economies fell after 1989 was caused by the CMEA's collapse, of course, as illustrated in Chapter 10. However, this foundering was not entirely an external shock nor can the bulk of the domestic economic decline in the members on the whole be attributed to the steep reduction in intra-CMEA trade. Both are usually ascribed to Gorbachev's posturing in early 1990. But that provides almost too convenient, indeed much too facile, an explanation. Some investigators have claimed to have detected a justified link, attributing nearly all of the domestic impact on output and employment of transformation policies to the CMEA trade shock (Rodrik 1992a, b). I find those sciolistic cause-and-effect stories, even if based on purported factual evidence, not persuasive.

The CMEA's collapse, that is, the putative external shock, could not possibly have constituted the alpha and omega of the transition rout in these countries, given the autonomy that had been preserved within each economy. Indeed, their considerable autarky had earlier been held responsible for much of the failures of inward-orientated economic administration! And, as argued, it could not possibly be considered a truly external shock for the central European countries for their policy makers in 1989–90 insisted quite vocally, come what may, on changing these intragroup relations very quickly, and dramatically so. When Gorbachev in mid-1990 decided to enact "world market conditions" in the CMEA as of 1991, that constituted only the rancid icing on the already thoroughly spoiled cake.

9.2 – World market conditions and their implications

The expression "world market conditions" refers to many things, but especially to four features: (1) transactions are negotiated by microeconomic agents on their own account; (2) market-clearing prices of a sort, given weak markets in the eastern part of Europe, are the terms at which transactions are concluded; (3) imbalances are to be settled in convertible currency on a current basis or, in the case of clearing, periodically; and (4) the usances of world trading, notably on payment conditions (that is, immediate payment for raw materials and fuels and short-term (perhaps 90 to 120 days) supplier credit for many manufactured goods), are henceforth to be closely observed.

The central European countries were adamant on instituting these features in intragroup trade. This was something that in the end could have helped to improve rationality in this commerce, and would thus have been crucial to those members then bent on restructuring their domestic economies so that microeconomic agents could soon play a critical role in resource allocation within a set framework (see Chapter 2). The failures of earlier reforms stemmed in part from the absence of a supporting framework in fraternal countries or in the CMEA organization itself. This experience had no doubt left many scars that the newfangled policy makers were all too keen to stress as excuses for abandoning CMEA economic relations at the first opportunity.

Even so, the implications of abandoning the former regimes in favor of moving to world conditions should be spelled out clearly in terms of various shocks. First, real demand and supply factors, both at home and from other CMEA countries, cause a volume shock. In addition, a terms-of-trade shock emanates from the discrepancy between CMEA and world relative prices and the different compositions of trade of the various countries. Furthermore, building up convertible-currency reserves for both precautionary and transaction motives from own resources is deflationary. Finally, disarray during hastily arranged transformation policies is bound to entail another shock. The latter could not have been entirely avoided for some period of time in consequence of the absence or poor functioning of the quintessential institutions supporting foreign transactions (such as for conducting payments, for arranging supplier loans or export credits, for acquiring convertible currency, for issuing insurance and engaging in rediscounting, and for expediting other services). This crucial issue has frequently been misunderstood, when not deliberately fudged, notably in the western advice rendered to the transition economies. The motivation may have varied. Even so, lack of an elementary acquaintance with, let alone interest in, the postwar institutions of the state-socialist economies was simply glossed over.

9.3 – Internal and external shocks

The four cited shocks can be separated only for heuristic purposes. In reality, they are intricately intertwined. However, in building up a scenario for the likely impacts of subjecting CMEA trade to world conditions at a time of transition, it is useful to bear in mind three moments. First, because of the sharp devaluation of the exchange rate in nearly all transition economies (Hungary being an exception to some degree), effective import demand at world prices gets curtailed; the same applies to total export revenue in the snort run because of inability to switch markets and the reciprocal compression of intragroup relations. In addition, the undervaluation of the currency destroys otherwise viable activities because of the sharply risen cost of imports and affords domestic monopolies a sizable protective cushion, thereby blunting the expected benefits of external competition. Furthermore, the policy stance taken by the new decision makers, in effect, discourages trade with the former, including "domestic," partners by economic and often indeed other means (such as tariffs, quotas and other NTBs, health-inspection regulations, exchange-rate manipulations, barter and bilateral arrangements down to the enterprise level, political invective, and outright export denial). Mostly ill-advised, one-sided demand-management stabilization measures sharply compress import demand and raise export supply, but temporarily more with the west. On balance, real effective protection against former partners rises sharply while that against the west is relaxed.

Second, the transitions have invariably proceeded with considerable chaos. It is arguably nowhere more pronounced than in the successor States of the Soviet Union and Yugoslavia. Even with limited distortion, as in the Czech Republic, economic turbulence in one country reverberates throughout the area. This has been notably the case for the former Soviet Union, given its pivotal role in supplying its former partners with fuels and raw materials and purchasing the latter's custom-made manufactures; the impact on the CIS States was bound to be even more pronounced. All this exerts a multiplier effect larger than one, guaranteeing a downward spiral for some time, although the initial phase of the transition is probably the worst time for this "imported" depression to manifest itself. Incidentally, this interlacement argues against the current mode in vogue of comparing individual country performances without taking into account that these cannot legitimately be treated as "independent" events, not even in the statistical sense (Ickes 1996).

Lastly, political obstacles have inhibited agreement on successor regimes to those anchored to the dinar, ruble, and transferable ruble. The inability to embrace "world market" conditions and the utter unwillingness to revive some organized form of intragroup cooperation have measurably exacerbated the impact of the disintegration of the former zones. Also, the startling lack of imagination on the part of otherwise well-intentioned western donors and assistance agencies has sharply understated the depth and breadth of interdependence among transition economies, both those in the vanguard of the movement and the more laggard ones. The assistance policies formulated under the circumstances have, at best, been poorly designed (see Chapter 11).

I do not, of course, suggest that all of the above difficulties encountered early during the transition, including in intragroup trade, could have been avoided altogether. This is a platitude as the transition could not possibly have been broached without negative implications on economic activity and employment (see Chapter 3). I do contend, however, that a considerable part of the collapse notably in intragroup trade stemmed from chaotic overshooting. That could have been averted to some degree without necessarily crimping the ability of the transition economies to explore other markets if effective successor cooperation mechanisms had been put in place. Not only would they have slowed down the contraction of intragroup trade, but also they would have bolstered the opportunities for trade creation (see Brabant 1990, 1991a, 1992b).

9.4 – An organized disentanglement?

From the transition's inception it was clear that the affected countries needed to disengage from the erstwhile unions that were either not politically desired or not truly based on economic factors. Less clear from an economic point of view was how best to divorce from this CMEA entanglement as well as from the erstwhile unitary economic spaces for the split federations. Opinions have ranged from emphasizing the maintenance of existing unions to their most rapid destruction. The latter point of view derives essentially from presumptions that in the long run – essentially the equilibrium position in comparative statics – most of the component economies would do better by seceding from the unions than from committing themselves to not very credible gradualism. The former position essentially rests on the argument that the costs of disengagement are so large, either because of true benefits forgone or because of the opportunities for gradual disengagement, that it would be sheer folly to seek rapid dissolution of the existing unions. Naturally, both positions are suspect. But I would ally myself more readily with the one advocating some gradual unwinding. The other evidently relies on the tacit assumption that "market-based" adaptations emerge quickly, hence that the short-term costs of complete destruction are inferior to the discounted costs of a gradual solution. The argument parallels those made for shock therapy (see Chapter 3).

Even if such a quick, moderately costly transition were feasible, I am suspicious of arguments that purport to be able to forecast the desirable trading and integration patterns of the transition economies some years hence and thus to chart a trajectory toward that desirable state with any degree of precision. This is especially the case for putative econometric "forecasts" based on gravity equations estimated for market economies (as detailed in Brabant 1992b, 1997c). For one thing, I find it all but ludicrous to entertain seriously any eventuality that the transition economies must return to their trading patterns of the 1920s, before either the Great Depression for eastern Europe or the emergence of state socialism in the USSR (minus the Baltics). Even the presumption that the trade orientation registered at that time was in any sense an equilibrium is suspect, if only because of the enormous adjustment difficulties encountered after World War I and the very substantial trade barriers erected by the successors to the empires swept away with the conclusion of that war. There simply is no reason to presume that the industrialization and related structural changes of the past half century have been all for naught, hence that each country would be well advised to return to its spuriously imputed prewar equilibrium.

That there would be a very substantial cost was entirely foreseeable. Arguments to the effect that the transition economies, unlike western Europe after World War II, could procure flexibility in established "open" trading and capital markets were theoretically correct. But the reality differed. As the course of events has shown, these countries were cut off for some time from private capital markets. It was essentially because of generous official assistance from bi- and multilateral agencies that some imbalances could be sustained. Also, the argument that the transition economies could jump into established open markets was simply ivory-tower rhetoric. For the products for which the transition economies possessed a temporary comparative advantage, these markets chiefly in western Europe simply were, and still are, not open. Not only that, the economic agents of these countries could not avail themselves of established trading networks. As a result, distress selling and retrogressing in terms of technological sophistication in exports have resulted (see Chapter 10).

9.5 – No future for regional trade?

Economics hardly played a role in the above policies, though some observers have argued that CMEA and interrepublic trade flows in the dissolved federations had little if any economic justification and that trade flows prospectively had to be west-reoriented in any case. The veracity of such extreme views, while they may be self-serving, is doubtful. With some effort, the large costs of rapid disengagement could have been anticipated and factored into alternative policy stances. Whatever the argument, policy makers sought rapid disintegration or allowed it to take place without any counteroffensive, thus exacerbating the economic depression. At the same time, the market institutions to decelerate and reverse rapid trade destruction have only slowly been crystallizing.

The recent tepid recovery in intragroup trade (see Chapter 10) and the regained enthusiasm for more intensive regional economic cooperation are welcome signs. It is not clear, though, whether these new trends stem from a shift in emphasis toward more businesslike relations with former CMEA partners. From the transition's inception, I have been among those who advocated that, from an economic point of view, there never was any reason to destroy the inherited trade patterns and levels that could be justified according to emerging economic-choice criteria. Whereas in the short run such cooperation would have been hampered by the deep economic, political, and social malaise in these countries, the latter's breadth and depth could have been alleviated to some degree by shoring up intragroup demand. Finally, the opportunities for reviving such economic cooperation in the medium to long run have always been considerable, regardless of the intensity of economic interaction with western Europe.

That is to say, ignoring the opportunities for intragroup trade might have been useful from a short-term political and security perspective. But it never had solid economic foundations. Indeed, the transition economies had been intricately interlaced for so long and their "natural proclivity" in terms of proximity and complementarity for close interaction was never zero. As a result, there must be room for relatively buoyant intragroup trade if accommodated. In the short to medium run, given prevailing conditions, this might have benefited from some policy intervention to restructure intragroup trade in an orderly fashion regardless of the sustainable level of such interaction in the long run. The point is that inherited specialization patterns without an economic rationale must be phased out and trading patterns warranted on economic grounds accommodated through some sensible coordination mechanism. Nonexisting or poorly performing markets manifestly do not provide that minimum degree of dovetailing. Of course, the instruments for such coordination must themselves be solidly anchored to market indicators, but conceived within an overall program of bold adjustments in economic structures and institutions.

9.6 – Trade diversion?

I submit that export growth to the EU has exceeded expectations both in terms of the speed with which such markets could be conquered and the extent to which trade was actually switched or domestic absorption curtailed to bolster exports. Recall that this stemmed in part from the impacts of domestic and external liberalization, including the sudden slack in domestic demand, the CMEA's disarray, the guarded opening of western markets, the entirely rational short-termist decision of SOEs to stress liquidity rather than asset value, and unusual temporary circumstances (including low-cost inputs available by decumulating inventories, currency undervaluation, comparatively easy access to inputs from other SOEs through either soft loans or established procurement channels, and newly gained discriminatory preferences in western markets). Full benefits depend on whether the transition economy can diversify its export supply beyond the products that enjoy such a one-off advantage. I return to these issues in Chapter 10.

Conclusions

Anchoring more effective relative prices and rapidly strengthening competition in domestic markets are essential in moving the transition forward at minimal cost. These tasks can be accomplished only by liberalizing the trade and foreign-exchange regimes. To do so in a precipitate manner, given the legacies of state socialism in terms of the rigidities present at the transition's inception, risks destroying needlessly a considerable proportion of the economy's productive capacity. Yet slowing down the transformation process too much through heavy explicit or implicit protection would clearly be counterproductive. Again, there is a tradeoff for policy makers to act upon.

One of the major lessons emerging from the transitions is that there is no quick and low-cost adjustment option when switching to relatively low protection and an undervalued exchange rate if there is a need for quick and massive structural adjustments – institutionally, organizationally, incentive-wise, and in the real production sphere. Given the defects of emergent markets in the transition economy, a judicious export-promotion strategy directed at all present and potential partners, perhaps in combination with some import substitution, in the context of an "orderly" disengagement of domestic activities, is advisable. This is especially the case when intrinsically unviable activities cannot be wiped out immediately for sociopolitical reasons. Of course, it is that only if appropriate governance capabilities can be mobilized at home and in the assistance providers as well. That has repercussions too for the stance taken on joining the EU (see Chapter 10).

Trade and foreign-exchange liberalization deserves to be promoted avidly, but only to the extent that its advantages are not hollowed out by the inflicted costs, which are far from zero. The purpose in principle would be to search for an export-led recovery and growth strategy. In practice, the core task of transition is building a strong market-based economy and solidifying democracy by identifying a new, sustainable growth path. That necessarily means breaking soon into global competition at a certain level of technological sophistication (in all of its dimensions), for which catch-up is required, or that can benefit from increasing returns, imperfect competition, economies of scale, externalities, and the economics of learning in all of its dimensions (see Chapter 12).

6

PRIVATIZATION AND THE MARKET ECONOMY

As indicated, I restrict the notion privatization to all means available to take the "state," including its serving bureaucrats and political actors, out of the allocation of most resources. Of course, the state has a role in steering resource allocation, such as through its macroeconomic policy (see Chapter 9). But it should not decide on the nuts and bolts of production and consumption, barring exceptional circumstances. On the transition's eve that is not the case, given the prevalence of state property. So one critical element of transition concerns what should be done with state assets to improve resource allocation soonest. One reason is that the state's potential function as owner is heavily contested in virtually any economic setting (Helm 1986; Kay 1986). The passions about divesting state ownership have been particularly virulent in the transition economies, although state owner-ship cannot altogether be avoided (Frydman and Rapaczyński 1991, pp. 254–5). Not only that, rapid progress with some classes of privatization *must* be made early on to anchor the rudiments of an emerging market economy and thus improve resource allocation.

This chapter presents the case for and against privatization from various angles. I first justify the choice of the compass of privatization advocated. Then I examine the motives for and goals of privatization pursued in transition economies. The alternatives to outright divestment are considered next. There-after I look at the obstacles to privatization. Following this, I sketch the various techniques of divestment in some sense used up to now. Before dealing with the remaining problems of privatization at this juncture, I assess the achievements to date.

Section 1: Privatization defined

Definitions should in the end reflect the type of remit the investigator finds most appropriate. Privatization has been used in a broad sense of fostering the market economy based on private property. This purpose of transformation is undoubt-edly important. But its broad canvas for projecting privatization is not quite congruent with the core tasks faced by policy makers in transition economies early on, given the legacy of nonprivate property. Certainly, private institutions and their legal foundations need to emerge. But the chief issues involved in that endeavor differ markedly from those pertaining to the core question of what to do with the stock of state-owned assets in order to improve resource allocation. Once the transition economy possesses clear property rights and adequate market institutions, the role of the private sector in determining how best the country should evolve toward a mature market economy becomes critical. Ensuring effective resource allocation under those conditions will primarily be a matter of incentives and how economic agents react to them. Just as I do not wish to deal with private economic undertakings as such, I do not intend to discuss under the label privatization the many ways in which the state can liberalize the economy or reduce the scope and intensity of, and modify, the regulatory control system.

Policy matters are vastly different when it comes to the utilization of existing capital assets, which are chiefly in the hands of the state and its agents, or entrusted in ill-defined ways to societal surrogates (such as enterprise, self-management, or workers' councils). These pose concerns with which the transformation *per se* has to come to grips in order to forge ahead with the core tasks at hand. Early on during the transformation, then, the key tasks consist not only of rapid divestment through outright sale or free distribution, but also ensuring more productive utilization of existing assets. Measures to be contemplated include the introduction of alternative incentive and governance mechanisms notably for assets that remain in the public sector (Gathon and Pestieau 1996; Morin 1996). Most SOEs on the transition's eve are going concerns that will quickly be confronted with a thoroughly depressed economic environment. This may pose insurmountable hurdles for those in rust-belt sectors, including metallurgy and heavy engineering. But most SOEs continue to operate and generate some profit, part of which is retained for amortization purposes and the rest for net savings. So, existing state-owned assets too may engage in new capital formation. And in some cases the transfer of these assets to private agents, possibly management, may be arranged by eliciting restructuring investment. Those cases too should be evaluated.

Many observers (see Blommestein and Marrese 1991; Blommestein, Marrese, and Zecchini 1991; Bouin and Michalet 1991) take privatization in transition economies to mean the irrevocable divestment of assets now held by the state and its surrogates, except in the case of nonphysical assets; for the latter privatization then refers to exploitation by nonstate agents. This transfer as a rule involves *all* property rights, including the alienation of assets (sale, destruction, inheritance, free distribution through voucher schemes, and others) regardless of their divisibility. Neither is necessary to improve resource allocation and delink the latter from political and bureaucratic controls. In fact, other methods must be embraced to expedite the exit of the state from most allocative decisions as speedily and widely as possible with minimal market and government failures because of time or format constraints. Deep divestment cannot be accomplished overnight. And no economy wants to divest all assets.

The frequent identification of privatization policy with asset sale is misleading for two reasons. As noted, outright sale need not at all be involved, as in the case of intangible assets. But it applies to tangible assets too: Privatization may simply divorce ownership *per se* from the exercise of most ownership rights. This can be easily seen when property rights are viewed as bundles of rights (see Chapter 7). The ultimate owner may not be the best suited to maximize anticipated property returns and may, therefore, temporarily entrust one or more elements of the bundle of rights to "other" owners. It is even possible (Blankart 1985; Swann 1988) to include under the label privatization enjoining SOEs to maximize profits; to provide goods and services only if the price covers the cost involved, such as through regulated user fees (Kent 1987b, p. 13); and to adopt cost-minimizing procedures in employment and procurement. In that sense, though ownership does not change, privatization alters the balance of power between government as owner and private agents as executors, giving the latter an important stake in selecting the best use of assets.

Second, even when asset sale or free distribution occurs, much of the impact of policy may arise from decisions about competition and regulation rather than from the mere transfer of ownership. The immediate effect of privatization is to substitute shareholder for governmental monitoring and control of the SOE's management. Its impact depends very much on the degree to which the new shareholders can motivate management to maximize net asset values. A simple exchange of title does not necessarily produce this effect. If actual shareholders do not succeed and others perceive they can do better, the impact of their monitoring stems from disciplining management, such as through takeovers. But the latter's operationality should not be exaggerated, not even for mature market economies (Corbett and Mayer 1991; Harris 1997; Stiglitz 1993).

Privatization, as a result, can be taken to encompass a wide variety of modifications to exercising control over assets by transferring to other agents the right of the state to influence directly the allocation of capital resources to nonstate entities. Some are concerned with alternative approaches to the supply and indeed financing of local and central government services. As such, privatization is an umbrella term for a variety of policies that are loosely linked by the way in which they are taken to mean the strengthening of the market at the expense of the state (Vickers and Wright 1988, p. 1).

In that context, I distinguish divestment from enterprise reforms that alter the legal position of the SOE from being a state agent into some joint-stock company. I call that "corporatization." But I do not equate it with profit making or maximization (Stiglitz 1997b). Provided there exists a legal framework for the firm, the incorporation process may be pursued rather quickly. With it, the state remains the owner but the usufruct accrues to the firm. Management becomes the agent and the state its principal. The latter needs to closely monitor the former. Given the convoluted situation in transition economies, such a legal context and appropriate monitoring are worth pursuing for their own sake, at least on an interim basis. When such corporatized firms are furthermore held to a "hard budget" constraint, that is, have to be profitable or otherwise be sold or dissolved, I invoke the notion "commercialization." This involves notably the fine-tuning of incentive schemes designed to motivate present or new management into maximizing net asset values on the strength of the firm's own and borrowed resources. Note that such resources may accrue from contractual compensation (hence not subject to soft budgets) for services rendered to the state or its agents that earlier were subsidized by government. Finally, the notion divestment includes the irrevocable release of all property rights from the state to another agent; this must, of course, be subject to constitutional provisions on condemnation for social purposes against some form of negotiable compensation or under untoward circumstances. Such transactions include outright sales through various channels, and I use here precisely that term. Divestment encompasses also programs that seek to distribute asset claims free of charge.

Asset sale in a transition economy is generally separated into the so-called "small" (or "petty") and "big" (or "real" or "mass") privatization. Three reasons explain this distinction. One is the goal of improving the efficiency of asset use, of buttressing private ownership as a key ingredient for strengthening democracy, and of rewarding the population at large with new forms of assets and risks. Another is that divestment of core industry can realistically be projected only over a protracted period of time, even if policy makers need not worry about proceeds and wealth effects. Finally, there are assets that should never have been arrogated by the state. This is certainly true for so-called petty assets. It applies too to the bulk of "large" assets, but the latter include also the production of public and quasi-public goods and services for which at least some SOEs will remain extant over the long haul or firms must otherwise be heavily regulated. Improving the former's governance regime and putting in place an adequate regulatory framework are crucial ingredients of building functioning markets.

The dividing line between small and large privatization is not set hard and fast. The first is essentially concerned with the sale to the public-at-large (possibly residents, nationals, expatriates, and foreign private and legal persons) of assets (including housing, service shops, retail outlets, catering establishments, small workshops, and similar productive units) for which the process of coordinating the embedded service streams can be ensured at least cost through private ownership. The owners in this case exert direct control and operate the assets for all practical purposes themselves. Such assets should be sold quickly through fair allocation mechanisms, such as auctions. On the other hand, "big privatization" refers to sale or the free distribution of shares to part of the state's *de facto* property rights to the vast bulk of SOEs that tend to be large, organized in conglomerates, and highly monopolistic. The objectives of such divestment and how to deliver on them are, therefore, considerably more complex than in the case of "petty" assets. Moreover, some will remain the state's for a long time to come. But that does not necessarily mean that the state itself should engage in direct production of goods and services (see Chapter 9).

The above categorization may seem pedantic at first glance. In view of the confusion in the literature, however, I deem it useful to confine the remit of privatization to the core tasks at hand, while considering all feasible policy options to forge ahead pragmatically, possibly on a transitory basis. I realize that the definition embraced gives rise to two concerns. One is the wide remit of the task envisaged. The other is the appropriateness of potentially confounding SOEs with the core of the future economic organization, which will be private ownership and control over assets. Although there is wide support for removing political interest groups from direct allocative decisions, the economic role of the state in transition economies (see Chapter 9) will remain considerable for decades to come and part of savings will be earmarked for upgrading these assets. This leads to a semantic problem when I use the notion privatization to encompass also public-sector reform. I have elsewhere (Brabant 1992a, p. 155) proposed makeshift solutions to this conundrum.

Two final conceptual remarks. In this chapter, I assume that clear property rights are recognized in society so that they can be enforced and protected in law, making them thus fully tradable in emergent markets; but I do not find it appropriate, as Cheryl Gray (1996, p. 2) posits, that clear property rights somehow presume the existence of owners who "have power, incentives, and capability to practice effective corporate governance." That would be a desirable characteristic, of course, and I thus include it under the privatization label. I also assume that a considerable degree of liberalization for entry and exit of firms and goods has been achieved (but see Chapter 5). In other words, I focus here on how best to reallocate assets in some sense owned by the state at the transition's eve. I do so for several reasons. My key point of departure is a proposition about how best to coordinate at least cost the service flows potentially emanating from assets. In some cases, this can best be assured by private owners internalizing the co-ordination process. Other instances are better (in terms of efficiency) handled through alternative property forms (cooperative, corporate, or state ownership). That implies that assets must be tradable, for which at least rudimentary capital markets must be innovated soonest (see Chapter 7).

Also, I am well aware that privatization, however defined, may be pursued for many other reasons than those leading to improving economic efficiency (see Section 2). One is that irreversibility of the transition needs to be safeguarded by placating the electorate into supporting "its transition." For that it may be desirable to divest quickly a portion of the capital stock through imaginative schemes other than outright cash sales and to foster the rapid accumulation of private property for economic reasons. Even so, I contend that privatization should first and foremost be an *economic* undertaking (Brabant 1992a). Much remains to be done to ensure that SOEs are restructured and to enhance the creation of new SMEs, especially in activities other than services and arbitrage. Particularly important is that the budding banking sector is not yet equipped to intermediate effectively between savers and new investors or to facilitate settlement of transactions. Yet progress with privatization in the sense defined *must* be made.

Section 2: Motivations for pursuing privatization

Privatization measures and their implications are rarely justified on economic grounds alone. Indeed, the driving force behind privatization, however defined, is nearly always political and nearly all such schemes arouse political controversy. But measures vary from country to country, and nowhere is the policy driven by one overriding objective (see Chapter 3). I consider here five clusters of motives.

2.1 – Economic objectives

From among the many angles, I suggest seven salient ones for transition economies. Foremost is improving economic efficiency, as noted. Because the size of the public sector is too large, it has led to intolerable inefficiency in production, in resource allocation, and/or in technological adaptation. The government has been neither a good manager nor a good monitor of economic resources. Its motive is not really – and cannot truly be – profit maximization. By divesting assets to privately motivated agents, economic efficiency is expected to rise, particularly if accompanied by strong procompetitive policies. It must be recognized, second, that there are areas in which government can deliver at lesser cost than the private sector, but possibly by worsening their delivery on unrelated tasks. Various schemes are available to separate the role of the government as producer from its other tasks in society, including contracting out or asking SOEs to keep the books of economic operations separate from transactions involving other tasks.

Third, privatization strengthens a shareholding culture. Divesting assets familiarizes the public at large with holding shares as part of wealth portfolios and may raise the intensity of the effort by which management is monitored. This may bolster absolute wealth, hence lower expectations regarding the state as a guarantor of social security and stability. However, the population at large may be so averse to diluting its wealth portfolio that it divests its acquired shares quickly. Nor is there certainty that private monitoring improves upon public monitoring. Also, fourth, divestment contributes to the development of financial and capital markets, thus propping up a growing "modern" sector. This is particularly important during the early stages of development. In any case, firms need primarily to be financed through capital markets.

Fifth, privatization promotes competition, which is so vital for a market-based economic system, provided product and factor markets are opened up. Liberalizing the foreign sectors and stimulating new investments from private and public savings may also improve competition. But more is required, including through deconcentration, demonopolization, and divestment of state assets, especially in economic activities for which the state does not possess a comparative advantage.

Sixth, divestment could raise revenue for the state, lower its outlays formerly required to finance loss-making operations, and modify its tax base. The latter may or may not yield higher revenues, depending on how quickly a modern fiscal system can be effectively completed. From a flow-of-funds' point of view, then, divestment through sales could help close the budget gap in the early phases of the transition. But it may also reduce actual or potential taxes. In this connection, finally, because it promises to radically change the prevailing penchant for the inflationary bias in the behavior of firms, privatization can help stabilize the economy in a flow sense. By soaking up money in circulation and streamlining it, privatization buttresses stabilization in the stock sense. Note that the latter requires divestment, but the former could be obtained by enforcing a hard budget constraint even for SOEs. That, after all, is the heart of commercialization and, in a sense, of corporatization.

2.2 – Political considerations

One is the role of the state in economic development. Liberty requires private ownership and the state's economic role restricted as much as possible to the enforcement of property rights, something that harks back to the Kantian enlightenment (Munzer 1990, p. 131). The state itself should provide public goods only when it has a comparative advantage; normally when there are market failures but no or less costly government failures (see Chapter 3). Another motivation is the need to strengthen democracy and shore up social stability by molding "a normal society." Many transition managers hold visions of an economic, political, and social order that is both free and prosperous. In some cases, these attitudes outlasted powerful oppression of those ejected from power under communism or survived in some form through "positive alienation" (Hankiss 1990, pp. 7ff.). Among the positive motivations are endeavors to enhance freedom and hence the democratic process. For that, some critical minimum of property rights' reform and divestment may have to be undertaken quickly. The reason is simple: Democracy without private property rights is unthinkable. To encourage the emergence of a middle class, quick divestment of a substantial part of state assets may be required. This contributes to rendering the political revolution irreversible and buttresses emergent markets.

Furthermore, by promoting shareholding in society, privatization may forestall social disorder as, in conjunction with democratic institutions and decision making, citizens now feel they have a voice in the way in which their society is run in marked contrast to the state of affairs under the previous regime. This includes getting even for the long years during which private ownership of many real and financial assets was denied and the state arrogated to itself the entire capital-formation process. Whether society will be willing soon to accept income and wealth differentiation with private ownership and market-based incentives is a question that may complicate property rights' reform (see Chapter 7). This is not a trivial matter when democracy is still shallowly rooted and it has perhaps been weakened, after the initial euphoria, by the disappearance of the organs of civil society under state socialism that triggered the political chasm (Bernhard

1996) without organs better attuned to the new sociopolitical context taking firm root (see Chapter 7). Reaching soon a critical minimum of nonstate ownership may play a crucial role in sidestepping some of the potential pitfalls. If investible resources are not available in the short run, or sales otherwise crowd out desirable startups, it may be desirable to divest quickly some portion of the existing capital stock through imaginative schemes other than outright sales.

A further political motive is coming to grips with old-style management and organization reserved for the Party faithful and their protégés. Taking the Party and government out of the decision making over the allocation of assets and removing the politically appointed SOE bureaucracy should help to focus more sharply on economic matters. Management appointed through the *nomenklatura* may have earned its spurs in Party politics or obtained its legitimation through the bureaucratic process; but rarely has it managed SOEs with a view to maximizing net asset values. This stemmed partly from the way the state-socialist economy functioned, but also from the state's grand failure over time to discharge its monitoring obligations (see Part I). Small wonder, then, that obliterating the overpowering influence of Party politics over economic affairs and curtailing the hold of the government bureaucracy over a highly monopolized SOE sphere provide one of the most cogent arguments for privatization in transition economies, even in circumstances where "market failures" exist and pure theory might suggest more nuanced positions (Lipton and Sachs 1990a). This may well be crucial early on in the transition to anchor the democratization process.

Once the new political structures are firmly in place, however, these abuses should be curtailed and altogether excised through the new political process. Economic arguments should receive a fairer, more technical reading. State-owned assets in essence represent societal savings enforced through socialist precepts. Society's custodians must, therefore, ensure that these resources are utilized efficiently, given the new allocative environment. This raises a number of technical issues, some of which I touch upon in the next two sections. One should recognize, however, that management and/or workers in SOEs have implicitly or explicitly accumulated property rights that cannot be taken away from them through an internal reform of the public sector. "Confiscation" of the property rights vested *de facto* with the *nomenklatura* might be counterproductive from the point of view of improving allocative and productive efficiency in the short run; it might also be unfair. The ability of the second-tier communist élites to transform themselves rather quickly, notably via privatization, into advocates of democracy and of the construction of a market economy (Bonnell 1996) may well fail to please those who suffered under state socialism. Attempts in some countries to exclude former "communists" from government positions via some "lustration" campaign create their own divisiveness. In the end, a thick line between the past and the future has to be drawn somewhere.

2.3 – Combating entrenched trade-union privileges

This may be quite important in countries (such as Poland and Yugoslavia) where these organs were active in SOE governance. By undermining, or at least seriously weakening, trade unions of the traditional mold or by eliminating an overly protective job-security system the state may help rearrange the social contract. Placing economic activity on an economic last requires a remolding of labor rewards according to performance and, at the same time, protecting labor from the potential abuses of capital. In countries where previously there was a tenuous relationship, if that, between labor effort and reward, the remuneration system needs to be restructured quickly. Furthermore, the implicit or explicit social contract may have to be renegotiated (see Chapter 8). To accomplish these more positive approaches to remodeling labor markets, cooperation among government, labor, and management may forge a more corporatist approach to reaching social consensus, notably on questions related to income distribution and wages. True, corporatism may not be very desirable in the long run, but an Austrian-type variant *may* yield a modicum of social consensus early during the transition (Henley and Tsakalotos 1991).

2.4 – Strengthening social cohesion

Societies that have a coherent framework on sharing and on how to navigate around sharp points tend to be more productive and stable than others in which the class struggle, even if under another name, continues to be a marked feature of interpersonal relations. Although the class struggle as an issue may have become remote in most transition economies, that of what to do with claimed property rights is not (see Chapter 7). It is especially critical to ensure that labor will not be the only sector to bear the burden of adjustment. A common understanding of what is required and an equitable distribution of the adjustment burden over a period of time may generate a positive motivation. This is as important prior to privatization as it is once the process gets under way (Buck, Thompson, and Wright 1991).

2.5 – Precepts on wealth distribution

Privatization may be directed at distributing society's wealth on an equitable basis and at providing new instruments for economic agents to diversify and enlarge their wealth portfolios. Because social property is considered people's property, transition society at large may claim its ownership. Various egalitarian distribution schemes are available. This may affect total wealth as well as its distribution. In turn, this may reduce future demands on government transfers for social programs. Individuals would more and more take care of their own intertemporal income distribution by voluntarily varying the level and composition of their wealth portfolios (see Chapter 8). Moreover, it might contribute to changing their time preference, thereby generating additional savings for development.

Section 3: Alternatives to outright divestment

Governments interested in ridding themselves of direct involvement in SOEs, yet bent on retaining ownership, can explore at least two alternative organizational formats once property rights are clearly demarcated. One is leasing SOE assets to the highest bidder or to a party determined as the most appropriate under the circumstances; another is to recognize the usefulness of management contracts, franchises, or subcontracting (Nankani 1988; Pannier 1996; Pannier and Schiavo-Campo 1996; Rapp 1986; Vuylsteke 1988, 1990). The advantage of proceeding in this manner is that the benefits of ownership are retained in the public sector, while the operations are in effect privatized. It gives the government time to decide on divestment while helping to establish the SOEs' comparative advantage. Alternatively, the government could make a genuine declaration to the effect that, irrespective of its ownership, it undertakes not to interfere in commercial decisions of the SOEs so identified. But that poses delicate monitoring issues (see Chapter 7).

For the above to be viable alternatives to divestment, criteria of managerial behavior as surrogates of markets that force an SOE to operate as if it were a private firm, thus bound by market disciplines, need to be operationalized (in investment, cost minimization, innovation, research and development (R&D), and pricing). These include specification of a minimum required rate of return on capital, of targets for overall and perhaps for disaggregated net returns, of unit costs and productivity, and of the obligation to procure funds in commercial markets. True, it is not easy to devise such criteria and apply them. But opportunities do exist (Backhaus 1989; Stiglitz 1997a, b). This leads to a paradox (Zeckhauser and Horn 1989, pp. 55–6): Although privatization may seem most appropriate for SOEs operating in competitive markets, these are precisely the firms whose internal performance can be most readily improved by reforming their public monitoring systems. Such would seem to be well suited for firms that remain in the public sector (Pannier 1996). Would it not make sense to conceptualize and apply managerial incentive schemes that remove a substantial proportion of the objections traditionally levied against SOEs, because of their relationship with government (Cook and Kirkpatrick 1988b, p. 32), often on rather flimsy evidence (Gathon and Pestieau 1996; Morin 1996; Pestieau 1989)?

In theory, it is possible to create the kinds of incentives that maximize efficiency under any type of ownership. Rather than it being impossible to design monitoring mechanisms and improve them over time, and indeed adhere to them through the political process, one should at least test the stability, reliability, and predictability of the political process during the transition in spite of the ascent of newfangled politicians. Note that the theoretically feasible is not what typically comes to the fore. As a commercial entity, an SOE must sell in the marketplace. As a public organization, it tends to receive other objectives and is exposed to pressure from sectional interests with political clout. SOEs are often operated as public bureaucracies with more attention paid to procedures than to results; the resulting ready access to subsidies tends to erode the incentive for managers to minimize costs.

Assuming that there will be a transparent and moderately stable political environment, an entire panoply of options on how best to mobilize the service streams of state-owned assets is available. These have unequal weights depending on the concrete types of assets and the motives that privatization is to serve. One could conceive of a "divestment function" with as arguments revenue generation, improvements in allocative and productive efficiency, contribution to stabilizing democracy, getting even with the Party and its associated bureaucracy, breaking the back of other interest groups, disbursing wealth to society at large to foster private ownership, and other goals to be served. Although this cannot possibly be a linear function, the nonnegative weights attached to each of the arguments must necessarily emerge in conjunction with the revelation of other preferences through the social consensus-building process. Seen from this angle, the *a priori* case for quick and cost-free divestment is weak. Likewise, any attempt to capture privatization campaigns in transition economies under a singular label (Grosfeld and Senik-Leygonie 1996) can at best provide a heuristic caricature. Not only that, given the complex tasks of how best to improve the allocation of state assets there, the importance of the various options is likely to shift as a result of evolution in various pragmatic, ideological, economic, and populist objectives.

The privatization motives that transformation managers may wish to pursue determine to a large degree the methods of divestment to be explored. Thus, if budget revenues must be maximized, assets must be priced at the highest feasible value. But if the prime motive is to buttress democracy or serve libertarian values anchored to private property, divestment through outright sale of or by giving assets away should be carried out as rapidly as possible. If those who can reasonably be anticipated to have an interest in exerting property rights for maximum economic benefit can be reached, so much the better; otherwise follow-up privatization measures aiming at endowing owners with power, incentives, and capability to practice effective governance (C. W. Gray 1996) are in order. Whether that should be done by giving each citizen an equal share in social property or through the creation of the institutions of the emerging capital market (including pension funds, insurance companies, holding companies, and investment or mutual funds) is something to be carefully pondered (see Section 5).

Section 4: Obstacles to privatization

From the beginning it was evident to those acquainted with state socialism that privatization would be a very cumbersome process fraught with perplexing difficulties even under favorable circumstances. But many issues have arisen that were not even imagined at the outset. These derive from the transition economy's social and political features, not just the legacies of forty years of state socialism.

220

4.1 – The salient policy issues

Once the decision to privatize in some sense is taken, at least four policy matters must be resolved: the speed of privatization, the identification of state-owned assets to be so earmarked, whether those so selected should first be restructured, and how to privatize (see Section 5). Speed of privatization is one of those chicken-and-egg problems that have bedeviled the transition debate and, even worse, policy resolution of how best to proceed with building market-based allocation. Indeed, the determination of the desirable speed depends importantly on the paramount aspects of solidifying and maintaining political stability. It is also a function of the chosen sequence of the transition and how it is managed. This leads to a central paradox: If politics permits proceeding quickly with privatization, chiefly in the form of divestment, there would be little point in hammering out a strategy *per se*. But precisely such a "plan" is required to ensure that the transferred resources are used to maximum economic, political, and social effect. Short of war, revolution, or profound civil disorder, rapid movement with privatization is by its nature bound to be relative. There can only be various degrees of rapidity with privatization, regardless of how expedient reaching that goal is judged to be. Policy makers can benefit society only by devising a clear strategy and by recognizing that fine-tuning and incisive modifications are likely to become necessary throughout the process.

Second, establishing some order of priority of remolding ownership and control over various state-owned assets does not conflict with rapid progress with privatization, even divestment; indeed that is desirable. In fact, there is little choice in moving first with small privatization. But whether that should be pursued through sales, thereby siphoning off savings that could otherwise be earmarked for new small firms, is not self-evident. Similarly, there are various alternative modalities to privatize, each of which has its own set of advantages and drawbacks. The implications and the best choices at each stage of the transition could be ordered differently for housing, land, small businesses, large SOEs, financial institutions, and public utilities, to choose only these six tiers.

In this connection, the third issue – restructuring – is especially important for SOEs and financial institutions. Improvements of land, including state farms, and of housing can best be left to individuals. But some farms are quite large and must first be broken up into separately manageable components. Improving public utilities must remain a task for government, though not necessarily by government producing the goods and services thereby targeted (Chapter 9). In the case of small undertakings, it is probably best to leave the restructuring up to individuals interested in operating those assets. It would seem advisable to transfer those assets as unencumbered as possible. Thus resolving the existing debt of and property rights to these undertakings is a priority item. This is even more the case for the financial institutions and the core SOEs. The balance sheets of these institutions must be cleaned up relatively quickly. Of critical importance is transforming financial institutions into viable entities, given their crucial intermediating role. But that does not warrant forgiveness of all debts contracted as of a certain date (see Chapter 7).

Another daunting task concerns how best to divide existing SOEs into various groups. Aside from identifying firms to be sold off relatively quickly and others remaining in state hands, firms need to be culled into those to be wound down, those to be divested as is, and others in need of some restructuring before they are privatized, regardless of the form in which this is being envisaged. Restructuring is especially important to take care of enterprise debt. No less important are the multiple questions that arise from the various policy objectives revolving around asset divestment. In the case of free distribution, should some voucher scheme be preferred over other ways of allocating state assets? If assets are sold, how should one best proceed with corporatization and commercialization? And once accomplished what is a desirable road to selling state-owned assets? Should such divestment be pursued with a firm reservation price? If so, how is this price to be set and modified depending upon the reaction of investors?

Also important are the issues pertaining to the envisaged role for foreign capital or managers in the transition process. Should residence be a criterion for allocating resources? Or would it be preferable for the sake of social harmony to focus on nationality, regardless of where the nationals have been residing? Would the circumstances of their departure matter, for example, in clarifying the issues involving restitution and compensation claims? And should those who changed their nationality, perhaps under force of circumstance, be entitled to reclaim their birthright, including to participate in privatization? Related to this is the role to be accorded to former owners, and where they reside or what their present nationality may be. Many questions of reprivatization, restitution, and compensation of former owners must be addressed.

Policy makers will have to decide upon the role of financial institutions, perhaps yet to be created or rendered operational, such as banks; mutual and investment funds; pension funds; insurance companies; holding companies; and stock markets, in driving the privatization process either on the supply or the demand side. Needless to say, areas of potential conflicts of interest need to be addressed as soon as feasible with a view to mitigating their scope and occurrence.

Finally, many issues pertain to whether the government should hold back shares for later sale, and in this case what its position in monitoring management should be. Another string revolves around whether it should strive to attain a stable core of investors soonest or later, once reasonable economic stabilization is gained. Another question relates to whether the stable core could conceivably consist solely of foreign owners, and for which type of assets such foreign participation would be acceptable. In this connection it may be useful to briefly ponder whether privatization should after all not be a very eclectic policy.

Even when these ideological, social, and political overtones of privatization have been diffused, reallocating assets can proceed only by resolving a great number of technical, economic, and managerial obstacles. I consider those in turn.

4.2 – Technical obstacles

First, market structures are key ingredients in arriving at any informed decision to divest, in particular when the campaign is aimed at improving efficiency (Fershtman 1990; Newbery 1991). Initially, most observers assumed all too facilely that the transition economy can quickly establish fair competition in privatized markets. Given the nature of these economies, this assertion threads shallow waters. Fostering private capital formation from domestic and foreign savings can enhance domestic competition; but FDI tends to be a lagging variable, given the uncertainty in transition. Substituting private for state monopolies is unlikely to enhance efficiency or increase the net worth of the firm as competitive bidding is virtually precluded in the process. Divestment of firms with market power brings about private ownership in precisely the circumstances where it has least to offer (Newbery 1991). The desire to sell off SOEs speedily, to widen share ownership quickly, and to raise short-term revenue should not detract from devising adequate measures of competition and regulation.

Second, privatization requires dissemination of information and a set framework. These are areas in which there is a great dearth in all transition economies, in part because of the legacies of state socialism. Accurate economic information on the value of state-owned assets is either not available or the little collected and released under state socialism is unreliable for the purposes at hand. Recall from Part I that SOE management faced an objective function that had little to do with raising net worth. Few managers had an incentive to do so on their own initiative. All this has made it difficult for outsiders to acquire a coherent picture of the survivability of firms.

Given the protracted time dimension of divestment, detailed analysis and classification of SOEs is highly desirable to enable decision makers to identify candidates for divestment, firms that can be sold immediately with success, those that need rehabilitation prior to divestment, those that must be retained in the public sector, and others that must be liquidated. Because of stringent limits on information regarding the true economic position of SOEs at the transition's inception such a preliminary classification can at best be very approximate. At the very least, steps must be taken to corporatize and commercialize SOEs that cannot be given away or sold off quickly. To sell SOEs, a proper economic assessment is necessary, although it may be very difficult. Furthermore, clear guidelines and administrative responsibility for program implementation need to be adopted. In that context, a legal and institutional framework may have to be developed to cut through the Gordian knot of the more intractable policy and administrative conflicts to be resolved in order to progress with the transformation. Finally, there is a severe shortage of trained human resources to prepare and negotiate divestment in the transition economy; underdeveloped capital markets and shortages of investment bankers, enterprise valuation experts, and similar personnel further compound matters.

Third, for privatization to work well an appropriate regulatory environment is required whenever private decisions tend to take inadequate account of the "public interest" (Breyer and MacAvoy 1987). It is notably directed at countering the adverse effects of monopoly power, at offsetting externalities, at compensating for inadequate information, and at rectifying unequal bargaining power. Such a regulatory framework is important also for new firms, SOEs to be prospectively privatized, and SOEs to be kept in public hands. Such a framework should be established, fine-tuned, and upgraded by an impartial body (see Chapter 7). Needless to say, a well-developed regulatory mechanism cannot be introduced as a *deus ex machina*. Rather, it evolves over time and rarely unidirectionally (Breyer and MacAvoy 1987; Collins and Wallis 1990; Helm and Yarrow 1988; Jenkinson and Mayer 1996; Kay and Vickers 1988; Stelzer 1988, 1989; Swann 1988; Vickers 1991, 1996).

Fourth, divestment is costly, lengthy, divisive, and yields mixed results. The costs can have various origins. One direct source is assessing the real worth of capital assets. Those managing the transformation should avoid a sellout at prices that deviate substantially from the intrinsic value of the assets being alienated, however approximately this can be gauged given weakly functioning markets (see below). The political backlash of underpricing assets as perceived by the electorate can be quite deleterious. This is not at all an easy matter as the price placed on a given firm varies greatly depending on the individual evaluator, the information that can be extracted from markets, the legitimate and other discreet information that can be brought to bear on the evaluation, and the purpose for which the exercise is being conducted. Bidders for assets in well-functioning markets generally have different ideas about what they can accomplish with them in terms of anticipated returns, given their management skills and anticipations about the best purposes for which the assets can be mobilized.

The situation in transition economies is far more complex. Without a rudimentary capital market valuation must be based on an assessment of how interested buyers may look at a company's economic prospects. That derives in large measure from their views of how the production process can be restructured, and at what cost, and the discounted net return on sales expected to accrue over the lifetime of the assets. Because the majority of SOEs are in need of major restructuring, there is little evidence of what kind of output and prices may prospectively emerge. Second-guessing the decision process of potential buyers is haphazard at best. As a result, valuation is perforce rather messy. Involving foreign experts at great expense may help clear up some points, but it cannot circumvent the pervasive uncertainty. Indeed, many foreign experts come to the valuation process with only the dimmest of knowledge of SOEs, the legacies of state socialism, or the macroeconomic and legal settings of transition economies. Matters are in fact still more complicated. Although there may be a veneer of greater rectitude in having values of assets ascertained by reputable accounting firms or western consultants, this procedure is necessarily slow and costly (either for the privatizing country or the assistance provider). In the end it is not clear that resources thus spent are well earmarked. This is certainly the case in economies experiencing rapid inflation. Any estimated value, no matter how accurately computed, will be well out of truck with present values when actual sale occurs.

Although free distribution of shares may, in principle, circumvent these convoluted issues, this holds at best at the time of divestment and even then only under highly restrictive circumstances. If the electorate has a longer memory, the backlash of giving away assets in such a way that considerable inequalities are generated is bound to be potentially explosive. This all the more so if the inequality results from the giveaway itself, particularly in an uncertain environment with asymmetric information; room for opportunistic behavior; and poor competition, rather than from the improvement in asset values generated by the emerging market economy. Policy makers and their advisers simply cannot ignore that their opponents, and perhaps the electorate at large, hold notions about the "fairness" of market value. The transition's highly convoluted sociopolitical environment further complicates this potential for future resentment about inequalities.

Recall that some valuation is necessary, regardless of divestment modalities. One reason is the need for restructuring virtually all SOEs. Potential owners or their agents must therefore obtain some idea of what is at stake. At least they need to estimate the likely reorganization costs. Perhaps more important, these assets are one of the few positive legacies of over four decades of state socialism. Whether or not a "fair" or "right" or "just" price exists, the population at large harbors expectations as to the valuation of the sacrifices it sustained. Assets may well be worth little in a market environment. But if the population feels that they have been transferred below their "proper" value in less than transparent markets, thus offering quick paths to riches even for the *nomenklatura* that ought to have been disenfranchised on ethical and political grounds, there is bound to be an unpleasant backlash. Trenchant political opposition only exacerbates matters.

Furthermore, the economic depression engendered by the transition depreciates the "real" value of assets. This makes it less urgent to embrace outright divestment of large SOEs as compared to reviving the economy through proper procompetitive policies. Not only that, the impact depends on the type of asset. Depression in the state sector may be accompanied by a booming private sector. The latter's assets and those that can be mobilized for private activities (rural land, urban real estate, some transportation means, and the array of assets that come in handy in bolstering the small-scale service and trade sectors) tend to appreciate relative to those in the public sector.

Some of the critical obstacles could be mitigated by privatizing state assets through other means than outright divestment. Separating ultimate ownership from the usufruct will not, of course, eliminate all of the key obstacles to divestment discussed here. Thus, leasing or contracting out operations to private managers requires that a "proper" rent accrue to the state. Also this needs to be established in an environment with deficient, unstable markets. But such contracting out leaves much greater scope for deciding on the ultimate disposal of state assets. At the very least, experimentation with determining the value of capital services through auctions, for example, could be subtler. Particularly at the outset, any auction is likely to be chaotic. But it need not be a game of *hazard*.

Finally, the starting conditions for divestment are not propitious also because of the potential incompetence, malevolence, or lack of control over rapid transformation on the part of those called upon to manage the process. Some transition economies have, perhaps unwittingly, allowed one group, usually managers in place, to transform part of their specialized knowledge into a property stake far beyond what may have been warranted by their quasi-legitimate property rights (see Chapter 7). This has arguably been most egregious during the initial phases of the transition, with those still in power capitalizing their property rights into a private stake in the new society. The process led to numerous complaints, particularly in Hungary and Poland (see Lee and Nellis 1990), and later in many CIS States, as well as Albania, Cambodia, Mongolia, and Vietnam, to name just a few.

4.3 – Economic obstacles

The primary motivation of privatization should be improving the allocation of existing assets, while protecting their value, and ensuring that new capital is formed and utilized as efficiently as possible, using the assignment rule associated with ensuring proper coordination of the allocation of the service flows emanating from state assets. Once these features are accepted, several technical economic problems can be readily discerned. First, on the transition's eve there is insufficient indigenous savings in spite of the "overhang," which precludes the outright purchase of a sizable portion of state-owned assets by domestic agents. The savings that remain after the burst of inflation could at best be earmarked for the acquisition of housing, small plots of land, small handicrafts, or service firms. In some cases, creating proper financial institutions (such as independent pension funds, insurance schemes, commercial banks, and the like to whom state liabilities are "sold") can facilitate intermediation. But it cannot be a panacea. Even if hidden savings are mobilized, those assets are tainted, arising as they do from illegal or barely legal activities under state socialism. It would be odd to legitimize them *ex post*, particularly if transition managers are concerned about equity and fairness. But even if enough savings were available, it is not self-evident that savers would be interested in acquiring existing assets without there first being substantial other institutional transformations.

Second, divestment has distributive consequences. Would it be useful to give part of these assets as shares to stakeholders, thus really socializing property? An argument can be made for an egalitarian distribution. But it reaches only so far: The confiscatory approach to wealth and capital formation under state socialism did not affect all citizens or workers equally. It certainly did not affect equally those presently alive; even if legitimate heirs are included, equal distribution on egalitarian grounds to the present population is rather suspect. But problems arise also in organizing a fairly egalitarian distribution of shares, even if essentially free of charge. A wide distribution avoids future resentment about giveaways to a favored class. It also elicits support for the temporarily painful austerity measures designed to render those assets more productive. Above all, it shores up democracy. But it cannot foreclose all resentment, especially if markets do not quickly take off.

Third, if revenue must be raised and concerns about improving resource allocation, property administration, and principal–agent problems loom large, perhaps "transparent" auction markets offer the most advisable route. Absent prior experience with such divestment, careful experimentation is warranted both in the methodology of organizing auctions and in phasing in the sale of assets. For one thing, transparency needs to be measurably enhanced by rationalizing SOEs at least to make their books reflect more accurately real values that can be audited according to internationally accepted norms. It is probably hopeless to aim at quickly implementing such accounting standards. The books in place reflect principles that diverge palpably from those required to impart pertinent information about a firm's value, as more or less standard in a mature market economy. Though auctions will at the start be rather wild, the state can provide some initial guidance, for example, by commencing the bidding process at the state's own expected rate of return and value of assets. Fair auctions can be looked upon as an investment in laying the foundations of a capital market, even if at the cost of lost budget revenue. The information gained in the process and the impetus extended to fostering market behavior may well be worth the revenue forgone. But auctions cannot possibly be a panacea for all assets to be divested, of course.

Fourth, whenever assets are somehow entrusted to other than ultimate owners, problems arise in ensuring that the agent is properly monitored. This includes protecting the integrity of assets through legal redress mechanisms, something that is not easily achieved in an economy with so few market institutions, including for risk. High inflation and economic depression erode real asset values, making it problematic how to select a standard for the agent's behavior. Pragmatism will therefore be required in more than one respect.

Finally, the early macroeconomic environment is not particularly congenial for divestment, even for assets with dependable property rights. Divestment was initially hailed as a cure-all for many macro- and microeconomic problems, as well as a device for resolving basic sociopolitical problems in the new societies. This is a highly simplistic way of looking at the multiple issues at stake. At the very least, the question should be turned around: To what extent can macro- and microeconomic problems be solved through outright divestment? Indeed, what are the micro- and macroeconomic requirements for successful privatization, particularly at a time of widespread turmoil? Without making substantial progress with other components of the transformation agenda, it is simply impossible to determine even approximately the efficiency outcome of any privatization campaign.

On the fiscal side, divestment changes the stocks of assets owned by the state. Without a shift in fiscal regime, it also changes the nature and size of the flows, that is, current taxes and subsidies. Privatization was at one point hailed as a generator of budget revenue, thus a channel to soak up any remaining monetary overhang or to fund state outlays otherwise difficult to finance. Much of this argument has a weak foundation in the stock and flow senses, however. Since the government's wealth portfolio is counterbalanced by a portfolio of liabilities, selling state assets unbalances this portfolio (provided it started from a sound level) unless proceeds are earmarked for retiring some of the state's liabilities or the latter can be wiped out otherwise. If assets are sold below fair value, the government is jeopardizing its future financial position. Should present and future generations of tax payers be held liable for present government liabilities? This is *prima facie* unfair. I am aware of the budgetary pressures during the early phase of transition, and indeed the inability of the leadership to quickly revamp fiscal systems, which are prejudging intergenerational transfers of financial liabilities. This does not augur well for credibility. Of course, it should not be exacerbated by falling into avoidable pitfalls of unsound privatization. Also, the future stream of revenues associated with SOEs vanishes, unless fiscal dues can be expected and collected.

4.4 – Managerial problems

The existence of management that holds a monopoly on information, because of widely dispersed shareholders or of a market monopoly, leads to potentially deleterious principal–agent problems. If the intensity with which management is monitored is low, those in charge have discretion to pursue their own objectives. The danger that the abuses of state socialism may be extended during the transition is far from imaginary. Stabilization of asset values can emerge only with the gradual institution of basic regulatory mechanisms, effective bankruptcy proceedings, rules on disclosure, adequate bank supervision, and other elements. None of this helps if the firm's monopoly of information is not broken, particularly as regards the potential for cost reduction. The problems of poor managerial abilities and aberrant behavior, and how best to intervene so that management acts on behalf of owners remain, of course, even in cases where the state retains control and directs enterprise management, for example, through management contracts. Monitoring problems are, therefore, important in structuring incentives to induce management to behave according to the instructions of owners (Laffont 1996).

Second, much has been made of the inefficiency of managers under state socialism. Some certainly maximized their multiple objective function and did very well, given the set tasks, although they may have done poorly in terms of maximizing profit. It is often assumed that new owners or managers of newly privatized assets by definition allocate the latter's service stream more efficiently than erstwhile state-appointed officials. There is no guarantee at all that this will eventuate so long as competition with flexible markets cannot be assured. Even so, few individuals in transition economies have had experience with proper management and such cannot be quickly assimilated. Managerial skills can be built up only "on the job," largely through trial and error.

Third, entrepreneurial management in established firms, as distinct from short-term intermediation and straightforward services, is perhaps the scarcest "production factor" during the early stages of transition. The same applies to enterprise monitors with a track record. To some degree there is, of course, an overlap between management and monitors; or, for that matter, managers and genuine entrepreneurs. But there are also palpable differences. This may be seen by looking at the requirements for good corporate governance, something that is almost as important as sane governance of the emerging polity (see Chapter 7). Good governance requires effective monitoring, if only to compel management to observe transparent criteria. Accounting and accountability through disclosure obligations should be clear and standard, and indeed public. Furthermore, it requires effective penalization of failures. Corporate governance, in other words, is what ultimately disciplines managers into acting on behalf of owners.

Fourth, many questions are connected with the order in which large privatization in particular should preferably be pursued to minimize transitional difficulties and cut short delays in getting the economy going again with more efficient utilization of available assets. Order matters notably when privatization aims at efficiency and raising revenue. Some transition economies place great emphasis on properly preparing the agents to be privatized. This requires in some cases demonopolization and deconcentration prior to the restructuring of firms. The latter encompasses measures that alter the "production technology" and help to manage it. These activities are undertaken with a view to ensuring that privatization takes place in as competitive an environment as possible. Other commentators prefer to leave even these tasks up to the private sector.

There can be no debate that petty privatization should be started quickly. When it comes to the core SOEs, however, more options are available. Whether first to corporatize or commercialize by setting the SOEs into a different legal framework and nominating corporate boards is something to be carefully contemplated. Once the legal infrastructure is in place, it can be accomplished as speedily as the available administrative structures afford. Key issues are the membership of the boards, how to exert control over firms, and how to avoid replicating the *nomenklatura* under a different guise. These firms can also be privatized by distributing or selling shares.

In looking at the managerial mechanics of privatization, there are eight: (1) the speed of privatization, the types of firms to be privatized, and the extent of restructuring to be undertaken prior to privatization; (2) whether to agitate chiefly through share sales or free distribution, and which method should be preferred in each case; (3) to whom privatization should primarily be addressed, including the role of foreigners and former owners; the desirability of spreading ownership; and the possibility of concentrating ownership by allowing those with financial clout to acquire real assets, no questions asked; (4) whether the implicit property rights of managers, the *nomenklatura* more generally, and workers (see Chapter 7) should be recognized and validated in full or only partially; (5) the role of financial institutions (such as banks, insurance and pension funds, mutual and investment funds, as well as holding companies) in intermediating between corporations and households; (6) the degree to which it is desirable for government to hold back shares for later sale; (7) whether a role for a stable core of investors should be entertained; and (8) whether it is desirable to pursue a rather eclectic approach to privatization as an alternative to a course motivated largely by ideological or technical considerations. Most of these issues have been looked at, when at all, in the context of ownership reform for industrial SOEs, and to some extent for financial institutions. This is a limited perspective. Parallel questions arise for agriculture, housing, some intellectual property, and land, and in some cases even for small privatization. These should be considered separately for each has a different bearing on improving resource allocation as one channel for alleviating societal upheaval.

4.5 – Attitudinal problems

One of the most important legacies of over forty years of state socialism derives from the behavior and expectations of economic agents. Given the paternalistic welfare state under state socialism, especially in the European countries, agents tended to be risk-averse. Although many individuals may appreciate the ideals of a market economy, they also may find it difficult in the short run to come to grips with bankruptcy and the attendant fluctuations in individual and collective fortunes. Related to this is whether individuals are interested in holding part of their wealth in the form of shares and will, in fact, rationally decide to exercise their ownership rights by monitoring management. That was never a realistic prospect. Neither was it realistic to expect individuals to remain dispersed shareholders. Participation and transaction costs may be very high. But apathy toward monitoring management and "appointed" directors probably plays a much more substantial role. So does "satisficing" of share owners by management in place. If any widespread distribution through sales based on undervalued assets or through giveaways induces new owners to seek quick divestment, adverse signals to the already weak stock market and inflationary pressures are likely to be exacerbated. This may have a deleterious impact on saving behavior as a critical variable in restarting these economies. But if such sales are prohibited, for example, by requiring new owners to hold shares for years, this too imparts adverse information.

Second, all transition economies have staked part of their programs on a sizable inflow of foreign investment. It can provide many tangible and intangible benefits (see Chapter 10). Whether these outweigh the perceived loss in sale revenue and people's reluctance to sell off society's assets to foreigners can be overcome, remains to be seen. Reaching a fair price is important in removing some obstacles. But there must be a limit to the dilution of economic sovereignty, particularly in societies whose scope for political autonomy and economic sovereignty was narrowly circumscribed for so long. The question is probably less whether to sell assets to foreigners than in what sectors, to what degree, and how foreign ownership will be regulated within the context of the broader aims of the transformation. Proxy sales of national assets to foreigners is something to be guarded against.

Third, it is especially important to recognize that thriving competition must apply also to the acquisition and disposal of private assets. Without this, it is impossible to institute proper monitoring and supervision. For that, it is necessary to have in place vestiges of capital markets, including proper safeguards and regulatory mechanisms against abuses of stock-exchange provisions and the like. As noted, such a market can function only if the regulatory mechanisms are in place and there is sufficient transparency in the market. This requires that firms adhere to certain supervisory and accounting rules that foster competition on the basis of actual and expected returns to capital. Once again, this can emerge only over time as the number of participants rises, coaxed through the rudiments of the capital market (see Chapter 7).

One of the key rules to be enacted concerns exit and entry of firms in response to the venturesomeness, thrift, and acquisitiveness of some layers of society in pursuit of their own interest. This is something quite new in these countries. Even if the state and its appointed officials were to withdraw quickly from microeconomic decision making, who would take their place? Even if replacements are available, can would-be managers and entrepreneurs successfully manage, or even protect, assets in the short to medium run? And perhaps most important, existing management embodies considerable human capital that should not be written off without further ado. That may fall short of the ideal of modern management. But linguistic and engineering skills, goodwill in markets abroad, acquaintance with the legacies of state socialism and its aftermath, and so on form all part and parcel of human capital. That is to say, for quite some time the bulk of inherited management will necessarily have to remain in place. Guiding those individuals into behaving more like managers of firms in a market environment is a major task that can be accomplished only gradually. Surely, once new transparent incentives and behavioral guidelines for management are in place, there is no reason to believe that all managers will necessarily fail to adapt to market-based criteria. But some will, and must thus be replaced. Yet, few are likely to voluntarily yield their entrenched power.

Fourth, although the means of production under planning were society's, in some countries legal ownership became blurred when SOE assets were simply turned over to management, enterprise, or workers' councils (see Chapter 2). These amassed various kinds of property rights (see Chapter 7), most of which cannot be expropriated or ignored. They certainly should not become the object of political bickering. A "neutral" quasi-state agency entrusted with fundamental aspects of privatization should preferably adjudicate these conflicting claims.

Finally, privatization is accompanied by serious conflicts of interest. True, the transition could not have been set off without replacing the top political leaders and the most nefarious links between the Party and the *nomenklatura*; likewise for the worst offenders of the various police organizations and economic sectors. But it would simply have been impossible, for sheer lack of even elementary talent, to replace the whole spectrum of society compromised in one form or another because of its allegiance to state socialism. In-between these two extremes, there is a wide layer of society whose overt collaboration with or tacit approval of the ousted regime should justify expulsion. Nevertheless, as the course of events has amply demonstrated, many of the élite under state socialism have now enthusiastically embraced the transition and its opportunities, particularly in the privatization campaign, with managers or bureaucrats privatizing themselves, politicians involved with privatization also being on company boards, and even banks being entrusted with the implementation and supervision of some aspects of the privatization of client firms. Arguably the worst instance of abuse potentially occurs when heads of privatization agencies are directly guiding the emerging stock exchange and/or steering management of commercial banks whose portfolio consists of tied debts owed by SOEs soon to be privatized, obviously after taking care of the bank debt. The potential for gross abuse is alarming. It is bound in time to set off political recriminations and social tensions, and may even destabilize the polity.

Section 5: On the techniques of privatization

Once the goals and order of privatization are set, preferably with sociopolitical support, managers must choose the "best" ways of proceeding with transferring operational control over the use of state assets to those who "promise" to be capable of maximizing net assets values and whose capabilities to do so can be challenged through incipient capital markets. One should harbor no illusion about the ability of the transition's leadership to embrace simple, professional, and technically competent solutions. Privatization is political economy *par excellence*. Even under the best of circumstances there is bound to be pragmatism, uncertainty, and arbitrariness – and indeed confusion and hesitancy – in the privatization campaign. Though the art of policy making is rudimentary in transition economies, progress must be made rapidly; hence polishing that art on the go is inevitable. Core guidelines should be minimizing the uncertainty and arbitrariness with a view to bolstering pragmatically the efficient utilization of capital assets, thereby strengthening the support for the transformation. Recall, however, that the environment for privatization during the transition may be very unstable, rendering support for the privatization mandate shaky. Policy makers must heed this reality or suffer sociopolitical backlash, as experience has so richly illustrated.

5.1 – Generic approaches

I consider four approaches with a separate comment on land and financial institutions. Spontaneous (or *nomenklatura*) privatization offers the first path toward privatization pursued almost by default. This means that those entrusted with the use of state assets somehow take possession of them. It takes on various forms that are best kept apart, given the negative aura attached to it. Very often it is indiscriminately treated as more or less sophisticated theft from the state, leading to highly contentious debates until the respective postcommunist governments put an end to the crassest abuses. Not all are illegal. All enable rapid progress with divestment and the creation of "clear" owners. It got under way because SOE managers or ministerial officials began to capture full property rights to assets placed under their control (see Chapter 2). The process is still evolving in one way or another in economies where the basic markers of the transformation are still hotly contested, notably in several CIS and Yugoslav States.

In countries where workers had considerable say in the management of "their" enterprise, some have advocated that they be finally entrusted with full rights to "their" firm. This has been contested because prior to the "1989 events" (notably in Hungary, Poland, and Yugoslavia) many abuses occurred in which manage-ment in place or enterprise and workers' councils turned SOEs into corporations that could seek recapitalization from new partners. Oftentimes, management, perhaps in collusion with workers, proposed to privatize the SOE either on its own or in collaboration with an outside investor, usually from abroad. In the latter case, management succeeded in trading off the loss in revenue in return for job security or other compensation as well as immunity from prosecution. Many cases are known in which management set up private firms that contracted out assets or business from the SOE – literally stripping the latter's assets or at least their service stream. This aroused political opposition to pursuing self-management to its logical end.

Turning the labor-managed firm into true workers' management has been contested on theoretical and practical grounds. Theoretically, it is presumed to be an inefficient organizational form as it tends to encourage maximization of income per worker rather than long-run profitability or asset value. On practical grounds, experiments with self-management especially in the former Yugoslavia turned out to be far from encouraging. However, many observers have argued that this resulted because self-management has not been pursued to its full internal logic (Comisso 1991; Estrin 1991a, b; Horvat 1991; Sacks 1983). This requires tradability of workers' right in some kind of competitive capital market (Nuti 1987, 1988, 1989). Note that this would eventually hollow out self-management as nonworkers acquire shares.

Second, the basic philosophy propping up free distribution asserts that state assets in place were obtained either through nationalization or public savings over which the population had little control, though it had ultimate title to the assets. With privatization, that property should finally be turned over to society

233

by distributing it free of charge. Several forms have been entertained, including giving away assets to decentralized government agencies, investment funds, mutual funds, holding companies, property funds, the financial sector (with a view to capitalizing or recapitalizing banks, pension funds, insurance companies, and similar institutions), and mass distribution of shares or vouchers to large SOEs. I cannot go into the details (Brabant 1992a). But a few remarks are in order.

Giving full property rights to workers differs from the labor-managed firm in that management can be separate from ownership but induced to improve the allocation process and render the firm profitable. Such distribution rests on a dubious assumption and is inequitable. For one thing, the value of capital per worker in SOEs varies a great deal for reasons that have nothing to do with the relative merits of the present labor force. It is also inequitable because all those not engaged in SOEs obtain nothing. Furthermore, it fails to generate income for the government, and it favors reinvestment in existing activities with the present workforce. But it might be useful to entertain some employee share-ownership program (ESOP), giving workers a material stake in their firm, especially if it can be coupled with promises to limit demands for monetary compensation, to foster productivity, to change work rules, and other measures that bolster profitability. Note that this option is available without outright privatization. All it requires is that the SOE be corporatized with performance incentives, including access to shares in the firm possibly below fair market value.

Property can also be distributed to society at large either on an individual basis or by households. The most important form has been distribution of shares or vouchers, perhaps at a nominal fee, which can subsequently be utilized to "purchase" shares in SOEs at a "price" in terms of voucher units bid in open or auction markets. Distribution can be to the entire population or to adult resident nationals. This is usually justified by the facile claim that, on equity grounds, it would be unseemly for the new governments to sell state assets "once again" to the population at large. Free distribution may seem to be the fairest and quickest way to privatize large SOEs: It establishes clear private owners, circumvents the problems emanating from limited savings, respects some egalitarian aspirations, and, if in the form of shares, it creates a critical mass for stock markets to be jump-started. But the merits of an equitable distribution on these grounds are debatable.

There are essentially four different classes that cover the variants discussed to date. Most logical is the free distribution of shares to society's wealth to the entire population, all adults, or some such well-defined category (usually restricted to resident citizens). The second approach taken in Poland and Romania is through the creation of financial intermediaries owned at least partly in time by the population at large. Third, the transition economy creates groups of firms whose private management is called upon to restructure or sell the firms to the benefit of their owners, who in most cases are the population at large or all adults; experiments have not been encouraging, however. Finally, the vast bulk of SOEs can be entrusted to local-level administrative organs (such as munici-palities), welfare organizations (such as hospitals), educational foundations (to foster training and R&D), and basic financial organizations (such as insurance companies, pension funds, and social-security institutions). Experiments have shown the financial and governance limits of such schemes.

The third generic privatization method is by way of divesting user rights through leasing, franchising, contracting out, and management contracts, all of which raise the role of nonstate decision makers in the allocation of the usufruct of state-owned assets and move beyond corporatization and commercialization. That is to say, private investors and managers take over the day-to-day affairs of the assets for which some contract is signed, usually involving the maximization of residual benefits after defraying operating and amortization costs, as well as paying the lease or contract fee. In some cases, these goods and services are delivered at a negotiated price, as in various forms of subcontracting. Or they are supplied at a fee as with leasing. Or they reward management according to performance, as in management contracts. Finally, franchising implies authori-zation to deliver goods and services in a reserved area. In none of these variants is there any transfer of ultimate ownership of the assets concerned. This is very important for state assets that cannot be sold. Such contracts in many other activities are constrained, however, by potentially insurmountable problems of defining the modalities of each operation, of protecting asset values, and of monitoring the implementation of the contract or lease (Brabant 1992a, pp. 218–20).

The final class is outright sale of assets. Credibly transferring all property rights to new owners at a positive price can take on many forms (Bouin and Michalet 1991, pp. 126–40). First, the divestiture of shares through capital-market opera-tions, while in theory available, cannot play a major role until a functioning capital market is in place. Floating shares abroad, as tried by Hungary, is difficult and expensive, and in the end disappointing given lack of western investor interest at a time of economic recession with tight monetary policy. A variant is the public offering of shares by inviting closed bids. Shares are sold not at a fluctuating price, as in a stock market, where underwriters are the only ones to get shares at a fixed price, but at one set by the seller with some rationing in case of oversubscription. This route has been explored by both Hungary and particularly Poland (and experimentally in some CIS States). The results have been mixed in part because of lack of experience, exceedingly thin share markets, and the protracted economic depression. If the stock-market option is feasible or if savers can be persuaded that there will soon be a formal secondary market for shares, a public offerings may be the preferred way of divesting large SOEs. It underlines the state's stance on publicly divesting to a potentially wide circle of shareholders at a price set on a "competitive" basis in markets that are equally clear (or opaque) for most participants.

Third, auctions offer the next best opportunity for selling assets, especially those that have to be transferred as a unit. Auction theory offers several variants, each with advantages and disadvantages regardless of whether a reservation price is set. Whichever one is chosen, a price needs to be set; hence again the problem of valuation crops up. Also, the auction needs to be carefully prepared and organized over some period of time, if only to determine potential participation and the conditions of financing and probity. Minimal information needs to be funneled to potential participants.

Fourth, private transfers are a discretionary form of divestment that may be initiated by any party. It may involve a negotiated transfer of a block of shares or the asset as a whole, just like in an auction, but the price is negotiated by other means than public bidding. Fifth, management and worker buyouts deserve to be entertained, if only because of the peculiar situation with property rights and the inability of most transition economies to replace entrenched management and overcome workers' rights. This may be the way to recognize property rights claimed by or vested in those employed in the firm (see Chapter 7), perhaps also via some ESOP. Sixth, unsubscribed capital expansion is like a partial transfer of assets because it dilutes the state's holdings. It might be useful given that many would-be purchasers lack capital to pay 100 percent. By acquiring stock rights, the private financier may contribute to raising the value of capital and thus finance his own involvement.

Finally, debt-equity swaps have been condoned as a way of cleaning up the books of SOEs, including banks, in several countries. There is nothing seriously wrong with this, provided the books are indeed cleaned up in the end. That has not always been the case. Instead, banks, which are largely state owned, become the "owners" of the former autonomous SOE, resulting in potentially "phony" divestment. Hungary has also encouraged cross-firm acquisitions by canceling interenterprise debt, usually in combination with an infusion of funds. True, cross ownership may ensure control. It is nonetheless mostly a more sophisticated variant of spontaneous privatization.

The privatization of financial institutions has widely been held to pose special problems. The preferred method for those aiming at divestment of existing banks is to sell off blocks of shares to foreign investors as an alternative to having foreign investors setting up altogether new institutions. But many transition economies initially prohibit, tacitly or overtly, the sale of financial institutions, probably because there are so few and all suffer from legacies discussed earlier. Some countries have more recently made progress with bank divestment. Elsewhere, however, financial institutions by assets and transactions remain over-whelmingly in state hands.

Also the question of land has aroused passions beyond those common in large-scale privatization attempts. Excepting Poland and Yugoslavia, where land was largely privately held, what to do with land in state and cooperative ownership has arguably been the most troublesome question in the privatization process. It remains a bone of contention in several large CIS States in particular. Elsewhere land has been subject to conflicting property claims. Particularly problematic has been what to do with agricultural collectives, whose property rights are in some cases highly uncertain because the socialist state had arrogated to itself only the usufruct of land, leaving property formally to the individual farmer. Some collectives also acquired their own land either from endowments of the state or through outright purchases. Similar questions arise with state farms, which have firm property rights. But the state has not been a good monitor for years. Even if land can be privatized, many people in the transition economies are not keen on returning to the land and working it. Similar problems have been observed with urban land. Absence of a clear-cut stance on property rights has been inhibiting the establishment of new firms or hindered notably the injection of new capital into those undertakings for lack of certainty about title and the firm's future.

5.2 – Advantages and drawbacks

The advantages and drawbacks of the various approaches depend on the, often implicit, privatization function for policy makers. Thus, if privatization must yield revenue to the government, modalities that leave the government without a financial return should be minimized. But if divestment helps to place the operations of these SOEs on a more efficient last, their future fiscal payments may well compensate the government for the loss of revenue in the short run. Similar benefits may be derived from other privatization forms that bolster economic efficiency by placing assets in the hands of those who either manage those assets themselves or who can and will monitor management, in which case concentration of ownership must be ensured. Divestment in either case would probably have to be undertaken through competitive bidding without which the transition's gains may seem hollow to vast layers of the population, even though such firms may soon provide higher labor reward and gratification to the population at large. On the other hand, if privatization's main objective is to create private agents, to buttress libertarian views about private property, to prop up democracy, or quickly to come to grips with the *nomenklatura*, privatization should proceed expeditiously and assets spread widely. That is to say, a single-mode privatization strategy is rarely appropriate. It is therefore useful to be aware of core advantages and disadvantages of the various options at hand.

The experience with spontaneous privatization has not been very satisfactory for financial, economic, political, social, and organizational reasons. Financially, it allows former management and possibly workers to become owners without paying a fair price, thus depriving the government of needed revenue. Economically, turning assets over to those who ran these facilities poorly under state socialism does not guarantee improved resource allocation. However, being entrusted with assets imparts different incentives to, and will most likely change the behavior of, management. Whether this will make a difference and entrenched management will do better than other asset holders are outstanding issues. Wealth effects may exacerbate already existing inflationary pressures (Nuti 1991). Politically, there is bound to be reprehension about the *nomenklatura* capturing property in a completely inequitable manner. Worker ownership might be fine for those employed in profitable or potentially profitable ventures, but not for those in persistent loss-making operations or not employed in SOEs. Finally, organizational problems arise. Under self-management those with the experience and knowhow of supervising the firm may be excluded from new management. Under management privatization, workers may be laid off as soon as politically convenient. Hence some symbiosis of interest must be strived for, and this may simply perpetuate old-style management.

Second, free distribution has frequently been touted as a way of socialist egalitarianism in reverse. But it may be quite inequitable. There are potential losers as well as beneficiaries. For example, the distribution of assets by states that are heavily indebted may diminish the prospects of repayment to creditors. Any attempt to allocate ownership in SOEs other than by completely distributing shares equally to all (adult) residents is bound to entail valuation problems. Because quick comprehensive fiscal reform is not feasible, free distribution also erodes the country's fiscal base. By depriving the government of future revenues from assets, free divestment should ideally be accompanied by the retirement of state obligations, either debt or other financial obligations. Furthermore, an equitable distribution of shares implies that a household holds only a minuscule interest in any one, leaving formidable principal–agent problems. The choice between the sale and free distribution of SOEs has other fiscal implications too. Thus, if a large part of socialist property can be sold only over decades and would be idle in the interim, the cost of giving this part away gratis now is small. Moreover, free distribution can partly substitute for other kinds of social policies. Furthermore, the efficiency gains of divestment will in due course yield more tax revenues, other things being equal. The most serious shortcoming of this approach is that it does not exert beneficial effects on management – normally the principal economic aim of divestment. This is even the case with the creation of funds, for who monitors the monitors (Bardhan 1991)?

Third, a lease yields revenue without divesting assets, provided asset stripping can be prevented, and it frees the state from responsibility for the enterprise's operating and capital-maintenance costs. Proper management may even raise the intrinsic value of the leased assets. But there are limits. Leases cannot possibly be of much help in privatizing complex firms. At the very least, competition at the tendering stage is limited. Setting fair leasing fees is not easy. But it may work in the case of comparatively small production and service firms. It is particularly apt to improve efficiency in many instances of "petty" privatization and the effective liquidation of the SOEs with buildings and rolling stock, for example, being let to private agents. Poland successfully leased trucks and related rolling stock from SOEs very early during the transition, thus erecting a substantially "privatized" road-transportation sector already in 1990.

But leasing is not without drawbacks. There are basically three. First, although in theory the expiry of the lease offers the state an opportunity to negotiate renewal from a strengthened position, the outgoing lessee has insider information and experience, thus a decisive advantage in submitting the next bid, even if disclosure rules are enforced. Second, adequate monitoring by the state or its agents is a must for otherwise the lessee has no incentive to divulge all the information required to make a fair evaluation by the state and potential competitors of the assets when they are up for lease renewal or perhaps divestment. This may sharply reduce the flexibility of the lease, particularly as an instrument of maintaining state property over time. Finally, the lessee has in the end little incentive to improve the capital stock and may be tempted to erode it, unless adequate compensation for capital gains and maintenance is embedded in the lease.

Management contracts require even more intensive monitoring and surveillance because of the financial-risk exposure involved. Management cannot be held responsible for the results achieved, except perhaps by forfeiting bonuses stipulated in the contract and the chance of contract renewal. As such, monitoring and supervision need to be more intense than in the case of a lease. For one thing, managers may tend to overinvest, including through reckless bank borrowing. But disincentive criteria may blunt this inclination. A second problem is how to avoid conflicts between management and the government as owner by setting explicit objectives and circumscribing the powers granted to the management team. The complexity of drawing up such contracts on a case basis tends to be the more time consuming the more complex is the SOE to be rehabilitated. Neither the lease nor the management contract (nor the franchise and contracting-out variants for that matter) can offer a panacea for any of the major obstacles to privatization touched upon earlier. What they do offer in some cases is a useful breathing space to move ahead pragmatically with taking the state out of direct management, pending the organization of divestment programs or to ensure proper use of many nonphysical assets.

Fourth, the variants of outright sales have their distinct advantages and drawbacks. Perhaps the greatest advantage of the share sale through subscription or in markets is widening ownership, which strengthens democracy and forestalls any criticism of the state encouraging the very rich, foreigners, or insiders to acquire real wealth at anything but a competitively determined price, given the circumstances. This may obviate future recrimination particularly if the assets can be quickly transferred into new operations and capital expansion. The cost of operating through this mechanism is appallingly high. Second, popular capitalism may instill a shareholder culture in the population at large and abate the strong risk aversion that is still pervasive in most transition economies. It may thus be an integral component of the attitudinal mutation required to reach a platform for launching self-sustaining modernization. But there is no guarantee that this will occur. Third, it provides a major fillip to capital markets by those having built up a financial interest from their own resources. Financial assets may be distributed over a more widely diversified portfolio, which itself feeds the demand for new securities. In time, this could ease public access to financing in open markets as alternatives to bank financing. But that benefit may accrue only once these nonbank financial markets become well rooted, which takes time. In the interim the commercial-banking sector continues to play the primary role (see Chapter 7). Finally, the democratic process gets strengthened politically but also economically. Widespread share ownership may be a powerful deterrent against any attempt to renationalize wealth.

Many of these advantages apply also to public bidding for undivided asset values, although it does not, of course, feed the shareholding culture and stock market. But auctions may foster participation in capital markets once the firms are taken public. Of course, how to set prices, including the reservation price, and how best to utilize proceeds remain poignant questions. Apart from the fact that auction markets have to be organized, the sale of state assets is hindered by low legal savings and it is uncertain whether society is prepared to put even these limited funds into company shares, thus possibly crowding out investment for new firms unless the state rechannels proceeds for specific commercial lending. But debt-financed auctions might be explored in some cases, the state becoming a rentier with the private sector ending up as debtor and capitalist.

The preparation of private sales may seem less complicated as it is both flexible and speedy. But it requires careful valuation and a credible reservation price, neither of which is easy. Private sales have their risks, of which three are worth pointing out. They tend to encompass the healthiest firms, saddling the state with the "basket cases" and possibly intolerable fiscal implications. Second, because of valuation problems and the lack of transparency, speed and pragmatism may be the handmaiden of nasty sellout insinuations, if not worse, levied later in the political discourse. Finally, private sales are usually arranged for substantial transactions and are tantamount to concentrating wealth in a few hands from the outset. This may leave a bitter aftertaste with the population at large.

An unsubscribed capital expansion might be useful given that many would-be purchasers lack capital to pay 100 percent. By acquiring stock rights, the private financier may contribute to raising the value of capital and thus finance his/ her own involvement. An unsubscribed raise in capital may meet the problems arising from the reduced equity resources of the SOE and the government's inability to increase authorized capital in advance. Of course, although it dilutes equity, it does not funnel revenue to the budget. But it does help recapitalize and finance investment of firms. Gradual dilution of state holdings has the parallel result of eroding the state's importance as financial backer of business. This withdrawal from the management and financing of the firm's operations is generally speeded up subsequently with a partial transfer to the private purchaser.

Worker and management buyouts are worth considering, particularly if coupled with firm commitments to limit demands for monetary compensation, to foster productivity, to change costly work rules, to abolish the job-security system, and to embrace measures that give workers a material stake in their firm. All it requires is that the latter become a joint-stock company whose performance incentives include obtaining a share in the firm's capitalized value, such as through some ESOP. Though there are limits to debt-equity swaps particularly among units belonging to the state subject to political interference, the advantages of this mode in terms of attaining control should not be ignored. Much depends on the government's determination to pursue genuine privatization in the sense defined. Finally, divestment through free distribution seems an egalitarian approach, but only in a narrow perspective. First and foremost is the issue of equity. There is no reason to claim that the present resident population solely contributed to the formation of these assets, let alone on an equal basis. Nor were these assets to be kept in trust on an egalitarian basis for society existing at any one moment of time. Should all but the adult resident nationals be excluded, except perhaps for purely pragmatic reasons? Clearly, a case could be made to distribute some shares to those who were earlier dispossessed, including those who emigrated after the first wave of property confiscation or forced savings. Perhaps more important than intergenerational equity is that state-owned assets have as counterpart state liabilities, which *in se* "belong" to the population at large as well.

Although free distribution of shares in SOEs is intuitively appealing, there are serious drawbacks of such divestment, apart from wealth effects. Some have already been touched upon, including *de facto* inequality, erosion of the government's taxing ability with fiscal reform being feasible only in the longer term (Borensztein and Kumar 1991), problems of retiring state obligations – including what to do with "merit claims" (Beckerman 1986, p. 10) such as pension rights, medical and disability benefits, rights to education, and claims on protecting minimal levels of living – little pressure on management to improve itself, no new financing, and so on. Monitoring mechanisms that rely on intermediaries are promising but only in the longer run, once capital markets and bankruptcy rules really begin to bite. Each of them exhibits its own drawbacks (Brabant 1992a, pp. 224–6).

Section 6: Experience with privatization since 1989

Although privatization has been at the center of the discussions around transformation, the progress made to date remains uneven. Except for a few spectacular sales, mostly to foreigners, and putting in place more or less rounded privatization laws, most action has been in the form of petty privatization and mass distribution of shares in one form or another; Hungary has favored sales, however. Sizable chunks of SOEs remain in the public domain in all transition economies. But far more so in several of the CIS and ex-Yugoslav States than elsewhere. Even less headway has been made in the Asian transition countries, except Mongolia with its genuine big-bang privatization.

Because it is impossible to seize up the situation in individual countries or even to draw a rounded picture of the various privatization campaigns, I point out some general features of the experience to date. First, whatever the ambitions for privatization held by managers of the transition early on have failed to be implemented. Privatization could not be arranged quickly or in a clean fashion with sizable revenues for the budget. No case is known in which privatization has been accomplished in anything like the record tempo held out at the outset. Second, "petty" privatization has provided the easiest path to getting a head start with divestment. Most of these assets have been sold through more or less transparent auctions; initially, many transactions passed through elementary leases and management contracts with the option to buy later. In a highly inflationary environment, these deals were exceptionally advantageous to the buyer.

Third, although at the outset of the transformation countries stressed different core ambitions of privatization (such as revenue generation in Hungary, public sales in Poland, endowing owners in Czechoslovakia and later the Czech Republic, and breaking the back of the entrenched *nomenklatura* in Russia), a much more variegated menu of privatization options has had to be adopted in practice. This is not always stressed. Thus there is a widespread notion even among those who ought to know better that the bulk of state assets of the Czech Republic were privatized via the two voucher rounds. Though these campaigns did indeed encompass a good proportion of state-owned assets, less than two fifths of the estimated value of physical assets in producing firms and some financial institutions were divested in this manner. At the same time, although sizable revenues have been obtained in a number of transition economies, it has proved rather haphazard to budget revenues from sales for current outlays. In fact, it might be best to think about privatization without from the start setting concrete objectives in terms of net revenues accruing to the budget.

Fourth, whereas in the beginning sentiment against management and worker buyouts ran deep in most countries, that has proved to be the most "successful" component of the privatization campaign other than asset transfers arranged via FDI. The latter have benefited from some "insider" advantages (in terms of management skills, market culture, technological knowhow, access to capital, and entry to export markets) that are not immediately available to domestic upstarts. Fifth, those that have tried to bring in foreign managers to rectify perceived domestic shortcomings have been sorely disappointed. Sixth, FDI has not been a leading variable of the transformation even with large privatization and is still at this stage entering these countries on a highly selective basis and in variable volumes that continue to trail well behind original expectations (see Chapter 10).

Seventh, no country has accomplished privatization without arousing political and other controversies. Many cases of less than fair dealing by the principals involved have become known, but not necessarily on account of malevolence by the state's agents. Nonetheless, many deals have aroused knotty sociopolitical problems. Eighth, the daunting nature and overwhelming range of obstacles inhibiting the multiple tasks of fostering a pluralistic market economy have affected privatization campaigns. Even a pragmatic, nonideologically motivated medley of privatization methods requires some order. In the meantime, very little has been done to protect the integrity of assets; but not necessarily out of malevolence or criminal activity. Shortsightedness, lack of knowledge, and almost pathological aversion to the state have been key (see Section 8).

Ninth, neither privatization nor divestment can be pursued solely for economic reasons. The political-economy process is bound to be messy, protracted, and costly even when a broad consensus can be forged. Without it, transformation in general and privatization in particular empower the coalescing political parties through "political rents." One can only hope to minimize the degree of political interference and avoid building up a new *nomenklatura*. This suggests that also sufficiently robust machinery must be in place to tackle unexpected setbacks or emerging problems while progressing with privatization. A strong government with a technically competent, well-motivated privatization agency (see Chapter 7) could facilitate rapid progress with corporatization and commercialization.

Tenth, neither sale nor free distribution obviates the need to come to terms with key obstacles to privatization. Purchasers may engage in strategic behavior on economically warranted grounds, given the option value of waiting under high uncertainty (Ickes 1996). This suggests that government may seek to stimulate private initiative on a selective basis by tackling not only wages but also the cost and risk of capital formation. With free distribution, thorough preparation is required to identify and reach the beneficiaries, to select the mode of distribution, and to elicit an active role from new owners in corporate governance. Even valuation cannot be sidestepped altogether, if only to come to grips with the need for restructuring, which influences expectations.

Finally, several transition economies still lack a consensus on privatization, let alone on divestment. These include in particular Belarus, Bosnia and Herzegovina, China, Croatia, Tajikistan, Ukraine, Uzbekistan, Vietnam, and rump Yugoslavia (especially Serbia).

Section 7: Outcomes of privatization

The verdict on whether the privatization pursued up to now has significantly improved resource allocation or not is still undecided, owing to the protracted recession (at times a veritable depression) and, at best, on the whole slow to moderate recovery therefrom. It is useful to look separately at what has happened to four classes of ownership. From all the evidence available, and much is admittedly still impressionistic or based on highly partial survey materials, in the reasonably successful transition economies especially in central Europe, the *de novo* private sector has been the most dynamic, largely uncontrollable force of economic renovation. It has boomed in part because of the advantages temporarily enjoyed precisely owing to the state's inability to integrate those private-sector activities into the "formal economy," notably making them fully subject to all the fiscal and social-security levies applicable to firms in the formal economy. Private-sector activities that have linked up with foreign producers and especially the new startups seem to have fared best. Least successful on average appear to have been the private-sector activities based on petty divestment of production assets (as distinct from all kinds of services). This may be due to the comparatively hostile overall climate for their expansion and growth, given the lack of effective intermediation both in acquiring new capital, leaving financing chiefly from retained earnings or funds raised in a narrow circle of family and friends, and in executing reciprocal claims (see Chapter 5); but also because of limits to managerial innovation and catching up with technology and effective marketing.

The real crux of this buoyant expansion, especially its sustainability, depends on two factors. One involves the gaps left by communist planning, particularly in service activities, and how quickly private initiative can mobilize resources to catch up and fill those lacunae. The other depends on the degree to which the private sector can mobilize resources to move into production sectors through various kinds of alliances, if warranted. The evidence is incomplete. In central Europe, the gaps left by state socialism have been filled rapidly but entry of those firms into manufacturing activities, oftentimes with new or newly designed products, has been much more gradual. Entry into manufacturing has been facilitated when the entrepreneur had contacts with SOEs, in some countries (Hungary and Poland in particular) already prior to the transition (Mickiewicz 1996a, b). With recovery of demand and the mobilization of chiefly domestic sources of finance, the future of these new, largely small firms looks quite bright until the next hurdle of corporate governance arising from the growing scale and complexity of economic activities will have to be faced. Overcoming these obstacles depends crucially on deepening and widening capital markets (see Chapter 7) but also on improving managerial skills.

On the other hand, greenfield operations in which foreigners have locked themselves appear to have been doing fairly well, no doubt in part because of the temporary advantages enjoyed by foreign capital. Access to outside finance, to managerial skills, to markets, to up-to-date technology, and to other resources, as well as in some cases being included in global marketing strategies of homebase firms, have all been critical. Few of these resources are available to "domestic" firms, at least for now. Continued expansion is largely a function of the buoyancy of domestic demand, the degree to which these countries can expand their economic performance most notably through intra-industry trade, and the successful merger of these economies into EU markets (Brabant 1995a, 1996).

There is scattered evidence that the state sector itself has vastly improved its performance even with the threat of privatization and the sacking of management in place, at least after a wait-and-see period to test the credibility of those threats and in spite of the rather adverse economic situation. Now that those political ambitions and threats have lost a good deal of their sting as a result of the transformation's sociopolitical complications, but also the inability to implement rapid divestment and ensure more constructive governance structures, it is clear that reasonably hard budget constraints can go a long way toward changing behavior in SOEs. This suggests that even within a "sea of state-ownership" there has been ample scope for dynamic new private-sector activity in countries that have not inhibited the sector. This is true even for the most "privatized" economies like the Czech Republic and Russia. This should not be read as an argument against divestment. Rather, it buttresses two policy points. One is the importance of fostering new private firms. At the same time, divestment of the large SOEs can be structured in a more orderly way provided governance capabilities are put in place or can be acquired expeditiously. On that score much remains to be done (see Chapter 7). But the lingering problems in the state sector are very considerable, in many cases owing to outmoded technology, a product assortment that lacks dynamic demand, crippling fiscal and social-security obligations that cannot be dodged, poor financing prospects, inability to invest in competing effectively in new markets, in some cases obligations toward workers in place, and other obstacles.

As pointed out, the divestment campaign, largely its informal and at times illegal components, has measurably reallocated both *de facto* and *de jure* income and wealth in most transition economies, thus influencing "winners" and "losers." First, the simple transfer of assets from the state to new owners changes the latter's income and wealth. Though the composition of the wealth portfolio is initially altered, in the aggregate nothing much transpires in the case of divestment through sale at "market-clearing prices": New owners swap financial assets for real assets of equivalent value as per their calculations, and their aggregate wealth portfolio stays unchanged. Likewise for the nominal seller: The state acquires financial assets in exchange for real ones, leaving its portfolio's size, but not its composition, unchanged. Note that although the transfer of assets from the state to private individuals may seem straightforward, it may deny property rights that some classes of individuals in society claimed for themselves or impose liabilities upon others that were previously society's. (see Chapter 7). Their assets and liabilities as per their evaluation are bound to undergo possibly considerable mutation both in composition and overall value.

When divestment in whatever form takes place without a proper price being invoiced, the balance of assets and liabilities changes and may become disequili-brated, notably for the state and claimants on present or future state resources, but possibly also for new owners. This is almost always the case, given limping markets. There may therefore be secondary effects on income and wealth directly attributable to divestment. New owners may simply come to realize that their new portfolio mandates reducing saving out of current incomes, possibly even dissaving in the sense that the wealth gain from unequal divestment partly funds current expenditure. This in turn affects sectors benefiting from the extra demand for current purchases. And the merry-go-round continues! Former claimants to imprecisely defined property rights lose and their portfolio becomes unbalanced. This may warrant supplementary savings to restore balance. Note that these claimants are unlikely to abide supinely by the situation. They tend to wage opposition to divestment in whatever form they can muster, including by hollowing out the transformation agenda. Hence the importance of appeasing those implicit claimants in one form or another, certainly legally and hopefully within the context of the prevailing sociopolitical consensus (see Section 4).

The literature has paid little attention to the disequilibrium into which the state itself may fall after divestment with its secondary effects and its implications for the reconstitution of household wealth portfolios. If state assets are divested below fair market value, however defined, state liabilities may exceed the value of the remaining assets. Without reducing its liabilities the transformation places a considerable burden on future fiscal revenues, hence indentures future cohorts for the sake of meeting the present one's expectations in an inequitable manner. Abrogating rights acquired under state socialism and dissuading citizens from maintaining earlier expectations on being provided for (see Chapter 8) that households continue to take for granted offers one channel for reequilibrating the state's portfolio. But that path is likely to be strewn with treacherous pitfalls.

It would seem prudent for private agents to include in their wealth portfolios the expected "certainties" to which the state has committed itself. An unbalanced state wealth portfolio should be offset by an unbalanced household portfolio of opposite sign. It is conceivable that some agents will be worse off after privatization below fair market value and certainly at fair market value, if revenues are not fully utilized to cover liabilities that are now no longer covered by the state's view of its assets. The cost to hedge privately against the disappearing certainties erstwhile assured by the state may exceed the cost previously incumbent on the state; it may be less as well in which case divestment is likely to lead to gains for households and positive wealth effects, ignoring for the moment the rentiers of state socialism.

Section 8: The remaining problems with privatization

As remarked earlier, privatization has consisted mostly of sales, including notably in the form of management and employee buyouts, or giveaways. Other forms, notably corporatization and commercialization, have not been explored to the extent feasible. Sales have focused overwhelmingly on the "better" assets, leaving firms in the hard core of state-socialist industry, particularly iron and steel and heavy engineering, in the public domain. The same applies to many utilities, financial institutions, transportation, and social facilities. Again it would be wrong to draw one line through the account for all transition economies. It is nevertheless striking that sizable chunks of state-owned assets in all countries remain in the public domain without having been subjected to adequate public-sector reforms to ensure proper corporate governance and monitoring. Most have been starved of funds and many continue to receive subsidies in one form or another. Even for many large and strategic, ostensibly privatized firms, the state has retained a considerable stake and the nexus government-management is by no means "businesslike." Yet, none of these economies has as yet adequate monitoring agents acting on behalf of the government or society. The initial argument that divestment would proceed swiftly, hence there would thus be no reason for intermediate solutions, rings particularly hollow after nearly a decade of divisive privatization campaigns.

In contrast to hiving off assets to nonstate entities, the underlying economic problem of ensuring that existing capital assets, the bulk of which is in the hands of ill-defined political surrogates, are utilized more efficiently remains as daunting as it was at the transition's start, albeit at a reduced scale. This is an area of concern that policy makers *must* tackle head-on to prop up sustainable growth through genuine restructuring. That remains an unnerving sociopolitical task, though alternative paths are available, as proposed earlier. They need not confound the agenda for transformation. A more reasoned approach is now being increasingly heeded particularly in countries where the disappointment about privatization as an economic instrument, as opposed to its political dimensions, has been considerable.

Can one determine which existing economic branches should be emphasized to the detriment of others and which firms deserve some support on a transitory basis? Clearly, if government decision makers knew with certainty the profitability of any given firm, it would be easy to divide economic activities into those that are now profitable, those that can be rendered profitable with suitable reorganization, and those that are hopeless loss makers. If so, government should try to disseminate that information as widely and as fairly as possible to nonstate agents; even incomplete markets might take care of the sifting of SOEs. Governance should then primarily be concerned about preserving state assets for now and ensuring that most are divested in an orderly manner in line with the capabilities of solidifying markets.

Even privatized assets, except those in which FDI has taken a considerable stake, are not necessarily being utilized more effectively than they were under state socialism. Productivity gains have remained small in most countries, Hungary and Poland being notable exceptions. Corporate governance remains in disarray. This has various origins, including dispersed ownership, the nexus between state banks and indebted firms, a poor legal environment for disclosure, entrenched management, an inadequate regulatory regime, and limping capital markets. Access to financing and technology by strapped firms acquired by domestic agents with limited means remains problematic.

The institutions to supervise remaining state assets to be privatized and public-sector assets that will be kept there, or to innovate regulatory regimes and deliver on supervisory functions, are not yet in place. This has various origins. All countries that have tried to set up such institutions have incurred setbacks for sociopolitical reasons. Tepid and partial public-sector reforms, if that, have not markedly improved governance capabilities. This has been aggravated by the weakness or inconsistency of parliamentary supervision and shallow governmental authority.

Finally, although the transition economies most advanced with privatization have paid attention to the rudiments of the capital market, skimpy regulation has been an open invitation to chicanery. At the least, potential conflicts of interest vest insider information and encourage shady deals. Charges of collusion have been levied, including for petty privatization. Whereas the political process should not get sidetracked by concerns about every single instance of such potential conflicts, the widespread malfeasance observed in these countries does not augur well for the chances of credibly maintaining the sociopolitical consensus. Indeed, the population at large can do next to nothing about these events, except at the ballot box. Greater skepticism about the alleged benefits of the revolution is likely to result. This cannot but further spread apathy toward promised political and economic progress than has been coming to the fore since the, admittedly exaggerated, euphoria engendered briefly by the "1989 events."

Conclusions

I have underlined in this chapter that privatization in transition economies is bound to be costly, protracted, and messy. No straightforward solutions to how best to divest the state of its influence over the allocation of capital assets are at hand. Pragmatism is the order of the day, given the multiple goals of and the many obstacles to privatization. Particularly important is that privatization arouses such passions on the part of large segments of the population. It may have had the wrong notions about society's wealth to be privatized to begin with. But that realization is not likely to mend the sociopolitical fabric without which adherence to the transformation agenda becomes illusory.

Apart from utilizing divestment for political purposes, which may be appropriate if democracy were to be in jeopardy or to kickstart the move toward the market economy, privatization deserves to be conducted in an orderly sequence and with as much governance as the state and its agents can muster, perhaps with external assistance, to seek efficiency, revenue, and equity in the process. That divestment process should proceed along with the creation of the appropriate market institutions, governance capabilities, and a redefined role of the state and its various agencies in managing society. But it would be hopeless to conduct an orderly privatization campaign in a highly unbalanced socioeconomic environment. It might then be better to just do it, and pray that a solid buttress for better corporate and state governance will emerge fairly quickly.

7

THE ROLE OF INSTITUTIONS
IN A MARKET ECONOMY

Once one moves beyond the confines of a contemporaneous exchange of the simplest kinds of goods, institutions are required to reinforce the validity of the contract embedded in nearly all forms of exchange in a market economy. Even in a viable contemporaneous market the "institutions" of credibility, trust, and reliability play an important role (Haggard, McMillan, and Woodruff 1996). These contracts need not, and usually are not, explicit. Even if they are, they rarely contain all elements bearing on the satisfactory execution of contracts or the resolution of related disputes.

It would be useful to have a comprehensive overview of the "institutions of the market." That alone might justify several tomes. This chapter can move only marginally beyond the core institutions introduced in Chapter 3. In this, I shall proceed relatively quickly with the legal codes and institutions required for protecting and enforcing contracts. I devote more attention to the institutions of functioning labor and capital markets and to the requirements for enhancing the collection, organization, and dissemination of various kinds of information. I touch in this context also on the notion of governance. But how this affects the state and the nonprofit institutions closer to the coercive state than the for-profit private sector I defer to Chapter 9.

After clarifying the nature of "market institutions," I start with the all-important subject of property rights. Next I give a quick rundown of the legal infrastructure. Then I proceed with the various layers of financial and capital markets; but I devote disproportionate attention first to having in place a viable commercial-banking sector. Thereafter I pinpoint the essential features of the institutions of labor markets and indeed of the social safety net, though the latter's details I explore in Chapter 8. The role of information, regulation, and supervision in a market economy is highlighted next. Before concluding, I set forth key notions of governance, though I take up the broader issues of governing the transition in Chapter 8.

Section 1: On the institutions of a functioning market economy

The concept "institutions of the market," as noted in the Introduction, encompasses broadly the infrastructure of a variety of physical institutions, of laws, of the attitudes of economic agents (whether private or not), and all the other elements that determine the particular shape of any one "market economy." In coming to grips with the creation of the institutions in transition economies appropriate to the emergent market environment, which itself is not a clearly defined concept, two critical issues need to be borne in mind. One is that the institutions inherited from state socialism are not particularly well suited to enhancing the allocation of resources via market channels. Yet those institutions linger on during transformation, in some cases for quite some time. Special efforts are therefore required to contain their negative influence on the transition and to transform the viable ones into full-fledged agents of civil society and the pluralistic market economy. Second, missing agents of the latter organization must be created in order to attain a viable market economy. But it is simply impossible to erect all and ensure their proper functioning in a short period of time. While simply borrowing them from abroad may look appropriate on paper, in practice this is not feasible for all too many of the institutions that identify a given market economy. As a rule it requires a long time, perhaps a generation or more in some transition economies, to have in place the rudiments of the institutions on which the proper functioning of a market economy is predicated. Not only that, the fine-tuning of institutions in breadth and in depth is necessarily closely associated with an economy's wealth-generating capacity and experience with "institutions." The task is daunting for the transition economies are asked to accomplish the features of reasonably mature market economies at a medium level of development over a period of time that is but a fraction of the two centuries or so of capitalist evolution, such as in western Europe.

Gradualism is inherent in building the institutions that enhance the allocation of resources in the senses of technical, allocative, and adaptive efficiency; I use the latter notion as coined in the property rights' school (North 1989, 1990, 1991). But for some a speedier solution can be found than for others. Consider, for example, the creation of simple but working commercial-bank intermediation (that is, ensuring effective payment transfers, collecting savings, and allocating loans for commercial purposes) as compared to having in place well-functioning financial and capital markets. Another implication is that for some time to come markets *cannot* function as they do in mature market economies for lack of the pertinent institutions. All this suggests that the proper sequencing and coordination of the establishment and maturation of these institutions with other components of the transformation agenda are of critical importance to the success of the entire undertaking. In and of itself, that has implications for the management of the transformation process, including possibly the state (see Chapter 9). I shall therefore focus here on the institutions that are most urgently needed and that can be innovated within a reasonable period of time, given political will, resources, and talents. Among the latter I definitely include assistance that can be obtained from the international community (as detailed in Chapter 11).

Section 2: Property rights

In a mature market economy, property rights as an economic category are rarely debated. Inquiries into the nature of property and its associated rights as a rule are the stuff of legal, political, and moral discourses whose outcome codetermines economic events. It is at that stage that the economist normally steps into the fray, taking property and property rights for granted because they have been well defined for some time, to inquire into their multiple consequences for resource allocation. The object for inquiry, then, is more the relevance of ownership to resource allocation than how to allocate property rights. Doing so in as convoluted a situation as in transition economies is a *sui generis* task well beyond this compass. This all the more since the existing theory of property rights exhibits much less of a consistent, self-contained, and comprehensive body of analytical insights than is the case with many other central topics of economics (Yarrow 1989, pp. 52ff.). To deal with the situation in transition economies, the economist has to borrow some notions of property and property rights from moral, philosophical, and legal discourses (Munzer 1990, pp. 23–5).

Property rights are important in an economic context because they are integrally related to incentive structures for decision making; these figure highly on the policy agenda of transition economies. Whereas I confine myself mostly to the multiple issues of the *economics* of property rights in these countries, it bears to stress at the outset the "messiness" of the issue. Any discussion of property rights in transition economies that sidesteps the multiple emotional, ethical, ideological, legal, philosophical, political, and social dimensions by focusing on detached, technical issues misses the point. Property and property rights as social institutions cannot really be looked at with cool detachment for they "can incite passion and be the stuff of revolutions" (Munzer 1990, p. 1). But it is not my purpose here to elaborate even a rump theory of property, even though the literature rarely agrees on *the* theory of property.

2.1 – Basic markers of property rights in a market setting

Emotive aspects of reordering property rights have been at the forefront of political disputes during transition in the eastern part of Europe; much less so in the Asian reforming countries, except perhaps for access to land. This stems in part from the fact that until 1989 most property was centrally owned, even if only nominally, with confined property rights for nonstate actors. Not only that, as shown in Part I, over time many of these rights had become blurred and uncertain. With transition there is urgency to reconstructing property rights as one critical cornerstone for laying the foundations of societal renewal.

251

Indeed, the essence of the market economy is the separation of economic transactions into mediated ones – the core of the division of labor. Markets accommodate the interaction of multiple economic agents whose purpose is exchange under various kinds of market structures, ranging from duopoly to full competition with many actors on both the supply and the demand sides. The latter case is, of course, the ideal paradigm of market competition wielded so ubiquitously in standard textbooks. Economic actors in such an environment should enjoy a great degree of sovereignty within a set framework, which itself should be predictable, reliable, and transparent. The emergence of such "rules of the game," which constitute the core of moving toward market-based resource allocation, may be spurred on via a purely technocratic approach or it may be filtered from bruising sociopolitical battles. In any case, in a market economy the reach of political authority is limited. Nevertheless, the latter is essential in establishing in a reasonably orderly manner the framework for market participants and in delimiting the evolving economic role of the state (see Chapter 9). Recognizing property rights and ensuring that they can be enforced are integral parts of moving toward the market environment. Furthermore, a market by necessity consists of conflicting interests to be reconciled through negotiations among agents, whose independence is bounded by some measure of sociopolitical and legal mediation so that one agent's sovereignty is not forcefully trampled upon by another agent while exercising that sovereignty.

For that state of resolution to come to the fore and underpin the more or less efficient functioning of the market, at least three conditions must be fulfilled. Politically, the establishment of the rule of law is necessary to protect individual rights, including economic rights and obligations, and civil liberties essential to democratic decision making (see the next subsection). For our purposes it may be taken to mean the organizing principle of society that determines the individual's expression of the key reference markers of sociopolitical precepts and how to enforce them. Unlike what some contend (Olson 1993), democracy as such is neither necessary nor sufficient to guarantee political stability, participation, or equality, in spite of exhortations to the contrary (Comisso 1991, 1992).

In the economic context, though, the conditions of liberalism may provide a highly useful ingredient for ensuring efficient resource allocation through operational markets. But it is by no means clear that they are either necessary or sufficient. Indeed, who among the various economic agents in society exerts control over resources, how those rights are acquired, and how those rights are exercised may impact on economic performance as critically as legally specified property rights. Establishing a regime that sets the latter unambiguously is by no means equivalent to formulating an appropriate economic policy. Thus it is essential to have a proper microeconomic environment to attain macro-economic stability. But the latter needs a few more ingredients than specified so far for it to crystallize into a constructive framework within which many economic agents can pursue their own interests without disadvantaging society at large.

Finally, it is necessary to have an unambiguous property rights' regime that differentiates between the state and economic actors (whether private, cooperative, corporate, or public entities without coercive powers) engaged in producing scarce goods and services. The polar case of a public good is full indivisibility over the whole society (Rawls 1972, p. 266). In turn, full divisibility provides the polar case of a private good. But in real life there are various kinds of public and private goods depending on their degree of divisibility and the size of the relevant public. Private goods are normally those for which most, but not all, benefits or costs associated with output are, respectively, collected or paid by private agents. In contrast, public goods are those that consist overwhelmingly of nonappropriable benefits (such as national security) or noncollectible costs (such as crime). Without a clearly delineated regime on property rights, it is difficult to carve out broad maneuvering room for voluntary transactions. And without the latter, it is all but impossible to meet the fundamental requirements for economic agents to partake in the benefits of the broadest division of labor.

2.2 – State socialism and blurred property rights

The construction of an appropriate property rights' regime in transition economies is a complex matter. Under state socialism, the situation did not even approximately reflect the conditions of an efficient property rights' regime (see the next subsection). It was profoundly confounding, certainly on the transition's eve. The reapportionment of property rights is a twofold task. One is a legacy of state socialism. If state socialism had delivered on its orthodox economic model, the prevailing principal–agent problems would have differed substantially from those typical of market conditions (Cheung 1987a; Niehans 1987). Some aspects thereof pervaded state socialism and must now be rearranged. The other is that the monoparty should have thoroughly monitored property rights free of any "competition." Such an in-growth, a failure to distinguish even nominally between government and Party, was often blurred. The consequence was either bad economic monitoring or neglect of monitoring obligations, as happened more and more under administrative reforms. This was especially the case for assets entrusted in one way or another to "private" ventures during the terminal years of state socialism. Effective monitoring by the legal owner, directly or indirectly and regardless of whether private or public, constitutes the central problem of ensuring efficient use of resources when property rights are unbundled.

Recall from Part I that on the transition's eve most assets are not privately owned; but many are not truly the state's either. Recall too that though the state was the dominant owner, as Cheryl Gray (1996, p. 2) notes, "the state itself was, always and everywhere, an amorphous collection of disparate interests." This derives from a variety of historical, ideological, institutional, political, and social factors. Society's wealth consisted of tangible and intangible (including notably technical and scientific progress) assets that had been either expropriated from former owners or built up on the basis of forced savings through tight control over wages and incomes more generally. In principle, this established clear property rights in favor of the state and its agents, who were called upon to properly monitor these assets to ease principal–agent problems. That requires putting in place the mechanisms and criteria necessary to induce agents to act on behalf and in the interest of their principals through incentives set by the latter (see Ross 1973; Stiglitz 1987). Note that these can vary a great deal and be coercively or, as in the market environment, voluntarily observed. One of the great problems with this type of distributional arrangement is that most assets are not really the state's, the government's, or society's but "communal" (Comisso 1991). Claims that the "people" own these assets are mostly fictitious as rights are exercised chiefly through a collective political process, which fails to recognize any individual's ownership of these assets. Many reasons are invoked, but most have an ideological twist or political origin (see Chapter 1).

Even under self-management in Yugoslavia or later in some of the reformed countries with state socialism, SOEs are essentially "political firms" vested with monopoly privileges, unclear and conflicting objectives, and a myriad of social and regulatory responsibilities. In actual fact, the jurisprudence on nonprivate property exerts only a limited effect on the allocation of scarce resources. Three such consequences are of sufficient weight to be highlighted here. One is that society's property needs to be monitored, just like corporate management, by real owners or at least by their elected or appointed representatives. This sets the ambit for corporate governance, regardless of the latter's monitoring mandate (see Section 8).

Second, administrative devolution transfers, at least implicitly, some property rights over resources to enterprise, self-management, or workers' councils; but not ultimate ownership. This is perhaps nowhere as egregious as in countries, notably Hungary, where the political cadres authorize managers to turn their enterprise into a corporation, whose shares can be signed away in return for some outsider, usually foreign, participation; but self-interested in-growth was not unknown (Bonnell 1996; Róna-Tas 1994, 1996; Stark 1992, 1996)! Because of inadequate monitoring by real owners, those entrusted with the user and some usufruct parts of the property rights, as examined below, utilize their position to capture all usufruct property rights, and some disposal rights as well, some of which they feel, not without some legitimacy, to be theirs. In many cases, privatization only exacerbates this (see Chapter 6).

Finally, property rights must be recognized for all assets of legal and private entities. That is to say, under transformation state, social, cooperative, corporate, and individual ownership (regardless of residence or nationality in most cases) *all* constitute potentially legitimate alternatives to the defunct system of "societal" ownership. Full legalization of diverse forms of ownership and control is crucial for the effective functioning of economic agents through increased competition, hence for fully reaping the latter's social benefits. Note that alternative property formats pose different issues in coordination and monitoring, and hence in the kind of outcomes that *can* come to the fore (Munzer 1990, p. 25). This applies to existing assets as well as to those to be created from new savings.

It is critical in this respect to distinguish sharply between ownership as such and resource allocation. Thus, the purported superiority of the capitalist economy is more an argument for the superiority of competition and regulation in full-fledged market economies as the central mechanism for coordinating decisions about resource allocation than for private ownership *per se* (Gathon and Pestieau 1996; Pestieau 1989). That competitive markets cannot operate properly in the absence of overwhelming private ownership was, with few exceptions, never more than an assertion. In any case, when it comes to assessing the efficiency of resource allocation, there is much empirical evidence in support of distinguishing private and public property from communal ownership, which blurs rights. Whereas it is clear that there can be no well-functioning dynamic market economy that explicitly precludes all but state ownership, private ownership by itself does not invariably guarantee the most efficient use of resources. Full divestment of state-owned assets to private agents is not really necessary to ensure a more efficient use of society's resources. The purpose of property rights' reform, as for privatization (see Chapter 6), should in any case be twofold: A sharp improvement in the efficiency of the allocation of the services potentially available from the existing capital stock and providing for new capital accumulation in multiple ownership forms to maximize present and future levels of welfare in society. There are many other objectives, however.

2.3 – *Ownership and property relations*

Stylized economic theory postulates the *homo economicus*, a standardized individual bent on maximizing a properly behaved "utility function" subject to clear "budget" constraints. This simplified world has been useful in deriving basic propositions in well-determined areas of economic discourse. But it should not be taken as the last word on how most economic agents in real societies can be expected to behave. Social interactions among individuals, corporations, and government agencies are indeed conditioned by two broad sets of constraints. One arises from physical limits on resources, including in many cases on the service streams emanating from reproducible assets, including over time. The other derives from various arrangements for mobilizing scarce resources. That is to say, behavior in society is also influenced by rules or institutional features, including property rights, that govern the choices of individual actors (North 1990, 1991). Because they shape the structure of incentives, institutions have a strong bearing on economic behavior. Depending on the cost of enforcing clear property rights (North 1991), if the social limits to individual behavior are well defined, hence rights are recognized and accepted as enforceable, social interaction materializes within an "order" that consensually reconciles the conflicting interests of various agents (Buchanan 1987); some time may elapse before this pattern of outcomes becomes tolerable (Kanel 1974).

To grasp the meaning of property rights it does not suffice to define them as "the behavioral relations among men that arise from the existence of scarce goods and pertain to their use" (Pejovich 1983, p. 42). Property refers to the present and expected relationship, usually of a legal nature, or one that can be legally enforced, between persons and abstract as well as concrete things in a realistic social situation. It is also of critical importance to conceive "property" as a bundle of normative incidents, which allows for powers to give and to sell anything that is transferable (Munzer 1990, p. 56). Property rights is a much narrower concept, referring chiefly to the positive sides of being an owner rather than the obligation of owners or the disadvantageous incidents of ownership (Munzer 1990, p. 240).

Whereas the literature on the nature of property rights and how they affect economic decisions (Alchian 1987; Demsetz 1967; Furubotn and Pejovich 1972; Pejovich 1990; Ryan 1987) has been fairly straightforward, many of its applications are not. In what follows, I consider a property right to be a socially enforceable right to select uses of scarce goods, but unambiguously placed within a concrete social setting. Recall the wide variety of property, not just tangible possessions, over which rights need to be structured. The essential idea is the exclusion of others from the use of a service or good and the transferability of this right according to prevailing institutional constraints. The essence of property rights is, therefore, the right to be protected in one's choice of permissible, mutually agreed contractual terms of the transfer (Munzer 1990, pp. 48–9). The crucial element, putting it in the context of Roman law, is the *ius utendi, fruendi et* (or *ac*) *abutendi*, that is, the right of use, enjoyment of the fruit, and (indeed) disposal of the object of ownership. Implicit therein is the right to exclude others. Property rights form a bundle of positive claims, some of which may be intangible. The unbundling of those rights through contracts or similar arrangements is a function of the institutional makeup of any concrete market economy.

The relationship between effort and reward is crucial in this context. In most circumstances, people do not make the necessary sacrifices to become owners in some sense unless they are confident of obtaining substantial control over the use and disposal of things; hence the need to establish and enforce clear property rights. Indeed, the creation of new firms requires the unbundling of property rights. The latter are claim rights to possess, use, manage, and receive income; the power to transfer, waive, exclude, and abandon; the liberties to consume or destroy; immunity from expropriation; the duty not to use harmfully; and the ability to execute to satisfy a correct judgment (Munzer 1990, p. 22). For property rights to be socially meaningful there must at some point be "an embodiment of a person in external things through an action done with an incentive to claim property rights that has effects recognizable by others" (Munzer 1990, p. 77). They need not necessarily be indivisible. But the value of property depends on the cost of acquiring other property rights over the same object that are socially recognized. The latter is important when it comes to reestablishing clear property rights in the transition economy and honoring explicit as well as implicit rights acquired by legitimate "users" of the erstwhile socially owned property.

256

As regards their effects on economic conditions, two angles of property rights need to be considered. One is that there are transaction costs to economic behavior that, in addition to intrinsic resource scarcity, codetermine outcomes (Cheung 1987a; Stiglitz 1987). Oftentimes, the magnitude of these costs can be verified only in the process of enforcing property rights (Barzel 1989), which infuses an element of uncertainty into exercising property rights. Those willing to take the risk must, therefore, be in a position to anticipate a reasonable return in the case of success, if at the risk of a substantial penalty with failure. Also, property rights are not always unambiguously delineated. If only for that reason, there often exists an opportunity to capture attributes of these transactions when they are not checked by the institutions in place. Certainly, alternative property rights exert different effects on the allocation of resources. That the owner should be entitled to the residual benefits of his property is also clear. But what does ownership mean and which residual benefits are targeted?

The conditions of an efficient property rights' system signaled earlier (Comisso 1991; Munzer 1990) are threefold. First, property rights must be lodged as much as possible in the hands of actors with purely economic responsibilities even though the consequence of indivisibility and publicness is that the provision of public goods must be arranged through the political process rather than the market. In a market context, such rights would of necessity be attributes of the behavior of private individuals. Although some will in time also emerge in transition economies, a good part of the existing public capital stock for years to come will necessarily remain with SOEs, even if corporatized and commercialized (see Chapter 6). Though ultimate disposal may still be the state's prerogative, all user and most usufruct rights *could* be vested in other economic agents.

It may be obvious to most observers that property rights have to be clearly demarcated for all actors. But this is still not so in transition economies. To meet some of the aspirations on economic gains and material well-being within a pluralistic polity, the limits to individual, corporate, or collective behavior have to be well defined and mutually recognized, possibly through a social consensus on the tradeoffs between private gain and social welfare. This takes time. When ownership of property is clearly defined and resides with specific economic agents, the owner benefits from using that property in the most productive manner or must personally bear the cost in the form of reduced returns (Alan Rufus Walters 1987, p. 36).

Second, property rights must be enforced by a neutral party based on an effective judicial system and modern civil and commercial codes. This should aim not only at issuing a guarantee that the state has no intention to nationalize property, barring extreme adversity. They must be constitutionally circumscribed and legally enshrined as clearly as possible. After all, the standard legal doctrine on property rights in mature market economies emerged precisely to counter-balance the capriciousness of royal favors under feudalism (Kanel 1974). It should also provide a guarantee about the framework, including the fiscal regime on the distribution of income and accumulation of wealth. Above all, administrative

257

institutions and Party organizations must renounce their powers of direct super-vision and restrictive regulation; in any case, the erstwhile tutelage should be abandoned at the earliest possible phasing of the transition. This is critical notably in the transition economy, where the "most powerful upper limit on accumulation is uncertainty and the fear of future nationalisation and confiscation" (Kornai 1990b, p. 11), as happened in the past, memories of such repression remaining very much alive.

Finally, policy-making authority, including the ability to prescribe the kinds of activities the bearer of property rights can engage in, must be entrusted to institutions that themselves neither exercise property rights nor enforce them. This role normally belongs to the legislative branch of government.

Property may be corporeal or intangible. In that sense, it can be looked at from three angles. First, in order to decide how best to allocate existing assets with a view to maximizing some returns, it is useful to distinguish between ownership *per se* and the usufruct component of property rights, given the overwhelming role of "state" property for years to come. But this should not be conflated with state power (Kanel 1974, pp. 828–9), as it was under state socialism. Converting this power into secure property rights protected by orderly judicial and legislative procedures limits arbitrary decisions by the powerful. Second, whatever rights are assigned and however they can be separated, mechanisms must be put in place to ensure that the value of capital assets is not eroded at the expense of the ultimate owner. This may necessitate the creation of insurance schemes in addition to legal redress. Finally, questions concerning the formation of new capital from public and private savings to maximum economic effect need to be addressed.

2.4 – Alternative ownership forms and their implications

From a technical point of view, it is *a priori* difficult to stipulate the most efficient property arrangement for any given set of assets. There are unquestionably instances in which it would be advisable to encourage private ownership, if only to mitigate the costs of ensuring proper allocation of user rights to state property. Examples would be housing, small retail outlets, or service firms – the objects of "petty" privatization (see Chapter 6). On the other hand, precepts on income and wealth distribution, and access to a certain social dividend, may well counsel for maintaining state property of basic sectors of economic activity. The same prevails in the case of market failure, notably externality and natural monopoly, in particular when the incumbent firm has irrecoverable costs (Thompson 1988, pp. 41–2). The core question should, then, be how to ensure the optimal service flow from such assets as measured by some objective function.

Property rights are important in explaining the direction and coordination of the use of scarce resources. Property rights that are as a rule partitionable, separable, and alienable (Alchian 1987, p. 1031) should be tradable, possibly in unbundled form, at mutually agreed prices in reliable contractual transactions that can be negotiated at a fairly low cost; this makes room for the organization of cooperative or joint production activities in highly specialized economic units, such as the complex corporation. Ownership affects allocative efficiency in the marketplace as well as internal efficiency of firms (Vickers and Yarrow 1988, p. 3), including adaptive efficiency or the best allocation of resources over time (see North 1989, 1990, 1991). Property rights define the feasible set of exchanges within a given economic system. However the efficiency function is specified, assignment of property rights determines the objectives of the "owners" of the firm, whether private or public (Nuti 1991); if the ultimate owner is not the manager, monitoring managerial performance plays a critical role. Public and private ownership differ in both respects. If transaction costs of operating an "organization" (Cheung 1987a, b) are zero, given Ronald Coase's theorem (Cooter 1987), alternative institutional or organizational arrangements would provide no basis for choice and, hence, could not be interpreted by economic theory. But normally a contract implies different costs of supervision, measurement, and negotiation (Stiglitz 1987). Also, the form of economic organization changes as does the function of the visible hand with the contractual arrangement chosen (Cheung 1987a, p. 56).

The efficiency implications of property assignments depend very much on the competitive and regulatory environment in which economic agents operate, with the latter two typically having substantially larger effects on company performance than ownership *per se*. These multiple determinants of a firm's performance also apply to the transition economy. Of course, by virtue of the nature of public enterprise in most market economies, the various weights of regulation, competition, and ownership differ from those in a transition economy. But ownership, competition (hence, the monitoring system), and regulation are essentially three shorthands for, possibly highly, complex sets of mutually interlocking influences. The efficiency implications of a change in one or more elements of one set is, as a rule, contingent on the other two.

2.5 – Property rights, privatization, and restitution

It is useful to distinguish property rights from privatization. The latter's fundamental aspects are rooted in the establishment of clear property rights for unambiguous owners. In that sense, the two are intimately related. However, the catalog of matters pertaining to property rights is vastly more complex than the issues that are pertinent to assigning property rights to existing assets. In some countries, an important concomitant of the transition takes the form of a socio-political consensus on restituting property that was earlier confiscated. Moreover, forced accumulation, meaning investments undertaken by the state that did not necessarily have the citizens' approval, may also cause problems. The overriding one is that the state itself cannot really lay claim to any assets, except those that would have been mandated, or approved *ex post*, by the electorate. In other words, most state assets are intrinsically owned by society and since the citizens have already "paid" for them, they should be returned to them on as equitable a basis as possible.

Although there are some grounds in state socialism for the first proposition, there is little merit in the latter, except on rather primitive egalitarian socialist grounds (see Chapter 6). Even more cumbersome is the presumption that confiscated assets deserve to be returned to their former owners through either physical restitution or some form of compensation. To be sure, restitution or compensation can be justified on many grounds. Morally, the events of 1989 were anticommunist, hence, against the confiscation through nationalization that had earlier been perpetrated. Furthermore, because the new societies want to emulate the *Rechtsstaat*, they can demonstrate their commitment to respecting the law by restoring private property through restitution or, at the least, adequate compensation. Also by infusing credibility into policy stances, legal recognition of the rights of former owners strengthens the position of the new policy makers.

Whatever the moral or ethical merits of restitution or compensation, their considerable drawbacks should be clear, particularly as regards efficient resource allocation and forging ahead expeditiously with the transformation. Identifying clear owners of confiscated property poses its own formidable hurdles. Even if former owners can be identified, can the usufruct since entrusted to or acquired by others be revoked without further ado? Matters become far more complex in the case of factories whose structure state socialism substantially modified. It is hopeless to resort to restitution when the essence of the confiscated property rights can no longer be separated from presently existing property rights, however inadequately state socialism may have monitored them. Particularly problematic has been land ownership (see Chapter 6). Without rapid progress in this domain the potential for output generation from the farm sector cannot be realized and it will be difficult to conclude viable contracts on real estate and land transactions. Likewise for urban land and housing.

The greatest danger of restitution in any but the most confined connotation (for example, the return of a confiscated painting) is that the already inadequate legal infrastructure of these economies gets hopelessly entangled in weakly enforceable claims and liens that bog down the exceedingly fragile civil society for years. In that respect, a commitment to compensate those whose assets were earlier confiscated is less troublesome. Of course, it too presents complications, notably in encumbering government budgets and ascertaining claimed property claims. Contentious moral and legal claims notably on the part of those who had been specifically disadvantaged under state socialism further complicate matters.

2.6 – Implicit property rights of administrative planning

Although the means of production under state socialism were society's, in most countries legal ownership became severely blurred over time. Schematizing the evolution of property rights under state socialism to the eve of the political revolution, the start and end consist of chiefly private property rights and limited public rights (see Brabant 1992a, pp. 119ff.). In-between, private property rights were confiscated and became overwhelmingly public property rights. These rights were initially monitored through the administrative and political processes in place. But the incompleteness of plan instructions to management and the gradual easing of the intensity with which the use of state-owned assets was monitored bestowed implicit property rights onto those called upon to seize initiative in executing the plan and did so successfully. During administrative decentralization this situation was further compounded by more sluggish monitoring of property rights, whose user and some usufruct rights had been entrusted to those managing state-owned assets. One might refer to these as *neglected* property rights. They consist of the implicit rights referred to earlier, as well as accrued and vested rights. *Vested* rights came about as a result of two factors. One was the transfer of responsibility for the proper use of those assets to decentralized agents, usually enterprise, self-management, or workers' councils. This conferred some usufruct rights on those directly involved in the production process. Though property remained collective, the inadequate monitoring by central or communal authorities of assets for which the *abutendi* powers had not been relinquished ensured that those entrusted with the use and usufruct of capital augmented their *accrued* and *implicit* property rights, in some cases to full ownership (Comisso 1991; Nagy 1991; Szálai 1991). In federally organized states, but also in countries that sought administrative decentralization, disputes have arisen over the respective rights of various levels of state authority. Finally, communist ideology emphasized the societal nature of property and the right of workers to the firm's assets. Even when rights were not explicitly vested in them, management or workers more generally may lay claim to accrued rights, for example, because their "firm" performed reasonably well over time.

Claimed rights became even more vested as a result of two developments. One was the emergence of new legal statutes for the SOE, entitling management, enterprise councils, or workers' councils to reconstitute the firm into a joint-stock company whose shares would not necessarily all be the state's. Another was the fact that the political leadership began to encourage SOE management to take initiative in restructuring their firm with a view to becoming profitable. As a result, those entrusted with the usufruct began to engage in "spontaneous privatization" (see Chapter 6). This together with the more general confusion engendered by the failure of administrative streamlining, especially during the latter part of the 1980s, led to unclear, overlapping, and even contradictory claims to almost every state-owned property. Another impetus has arisen from the disintegration of economic order, SOE managers essentially being left with a choice between doing nothing or seizing the moment, thus stretching their earlier discretion. Such legitimate claims, however ill-defined, by nonstate agents cannot all be swept aside. Indeed, management in place embodies human capital to be mobilized during the transition, possibly by recognizing some of their property claims. Even the more dubious claims cannot be removed by simply renationalizing assets as a prelude to transferring legal title to some central agency charged with divestment.

One critical question here is precisely how and to what degree these claimed and confiscated rights ought to be recognized during divestment campaigns. Resolving the issue as early as possible is useful to stave off potentially disruptive sociopolitical debates on the issue, thus being able to forge ahead with enterprise restructuring and divestment. Matters are clear when it comes to *confiscated* rights slated to be transformed directly through restitution or indirectly through compensation. Whereas *vested* rights may be recognized, at least in part, *implicit* and *accrued* rights will in time be distributed over the limited public and the unlimited private rights, but the proportions are offhand unknown. The presumption is that the proportion of implicit rights flowing back to the public domain, at least in the short run, will be larger than for accrued rights. But the real outcome eventually crystallizes through the shaky political process in place.

Section 3: The legal foundations of the market

With the transition, an infrastructure suitable to emerging market conditions and malleable to functioning markets over time needs to be erected almost from scratch and not only in the economic domain. That necessarily differs markedly from the constitutional infrastructure of state socialism. The "rule of law," and indeed law suitable to political pluralism and supportive of an emerging market environment, is not just about having the appropriate legal texts to refer to. Indeed, its essence is about the effective substance of these texts as applied in real life. This in turn can ultimately be guaranteed only by an independent judiciary, including in guarding the constitution itself and its principles, that is incorruptible and fair. This is not easy at all in most transition economies. The legal framework for the new societies elicits vast and complicated subjects on which economists have little to say, aside from affirming the importance of putting into place quickly robust regulatory and judicial frameworks. I shall nonetheless give a few comments on the economic aspects of the legal environment for markets to flourish.

Not only must all kinds of contract and bankruptcy laws be written into firm commercial and contract codes. Modern markets with their far-reaching division of labor and highly complex coordination tasks cannot function properly without a clear legal environment setting acceptable rules of behavior that can be enforced in courts. This is self-evident when it comes to exercising property rights. But more general, truly transparent civil and commercial codes ensuring that all agents can enforce their rights guaranteed by the constitutional infrastructure of a democracy are due. In addition to providing for clear property rights, this must include company, antimonopoly, bankruptcy, and foreign-investment laws as well as financial-sector legislation. Consistency across laws needs to be strived for. There is also a need to fill gaps such as in the commercial code, company law, securitization, and collateralization, legislation to that effect should be introduced quickly.

Precisely because some markets function better and emerge earlier than others, setting the limits to wild capitalism in society's interest is a complex undertaking. At some point, legislation on other matters such as labor protection, the social sphere, and the environment will be needed too, certainly if the transition economy wants to join the EU for which it must emulate the entire *acquis communautaire* (see Chapter 10). In addition, a corps of managers and individuals acting as closely as possible to the stereotype of the "profit maximizer" must be nurtured. The latter importantly contribute to changing the sentiment against market relations and the prevailing proclivity for egalitarianism. But more is required to ensure that economic agents who are not owners act in the latter's interests, that owners do not infringe upon society's prerogatives, that agents who feel their prerogatives have been trampled upon by other private and other agents be adjudicated, that some vulnerable layers of society are protected, and that core intermediating organizations are duly subject to an adequate regulatory regime. Recall that, especially in the case of financial institutions, such a regime encompasses prudential and supervisory regulations able to contain the failures endemic to financial markets (Sundararajan 1996) but also those deriving from the fact that for some time to come such markets in transition economies will be *in statu nascendi*. Of course it does not suffice to have these rules and regulations duly codified. They must also be applied and a jurisprudence built up for their expeditious enforcement. Erecting such "institutions" to the desired level of effectiveness requires time and effort, and experience. Because of the long gestation and the painful costs involved, this process must begin as soon as feasible after the transition's inception.

Of course, there is no need for each transition economy to draft such laws from scratch. Mature market economies offer several alternative codes that have served them well. To the extent transition economies desire to integrate themselves into the global economy in general and the EU in particular, they will in due course be required to render their legislation on a diverse range of matters compatible with the multilateral rules in place. Borrowing and adapting these codes as well as other institution-building measures under the circumstances are quite appropriate here. Adaptation must heed two influences. One is the traditions of the country, which may require special features for some legal aspects. The other is the ability to effectively implement the adopted codes and to build up soonest minimal jurisprudence. Without having an effective judiciary that can act in accordance with "modern" laws, it is hard to envision how the "market" can mature and yield sustainable growth at a fairly high level. This has implications for the speed with which legal harmonization and its effective application in practice can reasonably be assured.

In this connection just one word on the actors in the legal and paralegal sector. It does not suffice to have in place judges and courts without at the same time developing a "legal culture." That calls for educating people in a whole range of legal, accounting, regulatory, and supervisory skills. Some may be imported. Even if the latter is feasible, a flourishing domestic market economy depends intrinsically on a thick layer of domestic advisers. Their focus should primarily be not on the external dimensions of the transformation, but on ensuring that all domestic contracts are discharged honestly and in a timely fashion. Perpetuating the "wild east" in place in some of the transition economies does not augur well for the sustainability of the transformation agenda.

Section 4: Commercial banking

Financial intermediation in a market economy is essential if the latter is to encompass more than elementary exchange and the simplest division of labor. To foster specialization, the complexity of financial intermediation should be closely tailored to the actual and perceived needs of economic actors, the main impetus coming from market-revealed demands, perhaps in an anticipatory mode. Innovating this infrastructure and suitably extending it over time pose an array of daunting tasks if only because financial intermediation under state socialism was almost nil. True, promoters of administrative reforms indulged at times in schemes to reverse this situation. Because no commercially viable solution to tackling the engrained "bad" portfolio of assets and liabilities of state banks operating separately from the central bank was adopted, the unbalanced portfolio was carried over into the transition. These "commercial banks" are undercapitalized and woefully short of experience in debt management, in the collection of savings, in organizing an effective payment system, or in adjudicating loan requests (Bonin and Székely 1994). Because of the importance of commercial banking as distinct from other components of capital, credit, and risk markets, I discuss the latter separately in Section 5.

4.1 – The tasks of banking in transition economies

Transitologists are by no means unanimous on the tasks that banks should carry out during the initial phases of the transition. Most recognize the three or four elementary tasks specified below as crucial ingredients. Some would like to deny even these, constraining banking essentially to the clearing of payments (Rostowski 1994a, b) or to activities other than lending to decentralized units (McKinnon 1991a; 1991b, pp. 118–21); or to do so only within very strict quotas (Kornai 1990a, pp. 47–9). Still others want to move well beyond the tasks I emphasize and transform banks, among other aspects of German-style universal banking (Buch 1993b), into pragmatic agents of privatization (Bonin and Székely 1994); into self-interested conciliators with SOEs that have "bad debt" (Belka 1994; Slay and Vinton 1994); into agents that exert corporate control over privatized firms and, at least temporarily, over SOEs as well; or into institutions that take care of all kinds of risk in the emerging market economy (Guitián 1993).

About the minimalist position, one wonders whence, for example, the skills to assess creditworthiness will eventually be acquired for that must occur if markets are to take root. To confine enterprise financing to self-finance in a highly un-balanced environment is a chimera: An informal market is bound to emerge which, by virtue of its scale and deregulated nature, cannot but be less efficient than a well-constituted – read regulated and policed – formal market. The *métier* of banker is by definition learned on the go in an environment with adequate rewards and sanctions. Its fine-tuning takes time and requires an appropriate regulatory framework. That is to say, prudential regulation and bank supervision are central ingredients in adjudicating whether or not, and to what extent, banking intermediation can be permitted.

I have qualms also about the maximalist position. It would indeed be useful to have available the capabilities to ensure essential coordination of economic decisions through other layers than the compromised or inept bureaucracy, and leave all of these tasks up to "economic actors" motivated by profit. It might even be instructive to explore the respective merits of an Anglo-American (given the transparency and contestability) versus a German-Japanese (given the economies of scope and informational advantages) banking system. Beyond gathering knowledge about how well or badly existing banks function, the choice of ultimate system, once operational markets are in place, cannot motivate behavior in the short run. In other words, owing to the weak banking capabilities in place (in terms of management, infrastructure, skills, and experience), creating on short notice universal banks could be a leap in the dark, straining the competence of the existing bank management as well as of supervisory organs. It should, therefore, not rank high on the initial list of priorities. Likewise for the Anglo-American system: It requires capital investment and sophisticated specialization attainable once the transformation has progressed a good deal with building functioning markets. Formal training and readily transferred assistance do not as a rule provide much of a solid backdrop for managing "economic risk" in its diverse dimensions; restructuring the enterprise sphere far transcends the skills and resources presently available in the banking sector; and, in any case, bankers become sophisticated financial intermediators and trusted counselors primarily while learning on the job.

There is, however, no disagreement on the need to restructure the banking sector, to create a central bank with specific functions of monetary control, to restructure existing banks, to encourage the creation of new banks, and to exploit fully the knowledge that some banks possess about their clients. All that must necessarily take place while existing banks provide financial intermediation for the emerging market economy at least to *bona fide* firms. As far as the role of the central bank is concerned, until other specialized institutions are called for, its responsibilities include as a minimum keeping treasury accounts; managing official international reserves; providing interbank clearing facilities and, more generally, rendering assistance in the processing and settlement of payments; regulating bank liquidity and acting exceptionally as lender of last resort;

supervising bank operations and activities of other financial institutions; and taking responsibility for the conduct of monetary policy (Guitián 1993, p. 117). Note that this is far more encompassing than what can be accomplished via a currency board (see Chapter 4). By the transition's nature, ways and means of divesting the central bank of other functions, including being the state's fiduciary agent with a very close interlinkage between fiscal and monetary authority, must be found (IMF 1997b).

Commercial banks possibly to be created from existing institutions should be called upon to discharge three or four elementary functions: Ensure expeditious settlement of reciprocal claims, collect savings efficiently, allocate these funds for investment purposes on a commercial basis, and possibly market new financial instruments, including to finance any mandated budget deficit. Other banking functions can be added as the evolving market environment calls for them and regulatory mechanisms can be innovated and fine-tuned. Of course, commercial banks should not be clones. Rather, around a cluster of such general-purpose commercial banks various specialized institutions, including savings banks, agricultural credit cooperatives, and credit unions (Hannig 1994) will eventually be needed. Also these institutions should operate at their own risk and perform at best the above-cited three or four basic functions until the transformation is well advanced.

4.2 – Need for elementary but vibrant commercial banking

Just as the central bank should not act as the government's treasurer, commercial banks should finance endeavors at their own risk. For that constraint to bite with the establishment of independent commercial banks, financial restructuring is required (Carlin and Mayer 1992; Corbett and Mayer 1991; IMF 1997b). It is necessary to put in place stringent prudential regulations and surveillance rules to be exercised by a (fairly independent) central bank to ensure proper monetary control and coordination. At the same time, loan portfolios inherited from the monobank and the questionable loans granted during the "uncertain" phase of the transformation, including to private firms that in some countries have been a major contributor to the bad-debt situation, need to be cleaned out. New banks from domestic and foreign sources may have to be encouraged but within stringent rules. Existing commercial banks need to be recapitalized so that they can in principle intermediate on a strictly commercial basis. In all this, commercial behavior with hard budget constraints must be enforced soonest. Commercial banks should be responsible for their own profitability and fill lacunae as they emerge within the existing regulatory framework, which may need periodic fine-tuning. A viable commercial-banking sector is vital to successful transformation. The new private sector, not just as a result of privatization, needs encouragement and thus to access financial services, even if for some time their main funds are retained earnings.

From a purely technical perspective it would be useful simply to bankrupt and eliminate banks whose net worth is below minimum capitalization levels if new financial institutions could be expected to emerge quickly. There would be little merit in doing so otherwise. Domestic voluntary sources are highly limited and aversion to risky investment in the formal sector is acute. Likewise, foreign banks have low interest in performing banking operations, other than those required for FDI and trading, and perhaps meeting the needs of a few blue-ribbon domestic firms, during the initial phase of the transformation. This is due in part to the prevailing uncertainty and unfamiliarity with doing business in transition economies, thus making foreign banks arguably more risk-averse than domestic banks, at least until the recovery is well under way. These activities are very useful. But they do not quite meet the requirements for constructive intermediation during the transformation under difficult conditions. Scam financial schemes by domestic operators and services provided by foreign banks are altogether different issues. It is therefore doubtful whether new viable financial institutions will emerge quickly. For all practical purposes, then, the initial impetus to financial-sector reform must come from recapitalizing existing banks, chiefly from the public purse. Some have argued that those resources could be used to establish new state-financed or cofinanced institutions, presumably because government in effect cannot adequately monitor existing banks, but it might be able to do so for new financial institutions held to more rigorous surveillance rules. Some observers furthermore claim that such capitalized new banks will be unencumbered by the legacies of incompetence, institutional inertia, and principal–agent problems (Phelps *et al.* 1993, pp. 23ff.), presumably on the presumption that there is a layer of competent bankers available who for some reason are presently unable to take charge of existing banks or to found their own. Alas, *tabula rasa* solutions are rarely real options in the transition's context. Better risk management and intermediation at an affordable transaction cost need to be learned. Foreign banks provide some inputs and accelerate the assimilation process through training and transfer of banking technology. But that cannot substitute for experience and learning by doing overnight.

Once again, then, transition managers need to face up to the challenge of how best to work with the resources at hand: containing ill-designed new banks and improving the existing banking framework, among others, by focusing on supervisory activities and prudential regulations, and indeed by tackling the hard problems of unsound financial institutions in place. Managers face a painful dilemma in coming to grips quickly, radically, and credibly with the "problems" of the inherited banking sector: (1) redressing "old debts" of SOEs by offsetting in some pragmatic manner assets and liabilities of the state or society as a whole; (2) recapitalizing banks, thus making available the financial resources required to underpin the transformation; and (3) instilling "commercial rationality" and "discipline" into the behavior of existing banks through retraining, competition from new banks, joint ventures with foreign partners, and explicit rules on hard budget constraints for all economic agents that are effectively enforced. Oddly enough, in spite of these widely shared precepts, invariably policy makers have approached these "most urgent" and "chronic" issues much more slowly than any theoretical option called for. Even then, many have not succeeded. This is paradoxical, but it could hardly have been otherwise (Long 1993; Mayer 1993; Smith and Walter 1993)!

The expected value of assets, the nature and extent of "bad debts," the reliability of commitments made by the former regime, technology, ownership, moving toward a new growth path, and a myriad of other facets inextricably depend on societal change. There is therefore a built-in moral hazard in deciding what to do with existing commercial banks and how to encourage the emergence of new banks. No transition manager can easily sort out the various aspects of such nested uncertainty. Any decision affects the prospective behavior of agents. This in turn changes the quality of the debt portfolio, no matter how carefully the policy menu is chosen. Extreme views are as a result best eschewed. Rather, stringent prudential regulations with the maxim "no bailout," once rules are on the book and basic cleanup of bad assets completed, should be applied with determination. Penalizing institutions that assume too much risk, given their assets, should be more vigorous for existing commercial banks, because they are state-owned, than for new private institutions. Of course, the application of standard prudential regulations, such as the Basle rules, to financial institutions in an environment that is anything but a mature economy may well fail to avert premature bankruptcy. That too would be part and parcel of learning. Whereas risk by definition makes some loans uncollectible, the banking sector should be able to work off such *ex post* losses through its statutory capital, retained earnings, and current profits accruing from its other loans made against its own resources (deposits, borrowed money, capital, and retained earnings).

4.3 – Resolving bad debts

Bad debts pose a major policy problem to the extent that they cannot be resolved or, if cleaned up, threaten the viability of the banking system. This derives from the nature of these debts and the confined options available to redress the situation. The assets and liabilities that "commercial banks" inherited from state socialism change dramatically as a result of transformation policies. These assets were poor to begin with, consisting essentially of administratively allocated loans to support SOEs according to criteria that, on the whole, were well out of truck with market conditions. These were literally liabilities of one agent in the socialized sector to another. Those debts are now part of the portfolios of the so-called commercial banks. Their counterpart is the questionable debt of SOEs not carried by other SOEs or the state treasury. SOEs find it difficult to service these loans with the transition. In other words, "policies to deal with bank's balance sheets cannot be pursued in isolation from policies dealing with enter-prises' financial situation" (Calvo and Kumar 1993, p. 14), and indeed from other transformation policies affecting the economic buoyancy and the sociopolitical stability of the transition economy (Mates 1992). Furthermore, bank liabilities were essentially enterprise and household deposits implicitly guaranteed by government. Moreover, neither households nor banks (except the savings bank) had much experience either in collecting savings, in adjudicating loan requests, in marketing diverse financial assets, in effectively clearing reciprocal claims, or in discharging other, more complicated banking functions. As part of the transformation, then, bank capabilities must be drastically restructured and upgraded.

The problem cannot even be addressed until the notion "bad debt" becomes clear. This involves two rather arbitrary issues. One is the point in time at which managers of the transition decide that henceforth commercial banks should be responsible for their decisions and will be held to that constraint. Note that, inasmuch as the jump from state socialism to building markets cannot be accomplished from one day to the next, the cutoff date is essentially arbitrary. The other is what portion of the portfolio identified as "weak" should actually be cleaned up. Here two radically different approaches have been pursued: All debt before the decision to tackle the problem is bad or contaminated and should be removed from the books or bank assets should be marked to market.

The first approach is rather whimsical and almost certainly wrong. What good would it do to mark debt to market in a situation where such markets fail egregiously? Whereas it is difficult to estimate the size of problem debt, sheer logic suggests that it is a function of the course of the transformation, including any attempt to resolve the perceived debt problem. What is collectible depends on the eventual quality of the loan portfolio, something that is inextricably a function of SOE restructuring. Only once this is taken care of, preferably through a well-thought-out industrial policy (Brabant 1993a), can an informed assessment of potentially performing assets be undertaken. Furthermore, the banking sector itself does not claim that all are problem debts. Nonperforming assets are defined and measured variously, some on the basis of highly questionable approaches (see Brabant 1994c, pp. 24ff.). As a result, there is little point in seeking to redefine all assets and liabilities of banks and SOEs (Bruno 1992).

Though it would be useful to find a quick solution to the problem debt, the case for destroying what is in place is not particularly compelling for reasons already examined, but also because of the value of discretionary assets, which is the real bread-and-butter of bank capital (Buch 1993b, p. 81). Indeed, if governance capabilities are available, policy makers can best start with existing institutions, preferably without preempting future options. Whenever possible, an evolutionary yet expeditious approach toward applying prudential regulations and banking laws deserves to be adopted. In any case, old debts bear little relationship to how a firm performs under new, emerging market conditions. That includes the ability to service debts while moving ahead with restructuring in line with market disciplines and incentives. It might be useful to entrust *prima facie* problem debt to a specially created state debt-resolution agency, as in Czechoslovakia. This may assist banks but does not necessarily improve incentives for indebted SOEs nor is there any guarantee that the new agency will be better placed than existing banks to resolve the collection conundrum.

The second component of the debt has arisen in reaction to, in some countries overly, stringent monetary policies and related, largely experimental transition policies (IMF 1997b), including by banks themselves. Until bankruptcy procedures become a credible threat or the prospects for expansion and restructuring improve markedly, SOEs in particular grant each other credit simply by not honoring obligations, thereby rapidly escalating involuntary arrears. Similarly, initially SOEs increasingly flout their commercial-bank, as well as their fiscal and social-security fiduciary, obligations. The reasons are various but include bad policing of what is ostensibly still state property (see Chapter 6), inadequate prudential regulations, voluntaristic application of any regulatory regime in place, a thoroughly inadequate legal infrastructure to enforce bankruptcy, and political apprehension about massive SOE failure if such rules are available at all. In addition, existing banks have on the whole continued to lend to their established customers – by and large the less solvent SOEs with whom banks had built up firm relationships under state socialism.

Banks are not enforcing contractual loan obligations, not because they are simply perpetuating the passive adjustment of finance under state socialism, but for a number of good reasons. First, the expected value of the assets that can be collected may be less than the cost of enforcing the contract through cumbersome bankruptcy proceedings. Second, there may be an option value in waiting, given the pervasive uncertainty particularly during a severe downturn that government will have to help reverse, in which case new lending to "bad debtors" may be quite rational. Third, taking action against bad debtors may so weaken the structure of the bank that enforcement will be postponed. Fourth, any such action may alarm policy makers and regulators sufficiently to do something about the "signaled" contamination threat for the entire sector. Finally, banks may simply anticipate that there will be a bailout by government, in which case the incentive to seek liquidation is very small. Indeed, by making the collective problem more cumbersome to come to grips with, waiting with enforcement of discipline may compel government to bail out the banking sector (Brainard 1991, pp. 102–3).

A third component needs to be added. In many countries, inflation at the transition's inception all but destroyed the real value of existing debts. Because of substantial interest rates levied on arrears thereafter as well as punitive penalties for delinquency (Slay 1992, p. 36), total (including arrears and tax delinquency) outstanding debts in nominal terms tend to pile up rapidly. True, in many cases, interest rates have remained negative in real terms in a number of countries, thus reducing the apparent real present value of the debt. However, given the marked deterioration of the financial strength of many borrowers due to the transition's depression, it is not clear whether the ostensible reduction in the measured "real value" of an SOE's debt really signals that it is now in a better position to comply with its obligations. In any case, it is only in countries where interest rates have remained low (and will continue to be held down) in spite of inflation that the stock of debt inherited from state socialism has all but resolved itself.

4.4 – A nearly costless resolution of bad debts?

Many observers of the transition have argued that the state should quickly come to grips with outstanding debts essentially by "taking over," socializing, or confiscating these loans in true shock-therapy mode. The main purpose would be to enable both SOEs and banks henceforth to function on their own account without being burdened by legacies for which, in most cases, the indebted economic entity was not responsible; but neither was the new government or the rejuvenating society! Unindebted SOEs and banks that carry only performing assets on their balance sheets would not only be able to respond more constructively to emerging market signals; they would also be more attractive vehicles for privatization once the decision to divest them is taken. Otherwise, it is argued (Levine and Scott 1993; IMF 1993), there will be endless debates on the true value of the debt, hence on the purchase price of firms to be privatized or reconstructed. Although this might facilitate the sale, it would not necessarily eliminate moral hazard. It might be justified if the seller had "better" information on the true value of the debt than the potential buyer. But it would manifestly not solve the problem of the banks, unless the government were to reimburse the relevant bank whose debt has now been conflated with the sale of the SOE for the appropriate "real" amount. Likewise, piecemeal debt resolution does not eliminate moral hazard.

The proffered, ostensibly clean and encompassing, solutions (Begg and Portes 1992, p. 20; OECD 1992, pp. 48–50) render the problem deceptively tractable. Of course, matters are not quite so simple. The problem debt must necessarily be identified fully within the context of the needs for the whole society, including the economy, given the aspirations of managers of the transition and core features of these countries. Many observers (see IMF 1993; Levine and Scott 1993) have actually argued that debt could be transferred to the state without, in fact, yielding sizable obligations that will eventually have to be covered from fiscal revenues. To anyone with a double-entry bookkeeping mind, once the renationalization option is precluded as unrealistic, this cannot be true (Brabant 1994a, b). It is an illusion that fundamentally confounds stocks and flows, and perceives the debt of an SOE, whether with respect to the bank or another SOE, as something that will not be serviced. The latter derives from a misconception about the nature of bad debt and the phasing of the transformation.

To an omniscient planner or a sole western evaluator the washout solution would seem self-evident on his assessment of the state's net worth, provided these assessments of asset and liability values can be implemented in practice in all units thus affected. Only then is "renationalization" a simple matter (Brabant 1994a, b). The same applies to attempts to net out interenterprise debts beyond what can be accomplished voluntarily in a binary fashion (Brabant 1994c). But one is then not really addressing the debt problem! In any case, even though this solution essentially calls for a transfer within the state sector and might strengthen corporate governance by bolstering retained earnings, it would apply only to successful firms. It would be meaningful solely if otherwise "market discipline" were to be enforceable (Brabant 1994d). This is hardly likely to be the case, including because of diffuse property rights, bad monitoring, and poorly functioning markets. In addition, though this solution does not affect public-sector debt it does impact on the ability of firms and banks to operate to the extent that net assets of actually or potentially profitable firms and banks are offset against the liabilities of actually or potentially unprofitable entities, thereby hampering restructuring. In any case, wiping out deposits not only would hamstring SOEs in their day-to-day operations, but also it might debilitate them so severely that massive and largely premature bankruptcy becomes inescapable.

The washout solution normally has fiscal implications that cannot be belittled, given the tight budget constraints under which most transition economies labor and the growing number of tasks entrusted to them (IMF 1997b). It adversely affects the credibility of any stabilization program. Furthermore, there is no reason to presume that the legacies of chronic principal–agent problems under state socialism now completely vanish. Agents entrusted with SOEs during the transition are unlikely to be monitored much better unless public-sector governance is quickly upgraded. But this has not so far been adequately explored (see Chapter 9). Who then can be expected to make a wise decision about the washout (the stock problem) or prevent the problem from recurring by having all agents henceforth act responsibly on behalf of owners (the flow problem) – by necessity overwhelmingly still the state?

Though the "bad debt" problem has not been ignored in most transition economies, no country has thus far resolved the issue, let alone peremptorily. All have at least tacitly aggravated the problem by imposing high nominal interest rates with a wide margin between lending and deposit rates to enable banks to form contingent reserves for bad loans, thus discouraging private borrowers; by allowing banks to continue to serve their "best" customers, which are the traditional SOEs; and by acquiescing in the buildup of arrears by SOEs, including in relations among themselves, by not enforcing bankruptcy. This stark contrast between rhetoric and real choice is paradoxical, at the very least. An illuminating explanation must encompass more than lack of insight in what needs to be done on the part of the managers of the transformation. The seeming contradiction can be resolved only against the broader backdrop of the transition agenda and transformation policies. Only then will it become clear that cleaning up the "old debt" simply *cannot* be an isolated component of transformation policies. Rather, it is *one* critical element of a much more convoluted economic, political, and social situation. In that sense, the acuteness of the problem has markedly abated through direct and indirect government action on bad debts and indeed by the improving business climate in the more successful countries.

4.5 – Tackling recapitalization

Since the essence of proper commercial-banking behavior is to attract deposits (even if short term) and on-lend them (even if for a longer period) at some risk covered through the bank's own resources, any operation designed to cleanse "bad debts" that does not fully replace their "market value" in the affected portfolios weakens the bank's capital base or simply confirms its already weakened base. Under the circumstance, it is rather hopeless to expect that commercial banks adequately deliver on their crucial tasks in an emergent market environment. An inadequate capital base in conjunction with rather sluggish saving behavior, and even averse predisposition of savers to relying on banks, hinders commercial banking. Special incentives for savers in "familiar" institutions may provide some fillip (Hannig 1994). Barring private initiative, the state needs to issue special financial assets in exchange for the debt to be serviced out of future fiscal revenues and encourage further capitalization, perhaps by bringing in a foreign partner. This might enable banks henceforth to begin to discharge their critical intermediating role in constructively moving ahead with the transformation.

Given their narrow resource base, banks can engage only in the most secure projects, of which there are likely to be few during the most volatile phase of transformation when bank intermediation would be most helpful in eliciting market-based restructuring. This puts a damper on private-sector entry, slows down the divestment of state-owned assets, inhibits the effective adoption of sensible regulatory policies and bank supervision (EBRD 1993), encumbers the development of a sound financial infrastructure for modernization, and complicates the restructuring of SOEs, notably of the banks themselves. Furthermore, because existing assets are of poor quality, with borrowers wantonly disregarding their debt obligations, exit is being impeded. This in turn inhibits the restructuring necessary to regain a new growth path.

Banks cannot afford to enforce bankruptcy proceedings against their borrowers in technical default even if its legal infrastructure exists, thus compounding the task of discharging their proper intermediating role. The prevailing stalemate is particularly debilitating in that banks cannot, in fact, mobilize short-term savings and ensure their allocation to longer-term investment in profitable ventures, including notably for new SMEs. Most commercial banks are in any case not involved in retail financial services as households for now prefer to keep their savings either "under the mattress" or at institutions – the savings banks in some form – that are expected to provide, if only implicitly and perhaps irrationally, near-ironclad deposit insurance. For better or worse savers expect the state sector to be backed up by the good faith of the reform-oriented government; but that might not be a good "rule" for as long as prudential regulations and supervision cannot be effectively enforced. At least for now banks either have to attract placements of the institutions that collect savings or they have to confine their lending to what is prudently loanable against their own resources (capital, reserves, borrowed funds, and limited deposits). Since capital and reserves are generally low for the cited reasons, efficiency considerations have played at best a marginal role in bank lending to date. This is impeding in particular the emergence and restructuring of the private sector, which for now depends largely on "family" assets and retained earnings. This might provide one justification for desisting from forcing the less onerous second economy from being formalized until rules can be enforced. At that stage a well-prepared one-off amnesty for that sector might well be in order.

By now, virtually all transition economies have enacted some recapitalization of existing banks, allowed the creation of new banks even in the absence of adequate prudential regulations and effective supervision (Pitiot and Scialom 1993), and encouraged the entry of foreign partners for domestic banks possibly together with divestment. To date only a limited impact on domestic banking operations, as distinct from the functions noted earlier, has been exerted. The most common recapitalization format has been the transfer of "bad assets" from commercial banks to the government or a government-created agency in exchange for some government-backed debt instrument, but at less than face value and below-market interest rates. This form of replacement poses technical questions (Calvo and Kumar 1993, p. 14), but these need not detain us here. It is hoped that the banks' asset base can thus be strengthened, that the situation for SOEs can be cleared up more generally, and that restructuring and divestment is facilitated. The essential premise is that banks now have "better assets" against which they can contract new loans, particularly to new firms, if necessary by trading the state's debt instruments in secondary markets (Aglietta and Moutot 1993, p. 92). Of course, the latter need first to emerge.

A particular twist on this scenario has been pursued in Bulgaria: Government bonds emitted at well below market interest rates can be acquired and used at face value in the privatization process (Dobrinsky 1994). Note that this entails the *de facto* destruction of assets that, in fact, belong to the state (or society as such). Elsewhere, notably in the case of Hungary and Poland, some debt-swaps have been arranged, the banks in effect becoming part owner of the client SOE. In Poland, this way of proceeding has been tied directly to bank privatization as well as the reconciliation of the debtors with the banks' outlook; failing that indebted SOEs are placed in bankruptcy or liquidated (Belka 1994; Slay and Vinton 1994). Also in this case the government's wealth is deliberately sacrificed and other claimants on SOEs entering into conciliation procedures lose their priority claim, and often their assets altogether. Whether credible hard-budget constraints can henceforth be enforced, thus helping to lay the foundations for economic transformation and in that sense make the operation worthwhile, remains to be seen (C. W. Gray and Holle 1996a, b).

Whatever the form of recapitalization and cleaning up of bad assets pursued, usually conjointly, the volume and variety of loanable funds at commercial banks remain highly confined for now, and commercial banks, whether privatized or not, continue to be in need of further capital infusions. They also must deepen their loan activities. Some funds can be attracted from abroad. However, gaining greater confidence on the part of savers, to augment the mass of savings kept in the formal sector, and of depositors, to funnel their savings through the commercial-banking system, remains a high priority.

4.6 – Strengthening commercial-bank behavior

As noted, banking knowledge gathered under state socialism is not particularly useful for engaging in truly commercial operations, whether restricted to the four I have emphasized or not. As regards effecting smooth settlement of reciprocal payments, the transmission of payments within, and even more among, transition economies remains slow. Certainly, the acquisition of modern technology and automation may help. But more is required particularly in terms of organization and management so that up-to-date technology can be put to best use. Only then will the reciprocal payment system function at low transaction costs and contribute to formalizing part of the operations that are now conducted in the informal sector in cash or at usurious informal rates.

Because commercial banks in principle collect savings from multiple depositors and lend them to few investors, the safety of deposits depends on the ability and willingness of the banks to administer the funds in the depositors' best interest. Since this principal–agent problem is often overloaded with moral hazard, a substantial role devolves to the state to protect depositors through its supervisory functions and various prudential regulations, such as deposit insurance or minimum reserve requirements. These might reassure depositors in the absence of other capital markets, provided the risk commercial banks take is not too onerous for that would require government bailouts. That risk depends on the banks' "information capital," which must be deepened and widened. Because proprietary information is arguably the bread and butter of financial institutions, there is presently a very substantial backlog on gathering, processing, and applying elementary information and related skills. Filling this gap is critical in order to compress transaction costs and make a profit on loans in all transition economies. Moreover, impersonal transactions require costly specification and enforcement mechanisms such as rating and supervisory systems, whose informational needs transcend those invoked earlier. Because these systems too are in statu nascendi, many actors are for now sticking to well-established business routines with known clients.

Finally, even as concerns the marketing of new financial instruments, the drive to innovate beyond the commercialization of government-debt instruments has remained lackluster. Banks not only have to gain the confidence of savers, but also have to innovate financial-asset instruments in which savers want to keep some of their wealth. The road yet to be traveled until other credible capital-market intermediaries surface, remains long and arduous. Training and the transfer of basic technical assistance on these matters would be highly useful, though they do not by any means provide a magical solution.

275

4.7 – Enforcing discipline

Besides taking deposits and extending credit, banks normally carry out a number of other activities, such as in the areas of payment settlements, custody of assets, and management of investments (Guitián 1993). These can give rise to serious conflicts such as mismatch of assets and liabilities, low capitalization, and unduly risky asset portfolios. For that reason, banks are usually subject to official supervision and regulation. The aim is to promote bank safety and soundness and to maintain confidence in the financial system as a whole. Transition economies suffer from inadequate regulation, poor prudential regulation, ineffective supervision possibly for lack of trained personnel, and lack of experience with applying and enforcing the rules on the books. This is perhaps less the case for market-entry requirements and capital-adequacy rules than for balance-sheet control and application of prudential regulations. Depositor protection is frequently poor and systemic support from the central bank as lender of last resort suffers from the fact that it cannot be confined, as it should, to emergency situations and provided at a relatively high price, if only as an effective deterrent.

Even though banking skills may be slowly emerging, the importance of adequate prudential regulations and of applying strict banking supervision deserves emphasis. Both the central and commercial banks for now lack reliable information about the financial condition of firms and the banks themselves. They have limited experience in risk analysis of potential borrowers. Furthermore, they have limited knowledge about the intrinsic worth of their past borrowers, inadequate tax regimes for making loan-loss provisions, lack experienced supervisors and auditors, and prudential regulations leave a lot to be desired (Blommestein 1993).

Section 5: Capital, credit, and risk markets

Effective intermediation in resource allocation over time, other than through fairly simple commercial-banking operations, is the prime task of all kinds of capital and credit markets. The same holds for managing intertemporal risk via insurance markets. For simplicity's sake I lump all under the label capital markets. With a dose of stabilization, liberalization, and divestment of petty assets markets for goods and services can be expected to begin to function appropriately, if imperfectly (Sapir 1993). This cannot, however, be presumed to hold also for intertemporal allocation of assets and risks, if only because on the transition's eve capital and credit markets lack depth and breadth (Calvo and Frenkel 1991b) and abatement of uncertainty is a prerequisite for forging ahead with the tasks at hand.

The need for capital markets and the order in which they should be fostered may be envisioned by taking a step back and reflecting once again upon what markets should accomplish. The production process combines various primary and intermediate inputs with the goal of generating outputs yielding a "profit" for the producer and owner. Production factors can be viewed as potentially providing a sequence of services to be allocated in the most effective way to economic activities, whence the greatest profit is expected to be obtained. For most factors there is a foreseeable end to that stream, at least in probabilistic terms, as amortization in economic terms is unavoidable. The intensity with which this service stream can be produced during the lifetime of the "asset" as a rule varies. But there are several ways in which greater efficiency in the mobilization of these service streams can be contemplated. To do so one must be clear about the meaning of capital. It could be taken to mean physical infrastructure (such as the prodigious amounts of machinery, large-scale factories and plants, stores, stocks of finished and unfinished materials, knowledge, and skills used in modern industry) or material and other wealth. But then wealth itself depends on the value placed on its components, hence on what "capital" may mean.

Essential is that capital goods are utilized as inputs for further production. As John Hicks (1983, p. 97, original emphasis) put it, "capital, the *real* capital, of any economy extends the whole way from very durable instruments . . . to goods that are *in the pipeline*, goods in process of production." Because production evolves in time during which inputs are followed by outputs, capital is an expression of sequential production and, therefore, must have a time structure. This means that capital must belong to the *stream* of inputs giving rise to a *stream* of outputs. It is then the pricing of making available the particular elements of that stream of inputs expected to yield a stream of outputs that is at the heart of capital and its proper evaluation.

But capital need not be valued solely for its potential to yield goods and services as perceived by the present owner. Indeed, some components of tangible and some intangible (such as patents and copyright) wealth are appropriable by various agents. The institutions that enable trading in these real and financial properties are called capital markets. Property markets, as the name suggests, enable trading in real assets. Financial markets allow inside assets and debts to be originated and to be exchanged at will for each other and for outside financial assets. By convention, outside assets equal private net worth, consisting of privately owned items of national wealth, mostly tangible assets, and government obligations. These are as a rule held not directly but through the intermediation of a complex network of debts and claims, which constitute inside assets (see Tobin 1987, p. 341).

In this context, it is important to stress that tradability of capital assets and/ or of their service stream soonest into the transition is far more critical to the emergence of viable capital markets than having available the entire panoply of capital-market institutions. Specialization necessarily emerges, provided it is not inhibited, when a broader range of activities can no longer be efficiently catered to in one market that functioned relatively smoothly for some period of time. Equally important in ensuring such tradability is that the exchange can take place at a reasonable transaction cost, whose size relative to the perceived benefits of the transaction for those incurring the cost must be compressed over time. That, after all, is the essence of specialization.

Debates on the creation of a capital market have tended to treat technical matters with considerable political and ideological overtones. I shall avoid that. To my mind, the emergence of key capital markets for intertemporal intermediation (such as merchant and investment banking, real estate, stock exchanges, and insurance companies for all kinds of risk) cannot be a *deus ex machina*. Instead, the acute need for such instruments and institutions emerges gradually, in conjunction with the establishment of the proper "market institutions" with their enabling incentives. Critical here are market pressures associated with the path carved by the financial-marketing functions (including for public debt, enterprise bonds, debt-swaps in divestment campaigns, or even facilitating transactions on the stock market) performed by commercial banks early on in the transformation once they have gained control over the elementary tasks discussed earlier. In time, these tasks will surpass the capabilities of the banking sector. Proper "assignment rules" then call for establishing other components of what will in time grow into a full-fledged capital market. Their intensity and breadth depend on the nature and volume of transactions to be intermediated. Only in this way can the institutions that buttress a modernizing market economy be meaningfully completed. But markets may have to pressure government to create the enabling environment.

As the market economy develops, eventually there will emerge a competitive network of financial institutions of domestic and foreign origin placed within a sensible legal framework. Some are highly organized auction markets, such as for bonds, shares, overnight loans of outside money, standard commodities, and foreign currency including for futures. Here the concept of market is as its origin suggests. But many financial and property transactions occur in direct negotiations between buyer and seller. This is especially the case for goods and services that are not available in large tradable quantities or in precisely defined commodities or financial instruments. The concept market in this case is used metaphorically, of course. As the above suggests, capital markets may eventually become very complex institutions that play a central role in determining and bolstering the vitality of economic activity. They encompass many components, and it may, therefore, be useful to inquire into the order in which they should preferably be introduced, given the imperatives of the transition. Looked at in this manner, the desirability of moving forward with the various components of capital markets, once the rudiments of commercial banking are in place, can be ranked as follows: banking in all of its aspects, insurance markets, credit markets, real estate, money markets, and securities markets. The latter two could possibly be inverted.

Market pressures in and of themselves do not suffice to inaugurate functioning capital markets. Market failures are acute notably in capital markets, and they must be eased especially in the early stages of transition. Capital markets must operate to the benefit of society, while protecting the interests of all legitimate economic agents, in the first instance those directly involved in such transactions. Transactions must be transparent. In other words, the capital market must reveal information to economic agents, partly in response to the latter's insistence. For that regulatory powers have to be instituted, given asymmetric information, moral hazard, reputational problems, and adverse-selection problems to name only some of the more onerous facets of "wild capitalism" (Bohn and Levey 1991; Stiglitz 1991b, pp. 8ff.). These encompass prudential regulations and effective surveillance to ensure that transactions are actually in the reasonable interest of all potential parties concerned. It does not suffice to carefully draft rules and regulations. They must also be enforceable, for which trained professionals are needed who gradually learn on the job (Sundararajan 1996).

Much has been made of the importance of the stock exchange for emerging market economies. Indeed, such institutions might conceivably play a useful demonstration role (Atje and Jovanovic 1993; Harris 1997). But to expect them to perform wonders, especially in terms of yielding sources of finance for existing and new firms or of information about the worth of existing assets, transcends what can logically be derived from such "institutions." Even in a mature market economy, until recently relatively little capital has been raised through new equity issues. Also, little capital tends to be raised through secondary equity issues. Rather than looking at the stock market as offering mechanisms for raising funds for new ventures or even for expanding relatively new ventures, it should be treated, by and large, more as a facility for trading shares in secondary markets, certainly during the early phases of building a functioning market economy. This conjecture not only recognizes realities. Portfolio theory suggests that the best way for a new firm to finance itself initially is not through a public issue of stock, but by procuring funds through bank loans, silent partnerships of venture capitalists, or resources pooled otherwise. Stock flotations on a functioning stock market are rather rare. They are mostly confined to a certain category of capital funds. There is good evidence to presume that the more efficient contribution of the stock market in enhancing allocation is not in raising initial venture capital but in providing funds for activities that have already proved their mettle (Corbett and Mayer 1991; Singh 1990). Once the venture succeeds and its capital needs become too large to be financed (for example, by banks, venture capitalists, or partnerships) a public stock offering can be entertained.

Reflecting the frame of reference that runs through the above discussion, I do not rank very highly the creation of a securities market as an instrument for spurring on the transition. Essential transactions for commercial purposes, particularly for private portfolios of modest dimension, can be accommodated by channeling them through the commercial-banking system, once that becomes operational. Certainly, the stock market can perform a very valuable function at some stage of market maturity. But it cannot be very productive in terms of moving along the initial phases of the transition process and laying solid foundations for a new, self-sustainable growth path in a market environment until it can yield dependable, transparent, and adequate information for economic agents to act upon in their portfolio decisions.

Why is it appropriate to consider securities markets to be an important "market institution" at a more mature phase of building a vibrant market economy? Stock markets in particular, but also markets for fixed-income securities more generally, in essence fulfill at least three critical functions. They should provide vehicles for sharing risk and for guiding investment decisions. The latter applies in particular to outsiders. For now those managing firms base their investment decisions mostly on proprietary information, rather than on how their securities are faring. That information is, by definition, not readily externalized or, for that matter, available to outsiders. Second, securities markets should facilitate the measurement of asset values, in particular to outsiders, whether owners of securities or not. Finally, they should potentially raise the value of assets by providing "strategic information," that is, information that, if acted upon, increases the firm's value (Tirole 1991). Securities markets tend to function best when there is considerable certainty in the macroeconomic, political, and social environments. This is not so in the early stages of transition for reasons spelled out in Chapter 3. The uncertainty that prevails in transition economies, especially during the early phases of transformation, has implications notably for the functioning of securities markets. Four stand out.

First, the informational value of stocks for measuring managerial performance is very inaccurate. Price fluctuations under the circumstances of transition reflect more the "noise" in the firm's environment than the manager's ability to enhance the market value of the firm; and stock-market participants (and other economic agents) are more engaged in learning about emerging markets for goods, services, labor, and capital – and indeed about new government policies – than about how best to monitor managerial performance. Although this reduces uncertainty about the firm's exogenous environment and allows for better control of managers by core owners, the cost of this uncertainty is eventually borne by the firm's owners.

Second, market analysts depend on accounting structures (of revenues, sales, costs, depreciation, and amortization) that are reliable, undistorted, and relatively homogeneous across firms. It would be extremely naïve to expect these conditions to be met rapidly during the transition. There may be some room for western assistance in setting up accounting systems – a valuable educational experience (see Chapter 11). But it would not quickly solve the uncertainty that derives from the present inadequate state of accounting and disclosure of firm-specific information.

Third, it will take time to set up an efficient system of financial regulation. Thus, it will be very difficult to fight insider trading without having a modern system to keep track of transactions or to avoid a fair amount of trading being based on private information about forthcoming government actions without the government putting in place an infrastructure of safeguards. But the transition's managers have such a full plate of "very urgent tasks" on their table that I doubt they can be swayed early on to erect efficient financial regulatory mechanisms.

Finally, garbled stock-market prices may give the wrong signals to restructuring. True, there is no ideal way, in the sense of avoiding mistakes, in which the transition economies can be efficiently restructured. But there would seem to be fewer mistakes embodied in seeking restructuring through other means than the stock market. Historically, and logically, coming to grips with principal–agent problems through operations in securities markets, in particular stock exchanges, is essentially a luxury of advanced capitalism.

In short, I deem it appropriate to introduce with determination a stock market once the current noisy phase will have been surmounted. Even after the legal framework of ownership; contract, bankruptcy, and antitrust laws; disclosure rules; and so on will have been put in place, and professionals (auditors, analysts, managers, and so on) trained, securities markets will not run smoothly overnight. Opening stock markets to individuals, to newly created firms, to institutional investors, and possibly to foreigners as such is not likely to create the minimum liquidity required to motivate analysts into estimating the firms' values and discovering synergies. Without some viable trading, such as in the case of dominant shareholders, there is little incentive for analysts to "invest" in information on the basis of which they can trade themselves or persuade others to risk their capital. The consequences of immersing small investors in such an uncertain market can be devastating as many of the pyramid schemes in nearly all transition economies have quickly underlined.

In other words, in order for a stock market to play a constructive role in the firm rooting of the eventual complexity of a modern market economy, it must generate accurate and useful information about firm values; create an appropriate structure of control with large shareholders; give incentives for large shareholders or their agents to monitor and invest in information; and prevent the formation of cartels. None of these tasks can be accomplished in an orderly and reliable manner early on in the transition. In recognition thereof, the elements of the capital market for which this degree of uncertainty can be decreased expeditiously should be established first; hence my emphasis on commercial banking (Brainard 1991; Corbett and Mayer 1991; Levitas 1990; Rybczyński 1991a, b; Singh 1990) and building further on from there once procompetition and regulatory rules ensure the existence of a more or less stable environment for the stock market to play a positive role. Among the latter extensions I include the creation of private pension funds, including the management of assets presently held by state pension funds, and of a diverse range of insurance to cover most shades of risk. There is plenty of historical evidence on the evolution of capitalism that once all this functions satisfactorily, stock and bond markets that enhance the intertemporal allocation of resources and regulate the acquisition and disposal of wealth in all its forms discussed earlier are appropriate. For that to occur, financial institutions must eventually be permitted to innovate new instruments and emulate those already embraced in some mature market economies. But the need for diversity and variety in domestic capital markets at best emerges gradually.

Far more important than stock markets is to push for a reasonably functioning mortgage market. Very often, real estate constitutes the vast bulk of assets of households or of desirable portfolios. While real-estate transactions without a mortgage market are possible, the vast majority of households would be excluded from them without the ability to collateralize their real estate in some form. Although in the very initial phases mortgage loans can conceivably be arranged through commercial banks, this is likely to prove insufficient, particularly once "petty privatization" or restitution encompasses a considerable proportion of the existing housing stock. With the emergence of new firms, the need for commercial mortgages rises as well.

Given the prevailing uncertainty (see Chapter 3), an entire gamut of insurance operations must emerge in some fashion and rather quickly because of the lost certainties of state socialism and thus risks that now need to be covered privately. These range from transforming state-socialist insurance, such as for automobile and fire liability, to new kinds of risk insurance called for by the uncertainties and insecurity engendered by moving toward a market economy with exceedingly poor state authority for some time to come. One should consider here those risks that are generally covered in programs directed by the state. Pension, health, and unemployment schemes immediately spring to mind (see Chapter 8). These are quite different from the new kinds of insurance that agents in the transition economy may wish to consider. Surely, fire insurance assumes completely different dimensions with the privatization of housing and the emergence of functioning real-estate markets. Likewise, bank-deposit insurance in various forms must be made explicit, if desirable at all. Coverage for risk of portfolios held at brokerage houses will have to be considered to avoid the proliferation of all kinds of financial scams.

One way in which the capital market can be given a jump-start is by transforming existing institutions into capital-market actors or to create new financial institutions with the goal of fueling that market. The former could be accomplished by divesting the state of assets in return for taking over some of its liabilities. Candidates would be various types of insurance companies, social-security agencies, pension funds, and similar state organizations. The alternative is to create special mutual funds, holding companies, investment funds, or privatization agencies and entrust them with monitoring some category of companies as core investors, but whose shares could also be contested by other fund managers. Furthermore, the ultimate owners of such funds would be the population at large as a result of the free or nearly free distribution of shares or claims (see Chapter 6).

Section 6: Labor markets

The character, speed, and efficiency of the transition depend on the creation of effective labor markets. Fostering them is technically perhaps easier than introducing capital markets. At the same time, it is more difficult owing to the overprotection of labor under state socialism and the expectation of wide layers of the population to remain substantially insulated against untoward circumstances. The choice for workers between allotting time to work and leisure has by and large been uninhibited for years. Yet, labor markets prior to transition remained embryonic at best. There was little flexibility in negotiating labor contracts and accommodating in particular the tradeoff between leisure and work; the only option was joining the second economy, but that itself offered limited, if special, but in time expanding opportunities.

Promoting functioning labor markets not only involves the abolition of the job-security system and tailoring wages to effort and result, but also calls for putting in place safeguards against the most deleterious economic, psychological, and social consequences of involuntary unemployment and growing job insecurity; promoting labor mobility and retraining; and seeking a *modus vivendi* among effective labor unions, management, and government to ensure that labor rights are protected, yet not abused for whimsical reasons. Industrial relations need to be restructured with the recognition of genuine trade unions that take to heart the socioeconomic interests of their members as well as of the country as a whole. It is also desirable to foster greater cohesion among management. But one should have no illusion that collective bargaining, or other labor-market institutions, can be set up quickly or smoothly, given the experience of the trade-union movement in many mature market economies. Some form of worker participation in firms through profit sharing or even ESOPs may be desirable. Whether this emerges depends very much on the place and role of trade unions and societal preferences for the kind of industrial organization in core economic activities.

The process of establishing labor markets, then, includes the elimination of the drawbacks of state socialism, the creation of the institutions upon which flexible labor markets rest both on the side of the supply and demand for labor, encouraging the formation of trade unions that can genuinely represent their membership and take to heart the broader social interest of labor and the country, and to do likewise on the side of employers, and indeed for managers of the transition to structure the policies under their ward with a view to reaching high employment levels. Restructuring the negative aspects of virtually non-existing labor markets under state socialism is easy. Flexible labor markets under that regime were virtually redundant because of chronic overemployment, the poor link between effort and reward, and the state-socialist nature of virtually all economic operations. There are other features of inherited labor markets that need to be thoroughly restructured soon, hopefully in a socially compassionate manner (see Chapter 8).

The goal should be to arrive at flexible labor markets at the earliest opportunity. This requires actions on both the demand and the supply side of labor. As far as the demand for labor is concerned, institutions must be put in place that funnel appropriate information about job vacancies from employers to those seeking work or another job. At the same time, whereas employers should be able to determine by and large their firm-specific relationship between labor productivity and reward, a free-for-all is a recipe for depressing real wages to the lowest common denominator particularly at times of substantial unemployment (see Chapter 8). There may well be a need to institute something like a collective-bargaining process. The same holds for trade unions. They must genuinely take to heart the interests of their membership but are able and willing also to sub-ordinate their narrower interests to the overriding goals of transformation and wealth-generation over the longer haul. Without some concertation between demand for and supply of labor, possibly with the government or its agents as intermediators, however, it may be difficult to assure stability in the labor market and peace on the labor front while propping up aggregate demand at a high level.

The government has a special responsibility not only in facilitating the concer-tation between employers and employees. Indeed, its role in insuring against involuntary unemployment should be substantial. This requires passive as well as active labor-market intervention. Passive measures are essentially designed to ensure that the unemployed do not lose all sources of income and social protection. It is therefore necessary to put in place unemployment-insurance schemes, something that was all but unheard of under state socialism. Among the active labor-market policies (ALMPs), central and local governments need to create labor exchanges, where the unemployed or those desirous of changing jobs can register and obtain information on work opportunities. Training and retraining are also required to ensure that the unemployed have a decent chance of being rehired without losing all too much time being out of employment. The market environment requires in any case skills that in many instances differ from those needed under state socialism and that the formal educational system cannot provide to adults. While at least primary and secondary education is a public good from which present adults have benefited in the past, retraining those being laid off also constitutes a public good. It is in the interest of the transformation – economically, socially, politically, psychologically, and otherwise – to see to it that those being laid off get rehired at the earliest opportunity. Part and parcel of labor markets, though here one ventures into the more social aspects of the social safety net, is taking care of those who cannot be reemployed or employed for whatever reason. Whereas it is in the interest of society to encourage "churning," that is, to avoid long-term unemployment that renders the jobless eventually unemployable, managers of the transition must be aware of a category of people with skills no longer required and beyond training (see Chapter 8).

The above already suggests that government has a special place in rearranging labor markets through direct intervention. But it has also a unique responsibility in seeing to it that the economic environment stays buoyant for near-full employment. Macroeconomic policies need to be revamped in such a way that, once stabilization is regained, they encourage high levels of economic activity and labor demand. But also in other aspects of steering society, it is incumbent on managers of the transition to foster high levels of employment, to reduce the risks of unemployment, to minimize unemployment spells, to facilitate mobility of workers and their families, and so on.

With the transition's inception the emphasis is on deregulating labor markets soonest. Recall from Chapter 3 that policy makers expected the economic recession to be mild and to be comparatively short-lived. Once these hopes were dashed, and the depression worsened in depth and duration, with a potential calamity on the labor front in sight, measures were taken to alleviate the situation. This was at first conceived largely within the context of supporting the sociopolitical consensus rather than as a core component of managing the economy. Only later were more flexible methods embraced and targeted at stirring the unemployment pool from various fronts. As experience has amply demonstrated, forcing through rather liberal policies gives rise to peculiar behavior in SOEs, to social resistance to reform policies, to untenable levels of regional unemployment, to rapidly expanding social support that cannot be financed or for which there is no longer a minimal sociopolitical consensus, and to political disarray that weakens incipient democracy (Bresser Pereira, Maravall, and Przeworski 1993).

To characterize unemployment as a problem for policy makers, it must be clear who are the unemployed, why they find themselves in this predicament, and what specific remedial issues figure on the policy agenda. Individuals may intuitively be regarded as involuntarily unemployed if they are out of work but available for, and seeking, work at the prevailing wage, suitably normalized for productivity differences. From an economic perspective, the unemployed must, in some sense, be those whose reservation wage exceeds the prospective value of their contribution to production, when all measures are properly normalized and the unavoidable transaction costs of hiring and firing are taken into account (Lindbeck 1993). This may be because they confront a more confined choice set between work and leisure than the employed, perhaps because of the "wedge" driven between the net benefit of work to the individual and the marginal productivity of labor to the employer.

Aggregate unemployment derives to a large extent from underlying macro- and microeconomic conditions. As a rule, the real wage, employment, and unemployment are determined jointly within a setting of imperfectly competitive product and labor markets for both the employee and the employer. These clarify why real wages do not fall – at any rate, do not fall sufficiently – in the wake of involuntary unemployment, as classical labor theory would have it. Furthermore, even if employment growth were to outpace the labor force's, this would bring temporary respite only if the fall in unemployment itself had unsustainable economic consequences. Such an event may be associated with a wage demand that does not exceed the marginal product of labor at full employment, but there is insufficient aggregate demand to guide the economy back to full employment, as in Keynesian labor theory. However, if unemployment performs the disciplining function of staving off wage increases, thus pressure on the price level or on profitability, unemployment cutbacks could only be very limited or temporary, unless substantial changes in the patterns of wage- and price-setting were in prospect. This suggests that demand-management by itself cannot solve the problem. Streamlining the wage-bargaining process may significantly ease that managerial task, however. Three supplementary observations are in order.

First, to identify and explain the nature of the involuntary unemployed, it is important to recognize institutional and behavioral features of labor markets and to come to grips with the determinants of these phenomena as well as with the factors that undergird their dynamics. Second, it does not suffice to look only at the aggregate aspects of involuntary unemployment because neither the demand for nor the supply of labor is homogeneous. Firms seek specific skills for a particular job and the involuntary unemployed do not enter the labor market simply to seek a job yielding some positive wage. Finally, the category of the involuntary unemployed is not necessarily easily identified, either in theory or in practice. This complicates relevant policy analysis. These observations are particularly germane to transition economies, given the convoluted markets and the intransparency of labor markets in particular.

In all this one should recall that even in mature economies labor markets do not function smoothly if observed levels of unemployment are any indication. Particularly disturbing are the chronic long-term unemployed, the magnitude of youth unemployment, and the inability of workers once laid off to retrain themselves without some ALMPs, necessarily supported by government. Without such policies, given still inchoate markets, the sociopolitical costs of experimental transformation agendas turn out to be exorbitant. They therefore deserve to be contained through interventions that in fact amount to subsidizing employment. These can best be embedded in a purposeful policy directed at enhancing the transformation process through an orderly destruction of assets that cannot survive and the creative movement toward a new, self-sustainable modernization process (see Chapter 12).

For reasons of sociopolitical stability (see Chapter 8), employment in obsolete activities – the core of the "old" state sector, in some cases even after nominal divestment – cannot be eliminated in record tempo, employment creation in the private sector lags significantly behind the pace required to soak up desirable layoffs in the state sector and new entrants, and restructuring social-welfare provisions traditionally passed on through the socialized sectors has proved to be a cumbersome exercise (Boeri 1994, 1995; Burda 1995; Franz 1995). For these and related reasons, many transition economies maintain some subsidy. That is to say, policy makers have learned the hard way that labor-market pressures can be alleviated only over time and through compromise, involving a good deal of social transfers in order to maintain social peace (Moene and Wallerstein 1993; Przeworski 1993).

The measured elaboration and gradual implementation of a social-democratic labor-market policy would be desirable for reasons of history, fairness, and the type of society the transition economies appear to be aspiring to. I use the notion social democracy in its more positive sense, namely a society in which workers' power is exerted through strong unions aligned with, but preferably neither directly tied to nor dependent on the political parties dominant in parliament. Given the prevailing instability in party structures and in pluralistic decision making during transition, such comparative independence but willingness to cooperate and compromise, including with government and the legislature, is even more desirable than in a well-established democracy. Whereas it encompasses centralized trade unions and a system of regular consultation and cooperation among government, unions, and employer organizations, such a social-democratic labor-market policy should certainly not be structured so as eventually to give rise to corporatism or a misguided welfare state. Instead it requires a common understanding on the desirability of solidaristic bargaining; on access to basic goods and services as a citizen's right, perhaps reflecting some of the earlier traditions of these societies; and on a government's commitment to pursuing near-full employment policies, including through ALMPs with the social safety net explicitly tailored to the stage of transformation attained.

The emergence of such a flexibly managed market can be best pictured within an evolutionary perspective. It would by and large emulate the early postwar (say until the mid-1960s) policies of western Europe around a fundamental bargain among unions, which secure real-wage restraint; government, which seeks to prevent unemployment through its own economic and social policies; but also a host of NPOs other than the labor unions devoted to enhancing governance (see Chapter 8). A genuine industrial policy in the sense of government taking a proactive role in economic management, but not necessarily in specific SOEs, let alone intrusive interference in the private sector, may well be contemplated in this context. ALMPs would constitute one important component thereof (Brabant 1993a; Chang 1994). The emergence of corporatism and the welfare state with all of its potential excesses, and indeed the rupture of this implicit contract, should be prevented. The risk that such may materialize as a logical consequence of the inability to fine-tune the social contract with modernization gains is very real and cannot be ignored. Indeed, vested rights tend to become ossified if central decision makers hold on to policies that are no longer suitable to the situation at hand, until circumstances force a rupture of the institutions and policies distinctive of the cited social democracy. But those concerns, while they should be kept in the back of policy makers' minds, should not be too worrisome in the earlier phases of the transition economies. They should certainly not be an excuse for embracing unbridled liberalism as a panacea (see Chapter 8).

Section 7: Information, the market, and the state

I deal with the state as but one critical, though special, "institution" of the market in Chapter 9. It is appropriate to flag up here aspects of the economic role of the state that are not normally dealt with in the context of moving toward the market economy, that is the embedded role of information, the institutions that ensure coordination of several transformation tasks touched upon earlier, and the organs associated with generating and maintaining social cohesion.

7.1 – Quantitative and qualitative information

Coordination of the decisions of multiple agents via indirect instruments in a market environment hinges critically on the availability of accurate and ample information on economic and other matters (UNECE 1990, pp. 16–17). Not only that, such information must be disseminated on a timely basis as widely as resources permit. The considerable economic, political, and social uncertainty hanging over these societies (see Chapter 3) should at least not be exacerbated by the poor predictability, reliability, and transparency in the "information" disseminated by economic actors, including central authorities.

One of the critical props of the neoclassical paradigm is that information is readily available at no cost. That is simply not so in the real world. It applies neither to quantitative information nor to qualitative information, both of which are essential inputs in formulating rational decisions. The private sector as a rule does not provide such services; or if it does, it tends to focus on *ad hoc* inquiries motivated by private investment considerations. The provision of comprehensive and reliable statistics, for example, is a public good that is essential for the efficient working of a modern market economy. It must therefore be furnished by the public sector or it will not be available, or only inadequately, to agents. Producing such information depends in part on a well-trained, -organized, and -equipped public administration (see Chapter 9).

Whereas in mature market economies private firms often invest in collecting their own data, based, for example, on sample surveys that they finance, a considerable amount of market information is culled from official statistics; that is, statistical activities forming part and parcel of central governance financed largely through budgetary appropriations. The situation in the transition economies is such that few firms are for now able, both organizationally and financially, to generate such information themselves or to support the private provisioning of data collection, organization, and dissemination. At least for now, such information is either provided by government or not at all. In the latter case, a good deal of the uncertainty that has complicated transition policies will not be eliminated. Absence of such fundamental information heightens unrealistic expectations on the part of economic agents or distorts them. This exacerbates the degree of frustration in case of failure that would be considered normal under market conditions.

An efficient market economy not only needs accurate statistics on the variables covered under state socialism, but also needs different types of statistics for use in both public and private sectors, including NPOs. For one thing, macroeconomic policy relies on various instruments of fiscal and monetary policy, rather than on direct controls, and, as such, requires a broader menu of data than those useful under state socialism. Some can be generated from the primary sources only after the appropriate institutions, such as the central bank and the fiscal authorities, have been erected. Furthermore, reliable statistics as well as more qualitative economic and commercial information, in addition to data sets on other variables (such as demographics for market research), become essential for decentralized, not necessarily private, firms to reach their own production and distribution decisions, including notably on investment, in response to market signals.

Perhaps most important, the essence of the transformation is structural change in the enterprise sphere. Without the authorities having at their command comprehensive and reliable economic data it is difficult to monitor the progress made in shifting toward the market economy and to track the adjustment of behavior of economic and other agents to the new incentive systems. Such data are essential to assessing policies in place and refining them, perhaps also augmenting them with new policies, as the transformation is being implemented. Finally, effective participation of the transition economies in regional and global organizations depends on their willingness and ability to provide standard information.

7.2 – Institutions of supervision, coordination, and management

In the course of this excursion I have touched upon the need for setting up several state and related institutions to ensure properly functioning markets. These may be entirely temporary, such as an agency overseeing the divestment effort. Or they may be permanent, such as the institutions entrusted with enforcing and supervising bank regulations; the governance organs for SOEs that remain in the public domain or that will prospectively be erected by the public sector; and the quasi-insurance organs of government, such as pension funds, health insurance, and unemployment compensation (see Chapter 8). Some may be set up solely at the behest of government or parliament. Others are instituted to serve the political institutions. The civil service's role in economic affairs immediately springs to mind (see Chapter 9). I cannot here examine all of these organs. Some are the subject of the next two chapters and others have already been dealt with earlier. I should like to emphasize here the role of two important institutions.

One critical shortcoming of state socialism was poor monitoring of the state's assets; the comparable problem for the transition is how best to safeguard those assets until they can be divested or governance rules can be put in place for assets remaining in the public sector. If governance capabilities can be mustered, it might be useful to entrust state assets to some quasi-independent agency, perhaps subject to parliamentary supervision, to manage these assets and to take decisions on which SOEs to be privatized as distinct from others to be kept in the state's hands. The first could be placed under the supervision of a privatization agenda proper, which by definition is temporary, while assigning others to a state asset-management agency, which by definition will be more permanent.

The order in which these two agencies are set up depends, of course, on available capabilities as well as on the danger of "rent seeking" in the public sector. Thus the process could be started off by having a privatization agency as the first step toward severing the nexus between government and its clientelistic agencies from the decision making about the use of state assets. In its first order of business it would have to make a decision in principle about which assets to divest and others to be kept in the public domain. Alternatively, those decisions could be taken at the policy-making level, utilizing the privatization agency essentially as the executor of the political decision to divest and an asset-management agency as the guardian of SOEs selected to remain in the public domain.

It would be preferable to constitute the privatization agency as the executor of the political decisions to privatize. That is to say, it should not be in charge of writing a privatization law, let alone a reform statute for the public sector. That should ideally be the privilege of parliament in conjunction with a special ministerial portfolio, such as for privatization. The agency would then be entrusted with divesting the assets chosen by policy makers, including determination of the modalities and sequencing of privatization; with ensuring that in the interim these assets are used to best advantage, including by enforcing the corporatization and gradually the commercialization of SOEs; with putting in place rules on supervision and management, perhaps in coordination with the asset-management agency; and with exploring all forms of privatization other than divestment until the latter can realistically be entertained (recall that for some assets divestment is not possible, and so the agency would need to work out, for example, rules for leasing and management contracts).

Privatization in transition economies has been pursued in a highly authoritarian mode. Virtually all have entrusted at least one agency with privatization tasks, meaning as a rule divestment. This may be either a formal cabinet ministry or a quasi government agency with broad executive powers functioning under close supervision of the government and/or parliament. Few commentators have questioned the desirability of such a move as a first step in getting in particular divestment under way. But few have commented on what should be done to safeguard these assets in the interim, just like those remaining in the public domain. The agency has invariably been far more concerned with divestment modalities than with caring about the best use of its custodial assets during the divestment process. The reason has been various. But one erroneous assumption has been that divestment could be spurred along rather quickly and with minimal chicanery; hence that there would simply be no need for managing state assets to be divested.

Given the difficulties of divestment and the legitimate role for other forms of privatization (Chapter 6), the functions of a properly structured privatization agency should remain of some interest for some time to come. Assets yet to be divested should be better managed, just like assets remaining in the public domain are in dire need of different managerial and supervisory rules, if only to ensure an appropriate "destruction" as soon as the sociopolitical environment permits forging ahead with "creation." All legislative ambiguities about privatization, including restitution and compensation, and indeed recognition of the implicit property rights of managers, workers, and the population as a whole, should preferably be resolved at the political level, that is, government and/or parliament. The agency would "simply" have to see to the best implementation of the politically negotiated mandates.

The privatization agency should be staffed principally with professionals rather than politicians for it to become an effective buffer between the policy-making levels with their various clientelistic tentacles and users of state assets. It should have a managing and supervisory board endowed with incentives to render efficient resource allocation their main interest. Its tasks should be restrained to those cited above: the entire range of issues around divestment, corporatization and commercialization, nondivestment forms of privatization, working out rules of protecting assets to be privatized, elaborating lease and contract terms, liaising with the political bodies as well as related agencies (notably the one entrusted with management of SOEs remaining in the public domain), and so on.

Seen in this perspective, it is self-evident that the privatization agency's terms of reference are considerable and varying over time. Also, it would be unrealistic to expect it to be dissolved quickly. This does, of course, raise the issue of setting up a new bureaucracy with the ability eventually to develop tentacles throughout society, thus establishing a new power base. This would obviously be highly undesirable. One cannot preclude altogether this potential from taking shape. However, there are various reasons for optimism: With the proper design and supervisory dedication of the political bodies there should be ample room for ensuring that the latent danger of building a new power base can be contained. Surely it would not be perfect. Striving for perfection is tantamount to either wild experimentation or endless deliberation. The first order of business is to lay the foundations for improving resource allocation.

The basic safeguards against a power base would be fourfold. One is parliamentary oversight, which can be quite awesome if policy makers are determined to take to heart their true responsibilities. Privatization should not be used as a cudgel for settling political differences on how best to proceed with the transition, not even on how best to erase the "rents" inherited from state socialism. Second, because its mission to divest soonest is by definition temporary the agency's power base gets eroded as progress is made. Third, commercialization and corporatization, including interim rules on managerial behavior and supervision, should be inspired by preserving and where possible raising asset values. These rules would be transparent, and therefore limit the extent to which the agency could build up a power base. Finally, membership on the agency's board(s) should not be permanent. Key executive posts should be rotated. Members should be adequately compensated to offset the actual or potential losses sustained in terms of forgone private-sector salaries and/or capital gains. In return, the top leadership should be held to strict standards on conflict of interest, including full disclosure rules of incomes and wealth portfolios and desisting from acquiring privatized assets (excepts perhaps a home or similar petty asset under criteria to be specified). Once again, perfect professionalism is not something realistically within reach in real-life circumstances.

In many ways, the essentials of the agency charged with managing public-sector assets parallels the details on the privatization agency. By virtue of the fact that the public sector should *not* be a football for politicians and the agency's time horizon is almost limitless, there are qualitative differences to be respected too. For asset management, it will be mandatory that the agency come up with transparent guidelines for managing SOEs. Those must be more comprehensive and more finely tuned than what one might condone in the privatization agency, given its temporary character and the almost necessarily chaotic nature of whole-sale divestment over a comparatively brief period of time. There are plenty of precedents in market economies for enacting sensible public-sector reform. There is a fair consensus in the western professional community about the nature of the mechanisms and instruments of monitoring SOEs. They are not, of course, capable of squaring the circle, as most principal–agent problems will not vanish overnight and some simply cannot be eliminated. There will always be some leeway for managers in place to pursue their own agenda when surveillance bodies are not doing their job as well as private owners could have; as long as those are not dramatically out of sync with the preoccupation of owners, a *modus vivendi* can be worked out.

Like the privatization agency, the asset-management agency should be staffed with professionals and endowed with oversight mechanisms that rigorously enforce a code of conduct in line with the code of behavior of public officials of the highest integrity. The dangers of creating in the end new vested interests here are more pronounced, if only because of the absence of a clear terminal horizon for that part of the public sector; the comparable state of having completed divestment for the asset-management agency would be having succeeded in reaching near-perfect markets composed of private agents. Reform of the public sector therefore assumes considerable importance. Details of how this could be accomplished I cannot explore here, however (see Böhm 1990; J. A. Chandler 1991; Galal 1989; Gathon and Pestieau 1996; Ghai 1990; J. Gray 1989; Heath 1990; Morin 1996; Pannier 1996; Public 1990; Salamon 1989).

Section 8: Governance

"Managing" the transition, as indicated at several junctures, is typically a task incumbent upon government, and so I shall deal with governance in the broader sense in the next two chapters. Suffice it to emphasize here that governance issues emerge not only in the way in which the state "governs" society. It arises in all units that are not directly monitored by other institutions, such as the market or the pursuit of self-interest when principal–agent problems vanish. This has obvious implications, for example, in "governing" economic units with separate ownership from management. It also has clear repercussions on managing society through NPOs, the agencies of civil society in particular. I briefly discuss these two here.

8.1 – *Corporate governance*

This is not the proper place to delve in any detail into the multifarious problems of corporate governance (see Frydman and Rapaczyński 1993; Kester 1992; O. E. Williamson 1963, 1967, 1979, 1981). But I must flag up the entire range of issues pertaining to the truly important questions dealing with the internal workings of the corporation that are frequently ignored by economists (Dunning 1992b; Porter 1990; Sappington 1991; Simon 1991; Stiglitz 1991c), thus leaving the organization as a black box. I raise the issue of corporate governance in this context because, as Oliver E. Williamson (1967 [1986], pp. 46–7) notes, "virtually all of the interesting bureaucratic behaviour observed to exist in large government bureaucracies finds its counterpart in large non-government bureaucracies as well."

Corporate governance essentially means ensuring that assets are managed by "agents" in the interest of owners, whether private or not. As a rule that involves two tasks. One refers to the law on enterprises, including on disclosure of operations. The other consists of putting in place agencies that mediate between owners and management, such as a supervisory board possibly with a board of external directors. These are in principle called upon to ensure that management is doing its best for owners, who as a rule are represented on these boards; but not with dispersed ownership. One can in consequence view the structure of governance as providing the institutional matrix within which transactions are negotiated and executed in a wide array of organizations, including firms (O. E. Williamson 1979 [1986], p. 105).

There is by now ample empirical evidence that the problem of corporate governance is not limited to ensuring that principals work in the owner's interests. In addition, good corporate governance must come to grips with multiple layers of principal–agent problems that reach from top management all the way down to production and enterprise administration, and indeed ultimately to the single worker or employee. Seen in that light, corporate governance pertains to the nexus of explicit and implicit contracts that constitute a corporation. It is the process of optimally balancing the economics and hazards of transacting in the market with those of controlling the same activities within an administrative hierarchy (Kester 1992, pp. 27ff.). The central task of governance is to devise special incentives, safeguards, and dispute-resolution processes to promote the continuity of commercial relationships that are efficient in the absence of self-interested opportunism, but might otherwise fracture under the hammer of unassisted market contracting. Trust, in short, is a core ingredient of good governance.

Corporate governance encompasses the formulation, application, monitoring, assessment, and fine-tuning of all incentive mechanisms and behavioral rules pertinent to ensuring that managers, and their subordinated layers of decision making, of assets owned by others act as much as feasible in the latter's interest rather than overwhelmingly in their own. To satisfactorily ensure such congruence of interests, effective monitoring both within and outside the corporation is required. The first is the paramount issue of management, as distinct from engineering. Outside monitoring also calls for compelling management of firms with dispersed ownership to observe criteria of the greatest transparency as the law calls for; this at least encompasses fiscal regulations; but in most corporations also corporate law. Accounting and accountability through disclosure obligations should be clear and standard, and indeed public. Furthermore, it requires effective penalization in case of failure. Corporate governance, in other words, is what disciplines managers into acting on behalf of owners while respecting internal organizational requirements.

The matter is particularly acute in transition economies that have opted for insider or mass privatization. In both cases, corporate-governance rules need to be developed not only to protect owners but also to make sure that the enterprise functions appropriately within the "spirit" of the transformation. Insider privatization in particular may so entrench management in place that the assets in fact belong to it and are not being used to best capacity; they may even be eroded. Why should government be concerned about that? I see at least three reasons. First, the state must put in place the legal and organizational prerequisites for substantial ingredients of responsible corporate governance to emerge. Second, since the state at large has to remove itself from micromanaging the economy, it has to prove to be a good steward of resources entrusted to it by society at large until these resources can be privatized or firmly monitored otherwise. State desertion is, by definition, not a responsible policy except under circumstances where the ability to govern has all but completely dissipated. Finally, the very process of privatizing state-owned assets calls upon the state to put in place transitional mechanisms through which order and fairness can be imparted while steadily aiming at improving economic efficiency in privatized undertakings.

Whereas agency problems between managers and owners are always difficult, they are especially so with mass divestment. Dispersed ownership is unlikely to lead to proper monitoring and supervision of management. Various remedial formats have been proposed, entailing in one way or another the creation of intermediaries, such as investment funds (interacting actively with management), mutual funds (being mostly concerned with financial management), property agencies (in which state and private ownership is combined with the goal of divesting state ownership and enabling private owners in the property agency to acquire enterprise shares), or some form of holding company with a special mandate to oversee the operations of firms entrusted to it, including possibly divestment. Note that all these intermediaries have their own principal–agent problem. Who indeed will monitor these funds for as long as the market framework remains incomplete?

Although in principle corporate-governance rules and institutions could be transplanted from abroad, it is by no means clear that realistic governance structures can be envisioned as being independent of history and culture. Even if such off-the-shelf alternatives were readily available, monitoring would still be quite complex given the transition's context. Without firmly established and heeded accounting procedures; a record of corporate performance against which to measure the present actions of management; robust capital markets; specialized financial institutions engaged in assessing corporate performance; markets for corporate managerial talent; and many other institutions, it will be difficult to guarantee adequate monitoring. But at least a decent start can be made almost immediately through corporatization and commercialization.

8.2 – Agencies of civil society

Core aspects of the debates around transition have emphasized the need for a constitutional reform if only to remove the most noxious aspects of the inherited provisions. The other has been the priority of developing civil society both as a format that protects society against the usurpation of power by the few and as an instrument to help streamline the governance of the difficult passage to a functioning democracy and market economy. Why are civil-society organs so important?

A modern civil society encompasses a whole array of institutions. These include the intermediate groups and voluntary associations that broaden collective participation beyond the political realm of the state. For one thing, the government has, at best, a highly confined ability to meet the demands of a heterogeneous society. It can at best satisfy the median voter. This will leave a whole range of participants undersatisfied, even though they are willing and able to pay for these supplies. As a result, they can seek to establish other institutions, such as private firms, NPOs, or perhaps lower levels of government, to cater to their demands. Another justification is that consumers and donors are better able to monitor outputs and place greater trust in some NPOs as compared to for-profit organizations (Weisbrod 1988, 1989).

Certainly, because the coordination problem varies from country to country and remedial action in some has been farther-reaching than in others, developed countries have made very different choices about the size and composition of their nonmarket sectors. However, most such organizations in virtually all mature economies are engaged mainly in quasi-public activities. The development of these nonmarket organs is still in its infancy in all transition economies. Those that exist do not yet form an important bridge between the new élites and various segments of society. Moreover, many of these new organs have come about under impetus of the attempt of political parties and state institutions to establish direct links with the electorate. Because the parties themselves lack clear and consistent programs, and often depend on a single charismatic leader, with state institutions adrift, the associations they have sprouted are necessarily weak too (Comisso 1997).

A mature civil society cannot be created by any overnight decree. It takes years, if not generations, before a dense network of useful organs can emerge and assert itself in, on the whole, a constructive manner. The experience of mature market economies should be recalled here: Most of their NPOs antedated the modernization process, created as they were by philanthropy and charity to meet the needs that neither the for-profit nor the public sector would cater to; though the state may have encouraged their formation to exploit information in small organizations that a large centralized government may not be able to mobilize (see Chapter 9). Even so, a start has to be made. The way in which the process was put in train in most transition economies has not been the most desirable, however. This is regrettable since there are ample opportunities to redefine some of the societal organs inherited from the past into NPOs; others need to be transformed into for-profit organs or abolished; and indeed countries that had (usually illegal or barely tolerated) agents of civil society under state socialism have seen these structures fragment as a result of transition, thus enfeebling the foundations upon which democracy can be built (Bernhard 1996). There is insufficient appreciation of the advantages, and too many concerns about the disadvantages, of these organs in fostering along the transition. This state of affairs stems in part from misunderstandings of the concept and role of profit (Róna-Tas 1996), and how an NPO distinguishes itself from a for-profit firm. Many activities that could be undertaken by NPOs are now not being delivered by for-profit organs, and the state itself has become so limited in what it can prudentially undertake that it can no longer deliver those goods and services.

Conclusions

I have emphasized the importance of "institutions" in making a collection of individual agents with their peculiar private and collective behavior into a "market." Particularly in the context of the restructuring efforts of the transition economies they are arguably determinant in anchoring the emerging market economy and forging ahead with economic reconstruction, recovery, and eventually catch-up growth. From the few institutions of a well-behaved market examined in this chapter, the transition economies are most in need of precisely those that are the hardest to establish, regardless of available talents or access to foreign assistance. Certainly, the latter may be helpful in compressing the obstacles to "market making" in these countries. But they cannot innovate them in a hurry or transplant them from abroad lock, stock, and barrel.

As indicated, there are many such institutions of the market that deserve to be carefully examined. Some I deal with in other chapters. Others I have spelled out here, notably the requirements for capital and labor markets; the legal order; clear property rights; the role of NPOs and civil society in the modernization effort; the importance of quasi-state organs of surveillance, supervision, and jurisprudence, notably in financial markets, in coaxing along divestment, and in supervising assets that remain in the public sector. While all are critical to the proper functioning of the market economy, most will have to be nursed along within the context of the prevailing "culture." Others will continue to be buffeted by the political process. Transition simply cannot be conceived of without involving the prevailing political forces, whether in or out of power, and galvanizing them into a force supportive of some type of incisive transformation. It is perhaps easier to gain consensus on the tasks which must be delivered quickly and on those that cannot be engineered in a hurry than on what precisely to do about policy tasks that leave leeway for political choice (see Chapter 3).

8

TRANSFORMATION AND THE SOCIOPOLITICAL CONSENSUS

By all counts, state socialism in the eastern part of Europe provided cradle-to-grave social security. The policies followed in the other countries with state socialism were less generous, but contained major components of an eventual cradle-to-grave security blanket for particular categories of people – those employed in the state sector in particular. Though the latter countries, excepting perhaps Mongolia, have thus far been able to contain the impact of transformation on social-security provisioning, that has not been the case elsewhere. Many reasons help to explain this dichotomy.

In this chapter, I first examine the nature of the social-security blankets inherited from state socialism and why a large number of its components need to be thoroughly restructured and partly wound down. Thereafter I detail how best to reach a sociopolitical consensus, not just on the economics of transformation but also on the widely feared impact on social cohesion and well-being. Such a sociopolitical consensus has also to be sustained in spite of adverse developments, such as crime, corruption, nepotism, large unemployment, sizable income and wealth differentiation, ravaging inflation, and other emerging inequalities. This leads to a discussion of societal governance. Then I look at the unemployment conundrum seen against the backdrop of the legacies of labor markets under state socialism. Next I scrutinize the social services that SOEs used to provide and how best they can be organized under the new conditions. Pension reform forms a daunting task that I look at briefly thereafter. The relationship between budgetary stringency and social-welfare provisioning I consider before concluding with some tangents of corruption, crime, and personal insecurity under transition.

Section 1: Shrinking social security – expectations and realities

State socialism, especially in the more mature countries, eventually provided cradle-to-grave security to virtually the entire population. This blanket comprised a guaranteed job for life, fairly early retirement with dependable pensions (if low in real terms), large social transfers, generous maternity leave, comprehensive medical care, a variety of social services for the less advantaged (including children, the sick, and the handicapped), gratis universal elementary and far-reaching secondary education, free tertiary education, liberal abortion rules, preventive health care, continuing education for men as well as women, low-cost access to the arts and sports, privileged vacations, and social supports (such as kindergartens and child care) for a variety of production-related tasks. State socialism also ensured that society was provided with considerable personal security, such as in matters of crime, vandalism, drugs, and prostitution. The budget component for social expenditures was quite substantial.

János Kornai (1992) has termed this an instance of a "premature welfare state" in the sense that these countries attempted to erect a social safety net for which their level of development and wealth simply failed to provide an adequate support base. Much of this may have overly smacked of far-reaching paternalism, and some layers of these societies resented this lack of actual or perceived personal freedom associated with the cited security. In several instances, notably in central Europe and especially in Hungary (Kornai 1996a, b), this resulted from the "brokered" social contract that the leadership had felt it imperative to sustain for its own survival (Andorka 1996). Just the same, all this made these societies on the whole quite ill-prepared to face up to freedom, choice, uncertainty, and wrenching changes in almost every aspect of their lives.

Though some of the cited benefits have also been made available in the non-European countries with state socialism, the breadth of coverage and the depth of the cradle-to-grave security are rarely as encompassing as in the eastern part of Europe. However, lifetime job guarantees with some social amenities unrelated to production efforts have prevailed in their comparatively small state sector too. They continue to impinge upon the latitude of policy makers. Many of the policy makers concerned cling to the ideology discarded in the eastern part of Europe or succeed in their reluctance to disengage from absolute power. Because they have been more skillful at managing the social changes entailed by their own economic transition, they have not been able to avoid painful adjustments too in spite of the comparatively low level of social welfare provided at the height of state socialism. But social mutations have been managed and political changes largely contained to efforts from within the ruling Party under controlled conditions. It remains to be seen whether in the longer run these countries can navigate successfully toward modernization without introducing chaotic political mutations as well.

With transition, many of these social benefits are bound to disappear or shrink considerably. But this cannot be done overnight or applied to all components of the security extended under state socialism. This holds more for the eastern part of Europe than for other countries. For one thing, the former's cushion was much broader and thicker. Also, these societies had a long tradition of some kind of state paternalism in social affairs. Moreover, the vast majority of the population was not at all supportive of "wild east" experiments engendered by extreme liberalism with great uncertainty, inequality in incomes and wealth, marginalization of distinct layers of society that cannot make it in the transformation, and so on (Laski 1996).

As indicated earlier, policy makers have not been very good at managing the transition. This stems in part from the fact that the blueprint for transition toward political democracy and market-based resource allocation was never more than a vague conceptual framework of the diverse popular aspirations that welled up spontaneously or under the prodding of the dissident intelligentsia. In all too many cases, it embodied little by way of earnest contemplation of the feasible and realistic options. Popular support was mostly elicited for something that referred primarily to a broad guideline for the distant state toward which their respective polity should move. There never was more than a remote beacon by which the nearly rudderless state-socialist ship could be navigated through the transformation shoals. In many countries, with the notable exception of most CIS States, the enthusiasm for the twin goals of transition, when it erupted, was exceptionally wide among the population. But that too was based on sentiment rather than rational calculation; in many cases there was much more of the former in comparison with the people's feelings in the more western countries. Even the policies put in place in most transition economies were conceived more on the go, as it were, than from within the context of a well-contemplated strategy for change. Very often in drafting, implementing, and modulating these programs, it was forgotten that the pursuit of capitalism unconstrained by rules of equity and social responsibility is likely to undermine the very conditions that render capitalism and markets productive (Kuttner 1997; Silk *et al.* 1996; Weisberg 1996).

Even when one focuses on the technical aspects of the potential agenda for transformation, one cannot simply gloss over the fact that the initial, at times tacit, support for democratic decision making and embracing raw markets in transition economies has noticeably been weakening under force of circumstance. Particularly important has been the emergence of a number of economic, moral, social, and political phenomena that few, if any, observers had thought about in 1989. Crime, corruption, unemployment, poverty, destitution, and so on have all weakened the initial infrastructure for new political decision making. Extraordinary politics offered indeed an exceptional window of opportunity for those able and willing to seize the day. It was essentially a substitute by default for a sociopolitical consensus, regardless of whether and how this could have been galvanized.

The pervasive uncertainty unleashed by the transition has been exerting a palpable impact on political posturing. Its effect is arguably even more endemic to the economics of radical change, and its implications for sociopolitical stability in these countries, when the very foundations of a market economy are absent and these cannot be cemented in through a simple translocation, in nearly prefabricated modular fashion, of the institutions of the market economy that seem to have worked fairly well elsewhere. True, economic agents acting in their own interest now have to reach day-to-day decisions on resource allocation. But

300

they can do so only while the rules of the market game are still being thrashed out, at best assimilated, virtually from elementary principles. Uncertainty implies many things (see Chapter 3). In particular, the demand and supply pressures disrupting balances under state socialism are deeply embedded in the behavior of economic agents and cannot be rectified overnight. For one, the entrepreneurial élite was by and large appointed through administrative and political connections, rather than because of their demonstrated managerial aptitude. Moreover, the "animal spirits" of capitalist entrepreneurship are simply not present as the orthodox planning model fails to encourage the kind of decision making required in a market-oriented environment. Time is needed to inculcate this new spirit. Policy makers need to nurture along this transition process too.

Similar constraints arise for households as providers of labor services and as consumers. Having been exposed for so many years to relatively low and stable prices for a wide range of basic goods and services, households tend to be reluctant to part with implicit subsidies. This restricts the room for maneuver for policy makers bent on revamping the role of the government budget in steering in particular the economy and society more generally. The principle of wide income differentiation, after it had been frowned upon for so long, is not likely to be tolerated quickly by the vast majority of the population. Finally, households may be reluctant to give up full employment and other social-welfare and security guarantees.

The consolidation of fiscal revenue by minimizing distortions in microeconomic decisions, yet taxing economic agents equitably and delivering on social priorities, is an urgent task (see Chapter 4). This is especially so because reforms are being sought by societies that place a strong value on limited income differentiation, nearly free education and health services, fostering the arts for the wider public, and other social services. Recall that state socialism carried out these aspirations well beyond what people would have voluntarily endorsed. But many countries had such transfers already before the advent of state socialism. That fairness may distort economic efficiency needs to be factored into macroeconomic policy. To improve levels of living, it is necessary to use resources efficiently and for this purpose to reward persons unequally. To control income disparity, resource misallocation must be contained. The extent of income inequality and the means of keeping it within acceptable bounds are decisions that deserve priority attention to release creative ability, stimulate entrepreneurship, and exploit prevailing and emerging opportunities with the goal of attaining a higher, yet sustainable, rate of growth.

The duration of the transition depends on the initial conditions and the speed at which policy makers can succeed in implementing the transformation agenda. This can hardly be set once and for all. It is while moving away from the inherited structures that the agenda tends to be written and amended under direct influence of the transition (Chang and Nolan 1995; Murrell 1992, 1995; Nolan 1992; Pickel 1992). If only for that reason, except for the philosopher and the dreamer, the ultimate goal of the transition should matter much less in contemplating what needs to be done and how to accomplish it, than erasing the most venal legacies of state socialism as well as avoiding the less savory concomitants of raw capitalism. It is therefore of highest relevance that the transformation commence with those elements that can be obliterated most rapidly, given limited administrative, financial, legal, and organizational capabilities. At the least, this phase is likely to take a decade. This "near-term horizon" could in any case possibly apply only to the countries that have already gained a modicum of sociopolitical consensus on "what imprecisely" policy makers should strive for.

I emphasize the uncertainty about gaining a minimal consensus and the fundamental obstacles toward maintaining it through whatever feeble political decision-making structures may come into play (Comisso 1992). Though it may be inherently difficult to ask people to volunteer for sacrifice, this is not altogether impossible. In late 1989, policy makers of Czechoslovakia and Poland, for example, possessed such a consensus, even if only implicitly (Balcerowicz and Gelb 1994; Balcerowicz 1995a, b). But there never was a guarantee that this buttress for change would not crumble. The fractious political structures, the shift in sentiment when the population experiences the drawbacks well ahead of profiting from the benefits of transformation, when political promises made are not delivered upon for whatever reason, and other unforeseeable occurrences guarantee that the social consensus has shaky foundations.

Transition, and even more economic transformation, cannot be pursued without "events" in the social sphere. Some have a direct impact on economic affairs. Others affect the environment within which societal agreement must be thrashed out and maintained. For one thing, economic restructuring requires a redistribution of labor resources, and thus the abolition of job guarantees for life. Unemployment is bound to emerge, and workers expect the state to provide a safety cushion. Also, with the reorganization of state ownership, firms are likely to shed activities that have little to do with their core economic tasks. The question then arises whether these social props should be maintained; who should be entrusted with them; and in what precise form?

The cradle-to-grave social protection of state socialism undergoes various transformations with transition. For one thing, pervasive price subsidies have to be abolished, thus eroding liquid wealth (especially when held in local currency), wages, and fixed incomes like pensions. Second, transfers for explicit social-redistribution purposes and for insurance-type activities provided by the state as inherited from state socialism come under severe budgetary pressure on both the revenue and expenditure sides. Finally, some of the social-protection institutions inherited from state socialism are simply not viable in the longer run. There are, then, multiple reasons for knitting a social safety net during the transition. Most commentators have focused on providing support to those who lose from the transition and, even more, from transformation. These are new tasks for society that in time will disappear or shrink in acuity. But the social safety net has to be stretched so that normal life-cycle and other contingencies (such as old age, unemployment, child care, and family allowances) can be protected in an emerging market economy.

In either case, such protection must be designed in a cost-effective manner, possibly by revamping the infrastructure in place. Not only that, a fairly liberal market economy cannot deliver transfers to every claimant in society without some form of categorical targeting or means-testing. One can usefully distinguish here between primary and supplementary instruments or second-tier safety nets. Primary instruments in the form of price subsidies, targeted cash benefits (such as pensions, unemployment compensation, and child and family allowances), and the like tend to rely on categorical targeting to reach the majority of vulnerable groups through existing administrative arrangements. Supplementary instruments can comprise an entire gamut of measures such as public works, retraining, and social assistance. Such programs tend to rely on either self-targeting or local identification of beneficiaries in order to reach those inadequately covered by the first-tier safety nets.

Whatever measures are put in train, on balance transition benefits some members of society and disadvantages others. Benefits are unlikely to compensate for the actual or perceived costs inflicted by the transition in societies where categorical targeting or means-testing under state socialism was limited. Under the emerging market economy, at least until sufficient wealth will have been created, the previous type of social safety net simply cannot be afforded and governments cannot evade their responsibilities when it comes to remedying the situation for the more vulnerable groups during the transition. This forms an important ingredient of what is required to stretch and prop up a new sociopolitical consensus.

Section 2: Reaching and sustaining the consensus

The above elaboration begs a definition of consensus. Few analysts have ventured to make this explicit in an intelligible manner. But Jacob Viner's (1960) reference to a society that is "reasonably content" may be quite appropriate here. It implies that there is at least tacit agreement about the broad policies advocated, and undertaken, by those in power; that support for those policies exceeds what voters would be willing to grant the opposition, if a democratic outcome is available, and otherwise that they will not wage battles to undermine the regime in place; and that those in power, in fact, do not transgress on this confidence and trust on the part of the electorate or concerned citizens, and, if they must, that they can persuasively explain the unexpected state of affairs to the electorate at large.

An important component of that consensus concerns the burden of the transition from which three interrelated questions emerge: (1) How large is it likely to be? (2) How quickly will it have to be absorbed? and (3) Who in society will have to bear the brunt? Not only must there be a broad, basic understanding, tacit or otherwise, on how to proceed. The emergent new societies should also have in place a minimum of latitude whereby the idea of pursuing change

303

within consensual limits can be maintained in case of adverse development. The latter can be economic. But also the potential for political and social setbacks needs to be taken into account. They would rupture the consensus rather quickly, probably faster than the time required to construct some minimally coherent framework.

As far as I can make out only central Europe (Czech Republic, Hungary, Poland, and Slovenia, but Slovakia being not at all certain) could possibly be considered – and even then only with some hedging – as possessing a popularly supported workable consensus that might be sustainable; this was certainly true at the transition's inception. But policy makers even in these countries cannot sustain this continuing minimal harmony without engaging in painful compromises as the costs and rivalries unleashed by the transition become more tangible. Elsewhere, the transition may last several generations. The latter is almost certainly bound to be the case for most CIS States and perhaps even the economically more backward of the successor States of Yugoslavia. Not only that, but also there are good reasons to conjecture that the outcome is unlikely to be even a close image of the archetypal textbook market paradigm.

One can usefully distinguish among three levels of consensus at the transition's eve and during its initial organizing phase that need to be sustained during transformation. First is the degree of political consensus on unavoidable economic transformation, using the desired state of pluralistic democracy as benchmark; but other political arrangements could be imagined for moving ahead with far-reaching societal change. Without unambiguous political agreement on decision making by consensus, it is all but impossible to formulate a credible transformation agenda and embark on its implementation. This is particularly relevant to countries where the political process has not yet crystallized un-ambiguously in favor of a functioning democracy or where the sentiment for the latter has been eroded under vacillations brought about, among others, by the hardships of the transition. When political structures lose popular legitimacy, however expressed, yet new mechanisms of consensual decision making are not yet firmly in place, it is difficult to imagine practicable ways of forging a political consensus. This is still the case in countries such as Albania and all too many of the successor States of the USSR and Yugoslavia. But I submit that the question of political legitimacy and sustaining consensus is relevant as well for other transition economies, particularly those where a credible political process for reconciling conflicting views exists, but where the economic trauma of transformation may be so daunting that it makes that incipient democratic process rather vulnerable to setbacks of various origins.

In some countries, even at this stage, deeply rooted tensions between nation-alities and regions continue. These must be sorted out before any credible societal agreement (that is, one whose implementation can be initiated with wide support) on wholesale national economic, political, and social transformations can be hammered out. The key question in this connection is the degree to which political agreement on the transition, and economic transformation in particular, elicits wider popular support. The latter is undoubtedly easier to maintain in countries where policy makers have a popular mandate, whether tacit or explicit through democratic elections, than in countries where they are not directly accountable and may be swayed to impose change from above, perhaps in the erroneous belief that successful transformation will eventually broaden support.

But the latitude available to policy makers is not just a function of popular support, however obtained. Even with wide agreement on moving to market-based resource allocation at some point of time, circumstances may force the transition's managers to pursue other goals that possibly conflict with anchoring rapidly a full-fledged market economy. Thus, a commitment to avoid reschedu-ling foreign-debt obligations at almost any cost (as in Hungary) or the need to bolster domestic food supplies (as in Romania and the USSR in the early 1990s) tends to conflict with the rapid establishment of the essential institutions of a market economy. True, such decisions are intrinsically political. Yet, economists involved in managing the transformation, even at arm's length, should remain aware of the complex, often fiendishly difficult, political choices to be made in other domains than "simply" forging ahead with economic transformation.

International commitments too place boundaries on the room for policy flex-ibility enjoyed by transition managers. These can take the form of subscribing to economic regimes (such as in monetary, financial, or trading matters) with internationally agreed-upon rules that may not be the most advantageous from the point of view of moving forward rapidly with transformation. Even more than simply subscribing to a particular regime, joining binding arrangements, such as the EU with its *acquis communautaire*, imposes conditions that may not be supportive of swift economic transformation (see Chapter 10). Similar restrictions may emerge from pursuing transformation with foreign assistance (see Chapter 11).

Second, once most of the political obstacles to forging ahead with the destruction of the *ancien régime* have been overcome, those in the vanguard of the movement must be concerned about reaching a social consensus on the steps ahead. Even if such is reached at the transition's inception, including explicitly through the emerging democratic process, there is no guarantee that it can be maintained once the adjustment costs are to be borne. I return to this issue in the next section. That social consensus must refer, among other things, to the level, the distribution, and the time path of the costs of transformation, as indicated earlier.

A market economy is expected to yield considerable benefits to the population at large. And consensual decision making through the democratic process can only reinforce the robustness of these benefits. At the same time some groups may well fail to benefit, or to the degree they had anticipated, from these mutations, and disappointment, disgruntlement, and perhaps opposition set in. It is impor-tant that transition managers clarify as much as possible up front the magnitudes of potential benefits and the likely time scale for their emergence in order to obtain the widest possible support for transformation. Deceiving the electorate by populist promises may work once or twice. But it is unlikely to provide a solid platform supportive of change. In the first instance, the qualitative benefits, such as freedom of speech and movement, consumer sovereignty, increased choice in other matters, and the prospect of secure property rights should be stressed. But it is important that open discussion of the likely negative impacts of transformation not be skirted or minimized.

Even with all its benefits and the existence of firm rules for decision making through robust institutions, such as in the oldest democracy, there is still considerable uncertainty about the socially acceptable limit of policy change. More than marginal increases in inflation and unemployment, erosion of wealth, wages, and incomes, and so on have frequently led to changes in government. There is no reason to believe that the transition economy could find it easier to deal with such socioeconomic problems, irrespective of the longer-term benefits of transformation. As demonstrated in several countries, measures leading to economic chaos are unlikely to elicit a workable social consensus or to permit such a consensus to be sustained for sufficiently long to see the fruits of the steps taken benefit wide layers of society. But neither is erecting a halfway house: the collapse of state socialism and administrative coordination without another effective coordination mechanism being on the horizon; that is the case at least in several of the CIS States. Such a vacuum leads only to black markets, corruption, crime, and so on. Whatever measures are taken, increasing inequality, open inflation, rapid increases in unemployment, marginalization of layers of society, and impoverishment of many citizens cannot but engender disenchantment with the transformation process. Losers must be taken care of even if they can be considered responsible for their losses in the sense that they could have adjusted and chose not to; this is distinct from taking care of losing groups that cannot be held responsible for their plight (such as the elderly, children, unemployable, and handicapped).

Finally, as indicated, market-oriented transformation is by no means a process that can be embarked upon by following a well-rehearsed recipe. A consensus must be reached on the particular kind of social and economic protection that the majority of the population expects from the state, and thus to be embedded in the new market; on the role of the state in enforcing a "view" of what needs to be done and how; and on the degree to which economic liberalism can be circumscribed without running into debilitating sociopolitical problems or dysfunctional economic constraints.

Reaching and maintaining a social consensus is by no means an easy matter. For one thing, the range of perceptions of the positive and negative impacts of transition and transformation is wide, diffuse, changing, and often not explicit. This depends in part on what the population at large expects from society in general and from government in particular. Those benefits and costs cannot be confined to pecuniary ones, such as the taxes levied in exchange for the transfers made and services rendered by government. But surely those play a considerable role in gearing perceptions, particularly at a time of rapid societal change.

Government transfers can be roughly divided into socially motivated redistributions of income and wealth and insurance-type services that the private sector as a rule does not provide or can do so effectively only under stringent regulatory regimes. The pervasive price subsidies and taxes of state socialism entail a redistribution as well, chiefly motivated by political and bureaucratic reasons (see Part I). Since many of these subsidies are abolished rather quickly into the transition I focus here on the two cited categories. Examples of insurance-type activities are unemployment and health insurance or pension-type social security. Here there is a nexus between "contribution" and "benefit." Indeed a case can be made that such transfers should be self-financing; that is, the "savings" collected through mandatory or other retentions should be adequate to finance the discounted claims of beneficiaries. Examples of the socially motivated redistributions are welfare payments to the destitute or handicapped, child and family support, and other kinds of poverty alleviation. Here there is as a rule no tangible link between those contributing to and those benefiting from the transfers. Financing is as a rule part of the overall fiscal system or from some kind of "solidarity" contribution (Kornai 1996a).

Section 3: Governing the transition

Any sociopolitical system, including its economic organization, derives its ultimate *raison d'être* from its effects on human behavior – the incentives it provides and how economic agents are motivated by them with a view to generating steady gains in sustainable levels of welfare for the broad majority of the population. In other words, transformation is not only, and perhaps not even mainly, about productivity and income, or even about ways to remedy market and government failures. It is also about the core distributional questions so important to maintaining a sociopolitical consensus shaped in the context of the transformation agenda. If only for these reasons, exercising political power, thus mediating between interests and aspirations that find their roots both within and outside the individual polity, has become exceedingly difficult in many countries. These are frequently contradictory, incompatible, and not at all easy to assess. Steering the transformation process requires setting in motion a broad process of social learning, as well as establishing institutional arrangements to foster and exercise collective social responsibility. In short, it requires better governance, which should be the all-embracing reference point for transition managers.

3.1 – Governance and its meanings

Governance is paramount in managing economic, political, and social transformations. When put like this, most observers probably agree with the desirability of governing the transformation process. It is surprising, then, that even after nearly a decade of transition the issue of governance in the positive sense – that is, making best use of available resources and engaging fully in "creative destruction" in a manner acceptable to society – at whatever level has on the whole received short shrift in the debates. Even conceptually, it not quite clear what ideally needs to be done and what *could* be undertaken, given the sociopolitical environment for governing (Campbell and Lindberg 1991) at all levels of decision making. But I focus here chiefly on governing society as a whole (for corporate governance, see Chapter 7; elements of governing NPOs and international and regional agencies are discussed in Chapter 10).

Multiple questions immediately crop up when one advocates anything like "managing society." To many it smacks all too much of omniscient collectivist planning – echoes of the painfully long experiments with state socialism. Though historical experience should never be far from reflections on desirable and feasible transformation policies, equating governance with omniscient collectivism would be inappropriate. It is therefore pivotal to inquire briefly into what good governance in general and economic governance in particular may mean, and how they relate to the decision making about the form and implementation of the most promising transformation path, given the realities of the transition economies.

Governance is a term borrowed from political science (Hyden 1992). It is essentially the art of managing the affairs of society (Landell-Mills and Serageldin 1992, p. 304). But it is not quite congruent with the "task of running a government" (Hyden 1992, p. 5), with "good government" (World Bank 1992, p. 1), or for that matter with "the quality of the government bureaucracy, or alternatively, with the organizational structure of governments" (Frischtak 1996, p. 4). None of these concepts reflects satisfactorily how I view governance and its essential role in managing an entity composed of multiple actors with their tacit or explicit consent, or at least consensus on basic parameters of how their activities can usefully be meshed and for what specific purposes. Neither liberal theory nor collectivist thinking supplies a coherent justification for the asymmetric treatment of the state and the capitalist, or socialist, economy (Bowles and Gintis 1986, p. 66). The first notion captures at best only one part of what merits to be envisaged, and I return to this in Chapter 9. The second prejudices the issue in that governance is presumed to revolve solely around good (largely central) government, as a rule equated with the efficient delivery of public goods. In some cases, it also includes the correction of market failures. And governance cannot be confined to largely civil-service or ministerial-portfolio reforms. Other definitions of governance, as illustrated, cover a large palette, from public-sector policy making and management capabilities at one extreme to institutional pluralism, public participation, and human rights, at the other (Frischtak and Atiyas 1996).

In its most general setting, governance can be viewed as "the political and economic processes that coordinate activity among economic actors" (Lindberg, Campbell, and Hollingsworth 1991, p. 3). Alternatively, it can be seen as the exercise of political power and authority (Lindblom 1977, 1990) to manage a nation's social and economic affairs or those incumbent at a more decentralized or centralized level (Brautigam 1991; Landell-Mills and Serageldin 1991; Rice 1991). These include mechanisms that help decide the place and role of markets in generating and protecting economic wealth, and indirectly other assets, by fostering harmonious coordination, cooperation, and competition among various actors in society. Governance also helps in deciding the place and role of a wide array of nonmarket institutions and mechanisms. In essence it is the "capacity to mobilize, control, regulate, and coordinate to get things done" (Ibrahim and Lofgren 1996, p. 179). As such, it entails the leadership's mastery and deployment of the means of inspiration through vision as well as, in the case of state actors, the means of coercion with a host of other institutions and instruments in between (such as the legislature, the judiciary, the media, and civil society). That is to say, governance is a much broader concept than the state's role in economic affairs, which in fact is but one constituent part of economic governance.

Governance involves the steering and management of the affairs entrusted to the state and society – essentially the "public realm" (Hyden 1992, p. 7) – in accordance with the instruments at hand and institutions in place with a view to delivering in the best manner possible on the selected tasks through positive action by government and, in a wider context, nonmarket actors. It may also encompass instruments and institutions that need to be innovated, tested, and refined in order to meet prevailing expectations. Those tasks may have been set through a broad, democratically reached sociopolitical consensus. If so, they involve (Brautigam 1991, pp. 13ff.) accountability (which itself may bestow legitimacy and require institutional pluralism and participation), openness, transparency, and predictability (such as through the rule of law). Under those conditions, NPOs that do not form a formal part of the state, as defined, need to develop their own governance capabilities and structures in accordance with their smaller remit, given their specific mandate. Alternatively, the regime in place may have arrogated authority over the enumerated tasks to itself without there being visible opposition. In that case, the notions of legitimacy and coercion are pivotal. As the role of the latter wanes, the importance of the former ascends and may have to be heeded by instituting other features of more democratic governance (Lateef 1992; J. M. Nelson 1992).

Governance is, of course, a vastly broader subject than economic governance, or how best to steer and manage a nation's economy with the policy instruments and relevant institutions in place, or those soon to be acquired. That task includes the coordination of economic activities of all classes of agents, the initiation of positive steps to influence the way in which the economy is being coordinated, the monitoring and assessment of how the economy is faring, and indeed the initiation of remedial measures to correct failures early on or to reinforce promising activities as quickly as possible, including by hiving them off to nongovernmental agents at the earliest opportunity.

To elicit broad consensus among those watching the transitions unfold, it may be useful to distinguish four dimensions of the notion governance (GRADE 1992, pp. 4–12). These are: (1) the nature and functioning of the political regime in place; (2) the processes of economic, political, and social guidance – public as well as private and those situated in between – that are critical to charting the course for the country's development efforts and mobilizing support for them; (3) the government's capacity to design and implement policies and strategies, and indeed to monitor them for their performance with a view to putting in train, when warranted, corrective actions at the earliest opportunity, certainly within reasonable deadlines; and (4) the managerial and administrative capabilities both in the public and private sectors, including NPOs.

Addressing the core question of the relationship between governance and the political regime inevitably touches upon whether one type of political regime is more conducive to stability, economic growth, and social justice than another. This debate has focused on whether pluralistic political democracy fosters or hinders economic growth, whether economic freedom is the foundation stone for political freedom, and whether economic prosperity is a prerequisite for democracy (World Bank 1991, pp. 132–4). Whereas democracy allows peaceful and lawful change to take place gradually and in a consensual manner, it does so only when the basic elements of societal stability are in place and proper governance mechanisms can be activated (J. M. Nelson 1992). There are lingering doubts in the profession on whether there can be a tradeoff between democracy and economic growth, if only because of the formidable technical difficulties of capturing the "right" variables in determining the "better" alternative for pursuing modernization (Boeninger 1992; Frischtak and Atiyas 1996; Helliwell 1994; Hirst and Thompson 1996; Melo, Denizer, and Gelb 1996; J. M. Nelson 1992; Sah and Weitzman 1991; J. Williamson 1994a). Whichever may prevail or be desirable, it bears to stress the dynamic of political regimes. It is managing the transition to the "better" political constellation of forces, rather than democracy *per se*, that should be at the heart of this dimension of governance. That process has invariably proceeded with, at times daunting, conflicts, many of which could not be managed quickly or consensually.

Second, the relationship between governance and policy making deserves to be clarified. Many countries, including transition economies, are confronted with a rapidly changing and uncertain international context, marked increases in social demands and expectations, economic instability, and resource scarcities, in addition to the deterioration of physical infrastructure and the dramatic loss of human capital. In such a situation, priority setting, identification of strategic options, and a thorough review of alternative economic and social policies under prevailing circumstances become important. These cannot be confined to technocratic solutions by "technopols" (J. Williamson 1994a). Governance in this sense, then, refers to the capacity and ability of government to define objectives and directions, possibly as they emerge from sociopolitical priorities; to evolve strategies and set the course for government actions; and to gain acceptance and mobilize support for its development efforts. This is critical for "owning" adjustment programs and mobilizing political support for them. In this, credibility of the transition agenda, stability and predictability of policies, transparency and reliability of decision making, and accountability of the political leaders and their administrators are crucial.

Third, managers of a polity must analyze, design, implement, monitor, assess, and adapt themselves as well as influence the behavior of agents within their remit. These critical abilities of governance should be prevalent not only in the public sector but in all nonmarket entities, including private activities, professional associations, research centers, academic institutions, labor unions, and community organizations. This is required because the analytical and response capacities of public-sector institutions in many transition economies are limited. Even when broader capabilities are available it is not clear *a priori* that the public sector would be best suited, in a cost-benefit context, to take care of the assignment. Of much greater import is the capacity to process and arbitrate among competing claims in a pluralistic institutional setting. Under some conditions, this task could be best entrusted to a central guidance agency capable of complementing market signals. The essential point of departure should be the recognition that markets not only generate flexibility but also uncertainty and that not only government officials face difficulties in picking winners and losers, but also private business people (Wade 1988, p. 151), particularly in a confounding environment. Better policies and strategies are required to improve governance. The need for penetrating analytical and comparative studies that could shed light on the political and strategic options available to these countries remains acute indeed.

Finally, managerial and administrative capabilities are essential to translate policies into practice with multiple private- and public-sector actors. The public-sector administrative and managerial aspects of governance are well recognized. Issues that concern transition economies too are civil-service reform, review of public expenditures, administrative simplification, and regulatory improvements. These are the bread-and-butter issues of better public-sector management, of improved policy-making capabilities, and of introducing and fine-tuning a variety of institutional conditions (such as transparency, accountability, and the rule of law). Less recognized, however, is the importance of interventions that foster entrepreneurship, encourage risk taking, and enhance managerial knowhow outside the government sector in the strict sense. Topics such as information, training, technical assistance, research, dissemination of best practices, and others are critical here. In bolstering the opportunities for successful modernization, it may well not suffice to create the appropriate policy and institutional environment to elicit the necessary responses from private sectors.

3.2 – Why does governance matter?

Fostering coordination, cooperation, and competition among various economic agents is crucial when "markets" are immature. Governance issues have increasingly become recognized as central to dissecting and properly managing the development and growth processes in a vast array of countries, whether developed or not (Frischtak and Atiyas 1996); though insufficiently in transition economies. These stirrings have also called for placing a new focus on governance of the global economy, sort of finding once again a way to emulate the kind of multilateralism that prevailed in the postwar period (Bergsten and Henning 1996; Hirst and Thompson 1996; Ikenberry 1992; Kennedy 1993). It has also been common in a number of regional organizations, not the least the EU (Brabant 1995a, 1996) and indeed in the various regional-cooperation formats explored by subgroups of transition economies since 1991. They have come to the fore in political and business agendas for a variety of reasons. These include the new political demands imposed by the processes of internationalization and globalization, ecological concerns about the sustainability of development, the rise of ethnic and religious tensions, the development and assimilation of technology especially in a catch-up mode, the mixed success with the neoliberal agenda in reversing a long stretch of at best slow productivity growth since the early 1970s, and state socialism's collapse.

An explanation of why the rebuilding process in transition economies has been much more cumbersome than had earlier been imagined must be richer than the simple invocation of the legacies of state-socialist mismanagement, unless the latter is viewed in an all-inclusive deterministic fashion, in which case the inquiry becomes useless. Fundamental questions of the makeup of the new societies and polities derive from many other concerns, as highlighted throughout this volume. Stabilization, privatization, economic liberalization, and minimal government interference may have been useful stances to take, given the circumstances since 1989. But they have not brought back quickly a workable consensus; in many countries this is still lacking. Is something else required than uninhibited markets with completely self-centered, atomistic agents to ensure dynamic growth over the longer haul? This debate is being stoked, among others, by the sharp contrast between the growth in social demands and the capacity to satisfy them, and the critical need to marshal sustainable sociopolitical support for economic transformation.

3.3 – The agencies of governance

As already emphasized, issues of coordination, cooperation, and competition pervade the tasks of all organizations, not just the state or for-profit organizations. A modern economy depends on various links in finance, trade, technology, and production that are not directly scrutinized in the marketplace, yet do not form a component of the traditional state (Best 1990; Richardson 1972). This does not in any way seek to downgrade the vital importance of a competent and honest civil service (see Chapter 9). While an efficient central bureaucracy by itself does not guarantee successful modernization, without it sustainable modernization becomes elusive. The latter requires also other intermediating links in facilitating coordination, cooperation, and competition, hence in enhancing governance capabilities. I include associations, informal networks, and formal horizontal and vertical links among firms subject to antitrust laws, as well as between, say, firms and financial institutions. All agents involved in mediating economic activities for which they are not directly scrutinized through markets should figure prominently in conceptualizing and applying economic governance with a view to fostering dynamic development (Lindberg, Campbell, and Hollingsworth 1991, p. 5).

Generalizing, there are different forms of governance and each may play an important role in coordinating economic activity. Furthermore, these forms of collective action cannot simply be reduced to the paradigm of the public-choice school, though the dilemmas of large-group collective action must be recognized (Bergstrom and Stark 1993; Samuelson 1993; Wade 1986, 1987; Weitzman 1993). It is important to recognize the prevailing limits for what they are and to seize the opportunities for responding to other needs with a view to enhancing, rather than denigrating, governance capabilities. As time marches on the breadth, if perhaps not the depth, of demands for governance capabilities shrinks or expands, but the target will almost certainly get modified as well. That is to say, one governance capability should be the ability to adjust over time, depending upon the concrete sociopolitical and evolving economic situation.

3.4 – The tasks of governance and subsidiarity

The essential trait of good governance is managing change. Organs that find themselves the farther removed from the marketplace should increasingly be able to withdraw from allocative decisions once the market as a coordinating mechanism improves. It is incumbent upon good governance to put in train measures to ameliorate the functioning of markets as part and parcel of the development process itself (see Chapter 3). But there is little point in entrusting a given coordination task to an authority farther removed from the market-place when it can be accomplished at least as well by one located closer to it: Subsidiarity matters (Brabant 1993a, pp. 112ff.; 1995a, pp. 471ff.).

It would be a grave error, however, to hold that subsidiarity implies that decisions taken at a lower level are excluded from governance. At the very least, ensuring that this lower-level decision-making authority adequately coordinates the competition and cooperation among other agents remains an essential governance task. Thus, positive as well as negative feedback needs to be taken fully into account. Shifting circumstances determining whether or not a desirable level of coordination, cooperation, and competition can be reached by having lower-level organs take the "correct" decisions should be the motivating force for ensuring appropriate subsidiarity. Pragmatism and credibility are key qualities to be strived for. Insisting that governance in general and the state in particular be always right and demonstrate their comparative advantage before being granted authority to "intervene" is asking the impossible. For if the state, say, could undertake only what it knows to be superior, it should simply pass on that "knowledge edge" to the private sector. The point is that governance actions cannot invariably be successful, if only because of "external shocks" or events that

313

seriously modify the outcome of the envisaged policy measure. More important is the ability to diagnose the reasons for failure, assess what could be done to minimize the setbacks, examine other available options, and select the remedial policies to be put in train soonest.

3.5 – *Capacities to govern*

Coordinating various actors in a given economy is feasible only when there is a reasonable capacity to govern (Wade 1988). In the case under consideration that requires that cadres in the nonmarket segments, including an institutional capacity within government but possibly divorced from politics, can conceptualize, implement, monitor, assess, and correct on a timely basis the tasks of coordinating economic activities with a view to stimulating dynamic change over the long haul. Without it minimizing the damage of adverse developments and maximizing the gains from economic governance are not possible. This capacity presupposes that governance must be looked at from within a, possibly highly, dynamic perspective. It is the ability of those governing to adapt flexibly and responsibly to the requirements of the changing environment and of the partly self-chosen system that determines whether governance supports modernization (Frischtak and Atiyas 1996).

Better governance requires political accountability, freedom of association and participation, transparency and openness in most public activities, a sound juridical system based on the rule of law, accountability of the public administration, freedom of information and expression, and the ability of the government to deliver on its promises and to divest itself of tasks that eventually can be better executed in the private sector. Accountability in governance is critical and has at least three related dimensions. One is the existence of constitutional or legislated protection of the public interest through a code that regulates both public and private behavior. Another is the enforcement of such laws through specific institutions that receive adequate resources and are relatively independent of the political system. Note the "relative" qualifier for ultimately all offices in the public service have to be filled through the executive or legislative branches of government, and are hence affected by the political system in place. Finally, social expectations shared by rulers and ruled that provide the underpinnings of enforcement and compliance should be identified and widely relied upon.

One may harbor legitimate concerns about the ability of many transition economies to deliver even minimal governance in the sense defined. This is at the heart of the difficulties with formulating, implementing, monitoring, assessing, and adapting the transformation processes at this stage. However, absence of or poor capabilities is not a sufficient reason for shunning governance altogether. After all, capabilities can be acquired, in some cases rather quickly, provided the will to do so is present. This applies also to the commitment to deliver assistance via regional and international organizations (see Chapter 11). Not only that, many of the transition's problems cannot be resolved without a minimal degree of governance to hold together a workable sociopolitical consensus, and so assimilating these capabilities soonest should rank high on the assistance and transformation agendas.

Section 4: Overfull employment as a legacy for transition

As pointed out in Chapters 1 and 2, for over four decades in eastern Europe and nearly twice that long throughout most of the former Soviet Union (excepting the Baltic States), open unemployment was all but nonexistent. Until the late 1980s, not only was every able-bodied person above school and under retirement age entitled to a job. In many countries, it was a specific legal obligation for every such person to be gainfully employed, largely within the socialized sectors, though, after some initial hiccups, private agriculture remained dominant in Poland and Yugoslavia. As a counterpart, the state assumed responsibility for creating employment opportunities, primarily in the state sector. Not only was there full employment due to chronic hunger for labor inputs, job security was deeply anchored in the socialist welfare state, the stigma of being jobless was pronounced, and citizens had come to view this all-around social security as an acquired right largely independent of actual work performance.

Many implications of this reality can be specified. The salient ones for our purposes are eight. One striking consequence was exceedingly high labor-force participation rates, roughly 10–20 percentage points above comparable data for western countries, even though with variations among the countries. Although there was a decline in participation under state socialism during the 1980s and a rise in participation in western countries, notably for women, when the former collapsed the margin was still in "favor" of the eastern part of Europe by some 10 points; and more for female participation.

Another consequence was that the vast majority of new jobs tended to be created in heavy industry and in activities that with transition can no longer be sustained. Services not directly related to material production (the "nonmaterial sphere") as a rule received short shrift in development priorities throughout state socialism. Note that some countries had started to relax this bias well before the transition got under way. This explains part of the dynamics through which layoffs or quits in the industrial sectors have recently been absorbed chiefly in the emerging private activities, as detailed later.

Third, geographical labor mobility (as distinct from job hopping, for example, to beat rigid wage scales) under state socialism was limited. Even without formal constraints, labor mobility remained confined by the chronic housing shortage in urban areas and the housing-allocation system resorted to especially in industrial centers.

Fourth, some jobs were associated with low-cost housing, particularly in the state sector. State socialism also eased access to schools, to in-house training, and to medical care, including hospitals and sanatoria; and arranged for privileged availability of consumer goods otherwise in short supply, of health-care institutions, of child-care and nursery facilities without which female participation could not have been sustained, as well as of a variety of leisure activities. Note that the enumerated nonwage social and other benefits unrelated to actual job performance, at times correlated with the "type" of job (such as the privileged position of Polish miners), facilitated "organized" – read planned – labor mobility, but discouraged voluntary mobility. Except in Yugoslavia, migration was fully controlled through interstate agreements.

Fifth, this type of social-welfare distribution system had implications for policy formulation during the transition (see Chapter 3). No real-estate market emerged, lock-in of housing in SOEs was widespread, and throughout state socialism chronic undersupply of housing, certainly in urbanized areas, where policy makers tended to concentrate the vast majority of industrial SOEs, remained pronounced.

Sixth, with the redirection of resource allocation in tune with market-based decisions the activities of firms have become increasingly focused on their commercial tasks. On the whole, new or privatized firms do not provide their workers with social services that had traditionally inhered in being employed by an SOE. This is also occurring in the SOEs that still exist. These microeconomic shifts raise many vexing questions: Who will henceforth provide and finance these services? Who will be responsible for the associated assets? How can the population prospectively afford such (partially) commercialized services (notably housing, medical care, nurseries, some vocational training, and education above the primary level more generally)? I return to these issues in Section 6.

Arguably even more important than who will henceforth provide those goods and services effectively and how quickly this transformation can credibly materialize, are the prices at which these outputs will henceforth become available. The change in relative prices against the erstwhile free or nearly-free social benefits cannot but drastically affect family budgets. One should be concerned about how soon such market-based pricing can realistically be enforced for there is a limit to how much of the real cost the consumer can absorb in the short run. This is critical also with respect to the more humdrum aspects of enhancing labor-market flexibility (see Section 6).

Seventh, particularly in most CIS States the transfer of services still performed by SOEs to fully or quasi-commercialized operations has posed a major obstacle to economic restructuring. Many SOEs and even those ostensibly privatized (see Chapter 6) have been short of cash to pay the wage bill (not to speak of the tax and social-security bills) and have furloughed a sizable proportion of their workers. Most of the affected workers continue to be on the enterprise roll but not on the payroll if only to preserve access to several nonwage benefits (particularly housing, canteens, and essential medical services). Avoiding the stigma of unemployment, reserving one's right to shares in companies when privatization gets under way, and cherishing the hope of being rehired with better

316

times play a role too. In other words, most firms continue to be a repository of a substantial part of the real labor redundancies in these countries, in part because of inertia and strategic calculations regarding the benefits of preserving "human capital" and "worker support" for privatization.

Finally, creating new jobs during the transition, whether in the open economy or not, depends primarily on features of the labor market broadly considered that owe their existence on the whole to past developments. Of particular importance are the legacies of state socialism, in addition to the historical burden of agrarian overpopulation. But this is being compounded by newer developments that had not been anticipated on the transition's eve. Thus, new firms were expected to identify increments to their workforce essentially by hiring the unemployed, particularly those shed by SOEs in manufacturing and mining. Instead, new jobs tend to be filled by recruiting new entrants into the labor force or hiring away those in the state sector, perhaps because of the embodied knowledge that "insiders" can mobilize particularly in the context of massive divestment for new agents largely unfamiliar with the past, and often the current, business environment in these countries. In practice, those losing their job on the whole have tended to join the pool of unemployed, thus exacerbating the structural problems characterizing long-term unemployment. In short, these people become essentially unemployable, regardless of the measures initiated to improve the workings of budding labor markets.

Even with a vibrant new private sector, the employment problem can at best be tackled over a protracted period of time. Coming to grips with those central aspects of labor markets is a critical task of orderly transformation, regardless of the format that policy makers may favor for conceptualizing, implementing, and fine-tuning the transition agenda. First and foremost, apart from the social safety net, is the need to ensure that labor markets become more flexible all-around, not just for newly emerging private activities.

Section 5: Salient features of labor markets in transformation

Unemployment in the European transition economies has been exhibiting features that had not been counted on when the transitions were first inaugurated (Blanchard, Commander, and Coricelli 1995). Of special importance are ten. First, one of the more puzzling side-effects of the transition has been the rapid decline in absolute levels of total employment, from some 193 million in 1989 to 170 million in 1995 – a reduction of 11.7 percent; it declined further in 1996 but at the more moderating pace observed on average since 1994. The fall has been very steep – some 16 percent – for the smaller countries in eastern Europe, including the former Yugoslavia; similar declines are recorded, though more recently, in the Baltic States. The magnitude has been less – perhaps 11–12 percent – for the other successor States of the Soviet Union. Recall, however, that there are severe measurement problems (UNWES 1994).

Some shrinkage had been anticipated, given disguised unemployment under administrative planning, artificially high participation rates, and the anticipated "mild" economic downturn. A much sharper contraction became unavoidable, however, in the wake of the marked economic depression throughout these countries. The drop in employment cannot, of course, be equated with involuntary unemployment. Some of those ejected from the labor force have registered as unemployed or have been identified as being without work and actively looking for a job. Others have been discouraged, thus given up not only on registering in labor offices but also in looking for a formal job. Many are probably involuntarily unemployed. In the interim, some may have joined the informal economy, which by definition eludes official statistics. In several economies, women in particular have left the labor force, in some cases because child assistance previously provided by SOEs is no longer affordable, if available, or because maternity leave has been administered even more generously than under state socialism in a deliberate policy effort to disguise unemployment. Or the real problems have been deferred through various part-time jobs, sometimes subsidized from central budgets, and training and retraining programs. Also, some economies have applied early-retirement schemes and have forced out of the labor force workers above retirement age, thereby putting pressure on the country's social-security systems without counteracting the negative economic, psychological, and social impacts of the transitions. Some have voluntarily taken early retirement on the ground that prevailing social-security commitments would be honored once on the pension roll, whereas the benefits would in all likelihood be scaled down in the future. Real benefits have, however, markedly shrunk in most countries.

Second, open unemployment, measured by the number of those registered as eligible for some form of social compensation because they are looking for a job and need to be tided over, escalated during the first four years of transition in Eastern Europe from some 3 million persons in 1990 to about 8 million in 1993, but with a drop since then to over 6 million in 1996. In the Baltic States, the numbers of registered unemployed are still rather small, having inched up from some 7,400 in 1991 to 197,000 in 1994 and 240,000 in 1996. The data for the other successor States of the Soviet Union show only moderate open unemployment: from under 100,000 in 1991 to just over 1.2 million in 1993, but rapidly rising to over 8 million in 1996.

These data underline the escalation in the share of the labor force that is registered as unemployed but apparently willing to work – at present some 14 million. Actual shares and levels of unemployment, using labor surveys, tend to yield significantly higher magnitudes, particularly for the CIS States. In any case, measured shares range from a claimed roughly 0.4 to 4 percent in the CIS, except Armenia, to between presently 16 and 40 percent in the successor States of Yugoslavia. As regards the CIS, "latent unemployment" is vastly higher. In Russia in 1996 it was 9.2 percent of the total labor force, instead of the 3.4 percent registered as unemployed. Even among the eastern European countries,

318

levels of open and registered unemployment ranged in 1996 from some 3.5 percent in the Czech Republic to some 13.6 percent in Poland (well below the over 16 percent peak reached in early 1994). In the Baltic States, unemployment rates continue to be fairly low (between 5.6 and 7.2 percent), although real unemployment is probably much higher – between 10 and 16 percent – if the underemployed and those on short-time hours and on indefinite unpaid leave are included. The crest of unemployment now seems to have been passed except in countries where industrial restructuring has not thus far been effectively enforced. But even with the jobs created since 1994 and the withdrawals from the labor force, unemployment continues to be in the double-digit range, except in the Czech Republic and Romania, and is therefore a sociopolitical blight on the transition's record.

Third, those who are losing their job and are relatively unskilled tend to become chronic unemployed, thus exacerbating a "low turnover" or "stable pool" rather than joining a "churning pool" of unemployed, in part because most of the initial employment adjustment in the state sector was largely accommodated by direct flows to jobs in other sectors, allowing for those who quit the labor force through early retirement, discouragement, or disability. The pool of unemployed is being fed from both the state and private sectors, with the latter coming close in relative terms to the quits in the state sector as the initial adjustments in the private sector to fill obvious gaps left by state socialism are being completed. As a result, most countries have seen an alarming rise in the share of those unemployed for more than one year (now over 50 percent in eastern Europe, except the Czech Republic, Poland, and the Yugoslav successor States, but around one third and rising in the successor States of the Soviet Union) with regional concentrations. This raises the specter of large numbers of unemployable people, regardless of the measures initiated to improve labor markets. The threat is most acute for unskilled, manual, and female workers (Leven 1993; Standing 1994).

Excepting Hungary and Slovenia, more than half of the unemployed are female and in some countries this group tends to be affected earlier, as more traditional "female" jobs, such as administrative or secretarial posts in SOEs, are excised before "production" workers, largely male in heavy industry, are let go and the absorption in the newly emerging private sector has not yet fully got under way. This has been especially pronounced early in the transition in Bulgaria, Russia, and Ukraine, where the proportion of men joining the pool rose within one or two years following the initial runup in female unemployment (Beleva 1993; Dimitrova 1993; Kirova 1993). But the share of female unemployment in terms of the female labor force remains higher than that for men. The reverse situation in Hungary and to a lesser extent in Slovenia can be explained in terms of the early start with industrial restructuring and the emerging service sector.

Fourth, new entrants to the labor force, particularly those with lower-level and vocational training as compared to those with advanced degrees in most countries

319

(but apparently not in the Czech Republic), encounter obstacles in securing a workplace. Unemployment for those below 25 is particularly high, about double the average and in some countries, including Romania, nearly three times that. Measured magnitudes almost certainly vastly understate the problem in most cases. Most register as unemployed only when some compensation can be accessed and "transaction costs" are not forbidding. Those with advanced degrees are attracted to new private firms, oftentimes their own. Linguistic skills and *savoir-faire*, which unskilled workers as a rule lack, may play an important role particularly in entering employment in new foreign firms.

Fifth, labor shedding from existing SOEs has been much less, given the level of disguised unemployment through overstaffing and low labor productivity as well as the contraction in output levels, than had been anticipated. SOEs initially adopted a wait-and-see attitude in an effort to protect their labor complement even at the cost of an erosion in real wage and benefit levels. Even when turned over to private owners or to independent boards of directors, and in an adaptive mode for those not yet privatized, these firms have not infrequently maintained their labor complement in spite of redundancy. There are probably favorable externalities that explain this: Propping up morale and labor peace, preserving available insider information, being able quickly to take advantage of any upturn in the pace of economic activity, avoiding severance-pay liabilities, and the opportunities for existing workers and management to participate more actively in the *de facto* or *de jure* divestment of state assets. The degree of enterprise restructuring is positively correlated with the incidence of labor shedding in industry and indeed the rapid rise in productivity with economic recovery.

Sixth, the shedding of labor has had a differential impact on various social strata that used to be employed, including older workers, minorities, women, and the functionally disabled. Youth has found it difficult to gain entry into traditional manufacturing. Old prejudices and stereotypes have been reemerging in several countries, notably in hiring women or minorities (Sziraczki and Windell 1993), such as the Romanies (Blaha 1993).

Seventh, there has generally been a pronounced and worsening regional employment imbalance; at any rate, the degree of regional dispersion of unemployment rates in eastern Europe is large when judged by comparable magnitudes for western countries. As a rule, urban centers, such as state and provincial capitals and other centrally located cities, are faring much better than rural areas, in contrast to the typical situation in market economies, where urban blight and crime are frequently associated with high levels of unemployment and confined chances of emerging from the unemployment pool. In some capitals, such as Prague, it has proved difficult to alleviate an acute shortage of qualified labor resources because influx from high-unemployment areas is inhibited in part by lack of affordable housing. Furthermore, especially in central Europe, the situation suggests a sharp deterioration in opportunities moving from west to east. This owes a good deal to the CMEA's collapse. But it also derives from the buoyancy of trade and economic cooperation with, as well as FDI flows from, western Europe, particularly Austria and Germany (see Chapter 10). Regional imbalances have also become pronounced in the CIS States, owing to the advanced degree of manufacturing monoculture fostered under state socialism. The collapse of inter-republic trade ties has made this into an acute problem in the more outlying former Soviet republics.

Eighth, some short-term asymmetries in labor-market adjustments have been at work in the countries that have sought meaningful structural change, and they may last longer than those observed for developed countries: When aggregate demand increases, real wages for the employed and their productivity rise, but employment does not, or to a much smaller extent. This is in marked contrast to the association between decreases in aggregate demand and employment changes: Employment is compressed and wages for those remaining in the labor force are kept level or decrease only slightly with productivity declining less than the level of economic activity. This exacerbates the wedge between insiders and outsiders, thus magnifying chronic unemployment.

Ninth, output has dropped far more than employment in spite of chronic over-staffing in SOEs. This suggests that the true unemployment situation for many countries is bound to deteriorate for some time to come. It will also further worsen because of the disguised unemployment endemic for SOEs. Although it is a crude gauge, some idea of the former can be obtained by comparing cumulative declines in output and employment since 1989. A large discrepancy between the two suggests that average labor productivity declined as well because of "hidden" unemployment relative to the situation that existed prior to the transition. Note that those employed largely in SOEs remain there either because management finds it convenient, perhaps lucrative, to hold on to the labor complement or because workers are reluctant to give up the relevant nonwage benefits, both of which the state accommodates.

Seen over the period 1989–96, the degree of apparent hoarding has recently shrunk somewhat in several countries with incipient to strong economic recovery and contraction in employment levels, which may be indicative that enterprise restructuring is finally getting under way. But it continues to be quite large (over 10 percentage points) in countries such as the Czech Republic, Romania, virtually all the successor States of the Soviet Union and of Yugoslavia, excepting Slovenia, in spite of efforts to delay active transformation measures. These data suggest that the prospective dimensions of the unemployment problem, once enterprise restructuring finally affects nearly the entire economy, are daunting. This is notably the case, with hoarding magnitudes exceeding 20 percentage points, in Croatia, Macedonia, virtually all of the successor States of the Soviet Union, and rump Yugoslavia; there are likely to be other countries in this league. Unemployment in these countries in social, as distinct from statistical, terms is bound to worsen considerably in the future, even though the problem is already large, particularly when the above indicators are supplemented with reasonable estimates of traditional overstaffing in most SOEs. This cannot but further deflate people's expectations and aggravate disaffection with the transformation strategies. Note that in many cases this means more disappointment with the immediate consequences of the strategies pursued, and apparent inability of the new leadership to stanch the palpable socioeconomic hemorrhage, than a fundamental shift in sentiment as regards the nature of the desirable economic, political, and social remaking of their societies.

Finally, the ratio of the numbers of unemployed to vacancies in all transition economies tends to worsen rapidly after the first few months of transition policies. Virtually everywhere the number of vacancies is much smaller than the number of unemployed, sometimes by a factor of 50 to over 100. This may in part reflect some structural, rather than frictional, seasonal, or cyclical mismatch in labor markets. Only more recently has there been an apparent improvement in this situation notably in countries that have gradually been emerging from recession. But for some time the unemployment/vacancy ratio remains erratic. A more solid decrease thereof depends critically on having experienced growth for some time and indeed on embarking on a sustainable growth trajectory, when the process of economic restructuring through modernization opens up new jobs (see Chapter 12). The situation in most of the successor States of the Soviet Union and Yugoslavia is not encouraging in this respect, particularly when allowance is made for the difficult measurement problems. Moreover, particularly in the former, the combination of falling employment, rising unemployment, and increasing vacancies may indicate a structural mismatch in labor markets (UNECE 1995, p. 116; 1997, pp. 79ff.).

Earlier assumptions on unemployment being confined and transitory with markets clearing were simply naïve. Whereas part of the unemployment problem can be resolved with strong and sustained growth, entire layers of workers are likely to be excluded from the new job opportunities even if policy makers encourage job creation and prepare the unemployed for meeting new job requirements. It has also become clear that the way in which the pool of the unemployed has been taken care of through unemployment-insurance, and more general social-policy support programs, is not sustainable without a massive effort directed at reintegrating the unemployed, both those still looking for a job and others who have been discouraged but might be lured back if job opportunities were to emerge (OECD 1996a). ALMPs constitute one component of what should be done to ameliorate the situation, particularly to increase "churning" and thus compress the probability that the chronic unemployed become unemployable. In some countries (notably Poland and Romania) with positive demographic trends, indicating a rise in working-age population for the foreseeable future, measures deserve to be taken to prepare youngsters for a yet more demanding job market. Education and training can play some positive role here. In others with demographic trends indicating a rapidly aging population (including Bulgaria and Hungary), policy attention should be on coming to grips with a rapid rise in the number of aged persons relative to the working-age population (Boeri and Sziraczki 1993) with social-policy implications (see Section 7 and beyond).

For reasons of sociopolitical stability, employment in obsolete activities – the core of the "old" state sector, in some cases even after nominal divestment – cannot be eliminated in record tempo, employment creation in the private sector lags significantly behind the pace required to absorb desirable layoffs in the state sector and new entrants, and restructuring social-welfare provisions traditionally passed on through SOEs has proved to be a cumbersome exercise (Boeri 1994, 1995; Burda 1995; Franz 1995). For these and related reasons, while transition economies have eliminated most outright budget subsidies, many have embraced more subtle temporary transfers. Most common has been granting credit on a basis that has little to do with the borrower's creditworthiness; I include here the nonenforcement of arrears such as interenterprise debt, debt to pension funds, and unpaid tax obligations. But other facilitations, such as fiscal easements and larger import protection than decision makers would otherwise have preferred, have been accommodated. In some cases, early commitments to very liberal trade and exchange regimes have had to be reconsidered, pending greater progress with building a "normal market economy."

In other words, the transition economies have learned the hard way that labor-market pressures with marked downsizing of the economy can be alleviated only over time and through compromise. Even when embraced pragmatically, with the emphasis squarely on ALMPs, labor markets continue to experience pressures for years. Except for the speed with which it emerged, the features of unemployment, though not of labor markets as such, in the transition economies exhibit increasingly the familiar characteristics of structural unemployment in western Europe. Whereas the latter may well continue to muddle through for as long as the employed tax payers remain willing to fund the outlays that avert a social revolt, this stance cannot be replicated in the transition economies. For one thing, funding is simply not available to afford the unemployed the support cushion common in developed countries. Also, these countries have had a long history of social commitment to worker protection and some sort of social contract, often stretching back to well before the advent of communism; militancy for some form of codetermination remains pronounced. Expectations deriving from these and related realities cannot be wiped out by replacing administered markets with the neoliberal credo (Moene and Wallerstein 1993; Przeworski 1993).

As advocated in Chapter 7, it might be useful to elaborate social-democratic labor-market policies in part to solidify the sociopolitical consensus. That framework encompasses some of the measures that policy makers have been compelled to institute since 1989. Thus, there would certainly be room for affordable unemployment compensation, particularly when structured in a sensible manner with proper termination commitments and adequate support for a limited time, possibly made contingent on training or workfare programs. There would also be scope for social-welfare policy to take care of the weaker strata in society and those who, through no ill will of their own, simply find themselves excluded from labor markets due to the transition's vagaries.

Perhaps more important is the adoption of ALMPs for which in short order most outlays for unemployment should preferably be appropriated. This has thus far been underplayed in virtually all transition economies – Czechoslovakia and the Czech Republic being a major exception (Burda and Lubyova 1995; Ham, Švejnar, and Terrell 1995) – perhaps in the misguided expectation that markets would take care of reallocating labor resources. ALMPs are not a wonder remedy even if associated with the creation of new jobs; jobs need demand and that will necessarily have to come from solid economic growth in a more certain environment than prevails at this stage in most transition economies. Some active measures have been designed to alleviate the shortage of skills in demand; to combat the lack of mobility of the labor force for regional reasons or because of housing problems; to restore some measure of growth; and to foster the private sector, perhaps in combination with newly privatized state assets, so that new, fairly dependable, jobs will be created soonest. Another goal that deserves more than casual attention in ALMPs is to identify a new, employment-intensive growth path that can be endogenously sustained (see Chapter 12). I am thinking here especially of all kinds of education, the management of technological policies, the support of science, encouragement of entrepreneurship, and promotion of other policies that enable the individual to become and remain more productive, including from society's point of view.

Finally, I should like to flag up briefly the issue of industrial policy, which I view (Brabant 1993a, p. 49) as a strategy formulated, and possibly initiated, by the state (or on its behalf) that encompasses mechanisms by which the actions of various layers of decision making about resource allocation in an economy can be coordinated, monitored, evaluated, and fine-tuned. Clearly, suitable governance capabilities must be in place or quickly acquired, including perhaps through foreign assistance. These actions are designed to influence, by direct or indirect means, static resource allocation in and among economic sectors, and especially the pace and composition of dynamic economic expansion. The means used to reach this goal are selective commitments of resources to particular activities with a view to facilitating, accelerating, or retrenching their growth path, in the end yielding accelerated modernization.

Industrial policy is not an end in itself. Rather, if the principal purposes of the transformation are to catch up with the more advanced countries of western Europe and to strengthen the underlying foundations of political democracy, it is difficult to envisage how such a new growth path can be discovered, walked along, and sustained over the long haul by relying principally on stabilization, liberalization, and privatization. At the very least institutions need to be built, including revamping the role of the state in economic affairs and encouraging the formation of constructive trade unions. Also, efforts have to be marshaled to obtain and sustain a minimal sociopolitical consensus. Industrial policy deserves to be carefully considered in a pragmatic frame, rather than rejected out of hand on ideological grounds, if properly wielded by a governance structure that has clout and responsibility (Chang 1994; Wade 1990, 1995); that does not get captured by rent seekers; and that recognizes the merits of sharing the benefits of economic expansion. That would be particularly germane to meeting the requirements for regaining and sustaining growth by fostering market-conforming, -correcting, and -integrating measures. It could also help to solidify the sociopolitical consensus, including through direct actions to loosen up labor markets.

Unemployment is too high and entails a vast waste of scarce resources. Whether remedial measures can be activated depends first and foremost on political will, largely to conduct macroeconomic policy with a view to encouraging a more employment-intensive growth path. Of course, also the confined maneuvering room in transition economies stemming from the myriad of constraints on conducting the most desirable transformation policy, and on hopping onto such a recovery-to-modernization trajectory, must be duly considered. Recognizing these obstacles is quite different from simply deciding that nothing can be done to tackle them, perhaps out of misguided *a priori* ideological fear of corrupting transformation. This includes notably the creation of integrated and reasonably flexible labor markets within a sensible tripartite arrangement. Without such a policy stance, it is doubtful that the so vital economic, political, and social restructuring of the transition economies can prospectively be completed without jeopardizing core features of the "1989" visions.

The strategy pursued until now in many transition economies, either in the form of disguising or hiding unemployment or simply putting in place unemployment-compensation and social-support programs, will not do. I maintain this while recognizing the evident obstacles of commercializing the nonwage benefits of SOEs and of widespread unemployment, even if financial support can be mobilized. The markets for goods, services, capital, and labor in particular – arguably "the most important of all markets" (Burda 1995, p. 332) – in transition economies are still too fragile, incomplete, and unintegrated for policy makers to confidently predict that the employment problem can be solved spontaneously. Experiences of mature economies with labor-market failures should be heeded: Without positive policy intervention, the pool of unemployed becomes overloaded with the chronically unemployable, leading to economic and social, and indeed personal, ills that aggravate the sociopolitical concerns arising from the already unsettled employment situation. However, steps to reintegrate the unemployed should be carefully weighed and tailored to the requirements of readying workers for more durable jobs whose emergence, in turn, has to be fostered as well.

In a longer-term perspective, in which the economic restructuring issues ahead are fully reflected, much more encompassing ALMPs need to be embraced. Indeed, efforts to foster greater transparency and flexibility through retraining and mobility are required. These should preferably be strategic components of more forward-looking macroeconomic policies imbued with the goal of regaining growth, even though in and of itself this cannot be a panacea. This goal can be accomplished only when government plays a forward-looking role. In the interim, measures to enhance precisely that can take the form of some kind of industrial policy designed to avert pushing masses of workers out of a job through

325

targeted temporary subsidies directed at creating and sustaining employment, rather than through muddling-through strategies. Recall in this connection that creating judiciously chosen employment through some form of state support alleviates the state of the costs of unemployment and brings in new revenues, so that the net incremental burden of supporting employment expansion is inferior to the apparent wage cost – and revenue – of job creation. But this can only be a temporary solution. Only through active intervention could available resources conceivably be productively mobilized and the unemployment problem allevi-ated. Emigration may offer at the margin a temporary solution. But deliberately exporting excess labor, even through a cheap-labor export drive, is at best a cynical way of fostering markets supportive of political democracy.

Section 6: Social services and rearranging property rights

The transition induced firms to shed their inherited social obligations, as noted. Such institutional microeconomic reform poses many problems (see Section 4). It is not particularly useful to excise such benefits all at once early on in the transition. Nor can sudden commercialization of these services support the consensus. Clearly, some will continue to be performed in the public sector (such as access to schools, vocational training, child care, and kindergartens), and so the questions are who will do so and how will these operations be financed. Others can be provided in the private sector, including through NPOs. And a third category can simply be abolished (such as access to a wide variety of consumer goods in short supply, including canteen provisions, as well as leisure activities) or left altogether to the private commercial sector, perhaps in the for-mat of new small service firms. Proceeding according to this scheme presupposes that policy makers are able to conduct an orderly triage. Furthermore, since some services can be restructured faster than others (say the commercialization of vacation facilities as compared to lifting housing rents to market levels), policy makers must be in a position to draw up a strategy for social-policy reform; that should not, of course, be confined to the services typically provided through the SOE network. Finally, for services that will henceforth be commercialized policy makers must make their preferences explicit as regards minimum access for the layers of society that cannot be expected to profit from the transformation. Some means-testing will henceforth be required to assure delivery, notably low-cost housing, hospitals, nurseries, sanatoria, and health care more generally. Many of these services need regulations set by government.

Loosening up the ways in which some of these services were provided would be beneficial to economic transformation. An example may suffice to drive the point home. Low-cost housing allocated through the SOEs hindered labor mobility, as indicated. Given the various dimensions of the unemployment problem and the uncertain prospects for sustainable growth, mobility needs to be encouraged on a priority basis. For that a real-estate market must be allowed to emerge and rendered as flexible as possible. But that takes time and effort. It is sobering in this connection to reflect upon the following: Notwithstanding the most vocal free-market rhetoric of some policy makers, not a single transition economy has thus far succeeded in enforcing market-based rents, except in the thoroughly privatized sector, such as newly built housing, where owners can negotiate their own rental conditions. Even in arguably the most liberal economy, the Czech Republic, most housing rents will not be market based until well into the twenty-first century. Essential utility charges, such as for electricity and gas, in most countries continue to be heavily subsidized. All this complicates ensuring adequate availability of goods and services, given the parlous state of government budgets, and that those operations can be run profitably without creating socially destabilizing monopolies. The same holds for the link between a job-specific package of nonwage benefits, of course, since it makes job hunting into a complex operation that diverts attention from the specific choice between work and leisure at given labor-related remuneration.

Just as it is incumbent on good governance during the privatization campaign to ensure that state assets are kept intact and not siphoned off for private purposes, some instance must preserve at least the physical infrastructure of these social-service and -catering operations. As experience has demonstrated, the physical infrastructure of these social-service operations is frequently captured by those best placed in the "privatization" process and then exploited for private purposes, whereas the obligation to deliver the services ends up once again with government. Given the dire financial straits in which the state tumbles soon after the initiation of stabilization policies (see Chapter 4), this obligation is then frequently devolved to regional or local governments, ostensibly in order to downsize central government. But the budgetary constraints of these lower-level organs are arguably even tighter. Because the private sector is not equipped, at any rate not yet able, to provide such services on a commercial or voluntary basis, the result is often a marked decline in the availability and a deterioration in the accessibility of those services early on in the transition even without rationalization of the sector being attempted (Horton 1996; IMF 1997c). Paradoxically this occurs at a time when the need for a broad social safety net tends to be the greatest, if only to cushion the impact of those most adversely affected by the transition and to preserve a semblance of sociopolitical stability. Initially, this net should ideally also incorporate a weft for social functions that eventually need to be commercialized, and perhaps divested. Incentives to move expeditiously in that direction deserve to be reinforced. These transitory tasks are quite distinct from the social functions that properly belong in the public sector, whether completely (such as unemployment insurance and most forms of welfare support), in some form of surveillance and supervision (such as in the case of pension and health-insurance funds), or in a deliberate attempt to redistribute incomes (such as to alleviate poverty and take care of the helpless layers of society). The transition economies lag on both counts, albeit to different degrees. The proper role of the public sector in weaving the pattern and strengthening the warp of the safety

327

net according to revolving needs and resources has not received adequate attention to date. This is especially the case for those without gainful employment.

I cannot, of course, in what follows examine in detail all of the options for reform in these social-sector provisions, regardless of whether they were previously funneled through SOEs. I focus here on pension reform separately (see Section 7) from four other social-policy aspects: health care, medical care, education, and science (see Section 8). I return to other issues thereafter, particularly in discussing the link between budgetary stringency and social-service provisioning.

Section 7: Pension reform

By the end of state socialism, countries had gradually erected a very generous pension system on a pay-as-you-go (PAYG) basis. Generous refers to the statutory as well as the effective entitlement age and the size of the pension relative to the income earned during the later years of employment. In many cases, the system also tolerated pensioners who worked without losing their social benefits. With transition, the economic collapse and the sizable rise in pensioners have placed a heavy, at times an intolerable, burden on central budgets. The reasons thereof need to be clear.

7.1 – The state-socialist legacy

As part of the cradle-to-grave social-security blanket installed in particular in the more developed countries, policy makers tried to protect households from large fluctuations in real incomes. In a normal life cycle, people first consume. Once they start working they are expected to earn for a generation or more. During the final phase of the life cycle they normally wish to consume from savings. Under state socialism, for most individuals there was little chance to accumulate real and financial assets from which revenue could be derived to sustain old age without remunerative work or that could be passed on to heirs, possibly to fund the early-life stages of the next generation. In several countries and for some groups, such as farmers, for years the support of the retired came from the active population through the "family" system. For most workers, however, the financing of retirement coincided with accessing a state pension.

Pensions constitute by far the largest component of social expenditures throughout these countries. In the more developed ones, these outlays normally account for between two thirds and three fourths of total social-security outlays. Not only that, this publicly managed PAYG scheme often represents the single largest public-expenditure component. Pension expenditure in any given year is financed by that year's contributions in the form of payroll taxes. Any shortfall is covered by budgetary transfers. Whereas in the early stages of state socialism such pension schemes applied in particular to workers in the state sector, by the time state socialism was about to collapse in the late 1980s for all practical

328

purposes universal coverage prevailed. Also, as part of the social contract, especially in countries where policy makers felt compelled to trade off political acquiescence for social benefits, the statutory retirement age had been lowered over time and generous schemes were in place to permit early retirement, such as for disability; the number of disability pensioners in the total retirees tends to be very high, some 30 percent for Hungary and Poland, as compared to perhaps 10 percent in most OECD countries. This stems not only from the rigors of work in these countries; but also from rather generous regulations on disability retirement and lax enforcement of the rules in place. In addition, benefits relative to earnings during the latter part of productive life were raised several times.

Even before state socialism's collapse, the level of expenditure on pensions relative to aggregate output exceeded 10 percent, not unlike the situation in most OECD countries. Recall, however, that the share of labor revenue to GDP in these countries was well below that of developed countries. In other words, contribution rates tended to be rather high. This suggests that the statutory (and effective) entitlement age, the number of retirees, or the expected benefits relative to earlier revenues tended to be rather generous. In fact, the problem was a combination of these factors. Official statutory retirement ages, commonly between 55 and 60, were lower in countries with state socialism than in most other countries with a publicly managed pension system, where age 65 is a more common target. Effective retirement age, however, was much lower as statutory retirement was the exception rather than the rule. For example, Poland had a relatively high official retirement age of 65 for men and 60 for women; but due to early retirement and various allowances for disability, the actual age was closer to 59 for men and 55 for women. In a number of countries, furthermore, demographic pressures in terms of rising life expectancy and declining fertility rates were exacerbating the imbalance between pension revenues and expenditures, thus calling for rising contributions from the budget to support the PAYG scheme.

7.2 – The exacerbation of the situation during the transition

The transition has aggravated this situation in a number of respects. One could detail them by referring to the rising number of claimants and the diminishing number of contributors to the PAYG, the pressures on government budgets in general, and the inability of some countries to erode the real value of pensions, say, to the same extent that workers lost in terms of real wages. Poland is a case in point (Leven 1997). It is useful to distinguish between the factors that transition policies aggravated and the difficulties of the pension schemes due chiefly to the legacies of state socialism.

The economic collapse, withdrawal from the labor force, and substantial unemployment have removed many contributors and raised the number of claimants, hence total outlays from pension funds; the real value of contributions has also declined in many cases. This has been exacerbated by the booming second economy and exceptional rules even in the open economy regarding those subject to payroll taxes. The booming private sector, whether legal or not, contains a large component of revenue earners who do not contribute to the pension scheme. Note that part of the problem has been induced by policy makers to disguise the magnitude of the calamitous employment situation. Without such generous state actions during the early transition stages, economic depression and restructuring would have placed the social consensus under even more severe strains than actually materialized. As earlier indicated, the problem stems also from the reaction of those about to retire early on in the transition. In all likelihood they figured that commitments made by state socialism would be honored early on in the transition but perhaps not later. This was, in fact, made even more attractive by rather liberal regulations as concerns employment or work-related income earning after retirement. Even where that is not the case, pensioners receive generous revenues that tend to be untaxed and the inhibitions of working in the second economy are derisory. The present "dependency ratio," defined as the number of pensioners divided by the number of contributors, tends to be very high, certainly much higher than in many developed countries. Here lies one of the great difficulties that central budgets encounter early on in the transition. Furthermore, the hardships of the transition have in most countries further lowered fertility, although sometimes "compensated," as in Russia and Ukraine, by declining life expectancy, particularly for men.

As a result of this widening gap between pension revenues and expenditures, the distortions in labor markets caused by the wedge between takehome pay and labor costs and by the layers of society that contribute and those who do not is becoming intolerable. Moreover, with the additional personal income taxes faced by workers in the legal sector, and recently introduced unemployment benefits, those at the lower end of the labor market face high marginal rates of tax and benefit withdrawal. These tend to compress labor supply and raise incentives for benefit dependency and participation in the informal sector, further lowering the tax base. All this may eventually undermine the competitive position of these countries and fail to encourage workers to raise their labor productivity.

7.3 – Why should the state engage in some type of insurance activities?

Before exploring feasible and desirable reforms of the pension systems in transition economies, the rationale for state intervention in social security should be clear. This reaches beyond the provisioning of pensions, of course, as it could be applied to virtually all instances in which state-mandated and -operated insurance schemes are in effect, except when motivated by ideology as under state socialism. Unemployment and disability insurance are classical cases. Their origin harks back not only to the failures in insurance markets but also to broader objectives of saving and redistribution that the state may wish to encourage (Don and Besseling 1996). The two classical arguments for government interference with insurance against loss of income are to protect high-risk groups and to offer insurance where the private sector fails but a social need for protection is felt. The latter includes insurance against "collective risks," meaning that a large group of "clients" might suffer damage at the same time. As usual, this interference distorts the price signals to the market and hence tends to lead to a less efficient allocation of resources – a classical tradeoff between equity and efficiency.

Private insurance should be encouraged whenever egregious market failure can be avoided. But such markets are special as insurers face four types of problems. First, the cost of information required to write and implement a contract can be high. A uniform and collective contract, using rules on the provision of information set by government, may substantially alleviate this problem especially when clients fail to understand all the details of alternative insurance arrangements. Second, interdependent risks (such as natural disasters, inflation, and unemployment) hit many clients at the same time. A private insurer cannot offset one risk against another, and therefore may run a greater risk than his clients. A government may be able to do so, if necessary by making use of its powers of compulsion. Third, adverse selection, which occurs when one group of clients knows that their private risk is smaller than that of another, encourages the high-risk groups to seek insurance while the low-risk groups refuse to pay the "average" premium. This escalates premiums and drives out more clients. A private insurer may engage in premium rating, but that depends on costly information and it would not altogether avoid the in-group adverse selection. Finally, there is moral hazard because the insured may be "careless." A private insurer might institute all kinds of information and monitoring mechanisms, but ultimately less insurance is provided. The government may simply force all participants to pay when private monitoring is impossible, undesirable, or too costly.

7.4 – Possible remedies in a market setting

Because of the above distortions, responding to growing cost pressures by raising contribution rates is not a desirable option. At best it provides a short-term palliative. In the medium to long term it aggravates the competitive position of labor in these countries. However, benefits are often little above subsistence level, indicating that many pensioners rely on employment, preferably in the informal sector, as well as on intrahousehold transfers to avoid falling into the poverty trap. If poverty relief of pension schemes is to be retained, there is a limit to how much real benefits can be lowered. In other words, a thorough reform of the PAYG scheme is in order to contain costs, improve the targeting of benefits, and leave greater choice of lifetime savings to individual households. Two classes of reforms are being entertained.

One spectrum of remedies refers to streamlining the schemes in place, using the obvious options though none provides a magic solution in the short run.

There is by now fairly widespread agreement that PAYG pension systems are not viable, and perhaps not even desirable. This includes a wide range of countries where aging is a problem and thus net claims on state-run pension funds are rising. The remedies being considered include "shock therapy" by raising the retirement age by some five years, thereby increasing contributions and lowering claims (Fox 1995, p. 37). But that obviously can do the job only if employment opportunities in the formal sector can be widened significantly. The record of the past few years has not been very encouraging, and so raising the retirement age only swells the ranks of the unemployed, hence escalates claims on unemployment compensation or other social transfers. Furthermore, both opposition political parties and the individuals concerned reject raising the retirement age while pressing for further lowering the statutory retirement age. The Czech Republic may succeed in gradually raising the retirement age from the current 60 for men and 53–57 for women to 62 and 57–61, respectively, by the year 2006. But the political battle around this proposed law is far from over. Another powerful reform is to limit occupational privileges or at least to make them actuarially neutral, that is, lowering the pension claim or raising the contribution rates. Bulgaria and Romania have apparently succeeded in introducing higher contribution rates for those eligible for early retirement; Lithuania has been envisaging lowering the claims for those retiring early. A variant on this is to change the eligibility for disability pensions, which under state socialism were in fact related to sectoral privileges (the miners in Poland, for example). Poland has proposed to change the eligibility criterion for disability pensions from damage to health to inability to work. It has also been tightening the procedures for granting such pensions.

To discourage contribution evasion, the link between contributions and benefits can be strengthened, for example, by lengthening the base for calculating pension entitlement to cover a much longer working life span rather than, usually, the final three to five years of formal full-time employment. Thus the Czech Republic is gradually extending the base from the ten highest-earning years to the thirty highest-earning years. For that to work, however, the administrative infrastructure of keeping track of who contributed how much must be in place. In several countries, pensions were indexed to occupational uprating: If the wage scale got adjusted, so were the pensions for those whose reference wage for pension purposes had been earned in that sector. Indexing to prices so as to maintain purchasing power can be cheaper than indexing to wages. That is not so, however, when the authorities are able to erode real wages through inflation.

The other class of solutions envisages a different or at least one or more supplementary pension schemes to the beleaguered state-administered PAYG system (Fox 1994, 1995). These contemplated supplementary schemes are as a rule variants of, largely private, pensions schemes funded voluntarily or mandatorily. Current proposals aim at a two- or three-tiered system. On the contributory side, pension would be partly mandatory in state funds, partly mandatory but kept in private funds, and partly funded voluntarily. Mandatory state funds would disburse not only to those who had contributed but also to those who through no fault of their own become indigent once they reach retirement age.

Any reform of the pension system requires setting a cutoff date at which time the new system comes into effect. For those entitled to a pension, nothing changes. For those not yet in the labor force, they will enter with the new system. For those in the labor force who have contributed social security for some time, equity requires that their claims for past service, or at least a good portion thereof, be capitalized and funded by the state before being allocated to the "new" system. That can be a costly operation. These capitalized claims will eventually have to be funded from the taxpayers' pocket. But how and when this should be done are questions yet to be resolved even in the most advanced transition economy. That is not to say that none has made progress with pension reform. Indeed some have by cutting real entitlements or by encouraging present contributors to start saving for themselves in paid-up pension schemes, intimating that their past claims will probably be worth very little by the time they retire (Fox 1994, 1995). In several countries, Russia and Ukraine being notorious, pension payments have simply been withheld. A justification can be found in the fact that many firms collecting pension contributions have simply not passed on their revenue, thus adding to the tax and interenterprise arrears. But in several countries the payout has been delayed for months because it improves the budget situation, at least on paper since outstanding claims are not fully accounted for in the budget. Such a policy can at best be short term as sociopolitical dissatisfaction may spill over into dysfunctional political opposition to those in power and perhaps even rejection of the transformation agenda.

Several transition economies have introduced frameworks for the emergence and regulation of private pensions fully funded on a voluntary basis (Vittas and Michelitsch 1995). They are rather simple: An individual accumulates a fund over his or her working life. At retirement age, the value of the accumulated funds is available for withdrawal. As instruments to complement the public scheme, voluntary savings for retirement may increase domestic savings, thus fund domestic investment, provided private pension funds are appropriately regulated. This is by no means an easy task particularly during the early phases of the transition when capital markets are not yet in place. But vigilance in ensuring that private pension funds are not misappropriated is warranted, as the experience in a number of market economies has amply demonstrated (Don and Besseling 1996; Fougerolles 1995). Because these are often encouraged by tax incentives and state subsidies, an appropriate regulatory regime with prudential regulations and active oversight and supervision must be in place.

Private pension schemes funded on a compulsory basis remain as yet untried in the transition economies. But alternatives along such lines have been examined and debated in several countries if only because they may at some appropriate time replace the PAYG scheme altogether or accompany a much slimmed-down public PAYG scheme and voluntary funds to create a multipillar pension system.

Funded schemes can be more transparent than PAYG schemes, hence might eliminate the incentives for evasion and involve fewer distortions to the labor market, while stimulating savings and promoting capital markets. However, given the uncertainty in many transition economies, particularly during the early years, such private schemes are in need of strict regulation to protect the wider public against financial shenanigans, of which there have already been all too many. In this area, a large role accrues to the state in setting up a solid framework with supervisory institutions and mechanisms to ensure that funded pension payments are protected against misappropriation (Kornai 1996a). Whether the state should, within limits and well-specified conditions, offer state guarantees to pension savers presents a ticklish issue; it is probably the only path that will persuade the population at large to condone this kind of reform. Earning trust and confidence of the electorate in particular is something that accrues gradually, notably in countries exposed to the ravages of state socialism. Further, experience has been equivocal regarding the effect on saving rates. Private schemes may have high administrative costs and cannot ensure against high inflation or political interference at some stage.

The upshot of the pension debate is that there is no unique solution. Preferred alternatives are bound to vary among countries. Whether they focus solely on their existing PAYG systems or prefer to explore more radical reform options is immaterial. The point is that there is an urgent need to revamp the existing pension systems to safeguard the social-welfare component and security of citizens. The longer governments wait to implement change, the tougher and less palatable the required measures are likely to be.

Section 8: Budgetary policies, social security, and human capital

The magnitude of the pension problem in transition economies and the urgency of agreeing on sensible pension reform have multiple dimensions. One is financial: Government budgets in transition economies simply cannot be held captive to the needs of pensioners, yet the latter cannot be abandoned for political and social, not to mention ethical, reasons. Much the same comment can be made with respect to other insurance-type provisions (such as health and medical care) that state socialism made available through SOEs or its own social-welfare institutions. But there are other reasons for spelling out what needs to be done in these sectors. Finally, the financing problem also affects a range of socio-cultural provisions (including the arts, education, and science) that normally fall within the remit of government action. I can only flag up the problems and cite some of the possible solutions.

8.1 – The social safety net: coping with the adversities of transition

Once firms can hire and fire workers and regulate labor rewards chiefly on the basis of productivity, unemployment insurance and welfare reforms are critical in cushioning the transition's adjustment costs. Even though there may be agreement on the magnitude of the cost to be borne, the speed at which it should be absorbed, and the degree of equity with which it needs to be distributed, the transition inevitably exerts more adverse impacts on some layers of society than on others. The adversity may well exceed expectations in part because it is very difficult at the outset to be precise about the adjustment burden. But unexpected events may further perturb any estimate of corrective distributive action. Rather than allowing the potential for strikes, demonstrations, and other forms of social unrest to rupture the admittedly feeble sociopolitical fabric of the transition, it would be helpful to have in place a reserve to compensate for unanticipated adversities and to ensure that the transition's burden will not have to be borne chiefly by the weakest layers of society. The latter include labor, whose wages are in most cases nominally controlled, and those dependent on transfers whose real value inflation rapidly erodes. But key components of the excessive egalitarianism of the past cannot – and should not – continue.

Because attitudes change only gradually, a fairly comprehensive safety net must be put in place quickly, preferably prior to transformation, to bolster credibility of enunciated policies. This has distinct components. Some target easing unemployment, including by improving the functioning of markets and thus assisting the unemployed in their efforts to return to productive activities. As regards interim measures to cope with unemployment, the safety net could be stretched also to provide effective job placement and counseling, facilitate job searches, encourage retraining, allow recruitment and relocation subsidies, provide direct job-creation incentives to break radically with the inherited job and income security, and contemplate other measures. The package could preferably combine strict limits on the duration and magnitude of unemployment benefits with sizable expenditures on ALMPs. Structural unemployment needs to be alleviated as well. This particular module of the safety net could usefully be designed as comprehensively as circumstances permit. The basic motivation should be putting in place a fair and equitable labor policy that fosters market-conforming behavior and instills in workers a new attitude toward the workplace, including through work-related incentives.

The degree to which the ravages of inflation on labor and other incomes can be offset by income transfers from the safety net is a delicate issue. Those whose incomes fall below the accepted poverty line (including the handicapped, the elderly, children, and other indigents) need to be provided for chiefly through income transfers. Whereas needs are considerable, there are limits to what government can muster even with foreign assistance. It is utterly illusory to claim, perhaps for electoral purposes, to be able to protect nearly everyone against the inevitable adjustment burden of the transition; it most certainly would be futile to do so for its populist appeal. In fact, the limits are reached almost as soon as the socially more vulnerable layers of society are accommodated. Saddling the government with all kinds of liabilities, including social policy, financing compensation, correcting environmental degradation, and taking over bad debts of banks and SOEs, at a time that its fiscal probity is collapsing, is counter-productive (see Chapter 3).

8.2 – Restructuring other insurance-type government intervention

One aspect of the state-socialist approach to social provisioning was to have universal dental, health, and medical care at no cost to the user. Like pensions, these expenditures claim a substantial part of state budgets. In reaction lesser or poorer services, and in some cases a combination of the two, are being delivered. Wealthy individuals can now, of course, openly consult health facilities at their own expense, and many such providers have indeed privatized them-selves in every sense of the term. The point is that for the average citizen access to all health-care services has deteriorated substantially. Many policy makers agree that this is not a desirable outcome, but are powerless to enact quick reforms, given the parlous state of government finances. Another side of the coin, however, is that the transition leadership initially thought that reforms in these sectors would be induced by the dictates of markets, with NPOs intervening where individuals could not access desirable primary care. That has not been a very constructive approach. It could not have been that if only because of the asymmetric information available to users as compared to care providers. But a good many other reasons can be invoked. Primary health and medical care is an investment in the well-being of society in general and the productive contribution that workers can make to improving wealth in and welfare of their society.

Clearly, another road could have been traveled. Such a change in direction and pace has been overdue. But it will now have to be explored from a more rudimentary position than had been feasible with the "1989 events." Much of the services for dental, health, and medical care will have to be restructured, perhaps along the lines prevailing in western Europe, though even in these much wealthier societies these sectors have come under severe strain in recent years. One evident reform envisages replacing free access with a part-payment system. This can be on the side of the user, who absorbs part of the charges, the rest covered through some kind of insurance. It could also be covered by compen-sating dental-, health-, or medical-service providers according to the number of patients within their assigned ward. None of these options is free of abuse (with pay per service the provider's room for charges has to be reined in and with a fixed reward to providers other controls must be found to ensure adequate service delivery). None can guarantee that all individuals receive the kind of service that they feel entitled to. But some compromise needs to be worked out to avoid further deterioration in the health-care sector on top of the general deterioration in life expectancy because of the escalation of the incidence of physical and psychological diseases associated with the stresses and strains of the transition.

8.3 – Culture, education, and science

Relative to the situation bequeathed by state socialism, one of its crowning achievements was the emphasis on cultural enrichment, educational attainment, and scientific excellence. These may have been stressed for reasons that had nothing to do with altruism and the human face of state socialism (see Chapter 1). The point is, however, that particularly in the more backward countries, after a generation or less, they could boast nearly universal preschool, primary, and far-reaching secondary education, with free access to university for youngsters whom the system sought to promote for that distinction. That curriculum may have been spiced with propaganda and ideology. But few commentators would dispute the fairly high technical educational achievements, including linguistic skills, mathematics, the sciences, and the "classics."

Likewise, the leadership placed priority on nurturing and providing culture of its own choosing. That may have been very paternalistic. Nevertheless, access to arts and literature under state socialism was inexpensive and fostered by the state for the classics and the moderns when their visions could be mobilized to elicit regime adherence and doctrinal orthodoxy, such as through the largely failed attempt to exalt socialist realism. Many under state socialism may have availed themselves of culture "as a substitute for other desires, whose fulfillment they are denied" (Dahrendorf 1990, p. 68). Some reallocation of interests may have been unavoidable, indeed desirable. That some people may find gratification in cheap romance or utter trash cannot be interdicted. But to have the latter swamp the former without any restraint at all is leaning much too far in the direction opposite to what state socialism sought to propel.

As an extension of the promotion of universal education at no cost, the leadership also insisted upon having in place a broad network of scientific establishments. None of those employed there could pursue their endeavors without making some compromise on the subjects approved by state-socialist mentors. This was perhaps more stifling in the social than in the hard sciences. Even in the latter, state socialism knew how to suppress one line of research or another because it did not meet with the approval of the apparatchik or its tenets tended to run counter to the, at times fanciful, extensions of Marxist-Leninist dogma. One need only recall the approach to genetics or the skepticism toward stochastic statistics as a discipline.

Whereas the ideological inhibitions on culture, education, and science were nearly completely lifted with the onset of the transition (though remnants of the old-style *nomenklatura* in place have in some cases continued to exert restraint on the more enterprising staff), so were the material supports of these services. In some countries the delivery even of the basic educational equipment to youngsters has deteriorated sharply. School absenteeism on a scale resembling that typical of many developing countries is reemerging. Literary erudition has been replaced by a predilection for cheap trash. The glory of the musical establishment in many of these countries is now being replaced by kitschy commercialism and shoe-string delivery of the arts. The science establishment throughout these countries has seen its funding dwindle and stature in society severely erode. Surely, there is scarcity of funds. But that cannot be the sole explanation. There has also been a massive shift in priorities on the part of the new leadership as compared even to state socialism's nadir.

Ralf Dahrendorf (1990, p. 68) may well be correct in asserting that it is impossible to stem the tide of the ascent of shallow values and preserve "high culture." The point is not that the former should be heavily regulated, though one wonders at times where the permissiveness of the new societies should place a full stop. Rather, the "net social benefit" of such "culture" should be recognized and supported directly or indirectly from the social purse. That would certainly call, for example, for consolidating musea and orchestras, and undoubtedly reducing the number of chamber and folklore groups. It would also warrant raising private fees for such services. But it cannot mandate profit-based operations for that would toll the death knell of all too many cultural activities.

8.4 – Poverty as a blight on the transition's record

Whereas the number of wealthy people under state socialism was limited, however calculated, with the eruption of the transition the number of poor people escalates dramatically (Milanović 1994). Entitlements inherited from state socialism are in many cases and on the whole being eroded in an *ad hoc* manner, driven by the larger forces unleashed by the transition. This has often taken the form of inadequate funding or provisioning of extremely low pensions to those without another source of income (Krumm, Milanović, and Walton 1995).

Obtaining "objective" estimates of the incidence of poverty is by no means easy. Absolute poverty is as a rule defined as the number of people obtaining less than $1 a day. But that sum may be derisory in most open economies. Assuming that poverty can be identified by those obtaining less than $4 per day, the incidence of poverty in the eighteen transition economies for which more or less acceptable data are available grew from 4 percent in the years prior to the "1989 events" to 32 percent around the mid-1990s (UNDP 1997); the corresponding absolute numbers are 14 to 119 million people, respectively. The descent into poverty has been widespread across social classes. The poor encompass in the first instance those layers of society that were entitled to fixed incomes, whose real value inflation and budgetary stringency have significantly eroded. This applies especially to those who do not have the clout to force policy makers to provide adequate compensation. Thus, the retired in Hungary, Poland, and Slovenia have not fared too badly as compared with average incomes (Krumm, Milanović, and Walton 1995; Leven 1997). Elsewhere, however, particularly in Russia and Ukraine, and probably in other CIS States, they have not fared well at all. Not only has the real value of pensions been eroded. Oftentimes pensions are not at all paid or only with great delays, thus further cutting the real value of the money when received.

Poverty is not confined to those on fixed incomes, however. In many countries, the factually unemployed who do not join the second economy in anything like a regular working capacity have also seen their real incomes and wealth shrink dramatically. Likewise for households with large or extended families, or when headed by a single female. Worsening household poverty has been particularly pronounced for families with many young children even with working parents. Recall that whereas under state socialism clothing and feeding a child were often dramatically subsidized, prices of those goods and services are now multiples of what they were in 1989.

The "good" news about poverty in most transition economies, especially for the "working poor," is that it is shallow. Absolute poverty is not, at any rate not yet, very widespread. Most poor fall just below the relative poverty line. This suggests that with economic recovery, and indeed with explicit policies targeting a fair distribution of the benefits of the economic upswing, a sizable number of poor can be quickly moved above the poverty line. Until that takes place, however, it would be useful to consider means whereby the plight of the poor can be alleviated. This does not necessarily require more transfers from central budgets. Better targeting is feasible and desirable. Thus poverty in working households can be alleviated through family allowances (say, per child) without going through cumbersome means-testing, for which administrative and governance capacities may be inadequate.

Section 9: Corruption, crime, and personal insecurity

As mentioned (see Chapter 5), a good share of the so-called second economy is not just about dodging onerous economic regulations, or those perceived as such; it is outrightly criminal. Surely such instances of insecurity existed under state socialism. During some periods they were endemic, though not criminal in the Stalinist version of justice. Corruption in the sense of "the abuse of public office for private gain" (World Bank 1996, p. 95) was widespread, particularly at times of constraints with socialist incrementalism (see Chapter 1). As state socialism modified itself, corruption of this kind became endemic. Since the eruption of transition, however, this component of the second economy has assumed an altogether different character (Shelley 1997). For one thing, its magnitude has risen manifold. It has also become more blatant, visible, monetized, and by no means limited to the abuse of public office. Indeed, with the erosion of state power and the poor monitoring of assets at least nominally under state authority and with widely held share ownership, instances of abuses of office and of trust more generally have multiplied at a dizzying rate. It has also branched out into activities that previously had been unknown or were carefully wrapped in the state-socialist cloak. The internationalization of this part of the criminal economy and its coming to the surface in everyday life have by all counts risen dramatically. The criminal economy presently encompasses virtually all known areas of criminal activity: corruption, extortion, prostitution, drugs, protection rackets, murder for hire, theft, and what have you.

Since this is not a treatise on criminal justice but on economics, suffice it for me to draw attention to three negative aspects of this situation. One is the risen transaction costs for a wide variety of economic operations. The environment imposes a cost on doing business. When limited to its most "innocuous" variant, it takes on the intrinsic form of a tax on operations. But it is a taxing matter that by definition funnels uncertainty into transactions since the levy should ideally not be disclosed, certainly under normal intensity of law and order. In addition, the criminal tax skews decisions on resource allocation since it cannot be as easily imposed on "labor" as compared to other production factors. TNCs are often willing to absorb this levy as a business cost, and so distort the allocation process even more; but some FDI is altogether discouraged. Of course, none of this "tax" flows into the state's coffers and most of it may end up as capital flight.

Criminal activities in economic affairs also exacerbate insecurity and uncertainty. This is heightened by the fact that criminal corruption as a rule tends to run through various layers of society. Notably in several of the larger CIS States, including Russia and Ukraine, organized crime dominates the banking sector and the emerging financial markets, thus spreading the corruption germ through all layers of what should be intermediated in a market environment, but is in fact far removed from that. With the weakened state and the disintegration of law and order, albeit to various degrees, corruption in the broad sense is likely to pervade government. This further weakens the latter's ability to assure the protection to which its citizens ought to be entitled because tax revenues diminish, qualified people leave the public sector or do not even consider joining it, and the government's interest in discharging its societal mandate becomes very porous indeed. Ill-advised policies to downgrade the civil service in all of its facets only further aggravate the opportunities for corruption, frequently motivated by the sheer survival instinct of bureaucrats when their benefits are severely eroded by inflation and their prestige tainted by derisory policy stances. More generally, it eats away at the fabric of public life, leading to increased lawlessness and undermining social and political stability.

Finally, it cannot but be iniquitous, increasing poverty in many ways. Most directly it diverts resources to the rich, who can afford to bribe, and away from the poor, who are powerless when law and order disintegrate.

There is a wide range of this insecurity and uncertainty. Arguably one pole is formed by the marked rise in personal insecurity felt by economic agents, as well as citizens at large, thus further exacerbating the degree of insecurity that is endemic in the transition (see Chapter 3). The other is what one might term "contract" insecurity: Apparent terms for business in the emergent market environment represent only one side, and not always the operative one, for economic agents. This uncertainty is by no means restricted to the type of corruption and rent seeking that has been the subject of much searching investigations in the literature (Dawid and Feichtinger 1996; Mauro 1995, 1996; Shleifer and Vishny 1993): taking advantage of rent seeking due to government regulations or even influencing bureaucrats to decree regulations favoring one party or another. In most transition economies, particularly the less developed ones, corruption, nepotism, bribery, theft, and so on pervade the entire system, with particularly deleterious consequences for the establishment and growth of new small firms (EBRD 1995) and FDI (Shelley 1997). This is frequently all caught under the label "mafia," but that moniker is often misleading.

Of course, the situation differs from country to country, and all would like to ascribe the incidence of criminality to the "other," usually the Russian or Chechen or some other ex-Soviet mafia, putting it mildly. The fact is that since the transition the economic cost of criminal activities affecting all layers of the economy has risen exponentially. This cannot be confined to the direct cost of effecting a particular exchange; say, the price paid plus the bribe on obtaining "access" to a particular good or service. Indeed, the cost gradually pervades society. It may reach the highest levels of government and administration, in which case the probability of a solidly grounded market economy with a pluralistic democracy emerging becomes rather worrisome.

From a strictly economic point of view, the expenditures for the cited kinds of criminal activities are not a complete loss to society. To the extent these "revenues" are utilized to prop up domestic demand, especially for investment purposes, the offset may be considerable. Nonetheless, these incidences of crime distort resource allocation in a possibly insidious manner. Criminal capture of property rights may be so egregious that, rather than such property rights being eventually transformed into "legal" activity, the discord sown in society may be so large and so affronts the population that the elicited societal strife may mandate a "second" round of wealth redistribution, presumably one more attuned to what society condones as the limit. The eventual outcome may be quite sanguine. Nevertheless, the loss in time and resources, and indeed in human talent, can be staggering. This is perhaps nowhere more egregious than in most CIS States.

Conclusions

The sociopolitical pressures engendered by the transition are many. I have touched in this chapter on only some. One part of the discussion revolved around the construction of a sociopolitical consensus and how best to maintain it, including by fostering good governance throughout society. Another part examined the most important overall instances of actual or potential social discontent. I looked here at labor-market problems and passive and active policies designed to come to grips with unemployment. I also examined the state of funding of social programs, especially of pensions and the health-care system in the broad sense. I finally pointed out the pervasive costs, both in terms of money and uncertainty, brought about by the rapid rise in all kinds of criminal activities in economic affairs. Unless transition managers find a way to overcome these obstacles fairly quickly, and install a "society" deserving the label "good" (Galbraith 1996), one may legitimately question their claims to forging steadily ahead with laying the foundations of pluralistic democracy and a solid market economy. Indeed, the very prerequisites for embarking on a sustainable growth path may as a result be projected into a dubious light.

9

THE EVOLVING ROLE OF
THE STATE DURING
TRANSFORMATION

The recent near-global interest in "liberalization" policies has fired anew much ideology in riling against the activist state. In some of the more extreme cases, the position taken has slipped into libertarian, quasi-anarchist directions or even anarcho-capitalist dimensions (Buchanan 1987). This movement in market economies found an avidly enthralled, if on the whole naïvely informed, audience upon the transition's eruption. In rationalizing neoliberalism as a powerful ideology, indeed an instrument to influence events there, it has especially taken the rhetorical form of lambasting the role of the state. Its economic functions in particular have been under constant attack as being predatory, wasteful, rent seeking, too large, klepto-patrimonial, and so on. Efforts were launched from the beginning to compress the role of the state, in some cases with the explicit intention of reducing its economic involvement to that of the night watchman, that is, essentially protecting property rights and creating and maintaining the liberal market framework come what may (Sztompa 1996a).

Yet socioeconomic order without a functioning state is not readily imagined in the real world. Few would contest this position (J. Gray 1989, 1992). The market defects for which state intervention *may* be needed are perhaps nowhere as blatant as in transition economies (see Chapter 3). At the same time, the capacities of the state in these countries to fulfill roles that it would be accorded even in the more liberal market environment are rather limited, though varying by country. This poses a dilemma for policy making. The new leaders of the European, as distinct from the Asian, reforming countries, have displayed considerable enthusiasm for the market, private ownership, and privatization. This derives in part from the abundant support they have elicited from the most avid "free market" proselytizers in the west. But it stems also from the conjecture that "in economics and politics, as in religion, the new convert is often the most ardent in belief" (Galbraith 1990, p. 51).

In this chapter I examine why and when there could be a broader role for the state in formulating, implementing, monitoring, assessing, and fine-tuning the transformation agenda. This complements the introductory remarks on the role of the state in market formation of Chapter 3 and provides details on the governance issues broached in Chapter 8. I first briefly sketch the rationale for differentiating the state's economic role during the transformation and once the market economy will be reasonably functioning. As detailed next, both encompass more than what those intimately involved in the transition's *problématique* are prepared even to explore. Then I argue that the Manichean dichotomy between the rejection of "planning" and the embracement of the "market" misses the core economic issues at stake. Next I briefly examine a few crucial propositions on the state's economic role. Following this, I look at the major tasks that the state *can* perform in the years ahead. How this can be made acceptable is the next subject. Thereafter I discuss governance and managing the transition. Before concluding, I consider desirable and feasible improvements in governance, notably in SOEs and the civil service.

Section 1: The broad role of the state in transition

The state is often viewed as the quintessential Hobbesian organ. Its economic tasks are confined to specifying the rules, ensuring the transfer of property, and establishing procedures for arbitrating disputes about property relations (J. Gray 1989, pp. 29ff.). This is not a constructive option for transition economies. Seen primarily as an institutionalized structure of coercion and coordination of law-and-order and development types of activities, the state is an institution with distinct advantages and disadvantages as compared to private firms or NPOs formed voluntarily. Some of the differences often invoked are more a matter of degree than of substance, however. Thus, by creating proper institutional, monitoring, and incentive mechanisms in the public sector, typical performance discrepancies as compared to the private sector may be sharply compressed. But a class of differences cannot be glossed over. They follow essentially from the singular properties of the state as a universal organization with the attendant power of compulsion (Buchanan 1987, pp. 4–5), fiduciary responsibilities, and limits such as on property rights and commitment abilities (Stiglitz 1989a, b). Performance discrepancies are also often more illusory than real, owing to the unique feature of the state in governing the tasks incumbent upon a polity.

In examining the arguments mustered for and against a broader economic role of the state, it is useful to remind ourselves briefly about history over the past two centuries or so. That points to overwhelming state activity followed by abrupt, and at times violent, swings in the opposite direction (Heertje 1989). Indeed, the pendulum in the transition economies may initially have swung too far out toward where the state's role should be battered into the irreducible minimum that the more faddist liberal champions advocate (Dahl and Lindblom 1953, pp. 514ff.); hence the backlash that has taken place in many countries not just in verbal arguments but in actual policy making around the transformation agenda in particular. Adherence to such a vision from the transition's inception was bound to weaken the very platform for transformation policies for which market forces either are not available or not particularly well suited. It is an experience being belatedly recognized even by the World Bank (Chhibber 1997; World Bank 1997)!

Should there be a broader role for the state in transition? Is it because the state's capacities at the transition's inception are limited? No doubt, that is the case in all countries but with considerable variations. Furthermore, the capacity to acquire "governance" capabilities can be strengthened over time. In some cases good, if elementary, governance capacities can be secured rather quickly, although they need determined efforts at deepening and widening, and indeed streamlining, over time (Frischtak and Atiyas 1996). The alternative is either bureaucratic stalemate or deliberate state desertion. The former is counter-productive. The latter serves a useful purpose in the reconstruction of the eastern part of Europe only if there were no longer a political authority in place that can reasonably oversee moving toward democracy and market-based decision making. I include here the not-so-imaginary case where the authority in place, while still largely a remnant of state socialism, cannot even generate, let alone sustain, a tacit sociopolitical consensus and proceeds to agitate through violence, corruption, and other unsavory means of social control. Forcefully reducing the state under those conditions may be instrumental in tracing a firm course that holds the promise of building the foundations of the twin goals of the transition. Very quickly, however, the need for governance capacities by the state surfaces as a priority item, if only to hold together the sociopolitical consensus. If only because this requires action, it may be preferable to reform and build upon what is in place rather than to reinvent the state from the ground up, as it were.

Given the enormous undertaking that constitutes a sensible but vigorous trans-formation of these economies, the antistatist bent originally adopted is ill-advised for at least three reasons. One is that a modern market economy without a strong involvement of the state is unknown. Even in the most liberal market economy (say, Hong Kong) the state performs a role well beyond the night watchman's. Second, to the degree that belief in the spontaneous emergence of market forces and in the proper behavior of economic agents was rooted in ideology, hence beyond the arc of real decision making, many of the arguments mustered in the debates lack a robust rationale. To manage the transformation a strong state, but one obviously quite different from the remnants of state socialism, is required. Some central authority must necessarily formulate, implement, monitor, assess, and fine-tune the transformation agenda. Finally, inasmuch as no country has been able to initiate the "creative destruction" that constitutes the transformation without safety flags (such as social safety nets, continued subsidization of SOEs and state banks, and various price subsidies for utilities, housing, and trans-portation in particular), it would have been desirable to work toward a more streamlined public service from the outset. At the very least, such skills deserve to be upgraded on a priority basis if only to manage the funds thus earmarked by force of circumstance rather than to let these nonmarket interventions take their shape haphazardly. Under some conditions it would have been desirable to manage the process of "creative destruction" along the implied parallel track:

destruction of much of the existing assets and creation of new activities by sensibly rescuing existing resources and indeed by mobilizing savings for new firms.

The actual and potential role of the state in transition economies should be seen in the context of the market and government failures (see Chapter 3) and the need for good governance (see Chapter 8). One should look carefully not only at failures endemic in mature market economies. Indeed, it is critical to examine them against the backdrop of a dynamically changing societal setting and of economies whose aspirations are to reach soonest levels of development typical of western Europe. Abandoning the corrupt "old state" when the transition erupts in utter chaos is one thing. This cannot be ruled out, of course, as recent history has demonstrated, such as the Yugoslav hyperinflation of the early 1990s (Lyon 1996). However, assessing properly where the state can agitate and where it cannot, and ensuring that capabilities are amassed to facilitate intervention where warranted, constitute integral parts of the transition's tasks, given the immaturity or absence of markets (see Chapter 3). In the process one should also heed the reality that talents for the proper kind of public service in these countries were limited and that there existed considerable aversion toward purposefully strengthening the state.

The state's role in the transformation is particularly important in installing and maintaining the macroeconomic framework, in conveying appropriate statistical and other information to economic actors, in putting in place the basic constituents of the market economy through new institutions and legal codes, in ensuring property rights, in guiding the disengagement of the state in the economy, in fostering the other microeconomic foundations of macroeconomic stability, in forging ahead with incisive modifications of output, and in coping with many other aspects of the transition that I cannot examine in detail here. In short, it is impossible to envision an appropriate transformation agenda for a real-existing country without a functioning state. Even if society were to entrust a highly technocratic élite with major portions of the agenda, it is doubtful that formulating, implementing, monitoring, assessing, and fine-tuning that agenda could be safely left to "technopols" (J. Williamson 1994b).

Section 2: The state as market organizer

In delineating the potential economic role of the state, it does not suffice to be concerned about the gestation of functioning markets and how, at least in the interim, market failures could be remedied. The real task of transition economies is the identification of a new, self-sustainable growth path that generates sufficient wealth over a protracted period of time. Note that this path may be partly pre-determined by initial conditions. It may also exhibit path dependence in the sense that early choices matter for later outcomes. Policy makers also need to persuade the electorate at large that key planks of the transformation agenda to jump onto such a path are being delivered upon, if at a temporary cost. It is unlikely that such a new endogenous growth trajectory becomes available in a wholly spontaneous manner, even with full concurrence on the "Washington consensus," let alone in the context of ill-functioning markets. Provided governance capabilities are adequate, the state *may* become involved in identifying the growth path through appropriately selected interventions. In any case, orderly economic transactions require a broad network of stable "institutions" (see Chapter 7), which do not normally sprout spontaneously. Likewise, in seeking rapid change in income and wealth through market activities, markets need to be maintained and upgraded, including through proper governance (see Chapter 8).

Among the wide range of activities in a modern economy, some are universally recognized as the sole preserve of the state. Others are best left to private initiative. Between these two extremes, there is a vast area for choice. This not only applies to the tasks that should be entrusted to government, but also holds for resolving how government could best discharge itself of the functions that the sociopolitical consensus confers on it. Whereas the first topic has ebbed and flowed with the political outlook on the state's role over the long haul (Dahl and Lindblom 1953), the latter is of more recent vintage. Indeed, one concomitant of the stance on privatization has been the reignition of the debate on the alternatives for the delivery of public and semipublic services. Recall that the latter can take on various forms (Dasgupta 1986; Fine 1991; Helm 1986), including pure public goods (such as national defense), regulatory services (such as antipollution measures), quasi-public goods (such as education), and the administration of various transfer payments (such as unemployment insurance).

On the whole, government in market economies has tended to expand its sphere of activity for a variety of reasons (World Bank 1983a, 1991), including pressures from competing constituencies. Under state socialism, however, the proper role of the state was held to be the widest imaginable. Private economic activity was essentially relegated to areas upon which government could not fully impress its exclusiveness without severely debilitating that engagement. With transition, even the idea of "central planning" was overtly spurned. This stance has been based on incompletely validated principles. It also has ignored well-known defects even of a mature market. The role of "planning" in preparing well-founded decisions on tackling structural issues at this stage should be considerable. This deserves more than casual attention notably in areas where reinforced central coordination can demonstrably improve upon one or another kind of market failure (Brus 1990).

Much of the reluctance to endorse virtually any economic role for the state stems from the fact that the core rationale of past inefficiency in SOEs derived largely from the presumed omniscient control and intervention of the state *per se*. Sidestepping any serious search for feasible modifications of the existing order resulted from the bold presumption that the anthropomorphic state is a bad owner of property. In recognition thereof, most transition managers initially advocated, and in some cases still do even when their actions belie this verbal rhetoric, that a resurgence of state control must be shunned at all cost. In its stead, the wholesale embracement of the market has remained an *idée fixe* for all too long. This deep mistrust of the ability of the state, or government, to function effectively as owner or operator (Pannier and Schiavo-Campo 1996) has encumbered the appropriate fashioning of the transformation's architecture (Wünsche 1991).

Limiting myself to economic matters, the two sharply contrasting prescriptions of either the amorphous market or the unified central plan are myopic ways of coordinating economic decisions at some stage of development. Intrusive government intervention has been counseled to many countries in the process of emerging from rural underdevelopment, in some cases motivated by concerns about massive market failures (Killick 1990; Lall and Kell 1991), ranging from traditional public goods (such as infrastructure) to inability of the market to monitor entrenched management. Proponents of the market as an all-embracing remedy see government as a problem rather than as a solution. Their advocacy of what ought to be done revolves around unfettered markets and unleashing the dynamic forces of capitalism. As noted, such a stance frequently confounds the virtues of the market with capitalist ownership functions (Bardhan 1991; Comisso 1991). It also overlooks overwhelming evidence that pure markets can be stulti-fying, such as in fostering innovation (B. Johnson and Lundvall 1989) on which successful development and modernization are predicated. Mature market economies and now NIEs attained their present status through the articulation, at least in actual policy making, of an activist role for government (Bardhan 1990; Killick 1990; Lall and Kell 1991; Stern 1991). That role should, of course, change over time along with successful economic development (Panić 1992), even though it may be very difficult to wean government of initial tasks.

Second, proponents of "free markets" have a coherent conceptual framework at their command. But several of the assumptions upon which this sophisticated theoretical edifice rests are unrealistic; certainly inappropriate under a number of real-life conditions. Some of the ensuing policy advice has been invalidated in practice, thus tending to refute any extreme approach unless there is no alter-native to buccaneer capitalism. Aiming at the creation of pure markets can only be a costly pipe dream leading to cultural dislocation, unemployment, collapse of production and trade, and economic and political confusion. Especially when evaluation standards are not restricted to the assessment of material well-being and include various social and health gauges (see Chapter 8), purely free markets may serve a heuristic role in textbooks and structured undergraduate analyses. But their underlying libertarian philosophy cannot be the guideline for practical policy actions designed to buttress a harmonious social consensus for modernization.

Third, it is by now widely acknowledged that the private sector has various shortcomings in dealing with many economic problems (Kuttner 1997). Abundant examples can be extracted from the setting of public goods; situations of strong externalities; natural monopolies and other monopolies that are difficult, risky, and expensive to contest because of sunk costs; shortages of entrepreneurs and managerial talent; large inequalities in the distribution of incomes, achievements, wealth, and freedoms; missing markets; and violations of perfectly competitive behavior because of imperfect information, increasing returns, and entry barriers. "Society" may also harbor strong sentiments about poverty, deprivation, and other basic rights and equality of opportunity of the citizenry for which market solutions are illusory (Sen 1991). But not all market failures can be resolved through outright government intervention, as postwar experience has amply demonstrated. In some cases, interventions designed to correct market failure have exhibited even larger government failure. An appropriate regulatory policy or encouragement of NPOs may go a long way to easing market failure. More efficient, if imperfect, market outcomes can be designed through good contracting, providing incentives, shared risks, and protection against exploitation of specific investments (Jenkinson and Mayer 1996). These need not, of course, be formal contracts but rather perceived commitments based on reputation and trust, among other stabilizers of relations.

Even if the importance of the cited market "imperfections" is conceded, libertarian economists do not consider these "exceptions" the stuff of which the foundations for practical and durable policy making can be cemented in. Curiously enough, from the recent literature on the wholehearted embracement of the magic of the market, one misses at least a spark of recognition that the new political regimes in many transition economies differ from the old orders (see Chapter 3). Not only are there other actors, but also radically different policies and objectives of economic administration are being promoted. One may have doubts about the political abilities of these new teams and the robustness of the emerging institutions more generally. But should one prejudge them to be aiming at building up a parallel base to the corrupt administrations that eventually came to symbolize the worst emanations of state-socialist rule? Furthermore, the new governments cannot dodge all kinds of sweeping, mostly unpopular, measures that will deeply rut the sociopolitical fabric of these societies. At the same time, it would be naïve in the extreme to postulate that new governments will invariably behave in the best interest of society.

A suitable combination of "market" and "plan," and indeed a thick network of NPOs linking the market with the state, becomes all but unavoidable in actual policy making. One can only hope that such reconceptualization can be based on the respective instrumental virtues of these "institutions." One can be confident in principle that there has to be scope for government intervention. But it is a fairly diffuse and ill-defined role until the tasks at hand are clearly spelled out and the available capacities are thoroughly assessed and instructed. It might, therefore, be advisable to embrace a rather eclectic approach in which the aim is to endow government with a vital, if not necessarily very large, role in the development process.

The proper corrective action in the case of market failure is not always outright public enterprise or nationalization. There are many different competing forms that can be embraced short of entrusting government with the task of producing goods and services. At the very least, methods should be explored whereby markets can be rendered more effective. Various instruments are available that simulate market-based decisions also in the public sector. For one thing, at least three alternative allocative mechanisms as solutions to the problem of public and quasi-public goods can be explored (David 1992). One lets society provide independent producers with subsidies from general taxation, the goods then being made available freely or at a nominal charge. A second solution authorizes the state to levy general taxes to finance the direct participation in production and distribution processes, contracting where necessary with private agents to do the actual work. Finally, the state can create a publicly-regulated private monopoly, allowing it to charge customers prices that guarantee a "normal" rate of profit. Regulation in various forms can provide a useful intermediate format when imperfect information prevents the emergence of perfect competition (Stiglitz 1993; Veljanovski 1989; Willig 1993; Yarrow 1989). This may be required only temporarily until new market-based mechanisms can be innovated.

Of course, the latter solution can be carried one step further by entrusting the production task to an SOE that is entitled to make a "normal" profit or to capture the rents that government then earmarks for its own purposes. I realize that there is resistance to SOEs. Even so, perhaps the most potent argument is that SOEs exist and will continue in the public sector for years to come. Attitudes based on a "casual" reading of the past as a guideline for further actions are not helpful. It imputes gross incompetence to SOEs and their "old style" managers, who are also held to be incapable of restructuring themselves. Claims that all management of SOEs is corrupt, sycophantic, or most inept in managing scarce resources can be peremptorily dismissed as reflections formulated by those with a very short memory or too complacent to examine the record more closely. Even if correct, the question of what to do with existing SOEs that cannot be quickly privatized or that will not be divested deserves a candid answer. To ensure that such an SOE behaves like a "normal" production company, specific incentives have to be devised for management and workers, and appropriate monitoring mechanisms are required (Pannier and Schiavo-Campo 1996). Beyond that analysts and policy makers should still sift through the maze of options on how best to deliver public and quasi-public goods, all of which involve some economic role for government. This question is by no means settled particularly in the uncertain, at times highly convoluted, transition policy setting.

Section 3: Economic theory and the state

A discussion of the respective role of the market and the state can perhaps best be focused by recalling two theorems (Stiglitz 1989a, pp. 38ff.; 1991a, pp. 430–1; 1994, pp. 27ff.). The first contests fundamental assumptions of welfare economics. Its principal argument is that with incomplete risk or futures markets and imperfect information, markets are in general never constrained Pareto-efficient, assuming that government is subject to the same kinds of informational and/or incomplete-market constraints faced by the private sector. Once that is verified there is a potential for government intervention. Whether this potential should be realized depends very much on how governments can discharge those tasks. Greenwald and Stiglitz (1986) have in this connection developed the so-called fundamental nondecentralizability theorem. This posits that efficient market allocation cannot generally be attained without government intervention: Government has to deliver goods and services that markets cannot provide or only at an extra cost, thus yielding Pareto-superior outcomes (Datta-Chaudhuri 1990, pp. 27ff.). Such interventions render government policy consistent with the market approach. But they need to be carefully identified. Given the uncertainty and limited governance capabilities in transition economies, Pareto-efficient government actions are more likely with selective government intervention aimed at tackling the most egregious market failures.

The second theorem states that private production as a rule can emulate ideal public production only under highly restrictive conditions. That provides a weak intellectual foundation for understanding the precise roles of the government and the private sector. These and related considerations suggest that the appropriate analysis of the economic role for government should not be based on ideology, certainly not on its more vulgar variants. Rather, it can be more usefully constructed around a clear appreciation of the essential role of institutions and the various governance options available at alternative transaction costs, the galvanizing nature of government, and the unique function of the private sector, whether for profit or not, in society. Creating the proper institutional, monitoring, and incentive mechanisms in the public sector may remove or reduce some performance discrepancies (Pannier 1996). As noted, there is a class of differences following from the singular properties of the state that cannot be glossed over.

The conflation of moving as rapidly as possible toward a fully fledged market economy with the delivery of public and semipublic services is unfortunate for it can do justice to neither (Brabant 1992a, pp. 76–101). In addition, the debate has been phrased too much in terms of public and private actions, thereby not doing full justice to or ignoring the many other dimensions for categorizing or assessing intermediating instruments in society. Indeed, whereas we may be clear about what an individual is, the "state" is too vague a term when it comes to delivering goods and services in the most efficient way possible. By stressing the existence of options for the delivery of government services from among which policy makers can choose, the broader palette of tools of public action can provide a more appropriate backdrop for examining alternative means of realizing policy precepts (Kuttner 1997; Leman 1989; Salamon 1989). Notably in the transition economies, this debate has still some way to go before a workable consensus on the semantics of the state's prospective role can be hammered out.

Treating the "state" anthropomorphically is not very helpful. It consists of numerous formal and informal interest groups with their interlocking agendas. Each has considerable discretion over how best it can deliver on the items resorting under its responsibility. Just as these various levels of government have options with respect to the delivery of goods and services, so must there be ways of improving the public sector, in particular as regards the operation of SOEs (see Chapter 6). But there are also state-mandated or governance-related activities that cannot be reduced to the operation of some economic activity. This is notably the case for the civil service, on which more later.

To form a more objective stance, a basic understanding of what government can and cannot do must be gained. Asking it to undertake certain things in the most effective way certainly differs from simply asking it to provide specific goods and services. Although there is definitely an overlap between the private and public sectors for goods and services that are neither purely private nor purely public, the choice depends on the relative ease with which criteria of economic and social efficiency can be met within the context of generating and sustaining dynamic aggregate growth. Even once this is settled, how best to render the public sector more efficient remains a pivotal governance question. Modern governments have programs that already embody a significant component of the type of decentralization that "privatization" is supposed to achieve. Few deliver only services produced in the public sector. Instead, intensive use is made of precisely the type of private sector as well as state and local authorities that recent advocates of privatization and decentralization have tended to favor. However averse current policy makers in transition economies may be toward market intervention, the "institutions" discussed in Chapter 7 have to be innovated or transformed to enhance private- as well as public-sector performance.

A complete theory of nonmarket behavior requires more than what public choice provides (Wolf 1990, p. 6). Indeed, that theory typically inadequately explains the pattern of exclusivity (monopoly) in the conduct of nonmarket activities, the high degree of uncertainty surrounding the technology of producing nonmarket outputs, and the frequency of "derived" or unanticipated externalities resulting from these outputs. It also ignores the role of organizational inertia, tradition, and "standard operating routines" as contributors to non-market failures (Brett 1988). It is critical to be clear about what nonmarket activity encompasses. Aside from various levels of national, regional, and local government, it includes a host of NPOs (such as foundations, nonproprietary health-care institutions, and universities) whose operations cannot be reduced to the provisioning of private goods. Public-choice theory by itself is too restrictive to furnish an adequate frame of reference for this reality. Organizations whose suitable performance record cannot be reduced to a singular optimization function (such as profit making) tend to conform more closely to the characteristics of the nonmarket than to those of the market. They are hence more prone to the associated types of failures. In this respect, recall that private goods are those for which *most* of the benefits or costs associated with output are, respectively, collected or paid by the producer; but some are not. In contrast, the label "public goods" applies where most of an activity's consequences consist of non-appropriable benefits (such as security) or noncollectible costs (such as crime).

Before leaving this theoretical field, a word about the propositions elaborated by Ronald Coase (1960) is in order. He argued that those who are the victims of external costs can make these costs tangible to their sources by offering to pay the latter to desist or diminish the culpable activities (Cooter 1987); presumably the same option is available to the beneficiary of external gains to trade them. Whereas this should remind us of alternatives in which externalities can be resolved, we should also bear in mind that possibly formidable implementation problems arise here. No doubt, those "transaction costs" soar with the incompleteness of the "institutions," including information and commitment constraints, that buttress a properly functioning market (Vickers 1996). Those complicate the process of arranging the kind of bargain or contract between the sources and victims of the negative externalities envisaged by Coase. To the extent these formidable transaction costs can be avoided or surmounted, markets can overcome externalities and continue to function efficiently.

Section 4: The state as producer and the future of SOEs

Throughout the debate on the transition in general and privatization in particular, arguably no single organ inherited from state socialism, save the Party with its appendages, has come in for as much criticism as the SOE. Very often the poor overall economic performance of state socialism since the mid-1970s is attributed to the inefficiency of the state as a producer and to the dubious record of managers of SOEs. The poor impression many observers hold of the performance of SOEs in the market environment is as a rule invoked to lend further weight to this assessment. In other words, the SOE has come in for a slap that is often as unfair (Dornbusch 1991a, b; Frydman and Rapaczyński 1991; Frydman and Wellisz 1991) as it is applicable to the oversized nature of state intervention in many economies. This is especially the case for those undertakings coming within the purview of "large privatization," a sentiment that is widely invoked in the literature for all public firms. Rarely is it acknowledged that SOEs in market economies incur losses not because they are state-owned but often precisely because of the reverse: Most became state-owned because they were loss makers to begin with (Stiglitz 1986, p. 165). Of course, state socialism formed SOEs principally for ideological, political, and strategic reasons, rather than because of explicit concerns about market failures. Not all of these firms are loss makers in any case, particularly when full allowance is made for their *economic* performance as distinct from their many other roles.

Recall from Part I that management under state socialism was never called upon to maximize net asset value. Instead, it was expected to execute plan targets in accordance with prevailing rules on the administratively assigned allocation of inputs and outputs; among those "outputs" figured a range of deliveries that intrinsically had nothing to do with their main product. Moreover, at first management was monitored largely through noneconomic instruments and institutions, but over time increasingly left to design its own plans, given circum-scribed administrative devolution. Among those tasks figured all kinds of functions imposed by the Party or society that in a market environment with private ownership tend to be provided by other agents, possible for-profit firms, NPOs, or the state.

A review of the various empirical studies on the results of privatization, comparing the relative efficiency of public and private enterprise or the perfor-mance of pre- and postprivatized firms, is by no means unambiguously in favor of private firms (see Bouin and Morrison 1996; Cook and Kirkpatrick 1988a, 1995; Cullis and Jones 1987; Gathon and Pestieau 1996; Kent 1987a; MacAvoy *et al.* 1989; Ramanadham 1988; Suleiman and Waterbury 1990; Swann 1988; Vickers and Yarrow 1988; Yarrow 1986). They do suggest, however, that public ownership has the tendency to eliminate the threat of takeover and ultimately of bankruptcy, and the need to raise money in the market. Absent appropriate monitoring, public ownership provides incentives for seeking a comfortable life and destroying the commercial ethic. Also, these studies find that it is primarily competition rather than ownership that is the major force influencing perfor-mance. This suggests that there are instances where economic liberalization without change of ultimate ownership *could* confer substantial benefits. Yet, divestment has been upheld as a magic wand for raising efficiency through the changed incentives of firms in private ownership and for separating political tutelage from the microeconomic sphere (Hemming and Mansoor 1988).

But to a large extent the perceived "inefficiency" of SOEs results from judging them by criteria that only partially correspond to their policy objectives (Commander and Killick 1988). SOEs have had many tasks that are far removed from pursuing profit-maximizing behavior. Thus, they are present in some indus-tries where, in the absence of state dominance, they would provide essentially similar services at vastly different prices to different markets in mature market economies (Peltzman 1989, p. 71). State intervention has sought to suppress these differences, usually by creating monopoly rents that partially cross-subsidize high-cost customers; government has been motivated by concerns about preserving the social peace in "guiding" SOEs. In that sense, the movement for divestiture tends to be symptomatic not merely of a change in values but also of what SOEs are expected to target. Generally speaking, they have multiple and variable objectives.

There are good theoretical reasons why one may presume that a private firm, other things being equal, tends to be more efficient in terms of generating returns to assets than an SOE. It is by now commonplace to invoke principal–agent problems. Managers of private firms are presumed to be subject to three types of contractual discipline. One is enforced by shareholders interested in seeing managers maximize the net value of their assets at the penalty of being fired with poor performance. Second, management that cannot ensure adaptive, allocative, and productive efficiency is subject to takeovers by participants in capital markets who believe themselves able to generate better yields from the assets in place.

Finally, to the extent that managers borrow they are under the scrutiny of lenders as well as owners legitimately concerned about leveraging. If they fail to pass the scrutiny of financial probity, the firm will simply be denied loans, thus crimping its ability to expand and reap profits for owners as well as gains in income, stature, market power, and the like for management. If loans are mismanaged, the firm may be forced into the ultimate discipline of bankruptcy. Because they are not subordinated to economically motivated shareholders, managers of SOEs are not subject to such disciplines. They tend to have a monopolistic position and are protected from potential takeovers by private-sector agents. Most SOEs obtain privileged access to financing, such as through subsidies or soft loans, from the state sector. This is often consolidated by various clientelistic relations resulting from coalition building.

Whereas these principles may be impeccable in theory, their importance in real life should not be exaggerated. Thus, with dispersed ownership the owner as a rule cannot afford the cost of monitoring and free-rider problems are pervasive. Monitoring occurs only by core owners or their financial agents. But this does not completely eliminate the free-rider syndrome. There are indeed pervasive problems with effective monitoring of management also in mature market economies (Stiglitz 1991b, c), even if meaningful contracts for the medium to long run could be specified (Jenkinson and Mayer 1996). Most intractable are those associated with proprietary information held by insiders. Also, while the takeover threat can be a potent weapon, its role should not be exaggerated. Takeovers are most effective in firms that are already on the brink of failure (Ickes 1990). Likewise, to the extent the aspersions cast on the public sector in principle are valid, instruments exist to mitigate the worst problems.

The expansion of the tasks of SOEs and the quest by managers for access to and autonomy from the state generate pressures within the state to recast the relationship. Not only that, under some realistic conditions SOEs *may* be more efficient than their private counterparts (Greenwald and Stiglitz 1986; Sappington and Stiglitz 1987; Shapiro and Willig 1990; Stiglitz 1991b). The superiority of private enterprise is indeed in large measure a function of market structures, including the foreign-trade regime, rather than ownership as such (Cook and Kirkpatrick 1988b, p. 20), and the ability to enforce a suitable regulatory environment. Simple assertions that SOEs are inefficient or convenient theoretical arguments that ignore market structures and failures will not do. Private monitoring of managers is more effective than public monitoring in the absence of market failure (Yarrow 1986, 1989). Any privatization must take account of both the relevant market structures and the competition and regulatory policies that are being simultaneously pursued. These are all more important determinants of economic performance than ownership *per se*; productive efficiency is in large measure a function of the efficient monitoring of management rather than denationalization (World Bank 1983a, b; 1988). Also, SOEs need not be shielded from competition, such as in the case of subsidized financing and monitoring, including through simulated takeovers. Oftentimes

355

these results can be implemented through the privatization of management rather than of ownership (Pannier 1996). A government looking with an open mind to such solutions, rather than being bent on amassing political rents, may well derive some benefits from takeover threats. Thus, while it is true that constraints on the behavior of SOEs are "deeply rooted in the ownership and control structure" (Frydman and Wellisz 1991, p. 141), it is especially the control structure deriving from the peculiarities of ownership under state socialism that is at stake (C. W. Gray 1996).

The question of control over SOEs is a critical one. This holds true even after divestment for all firms in which private owners do not actually exercise full ownership rights. The crux of the lingering inefficiency lies in the fact that many firms lack a well-defined owner seeking to maximize the present value of the returns on capital and able to influence the use of resources, including by declaring incentives for agents (Frydman and Wellisz 1991, p. 154; C. W. Gray 1996). This situation is perpetuated through all forms of divestment that essentially envisage insider or mass privatization yielding dispersed ownership. Prior to divestment, however, the poor exercise of ownership functions by the state or its agents typically enables those in physical possession of the assets to build up further property rights and to capture them with impunity (see Chapter 7).

Are SOEs intrinsically inefficient because their management leaves a lot to be desired? Though the presumption for this is strong, the evidence is not particularly compelling (Chang 1994; Chang and Singh 1991; Pestieau 1989; Stelzer 1988; Wade 1990; Yarrow 1989). SOEs tend to exploit government-imposed constraints and regulations to their advantage, in the process frequently generating socially inefficient outcomes. The central problem is that SOEs often suffer from poorly defined objectives and limited operational autonomy. Both inevitably exert an adverse impact on the internal operations of SOEs (Cook and Kirkpatrick 1988b, pp. 12–13). Failure to set specific goals for SOEs and, even more, negligence in monitoring them can lessen the incentives to pursue productive efficiency by management (Zeckhauser and Horn 1989, pp. 8ff.). Inadequate state incentives suggest that managers in SOEs pursue goals and set agendas that maximize their own well-being. The chance that the manager's own agenda replicates society's is pretty remote (Murphy 1989, pp. 59ff.).

Whereas the key problem of the performance of SOEs lies in control and effective monitoring, palpable informational and incentive differences are to be taken into account (Shapiro and Willig 1990, pp. 55ff.). At a fundamental level the intrinsic differences between public and private firms must derive from incentives, and these in turn are based on available information. The shift from public to private ownership alters the structure of information, incentives, and controls facing the individuals operating the enterprise. These in turn determine the firm's operating decisions, hence its economic and social performance. Neither public- nor private-sector firms operate perfectly. It is, therefore, necessary to look at the alternative conditions under which it is possible to predict that one performs better than the other. Once this is accomplished the distinction between SOE and private firm "is not nearly so stark or so inevitable as it might appear upon casual consideration" (Shapiro and Willig 1990, p. 57). It can be demonstrated that under remarkably general conditions, there is *no difference* between the performance of an SOE and that of a private company subject to optimally designed regulatory and tax schemes. The essential difference between the two is the location of private information about cost and demand.

In any case, even where there is a sharp deviation between public goals and profit maximization, private enterprise can be subjected to various regulations to make it better serve public goals. Simply privatizing SOEs without establishing any regulatory oversight has a substantial effect on the allocation of resources because an unfettered, but governed private company seeks to maximize share-holder profit, whereas an SOE is likely to be operated to serve social, and perhaps political, goals apart from profit maximization. If market failures are severe, privatization without regulation may well be inferior to restructuring SOEs. But there is a tradeoff. Privatization has the undesirable effect of raising the cost to the public official of inducing an enterprise, via regulation, to serve legitimate public-interest goals. These costs are an obstacle to coordinating the public official's information with the owner's to achieve the socially preferred outcome. This suggests that the conditions necessary for divestiture to be both appropriate and successful are rather restrictive (Commander and Killick 1988, p. 120) and that private enterprise is going to be superior over any kind of SOE only in a rather narrow range of circumstances, whose scope is however likely to increase as development proceeds. But the acuity of new public concerns may then come to the fore and legitimize public-sector undertakings to produce activities that were previously not even called for.

In sum, the newer literature on enterprise design and performance in connection with principal–agent problems demonstrates that discretionary regulation of private enterprise is more desirable in comparison with discre-tionary public control the more salient the private agenda of the public official and the less significant the private information concerning profitability. A poorly functioning political system, or the absence of substantial information at the firm's operating level, implies that private enterprise, and thus privatization, is superior to public enterprise.

Just as few of the above arguments have been accepted by transition managers as an inducement to restructure SOEs through corporatization and commercial-ization, little thought has as yet been given to the restructuring of SOEs that remain in the public sector. In fact, it is surprising how little attention this question has elicited to date (Pannier and Schiavo-Campo 1996), especially in view of the very sizable size of the public sector for years to come. Such trans-formation could have been enacted fairly easily once an enterprise law exists. Unfortunately, this option has not been pressed as vigorously as desirable to dilute the role of noneconomic actors. Various explanations can be invoked, including the initial enthusiasm for irrevocable divestment and the expectation that this could be accomplished in record tempo (see Chapter 6), lack of understanding of the importance and possibilities of reaching improved performance in SOEs, skepticism about the capacities of the state to introduce such changes, obstacles to designing appropriate incentive and control schemes, fear that SOE restructuring would undermine the privatization drive, and generally negative attitudes on the part of assistance providers and outside advisers for the public sector or its restructuring.

I am skeptical about the true intent behind this negligence. The foregoing "excuses" should certainly not be invoked as sensible explanations for the delays in clarifying property rights and separating – at least distancing – the state from the economy. Ensuring proper corporate governance in public institutions too – that is, installing the mechanisms and setting the behavioral rules that ensure that managers of public institutions act on behalf of the "public" rather than themselves or their political masters – is something that must be built up quickly, regardless of economic circumstances. That remains an important prospective task of government.

Section 5: The desirable role of the state during the transition

Given its earlier thoroughly overbearing presence, defining the state's role in the "new" societies is pivotal. The solutions proffered so far have not always heeded prevailing economic, let alone social, needs and possibilities. Key is to identify, and capitalize upon, the benefits that the market may derive from an activist government, including through some form of indicative planning or structural policy. That can only emerge from "painstaking pragmatic tests of validity of government intervention in particular areas of economic activity under particular circumstances" (Brus 1990, p. 343). In this connection, recall that governments have always been central to the modernization process whether "as economic ringmaster in the laissez-faire Britain of the past century or as central planner and provider" (World Bank 1987, p. 58) elsewhere. But other governance mechanisms deserve to be explored for they simply exert a different influence over how well the various actors in society are coordinated, goaded into cooperating, and induced to benefit from competition.

At the least, one should separate conceptually the tasks ahead *during* the transition process from those that may be incumbent on the state once the basic elements of the transition's ambitions will have been realized, even though path dependence introduces significant modifications *during* the mutation itself. Unless governance capabilities are simply altogether absent, it is hard to imagine how a far-reaching libertarian government policy can be justified and sustained. Formulating policies, creating institutions, and embracing instruments that help coordinate economic decisions through indirect means on the basis of what is in place are by no means readily transparent or easily discharged tasks. Furthermore, the way in which these assignments are tackled, including through desistance on the part of the state, reflects upon the premises for maintaining consensus on forging ahead. That does not, of course, imply that state involvement take the form of bureaucratic administration, let alone production.

Opinions on the role of the state in the transition straddle an especially wide range. There is little dispute about having government concentrate on sheer governance – in its most austere version equated with playing night watchman (Helm 1986, p. xi). This includes the provision of pure public goods, such as national security, defense, law, and combating crime. The first and the last are the quintessential public good and bad, respectively. As far as economics is concerned, there is broad consensus that the state must be involved in identifying, establishing, protecting, and enforcing all property rights, in creating and maintaining a stable macroeconomic environment; and in promoting the institutional framework that is essential to ensuring an economic order for market operations. All other functions, including even regulating economic affairs and redistributing incomes (Wünsche 1991), are heavily contested. Indeed the role of new governments even in weathering standard market failures, given the confined room for efficient contracting in the short run (Jenkinson and Mayer 1996), is doubted by many (Lampert 1990; Wolf 1990). This is so even when one realizes that from its inception *laissez-faire* has led to structural problems that the market could not rectify (Bihr 1992; Delorme and André 1983; Polányi 1944; Stiglitz 1997b). Emotional concerns may persuade transition managers at first to eschew anything that is not purely "free market." But this stance cannot be sustained for long as outcries for regulation fuel unsettling political debates. If the roundabout way can be avoided, it is preferable to address the pivotal transformation issues pragmatically.

Aside from the generally negative attitude toward letting the state undertake anything other than delivery of pure public goods, there has on the whole been little genuine discussion of the possible role of the state either in the transition or in the coveted market (Tanzi 1991). Three reasons may usefully be ticked off. One is that the state has been so largely discredited in these countries that the very idea of assigning it a specific role, such as in economic affairs, echoes perversity. Another is that the new governments and their bureaucracies have coopted, in some cases reluctantly, large segments of the core politicians and bureaucrats below the top rungs of the *anciens régimes*. This gives inevitably rise to skepticism as to whether these individuals see the role of the state, hence their own, in much the same way as it is in mature market economies. There is also a considerable degree of naïveté, sort of the obverse of the long-standing commitment to socialist ideals (Wolf 1990, p. 47). Finally, the population at large may favor the market economy in the abstract without really being cognizant of its implications, such as unemployment, redistribution and polarization of wealth, instability in incomes, and erosion of social certainties. Once these come to the fore, large segments of the population may resist the changes required to realize such a socioeconomic construct.

Whatever the consensus may entrust to government, some mix of market-based decisions with some form of "planning" is required. Extremist arguments are not particularly helpful. Cogently strengthening the case for a mixed solution, with changing proportions of "market" and "plan" as development proceeds and governance capabilities are required, has yet to elicit strong support by policy makers. This in spite of the fact that prevailing economic theory has failed modernization ambitions in transition economies in more than one respect. I argue this position well realizing that government can be a coercive instance that further distorts market-based incentives. But this need not be so: With proper governance, a solution, however partial and temporary, to market failures *may* be engineered, possibly through regulation rather than outright state activism. Of particular importance is the classical case for the state's role in the economy: providing an efficient legal and institutional system that sets out clear rules of property and commerce, and the respective roles of public and private sectors. This is especially vital to modern economies and to those bent on rapidly reaching this stage. Evolving a system of laws in which private ownership and freedom to dispose of property are guaranteed also provides some security against arbitrary seizure or punitive taxation by the state. It is furthermore conducive to reaching workable contracts that can be upheld in law by private individuals or privately owned firms.

The state's role as regulator, initiator of codifying the rules and regulations pertaining to market behavior, and guarantor of institutions (such as in preventing unfair practices) is beyond dispute even in transition economies. The tasks ahead under this rubric certainly encompass contract enforcement, but also the widely accepted responsibilities of state bodies in market economies: promotion of competition; monitoring the operations of market institutions; guarding the balance between the right to commercial discretion and public accountability; and helping the consumer, who is sovereign at best in theory, to stand up to unscrupulous producers and traders. Without acknowledging the need for judicious intervention when governance capabilities are available and guidelines regulating its application and defining its purposes are not established, there will be intervention in practice anyway, most likely of the injudicious kind (Bruno 1992).

The paradox of the transition's setting is that only appropriate regulation can mold the real market, including eventually deregulation, in such a way that the advantages from it closely approximate its theoretical virtues (B. Johnson and Lundvall 1989). One may harbor legitimate doubts that any well-developed regulatory mechanism can be introduced as a *deus ex machina*; I consider it most implausible. In mature economies, existing regulation has come about in response to felt needs (see Breyer and MacAvoy 1987; Collins and Wallis 1990; Helm and Yarrow 1988; Kay and Vickers 1988; Stelzer 1988, 1989; Swann 1988; Vickers 1991). These have at times been highly conflicting, thus necessitating regulatory change over time, perhaps to ensure that government, and its interest groups, do not become subservient to the regulated groups. But there are no obvious ways in which this outcome can *a priori* be averted (Laffont and Tirole 1991).

Whatever the initial stance adopted, the role of the state in the transition economy will in due course inevitably be greater than in mature economies (Stern 1991); this is likely to endure for as long as the transition is still in search of reasonably functioning markets. From the point of view of income distribution and protection, government ought to be active in ensuring at least minimal social security. From the point of view of "positive" rights (Dasgupta 1986; Sen 1991), it ought to be active in education and health. From the point of view of market failure, it ought to be active in infrastructure, roads, power, and so on. Where government should not normally be active, because none of these arguments can conceivably apply, is in the production of hairpins, motorcycles, bread, and the like. Even the infant-industry argument holds only when there is an inadequate capital market for risky ventures with a payoff at best in the long run that can be expected to exceed the prevailing rate of return on capital. But even then it is not necessary for government to eschew *per se* indirect means of coordinating these decisions (World Bank 1987, pp. 69–71). At the very least, governance capabilities to ascertain the validity of the infant-industry case and ensure that the infant will expeditiously mature, or be discontinued, are required.

At least initially, the above agenda for government action in the transition differs qualitatively from steering mature economies. The entire wherewithal of market institutions in their broad setting needs to be put in place quickly (see Chapter 3). This maturation can hardly be left to the magic of the nonexisting market. Precisely because the market performs an important function in disciplining economic agents against wasteful resource use, the required changes in the institutional environment must be brought about quickly and without building up new constituencies in government. Markets are unlikely to do so automatically (Datta-Chaudhuri 1990, p. 38) or quickly. The core question now is to what extent its germination can be "forced," necessarily through state intervention. This role for the state is hardly in conflict with the market. In other words, while "the invisible hand of the market is adept at dealing with [the] complexity of [market coordination], the visible hand of government needs to provide the rules of the game for markets to work" (World Bank 1987, p. 58). But the World Bank has not always read its own counsel (World Bank 1983a, 1987, 1988, 1991, 1997), reflecting in part the winds of political change in its constituency (Biersteker 1990; Williams 1996).

Second, state agencies have played a major role in providing important parts of the economic infrastructure on which progress in the rest of the economy so heavily depends. These include transportation networks in the broad sense (roads, railroads, port facilities, navigable rivers, water management, power grids, and many others). They also encompass health and educational services. Note that historically some of these services were at first undertaken by private enterprise or by voluntary, charitable organizations. Many gradually reverted to some public agency because self-regulated coordination among private actors simply did not function as expediently and efficiently as circumstances required. Recall that not all goods and services need be "produced" by government, however.

NPOs, possibly situated largely in the public sector, must take care of one aspect or another of the above-enumerated tasks. This applies to all countries.

One particularly important case is education, including in support of encouraging behavior on the part of economic agents that is in broad conformity with the requirements of the market-based system (Cook and Minogue 1990). The need for national education standards and for civic responsibility implies public-good elements. Trying to arrange this at all levels through monetary discrimination by giving free choice (J. Gray 1989, pp. 51ff.) is, in my view, a serious mistake. When educational benefits can be captured by those being exposed to them directly (the student) or indirectly (the firm sponsoring the program), user fees may be the better way to proceed. When capital markets are poorly organized, the state may initially have to make arrangements to permit private-sector agents to finance the acquisition of special skills since they will not normally be able to mobilize collateral to cover the risk of private lenders. This is certainly true in the eastern part of Europe, in some contrast to the Asian transition economies. In the first, a good deal of formal training from the infant's first step to higher education and research during state socialism was geared toward instilling values in people that are now no longer applicable; most cannot be validated in mature markets, let alone in the limping markets typical of the transition.

Not infrequently precisely the erstwhile negated values are now deemed to deserve emphasis. Although people well educated under state socialism may possess the basic skills coveted by new or restructured firms, their training has essentially been in technological processes that are now no longer desired. The proper reaction is not, as has been the case in many countries, to pare these services to the bone through state desertion. Salvaging valuable human capital perhaps through retraining is an urgent task. Likewise, cutting severely into elementary education even at the primary level, as in several Asian transition economies, is not the proper response to fiscal crisis. The state *must* play a galvanizing role in helping with the acquisition of the skills necessary to operate new techniques of production and management, to quickly modify input or output mixes in response to the changing economic environment, to reduce costs, and to improve the quality of innovation under an emerging market environment.

A related element is technological upgrading for countries lagging behind world standards. This knowledge can be reproduced at a fraction of the cost borne by the leader countries that devised them. But even in leader countries, technology in some cases is akin to a public good. Technological knowledge is already reproduced as a free good by universities, publicly subsidized laboratories, or private foundations. When this research becomes less "pure," but more applied as well as product- and firm-specific, its benefits can be earmarked to finance research expenditures. Again, for this to work linkages between firms and research centers, possibly through the intermediation of financial institutions, must be forged. Among others, appropriate basic standards need to be set. Examples are metrics for weights, ensuring dependable inspection and enforcement of regulations, and setting rules against hazardous materials as in the case of polluting agents, safety, health, and so on. In a number of cases, these public goods can best be provided by regulating private transactions rather than through government production.

Third, governments often intervene in markets to improve economic performance, to limit abuses because of egregious differences between social and private costs (such as through fraud, pollution, and endangerment of health), or to promote the welfare of the disadvantaged. Careful intervention in these areas is particularly relevant. It deserves to be taken as close to the source of failure as possible. Even in the most libertarian economy, nearly complete withdrawal of the state in favor of passive acceptance of the results of spontaneous market forces is a very rare event that, as a rule, lasts only a few years. In no case in modern history has there been a complete eschewing of the state; anarchy pure and simple would have resulted. In fact, government intervention in organizing markets for executing private property rights has come about largely in response to the *dis*satisfaction with the prevailing distribution of income and perceived lack of social justice, hence the alleviation of poverty and the reduction of income and wealth inequalities (Helm 1986). Some measure of "distributive justice" is required to attain a minimum of contentment in society (Viner 1960, p. 68).

The role of government in formulating and implementing macroeconomic policies centers on putting in place what is required to effectively coordinate microeconomic decisions and ensure that stability, reliability, and predictability of the institutional environment reign supreme. In some cases, it may even be entrusted with promoting capital formation and job creation, certainly in light of the socioeconomic calamity engendered in nearly all transition economies. Government must assist in mobilizing savings through its own net saving behavior, by creating financial institutions, by formulating state policies that encourage individuals to be thrifty, and by setting a macroeconomy that encourages behavior on the part of individuals so as to promote a dynamic of self-sustainable economic growth. State desertion, such as through rapid divestment, cannot accomplish these core tasks (Carlin and Mayer 1992). Given the crumbling infrastructure, the lack of pollution safeguards, technological backwardness, pervasive macro- and microeconomic imbalances, and the absence of various other safeguards on the transition's eve as well as the daunting tasks ahead, in many ways macroeconomic policy in these countries must for the near future by necessity be more encompassing than this has recently been the case in most mature economies. In view of the weak civil service, the real political challenge is to construct a durable and broad coalition of modernizing interests on the basis of the tradeoff necessarily involved in the boundaries of government competence and the market failures that are bound to accompany rapid economic liberalization.

One of the most critical economic tasks of government in transition economies is protecting the "social wealth" embodied in state assets (see Chapter 6). It is simply not true, as some contend (Blanchard *et al.* 1991; Dornbusch 1991a), that the assets inherited from state socialism are worthless. State-owned assets are one of the few positive legacies of over four decades of communist rule. In this connection, it is useful to recall that the transition has proceeded with a severe economic downturn that depreciates the "real" value of assets. This makes it less urgent to embrace divestment particularly of large SOEs and more urgent to revive the economy through proper procompetitive policies. Furthermore, the impact will be differentiated by asset type. Thus, in the early phase of transition the private sector is relatively booming, largely through arbitrage, while the public one is languishing. Assets employed in the private sector are therefore appreciating in terms of those still in the public sector. This is notably the case for rural land, urban real estate, means of transportation, and the entire array of assets that come in handy particularly in bolstering small-scale service and trade sectors.

Fourth, the paramount economic task ahead is wholesale restructuring. It would be naïve to pretend that this can be left to the magic of the market. If neither the state nor the market can be relied upon in shaping future economic structures, can one believe in the Schumpeterian type of "creative destruction" to nurture the transition economy into the mainstream of the world economy? True, the state is not sufficiently omniscient to pick the winners for a new market-based environment at every turn. But successful economic development of many mature market economies, let alone many NIEs at this stage, would have been unthinkable without an active government policy. The instrumentality of giving government a stake in the modernizing efforts through joint research, risk sharing, fostering development projects, and other means must be recognized. This has implications for entrepreneurship in the transition. That should focus on capitalizing on the talents in place, however badly state socialism distorted them, such as through the second economy, in order to generate sustainable development and attain prosperity (UNWES 1992, pp. 139–80).

Even for the most liberal transition economy, the paradox of the present situation is that the transition to economic liberalism requires strong state involvement, almost regardless of the efficiency of governance. Not only that, for the proper working of the market to be maintained, streamlined, and in many cases expanded, state intervention of the right kind, in the right areas, and at the right time is necessary. Perhaps most important, for the transition economy to regain a sustainable growth path in an open environment pervasive changes in traditional behavior and thinking are inevitable. Forceful political action is required over time, and that can only come from the state.

Finally, virtually all governments provide at least some commercial goods and services, notably power and telecommunications, through SOEs. The record of performance of such firms has not, however, been outstanding in the sense of having delivered the mandated goods and services at least cost (Sah and Weitzman 1991; Singh 1992a, b). But I would not without qualification emphasize that SOEs "have failed to play the strategic role in industrialization that governments had hoped for" (World Bank 1987, p. 66). Indeed, firms may be publicly owned, yet subject to the discipline of a competitive market and be required to realize a profit if they are to grow and the tenure of present management is to be renewed. Such profit-making SOEs are perhaps rare in market economies. But they do exist. Not only that, one should be able to devise criteria by which this outcome may be ensured, such as through precommitments (Sah and Weitzman 1991), particularly in emerging democracies bent on eradicating the vested interests of the old regimes as quickly as circumstances permit. This is even more the case for the provisioning of public and quasi-public goods (see Chapter 6). But execution may be delegated to private activities, provided the government is able to enforce a proper regulatory framework.

Section 6: Legitimizing the new role of the new state

The argument so far has been that the choice between markets and various kinds of government interventions is not a choice between perfection and imperfection, "but between degrees and types of imperfection, between degrees and types of failure" (Wolf 1990, p. 87). In many instances, it may simply be a choice between the disagreeable and the intolerable. Even if the preferred choice favors the market, a significant role for the nonmarket, including government, exists. This role relates especially to the delivery of public goods, establishing and maintaining the legal and other environments essential for the continuing functioning of markets, and providing the necessary redistributive services and programs that constitute an acceptable safety net for society and that reflect the standards of "distributive" justice with which that society is, as Jacob Viner (1960, p. 68) put it, "tolerably content."

The purpose of statewide economic policy depends on two overriding priorities concerning rules of the game. One focuses on the extent to which the individual is subject to the state's authority. Conversely, this calls for delimiting the perimeter of the individual's private sphere, that is, an action range that is not subject to state usurpation. The other centers on the structure of the decision-making process through which the state's authority is exercised and the degree to which an individual can influence that process. Clearly, rules that constrain the potential exercise of state authority are "categorically of greater import than any guarantee of voting franchise within a given constitutional structure" (Buchanan 1987, p. 6).

In pondering the evolving role of the state in the transition, it is instructive to bear in mind that the issue is rarely discussed dispassionately or rigorously. Polarization is especially pronounced in transition economies, even in those that have in principle charted the fundamental directions of moving toward a desirable state of markets and political pluralism. The range of issues voiced elsewhere understandably continues to be much wider and less crisp. There may be broad agreement on the desirable division of priorities and responsibilities. But rarely is it realized that writing a new framework for macroeconomic decision making within the context of altogether new economic governance, and indeed governance more generally, must necessarily emanate from the economic structures, institutions, and policy instruments in place; it cannot be decreed as a *deus ex machina* (see Rausser and Johnson 1993). The role of the government especially as provider of goods and services forms part and parcel of this unsettled debate.

The drift of the discussions about economic policy in particular since mid-1989 at first swelled in favor of a new orthodoxy advocating the myth of a natural order emerging in full glory – including stability, prosperity, and welfare – upon removal of the shackles of public ownership and state regulation. Liberalization in its extreme, "irrealistic" formats triumphed (Sztompa 1996a, b). This new ideology is potent, though presently more limping in view of the adversities experienced. Because it confounds the goals of a balanced and healthy economy, and society more generally, with the means, such as privatization and markets, it prejudices the future of these societies and may even jeopardize reaching the destiny they covet. It furthermore ignores history and misreads the nature of economic organization in mature economies. It also disregards regional statist traditions dating back to the beginnings of the modern era. It blithely under-estimates the role of social preconditions for the establishment of a capitalist order and simplifies the relationship between market and prosperity. In the final analysis, it is the dogma of ivory-tower or doctrinaire economists (Soros 1997) bent on curing the ills of the eastern part of Europe with the same medicine they have applied so unsuccessfully to the Third World and of their local acolytes whose experience of capitalism is confined to dreams and textbooks (Liebich 1991).

Among the many concrete tasks that could be addressed, it would be very helpful if the undoubtedly essential role of government in initiating and providing momentum notably to modernization in most countries were recognized, warts and all: Countries develop by deliberately transforming their comparative advantages, that is, by being more interested in generating specific dynamic comparative advantages than in simply exploring the benefits emanating from differential, but passive resource endowments. This has certainly been the case in the more successful Asian NIEs, where government has actively intervened in various ways to facilitate jumping into the virtuous circle of intra-industry trade by promoting exports of specific manufactures of ever-increasing technological sophistication. Historically such activism has even been endemic to what are now the mature market economies, including the fiercest advocates of privatization.

Perhaps some agreement could be construed around the role of the state in governing an economy in general and the transition economy in particular (Brautigam 1991; Rice 1991). The state intervenes in an economy in a number of distinct ways (Biersteker 1990, pp. 480ff.; Wolf 1990) with a view to influenc-ing, mediating, distributing, and producing goods and services. The nature of this intervention may range from sheer *ad hoc* measures to a well thought-out, formally elaborated strategy. The latter should reflect characteristics of time and place and recognize that changes therein are bound to occur with development

(Panić 1992), and thus should be accommodated. It is entirely possible for the state's role as producer of goods and services to be rising in a particular phase while its role as mediator may be shrinking.

As regards its role in *influencing* the behavior of private, and perhaps other, agents, including local governments, the state conducts certain monetary, fiscal, investment, and trade policies designed to enhance behavior and thus lift economic buoyancy. In some cases, corrective actions may be required that temporarily compress sustainable economic activity. But even then the goal is to bolster the pace of economic growth. Resorting under this rubric is also a battery of policies that regulate or constrain the behavior of economic agents so that an acceptable reconciliation between private and social costs and benefits may be within reach. Examples are pollution controls, worker-safety programs, and minimum-wage legislation. Note that the range of options here extends all the way from the "minimalist state" to what is in essence the "incorporated state." The former employs limited fiscal or monetary instruments and relies on modest regulatory policies and distributive programs. The incorporated state, however, is very interventionist.

In its role as *mediator*, the state tries to alleviate distributional conflicts between capital and labor through interventions that may range from loose cooperative strategies to formal corporatism. An activist state may seek to influence the ultimate *distribution* of national income and/or wealth through the use of subsidies, transfer payments, location policies, rules on inheritance, and other means. Finally, the state may also be the *producer* of goods and services. It can do so directly through SOEs or indirectly by subsidizing the infrastructure necessary for the expansion of national production or by embarking on high-risk or capital-intensive projects by financing and creating SOEs.

This taxonomy could be applied to a wide variety of issues pertaining to the government's involvement in economic affairs. Take industrial policy as a possible field of operations (Brabant 1993a). The key elements thereof are selective mechanisms to influence directly or indirectly resource allocation with a view to bolstering aggregate economic growth and sustainable levels of welfare over the long haul. Mediating among the various government, other nonmarket, and private-sector actors is critical in nurturing the modernization process along. This mediation can be conducted through various means of persuasion, of which actual outlays of public funds do not in every instance have to constitute the most important component. When uncertainty, transaction costs, and inertia are very pronounced, industrial policy can be enhanced through SOEs or other forms of direct involvement of the state in production to overcome initial impediments to modernization.

Although certain elements are common in all desirable formats of governance, distinct country-specific tasks arise in the development process. For the transition economy the agenda is a special one, sort of a varying amalgam of the tasks incumbent upon good governance in developing and developed countries. In the former, the essence is generating sustainable modernization at a fairly rapid pace by absorbing as many available resources as possible in the production process without becoming stifled by the legacies of factor availabilities. For the latter, good governance consists chiefly of managing structural change while ensuring fairly dynamic economic expansion. For that markets and institutions must remain as buoyant as possible. Governance should also aim at bolstering the pace of dynamic economic change which, if successful, consists of diverting resources presently allocated to senile activities to the more promising, dynamic activities.

In transition economies the tasks ahead are a mixture of the two because vestiges of state socialism have to be removed one way or the other, including through incisive structural change. For the more developed countries this implies orderly destruction of nonviable activities to be followed soonest by catch-up modernization largely through the type of governance suitable to countries that have all but accomplished this modernization. In the more developing transition economies, the order of priority, once the destruction has taken its toll, should zero in on the modernization tasks that parallel those of more orthodox developing countries.

Section 7: Governance and managing the transition

Regardless of the leadership's precepts on the government's eventual role in the economy, for now the basic questions revolve around how best to manage the transformation, given the fluid situation in these countries. Transforming the agreed-upon long-term tasks into policies, institutions, and instruments to co-ordinate economic decisions indirectly on the basis of what is in place is neither well defined nor easy. To place the state in the new environment, it may be instructive to inquire into what government is, in which activities it may find its comparative advantage, into the dynamics of government intervention, and when and how alternative policies crystallize.

Clearly, egregious differences between social and private preferences need to be bridged by guiding or intervening in purely privately motivated decisions. Also, sociopolitical preferences need to be safeguarded centrally. But this must be accomplished through new, possibly market-type, rules of the game, not necessarily through SOEs. Because the social-service sphere remains largely under central control, the government simply cannot refrain from managing these activities until other agencies jump into the fray (see Chapter 8), possibly for profit. Furthermore, infrastructure works and other crowding-in capital projects need to be initiated by the center, but not in an economic vacuum. There may be wide agreement about this division of priorities and responsibilities. But rarely are the institutional implications of such a new arrangement, which moreover must be grafted onto the economic model in place rather than introduced in a vacuum, assessed fully.

All these activities form part and parcel of the idea of "governance" (see Chapter 8), but here focused on the state sector. That includes notably engineering the place and role of markets in generating economic wealth. Because of the contestation of what government should be all about since 1989, there ought to be increased interest in these societies in deciding how best to design alternatives to the failures of state socialism. Of particular importance is improving macroeconomic administration, removing abuses of authoritarian power, and ensuring the appropriate dovetailing of the state's economic functions with market-related incentives, institutions, and instruments. This is salient because, in the end, government determines how well or how poorly markets function. Better governance requires political accountability, freedom of association and participation, a sound juridical system based on the rule of law, full accountability of the public administration, freedom of information and expression, and the ability of the government to deliver and divest itself of tasks that eventually can be better executed in the private sector. I realize that the latter mutation may be costly, time consuming, and politically bruising (Starbatty 1996). But it *must* be provided for.

In this connection, it is critical to bear in mind a number of features of government. First of all, it does not consist of selfless, benevolent public servants whose activities are virtually costless. Whereas it may have been useful at some point during state socialism to project the state as an anthropomorphic agency, but there are doubts that this is appropriate for most of the period (Hankiss 1990; Winiecki 1991), this clearly will not do for the market environment. The "state" consists of multiple actors. It is naïve to assume that these agents simply maximize their own welfare like the *homo economicus*, as posited in public-choice theory (Elster and Hylland 1989; Mueller 1989). But it is equally unhelpful to posit that they act out of sheer altruism. It is often ignored that there are politicians whose career depends on events that differ from the determinants of the careers and interests of the civil service. There are also pure technocrats, whose mandate is fairly well defined and who are challenged by the purely technical aspects of the mandate, on which they deliver "efficiently" (Breton and Wintrobe 1986). Of course, there are many divisions within each of these groups, and it is rare that any one is unconstrained in discharging its responsibilities.

Finally, the guidance that economists can provide to government is limited (Cairncross 1985). They can point out the informational costs of alternative policy options. Those with high costs usually have obscure constituent elements, hence yield an opportunity for collusion of special-interests in the private sector. In turn, this enables administrators to exploit those policies to their advantage without incurring the opprobrium of voters and other interest groups. To mitigate this, criteria or rules by which government intervention is administered and in what form need to be specified. Only then can one estimate the costs involved. But there cannot be any blanket guarantee. The less deeply rooted an administration the greater the opportunity that the least costly alternative will be chosen. Nevertheless, the political and administrative process offers many instances of rents simply because devising adequate incentive criteria for public servants is an unresolved task. Economists can assess potential rents and warn against the probable cost of their exploitation to the detriment of the public at large.

At the same time, the presumption that everything requiring bureaucratic administration should be executed in the government sector is fallacious. At the very least, there are direct and indirect costs of such activities. The comparative advantage of government depends not only on the nature of market failure, but also on the cost of rectifying it, particularly when the government sector drains scarce administrative and organizational resources from the private sector and it is offhand unclear whether these individuals are best suited to provide effective public services. That is, government failure may arise as much from negligence in providing the needed infrastructure for activities in which government has a comparative advantage as it has in providing poorly things in which it does not have a comparative advantage (Krueger 1990).

As regards the difficulty of realizing whatever compact can be agreed upon, the many issues involved are not simply confined to the techniques of replacing one model with another. Market-oriented coordination can succeed only when economic agents have confidence in the framework within which they can pursue their own interests subject to rules and regulations set and enforced by central policies. Policies must be credible. Strengthening confidence of economic agents in the government's transformation policies could help mobilize additional indigenous resources for bolstering development. If only for that reason, continuous government activism is required to successfully steer the transition to even the most liberal market-economy variant. At the same time, central authorities need to encourage the renovation of institutions and instruments, and indeed the rapid emergence of new ones, to facilitate the smooth distribution of savings to viable projects. But there are also a host of operations in which the government should not get involved, particularly given the weak markets in place and the legacies of the protracted state-dominated development. There is, however, ample room for government to innovate and coordinate macroeconomic policies, to see to the emergence of "institutions" of the market, and to improve the instruments of policy making.

There are, of course, also areas in which the state cannot get involved, given the basic change in political framework and the limited arena within which it can finance itself. Seen in that perspective, the many gratuitous suggestions by commentators throughout the transformation exercises have often been seriously flawed, even if well intentioned. Those bent on advancing the implantation of market-based economic systems as quickly as possible argue, for example, that the state take over the bad debts of banks and SOEs, set up adequate safety nets, compensate former owners, enact low external tariffs, keep domestic fiscal systems procompetitive, capitalize state liabilities (such as for some social-security tasks), and underwrite what is required to redress the environment. Oftentimes, only one or more of these alleged tasks for government are addressed, but the outcome is the same: The state should assume greater responsibility for shouldering the bulk of the costs inherited from state socialism even though its revenue base is being severely eroded. There is a basic incompatibility between allotting to the state only a minimal role in economic affairs and, at the same time, offloading onto it liabilities that, by necessity, will force it to violate budget discipline or jeopardize the social consensus. Neither will be constructive steps to spur on the desired transformation.

Section 8: Improving governance capabilities

The more self-evident reforms of the public sector that I have treated earlier encompass three: liberalization, privatization, and social-welfare provisioning. In many of these endeavors, the state is expected to, or simply must, retreat, perhaps after the proper transfer of the tasks to other actors in the economy. There are, however, activities in which the state retains control and for which reforms must be introduced soonest. Public-sector government over SOEs that in time will be hived off to the private sector can be handled, when at all, through corporatization and commercialization (see Chapter 6). This has not been pressed to even its minimal logical state (see Chapter 7). Among the many other public-sector activities for which reform is urgently required (Winiecki 1996), I discuss here three: overseeing SOEs that will not be divested, reforming the civil service, and improving the volume and variety of public information. I close this with a brief remark on the role of the state in fostering civil society, at least the components that bear directly on the provisioning of quasi-public goods. The principal argument is that if the state is to play a useful role in governing society in general, and in economic affairs in particular, it needs capabilities. These are as a rule embodied in the civil service in the broad sense as the backup of the governing policy makers and their immediate advisers.

8.1 – SOEs that remain in the public domain

All kinds of public-sector production activities are unlikely to be turned over to the private sector given the state's mandate. The state retains control over these activities perhaps because they encompass SOEs that produce typical public goods (defense sectors) or exhibit monopolistic tendencies or externalities (such as many utilities). There is no reason to believe that those SOEs were run any more efficiently under state socialism than their counterparts now being privatized. Not only is there room for divorcing the political process largely from its immediate involvement in the management of these activities. Those need to be regulated better than in the past through parallels to corporatization and commercialization in the privatization process to improve management, thus technical efficiency, of these firms and to ensure that the "state" as societal arbiter is concerned about the proper "corporate governance" of these institutions.

After nearly a decade of transition and debates on divestment, one must wonder how much of this rationale can still hold water. Certainly in the transition economies where the battle against the old plutocracy has been won through a preemptive strike, as some see the core task of transformation (Åslund, Boone, and Johnson 1996), the only remaining valid reasons would be ignorance and distaste for the public sector. That is a naïve, unimaginative way of policy making. Although one might not have reckoned with a comprehensive restructuring of the SOE sector, the topic should at the least have elicited more than casual interest. Some restructuring steps should have been introduced, especially in countries where this sector continues to absorb scarce financial resources at a cut rate, whether by design, by default, or for lack of the appropriate enforcement mechanisms (including bankruptcy).

Clearly, there are other factors at work than economic efficiency to influence the nature, pace, and extent of SOE reform (Campos and Esfahani 1996). I would attribute the major problems to the inability, or unwillingness, of the political leadership to divorce itself from fairly direct involvement in economic affairs. One could indeed conceive the relationship between policy makers and the public sector as a set of contracts between the government and various socio-economic interest groups. These address problems of market failure as well as demands for resource redistribution. SOE restructuring, then, involves the renegotiation of contracts. In transition economies that entails direct government involvement. More efficient, market-oriented behavior can emerge only if the other social and political parameters of the nexus SOE and policy making is considerably loosened.

Improved corporate governance in SOEs is particularly important in transition economies because other "institutions" that provide checks on the behavior of managers, such as rating companies, brokers, financial investors that assess the performance of firms, and the capital market, continue to be rudimentary at best. Elements of encouraging such a corporate-governance culture can be readily discerned (see Chapter 6): corporatization and commercialization, meaning cutting off all *ex post* subsidies, regardless of their origin. In addition, policy makers need to select an agent to represent the state as owner (see Chapter 7). That should be concerned about putting in place mechanisms that elicit improvements in management culture, including through various oversight boards. True, writing meaningful performance and management contracts given the convoluted transition is difficult, but not impossible. At least a first stab at such control mechanisms could have been set, even if in the end the contracts would have had to be renegotiated.

Often one hears objections to the effect that "old style" management would not be capable of restructuring "its" firm and be guided by profit-based considera-tions. Much of this stems from prejudice. Although some political managers can probably not reform themselves and revamp their firm to profitability, to apply this sentiment in one full sweep to all old-style management is not very sensible. At the very least the hypothesis should be tested. With a few demonstration cases of management in SOEs being effectively removed through the above-cited governance mechanisms, one could elicit some movement in the SOE sphere more generally. In any case, it is not particularly useful to expect that soon there will be a new class of managers. Policy makers have to work with the resources at hand and aim at some more gradual changes.

8.2 – The civil service

To the extent that the state has to play a positive role in society, not just in economic affairs, there is an urgent need to reform the civil service. Governance is not feasible when seen solely in an ideological, value-weighted scheme of things. Good governance can be ensured only when the prevailing sociopolitical consensus translated into some strategy on how to govern is implemented by the rulers. That can be done only when an amenable civil service is in place.

A civil service, which separates fiscal appropriations from private property of those staffing the service, is a product of long development (Weber 1946, p. 197). Although it may be extant at some point in time, when the sociopolitical consensus as well as the rulers change there is a need for placing the civil service on a new last. Also this cannot be done at once. Mobilizing the bureaucracy's loyalty, trust, and commitment to a new government's program is vital. This simply cannot be achieved by maligning the civil service. To recruit and retain qualified, competent, and honest civil servants, adequate salary and associated perquisites are minimal requirements. The shortcomings of an unprofessional civil service, with recruitment and promotion criteria frequently based on political patronage, figures prominently among the ills of the state (Frischtak 1996). But more than monetary emoluments are needed to sustain a well-functioning civil service (Weber 1946, pp. 198ff.). Indeed, the recruitment of and ability to retain highly qualified civil servants is "decisively influenced by considerations of vocation for public service, political commitment, and the professional status of civil service" (Boeninger 1992, p. 274). These values can be furthered only by strengthening the commitment to the public service and granting nonmonetary rewards for performance.

Whereas in the private sector, particularly in corporations of rather individualistic societies, virtually all rewards for competent and effective work are translated into pecuniary magnitudes, efforts to emulate this modus in the public sector have foundered. Indeed, the public service in these societies tends to be weak; frequently it is a preserve for those unable to make it in the private sector or for rent seekers. The former will tend to stay in the public service, and for that purpose insist upon being granted long-term contracts bordering on lifetime tenure. Rent seekers, on the other hand, join the public service, and perhaps even the government, simply to build up "contacts" that can be translated into pecuniary benefits when they rejoin the private sector. This does not materially differ from the way in which prebendal officialdom, from early history up to the threshold of modern times, operated (Weber 1946, p. 199). In such situations, the more cogently argued rhetoric of the public-choice school is fully applicable. Governance in the sense defined here will not only be difficult. It is also unlikely to remain fair.

Executing the tasks of governance through a civil service differs intrinsically from managing private economic affairs (Dahl and Lindblom 1953, pp. 233ff.; Weber 1946, pp. 198ff.). On that score, opinions formulated by those steeped in

373

the European tradition differ sharply from those held, say, in the United States (Weber 1946, p. 198). That is not to deny that opportunities exist for slimming down government and decentralizing activities; any rounded treatise of reform of the public service provides a cogent review of the multiple issues (Osborne and Gaebler 1992; Salamon 1989). Under proper conditions, this may provide better pecuniary incentives to delivering quasi-public goods and services with greater efficiency than this is intrinsically possible in the public sector, once the conditions of time and place are well identified. What matters for our discourse, however, is that the tradition of the civil service and the expectations of the population at large with respect to the governance of the state in virtually all transition economies tend to be much closer to those held on the European continent than those propounded, say, in the United States.

The trend since the mid-1970s has been to malign the civil service as a rent-seeking class. Advocacy of such a slimmed-down public service entrusted with the smallest number of assignments is not necessarily sound advice for transition economies. This is particularly so when its normal functions are being captured by a highly centralized, narrow élite reminiscent of the old *nomenklatura*. For one thing, the transition is very complex and the trajectory should be made the shortest and least costly. Also, most of these societies attach a positive value to public service and expect the state to deliver far more "security" than, say, in the US framework. Finally, reform of the public service is unquestionably required. In a number of transition economies the temptation has been very pronounced to settle accounts and all but rid the country of the public service, not just the civil servants inherited from state socialism. Instead of searching for constructive reform, many transition managers have outrightly spurned the public service as intrinsically providing questionable assistance at best in moving along the transition processes. They have done so, among others, by keeping salaries in real terms very low, by relying on other channels for governance; and by otherwise downgrading the public service. The policies implemented since 1989 have left the civil service in many cases in appalling disarray.

Budget parsimony is the order of the day for public institutions. Its indiscriminate application, in lawn-mowing fashion, is particularly misplaced especially in this instance. "Putting private enterprises on a pedestal tends to lead to the disintegration of the public service" (Boeninger 1992, p. 278). The pre-ordained result is demoralization of the public service, good people leaving for the private sector, and difficulty in recruiting motivated and qualified replacements, leaving behind in some cases a dysfunctional class of rent-seeking, corrupt officials preying on the private sector in what George Soros (1997, p. 55) has labeled "the gangster state." It is a tragedy simply to destroy what is in place, thus impairing governance, for the sake of safeguarding questionable market freedoms that soon have to be regulated, including by rebuilding the civil service.

Much abuse occurred under state socialism. Its highly bureaucratized administration offered many opportunities for maximizing private gains as well as perpetrating all kinds of wrongs. But not everyone in the public service was tarnished in this way. Certainly, a good deal of what was positively valued in the public sector under state socialism has now lost its potential and may in fact have become a liability (Michnik 1993). The inherited civil service is not very well suited to discharge the functions incumbent upon a civil service in a rule-bound society with a market-based economy. But it is a fundamental mistake to assume that the shadow value of human capital in the public sector in 1989 or so was zero, let alone negative, hence that these ranks must be rapidly thinned. The challenge instead should be how best to mobilize most of the existing public service for the new economic, political, and social tasks. Inertia may be taken to mean opposition to the new trends. In some cases, this may well be so. In most others the inertia is genuine and quite human. The public sector too requires an enabling environment. To be effective, it must be endowed with dignity, social recognition, reasonable stability, and adequate compensation. Furthermore, above-average performance should be rewarded with appropriate career-advancement chances. Because comparable metrics to those of the private sector are often lacking, it is difficult to evaluate and reward public-sector performance. But also this should not be exaggerated, given the multilayered principal–agent problem in *all* organizations.

Surprisingly little has been done in recent years to strengthen the capacity of the state so that it can discharge the functions that are commonplace in even the more liberal market environment. This is ironic especially in transition economies. Let me briefly touch upon three areas in which the civil service must play a crucial role during the transformation process, but there are others among which the "information" issue of the next subsection figures prominently (Verheijen 1996). First of all, managing the transformation requires governance. Throughout the volume I have argued the case for orderly transformation, a process that can only be ensured via government action, provided governance capabilities are available in the state sector or can be acquired expeditiously, possibly with foreign support (see Chapter 11). The alternative is quasi anarchy. Without going into the finer points (see Brabant 1993a, pp. 142–70), the capacities of the state to govern also economic affairs, where it has, or should hold, a comparative advantage, must be transformed. The capabilities for good economic governance still within reach need to be mobilized to navigate the more socially corrosive passages of the transformation agenda.

Rethinking the new role of the new state in all of its dimensions is not something that can be postponed until the rudiments of incipient capitalist markets will have been assimilated and the needs for reining in the wilder sides of such an environment will have been forcefully expressed once again. Rather, it is urgent to forestall the eventuality that these economies retrogress into primitive capitalism (Soros 1997). Ideological stances are unlikely to be very helpful in this regard. Determined pragmatism on the part of all actors involved in transformation policies is urgently needed. Under some conditions, only an authoritarian intervention in economic affairs, such as the so-called shock therapy, may successfully inch forward, and perhaps guide the process, toward the coveted new development path. But there can be no guarantee that this outcome emerges from the shock (see Chapter 3).

Second, whenever a decision is made, perhaps for critical social and political reasons, that the process of "creative destruction" cannot be unleashed without some temporizing, the mutation can succeed only if the state adopts some form of industrial policy. In this connection it may be useful to focus civil-service reform on properly staffing activities for which the state decides not to leave matters to whatever market forces are in place. Orderly privatization, strategic thinking about the new growth trajectory to be located, proper governance of remaining SOEs, fostering public saving institutions and development banks, managing a debt-resolution agency, and many other tasks immediately spring to mind. Some may be fashioned out of existing organs while others should be cast almost *ab ovo*. Presumably this offers a chance not to infuse these organs with many of the defects of public agencies that have come about in market economies as a result of historical accident, coincidence, or pragmatic need.

Third, most transition economies want to forge close ties with the EU, and at least ten covet full membership in the near term (see Chapter 10). In preparing for accession negotiations, the civil services appear to be overwhelmed by the tasks incumbent upon seeking membership, let alone in eventually operating constructively within the EU's single market. To participate fully in the EU, a member must have a civil service that can incorporate the *acquis communautaire* into the national legislative framework and public institutions, apply it reasonably smoothly, supervise implementation of these rules in a market context, and work positively within the *modi operandi* of the EU. That presupposes a substantial and effective role of public agencies in socioeconomic life given the difficulties, and sometimes the costs, of observing the regulations of the EU club (Brabant 1996). It is critical to have appropriate capacities when, for example, concrete negotiations for membership get under way. The comparative disappointment with the Europe Agreements negotiated early in the transition stemmed in part from the weakness of the civil service that negotiated these instruments (see Chapter 11).

8.3 – Quantitative and qualitative information

As discussed in Chapter 7, coordinating the decisions of multiple agents in a market environment hinges critically on the availability of accurate and ample information on economic and other matters. This has the character of a public good, particularly during the early phase of the transition, given the prevailing uncertainty, and the poor capabilities and interests in the private sector to invest in the collection, organization, and dissemination of information, except when it has a direct private interest and the cost is limited.

It is perhaps easier to deal with quantitative information, if only because the state of statistical information provided by and available about the transition economies has been the subject of so many commentaries (see Chapter 3). The statistical legacies of state socialism are certainly many, in terms of coverage, routines for assembling and organizing the data, and indeed the habits to divulge the information at low cost to the user. Different types of data are required for a number of reasons. One is that macroeconomic policy in a market economy relies in the main on instruments of fiscal and monetary policy, rather than direct controls, as under administrative planning. As such, it requires different data from those utilized by a central planner. Some can be generated only once the new institutions, such as in the area of steering monetary policy or revamping fiscal systems, will have been credibly put in place.

Arguably even more essential is that a market economy thrives on coordinating decisions of independently functioning agents subject to competition or liberal entry-and-exit provisions. Reliable statistics, as well as other kinds of economic and commercial, and in some cases political and social, information, become essential to individual firms, especially new ones. In this respect, priority deserves to be accorded to collecting, processing, and disseminating appropriate information on the newly emerging private sector and the gradually legalized underground economy. Both types of activities were largely ignored in data activities for policy purposes under state socialism. But they are paramount in carrying these societies onto a new, endogenous growth path (see Chapter 5). As a result, better ways to include comprehensive information on these sectors in statistical reporting for policy purposes must urgently be found so that decision makers, whether in the private or public sector, can properly steer the transition by adopting pertinent policies or remedial actions on a timely basis.

The transition economies also require statistics to monitor their progress toward a market economy and to track the adjustment of economic behavior to the new incentive systems. Such data not only are necessary to formulate and implement proper policy measures, but also are even more essential in order to monitor, assess, and fine-tune particular policies. They will also be required to enable providers of international assistance to ensure efficiency in their assistance policies and indeed to justify their activities to their own national or multilateral constituencies. Finally, accurate and detailed statistics are a vital source of information to facilitate the integration of the transition economies, including their economic agents, into the international economy.

8.4 – Fostering agents of civil society

At first blush it may seem perverse to call for state involvement in the establish-ment and development of the agents of civil society (see Chapter 7). Indeed, there is much to be said for eschewing any attempt to deliberately construct the "creative chaos of organizations, associations, and institutions" (Dahrendorf 1990, p. 103). Normally this would lead at best to an artificial construct from whose nooks and crannies people yearn to escape for the real thing. However, there are two features of the transition economies that *may* call for special measures on the part of the state to nurture NPOs. One is the agencies left from communism that are no longer warranted, hence must be dissolved, or that may be suitably restructured into NPOs. Second, for the time being the contributions from private individuals and corporations to nonmarket organizations are likely to remain subdued, given the adversities of the transition. Private initiative may be seized to encourage the formation of NPOs, but this may come about too slowly and perhaps in a skewed manner. Encouraging variety, the central task being one of deliberately enabling or empowering nonstate agents rather than planning or even building civil society, may therefore be warranted. This need not be a costly adventure. In fact, government in these economies should address in the first instance the legislative environment required to nurture NPOs. It should also disseminate information about the advantages and drawbacks of NPOs abroad at fairly little cost. As already argued, it could transform a number of existing cultural, educational, scientific, welfare, and related budget organs without having to provide *incremental* resources from dwindling fiscal revenues. This is important because it would not be in the state's best interest to let these organs atrophy under impact of shrinking real resources and lucrative private-sector opportunities.

Conclusions

Barring an anarchic transition, the role of the state in reality will have to be much larger than the advocates of neoliberalism like to admit. Its central focus should be providing order to the transformation commensurate with the capabilities that the state has at its disposal or can quickly acquire. The state can do so through various means, including by wielding its coercive prerogatives. But these are better used sparingly. Instead, policy makers should be concerned about actively promoting governance capabilities for the major tasks at hand. Aside from the humdrum aspects of presiding over the society, during the transformation these all revolve around the orderly destruction of assets in place that become superfluous in a market context and the encouragement, within a set framework, of creative activities, particularly through new small firms.

Apart from aspirations for minimal government, the maxim to be heeded should be that government intervenes in economic affairs only where market failure is most pronounced and even then only in a guarded manner, that is, when the risk of even larger government failure is tolerable. When governance capabilities fall short of what is deemed necessary to maintain order in the transformation, it behooves those managing the transition and their advisers, as well as assistance-delivering agencies, to explore with determination ways and means of upgrading and extending governance capabilities. Only in this manner can a sociopolitical consensus be forged and sustained through the hobbled path leading toward the realization of the transition's goals.

Part III

TOWARD SUSTAINABLE GROWTH AND GLOBAL INTEGRATION

The following three chapters examine several external dimensions of the transformation leading up to a consideration of the sustainability of the gains booked to date, of accessing a modernization path, and of staying on it for some period of time. These elaborations complement in particular the discussion of Chapter 5. They can be located around international assistance for transition policies, fuller merger into the global economic framework through multilateral organizations, working toward meeting the requirements of EU entry and elaborating a constructive relationship with the EU, and how all of this plus the transformation agenda itself is shaping up with respect to the sustainability of the transformation under way so that "modernization with catch-up" can be assured.

Economic progress as such deserves to be applauded and gains in material welfare are important, including for the electorate. But those benefits attained in some countries do not yet signal sustainability and modernization even for the economy the most advanced with its transformation. I maintain this in spite of the widely held expectation that all transition economies will before long emerge from their protracted depression, thus perhaps mutually reinforcing recovery impulses. Neither can sustainability be equated with reaching positive growth of a few points above the "normal" pace for mature economies. Indeed, the material achievements recorded should at least be contrasted with the protracted societal depression, including the steep decline in the economic and social fortunes, of these countries over the past decade, and longer in some cases. Rather, the current progress booked or expected to materialize soon is significant for completing the intermediate stages of political pluralism and market-based resource allocation. The ultimate aim of the *annus mirabilis* in most countries revolves around broader societal renewal than just expanding economic wealth: These countries want to emulate key features of wealth, productivity, and incomes held to be "normal" for a mature market economy.

10

TRANSFORMATION AND INTEGRATION INTO THE WORLD ECONOMY

"Full integration into the world economy" has been one of the insistent mantras purveyed since mid-1989 throughout the transition economies. Its meaning is not always clear, if only because of the notion's multiple dimensions and policies have often diverged from enunciated intentions. One aspect pertains to opening the domestic economy to external competition for goods, services, and production factors (certainly capital inflows) facilitated through various domestic institutional arrangements and possibly positive policy measures (see Chapter 5). A second is joining global economic organizations and subscribing to their underlying regimes. A third one uppermost on the minds of policy makers, especially in the more western of the transition economies, is joining the EU. One may well ask whether such forceful meshing with the world economy is the best course to pursue, given the state of affairs in these economies. The controversy over short-term foreign economic policies I highlighted in Chapter 5. Here I consider the question from the perspective of the core task of the transformation: Engineering rapid catch-up with average levels of development typical of the advanced "western" countries, such as in western Europe.

This chapter focuses on dimensions of opening up seen largely from the point of view of autonomous decisions by transition managers. The "views" of other countries and the organizations themselves are dealt with in the context of Chapter 11. After inquiring into the meaning of "integrating into the world economy," I debate the desirability in principle of the transition economies' joining the multilateral organizations in light of the latter's universal ambitions. Next I examine the role of the transition economies in the global economic organizations and the desirability of subscribing to their underlying regimes. Thereafter I look more closely at the advantages and drawbacks of attracting foreign investment, FDI in the first place. But I focus on the realism of utilizing FDI as a substitute for or complement to domestic savings, and on the implications of subscribing to the implicit "international regime" of TNCs. Before concluding I clarify the central questions of the relations between the transition economies and the EU. External assistance for the transitions I deal with in Chapter 11.

Section 1: Integrating into the global economy – its meanings

A country merges into the world economy through a variety of channels. It becomes ultimately "fully integrated" as a result of administrative decisions affecting domestic and external liberalization (see Chapter 5); of international agreements with countries and regional and global groupings; of membership and participation in multilateral institutions, and indeed of subscribing to and abiding by their regimes; and of the spontaneous trade, technological, financial, communication, and other links created by the interplay of market forces. The latter's dynamics depends not only on the domestic institutional transformation, but also on the policies and economic vigor of partner countries. In particular, a buoyant international economy characterized by vigorous growth and balanced macroeconomic policies in conjunction with increased access to markets can speed up the process of dovetailing the transition economies with the world economy. Still, international cooperation policies have a major role to play in expediting that process.

At the inception of the transformations, national policy makers, executives of multilateral organizations, and many commentators held ambitious targets on finally merging the eastern part of Europe into the global economy. These ambitions, even if tempered over time, have since been frustrated in all too many countries. In fact, they were patently out of touch with the transition's realities, at least during the initial phase. This incongruity arose because the cited aspirations did not sufficiently reflect the ability of the transition economies to absorb adjustment costs, undertake quick and substantial changes in institutions, modify behavioral patterns of their agents, and attract sizable private as well as official resource inflows. Yet, several economies have made major progress on several fronts. Elsewhere, however, the core questions of the desirability of actually merging into the international economy on favorable terms remain unsettled.

1.1 – Foreign trade flows

Mixed tendencies have been observed since the inception of market-orientation in 1990 throughout the economies in transition. For what official numbers are worth (see Table 10.1), trade by now has surged ahead at a very fast clip, at least in nominal dollar terms. In 1996, for example, total exports for eastern Europe reached $96 billion and imports $130 billion. The corresponding data for the former USSR are $94 billion and $60 billion in 1996 as compared to $59 billion and $65 billion in 1990, respectively (UNECE 1997). In other words, official imports into former USSR have not yet matched the 1990 level, but exports have surged ahead albeit at a slower pace than in eastern Europe; however, informal imports in 1996 may have reached anywhere between $10 billion and $25 billion, with the former amount apparently for unreported imports from Turkey alone! Also, whereas eastern Europe has been running a sizable and growing

Table 10.1 Total trade and trade shares by broad partners groups (billions of dollars and in percent of current values)

	1985	1990	1991	1992	1993	1994	1995	1996
				Eastern Europe				
Exports								
bi. $	55.0	61.7	57.1	59.5	61.3	71.4	95.2	96.1
ex-USSR	28.5	22.3	17.9	12.3	9.2	8.6	8.3	9.0
EE1	16.2	12.7	7.7	6.9	7.1	8.2	8.4	n.a.
EE2	16.2	12.7	7.7	6.9	16.7	15.1	14.8	15.3
OSots	5.4	6.1	4.4	5.0	5.1	3.5	3.4	3.3
DME	35.9	49.5	59.8	63.2	58.0	62.5	64.4	63.6
DE	14.1	9.4	10.2	12.7	11.5	10.2	9.1	8.8
Imports								
bi. $	53.9	63.4	61.5	68.3	74.3	83.7	116.6	130.0
ex-USSR	32.2	18.3	20.2	18.0	16.1	13.9	12.9	12.5
EE1	17.6	12.5	6.3	5.6	5.0	5.6	6.0	n.a.
EE2	17.6	12.5	6.3	5.6	11.9	11.1	11.2	10.8
Osots	5.3	6.0	2.8	2.3	2.2	2.4	2.3	2.5
DME	32.9	53.3	58.3	64.1	61.6	65.0	65.8	66.2
DE	12.0	9.9	12.4	10.1	8.3	7.8	7.8	8.0
				Former Soviet Union				
Exports								
bi. $	57.3	59.1	46.7	53.7	56.7	67.0	85.3	93.8
EE1	31.6	18.8	22.9	17.7	17.0	14.1	16.2	13.0
OSots	9.7	7.1	7.0	13.0	9.3	9.7	10.0	13.1
DME	38.7	49.5	56.5	57.9	59.7	62.0	59.9	58.0
DE	20.0	24.6	13.5	11.3	14.0	14.3	13.9	16.0
Imports								
bi. $	54.8	65.0	45.4	44.2	37.5	41.7	52.5	59.7
EE1	32.1	23.2	24.5	12.1	10.7	11.7	15.5	8.9
Osots	9.1	6.2	6.9	11.6	11.4	7.1	6.7	9.1
DME	42.1	52.9	58.1	62.4	60.6	70.3	69.6	67.3
DE	16.7	17.7	10.4	13.9	17.3	10.9	8.2	14.6

Source: UNECE 1996a,b; 1997.

Notes:
EE1:   Traditional eastern Europe without 'new' trade; former Soviet Union, all trade.
EE2:   Eastern Europe, including 'new' trade.
OSots: Other socialist countries, including China, Cuba, (north) Korea, Mongolia, and Vietnam.
DME: Developed market economies (nonsocialist world minus traditional developing countries).
DE: Traditional developing countries.

trade deficit since 1990, amounting to $34 billion in 1996 as compared to $1.7 billion in 1990, former USSR has been running a huge export surplus since 1992, amounting in 1996 to $34 billion, as compared to a deficit of $5.9 billion in 1990. The countries with large deficits relative to exports (but omitting the "bizarre" cases of Albania, Macedonia, and rump Yugoslavia) are on the whole the fastest reforming central European countries, but also Croatia. The huge surplus in former USSR is essentially on account of Russia ($37.4 billion in 1996, or some 54 percent of reported exports).

These changes in nominal values do not tell us much about the real changes in trade observed, given the shifts in relative prices and exchange rates over the period. Unfortunately, the data here are especially unreliable. At best one can construct some approximation (as regularly reported in *Economic Survey of Europe* . . . and *Economic Bulletin for Europe* on whose data I rely extensively). The general trend has probably been quite a bit more mixed than nominal values suggest. After an initial contraction due to the plummeting trade with CMEA partners, as a result of the liberalization and stabilization policies embraced the more successful transition countries registered a surge in real exports along with a sharp compression of real imports. The former arose because of the need to compensate for terms-of-trade losses but also export-price erosion because of switching from CMEA or domestic to EU markets in particular, and variable exchange rates. Declining domestic demand created room for exports from inventories and running production at whatever price supported liquidity largely for SOEs. Imports contracted in real terms because of the sharp drop in domestic demand and rising prices for fuels in particular. The former USSR also encountered real losses notably on the export side, but the fuel exporters in particular benefited from terms-of-trade gains though available volumes shrank; the sheer collapse of imports suggests real losses were probably sustained as well. But the data are very uncertain. About one to two (and longer for former USSR) years into the transition, most of these countries began to experience difficulties in maintaining balance in their external accounts. Exports fell or stagnated, among others, as a result of the further erosion of the reserved CMEA "markets"; the severe recession in western Europe in the early 1990s and again the milder contraction at mid-decade; and the absence of strong export-oriented policies, while imports generally soared under pressure of shifts in domestic demand, especially for consumer goods.

Perhaps the most spectacular facet of developments since the late 1980s has been the reorientation of trade from eastern to western markets, but there has in fact been little trade diversion. Indeed, the vast bulk of export gains stemmed from forced sales from domestic inventories or current output for which domestic demand had vanished. Within a record short time span, the most important trade partner of all economies in transition, save some of the more remote CIS States, became the EU with Germany in the lead (Brabant 1997c; Kamiński, Wang, and Winters 1996; Landesmann and Székely 1995). Both exports to and imports from the latter have continued to surge, although unsteadily in part because of the above-cited recessions in western Europe, Germany in particular. Thus, whereas for eastern Europe in 1988, the developed countries (almost identical with the EU) accounted for 39 percent of exports and 36 percent of imports, by 1996, these magnitudes were 64 and 66 percent; a similar but much smaller shift occurred for former USSR, with Russia in the lead (UNECE 1997).

Especially in relations with the EU, the deficit for eastern Europe has become very large indeed; it was about $25 billion with developed market economies in 1996. Matters are more balanced for former USSR, Russia in particular. But it recorded a not insubstantial deficit of $5.7 billion with developed countries in 1996. There has been considerable apprehension in policy circles about the sizable deficit that many of the economies in transition have incurred with the EU in the past few years. In and of itself, this would not be too worrisome if countries were raising capacity utilization, expanding capacity, and net capital inflows continued to be positive – after all, that is precisely one essential component of what the transformations in the eastern part of Europe should be all about. It would be more positive if with idle capacities these countries were financing the capital reconstruction from both domestic savings and net FDI. Bringing about the latter favorable conjuncture, however, has taken time and only few countries, perhaps the Czech Republic and Poland, reached it by 1996. Elsewhere much of the capital inflow is speculative, FDI targets domestic consumer markets and is not necessarily strengthening the export capacity of most countries, and a good proportion of the external deficit, including with the EU, is on account of imports of consumer goods. It is also worrisome that several countries have at some points since 1989 experienced problems, actually or in a contingent mode, in accessing EU markets for the products for which they possess, at least for now, excess capacity and a comparative advantage.

The economic resurgence in western Europe and the improved market access provided in the context of the various trade and cooperation agreements under implementation should improve matters prospectively (see Chapter 11). To gain maximum benefit from these markets, the transition economies themselves need to bolster their export offer of competitive goods, including via diversification of export supply, which has been difficult because of low domestic investment levels and much smaller than expected inflows of FDI (see pp. 390–2). In any case, a reversal of policy toward greater export orientation remains contingent on the adoption of appropriate domestic policies broadly supportive of a determined export drive.

In a rough-and-ready assessment, whereas the primary beneficiary of the recent surge and diversion of trade of these economies has been the EU, the large loser has been the former CMEA and interrepublic partners. Trade buoyancy in these relations has savagely shrunk. Thus, for eastern Europe, omitting the "new" international trade (for the former Czechoslovakia and Yugoslavia), shares dropped from a high of 19 percent in 1986 to a low of under 7 percent for exports in 1992 and 5 percent for imports in 1993, and have been recovering only slowly since then; unambiguous trends are difficult to discern, however. Similarly for eastern Europe's former trade with the former USSR: From highs of 31 percent for exports and 35 percent for imports in 1986, the trough was 8.3 percent for exports in 1995 and 12.5 percent for imports in 1996. Although some recovery of trade with the core CIS States, notably Russia and Ukraine, has recently taken place, it is even more difficult to dissect clear trends here than for eastern Europe's intragroup trade.

The recovery of trade among the former CMEA members since about 1994–5 has been confounding those who had earlier posited that there would be no "future" in propping up and bolstering intragroup trade as one lever for shoring up demand during the transition. But it would be premature to affirm that there is as yet an unmistakable trend toward "normality" in these relations (Brabant 1997c). Though it has proved to be unfashionable to stress this in recent policy making, with few exceptions, there continue to be opportunities for expanding trade and cooperation among the transition economies. Recovery and expansion of regional trade would be of particular importance for the members of the CIS, which at least for now have limited possibilities of establishing free-trading agreements with western Europe. But the market institutions for facilitating intra-group trade and broader economic cooperation, even when some free-trading arrangements are in place, such as in the context of the Central European Free Trade Agreement (CEFTA), which came into operation in March 1993 and now encompasses also Romania and Slovenia, soon to be joined by Bulgaria, continue to be rather primitive. This not only applies to export-insurance and -guarantee facilities, but also pertains to the expeditious clearing of reciprocal settlements and, even more, to the regular financing of trade. If the latter avenues are to be used to smooth exports, for now they have to be procured at considerable transaction cost from western European intermediaries.

Also trade with the traditional partners among developing countries all but collapsed as did eastern Europe's trade with other socialist countries, in marked contrast to the former Soviet exports, but not imports, which have been very unstable. However, there has been more buoyancy in economic relations, once the initial stages of the transition are overcome, with other developing countries, especially the more dynamic NIEs in east and southeast Asia as well as China. Nonetheless, as a group the developing countries have not done particularly well: Their trade share dropped from a high of about 13–14 percent for eastern Europe to the trough of 8–9 percent reached around 1995. Data for the former USSR for these relations point to an even larger collapse, if only because trade with the former developing-country client States all but vanished.

One of the crucial markers of progress toward modernization is the restructuring of the composition of exports, and indeed the nature of the imports, particularly when a deficit is being financed from abroad, as noted earlier. Unfortunately, we know fairly little about the commodity composition of trade among the transition economies as the available data are unreliable, incomplete, and issued with great delays. Some impression can be gained from the composition of trade between the EU and the ten transition economies with a Europe

Agreement (Bulgaria, the Czech Republic, Estonia, Hungary, Latvia, Lithuania, Poland, Romania, Slovakia, and Slovenia). Presumably trends observed there, particularly EU imports from these countries, are indicative of changes that have been taking place also in intragroup relations. The data produced by the EU (European Commission 1997b; see also Hoekman and Djankov 1996; Messerlin 1996; UNECE 1996b) make it immediately evident that manufactured goods account for the bulk of the exports from the transition economies, and that gains there have been at the expense essentially of agricultural products and fuels, and to some degree chemicals. The crisis of agriculture throughout the transition economies and the elimination of subsidies for the reexports of fuels from former USSR to western Europe is partly responsible for this shift. But a major impetus to bolstering the exports of manufactures has been imparted by foreign invest-ment, including the more footloose kind that is meant to be a substitute for labor migration. In the absence of very detailed commodity data, it is not quite clear what kind of "new" goods might have been emerging. But some perspective can be gained by examining the EU's data of trade with the privileged transition economies (European Commission 1997b). The truly sharp gain in imports by the EU from the ten privileged transition economies since 1991 has been, apart from resource-based goods, in miscellaneous manufactured goods and in machinery and equipment, starting from a very low level (European Commission 1997b). One can speculate that the latter gains stem largely from the vertical integration that FDI has brought about in the more advanced countries. The former depends crucially on export gains for clothing, footwear, travel goods, and furniture (Hoekman and Djankov 1996, p. 11) as the bulk of manufactures. These are all low-wage goods, the bulk of which is "exported" through outward processing, a polite form of exporting "cheap labor." That would also appear to account for the high levels of apparent intra-industry trade in these relations.

Second, from detailed analyses of the commodity composition of trade with the EU (UNECE 1996a, b; 1997), there is evidence that the gains made in manufacturing have more generally tended to be in the more resource- and unskilled-labor-intensive production lines, rather than in high value-added activities. The bulk of exports to the EU appears to consist of resource- and labor-intensive products. Indeed, outward processing accounts for a sizable component of some categories, textile and clothing in particular. This is useful in the short run since it props up aggregate demand and provides foreign exchange. It is not sustainable, however, once the "assistance sentiment" shifts, in the EU in par-ticular, or real wages in foreign currency, as has happened throughout the western transition economies. Difficulties in managing exchange rates offer only one explanation. Several countries have recently seen their competitive position weakened by a real appreciation of the exchange rate that is not justified by factor-productivity performance.

All in all, one has not yet seen a dramatic shift in the composition of exports away from low value-added goods; similarly, imports are in few cases dominated by investment goods. In fact, even in intragroup trade, many of the high value-added traded goods, such as for cars, have been severely compressed as consumer tastes, policy orientation, and the asymmetric playing field have been favoring western imports. Finally, although the evidence is not overwhelming in part because documentable trade categories remain rather coarse, "new" products have been entering trading markets, and presumably domestic production, only very slowly. This evidence for trade with the EU has probably a direct bearing too on the type of goods entering intragroup trade.

1.2 – Capital inflows

Other than trade channels for anchoring the economies in transition more solidly into the global economy at an early stage have not been functioning as smoothly as it had earlier been envisaged. The effective magnitude of delivered assistance has lagged well behind expectations (see Chapter 11). Anticipated private flows, notably FDI, have far exceeded what has, in fact, materialized. The data on the relevant gross and net variables by type of capital flow are, however, far from reliable. Nonetheless, especially in recent years, net capital inflows into the transition economies have risen markedly, albeit with great variations among types of inflows, volumes over time, and distribution over the various countries. From a negative magnitude in 1990, net capital inflows into eastern Europe rose from $3.5 billion in 1991 to some $22 billion in 1995 but then dropped markedly to some $15 billion in 1996. Net inflows into former USSR have remained very small, however (UNECE 1997). The rapid rise in capital inflows for eastern Europe stems essentially from net additions to the stock of FDI, on which more below; but also a spike in portfolio investment in 1994–5 and indeed renewed medium- and long-term borrowing in international financial markets for the more creditworthy countries, and their number has risen to 13 in 1996 and 16 in mid-1997 (but a much smaller number enjoy an investment grade). Especially in 1995, there was also a sharp rise in short-term, speculative funds particularly in countries, such as the Czech Republic, where policy commitment to a narrow-band fixed exchange rate invited speculation, which was subsequently defused by decreeing a much wider band. Note that capital flight has been considerable in some countries, especially Russia and Ukraine. Also for several countries, notably Hungary, debt service has been considerable, thus offsetting some of the potential gains from capital inflows.

1.3 – Financial flows other than FDI

Given the magnitude of the need for capital renewal and expansion, financial flows into the economies in transition have on the whole remained sluggish, especially from private sources. Only central Europe is able to borrow on invest-ment-grade terms. For the others, private financial markets remain closed or are very expensive. This stems from the generally negative perception of the area by creditors, a sentiment that is being driven in part by levels of indebtedness and uncertainty about how and when these economies will succeed in reestablishing the economic, political, and social stability that is so necessary for inspiring confidence. As a result, the inflow of private capital has continued to play a marginal role in mobilizing funds for economic restructuring in all but the Czech Republic, Hungary, and Poland. Improving this situation for other countries hinges critically on regaining stability and growth. Among other factors, the lingering crises of various origins will need to be overcome, more progress (and in some substantially more) will have to be recorded with the implementation of the transformation agenda, and countries will have to show that their stability is translating into growth resumption.

Financial flows can be disaggregated into official and private flows, with the former into grants and loans (from bi- and multilateral agencies). Private flows consist of debt flows (mainly loans from commercial banks and bonds), FDI, and portfolio investment. Although gross annual flows of finance into the economies in transition as a group have been considerable in recent years, on a net basis they have been much less impressive. Depending on the measure used, and bearing in mind the considerable uncertainty that surrounds the available statistics, the net transfer of resources was actually negative in 1991–2; it became positive only in 1993 for most eastern European countries, but it remained largely negative for Russia, which, in addition, experienced considerable capital flight, as noted.

What really matters from a flow-of-funds' point of view is net financing from various sources. As regards funds raised in capital markets, very little materialized until 1993 and on a net basis until 1995. This is partly explained by the fact that some countries, including Bulgaria, Poland, and the Yugoslav successor States, regained access to capital markets only after they had worked out deals with the London Club. Until these arrangements were fully in place, only the Czech Republic and Hungary were able to use a wider range of both public and private sources of funds, including from commercial banks. Note that increasingly the latter type of financing has been shifting from sovereign to commercial borrowing by blue-chip firms and banks in the countries more advanced with their transformation; some of the latter have also entered the international equity market and, of course, some western investors have funneled considerable resources into domestic equity markets in these countries in addition to participating in various privatization deals under FDI formats. Other countries have either encountered obstacles in servicing their external debt or they have been unable to dispel uncertainties for investors about the future course of their economic policies and indeed the broader dimensions of the transformation process.

Although much has been made of channeling official funds from bi- and multilateral "donors" to transition economies, the net flows have remained very small; much of the activity has taken the form of debt forgiveness, rescheduling, export and loan guarantees, and so on, but the largest amounts have been for arrears and debt deferrals, which at their height in 1990–1 reached about $10 billion per year for eastern Europe and $15 billion to $17 billion for Russia in 1992–4 (UNECE 1995). Grants were important in the early 1990s for eastern Europe and a bit longer for the former USSR, Russia in particular; but they never exceeded an annual $2 billion for the former and $3 billion for the latter. Bilateral loans were substantial notably for Russia. Given the generally modest flows of private capital until recently, and then only for some countries, official funding will continue to be a key element of support for these economies for years to come. Large commitments have been made by the EU and individual western countries, in the form of export credits, guarantees, and grants, and to some degree from the European Investment Bank (EIB), principally for infrastructural projects. Also the IMF and the World Bank have continued their support, using a variety of facilities.

A solid recovery in the economies in transition remains predicated on a revival of productive investments. That depends on an upturn in domestic and foreign demand. Access to markets, particularly the EU's, for the goods for which the economies in transition have spare production capacity and, at least for now, a comparative advantage, continues to be hindered by various protective measures, as in agriculture, or the threat of contingent protectionism for a number of "sensitive" manufactures (such as clothing and textiles, chemicals, footwear, iron and steel, and motor vehicles), in spite of considerable relaxation achieved in the context of the various trade and cooperation agreements recently signed between the EU and EFTA, on the one hand, and various groups of economies in transition, on the other (see Chapter 11).

1.4 – FDI

At the outset of the transitions, many observers felt that FDI into the transition economies would impart a sizable impetus to transformation. Policy makers in the area were certainly keen on obtaining access to this additional stream of finance, but not only in order to finance capital reconstruction. Nevertheless, the expectation was widespread that mobilizing FDI would muster the resources required to finance a good part of the transformation effort. In conjunction with the operations of TNCs, it was hoped that FDI would also usher into those countries modern technology, more up-to-date management, and organizational methods as well as provide access to western markets. Some even feared that the attractiveness of the region, because of low wages; the generally highly skilled labor force; and geographical proximity to EU markets, might divert FDI flows away from other destinations, including from developing countries.

Neither has the required or anticipated inflow of resources in the broad sense been reached nor has the diversion of FDI flows from other regions materialized. The economic recession, the confused state of property rights, the poor regulatory framework in most economies in transition, and the pervasive economic, political, and social uncertainty together are partly responsible for the lack of significant investor interest and the low levels of FDI inflows into the region until very recently. Those who had placed high hopes on FDI leading the turnaround in the transition economies were sorely disappointed. But could it have been otherwise except in an ivory-tower scenario? For the group as a whole, until 1994, volumes of FDI remained comparatively small and its beneficial effect on the potential for resuming growth was in several cases offset by capital flight or debt-service flows. More recently, once growth resumed notably in the more developed transition economies, capital inflows, including FDI, have surged. Elsewhere these flows remain minimal.

Reliable data on FDI in order to assess its impacts on production and exports of transition economies are not easy to come by. Taking 1988 as base and counting only FDI figured in the balance of payments (that is, actual financial flows on a cash basis), the stock of FDI in eastern Europe rose from $1.1 billion in 1990 to $10 billion in 1994, but then surged to some $30 billion by 1996, the major impetus coming in 1995; the corresponding data for former USSR are very little in 1990, perhaps $5.5 by 1994 and some $15 billion by 1996. That is to say, despite the growth of FDI in some privileged countries, on which more below, inflows into the transition economies in comparison with global or even developing-country flows remain small. In 1996, for example, total flows into developing countries amounted to $238 billion, with China one of the largest beneficiaries, in contrast to perhaps $12–13 billion into the transition economies. For some countries, however, the share of FDI in GDP, and thus in investment activity, has been quite considerable. This has been especially the case for the Czech Republic and Hungary: At their peak in 1995, FDI amounted to 5.4 and 10.1 percent of GDP, respectively. Also in the Baltic States the shares are about 4–6 percent of GDP, but elsewhere they are much smaller, between very little to several percentage points (notably in Armenia, Kazakstan, Kyrgyzstan, and Moldova).

However, the potential for imparting a significant fillip to FDI inflows in the future, with greater economic, political, and social stability, given the nature and location of these economies, remains considerable. The more successful transition economies have demonstrated FDI's potential contribution to growth and exports, but also its challenges ahead. The upsurge experienced in the Czech Republic, Hungary, and Poland in particular since 1994 and in the Baltic States more recently has underlined the potency of such flows in stimulating domestic demand; but also the dangers and pitfalls. Especially the experience of the central European countries, and indeed of some of the Baltic States, has shown that FDI inflow is a lagging phenomenon: Incipient to strong economic recovery while regaining some measure of economic, political, and social stability sets the pace for, at times massive, capital inflows relative to the absorptive capacities of these countries. Among the latter I count the rather primitive instruments at hand to come to terms with the more speculative type of capital inflows that can play havoc with monetary policy as well as be very cumbersome and costly.

These flows have been highly differentiated among the various economies in transition and by types of economic activity. Generally speaking, the Czech

Republic, Hungary, and Poland account for some 63 percent of total inward investment, Slovakia and Slovenia for another 7 percent, and Russia for some 14 percent. The remainder 16 percent went into nearly all other countries, but proportionately more into those with comparatively rich natural resources, oil and gas in particular. Some have received rather little: Ukraine, which is the second largest of the transition economies, had by 1996 obtained only $24 per capita; Hungary by contrast reached some $1,300 (UNECE 1997). Most of these flows, with the exceptions noted, have been earmarked for manufacturing activities or, in some countries, services, generally for projects that on average are significantly smaller than the average value of FDI projects in other countries. Given the size of some projects, such as in the automotive and chemical sectors, the distribution of FDI across the various manufacturing sectors has been quite uneven throughout the transition economies.

FDI inflows in part reflect divergences in economic performance and progress with economic transformation. But they also explain part of the differences. For example, a good proportion of the initial export boom and the industrial revival in Poland since 1992 has been due to the operations of two major foreign investors in the automobile sector, both of which have included Poland in their global marketing networks on the input (for example, motor production) as well as on the output side (including Polish-produced vehicles in their international line-up). This phenomenon has not been limited to Poland, however, thus accelerating the integration of these economies into the world economy. To the extent that trade plays an important role in promoting growth and in easing the adjustment process, the role of TNCs and of being inserted into their global strategies has been larger than what other indicators of the importance of FDI in these economies appear to suggest.

1.5 – Participation in international and regional organizations

Most economies in transition set steps to join the existing IEOs or upgrade their participation early on in their transition. The initiatives taken envisaged gaining full accession to or activating and regularizing their participation in the regimes in place – notably the Fund, the World Bank, and the GATT/WTO. Whereas nearly all are now in the first two organizations, full accession to or regularization of their status notably in the GATT/WTO, has been taking more time than policy makers of these countries had been counting on. Thus, only three economies (Bulgaria, Mongolia, and Slovenia) have acceded to GATT/WTO since the "1989 events." All transition economies that desired to become observers have done so quickly. This process accelerated notably after the conclusion of the Uruguay Round because the transition economies are expecting that it impart a new impetus to a rule-based multilateral trading system. Greater transparency and predictability in global markets should enlarge the scope for fair competition (see Section 4).

As concerns the Bretton Woods institutions, all countries sought to join the IMF and World Bank, or regularize their participation therein. Many desired to do so in order to gain access to assistance funds and loans from the World Bank. But that channel becomes available only by first joining the IMF. Assistance efforts from the global community were in any case predicated on first agreeing to a supervised stabilization policy; an IMF agreement was as a rule a non-negotiable prerequisite. All are now members of the IMF, the exception still being Yugoslavia. It tried in vain to succeed to ex-Yugoslavia's status in all IEOs. After long claims and hesitation to apply *de novo*, if only because success for such a *démarche* remains predicated on resolving the tricky issues of dividing the former Yugoslavia's international debts and assets, with some good will a solution now seems to be in the offing.

1.6 – Rapprochement with the EU

The relationship between the transition economies and the EU has been complex, driven by the EU's role in assisting especially the more western of these countries (the CIS being serviced primarily through the IMF/World Bank) and the aspiration of many countries to gain EU entry "soon." As an interim solution, the EU proposed so-called Europe (or association) Agreements for selected countries; Partnership and Cooperation Agreements (PCAs) especially with CIS members; free-trade agreements with a number of countries, in particular those whose Europe Agreement has not yet been ratified; and more conventional trade and cooperation agreements with other countries.

There are presently ten countries with an association status, as noted. The first ones signed and ratified were with the central European countries, those with Bulgaria and Romania more recently. But ratification, which has turned out to be a very protracted process, of the other four is still pending. In the interim, the trade parts of the agreements, which do not need ratification since they come under the European Commission's trade mandate, became operative soon after signing of the agreement. All of these countries have applied for full accession to the EU, negotiations for which are now expected to commence in early 1998. The first rush of countries (central Europe plus Slovenia but perhaps without Slovakia) into the EU is likely to occur at the earliest sometime around the middle of the first decade of the twenty-first century; the others will enter, if at all, only much later. Whether an association agreement will be extended to other "European" (largely the Balkan) countries is by no means a forgone conclusion. I detail the backdrop and extent of PCAs in Chapter 11 as they contain a considerable element of EU assistance. Free-trade agreements between the EU and the Baltic States as well as Slovenia came into effect as of 1995, but have since been overtaken by the trade component of the Europe Agreements; Slovenia's came into effect in 1997.

1.7 – Other regional agreements

Since the transition's inception, an altogether new system of alliances for countries wedged in the corridor running from the Baltic to the Adriatic and the Black Sea has been crystallizing. The efforts have been various and include most notably the Baltic Sea States Council, a sort of outgrowth of Nordic cooperation, which has found it difficult to fuse the Baltic States with the established Nordic Council, and the Baltic Council, which has been in need of credibility; the dormant Visegrád forum with the CEFTA; the Baltic Free Trade Agreement (BFTA); the Central European Initiative, which was preceded by the Alps-Adria initiative (with Austria, Hungary, Italy, and the former Yugoslavia, and in 1989 also Bavaria) and the *Pentagonale-Hexagonale* (the *Hexagonale* with Poland; the *Pentagonale* with Czechoslovakia and the four Alps-Adria participants); and the Black Sea Economic Cooperation Region. A number of subgroups of the CIS members are searching for various kinds of more or less formalized economic cooperation in the form of free-trade arrangements, customs unions, economic unions, and so on. However, none appears to be functioning in a reasonably stable manner to date.

Most of these regional formats have remained very weak and fragile. One should best look at these undertakings as potentially affording interim forms of economic and related cooperation that may or may not survive evolving events. Most probably will not as stronger ties are forged over time with core cooperation partners. Unlike others (see Baldwin 1994) I do not see much purpose in promoting new institutions of either intragroup or east-west cooperation. Exceptions for intragroup trade are to level the playing field as discussed earlier, and here proposals have ranged from streamlining and expanding CEFTA to emulating the Asian-Pacific Economic Cooperation initiative (Messerlin 1996). Cooperation in the EU framework I deal with later.

When all of the above are duly considered for their economic significance, the most important arrangements are those seeking to foster free trade, such as with EFTA and Israel. Several such agreements between pairs of transition economies or one transition economy with a developed or developing country have been signed. CEFTA was expanded in 1996 to include Slovenia and in mid-1997 Romania; and soon perhaps Bulgaria. In the meantime, the Czech Republic, Hungary, and Poland have joined OECD, and Slovakia may follow in 1997. The Baltic States are working together in the BFTA and may soon seek a rapprochement with CEFTA, once well on their way into WTO.

Section 2: Multilateral institutional integration

Not every observer is persuaded of the usefulness of the international economic regimes and their custodial IEOs. Some even argue that the postwar infrastructure meant to "manage" the global economy has hampered sound global economic relations. Others fundamentally accept that, in principle, some positive benefits derive from having predictable, transparent, and reliable rules and regulations for international trade, finance, investment, the monetary framework, and so on. But they may not be completely pleased either with the regimes as originally set up or with their implementation and evolution; some see primarily problems with one or more IEOs rather than their underlying regimes (Gilpin and Gilpin 1987; Keohane 1984; J. Williamson 1985). Those commentators would not, however, contest that a search for multilateralism may yield positive benefits, particularly for small and medium-sized countries. I share this view. But I also advocate that there is cause for continually honing the existing *modi operandi* (Brabant 1991b; 1993b; 1995a, b; 1997a, b).

During World War II and in the ensuing two decades, many foreign-policy and economic analysts looked on the whole positively at the promise of "global economic management." This derived not only from the generally progovern-ment attitude prevailing after World War II, but also from the profound belief that markets alone could not sustain buoyant growth, transparency, stability, predictability, and equity in the world economy. Hence the attempt, in the absence of global government, to entrust responsibility for the global economy to IEOs for which "regimes" were developed. That enthusiasm has since waned considerably. The reasons are legion. They include vastly exaggerated hopes of what can reasonably be accomplished in the context of essentially an inter-governmental body. There are two sides to this. One is divergence of views among the membership on what precisely they wish any one IEO to undertake. How best to coordinate the activities of the various IEOs, let alone of the many regional ones, remains to be addressed for good multilateral governance is a rare commodity indeed. There are evidently issues related to translating this assignment into the IEOs' operational activities. But skepticism about global cooperation since the early 1970s also derives from equally mistaken views that IEOs are not particularly useful or cause more harm than good.

I do not subscribe to either extreme view. I simply assert here that the existence of IEOs in which many countries participate and air their own interests, as well as their perceptions of more global issues, is an essential ingredient of a "normal" state of affairs in an interdependent global economy. One must recognize that the various actors have their own interests that diverge and even conflict, and this may call for instituting transitional regimes (see Brabant 1991b, pp. 215ff.; Drábek 1996). But they also arise because the various actors have their own ideas, values, norms, and assumptions (Williams 1996), all of which influ-ence their behavior. Needless to say, this considerably complicates governance of the regimes for which these IEOs act as custodians.

It is useful to be clear about the meaning of an "international regime" and why countries may wish to partake in organized international relations and submit to the regime's rules even though the regimes have really been neither global nor have they brought "order" in global economic affairs (Brabant 1991b, pp. 11ff.). Nonetheless, an international economic regime can best be thought of as a set of gradually accepted rules and conventions on how countries are expected to conduct their economic policies that have significant external repercussions. As a rule, this order needs to be endowed with full-fledged organizations or state arrangements through which the agreed-upon rules and conventions can be enforced in a predictable and reliable manner. Without such accommodation, an international economic order is likely to fragment quickly into a state character-ized by, at best, weak rules and light-hearted breaches thereof as countries adopt at their own discretion policies that have pronounced international repercussions; paralysis in IEOs and "market anarchy" would be the worst outcomes.

As such, a regime consists of "explicit or implicit principles, norms, rules, and decision-making procedures around which actors' expectations converge" (Krasner 1982, p. 186) on a component of the international economic order with a view to coordinating their behavior (Krasner 1983). *Principles* are essentially beliefs of fact, causation, and propriety or rectitude. In contrast, *norms* are standards of behavior set in terms of general rights and obligations. These two terms constitute the fundamental traits of a regime and are consistent with a variety of rules and decision-making procedures. *Rules* are specific prescriptions or proscriptions regarding behavior for action. Finally, *decision-making procedures* are existing practices for making collective choices and implementing them. This should also include assessment of results and consideration of how best to fine-tune the rules and procedures, and perhaps even the principles and norms, when warranted. In any case, a regime is by its nature distinct from a temporary arrangement that can mutate or is modified with every shift in power or interest. It cannot be based chiefly on short-term or unilateral calculation of interest of one or a few actors.

A regime's usefulness derives from the fact that it smooths the intermeshing of the behavior of individual states, or élite groups within states, upon what can be achieved when the latter act through uncoordinated individual calculations of self-interest. Because it may satisfy the realization of a common purpose beyond what individual actors can attain by themselves, a regime is essentially a vehicle to maximize the benefits derived from a public good according to some accept-able understanding on the sharing of benefits and costs. The importance of the externalities that affect the welfare of individual actors or well-defined élite groups is likely to grow with rising interdependence in the world.

Membership in IEOs entails a variety of direct and indirect outlays: Contribute to the organization's regular budget, participate in meetings, main-tain some representative office, and submit to explicit or implicit constraints on the member's behavior in international relations. For better or worse, the IEOs may be seen as potentially meddling in the internal affairs of members. To be sure, this affords a particular negotiating posture, including in domestic squabbles over reform. Such is likely to be especially touchy during ongoing debates on the depth, breadth, and pace of economic transition, when even highly technical proposals have political overtones and social implications are likely to be contested. Political entanglements also crop up once the reform enjoys firm consensus and is being implemented. Because some IEOs, especially the Fund, deal essentially with government bureaucrats, they cannot avoid having to walk a highly sensitive tightrope. But these obstacles should not be blown out of proportion, as they have on occasion in some transition economies. With a bit of good will and recognition of realities, solutions are in principle within reach.

To justify these and related costs, the country seeking membership must perceive palpable advantages and, depending on its political organization, may have to be accountable for them. Benefits can take the form of an enhanced status in global affairs or opportunities for policy makers and civil servants to travel abroad and establish "useful contacts" for themselves, their interest group, or their perception of national needs. Second, a country's view on some problems at times cannot attain the desired visibility without an affirmative presence in the appropriate forum. Third, being an insider may yield valuable intelligence and other information that supplements and, from an individual country's perspective, complements what can be obtained from public and not-so-public domains. Oftentimes such insider information can be accessed faster than via the usual media, and thus permits timely reaction if necessary. This includes advance information on what actions nations and international secretariats are proposing; forming judgments on the merits and strengths of such proposed actions well before they can be implemented and assessing the likelihood that they will be carried out and when on the basis of "adequate" information; and gaining access to a plethora of political, economic, administrative, scientific, or technological background papers and documents prepared to facilitate deliberation about the proposal in question, and perhaps even technical assistance and financial resources. Fourth, membership may confer tangible economic, strategic, and other gains. Finally, some desirable actions cannot be undertaken by any one country in isolation. Note that adherence to a particular regime may yield benefits and costs that are quite visible. There may also be future costs; these, I submit, are rather small. Much more significant are the benefits that accrue only indirectly, thus not readily identified as such, or that materialize only in a roundabout way.

It bears to recognize too that the existing regimes are essentially public goods, thus by definition indivisible. Yet, one critical aspect of maintaining a regime is to ensure that costs and benefits are fairly parceled out in spite of the potential for free riding (Keohane 1986). In some cases benefits cannot be apportioned to members that contribute to maintaining the public good. It may even be impossible to limit them to the group, in which case there may be an argument for ushering many countries into the regime. There cannot be perfect symmetry in sharing costs and gains, however, let alone in tying the latter to the former. Smaller countries benefit proportionately more from such a public good than large countries. Yet the effective operation of the existing regimes and the ability of IEOs to function properly can be ensured only if major actors provide continued support and positively participate.

But there are other reasons for drawing all major actors of the world economy into a coherent, common framework for examining and devising acceptable solutions for problems besetting international economic interdependence. One certainly is that international economic relations are not a zero-sum game. This implies that international behavior cannot be steered by one single country but must be managed cooperatively. Another derives from the proposition that a well-organized regime is likely to curb the power of big members by transferring some decision making to forums governed not by the will and in the interest of one state, but by a multilateral complex of interests, checks, and balances. As the past has amply demonstrated, the greatest danger to international stability often arises from those actors whose real power is inadequately reflected in both the relevant parts of international arrangements and symbols of status therein. That is not to say that stability is predicated on universal organizations with equal or even proportional representation in all cases adjudicated within a given regime. Yet, imaginative mechanisms for balancing universalism with the need for operationality of the regimes deserve to be devised. For all these reasons I deem it useful to try and draw all major actors of the world economy into a coherent, common framework for examining and discussing problem areas that inhibit the smooth conduct of trade with a view to devising all-around acceptable solutions.

Yet, one must recognize that there is an inevitable conflict between universalism and efficiency in managing an international regime. But meaningful, intelligent solutions may be found pragmatically. The argument can be phrased in two different ways. One depends essentially on the pros of multilateralism. A firm commitment to multilateralism is an essential ingredient in maintaining peace, transparency, stability, predictability, security, and reliability in international affairs. Participation in one or more mutual security organs ought to be fostered to the extent that it does not compromise either the basic principles upon which these institutions act or the functional degree of cooperation that can be ensured by expanding membership. In addition to the adjustments that potential applicants may have to engage in, universalization may require some modification on the part of the present membership and perhaps even in the particular focus of the activities of these organizations. This does not mean, however, that there would be no room for smaller steering groups exerting representative governance when universalism proves to be too unwieldy to manage decisions.

Section 3: Universalism ʌnd systemic differences

Until recently, since their establishment during and after World War II, the IEOs remained less universal than intended largely because the state-socialist countries shunned participation. They did so for a variety of economic, political, security, technical, and other reasons (Brabant 1991b, pp. 62ff.). Putting it briefly, the IEOs at the time had little to offer to economies with comprehensive physical planning, that adhered to strict commodity and currency inconvertibility, that practiced rigid bilateralism, and that operated with notional exchange rates, thus further segmenting domestic from foreign markets. Also, given the rapidly deteriorating east–west environment in the second half of the 1940s, the state-socialist economies decided that it was not in their best interest to provide extensive economic intelligence to the IEOs. Furthermore, they had no reason to subject their exchange regime and broader macroeconomic policies to Fund surveillance, for example. Finally, though they coveted access to finance from the World Bank, this was obtainable only through Fund membership for which the price to pay was deemed to be excessive.

The shifts in the makeup of eastern Europe, and indeed Europe as a whole, have yielded new opportunities for completing the universal vocation of the regimes in place. One is that the countries that spurned the IEOs in the postwar period, or participated in the regimes only perfunctorily, have rapidly merged themselves with them. As a result, the "Bretton Woods" precepts on global economic management might now be implemented. Unfortunately, such would hardly be very relevant to the problems now confronting the world. Thus, all efforts to introduce special arrangements for the former state-socialist economies in the context of the IEOs where these economies are not yet admitted, notably the GATT/WTO, are now taken to be all but superfluous. The real motivation underlying these efforts (see Brabant 1991b, pp. 116ff.) has not, of course, been completely overtaken by events as the transition economies encounter difficulties in playing a constructive role in some of the IEOs, even as beneficiaries of global economic management. Indeed, the original aspirations of the Bretton Woods system are still relevant to the countries under consideration. Recall the active search for flexibility in economic policy in the late 1940s, but soon thereafter abandoned. Incidentally, this spirit of Bretton Woods addressed a far more comprehensive world than the negotiations that led to the mandates and tasks of the two Bretton Woods institutions. Once the transition economies succeed in implanting viable markets, their role in IEOs will be quite comparable to that of market economies roughly at a medium level of development. Until that platform can be reached, however, it remains useful to seek some accommodation in trade, in finance, and in monetary, and perhaps in other multilateral, affairs.

Reviving Bretton Woods would not be very relevant at this stage, however. For one thing, the universality of the IEOs has become too unwieldy. Some "representative governance" by other means than sheer economic or political clout will have to be increasingly explored. In addition, many aspects of rendering development assistance, including for transition economies (see Chapter 11), deserve to be reexamined in the light of "appropriate development strategies." Furthermore, management of the global economy cannot be based on either fixed or flexible exchange rates. Another system is yet to be designed lest the present *de facto* arrangements revolving around the shaky yen–dollar–ecu axes will become the norm for lack of imagination and political will. Finally, global economic management at this stage must be tailored to present and prospective views of how the world economy functions, with multiple trade blocs, with particular attention to the core issues of economic development, structural adjustment, and catching up.

The other reason for guarded optimism is that this universal nature of the IEOs, if only by confronting them with the complexities of the transition, is offering an opportunity to improve the regimes and their management with a view to heeding the needs of the 1990s and beyond. I include in this the remaking of Europe, largely within the EU framework. The latter is of more than passing importance not only because of the historical opportunity offered by the "1989 events," but also because from their inception arguably the most important foreign-policy goal of the transition economies, aside from obliterating the CMEA and seeking new security arrangements, has been full integration in the EU, which is not possible without modifying the latter's regime. Such renovation would be useful. But other measures are required to ensure that the diverging interests among the members are respected. It is especially important to undertake such reforms with a view to coming effectively to grips in a more coherent and consistent manner with the salient international economic problems that confront the global community on the basis of broadly agreed-upon development priorities. For now, however, far-reaching concertation of policies remains a distant goal. Other countries too stand to benefit from such a better focusing and concertation at the global level. But this outcome can materialize only in a more distant perspective, if only because resolving deeply rooted structural problems, and thus converting the transition into market economies, requires considerable commitment and societal forbearance. It will also lay claim to vast outside financial and other assistance to alleviate the adjustment burden and anchor the emerging markets more firmly within an acceptable time frame.

Recall in this context that the existing global order in general and its economic component in particular were largely put in place for the benefit of countries that possessed on the whole fairly integrated domestic markets and were prepared to open them up to outside competition, albeit with considerable restraints. That system has not shown itself quite adept at dealing with problems of a rapidly widening range of developing countries. Though there may be broad "consensus" on what needs to be done (J. Williamson 1993; 1994a, b; J. Williamson and Haggard 1994), experience indicates that assisting countries at greatly varying levels of economic maturity requires a broad measure of flexibility not only in the *modi operandi* but also in the philosophy and by existing organizations to approach the problems at hand.

Remaking global relations in line with present and emerging conditions is not just a task that can be left to diplomats. Neither can it be entrusted to one or a few key industrial powers. Certainly, hegemons may play a pivotal role in this process. But there are presently few that can – indeed are willing to – assume that role with all its incumbent responsibilities. Other solutions must therefore be explored at the earliest opportunity in order to answer the question whether there is "nonetheless a set of practices, a system of behaviour, which one or more major powers can follow in order to induce co-operative behaviour on the part of others" (Marglin 1990, p. 38).

Without proper adaptations of the prevailing international regimes and their associated institutions, given that they have by now to some extent fallen out of sync with reality, it is difficult to envision how a more harmonious world could be constructed by making hay of the cited historic chance. This applies nowhere with greater force than in Europe. With the prospect of establishing pluralistic societies anchored to market-based decision making throughout most of the eastern part of the continent, the postwar divide in Europe could be closed over time but only if its roots in a much farther-reaching history, and a sad one at that, are better understood. Eventual fusion of countries into all-European co-operation requires several actions that could quickly enact positive changes in the landscape of the transition economies. But it also exerts negative effects. Transition managers appear to be persuaded, however, that the former outweigh the latter by a substantial margin.

The circumstances under which the international community could be persuaded to innovate international regimes, and the institutions entrusted with guaranteeing them from the ground up, as accomplished after World War II, are not likely to resurface any time soon. At the same time, it should be crystal clear that the existing multilateral institutions and their respective underlying regimes – and even their ultimate rationales – are no longer well tailored to the needs of the day. Judging by the rapidity with which the states that had traditionally shunned that order have clamored to come on board in recent years, nearly all countries may presently be prepared to work within the existing order and endow it with a new mission by meaningfully updating its "regimes" from within the presently prevailing deliberative arenas.

So what could prospectively be done, given prevailing realities and opportunities? I conjecture that the transition economies can be full-fledged participants in the international regimes and their supporting organizations only once their transformation will have been reasonably completed. In the interim, adapting the international regimes so as to better accommodate these countries' needs deserves to be explored. The international community has thus far paid rather scant attention to the specific requirements of the transition economies as compared to the nearly standard menu of, say, Fund orthodoxy (on macro-economics but also on privatization, liberalization of markets, on managing SOEs, and on industrial restructuring), and how programs formulated in the mode of the standard recipe have performed in a wide range of countries whose economic structure diverges in major respects from that of the paradigmatic fairly mature market economy.

Even when this art of the possible is acknowledged, at the very least there should be room for suitably reinterpreting existing mandates with a measure of urgency and determination warranted by present circumstances. Yet, when all determinants are factored into our probability function, one cannot be too optimistic about the outlook for proceeding in this fashion because key actors are no longer genuinely committed to utilizing multilateral organizations for the purposes for which they were ostensibly set up, as distinct from how these organizations might be mobilized to enhance the perceived "national interest" of some participants. This includes entrusting the IEOs, but also other institutions, with mandates that cannot be adequately addressed in the national context, yet without obligating the means so that the IEOs can adequately discharge them. If only because of national jealousy, it is symptomatic that the IEOs have been kept weak, both in terms of the elbowroom that members allow them and the way in which they are enabled to be managed internally. True, some are undoubtedly run better than others. Some are utilized productively too; but on the whole only when it suits the interests of a major member. The former appears to be a direct function of the organization's technical nature. In spite of this skepticism, with leadership and political will, notably on the part of key actors, some constructive, if modest, reconceptualization could realistically be entertained (Kennedy 1993).

Section 4: The desirability of joining the IEOs

If the transition economies are not yet reasonably integrated market economies and the regimes in place are designed to cater chiefly to fairly integrated market economies, one ends up with a dilemma: Why should these countries suddenly rush into the IEOs? What benefits can they expect from membership? The most obvious answer, pertinent to the current efforts, is, of course, that international assistance has been predicated on joining the Fund in the first instance, and by implication seeking a rapprochement with other IEOs (see Chapter 11). But this does not explain why some countries already in the 1950s began to explore membership or, for that matter, what other benefits the transition economies may expect to derive at this stage. In this context, it is instructive to reappraise in the light of experience how members can fully benefit from the international regimes in the process of undertaking massive structural adjustment.

4.1 – The IMF

The experience since 1989, given the involvement of the IMF with the issues of transition and transformation of former state-socialist countries, suggests that the salient technical problems at the roots of why these countries in their earlier incarnation shunned the IEOs are being replicated, albeit on a different plane, during much of the transition (Brabant 1991b; 1993b; 1995a, b). One was the issue of currency convertibility and how best to manage adjustment with external financial support. Rather than relying primarily on demand-driven adjustment programs, the proper menu of policies that transition economies could profitably explore must include a component that fosters positive supply actions. Given the still poorly functioning markets in these countries, it is hopeless to anticipate that their economic agents will even come close to behaving according to the precepts of markets championed by the Fund and other organs. In an environment with serious market rigidities or where markets are not fully free by policy design or legacies of past developments, output losses may result that far exceed any efficiency gains from better resource allocation. In some cases, the mandated curbing of demand may be so counterproductive, for lack of a response on the supply side, that the transition economy may sink into a low-level equilibrium trap for an extended period of time. The real tradeoff between adjustment and growth that exists in many economies that have embraced Fund-mandated adjustment tends to be considerably magnified in the case of transition economies. This potential outcome should be fully heeded in conceptualizing adjustment programs if constructive balance-of-payments assistance is to be earmarked for these countries. More appropriate programs than "proven" menus can be innovated for classes of countries facing special problems, such as those on the transformation agenda. Note that this, once again, may justify "transitional regimes" (see Section 3).

Because of the conflict between static efficiency and sustainable growth, a program for adjusting to external or domestic pressures in transition economies, and for monitoring its performance, must necessarily be phrased differently from the way in which stabilization has traditionally been accomplished in either market or state-socialist economies. Two fundamental reasons deserve to be borne in mind. One refers to the pervasive legacies of state socialism, the sort of specific policy and systemic antecedents of these societies that are readily ignored, yet deserve to be clearly understood and factored into the policy deliberations and the package of measures ultimately agreed upon. The other recognizes that, in part because of these legacies, macroeconomic management must include active intervention on the supply side to sensitize economic agents into under-taking the structural changes required to install the rudiments of the coveted markets. For the foreseeable future, adjustment even in the more advanced tran-sition economy requires a much more varied policy regimen and institutional setting than envisioned in orthodox policies (Brabant 1990; 1991a, b). I include here the need to be "involved" in the transition on a much more immediate, day-to-day basis, and for far longer in a coherent framework, than the IEOs have so far been willing and able to undertake, perhaps for diplomatic reasons. This is particularly important in modulating assistance strategies, and I return to this broader set of questions in Chapter 11.

4.2 – The World Bank

Much the same type of comment applies to the World Bank's agenda. Its shift away from project financing to structural-adjustment programs has entailed a particular development philosophy (Williams 1996). That rests primarily on a pronounced advocacy of private enterprise and privatization of SOEs; strengthening the role of all types of market forces through substantial internal and external liberalization and the downsizing of government; improving the governance capacities of central actors while emphasizing the role of civil society in all of its dimensions, including empowering all legitimate actors in society; and so on. Note that this on the whole endorses the demand-driven approach favored by the Fund. In addition, it recognizes the longer-term nature of meaningful structural adjustment and the urgency of tackling supply rigidities of various origins (history, regulatory regimes, protectionism, inward-orientation, feudal land arrangements; reforming overly generous entitlements and steering them better through means-tested and categorical benefits; and so on). Similar comments apply to the World Bank's pronounced advocacy of dismantling institutions, policy instruments, macroeconomic policies, and behavioral guidelines that are perceived to hinder market-inspired entrepreneurial activity, whether of domestic or foreign origin.

It is much more difficult to speak of a Bank than of a Fund recipe if only because the latter's activities tend to be much more focused than the former's disparate approach to tackling sectoral issues, which may or may not form part and parcel of a more comprehensive structural-adjustment program. Moreover, there has been quite some vacillation in advocated policy stances with the pendulum now apparently swinging back toward greater appreciation of the role of institutions, including governance and the state (Chhibber 1997; World Bank 1997). In any case, the approach adopted by the Bank for transition economies has had disastrous consequences especially during the early phases of the transition. It would seem hopeless to anticipate behavior on the part of economic agents conforming to market criteria when markets do not exist, or can be expected to perform poorly, at least in the near term, and economic agents are bewildered by what the market is all about.

4.3 – GATT/WTO

Since the transition's inception, several changes have occurred in the relationship between transition economies and the GATT; since 1995 the WTO. It is important to bear in mind three types of approaches with their implications. The first has been regularization of the position of countries that were a Contracting Party (Brabant 1997b). Transition economies that had previously not fully benefited from the provisions of the General Agreement (Hungary, Poland, Romania, and Yugoslavia) or that had kept their membership dormant (Czechoslovakia) were keen on being recognized on a "normal" basis; presumably Cuba would wish to do so too if it were to opt for creating a functioning market economy. For Poland and Romania this required the renegotiation of the entry provisions on reciprocity. For Hungary and Yugoslavia it entailed in particular the abolition of discriminatory quantitative restrictions (QRs). With the exception of Yugoslavia, this was fairly swiftly enacted; even the successor agreements for the Czech Republic and Slovakia were negotiated quickly. The Yugoslav case is special as the dissolution of the old federation has been viewed by all IEOs as a final breakup. As a result, all successor States have had to approach the GATT/WTO as if they were new applicants almost *ab ovo*.

Note that the recognition of the above countries as "market economies" for GATT/WTO purposes does not remove the residual need to come to grips with the discriminatory trade regimes of the countries not yet committed to opening up their economies on a fully competitive basis. Bulgaria's accession on 1 December 1996, for example, at a time of severe economic crisis with foreign sectors in appalling disarray offers an extreme illustration of what seems to be required by way of continuing surveillance and guidance to ensure that the domestic transformation firms up, rather than loosens, market-based foundations, a guideline that applies as well, albeit to a lesser degree, to many other transition economies. This too needs to be carefully monitored to ensure that trade liberalization and domestic structural change remain mutually supportive without harming the interests of other WTO members.

Second, the countries that were observers in the GATT one after another requested that the process of preparing for full accession be initiated fairly quickly. But accession has continued to be a very protracted process, particularly for countries undergoing radical shifts in economic structure and macroeconomic policies and institutions. GATT/WTO would prefer to usher countries under its wing only once the transformation is well under way. But this creates obvious policy and technical dilemmas, and indeed time inconsistency: If the transition economy needs the IEOs to engineer the transformation agenda, early membership is desirable but that can be accommodated only via a transitional arrangement. Since the transition erupted, only three countries – Bulgaria, Mongolia, and Slovenia – have been admitted. There are then eight transition economies as full members as of mid-1997: Bulgaria, the Czech Republic, Hungary, Mongolia, Poland, Romania, Slovakia, and Slovenia.

Finally, the transition economies that were not associated with the GATT one after another requested, and were granted, observer status. Most have since submitted their request for full accession, and the various procedural steps to reach that stage have been under way for a number of these countries. As of end 1996 (WTO 1996) "accession parties" existed for eighteen transition economies (Albania, Armenia, Belarus, China, Croatia, Estonia, Georgia, Kazakstan, Kyrgyzstan, Latvia, Lithuania, Macedonia, Moldova, Mongolia, Russia, Ukraine, Uzbekistan, and Vietnam; Mongolia's has since been terminated with the country's accession in mid-1997). In time these countries will presumably be able to join the WTO. Finally, Azerbaijan, Tajikistan, Turkmenistan, and, following the end of the sanctions, rump Yugoslavia are observers. Since the latter has accepted the procedures for readmission into the Washington IEOs, the same will soon probably apply also with respect to WTO.

Apart from delivering the kind of services GATT/WTO is entrusted with, the secretariat has been providing technical assistance concerning the international trade regime in place, including the follow-ups from the Singapore Ministerial Meeting, and how it is being administered. But it has also assisted with the broader aspects of preparing a viable application for accession. Among the latter, the desirable features of trade and foreign-exchange regimes to function appropriately within the context of the GATT/WTO have been clarified through various training seminars. The accent has been on trade policy, that is, essentially the meaning of reciprocity and most-favored nation (MFN) status, as well as the institutional requirements for operating such an open trade regime and participating in the GATT/WTO.

4.4 – Room for transitional regimes in IEOs?

To be able to function as a "regular" IEO member, the transition economies have to resolve, mainly on their own strength, the wide range and depth of their transformational difficulties. The multilateral agencies could help out by adapting their mainstream *modi operandi* and precepts to the immediate and evolving tasks at hand. This applies as much to the IEOs as it does to the ongoing debates in the EU on forging ahead with its own integration plans and coming to grips with the new realities in Europe (see Section 6). Such modifications in "proven menus" are all the more desirable since it is not easy to create more appropriate institutions *ab ovo*. In fact, the international debate since the early 1970s suggests that accommodation for countries that fit incompletely into the existing regimes and their underlying institutions needs to be sought from within the various organs in place. Only in this manner is there hope of maximizing the regimes' benefits for the largest number of participants, including transition economies.

One bundle of issues concerning ushering the transition economies into the international regimes revolves around how to adapt the latter's *modi operandi* temporarily to the "transitory" needs of incisive society-wide transformation. The other is to what extent the newly gained proclivity toward multilateralism can be exploited in order to update some of the regimes and thus strengthen global economic management to the benefit of a wide spectrum of countries that have yet to restructure themselves into functioning market economies. This requires essentially infusing a greater degree of transparency, predictability, and reliability in international economic relations, indeed international relations *tout court*, than would occur spontaneously by countries engaging themselves for their own interests in the international economy. Successful conclusion of any such deliberations by necessity depends on creative, imaginative proposals formulated by all parties involved, including the targeted countries, the IEOs, as well as the insiders. In all this, the question of where the more advanced transition economies fit into these international-management and -assistance efforts, once their transformational difficulties will have been surmounted, deserves at least to be flagged up. But I cannot address it here with the nuancing it deserves.

All things considered, the international debate since the early 1970s or so, and the erosion of the commitment to multilateralism on the part of key actors in the global economy, suggest that there is little chance of obtaining a broad consensus among key actors in the global economy on remaking the basic framework of global economic cooperation, institutionally and conceptually. The search for ways of coming to grips with the breakdown of the Bretton Woods system in the early 1970s, the recriminations around the creation and early operations of the European Bank for Reconstruction and Development (EBRD), and the disputes about WTO even before its establishment have amply demonstrated this reluctance to re-create the global economic system *ab ovo*, as it were. One must therefore proceed with the resources at hand or do nothing. The latter I deem to be unacceptable for reasons given earlier. The former deserves to recognize that fuller accommodation for countries with less than integrated, functioning markets into the existing international regimes could benefit from transitional accommodation until their demand and supply will respond more flexibly to shifts in a predictable manner, as seen from within the orthodox paradigm. The advantages would be reciprocal: Insiders gain assurance that new applicants embrace realistic policy measures and that countries previously unable to fully adhere to the agreed discipline harmonize their systems with those of the regimes in place and the major actors therein.

In this way, the international community could avoid deliberately, or by default, undermining support for the ongoing reform process in countries with less than integrated markets. It would also provide some assurance that transition processes stay on course and eliminate what needs to be jettisoned, correct and repair what presently exhibits shortcomings, and better harmonize the more enduring economic features of the transformation that now inhibit fuller partici-pation in the international economy. Because this is largely uncharted territory, successful deliberations depend on creative, imaginative proposals formulated by all parties involved – insiders, the transition economies themselves, and the multi-lateral organizations – and a commitment to pragmatic policy making rather than enforcing blind adherence to a stale ideology. Simply entrusting the global and regional institutions with tasks motivated by the political desiderata of main members that do not foot the required bill in terms of domestic-resource appropriation does not belong to the proper pragmatism I advocate. The example of the Fund's involvement with Russia is symptomatic.

There is ample room for improving "governance" of these institutions through more congenial attitudes on the part of the membership as well as by embracing a broader approach to global economic management by these institutions them-selves, in spite of the fact that sovereign states are reluctant to yield voluntarily even part of their autonomy to higher authority. Two ways out of the apparent dilemmas associated with revamping the IEOs from within can be readily discerned for transition economies. One is through technical-advisory services, ensuring that policy makers in transition economies are fully conversant with the various implications of their favored transformation strategy. That requires "education" in the broad sense so that managers of the transition understand the options available with their respective advantages and drawbacks. It might justify possibly intrusive, hands-on engagement in the formulation, implemen-tation, monitoring, assessment, and fine-tuning of the transformation agenda if and when managers of the transition appreciate and condone such assistance. The other is by providing external financial support for easing the burden of the endorsed transition strategy. Whereas the latter is very important as it provides in principle additional degrees of flexibility in adjudicating policy options, the primordial importance of the former should rule especially because "financial assistance" generally means obtaining access to loans at near-market interest rates and other transaction costs. The borrowers are certainly expected to service those debts. That can reasonably be assured only once the transition begins to pay off.

4.5 – Advantages for transition economies

It is in the nature of the international economic regimes that they border between economics and politics, and some may well have a heavier touch of the latter than of the former. This is perhaps more the case for the trade than for the monetary and finance regimes. From an economic point of view, particularly for countries bent on pursuing an outward-looking economic policy, the benefits of belonging in the IEOs, even without transitional regimes, in the medium to long run generally outweigh the drawbacks. These net benefits would also accrue in the short to medium run if the IEOs were to embrace formally or otherwise flexible transitional regimes for countries that are not even remotely comparable to the paradigmatic integrated market economy. Membership is important if only for the political endorsement, credibility, and reliability that it conveys to partner countries as well as to those managing the transformation with respect to their own domestic support base. That could be reinforced with suitably configured transitional regimes.

For the transition economies to leverage their membership into fully equivalent participation will take more time, effort, and imagination than has on the whole thus far come into play. This will no doubt be more difficult for the monetary and especially the trading regimes than for the financial regime. One may at least query, though, whether by committing themselves to strict rules early on, such as those of the GATT/WTO, the managers of the transition are jeopardizing policy credibility. An accession transition regime might therefore be useful (Drábek 1996) for much the same reasons that it would earlier have been desirable for other groups of countries, including those that still maintain vestiges of state-socialist administration (Brabant 1991b).

Section 5: The TNCs, modernization, and the transformation

Cobbling together a new growth strategy in transition economies with massive resource mobilization is justified for at least two reasons. One is the need to come to grips with the capital losses, physical and human, sustained as a result of the *de facto* collapse of many structures built under state socialism. One main goal would be preventing levels of living from crashing, and perhaps remaining stuck for years at a low equilibrium, thus fomenting sociopolitical discord. Substantial fresh funds are also required to start off along the new growth trajectory and build upon this momentum through cumulative causation (see Chapter 12). Such resource mobilization, the transitology literature emphasizes, should primarily originate from private sources abroad, possibly initially paced by official transfers. Can this resource flow realistically be expected?

5.1 – Initial expectations and reality

FDI in greenfield operations, for joint ventures, and through privatization in particular was expected to provide modern managerial expertise and corporate-governance structures, fresh financial resources and access to modern technology, an impetus to exports and marketing skills, market access by merging into an existing marketing infrastructure, substantial new jobs, a dramatic change in business culture toward the market-oriented modes of operation, and inhouse training to hone the human capital inherited from communism to the require-ments of a new, dynamic growth strategy (Lankes and Venables 1996). Responding to the multiple needs in this fashion, it was thought in a rather dirigistic manner during the early phases of the transition, would short-circuit the "learning process" on whose basis sustained economic growth is predicated. Because the domestic environment was considered comparatively hostile to foreign investment, FDI in particular, it was thought useful to grant such capital formation all kinds of privileges in terms of import-duty rebates, tax holidays, favorable investment regulations, labor rules, and so on – a better-than-level playing field as compared to potential domestic investors.

The above expectations were based on two broad assumptions. One was that liberated financial markets are efficient, almost as in the textbook (see Chapter 5). Naturally, this was highly unrealistic. The other was that these economies offered massive opportunities for foreign investment, particularly FDI. Not only was it an act of faith that ample inflows would be forthcoming. Also little concern was expressed about the ability of these economies to absorb such volumes productively to benefit the mutation toward a new growth trajectory, especially in view of their weak financial infrastructure (see Chapter 7).

As documented in Section 1, the attracted volumes have exhibited various features at odds with the above optimistic scenario. Absolute volumes have lagged far behind expectations. Also, the pace of inflows has been quite uneven over time even for the best-positioned economies (the Czech Republic and Hungary) and over various sectors. Furthermore, some foreign investment has entered these countries with motivations that have little to do with the desire of policy makers, or the fundamental needs of the transition economies, to raise efficiency and accelerate toward a durable growth path. With some notable exceptions, it has not brought in the latest technology and it has been concen-trated geographically and sectorally. Moreover, many actual and potential investors have been disappointed with the results recorded to date. Finally, the labor force has on the whole not been very pleased about new job creation or the lagging gains in remuneration for those able to hold on to their position.

Most of these results, if not their precise details, could have been anticipated. Theory and practices in the global economy would have been useful vehicles to construct better scenarios than were held out with such levity in the early 1990s, and in some cases are still being peddled to countries that have not yet made the transition, in spite of earlier efforts, to growth resumption. Although our general knowledge about the precise determinants of foreign investment is neither very deep nor reliable (Lankes and Venables 1996; Markowski and Jackson 1994; UNCTAD 1993), there is evidence that a country's size, its expected pace of growth with its likely variability, and prevailing imbalances (in external payments, in exchange rates, in domestic budget finances, and in consumption) relevant to the determination of foreign-exchange risks are in general the major determinants of foreign-investment inflows. Political stability, a predictable regulatory environment, proximity to major developed markets, size of the local market, and the degree to which skilled labor is available are also important factors entering investors' considerations, especially in the case of capital movements designed to bolster the recipient country's export capacity. For smaller and less developed countries, in addition the level and stability of the exchange rate, external indebtedness, and the degree of openness too have a bearing on the volume and kind of foreign inflows. Of particular importance for productive investment, then, are two critical factors: the expected rate of return on such investments and the anticipated variability or the associated risks.

Any cursory analysis of foreign investments, but especially FDI, since, say, the early 1970s would have buttressed a number of the more practical features regarding desirable investment environments. Low political and economic risk appear to be crucial. So is the prevalence of externalities associated with the presence of FDI. One can expect geographical and sectoral concentration as well as shifts in type of FDI regime as experience with investment and with the structural-adjustment package is gained. Without imposing guidelines on capital inflows, congruence of domestic and foreign interests is fortuitous as foreign capital enters for its own reasons, motivated largely by cheap labor or easy resource availability.

On both theoretical and practical grounds, then, the transition economies initially were not particularly attractive sites for FDI for some time to come; this feature still holds for all too many countries. Expected rates of return depend on progress with the structural transformation, including regaining positive growth. Risk abatement is in addition a function of the restoration of economic, political, and social confidence in these countries. Substantial progress with stabilization and the establishment of the "institutions" of a viable market economy, in addition to liberalization and privatization, are critical. Risk-averse behavior on the part of the "better" kind of FDI should be reckoned with. This suggests that policy attention to transparency, stability, and predictability of the economic environment deserves priority over "cheap" resources as pole of attraction of FDI.

5.2 – *Motivations of foreign investment – expectations and realities*

When growth is being in part accounted for by FDI utilizing cheap labor one should be cautious about assertions that cite any such phenomenon as the first harbinger of a sustainable catch-up recovery and growth dynamic. It may only be indicative of the externalities available to small new investment once the overall economic, and particularly the investment, climate begins to improve. Without having anchored the foundations for a sustainable rise in factor productivity with foreign investment fully integrated into this strategy, turning these incipient gains into sustainable growth is a crucial maneuver. To pace such a trajectory by exploiting cheap labor or relying on readily available natural resources is unlikely to be fruitful. To try and do so with FDI may in time, as wages move up (Wade 1995), lead to "little but abandoned factories and unemployed low-skilled labour" (Kregel 1994, p. 37). This reality of history is indeed the heart of the proposition that I should like to buttress in what follows as a crucial input into the discussion on sustainability in Chapter 12.

In appreciating the contribution of foreign investment in general and FDI in particular, it is important to be aware of different strategies pursued by foreign investors. Even when targeting investing abroad for productive purposes, as distinct from simply mopping up rents or wagering on speculative gains, one can separate investments into three categories according to their main functions: (1) to ensure distribution via an appropriate marketing and sales infrastructure in lieu of direct exports from the home base; (2) to produce for the local or regional market, or horizontal integration; and (3) to configure the foreign firm as fully as feasible within the broader corporate strategy by promoting exports from the foreign affiliate, or vertical integration (Lankes and Venables 1996). Very rarely, and then mostly when considering FDI in developed countries, are the TNC's fundamental research and decision-making functions in the broad sense – all associated with high value-added, well remunerated jobs – moved away from home base.

Recent research on FDI flows into transition economies has documented a more complex picture than simply relating FDI to the state of the transition in the host country. Since the first goal of FDI – essentially distribution abroad when direct export costs can be saved – is by definition a simple extension of a firm's export strategy, such flows tend to materialize well before the other two kinds. Especially export-oriented FDI often involves a refinement, or reconsideration, of corporate strategies and thus as a rule leads to relocation or extension of activity. This is distinct from the second purpose – catering to local or regional markets – for that in essence involves a replication of the TNC's activities elsewhere and as a rule for a new or growing market. Carving out market share, or securing first-mover advantages, is a prime FDI motive, particularly at the early stages of transition. In addition, factor costs are less important than having available a suitable investment climate and skilled labor in the third category of

FDI motives. Furthermore, FDI projects in the more advanced transition economies tend to be more export-oriented and more integrated into the TNC's global production process and more likely to exploit the host country's comparative advantage. Moreover, the control mode pursued in FDI tends to be closely correlated with the host country's transformation progress, and thus the more vertically integrated type of FDI motive pursued. Finally, the export-oriented FDI tends to be associated with a much farther-reaching product integration within the TNC on the input or output side, and possibly both.

FDI according to the first two functions – distribution/sales and production for local and regional markets – is useful in delivering several advantages of FDI, particularly when the new activities complement or qualitatively improve local availability and create new jobs. Such FDI may simply replace domestic activities and worsen the employment situation. Without a reasonable degree of competition, there are "rents" to be blotted up in the transition economies. FDI with such a focus is not necessarily the best sort of investment for recovery and catch-up growth. If FDI enters solely to take over existing operations, the advantages for the host country derive essentially from the transfer of business acumen to this particular operation. Workers and employees may gain useful "technical assistance" from such experience. Consumers too may benefit in terms of presentation, quality, and perhaps price. But this FDI is not necessarily accompanied by inflow of technology, by new finance, or by access to export markets as it would cut into the investor's prime market. Of course if FDI enters basically to cater to the local market with products that were previously not available or in that type of quality, broader benefits can be reckoned with. There may be financial and technological inflows, new jobs may be created, the consumer may benefit from lower prices though the treasury forfeits import duties, and so on. These benefits should not be belittled, but neither should they be exaggerated.

The third type of FDI by function would, then, seem to be of crucial importance in appreciating the role that FDI can play in mobilizing resources for identifying, jumping onto, and staying on a sustainable growth path. That goal cannot be reached automatically. It becomes more predictable the more of the usual functions normally kept at the TNC's home base become integrated with the foreign operation. Such usually warrants transfers of technology and perhaps capital, thus ensuring transformatory production within the context of the global corporate strategy, rather than simply exploiting temporary comparative advantages.

Given "strong support for the proposition that progress in transition is associated with a changing mix of project types, away from projects that are designed to serve local markets, and toward export supply projects" (Lankes and Venables 1996, p. 343), FDI is essentially a follower rather than a leading sector in modulating the transformation. Other evidence along those lines can be gathered from the preference of foreign investors for a host country with political stability, particularly in first mover FDI, that is, for distribution purposes, where supply-side considerations or factor costs are perhaps most important. More significant, particularly for FDI serving the third function, is macroeconomic stability and the regulatory environment, as well as broader demand considerations. Of course, whatever its functions FDI *could* be useful, depending on circumstances, and one should therefore look concretely on a case-by-case basis at the contribution of a given project to the particular stage of the transformation. That too requires governance of the transition!

Nevertheless, the above summary suggests that, even during the early stages of transition, provided governance capabilities are at hand, capital-market policies in transition economies should be focused. The primary purpose at the early stages is to scrap in an orderly manner obsolete human and physical capital, while encouraging rapid technological upgrading and modernization. FDI is not very likely to be interested in the former, except in strategically removing an actual or potential competitor, as happened in a number of cases in the former GDR and, one suspects, in some other transition economies. If such destruction is not directly tied to the setting up of modernized or modern operations, then the FDI inflow is unlikely to be beneficial to the country as a whole.

Bearing in mind the overall contribution of FDI to discharging the transformation's agenda certainly warrants more than casual attention, even if limited to the economics of such operations. But it is also crucial for meeting as much as possible the conditions for moving toward, and maintaining, considerable stability in political and social affairs. At a later stage, the primary motive should shift toward carving out and successfully implementing the catch-up strategy. Under those conditions, domestic and external finance should serve the modernization objectives rather than the other way around (see Chapter 12). These justifications of economic policy provide the logic for intervention and control over financial activities as earlier intimated (see Chapter 5). They also help to rationalize intervention modalities and justifications by upgrading governance capabilities, including through foreign assistance, as an alternative to simply abdicating economic policy to the at times spurious "free-market benefits."

5.3 – Some illustrative negative aspects of capital inflows

I do not want to bias the case for or against foreign investment in "assisting" the transition economies in their efforts to regain sustainable growth, and ultimately lift welfare. The earlier assumption that massive FDI flows would enter these countries, predicated on an abundance of cheap skilled labor, proximity to vibrant western markets, the potential for substantial growth of internal demand, and liberal commercial legislation, has not well withstood the test of time. In fact, there has recently been a slowdown in FDI inflows, perhaps because the "crown jewels" have already been picked off; strategic investment positions have been taken without really resulting in benefits in terms of capital, market access, upgrading of human-capital skills, broadening and deepening technology, improving management, marketing, corporate governance, a market-oriented

413

business culture, and so on; and, with few exceptions, the rather slow pace of recovery has not encouraged follow-on investment, even if committed, precisely because of the prevailing uncertainties. With growth now under way in several countries, particularly in central Europe, this sentiment may be changing for the better. But there can be no guarantee that once buoyancy is regained the pace of economic growth will be sustained for a protracted period of time. This holds in particular if merger into the EU economy were chiefly based on prevailing demand and supply. The business cycle is bound to crimp the chances of reaching sustainable growth by simply displacing other exporters to the EU on the strength of prevailing comparative advantages.

One should be aware of several adverse impacts of foreign investment experienced in a number of transition economies. They have various origins. Most important has been that these countries are not (yet) equipped to manage such inflows in harmony with the envisaged growth trajectory, or one yet to be elaborated, and that foreign investors are frequently motivated by strategic behavior and rent seeking. First of all, FDI has been heavily concentrated not only geographically but also sectorally, suggesting that carving out market shares and rent seeking have been prime movers. Foreign capital has not been an integral part of available savings to be allocated to the most promising ventures. One cannot blame TNCs for grabbing activities with a high-rent potential, owing to monopolistic positions and special arrangements with host governments (for example, in the automobile sector), such as on customs duties, tax regimes, QRs on competitors, and cofinancing. Managers of the transition should have refrained from such behavior.

Second, strict monetary policy has been an adage that central banks are expected to observe. With rather rudimentary financial markets in place, short-term speculative capital inflows in particular have at times threatened to undermine the capacity of central banks to keep money supply in line with anti-inflation stances. Sterilizing such flows, because they cannot be productively invested in a noninflationary manner, has its limits, given the narrow arsenal of monetary-policy instruments even in the more advanced transition economy. It is also a costly operation as central banks as a rule earn only the foreign interest rate but have to pay the high domestic one. Monetizing such inflows provides downward pressure on the real appreciation of the exchange rate, but it tends to stoke inflation.

Third, domestic banks on average have been sitting on sizable local-currency deposits that should be mobilized for onward lending to domestic users. Because of capital inflows the larger domestic banks are being further squeezed into insolvency, given their asset-liability structure (see Chapter 7). Blue-chip domestic firms can borrow directly abroad. Foreign banks can do so in order to on-lend to domestic corporate borrowers. In a number of cases, these funds can be provided with a competitive edge because foreign lending is not fully subject to domestic fiscal rules owing to loopholes.

Fourth, speculative capital inflows are to some extent related to the still shaky foundations of the banking sector in the transition economies. The many new private banks, though small in terms of assets and liabilities, are as a rule under-capitalized and poorly equipped to manage risk. They are thus contributing to double jeopardy because of the limited room for assimilating the art and skills of risk assessment (see Chapter 7) in its incipient phases.

Fifth, monetary policy in many transition economies has remained stringent with high domestic interest rates and in many cases undervalued exchange rates. Once these countries regain a modicum of confidence in international credit markets, speculative funds tend to enter for two reasons. One is that foreign lenders are eager to expand their business, and indeed to carve out market share, at attractive interest rates in foreign currency, thus avoiding any foreign-exchange risk. Domestic borrowers with some positive credit rating can attract foreign-currency loans from abroad at interest rates that are considerably below domestic ones and, furthermore, in the expectation that the exchange rate under pressure will be revalued, thus lowering their domestic borrowing costs. And this pressure derives precisely from capital inflows, not stellar export performance.

Sixth, in many transition economies, even if adjusted for productivity differentials, wages are but a fraction of labor costs in developed countries. Foreign firms are therefore likely to offer rather generous wages as compared to prevailing norms. When labor markets are managed with rather low short-term unemployment, the wage stance adopted by FDI in particular may begin to exert pressure on local wages before such raises can be justified by real, sustainable productivity gains. To the extent that wages are sticky downward, this may complicate policy making particularly if the incipient signs of economic growth are not really the harbingers of having jumped onto a sustainable catch-up path.

Seventh, countries with a fixed exchange rate, notably in the form of a currency board, have encountered problems in working off pressures stemming from capital inflows because adjustments can no longer be engineered by changing the exchange rate. Instead, domestic wages and prices, which may be sticky downward, and interest rates, which cannot diverge too much from those in the markets of the vehicle currency to which the rate is pegged, need to be adjusted (see Chapter 4).

Finally, particularly in the CIS States, FDI inflows have been heavily concentrated in mining and raw materials. Although available information remains scanty, one must doubt that these investment projects, if indeed started up, are knitting forward and backward linkages, notably to new small firms, through which the cited benefits of capital inflows will be transferred. History teaches that very few countries have modernized on the basis of rich natural resources (see Chapter 12). One cannot be confident that these transition economies will fare any better.

I am singling out these features only to underline the limits of utilizing foreign savings as a basic source for domestic modernization and to remind ourselves that policy makers ought to place greater emphasis on policies designed to mobilize domestic savings, including repatriation of resources parked abroad, for modernizing investment projects. By being cautious about the benefits of capital inflows, I do not, of course, wish to deny that such net resource increment can in principle bolster demand and change the supply in transition economies. It may even impart an impetus to economic recovery and growth for a while, particularly if complementary activities are embraced. However, unbridled capital mobility is not necessarily a blessing given the transition context, especially its phased "destruction" and "creation" tracks, as discussed.

Section 6: The transition economies and the EU

Following the "1989 events," the smaller and more western transition economies began to air their strong desire "to return to Europe." This expression has meant many things, frequently confounding the "idea of Europe" with the EU (Havel 1996). This is not helpful. For the purposes at hand, however, I take the expression to mean the ambition to seek, as quickly as possible, close economic, political, and security ties with the "west" and to join the EU at the earliest opportunity. These ambitions crystallized for economic, ideological, political, security, and undoubtedly an entire array of other convoluted reasons (see Brabant 1990, 1991a, 1995a), whose foundations are at times difficult to grasp. But they could hardly be reconciled with the neoliberal stance the transition's leadership professed to adhere to. Nor is it self-evident that membership *could* be arranged while maintaining and extending provisions conducive to sustainable growth (Brabant 1995a, 1996).

6.1 – Initial approaches

The "1989 events" have confronted the EU with the opportunity to recast its working horizon in terms of "all Europe," a possibility that had been very remote from European thinking for well over four decades. Such a broadening of perspective was necessary to strengthen both the political transitions in eastern Europe as well as their economic foundations while these countries move toward full-fledged, market-based resource allocation. Given the very complexity of any earnest attempt to reconfigure the continent, it would have been useful if the EU had developed a long-term strategy leading up to this "new Europe." That remains a daunting assignment to date.

Initial reactions by EU policy makers to the "events" and to the requests for a rapid, comprehensive rapprochement by many transition economies were singularly qualified by the perceived need to strengthen the depth and scope of integration policies among the (then) twelve EC members, rather than to widen membership. Faced with such a diversity of potential partners, it was feared that the very idea of "Europe" as a common economic area and, increasingly, as an integrated political space might get lost in the process of enlargement, a development that would serve neither present nor potential members. The initial reaction consisted of improvised attempts to assist the transition economies while holding them off any accession track, including by offering them an ill-defined association status with the so-called Europe Agreement as an alternative (see Chapter 11). However, circumstances prompted the Twelve in mid-1993 to entertain a credible request for membership with the ten transition economies identified earlier, once candidates fulfill a number of conditions. Negotiations are currently slated to be started in early 1998.

Up to that point, little thought had been given to the need to prepare the candidates in any foreseeable future for inclusion in the EU framework. In many respects, such a strategy is still lacking. Initially it was generally assumed in EU circles that any expansion toward the east would become topical at best only after these countries had been embarked for some time on a rapid and endogenous growth path opened up by the liberalization of their societies. It was taken as axiomatic that they would eventually come to resemble western European democracies. They would be at the lower end of the scale of wealth in the EU, of course. Just the same, they were expected in due course to become vibrant market-based economies with a solid democracy animated by a lively civil society. Once that stage was reached, so the expectation went, integration into the EU framework could be arranged in much the same way as in earlier enlargements. Of course, we now know that many of the assumptions on which the EC's initial standoffish attitude had been predicated, were patently wrong.

And so the remaking of Europe continues to be, without exaggeration, an unprecedented historical event that deserves a better-fashioned approach at least on the part of the EU. What is really required is a more comprehensive, strategic, and longer-term framework to permit a broader coordination of the EU's policies with respect to the economies in transition, even if accession for some were feasible by the year 2000 or soon thereafter, which I frankly doubt. Such a strategy should preferably avoid excessive bilateralism, move well beyond providing financial or technical assistance on an *ad hoc* basis, insist upon effective surveillance, and promote a revival of economic ties among the economies in transition themselves. It should also aim at imparting further credibility to the transformations as well as at bolstering security in other domains. Furthermore, it should be cast against a longer-term horizon with, for most transition economies, membership of the EU or, for others, a well thought-out preferential arrangement as the end target. Such a strategy should be looked upon for what it truly is and intrinsically hopes to accomplish: a set of guidelines for mobilizing with maximum dispatch all available resources to assist the process of enlargement and make it come true at the earliest opportunity.

Regrettably, the EU continues to waffle. This suggests that its interests and those of the candidate members are not quite concordant. This is important for these differences influence the tone and conduct of the forthcoming accession negotiations. Unfortunately these interests are not well defined let alone spelled out in anything like a strategy for moving forward with integration and enlargement. Moreover, they range over cultural, ecological, health, economic, political,

417

security, social, strategic, and other domains. Attaching a realistic weight to qualitative assessments in order to assess priorities or reach an aggregate benefit-cost calculus is by no means easy (Brabant 1996). But I can tick off here only its most important aspects.

6.2 – Interests of the transition economies

They are perhaps easier to identify. Quite apart from "rejoining Europe," these economies have assiduously sought entry into the EU for economic, political, and security reasons; cultural, scientific, educational, and other interests are also at stake, but these I shall not pursue here, although I do not in any way minimize their intrinsic importance. Given the fragility of the political situation in all too many transition economies and the widespread apathy toward any old or new regional economic or security arrangements, even if supported by the EU or another international grouping, the preference of policy makers in eastern Europe for seeking closer affiliation with "western" institutions is straightforward. If the EU had succeeded in strengthening its second "pillar" (that is, the common foreign and security policy), EU affiliation would have been a natural objective of many of the smaller transition economies to anchor their security. Without such a strong pillar, and the present one hardly exists, it is doubtful that the EU can meet such expectations.

Strengthening the credibility of transformation policies constitutes a second set of preoccupations. Given the considerable costs of transformation, not just in terms of output forgone but also in terms of dislocations, increasing inequalities of income and wealth, and the considerable exacerbation of personal and economic insecurity (see Chapter 8), it is crucial for transformation managers to gain the approval and support of key policy makers in "successful" market economies. Because the European Commission was chosen as a central co-ordinator and deliverer of assistance to the transition economies (see Chapter 11), building and maintaining good relations with the EU can provide a "seal of approval" for policies that are domestically unpopular. This is all the more important since convergence toward the minimum criteria for EU accession is bound to inflict further costs, and these must be borne mostly before the more tangible benefits of EU accession can conceivably materialize.

Undoubtedly a major interest of the economies in transition at present lies in the broad area of economics. It is here that access to markets in the EU, in the first place for their present exportables, which does not necessarily require full membership, is a critical factor; never mind how long that comparative advantage will hold up. It is arguably no more crucial than in propping up demand for products coming from an area that has been going through a wrenching socioeconomic depression. Aside from lifting aggregate demand, this buoyant interaction has also imparted a greater degree of confidence in trans-formation policies, strengthened the conditions for resuming investment largely on the basis of domestic savings, and supported the fledgling private sector. In time these factors will undoubtedly help to mitigate most of the social discontent aroused by the adverse effects accompanying transformation policies. Moreover, easing the relationship with the EU should strengthen the inflow of private capital, though in some countries a too rapid expansion thereof can be a decidedly mixed blessing. Finally, smooth relations with the EU as an organization form part of the integration of the economies in transition into the global economic framework.

Formal accession to the EU, at least in the first few years, will not add too many gains in addition to those from which the transition economies have been benefiting since the early 1990s. More is potentially available with even closer affiliation with the EU, short of membership. The obstacles to market access for some "sensitive products," notably agriculture, would be reduced and the threat of contingent protectionism for other "sensitive products" (such as textiles, clothing, footwear, iron and steel, automobiles, some chemicals, and so on) would vanish. Labor migration from the economies in transition would in all likelihood become feasible only after a protracted adjustment period. The same applies to accessing fully the EU's transfer programs.

Perhaps the single largest economic benefit for the transition economies derives from the credibility of a firm commitment to eventual EU membership: Based on a coherent accession strategy, it would hold both the EU and the potential entrant(s) to effectively observing closely monitored convergence criteria (Brabant 1996, pp. 212ff.). This could inspire much greater confidence on the part of economic agents, including foreign investors, particularly in economies where the transformation has so far been wobbly at best. Such a blueprint would contribute to reducing the still pervasive economic, political, and social uncertainty in transition economies, thus imparting a positive fillip to the domestic investment climate. The prospect of becoming EU rule-bound economies could only enhance matters. Such a development would enable foreign investors to configure the potential entrants as part and parcel of the "single market" in their broader investment and distribution strategies (see Section 5).

A more effective allocation of the resources at hand across and within sectors and regions in the economies in transition, given the still distorted nature of resource allocation, should provide a significant, positive impetus to growth based on technical and allocative efficiency gains. As explained, it could also strengthen the basis for identifying a catch-up strategy based on dynamic efficiency gains, which will be critical to facilitating EU entry, if only by compressing membership costs, financial and otherwise. Economic recovery and sustainable growth at a rather high rate are desirable in themselves, if only because they help to satisfy widely held popular expectations of gaining soon improvements in levels of living, particularly if the benefits can be shared fairly widely. But it would also encourage steady convergence between the potential entrants and the average level of development in the EU, thus easing pressure on EU budgets and dissipating the potential for discordance in the "single market."

419

The potential gains from rapid trade expansion are considerable. However, offhand it is not clear whether the recent growth in exports provides a firm basis for predicting further steady economic gains (Chapter 12). The recent output growth obtained in most of the more western economies in transition continues to be fragile. It has been bolstered primarily by labor- and resource-intensive exports and pent-up domestic consumer demand rather than, with few exceptions (notably Poland), strong gains in productive investment and restructuring. The latter will be required to carve out dynamic comparative advantages, in part by inserting these economies more fully into the international division of labor, notably in intra-industry trade. That dynamic, I submit, will be determinant of the size and distribution of the economic benefits of participating in Europe's single market. But I see them neither in terms of the trade creation-diversion calculus nor of other economic benefits (Olson 1984, pp. 118ff.). The contribution to growth of direct net trade gains has historically been assessed as being surprisingly small (Brabant 1995a, pp. 38–46). Far more important, I contend, is the impetus to buoyancy due to the greater certainty imparted by a transparent, rule-bound regime applicable to a vast area with a substantial demand of some 380 million consumers; with eastern accessions the market's size may expand to some 480 million individuals, and even more if CIS and other Balkan States will eventually be adjudicated as qualifying in principle for EU membership.

It is important to bear in mind that accession to the EU entails not only benefits, which may be substantial for successful transition economies, but also costs. It is impossible to list all of them here without assessing them for individual applicants. But it may be useful to look, at least qualitatively, at five such costs categories. First, full adoption of EU competition policies exposes the more fragile and marginal economic operations, especially those being restructured, to sophisticated competition, which may drive these operations prematurely out of business. Inasmuch as these economies *must* make significant headway with economic restructuring and with the acquisition of robust capacities to compete in intra-industry trade, particularly in manufactures, some degree of protection may be desirable. But that would simply be incompatible with the *acquis communautaire et politique* (henceforth *acquis*). This is one cogent reason for forging ahead as rapidly as possible with industrial restructuring before entering the EU.

Second, agriculture throughout the transition economies has been weakened in general by transition policies, but especially by the destruction of the co-operative infrastructure before new distribution networks, for inputs as well as outputs, could be cobbled together (Comisso 1997). In some countries, Poland in particular, agriculture suffers from rural overpopulation and low productivity. The transition economies therefore have to face up to launching painful rural restructuring similar to western Europe's efforts in the 1950s and 1960s. This will cost money before the productivity gains obtained and diffused to wide swaths of the economy begin to alleviate matters.

Third, converging toward the Maastricht criteria for admission to the monetary union is a costly exercise. The more advanced transition economies have made significant progress in correcting public-sector deficits, lowering inflation, and ensuring exchange-rate stability and currency convertibility. However, in many countries capital mobility needs to be further liberalized to conform to EU standards, and both interest and inflation rates brought down to much lower levels feasible at the present time without nipping in the bud the recovery of output, still incipient in many cases, and exacerbating the already calamitous employment situation in many countries. In some, Hungary in particular, levels of public-sector debt are too high to be brought down quickly to the convergence criterion. In this it is important to recall that, although joining monetary union is not a precondition for EU membership, the members of the monetary union insist upon fairly demanding macroeconomic convergence policies in other members, including new entrants.

Fourth, entrants have to introduce the regulatory framework of the *acquis*, notably as regards standards for health, the environment, safety, and social conditions. How the fresh entrant could or should conform to set norms tailored to the needs of more advanced economies with precepts that differ from prevailing realities in the transition economies remains a challenge. Doing so rapidly would only exacerbate the overall cost of conforming. Some of the present comparative advantages benefiting these economies will partly be eroded. Whether it is wise to impose such costs on economies whose recovery is in many ways still fragile, is obviously a matter of judgment for policy makers. But the alternative policy options at hand should be carefully set out and weighed before pointed decisions are taken. I return to this in Chapter 12.

Finally, membership of the EU will inflict a costly budgetary burden. There will be a loss in customs receipts because of the elimination of internal tariffs and of conforming to the lower common external schedule (Messerlin 1996); and the assistance programs in place will be discontinued. These losses may be small in relation to the benefits and other costs mentioned above, but several billion dollars are at stake. Such magnitudes are not trivial. They cannot simply be ignored.

6.3 – Interests of the EU

The interests of the EU in bringing the transition economies into its fold are also spread over economic, political, security, and other areas. But there are palpable differences. For one thing, the relative weights of these considerations differ markedly between the EU and the potential entrants. Also, the EU has other interests, such as the environment, health, cultural diffusion, and foreign policy, that, at least for the present, would seem to carry a much lower priority in the ranking favored by policy makers of the transition economies.

There is a marked asymmetry in the relations between the EU and the economies in transition. In contrast to the weight of the transition economies relative to the EU (the aggregate GDP of the ten transition economies with a Europe Agreement, which is not easily estimated because of severe data problems, may in 1996 have added up to between 4 and 8 percent of the EU's

421

total GDP evaluated at market exchange rates), the EU constitutes a vast and wealthy market for the economies in transition. Admittedly, having buoyant markets at the EU's eastern frontier at a time of slow growth may on the margin provide a welcome lift to aggregate demand. For some time to come, however, its overall effect on EU activity remains confined. The EU has already access to capital markets in the eastern part of the continent (as enshrined in the various agreements). Given its employment calamity, it would wish to defer the opening of labor markets for years to come.

Much more important than the eventual trade and capital-market benefits is that, at least initially, another enlargement is likely to impose considerable net adjustment and budgetary costs on the present EU members. In the first instance that means present net contributors to the EU's budget. But enlargement also affects present net beneficiaries. Not only would they lose in relative terms (because economies in transition enter well below the average level of per capita GDP in the EU, even when reconfigured), but also it is not at all clear that the aggregate volume of transfer payments could be raised sufficiently to compensate losers to a politically acceptable degree.

From a strictly *economic* point of view, then, unless there were to be a very rapid rate of income and structural convergence by the time of accession, the potential material benefits for the EU from another enlargement are not very pronounced, certainly not in the short to medium term. But the EU has much stronger environmental, health, political, security, and other interests. Some members are also keen on propagating their language and cultural heritage. Since environmental problems do not respect borders, the EU is naturally concerned about mitigating spillovers. It also has a vital interest in ensuring stability and predictability on its eastern border; indeed, this interest applies to just about all economies in transition. Finally, inasmuch as the EU seeks to project itself much more forcefully in international affairs, its foreign policy can be better informed by having a close relationship with the transition economies.

Since the Copenhagen commitment on bringing into the EU up to ten economies in transition within the foreseeable future, the EU's stance has been, in the words of the decision of the Madrid Council in December 1995:

> Enlargement is both a political necessity and a historic opportunity for Europe. It will ensure the stability and security of the continent and will thus offer both the applicant States and the current members of the Union new prospects for economic growth and general well-being. Enlargement must serve to strengthen the building of Europe in observance of the acquis communautaire which includes the common policies.
>
> (European Commission, 1995b, part III, p. 1)

When this sheer rhetorical hyperbole is contrasted with the EU's actions regarding the transition economies, it quickly becomes evident that a real base upon which the political necessity and the historical opportunity could be solidly grounded remains to be forged.

6.4 – Would membership be beneficial for transition economies?

Surely, ties with western Europe can facilitate the transformation process. Aside from the kind of assistance rendered since 1989 (see Chapter 11), the benefits of trade and cooperation accruing with EU membership other than those presently derived from the Europe Agreements depend in good measure on what the EU has to offer and what the transition economies have to concede in order to be admitted. How policy makers, producers, and consumers in the EU as well as in transition economies react to liberalization, what the latter countries presently can offer and can realistically hope to table in the next few years, and what they can gain from trade expansion are critical determinants of the transformation's success or failure.

Enlarging membership has economic consequences. Though the opportunities are favorable for trade creation and the diffusion of western technology throughout the new entrants, they cannot bear fruit immediately. Bringing poorer countries into a wealthy club dilutes the wealth of those asked to share the burden of leveling. In the past, the EU has invariably opted for spreading the implied costs of structural adjustments over a considerable period of time. Even if it were to consider such a solution for the transition economies, despite the fact that there are no longer the same strategic and political reasons for burden sharing, such an accession strategy is not likely to be embraced very quickly. The transfers from the agricultural, regional, social, and structural funds required for the candidate to reach the median levels of income and productivity for Europe soon are likely to test, and perhaps stretch, the patience of European taxpayers.

Some compromise solution will necessarily have to be thrashed out, lest the transformations of the eastern part of Europe fizzle out for lack of political foresight and will. A combination of greater self-help by the transition economies individually and as a group; a bold, if gradual, revision of the EU's philosophy; and a much more target-oriented EU strategy toward the transition economies in general and the ten candidates in particular offers the only realistic course. Whether such a cooperative strategy will permit these countries to adopt pluralistic market systems that enjoy a sociopolitical consensus remains to be seen. Incidentally, this situation should be the subject of good regional governance and solvable in the EU context, given the comparatively small number of actors and the greater degree of commonality in obtaining the particular public good that EU integration provides. In principle this should offer greater opportunities for molding the regional regimes and appropriately reflect the current and prospective interests of the transition economies (Brabant 1995a, pp. 504ff.).

6.5 – How best to forge ahead?

The EU has been putting in place its preaccession strategy at least since early 1995. To the extent that it does not focus on preparing its own institutions and programs for another enlargement, this strategy is largely geared toward acquainting the transition economies with the implications of EU membership, notably the obligations of the *acquis*, and with how the EU functions (Brabant 1996, pp. 168–73). None of the measures taken to date is likely to have a major impact on the more fundamental problems of accommodating new members unless a more active and engaged stance by Brussels will be promoted. Thus, although the White Paper prepared for the economies in transition in 1995 has been most welcome, complying with all the legislation around the single market, which is deemed to be a prerequisite for accession, will take many years. As with so many other aspects of contemplating accession, the White Paper can be invoked to accelerate the process or to slow it down, depending on how lenient the interpretation of "minimal compliance" will in the end turn out to be. Several initiatives on how best to map the future of the more likely entrants within a "European" context could usefully be embedded in a more coherent and strategic – as well as ambitious – framework designed to address problems systematically over an extended period of time.

Without resorting to economic determinism, economic interests as well support the claimed justification for innovating a more active, strategic approach to assisting the economies in transition in general and facilitating accession of the ten in particular (Altmann, Andreff, and Fink 1995; Altmann and Ochmann 1995; Baldwin 1994, 1996; Brabant 1996; Ludlow and Ersbøll 1996, pp. 59–61; Weidenfeld 1995a, b, c; 1996a, b). Without the economies in transition benefiting from a solid economic recovery that can be sustained into some catch-up dynamic over a substantial period of time, it is hard to see how the interests of the EU can be blended with those of the candidates for entry in particular. But it might be constructive also to favor a broader scope and extend the approach, at least conceptually, to other transition economies.

For the economies with a Europe Agreement the framework should preferably amount to a strategic sequencing of measures to be enacted in both the potential entrant and the EU, with as end result swift EU entry. Fixing an entry date up front may be useful for public relations. But such a calendar deadline is not very meaningful from the point of view of the broad political economy of EU accession and membership without having in place a credible strategy for meeting it. It is of course necessary to monitor, assess, and fine-tune a constructive strategy in the light of actual events, including those originally not foreseen. Given the importance of what is at stake, the course ahead needs to be sensibly steered with a degree of flexibility, pragmatism, and purposefulness that has been sorely lacking to date. Indeed, the EU could usefully elaborate such a strategy to clarify its own priorities and obligations at this stage. Such strategic planning could also provide the potential entrant with a clearer vision of what it needs to accomplish in the near term, how to obtain appropriate assistance from abroad (including from within the EU) to support the action-oriented agenda when desirable, and how best to mobilize the limited domestic resources to adhere to such a commitment.

I am advocating this way of approaching the problem not solely to render membership of some transition economies in the EU feasible against a realistic horizon. Indeed, the remaking of Europe is at stake; this requires far more than "simply" engineering another EU enlargement. It focuses first and foremost on strengthening the integration achievements booked to date with all of their drawbacks and advantages into a robust edifice that can act not just as another intergovernmental body, albeit a special one. That was the original purpose of the 1996 Intergovernmental Conference (Brabant 1996); unfortunately, its outcomes in mid-1997 fall far short of even minimal delivery on these expectations. Remaking Europe also includes building prospectively a constructive relationship with the eastern part of Europe. The latter must be motivated not only by the interests of the present EU members, but also by the real needs of the "other" Europe. Such a strategy will therefore exhibit for the foreseeable future more of the character of foreign assistance than of a joint approach to tackling continent-wide problems in economic, political, social, strategic, and other domains. I shall therefore spell out what could reasonably be undertaken in Chapter 11.

Conclusions

Managing economic, political, and security changes and remaking global relations in line with present and foreseeable tasks are two of the greatest challenges facing the global community at this juncture. This cannot be just a task for diplomats. Neither is it something that can be entrusted only to one or a few key industrial powers. Certainly, hegemons may play a pivotal role therein. Without proper adaptations of international regimes and their associated institutions, however, it is difficult to envision a more harmonious world resulting from seizing the historic opportunity offered by the demise of state socialism. What is required is the concentration of national, regional, and international efforts on rebuilding a method of conducting international relations (including finance, trade, and payments) that would function as easily and successfully as the one that was slowly regained in western Europe after World War II. In the broad sense, the daunting transformation agendas in the eastern part of Europe for some time to come could only benefit from far-reaching reform of the global economic framework and its main institutional pillars. That cannot be achieved quickly, certainly not within any reasonable time frame for moving forward with democracy and anchoring "market institutions" in these countries.

Some of the more transitory costs of adhering to the regimes in place derive from the fact that the latter cater to a paradigmatic type of economy toward which the transition, and indeed several other, economies aspire. But they tend to be too inflexible to accommodate the *sui generis* transitory needs of these countries. Even if the regimes in place could be reconstructed within the context of opening up the eastern part of Europe and some Asian countries, one must remain cognizant of the range of advantages and drawbacks, with the costs being palpable in the short to medium run and more tangible than the eventual benefits, which prove to be considerable. I have emphasized in particular the sizable costs and benefits, with their asymmetries across countries (individual members as well as candidates) and over time, of arranging EU membership for the privileged transition economies. A sober analysis is warranted: Accession negotiations are bound to be complex and difficult, given the historical, institutional, logical, and other evidence that bears on the issue. This is not an unduly pessimistic, but a realistic picture of the situation at hand. With a purposeful preaccession strategy (see Chapter 11) the promise of another enlargement can be turned into reality without rocking the delicate EU boat to the point where it may have to be scuttled altogether or imposing an insuperable burden on the candidates.

11

TRANSFORMATION AND INTERNATIONAL ASSISTANCE

One of the greatest challenges facing the global community since 1989 has been the management of the multiple economic, political, and security changes, in some cases of seismic dimensions, due to the demise of state socialism. Of course, many other changes in the global context have transpired, but I focus here on "transition." The ensuing management tasks include not only coming to grips with these mutations as they crystallize or threaten to erupt. It may arguably be even more important to be in a position to address in an orderly manner the repercussions emanating from these, as well as other, changes through various foreign interactions. These include the remaking of the postwar monetary, financial, and trading regimes without which the world order will once again come to rest on the hazards of intergovernmentalism. In a world without clear hegemons this spells broad immobilism and ultimately inability to avert, or even to cope with, open conflicts.

Without a doubt, the tasks of managing the post-Cold War world have become more formidable. The magnitude and scope of the problem are presently arguably more complex than was the case even a few years ago, given the disintegration of collective security, the reluctance or inability of the big powers or those aspiring toward that status to influence events, and the broad apathy of a world becoming seemingly inured to regional conflicts, even mass slaughter and starvation. Even the most tentative of answers to any of the many questions is still outstanding. If only for that reason, it should provide the rationale for qualifying the cited challenge of managing global economic, political, and social affairs as "the greatest."

The purpose of this chapter is not to engage at length the whole debate, but to provide a summary view on managing assistance to transition economies and the lessons that can usefully be drawn from this experience. After looking at the stance taken by the international community since 1989, I adduce a rationale for it as well as a framework for best-practice assistance delivery in general. Thereafter I examine its institutional arrangements. Europe's early assistance approaches, and the hopes and disappointments around the Europe Agreement, are detailed in the next two sections. Then I spell out how assistance to the transition economies could prospectively be improved with implications for rendering a helping hand, and dollar, to other countries that may eventually have to face the tasks incumbent on wholesale socioeconomic and political transformation. Before concluding, I briefly address the remaking of the EU's assistance programs with a view to cobbling together a more coherent, strategic approach to eastern Europe.

Section 1: Transition and international assistance

In treating the transformation of the eastern part of Europe as a millennial event, whose full dimensions and repercussions are yet to be ascertained, I am not exaggerating. Its actual and potential benefits, even if configured solely in materialistic accounting, are likely to be quite considerable in the longer run. Yet one cannot gloss over the fact that the magnitude of the adjustment costs involved, however configured, has been staggering, and climbing.

Soon after the "1989 events" the international community was asked to provide – and indeed magnanimously volunteered – various kinds of assistance to the transition economies. Initially, western governments and regional and international organizations offered to provide financial, technical, humanitarian, and other assistance to speed up the transition process, if only to ensure its irreversibility, and, where possible, to help work off part of the adjustment costs faster than these economies would have been able to support on their own strength. The core assumption at the time was that a successful economic, political, and social turnaround in these countries could be engineered fairly quickly and smoothly. We now know that this was a false premise. The transitions can be seen through neither quickly nor without engendering costs that may be socially and politically destabilizing. There is bound to be path dependence. Outside financial assistance can at best ease its vagaries on the margin of what were earlier deemed to be the moral and political imperatives.

Just the same, the core questions remain: Could more have been done and in a different manner, given the volume and diversity of the appropriated resources and the apparent needs of the transition economies? Indeed, why should the international community feel compelled to assist these countries and for how long should this effort be sustained? What is the desirable degree of governance that should be available in, or that should quickly be built up by, multilateral organizations, particularly with a view to facilitating the process of fusing the two parts of Europe eventually into a continent remade? Could better results have been obtained from this generosity? These questions should figure prominently in debating the pros and cons of assisting transforming countries. They are also germane to the discussion of merging the transition economies into the existing international regimes and their custodial IEOs (see Chapter 10) while heeding their peculiar "transitional" economic, political, and social problems. They deserve to be examined against the backdrop of the expectations of wide layers in these countries, and elsewhere, and the resources appropriated and disbursed, relative to their needs.

The transition economies are all countries that encounter temporary adjustment problems, albeit in some cases very severe ones, deriving from the need to switch from an administratively steered economy largely segregated from the world, but well embedded in the CMEA framework (except Albania, China, and to some degree Yugoslavia), to market-based resource allocation pursued in the context of global competition. Note that these countries fall into two broad categories. One comprises those on a medium level of development (most of eastern Europe proper except Albania, Bosnia and Herzegovina, and Macedonia, plus most of the western successor States of the Soviet Union, including Russia). The other countries by any measure belong in the category of developing countries. For them the orthodox criteria on providing international assistance can be invoked without much further ado (Berthélemy and Varoudakis 1996), though with two provisos. One is that claims on international assistance resources are now rising while donor fatigue and budgetary stringency in major donors are taking hold, severely curtailing official development assistance (ODA). The other is that many of these new developing countries do not start their modernization drive from a low base in terms of, say, education, infrastructure, industrial islands, and other legacies of having been part of a broader setting for state socialism. Rather, they too will have to reposition their structures inherited from "equalization attempts" before their takeoff for more appropriate modernization can dependably be launched.

Of course, those opposed to providing international assistance by transferring real resources other than what markets elicit, or national-security priorities warrant, would deny the right to assistance for these countries for the same reasons advocated in seeking to withhold it from the more orthodox developing countries. For the other countries, however, the core question on justifying assistance remains: Why should the international community earmark its scarce resources to help them and in what form (volume, composition, conditionality, and timing) should it preferably do so?

It is by no means self-evident why the transition economies, particularly the more developed ones, should be entitled to economic assistance from the global community. I prefer to place it squarely within the context of the political-economy response to the "1989 events." This justification offers one concrete illustration of the position advocated in Chapter 10: The need for flexibility and adaptability in the programs pursued by multilateral organizations with respect to members that cannot fully participate in or benefit from the regimes in place. With proper governance in these organizations such a more pragmatic approach, rather than one steeped in ideology or congealed around standard adjustment recipes, could be of strategic importance in enhancing coordination, cooperation, and competition in the global economy. Of course, the arguments I develop here apply only *mutatis mutandis* to categories of countries other than the more developed ones.

One could set forth a litany of reasons for assisting the transition economies. I do not, of course, wish to deny that one finds occasions where altruism motivates assistance flows. Emergency situations as a rule elicit a magnanimous response in the international community. Even so, I am generally skeptical of appealing to such a rationale. I am even less swayed when observers invoke some kind of historical, ideological, natural, political, or strategic "right" to assistance, sort of a compensation for past wrongs, such as for having been "abandoned by the west" or "forced to endure communist oppression" in the case of the more western transition economies. Policy makers in donor countries are not generally swayed by such arguments. But I can discern at least two groups of more compelling justifications for assisting the transformation.

One revolves around expectations. Particularly during the first year or so of transition, western and also some eastern policy makers, as well as managers of multilateral organizations, were quite optimistic about the future of steering global economic and related affairs in general and of managing the relationship with the eastern part of Europe in particular. The reasoning went as follows: If the transition economies could quickly play a more constructive role in the global economy by forging new commercial and financial linkages as well as through more active participation in the multilateral economic dialogue, benefits would soon accrue for the global economy. Such new links would be particularly useful to trading partners able to position themselves quickly in these liberalizing markets. The advantages would rapidly become visible in western Europe. With more access for these eastern countries to European markets, favorable spillovers should also appear fairly soon for other partners willing and able to compete openly in such markets. The more developed countries were expected in due course to revamp their development-assistance posture with positive benefits for the less developed countries. On these grounds, official assistance to transition economies was held to be confined to a comparatively short period of time and be of limited dimensions. Indeed, it was anticipated that these countries would soon begin to contribute to the global community's capacity to deliver "better" and "more" assistance, including through ODA, to the orthodox developing countries.

After nearly a decade of transition policies, we now know that these benefits have been materializing much more slowly and far more haphazardly than had been anticipated at the transition's inception. Nonetheless, the fundamental reasoning on which the above stance rests has by and large remained unchanged: With vibrant economies emerging in the eastern part of Europe, given the size of the population and the potential for raising purchasing power, a major impetus to global demand and supply can in time be anticipated. Once these magnitudes crystallize, they are bound to affect positively all facets of international economic intercourse. The virtuous circle of export-led expansion could be expanded, provided myopic protectionism and lack of imagination in partner countries, western Europe in particular, will not nip these forces in the bud. If the latter threats can on the whole be successfully weathered, economic self-interest, if nothing else, should favor continuing, and indeed strengthening, the effort to integrate the transition economies into the global economy with tangible deeds. Of course, private initiative should take over from public efforts once the uncertainty and risks of the transition abate. This juncture may now be within reach in the transition economies that have been reporting fairly robust growth.

The other group of arguments invoked by way of justifying international assistance hinges on security issues: Weakening the military (but also economic and social) threat of the eastern bloc by fragmenting its cohesion and reducing various instances of actual and potential east–west tension can only benefit the overall global economic, political, and social environment, though not all partners would on balance share to the same absolute or relative extent, of course; some might not gain at all. These more political and strategic considerations grew in importance as the exuberance aroused by the "1989 events" waned and the fundamental aspects of how best to conceptualize, implement, and steer complex transformations over the longer haul came to dominate the international political discourse. Adjustment costs in transition economies will in the end be staggering, regardless of what happens to the sociopolitical consensus on which steady progress is predicated. This has weighty implications for the stability of the region, for booking further progress in moving toward civil society (Gellner 1994) and pluralistic democracy, and in ensuring that the transition economies pursue a more constructive role in European and global affairs (Bernhard 1996; Ignatieff 1995). In turn, all this affects the security situation – sort of the emerging new constellation of what used to be the "east–west conflict" in a wide range of endeavors.

Although some of the most critical security concerns manifested in the early 1990s have found their potency blunted, the range of acute conflicts has augmented significantly and they have become messier, less tractable. Regional strife, deteriorating nuclear safety, ecological insecurity, disintegration of existing polities, a weakening commitment to democracy, and many other, less well defined concerns, in addition to the defused potential for global military conflict, have gained attention, if perhaps not intrinsic importance. They too continue to justify assistance with the transformation strategy on the part of the international community, if only because of selfish concerns. In what follows, I zero in chiefly on the more economic aspects of rendering multilateral assistance.

Section 2: The case for assisting the transition economies

At the inception of the transformations in the eastern part of Europe, several assumptions were invoked by the international community, and indeed by the leadership of the transition economies. One was that the net results of the impending systemic changes would be positive and sizable for the transition societies, and in due course for their outside partners as well. Another was that these benefits could be obtained quickly and without provoking major social or political upheavals. Western assistance, aside from resources appropriated for humanitarian and emergency purposes, was meant to alleviate some of the

431

socioeconomic costs of transition and to provide financial resources and technical knowhow to accelerate the process of economic restructuring. It was always clear that such a large-scale transformation would have to be accomplished largely on the strength of domestic efforts. That should quickly yield results in view of the presumed more efficient use of resources, in the allocative as well as technical senses, now feasible. It was taken for granted that, after a fairly brief tumult, these societies would embark on a self-sustainable growth path with substantial gains in per capita income. The principal driving force was expected to be the opportunity and challenge of starting to close the pronounced gap between their levels of wealth, technology, productive capacity, productivity, and income and those of western Europe through imported technology and foreign investment. The rapid assimilation of up-to-date western technology would be spurred on via large private capital inflows, though initially stimulated by official transfers, which would lubricate the adaptation and catch-up processes to bolster the credibility of transformation policies. I return to this issue in Chapter 12.

Most of these assumptions have not been borne out in practice. The transition process has been much more cumbersome and confounding than initially assumed, in terms of the depth and breadth of its complexity as well as of the time required to assimilate all the required changes and innovations. In many ways, this still holds today and suggests that the justification of the early forms and quantities of assistance (other than humanitarian and emergency aid) just quoted may well have been wrong. Likewise, the expectations of a quick revamping of the eastern economies and societies with a swift economic recovery have not been validated, thus raising again the fundamental questions of transformation and prospective assistance. Because other anticipations of the trajectory of the transformation have been frustrated, a reappraisal of what is feasible could best be placed in a broader context, now more relevant to the real *problématique* of conceptualizing and carrying out incisive structural transformation.

Many reasons could be cited in support of providing a helping hand, and money, to the economies in transition, including altruism, compassion, and guilt. Certainly of equal weight is the following: It is ultimately in the genuine self-interest of the global community to compress the acuity and length of the period of adversity in the eastern part of Europe. That can be argued on the basis of a wide range of economic, humanitarian, political, social, and strategic features. Whereas these factors prevailed from the transition's inception, they have arguably gained in pertinence as a result of the rocky progress with implementation of the transformation agenda. The realities of the transitions have amply negated the simplistic assumptions on built-in stabilizers and automatic adjustments, of smooth corrections of imbalances, soon after launching a credible transformation commitment.

The particular configuration of the magnitude, timing, and composition of the assistance, and by whom, should preferably have been decided against a realistic backdrop of the envisaged transformation policies with their associated sizable adjustment costs. These were predictable, given the various instances of supply inertia, which could not but inhibit a quick reallocation of intrinsically still-valuable resources and dampen new resource mobilization to finance restructuring. Real demand in official and other markets was bound to shrink because of the erosion in wealth for many households, of the drop in real incomes, and of the desire to rebuild precautionary savings. Moreover, substantial inflation was resorted to, perhaps deliberately, to confiscate most of the monetary overhang in countries where that was considered a serious policy problem. In some cases, the emergence of hyperinflation should have been reckoned with, rather than its dangers underplayed, from the beginning by realistically appraising the chance of regaining control over the money supply.

The critical policy questions are four-fold. One set is addressed almost exclusively to domestic managers. It revolves around the determination of the precise size of the adjustment burden (say, the percentage drop in levels of living and of wealth, as well as their distribution over time and over various social layers or interest groups) that can be inflicted upon their societies without generating dysfunctional sociopolitical disaffection with the overall drift of the transformation. A second set confronts domestic policy makers and assistance providers alike. Once the latter are prepared to alleviate the adjustment burden, the key issue is whether such foreign assistance could have mitigated the adjustment burden, while perhaps speeding up the transition. A third set is primarily addressed to assistance providers. The crucial questions are who best to entrust with the task and which governance regime to choose for the envisaged action, given prevailing realities. Finally, assistance has to be seen against the backdrop of the limited capacity, and indeed lukewarm will, to mount new assistance efforts within the donor community. Those questions arising primarily for assistance providers revolve around whether resources could be diverted from traditional clients without harming the interests of donors, recipients, or the global community at large. The first two sets of questions are not really the proper issue here. But they are not completely irrelevant in determining who should be entrusted with the task of coordinating assistance, of how to ensure that this process remains governable and be best governed in the light of available capacities, of who would be harmed by the potential diversion of resources, and of the degree to which the worst adverse effects of this reallocation could be alleviated.

The second reason for providing assistance is self-interest. This has various facets. One certainly is the potential for retreat from reform in the transition economies and its implications for other countries. The issue is manifestly *not* whether political forces may revert to state socialism with its attendant implications. Rather, the point is that policy reforms anchored to a sharp devaluation of the exchange rate and far-reaching price and trade liberalization usually generate sociopolitical resistance, if only because of asymmetry and time inconsistency in costs and benefits; so does uncontrolled privatization and eroding the sociopolitical certainties of yore. Replacing the safety and certainty of the old with the quite palpable hazards of an emerging society new and wobbly in so many respects cannot but be unsettling. The minimal critical shock required to elicit a

433

favorable response to the economic, political, and social aspirations of those advocating positive changes may well exceed the magnitude of the transition's burden that the electorate at large is willing to support for any length of time.

Related to this, also in the self-interest mode, is that western governments and multilateral organizations had predicated their initial stance in part on the potential impetus to overall demand that the transition economies could impart to global growth. Following a comparatively brief adjustment period, these countries were expected – and indeed encouraged – to reroute their commercial interests to the west, particularly for the importation of capital goods to shore up their industrial conversion and in time to buttress the new catch-up growth path. This expectation has in the meantime been frustrated in a number of respects. The downturn has been wrenching by any measure. True, the prospects for solid economic recovery in many eastern economies have improved markedly, at least soon to compensate for the losses sustained in the transition and, in many countries, the preceding years of stagnation and decline. The pace of gains has been slow to moderate at best. For example, only in 1996 did Poland surpass its 1978 GDP. Positing the recent growth gains as *real* gains from what would have prevailed without the transition experience requires an *anti-monde* in the *post hoc ergo propter hoc* fashion that at least this observer, deems not to be a very logical way of adjudicating success. Furthermore, it is as yet unclear whether this recovery can be sustained into catch-up growth (see Chapter 12). In other words, I see little ground for complacency. The potential is there, but as yet in a rather far-off future. Given the salience of successfully engineering the turning point from recovery based mostly on mobilizing previously idled resources to sustainable catch-up, many justifications can be invoked to argue that propping up recovery, or ensuring that it will be around the corner fairly soon, would be wise policy making, particularly in the international community. It would also be to the latter's advantage to properly target available assistance resources in harmony with agreed-upon transformation policies.

Once a decision is reached to render assistance, it is important to gain concurrence on the organ to be entrusted with the conceptualization and delivery of the assistance, that is, with elaborating a strategy for underpinning the transition and ensuring that the delivered help is actually put to best use. This raises a number of issues. Particularly germane to the present discussion is the following: Mobilizing international assistance as effectively as possible presupposes that there are sufficient capabilities available within the various bi- and multilateral organs entrusted with assistance coordination; or that such capabilities can be built up rapidly. I contend that the international community was woefully ill-prepared to assist the transition economies in establishing functioning markets in a coherent manner and in holding adjustment costs within manageable dimensions, while ensuring steady progress toward pluralistic political systems.

In any restructuring effort, it is necessary to identify resources, desirable output targets, need for import substitution or export promotion, and other decision-making parameters to address systematically the core tasks at hand and reach some modicum of order. The instruments through which these modifications should preferably be brought about in transition economies must themselves be solidly anchored to market indicators, but conceived within an overall program of bold adjustments in economic structures and institutions. These include the conceptualization of new arrangements to whittle the economic relations in regional arrangements or federal structures that are economically not warranted. Bolstering economic cooperation among these countries, old and new, to prop up demand and alleviate the snowballing effect of simultaneous structural adjustments with considerable political overtones deserves to be explored with determination. If only for reasons of managing the process of change and reinforcing reciprocal confidence, thus avoiding a steep downward spiral, they deserve outside support.

To accelerate the transformation process, or cajole it into a virtuous orbit, proper policies motivated by the need to identify a new, sustainable growth path in the transition economies are required at the earliest opportunity. Although the agenda for the transition was complex from the very outset, that confronting the international community at this stage, when fundamental issues of the purposes of the transformation remain unsettled in many countries, is utterly bewildering. Even so, all transition economies deserve considerable attention on the part of the international community and the EU in particular. Why this is so and what can realistically be accomplished in spite of all the hazards I address below.

International assistance should not, however, be conceived as a one-way street. From the beginning of transition, the countries have been in need of all the self-help that they can reasonably muster by themselves, possibly with international support. The main objective is how best to enhance the usefulness of outside assistance, however delivered, and of domestic transformation policies. There never was an economic justification for artificially obstructing intragroup trade and other forms of economic collaboration based on emerging market criteria. Political and economic cooperation among the former CMEA members has been chaotic since early 1990; even the formal commitment to central European cooperation in the Visegrád and CEFTA contexts has amounted to little more than formal diplomacy with useful exchanges of information, but few hard policy decisions with a discernible follow-up (see Chapter 10). Yet the structural mutation could have been smoothed and integration into the international economy facilitated if the transition economies had maintained and expanded intragroup economic links based on market principles. From the outset of the transition opportunities for sustaining trade and cooperation among those countries existed. This has been so regardless of whether quick accession to the EU, which was never plausible, could have been arranged. Reinforcing mutual commercial ties on economic grounds would have supported the reform trends from within. It would also have transferred western assistance in a form that least interferes with the emerging economic incentives for microeconomic actors. It would furthermore have smoothed the adjustments to be undertaken by the EU to accommodate trade by the transition economies and eventually accession or close association.

Section 3: Institutional arrangements for assistance delivery

There can be no doubt that the response of the international community to the adversities in the eastern part of Europe has been generous and substantial (UNECE 1991a, b; 1992, 1993, 1994, 1995, 1996a, 1997). Whether it has been sufficient to prop up wobbly transition policies, whether a more magnanimous stance (on the order of the postwar Marshall Plan, for example) could legitimately have been anticipated, and whether the assistance could have been delivered more effectively in the global sense that I advocate are all appropriate questions in their own right. But they should not detract from the fact that the initial response of the international community was quick, sizable, and generous. Not only did many countries pledge assistance, they also singled out two focal aid-coordination organs – the Fund and the European Commission – to take charge of the formulation, implementation, and fine-tuning of assistance efforts. Other institutions have, of course, also been playing a role, but at a decidedly secondary level. The key question in this connection is whether these organs, in the first instance the Fund and the European Commission, can efficiently execute these new mandates. Let me start with the Fund, but without rehearsing again its more general role for transition economies (see Chapter 10).

Virtually all western assistance, other than that rendered for emergency and humanitarian reasons, has been pledged for release only after the potential beneficiary has reached an agreement with the Fund on macroeconomic stabilization. For members this is a regular Fund program. For others, the potential beneficiary has to commit itself to seeking accession (or re-accession in the case of rump Yugoslavia) and having come to some understanding with the Fund. In the latter case, Fund discipline is due as part of the accession negotiations. This holds even with respect to disbursements of funds in support of various kinds of technical assistance for the transition, not just providing stabilization loans, more general support for external payments, or funds to prop up a commitment to current-transaction convertibility. Once this platform is reached, the key to unlocking the assistance pledged chiefly by and through the EU in the case of eastern Europe, including the Baltic States, and to a lesser degree also the CIS States as well as Mongolia, can be turned. The European Commission is indeed acting on behalf not only of its members but also of the rest of the so-called Group of Twenty-four (G-24), essentially the OECD countries prior to the accession of Mexico, in coordinating assistance to eastern Europe, including the Baltic States.

Meeting the assistance needs of the CIS States and Mongolia was initially dealt with within the so-called "Washington Conference format," meaning essentially that they are within the ward of the Group of Seven (G-7) industrial countries, and thus the Fund, which serves as its secretariat by default. The designation "Washington Conference" stems from the fact that the disintegration of the Soviet Union in late 1991 led the United States to convene a conference in Washington, DC, 22–23 January 1992, on conceptualizing and streamlining assistance to the CIS States among the principal multilateral agencies and donor countries involved. This was followed by a second meeting in Lisbon (23–24 May 1992) and a third in Tokyo (29–30 October 1992). Since late 1992, however, the format has turned more and more to the deliberations within the G-7 and the national coordinating centers erected in an *ad hoc* format.

Reaching an understanding or agreement with the Fund involves a good deal of policy synchronization and indeed thorough exchanges of views on what constitutes proper transition policy. These include in particular coming to a working arrangement with the Fund mission on terms for eventual accession, on domestic policies to be pursued, and possibly on Fund loans granted in the context of restructuring the external-payment situation of the potential beneficiary. In the course of the exchanges of views on macroeconomic policies, as well as considerations about the underlying efficiency of the microeconomic sphere (particularly as far as prices, interest rates, wages, and exchange rates are concerned), all mostly formulated in monetary rather than real terms, there is ample scope to pass Fund precepts on to local decision makers.

To assess how well the Fund as the central organ in animating the disbursement process can perform this task, it is instructive to recall key features of why, in the past, the relationship between the state-socialist economies and the Fund, and to some degree also the other IEOs, was at times beset by serious conflicts and controversies, and why these countries otherwise remained on the sidelines of the policy debates (Brabant 1991b; 1993b; 1995a, b). It would have been useful if the international community had recalled some of the critical technical reasons, as opposed to political and ideological posturing, that help explain why state-socialist economies had shunned the IEOs in the early postwar period and why those that actually joined encountered more or less severe problems, unless state-socialist policy makers had themselves in essence already opted for something akin to the standard adjustment package of these IEOs, notably the Fund – a very special case of "owning the Fund's program." Of course, one must be a bit more forward-looking than the attitude that outsiders are assumed to be capable of, presumably because IMF consultations with governments are "highly confidential; they're negotiating for money. You wouldn't want your banker going out and telling all your neighbors about your negotiation for a mortgage" (as claimed by Ms. Pamela Bradley, Chief of the IMF's Public Affairs Office in New York on 14 September 1993).

The custodial institutions entrusted with assistance delivery accomplished the tasks sketched in Section 2 largely in a muddling-through modus. This was particularly so during the earlier phases of the transitions, when outside assistance would have been most welcome but delivery capacities in the chosen institutions were at their low, if extant at all. Without reliving history, the path followed has nonetheless implications for the future. Because incisive structural change, on which gaining sustainable growth remains predicated, will come to the transition economies at best very slowly, claims on global assistance from official sources have continued to be sizable. This will remain the case until private capital markets can take the relief. Benefits from increased trade and finance will jell for parties other than those directly involved in providing assistance only once a solid, sustainable recovery in the transition economies gets under way. This is particularly the case for foreign investment, which in the form of FDI will provide dependable relief on a substantial scale only upon the restoration of greater economic, political, and social stability.

Section 4: Europe's early assistance approach

There can be no quibbling about the fact that western Europe initially responded quickly and magnanimously to the requests for assistance from the economies in transition; in some instances, western Europe even volunteered and it took the lead in the global assistance effort. The response was largely motivated by the hope of thus consolidating a decisive turn away from state socialism, and indeed from dependence on the USSR, and ensuring that these changes would be irreversible. But the assistance efforts for a long time were largely improvised; in some respects they continue to suffer from this inability to take a longer and more coherent view of what has been at stake in the eastern part of Europe since 1989. Such a piecemeal approach was probably unavoidable at the start of the transition, given the sudden and extraordinary turn of events, the limited information upon which assistance providers were initially acting, the poor intellectual and practical infrastructure for comprehending events in the eastern part of Europe, and the fact that the European Commission was at that time overloaded with its own agenda (Brabant 1995a, pp. 285ff.). In the process, substantial resources have been misallocated, some utterly wasted (Kaminski 1996).

4.1 – Evolution of assistance

The EU's assistance activities in favor of the economies in transition date from the G-7 summit in Versailles in July 1989. It was in consequence of the decision in principle reached there that the G-24 donor countries decided to support the nascent reform efforts; this was subsequently extended to all economies in transition save the CIS States and Mongolia, and to help these countries integrate themselves into the world economy. The European Commission in that context was entrusted with the task of coordinating the efforts of individual donors, the multilateral financial institutions, and its own activities. The latter included the so-called PHARE program (for *Pologne/Hongrie – assistance à la restructuration économique*), lending by the EIB, and other types of assistance within the perimeter of EU activities. PHARE is essentially grant aid designed to support technical assistance of the most diverse kind. Its resources have more recently been reconcentrated on supporting infrastructure and on facilitating EU accession by the ten candidates (see Section 5). The EU has also participated in delivering emergency and humanitarian aid to the few countries that required it.

In early 1992, following the fragmentation of the Soviet Union, the EU established its TACIS (Technical Assistance to the CIS) program, similar to PHARE, to assist the former USSR (other than the Baltic States) and Mongolia in their reform efforts; but in the USSR's case it had already before the country's implosion extended a helping hand. This too was part and parcel of a broad international effort, this time led by the United States, as explained.

At the turn of the 1990s, the EU joined other donor countries in granting GSP (or Generalized System of Preferences) privileges to economies in transition, which were subsequently incorporated into the Europe Agreements, and in removing those QRs that had specifically been imposed upon so-called "state-trading countries," as defined in the context of the GATT at the height of the Cold War. It also granted some transition economies privileged access to its markets for sensitive products and tariffs cuts (see European Commission 1995c). Furthermore, the EU has extended loans directly and through the EIB, and some grants, in support of stances on macroeconomic policy in several economies in transition, supplementing the resources of the IMF and the World Bank. The latter in particular as well as the EBRD, of which all EU members and the economies in transition are shareholders, have provided sizable loans for restructuring.

It is by no means easy to track how much each transition economy has received, when, and for which particular purpose. By its own reckoning (European Commission 1995c, 1996), the EU granted over the five years 1990–4 to the ten economies in transition with a Europe Agreement as well as Albania and Macedonia (which are the twelve beneficiaries of PHARE) some ecu 33.8 billion – about $44 billion in early 1996 dollars – or 45 percent of the total assistance these countries received from the international community. Grants constituted some ecu 13 billion. Of that total some ecu 4.3 billion was committed under PHARE. Another ecu 1.2 billion was appropriated for 1995 (OECD 1996b, p. 69). A slightly higher annual average has been budgeted for the second half of the 1990s (ecu 6.7 billion for 1995–9, according to Vrbetić 1995, p. 7).

The EU has also provided substantial resources to the CIS States (European Commission 1995c): During 1990–4, ecu 59 billion in aid out of a total worldwide of ecu 98.3 billion, or 59 percent. Of the EU's delivery, however, a comparatively small share was for technical assistance (for the period 1 September 1990 to end 1994, ecu 2.6 billion out of total technical assistance of ecu 5.4 billion). The vast bulk has been in the form of loans and guarantees as well as strategic assistance in facilitating the withdrawal of Soviet troops from the former GDR in particular.

4.2 – Evaluation of assistance to date

There seems to be broad consensus among outside observers and policy makers in the economies in transition (see Altmann and Ochmann 1995; Havel 1996; Hutchings 1994; S. Richter 1996; Weidenfeld 1995a, 1996a; Weiss 1997; WERI 1995), as well as in some cases among critical observers from within the assistance-delivering institutions (European Commission 1995a, pp. 8 and 201–28), that western assistance has trailed well behind expectations. A Polish commentator has opined, somewhat irreverently, that it has amounted to little more than "lunch and dinner diplomacy" (WERI 1995, p. 188). One can usefully assess the disappointments at three levels: (1) the mobilization of assistance from bi- and multilateral donors; (2) the precise targeting of that assistance toward the real needs of the economies in transition, as seen from within their own societal contexts; and (3) more effective and better coordinated delivery of assistance, given resource commitments and the recipients' needs. (For an early discussion of the need for a coherent framework for providing western assistance to the transition economies, see UNECE 1990, pp. 5–26; 1991b, pp. 7–9.)

Although the volume of bi- and multilateral assistance rendered to the transition economies has been substantial, two observations are in order. As noted, the total delivered has lagged well behind initial expectations and much has been in a form that does not directly contribute to propping up the desired structural change. Perhaps more important, the vast bulk of this assistance, but less so for that rendered by the EU, has been in the form of loans at commercial interest rates. These loans must eventually be repaid and current service must be assured. To live up to those obligations, even if the international community may be well disposed toward the countries that adhere to the "Washington consensus" to renegotiate loans, that is, enter swiftly into *de facto* rescheduling, in the end the ability of these countries to discharge their foreign financial obligations depends on their capacity to generate export revenues over and beyond import requirements. As shown in Chapter 12 that depends importantly on whether countries succeed not only with transformation but indeed on their ability to embark on catch-up growth, thus entering into the virtuous circle upheld by the neoliberal proponents of all-around stabilization, privatization, and liberalization.

The delivery of various types of assistance is widely judged to have been carried out in a rather haphazard fashion with much of the mobilized resources "captured" either by the delivering institutions' formidable bureaucracies or their associated rent-seeking advisers and consultants, from both sides of the divide alike but vastly more from the latter than from the former (Kaminski 1996; Weiss 1997), and with limited delivery on the ground, as it were, thus confining the positive impact of assistance for the beneficiary countries. As a result, the record of nearly a decade has not been particularly encouraging. It has certainly not impressed those who had hoped for a decisive breakthrough in the remodeling of Europe.

4.3 – Types of relationships

The variety of responses cited above has given rise to a complicated structure of relations between the EU and the economies in transition. It now consists of bilateral Europe Agreements with ten eastern European countries, bilateral PCAs with CIS States, and bilateral free-trade or second-generation trade and cooperation agreements with other economies in transition, including Albania. Note that the Europe Agreements (see Section 5) take a long time to be ratified and four are still to reach that status. For the latter only the trade components of the agreements are in effect (see Chapter 10). Furthermore, PCAs exist at least for Armenia, Azerbaijan, Belarus, Georgia, Kazakstan, Kyrgyzstan, Moldova, Russia (for details, see Borko 1996), Ukraine, and Uzbekistan (European Commission 1997a). However, these too need ratification and for most this process has not yet been completed. In the meantime, then, only the "interim" trade part of the agreement is in effect in only some cases; for most even that component is still pending. Albania has a more limited kind of cooperation agreement. With the normalization of ties with the other successor States of Yugoslavia, a renewal in some form of the trade and cooperation agreement extant before the breakup of the federation was completed with the April 1997 agreement with rump Yugoslavia.

Just one word about the origin of the PCA. This came about because most of the CIS States will never be eligible for full EU membership and others may not qualify for several generations to come. Yet, events in those parts of the world could not be left in a state of considerable economic disarray and sociopolitical instability. The latter might elicit the adoption of a strategic reaction to being "isolated." At the very least, events in that part of the continent impact on the robustness of the eastern flank of the "Europe" of principal concern to the EU. If only because pressures for migration into the EU or the transition economies to the CIS's western borders were bound to become aggravated over time, the EU felt compelled to transcend the strict economic formats of trade and economic cooperation, and thus suggested the PCA. Like the Europe Agreement, this is not solely about trade or broader commercial and economic relations. Indeed, specifications on human rights, on protecting FDI (at least from the EU into these economies), and on safeguarding intellectual property rights (again, at least those from the EU introduced into the transition economies) are also included. These elements form currently part of the agreements with the cited countries and are envisaged in agreements with some other CIS States. But information on the details and on the repercussions of these agreements remains sparse at best (for Russia, see Borko 1996).

In any case, most agreements of the EU with the various transition economies have not been particularly innovative (Altmann, Andreff, and Fink 1995; Balázs 1996; Kramer 1993). They have proved insufficient to meet four identified and widely accepted needs: (1) to provide economic, political, and strategic security to the eastern partners; (2) to respond strategically to formal requests for accession lodged since April 1994; (3) to strengthen economic and political rela-tions with the western CIS States; and (4) to hold a constructive dialogue on strategic cooperation in economic, but also in political, defense, environmental, health, and other affairs with many other economies in transition.

Section 5: The Europe Agreement: hopes and disappointments

Although it quickly became clear that most of the premises on which global assistance to the transition economies had been predicated were questionable, the European Commission hesitated for a long time about what could and should be done for these countries beyond a number of programs for humanitarian and emergency purposes. Absent a coherent strategy, the vast majority of the assis-tance efforts were hastily cobbled together in 1989–90 and gradually extended, particularly following the August 1991 coup in the Soviet Union (Reinicke 1992, p. 94), to other transition economies under its ward. Later on, these efforts were rationalized in the Europe Agreement for all but Albania and Macedonia.

5.1 – Origin of the Europe Agreement

In 1991, the EU innovated a sort of halfway reply to the "return to Europe" aspirations by extending to the more developed transition economies an associate status based on the so-called Europe Agreement. This was conceived under article 238 of the Treaty of Rome, which does not confer the expectation of eventual membership. In fact, at the time little thought was given in EU deliberations to whether and when the economies in transition could eventually be brought into the EU. This *démarche* not only was prompted by the insistence for recognition on the part of the western transition economies, but also, indeed, it was inspired by Brussels's growing awareness that the transformation would be more problematic than originally thought in 1989–90, that many of the western economies in transition were bent on full membership, and that its own efforts at assisting these countries directly and indirectly were less than visionary.

However, policy makers in many of the transition economies persisted in arguing their case for "Europe" status and eventually managed to persuade the Twelve to change their deep-seated reluctance to contemplate yet another enlargement. They did so in part because of the unanticipated effects of transformation policies throughout the area. The sharp curtailment of economic activity, especially during the first years, and impact on income and its distribu-tion were fomenting rising social discontent after a short period of "extraordinary politics." They thus threatened not only the future of structural transformations but also the stability of the entire region. That is to say, the Europe Agreement was invented largely because of the EU's own interest.

5.2 – Toward the Europe Agreement

This instrument revolves around asynchronous and differential trade liberalization for most manufactures. That is to say, the EU gradually removes its import duties on the products shipped from the partner country, initially foreseen over a five-year period but since advanced to three years (European Commission 1995c, p. 10). The eastern signatory has to reciprocate usually over a similar period (original schedule), but chiefly during the second half of the 1990s. This asymmetry suggests that the partner temporarily gains a relative competitive edge over EU producers and outside competitors. Thus, the central European countries signed their Europe Agreement in December 1991. The trade provisions came into effect in March 1992 (for Bulgaria and Romania this happened only in February 1994, after several delays for political reasons), pending ratification of the agreement by all national parliaments, which was concluded in February 1994 for Hungary and Poland and February 1995 for the other four countries; similar arrangements have more recently been established for the Baltic States and Slovenia. Eastern Europe has worked out a similar instrument with the EFTA, naturally chiefly for industrial goods. However, since EU tariffs on average now amount to less than 3 percent *ad valorem*, down from about 5 in the early 1990s, one should not exaggerate the export-revenue benefits obtained (WERI 1995, pp. 181ff.), particularly in the light of the considerable fluctuations in exchange rates; on the other hand, the eastern partner has been spared outright competition from EU agents for some period of time. The psychological impact of these agreements has probably been much more important than the benefits from tariff cuts and the alleviation of QRs.

The fairly standard Europe Agreement represents a very complex, voluminous exercise in commercial diplomacy. The key provisions of the original three treaties, which reflect the EU's strong bent on obtaining markets and production facilities in the eastern part of Europe; on managing access to its markets; and on avoiding serious levels of immigration, are set forth below. Those for Bulgaria and Romania, the Baltic States, and Slovenia and the successor agreements for the Czech Republic and Slovakia are quite similar. Exceptions are in the less generous access provisions for some quotas, notably for agriculture; on the commitment to the enforcement of human rights; and in some the statement that the Europe Agreement is a prelude to membership if the partner country so desires.

5.3 – Principal features of the Europe Agreement

Although there are some differences in the details of the various agreements since they are negotiated bilaterally, they exhibit chiefly common features. From the economic point of view, eight are most pertinent. First, the transition economies must open their markets to EU manufactured goods within ten years. Tariffs are to be eliminated over a period stretching from four to ten years. QRs against EU exports too are to be abolished but only by the end of the transition. If the transition economy maintains import restrictions thereafter, its commercial policy needs to be formulated in an explicitly discriminatory fashion so that the EU will not be in a worse position than the MFN partners as per the preferential arrangement. In principle, no new customs duties or QRs can be introduced, except in the case of infant industries and sectors undergoing restructuring in the transition economy.

Second, the EU opens its nonsensitive markets virtually immediately, with tariffs being abolished over a period varying between two and five years (later reduced for most products to between two and three years) for products with at least a 60 percent "local" content – a rather restrictive condition. Many tariffs for nonsensitive products are abolished upon the introduction of the commercial component of the agreements. QRs not governed by international agreements, as in the case of the Multi-fibre Arrangement (MFA), too are eliminated upon the entry into force of the commercial part of the agreement. The aim is to remove all trade barriers. But the agreements maintain rather elaborate antidumping and safeguard clauses – "contingent protection," in other words, which can be quite deleterious to investment decisions (WERI 1995, pp. 181ff.), hence exports and growth (Švejnar 1995, p. 14) – and in "sensitive product" sectors they offer only a gradual approach to free trade. These include in particular textiles, clothing, footwear, some chemicals, and iron and steel products. However, duties on outward-processing trade are abolished immediately. Safeguard clauses are included but there is a guarantee that after ten years (that is, at the latest in early 2002) these products will not be given different treatment than other industrial goods. For iron and steel products, improved transitional "voluntary export restraints" have been arranged.

Third, the EU offers concessions in agriculture, but nothing like free trade (Tangermann 1993). Previous facilitations for exports of foodstuffs have been consolidated and reciprocal concessions for specific products granted. These have been restricted to a subset of commodities, and then only for within-quota limits. The latter are set to grow by some 10 percent per year from 1990 levels. Variable levies, which are among the protective devices for price equalization within the arsenal associated with the common agricultural policy (CAP), will fall at most by 60 percent over a period of three years; in some cases by only 30 percent. Outside the quota limits, however, for now full tariffs and levies remain in effect.

Fourth, the transition economies must adopt EU competition policy within three years, during which GATT/WTO rules apply. For the first five years the countries are regarded as "backward areas" for EU purposes, which permits some relaxation of competition rules. The Association Council, on which more below, is empowered to extend this period by another five years. The transition economies must also adopt the EU's policy on intellectual-property rights within five years, converge toward EU standards on environmental protection, and make best endeavors to approximate as closely as possible the other legal elements of the *acquis*.

Fifth, products from the transition economies remain subject to key provisions of the EU's protection policy. As noted, many antidumping and safeguard clauses have been retained in the agreements even for products for which imports have been completely liberalized. Moreover, the EU appears to be using a criterion for assessing the imposition of punitive measures that is not quite appropriate (Vandenbussche 1996). These clauses are rather vague, hinging as they do on "serious deterioration" in the economic situation of an "EU region," but that concept is left undefined. These escape rules are perhaps most ominous for "orthodox sensitive" products, as enumerated earlier. But there is nothing in principle to prevent the EU from denominating other goods as "sensitive" if it deems that "its market" in some region has been seriously impaired. Contingent protectionism imparts an unnecessarily large element of uncertainty to the relationship between the EU and transition economies.

Sixth, no special provisions for labor mobility are included, other than that "essential" personnel (managers, supervisors, staff personnel, highly qualified workers, and professionals) in case of FDI into the EU can be mobile. But individual EU members can contract bilaterally, particularly for skilled workers from transition economies. This provision, together with the rules embodied in the agreements in case of inward FDI into the EU from the transition economies, may encourage brain drain. Of course, it also permits the EU to ward off export of the factor – unskilled, manual, and related "unessential" labor – in which the transition economies have a surfeit and for which the EU States are confronted with a severe sociopolitical calamity.

Seventh, the agreements strongly encourage and protect FDI from EU members in the transition economies. They do not incorporate special stipulations for financial cooperation in official flows, but they potentially provide the framework within which PHARE assistance is conceived and executed. There is also some promise to the effect that the EU may favorably consider further assistance, if necessary, to support currency convertibility or to buttress economic restructuring or prop up the balance of payments.

Finally, instruments are put in place to maintain a "structured political dialogue" between the EU and each transition economy, chiefly through the so-called Association Council. This is a bilateral organ between the EU and each "associated" country that is not, however, particularly well structured. Thus far it has been essentially a public-relations organ.

5.4 – Beyond the Europe Agreement

Whether the Europe Agreement reasonably provides the best offer that the EU could have proffered and the transition economies could have legitimately hoped for are quite distinct matters. These in turn stand separately from the best mutually acceptable solution at this stage, given the commitment to work toward full membership. Many leaders of the transition economies bemoan the fact that so far outright membership in the EU has been withheld and that the Europe

Agreement has not been transformed into an instrument to expedite the timing of such accession. I deem it more useful to take the Europe Agreement as a given for now and look ahead toward the future by assembling positive proposals on what can reasonably be done with the instruments, including financial transfers, in place.

All things considered, the beneficial economic nature of these agreements, as distinct from the political and psychological gains they undoubtedly impart, should be neither exaggerated nor downplayed. Improved access to developed-country markets is pivotal to successful transformation, particularly for the smaller transition economies. In that sense, lowering tariff barriers and removing some QRs rank among the most crucial forms of assistance that developed nations can extend to the transition economies; on balance, it is also the least costly. That assistance channel could usefully be widened by removing the contingent protectionism, including for agriculture, with on balance little loss to individual EU constituencies if handled intelligently. For many of these "sensitive products" the transition economies, at least for now, hold a comparative advantage. They constitute a sizable proportion of their total trade with the EU (see UNECE 1992, pp. 79–81; 1996a, pp. 110–17). Exploiting these comparative advantages while building toward a sustainable growth path with new dynamic comparative advantages constitutes the only feasible catch-up path (see Chapter 12).

It is in the latter spirit that I advocate exploring with determination policy steps that can be put in train to facilitate expeditiously the entry of some of the transition economies into the EU. Such a positive stance is far preferable to the cheap carping about being ostracized because the EU is allegedly not ready, or willing, to cope with transition economies. The Association Council, particularly if multilateralized for most purposes, could, in fact, become the chief mediator between the two sides in order to innovate a constructive relationship of assistance and cooperation, leading up to full membership as soon as feasible. Such an act of statecraft would also provide the EU with a forum for its assistance, advice, and surveillance to ensure that intragroup cooperation is meaningfully exploited as a force to *accelerate* the stage at which credible accession can be arranged. It would in particular be able to work concretely toward mutually acceptable and feasible admission criteria, and seeing to it that they are implemented as expeditiously and generously as possible.

Section 6: How best to assist transition economies

Mounting western assistance, other than for humanitarian or emergency purposes, calls for reinforcing the coherence of economic transitions through proper policies and appropriate institutions as quickly as possible. The principal purpose should be eliciting at least elementary modifications in the behavior of economic agents to help move the transition ship toward the distant harbor in spite of stormy seas and treacherous shoals. The program should also

446

incorporate features that make the cataclysmic mutations worthy of costly support to the electorate in donor countries as well as justify the forbearance of others that may be adversely affected in the process. For the rest, the automatic stabilizers of the market environment, once it gathers sufficient strength, should take care of adjustment (see Brabant 1990, 1991a). This is largely a matter of national governance in the case of bilateral assistance and of good multilateral governance otherwise.

The single most critical economic element of the transition should have been proper policies motivated by the need to identify a new, sustainable growth path in the transition economies. Because markets in these countries either are lacking or remain quite primitive, such a path needs to be identified by different means (see Chapter 12). International assistance suitably modified could have played a key role therein. Unfortunately, delivery of assistance by the international community, as argued, has remained well below anticipated volumes, disbursement has been delayed by too many bureaucratic squabbles, and much assistance has not really been targeted at the real source of the deep-seated structural-adjustment problems of the transition economies, namely marked supply inertia in the real sphere inherited from state socialism. The introduction of far-reaching structural change in transition economies, necessarily at the microeconomic level and in the institutional makeup of these societies, deserves comprehensive international assistance. And this could never have been confined chiefly to a standard demand-management stabilization-*cum*-assistance program running one to three years. The focus of assistance has been too much on macroeconomic policies and institutions, or nominal monetary policies. It is indeed in the very production process – the real microeconomic sphere – that right after demand stabilization remedial action should have been enacted soonest, where possible with outside assistance (see Part II). This seeming truism in the early 1990s still holds in the late 1990s, particularly for countries that have not yet resumed growth in spite of national efforts. Growth with equity must provide the principal impetus. Better, well-targeted, and timely delivered assistance could have made the difference. It still can. A change in policy stance not only on the part of transition leaders but also in the international community is required to bring this about.

In all this it is important to recall that much more is involved than simply transferring vast financial resources. The bulk of appropriated assistance should act as a catalyst, both to impart credibility to the transformation processes and to cement in the groundwork for mobilizing private initiative, including FDI. In any case, that assistance needs to be managed so as to impart best-practice positive effects to the transitions, while containing negative repercussions for all partners involved. Those considerations should have played a critical role in choosing delivery organs and in formulating and implementing the assistance conceptions.

I have earlier aired my concerns about entrusting the international assistance efforts largely to the Fund and the European Commission. As far as the Fund is concerned, my qualms stem largely from the specialized nature of that organization. It is at marked variance with the unprecedented changes in the eastern part of Europe that need to be fully factored into assistance packages. A substantial part of the skewed policy advice extended to these countries, whether with or without the full concurrence of the client government, derives from that particular feature. By its very nature the Fund was called upon to steer the transformation by managing demand and closing the foreign-exchange gap (see Chapter 4). This was shortsighted. Anything beyond that mission would have transgressed on the Fund's fundamental mandate as custodian of a special monetary regime. The Fund should have denied its support for any such venture, however "good" it may intrinsically have been. As an example, its early support for Russia through thick and thin was, in my view, not within the Fund's mandate. If for political and strategic reasons the international community felt Russia deserved its financial and other support, the assistance should have been earmarked from appropriate resources, not those entrusted to the Fund, the World Bank, or the EU for discharging well-specified tasks related to managing the global or European economy.

Putting it bluntly, the Fund's mandate and credo run fundamentally counter to managing operational, customized assistance programs, if only because of its main mission, time horizon, and financial resources. This is manifestly not meant to denigrate the professionalism of the Fund's staff. The Fund never cared much about supply management and it had little experience in assisting these countries prior to the transition. Traditional Fund programs do not function well in economies that lack reasonably integrated markets, where demand and/or supply responses are at best sluggish, where the resource gap is very substantial relative to the overall resource base of the economy, where export revenues are unpredictable or import costs subject to wide fluctuations, when much time is required for engineering a turnaround, and where economic, political, and social relations are in very considerable flux. Estimating for such countries a reasonable resource gap to be financed in a credible manner as part and parcel of a return to sound external accounts can only be a daunting assignment. It was bound to exceed by a wide margin the Fund's mandate, resources, expertise, and commitment. As argued, the real problem was not the external resource gap. Rather, it was bringing about incisive structural change in these economies

Because of the evident conflict between static efficiency and sustainable growth in orthodox demand management, a program for adjusting to external or domestic pressures in the transition economies and monitoring its performance must necessarily be phrased differently from the way in which the Fund has traditionally sought to accomplish stabilization. There are two fundamental reasons for this. One refers to the pervasive legacies of state socialism which have been all too readily ignored, yet must be clearly understood and factored into the policy deliberations and the package of measures ultimately agreed upon in order to improve the chances of success with structural adjustment. The other recognizes that, in part because of these legacies, macroeconomic management must include active intervention on the supply side to sensitize economic agents into undertaking the structural changes required to begin to solidify the rudiments of the coveted markets. For the foreseeable future, then, adjustment even in the transition economies that are already growing will require a much more varied policy regimen, a longer time horizon, and a much more encompassing institutional setting than envisioned in orthodox macroeconomic policies, such as the Fund's (Brabant 1990, 1991a).

In much the same vein, it was a serious error of judgment to entrust the coordination of the efforts of the G-24 to the European Commission at a time that this organ was already overloaded with its own agenda (Kramer 1993). It had even less experience than the Fund or the World Bank in dealing with state socialism and its legacies. The Commission in particular lacked an insight into the fundamental development *problématique* of these societies, and was thus unprepared for discharging the tasks the international community entrusted to it; indeed, that it had avidly sought to undertake. It may have seized upon the sudden opportunity to pursue its buoyed claims on playing a centralizing role even in foreign-policy and security matters. This was not only misguided but also quite premature as the chaotic behavior of the Commission and some of its members has since borne out, such as throughout the Yugoslav conflict. Small wonder, then, that its response has been neither "innovative" nor "daring" (Kramer 1993, p. 234). A constructive assistance package must consist of far more than simply keeping record of who is giving what to whom at which particular point in time. It also requires more than mounting mission after mission ostensibly to find the facts that should enable the Commission or other assistance providers to aim at efficient delivery of assistance. Relying primarily on channeling research and consultancy funds to western agents, most of whom had no particular knowledge of the beneficiary countries in any case, cannot constitute the best policy choice.

From early on in the transition several commentators, including this one (Brabant 1990, 1991a), and institutions, notably the Economic Commission for Europe (ECE), have argued that the complexity of the transition justifies the adoption of a much more modulated, intrusive, and hands-on approach toward assisting the transition economies than what has thus far come to the fore. Such a revised stance should permit each of the existing IEOs, and even some regional organs, to play its particular role. For example, the IMF should focus on current-account stabilization, the World Bank on structural-adjustment lending, the GATT/WTO on overseeing the evolution of the trade regimes, some institution on ensuring that the transition economies get ushered into the "European" fold, and some payments institution on managing temporary derogations from the accepted multilateral regime. Of course, this agenda in its entirety is no longer applicable to the more advanced transition economies. But it is still relevant to the vast majority of those struggling with emerging from the transitional depression. And such an institution could play a critical role in facilitating accession of privileged transition economies to the EU as well as elaborating a more perspicacious relationship between the EU and other transition economies (see Section 7).

These efforts could best be coordinated by a special *ad hoc* organ endowed with considerable policy discretion, competence, and flexibility, and specifically created to deal pragmatically and strictly on a temporary basis with the particular complexities of the transitions. This approach would lower the overall cost of the transition for all involved as compared to what has been coming to the fore to date and appears to be in the offing on present policy stances. Such an organ would have three vital tasks that any of the existing specialized agencies find it difficult to accomplish. First, it would have to ascertain what the transition as a complex, protracted, and uncertain process is all about. This includes verification of whether there is a reasonable sociopolitical consensus in each country to forge ahead with the realization of these aspirations and at what speed these objectives can best be pursued; failing that, there is a need to ascertain whether such a minimal consensus can be brought about in due course, perhaps with the diplomatic negotiating skills of the assistance provider. Second, it would have to assess to what extent these programmatic policies hinge on obtaining external resources, financial and others, and whether potential donors can muster sufficient support, including among their electorate, to mobilize these means. Most importantly, the coordinating body would have to ensure that appropriated resources will be mobilized in the most effective way, as measured by the degree to which they are fully blended in with the envisaged transition agenda and indeed help speed up its implementation as well as extend its remit.

Management of the policies underlying such an approach should preferably be entrusted to a fairly small group of skilled economists and financial diplomats acting on the authority of some outside organization. This should be intimately involved in transition affairs, not just assistance delivery, on a day-to-day basis, certainly during the early phases, rather than intermittently in the jet-set fashion; and in fine-tuning the transition's agenda, rather than issuing *obiter dicta* and platitudes, particularly during the early phases or when things go awry. Its authority would necessarily have to devolve from the major funder or coordinator of the resources mobilized in donor countries to the benefit of the transition economies. One could argue that this task is incumbent on the EU (but manifestly not the Commission) because the remaking of Europe is, after all, a supreme European task. Others have argued that the organ should be truly international or at least be responsible to a broader range of actors in the international economy and international affairs. Regardless of the umbrella authority to which the assistance agency must be held answerable, such a temporary institution could provide the vital ingredient to untie resources that politicians can and might prospectively be willing – and able – to muster for the sake of political gains, including the peace dividend; staving off a new military buildup because of serious ruptures in the transition process (in Russia, for example); or maintaining support for a concerted global approach toward resolving regional conflicts.

The western assistance mobilized in this manner would differ in more than one fundamental respect from what has thus far been transferred to transition economies, at least in "quality" if perhaps not in volume. It would call for a much more involved, comprehensive, and hands-on approach to managing global economic interdependence in general and on resolving the question of how the transition economies can be constructively ushered into that regime's architecture. This would require fuller commitment to jointly shaping the transitions on the basis of domestically innovated programs, possibly through an industrial policy as but one instrument of governance. Gaining current-account convertibility at near-full employment in old and new transition economies, rectifying external imbalances, or pursuing domestic liberalization measures, for example, should then form core components of a much more demanding, dovetailed, and appropriately-governed transformation agenda to be assiduously adhered to in all countries bent on restructuring their economy and broader society (see Chapter 3).

The principal elements of this agenda should consist, on the one hand, of economic stabilization. There can be no doubt that the first task of governing the transition economies is to stabilize the economic situation, thus crimp uncertainty. The core modalities thereof may or may not coincide with the programs that have recently been applied. By that I do not simply mean macroeconomic stabilization, or the removal of imbalances in internal and external sectors through Draconian monetary policies. Under some conditions (see Chapter 4) this may well be the first order of business to break the back of a near-hyperinflationary situation. But this should only be a prelude to setting forth, once a firm grasp over the socioeconomic situation is gained, the real order of transformation. Adhering to policies to stamp out all vestiges of inflation when exchange rates are fluctuating and some prices for important services are still being gradually relaxed is not necessarily the best route to opt for (Stanners 1993, 1996).

Whereas it may be constructive to have credible policies in place and hold on to them, adhering at all cost to policies that are not working or that are inhibiting the realization of other components of the transition strategy for the sake of ephemeral credibility is not conducive to proper governance. Central on the transition agenda should be sound macroeconomic management, including in fiscal and monetary policies as well as with respect to external liberalization, and a vision of the broad direction into which structural change should preferably evolve, while defusing any suspicion that the current transformation process may be retracted. It is hard to envision how this could be accomplished without an activist government – obviously one markedly different from the remnants of state-socialist control. If governance capabilities are available at all, there are some areas for which the state possesses an intrinsic comparative advantage. If minimum capabilities are lacking, they should be built up at the earliest opportunity (see Chapter 9).

In any case, such a stabilization package should be immediately linked to broad-based structural transformations. These must constitute an integral part of the policy goals that inform the specific shaping and fine-tuning of the stabilization agenda from the very inception. It would include rapid divestment of petty assets as well as removing the political and state organs and their various interest groups from micromanaging; corporatization and commercialization of SOEs while ensuring better corporate governance; attending to the rapid development of the financial infrastructure, starting with agencies to collect and channel savings; establishing firm property rights, notably seeing to it that public property rights are carefully monitored; and many other aspects of remaking the eastern part of Europe touched upon in Part II. In such a broader tackling of the full range of issues at hand, a coherent and well-defined assistance program could play a critical role in improving security and confidence on the part of economic agents and in seeing to it that proper adjustments are introduced when the original planks are no longer realistic, for whatever reason. If feasible, all this could be poured into a mold for "a second recovery program for Europe" (see UNECE 1991b, 1992, 1993). Particularly if the first impetus to such a program could emanate from within the transition economies, were based on exploring fully all opportunities for regional cooperation, and then coordinated with the committed participation of the special organ entrusted with delivering assistance, the potential for success could provide the psychological booster shot to impart an élan to transformation policies, thus offsetting the presently prevailing ills – fatigue, disappointment, and impatience. It would be an impetus that the transition economies by themselves, regardless of the assistance mustered, cannot plausibly mobilize.

It would, of course, be foolhardy to count on any such organ being in a position to reach optimal results or to expect it to concertize completely the various recipients and donors involved. There would not even be any reason for a high degree of centralization. What is primarily required is commitment, coordination, and cooperation. A credible organ entrusted with these tasks, I submit, would muster the support of existing multilateral organs for their instrumental value within their respective fields of authority. It should also be able to persuade bilateral donors that assistance efforts minimize duplication, be targeted at the core supply problems in transition economies, be appropriately direct for relieving these bottlenecks, and be made available on a schedule and in a form most conducive to implementing the agreed transformation agenda. Furthermore, the organ should be able to induce national policy makers to assist in tailoring each country's program according to local conditions and to extract as much group cooperation as economically meaningful and politically feasible.

Section 7: Shaping the EU's prospective relationship with transition economies

Wherever the EU's eastern borders may eventually be drawn, coming to a constructive relationship with the continent's eastern half is integral to the EU's

Europeanness. That consists for now of a set of countries – the ten with a Europe Agreement – that may eventually join the EU; another set – Albania, the successor States of Yugoslavia other than Slovenia, and perhaps some of the western CIS States (such as Belarus, Moldova, and Ukraine) – that in some distant future too may be adjudicated as intrinsically entitled to work toward EU membership, if so desired; and a third set – Russia and the Asian, probably the Caucasian, and perhaps other CIS States – that will not qualify for membership because they are not European or may not wish to seek EU membership for their own reasons. All are presently benefiting from one EU assistance project or another. It would be useful to streamline these programs in such a way that they form an inherent component of the constructive relationship on the continent yet to be worked out.

In working toward a useful preaccession strategy for the ten privileged transition economies, three aspects of such a coherent policy package deserve to be highlighted: economic benefits, gaining greater security in various dimensions, and strengthening and maintaining economic and political credibility for implementing the drawn-out transition agenda. These have been the root aspirations of the transition economies from the moment they declared themselves keen on entering the EU. Among the economic benefits to be expected, transfer gains can be separated from other economic advantages. There is good reason to believe that the transfer bonus will not materialize soon. But economic advantages from liberalized trade and capital movements can be quite substantial for the economies in transition and, on balance, significant for present EU members as well, regardless of the institutional and conceptual assistance frameworks envisaged; labor mobility opens a different set of questions, however. Those beneficial channels deserve to be accommodated soonest, especially to solidify the foundations for sustainable catch-up growth in the transition economies.

But these gains are not simply there for the taking. Successful transformation in the eastern part of Europe hinges critically on the ability of these economies to penetrate world markets on a competitive basis. That depends importantly, but only in part, on the domestic economic restructuring under way in these economies, including the policies, instruments, and institutional supports on which the transformation's successes and failures are predicated. It is also a function of the buoyancy of world markets and their openness to fair competition on a predictable basis. Much remains to be done in the latter respect. Some efforts have been made, notably in western Europe, to eliminate altogether discriminatory trade restrictions and indeed to grant these countries in turn discriminatory preferences. But more could and should be done by restoring and reinforcing basic elements of a multilateral trading world. Furthermore, trade can be hindered or promoted by various measures, many of which are not immediately identifiable – the intransparent, more qualitative NTBs in particular.

In addition to seeking trade and other economic gains, the transition economies also desire a greater degree of stability and security, and indeed credibility, for their ongoing transformation programs. These aspirations definitely should not be disregarded. Considerable benefits, including increased security and policy credibility, as well as economic gains, can be safeguarded without rushing into hasty accession negotiations. Accordingly, a coherent preaccession strategy reaching well beyond the EU's assistance efforts mustered since 1989 deserves to be worked out already prior to the start of accession negotiations. The more strategic approach advocated here could have a major impact on strengthening expectations both in and toward the transition economies. This should be supported by well-targeted assistance on a much larger scale than has been forthcoming since 1989. Major new funding might be welcome for some economies, of course. But it would not be necessary for the most credible candidates. I contend, then, that major gains can be made for very little, if any, extra budgetary expenses by the EU.

Arguably the most important benefit of such an approach would be confidence building. Expectations of policies and their likely outcomes are very important in stances that economic actors, investors in particular, take. Enterprises in the transition economy and potential foreign investors should be more confident about the success of the transition process and of the country's eventual EU entry if such a process were credibly elaborated in a coherent preaccession strategy, one that is furthermore steered in a confidence-inspiring mode. If expectations of households in the transition economies stabilize around steady gains in their levels of living, however slowly accruing at the beginning, the social and political pressures on governments to abandon or dilute their transformation programs will be much reduced, thus freeing up valuable resources in strapped civil services to get on with the tasks at hand rather than finding ways and means of acting in a more cautious, at times even surreptitious, manner. A well-organized and strong commitment by the EU to such a strategy, possibly around principles and components that I have detailed elsewhere (Brabant 1996, pp. 212ff.), could therefore play an important role in supporting and strengthening the credibility of transformation policies. Underlying this advocacy is the contention that the EU constitutes a natural center for exerting "subtle" pressures on the transition economies perhaps in exchange for a commitment to broader assistance from and collaboration with the EU. This could most fruitfully be formulated to shore up and impart a new impetus to intragroup cooperation, while smoothing whatever rough edges there are for now, linked directly to the integration of these countries into the global community in general and into "Europe" in particular. Providing support for intragroup cooperation through financial transfers, macroeconomic surveillance, and diverse forms of technical assistance would in and of itself inject a crucial measure of credibility into intragroup cooperation at this juncture, prior to merging more fully into the EU.

Adherents of the notion that it is desirable to foster only the purest market relations may object to such "intervention," particularly since it emanates from the outside. Naturally I disagree with this stance in principle. On reasonably realistic grounds and historical experience, the advocated measures can be considered an integral component of good regional governance and indeed of just plain good policy making in the economies in transition. Positive intervention where warranted by the adversities and distortions of the transitions, not to forget by the various instances of EU discrimination in favor of the eastern economies, could be particularly appropriate in the context of easing these countries into the EU. Of course, such should not even be contemplated simply for the benefit of reviving intragroup cooperation. Rather, it could be an integral element in the strategy for strengthening democracy and market-based decision making in the eastern part of Europe. It would play a similarly seminal role in preparing these countries for moving eventually more fully into the global economy in general and the EU in particular to obtain especially economic security, but also some measure of political and military security.

It should be clear, however, that such an assistance package, including its domestic requirements, cannot be foisted upon any transition economy. But unwillingness to cooperate on the latter's part would diminish its claim for assistance beyond the level that the EU may wish to safeguard for reasons of "national security." This approach too forms part of good regional governance and of what is required to facilitate, not to delay, the entry of economies in transition into the EU. The EU leadership's attention in particular should be better attuned to what can and should be accomplished in terms of forging a more realistic rapprochement with the economies in transition than what has been undergirded since 1989. This is quite germane to facilitating another enlargement.

The suggested proposal is not, of course, prescriptive. Nor does it aim at centralizing all western assistance under the EU's umbrella. There is just no need for that. Quite the contrary: An articulated strategy that is comprehensive, well coordinated, and credible is required. By leading up to the accession of the transition economies with a Europe Agreement, but not necessarily at the same date, such a program will, in and of itself, act as a coordinating mechanism. Other partners in global cooperation are likely to pay attention to the program's components of direct interest to them and their repercussions. Since they support the basic objectives of the transition process anyway, they should see the advantage of orienting their own efforts to its basic structure, if only because the latter forms the *raison d'être* for the preaccession strategy to begin with. As a result, rather than aggravating bureaucratic turf battles, wasting assistance, or creating overlap in different approaches, such a coherent program would provide the basis for a more spontaneous format of coordination among the various actors assisting the transition process and preparing the EU for enlargement.

There are at least two other groups of economies in transition of strategic significance to the EU as a whole or to selected members (Austria, Finland, Germany, and Sweden in particular). One consists of Albania, the successor States of Yugoslavia other than Slovenia, and perhaps some of the CIS States. Presumably after suitable socioeconomic restructuring and the normalization of relations in the Balkans, these countries too will eventually seek EU entry, and be allowed to do so, once the next round(s) of enlargement will have been concluded. The obstacles to recovery and sustainable growth that these economies face are quite different from those prevailing in the EU candidates.

In the Balkans, several successor States of Yugoslavia have an immediate need for societal reconstruction and basic development as well as for making headway with the rudiments of a coherent transformation agenda (notably stabilization, privatization, fiscal reform, governance issues, financial markets, and restructuring). Their potential for being brought under the EU's umbrella as full partners is therefore latent at this stage. But at some future point these countries too will, on present policy stances, hope to become credible candidates for entry. In that perspective, it might be useful for the EU to think more strategically about how best it can earmark available funds, even if only from within existing assistance budgets, and target them at expediting economic recovery in the area; establishing a democratic political culture with at least minimal respect for human rights; accelerating the sociopolitical and economic transformation processes, including the role of the state and the public sector in economic affairs, in such a way that the countries will be able to deal constructively with the prospect of eventually merging with the EU; and regaining sustainable economic growth with substantial structural change over the next several years. In terms of economic development, these countries are now even less capable than the present candidates for EU membership of engaging in open competition in the EU's single market and of jumping into the virtuous growth circle around vibrant intra-industry trade. A priority therefore is to construct programs that contain the risk of peripheralization.

There are other economies in transition, notably in the CIS, that are unlikely (especially those that can hardly be classified as European) or unwilling for their own reasons (for example, Russia) to consider membership. Especially the western countries – notably Belarus, Moldova, Russia, and Ukraine – are strategically located *vis-à-vis* the EU. Some are large and potentially significant trading partners for the EU. All have been benefiting from some types of EU assistance, notably via TACIS. Streamlining the present assistance approach toward these countries into a constructive partnership for years to come can be easily justified: The EU has fundamental interests in commercial, environmental, human rights, health, foreign policy, cultural, transportation, security, and related matters at stake that cannot be ignored.

The tasks at hand in forging such a relationship are in some ways comparable to those advocated for the second group of countries. At the same time their nature differs. Of course, if there were to be any likelihood of some of the western CIS States being eventually considered for accession, and some like Moldova and Ukraine have already underlined their desire to be so chosen, those countries could be dealt with separately from the other CIS States that cannot or do not wish to be so treated. Comprehensive trade and cooperation agreements are probably the most useful vehicle for tackling the core issues at stake in a first revamping of their relations with the EU. These also seem to offer the most suitable way of assisting the western CIS States over the next several years. But eventually more substantial assistance may be required to check the decline in support for economic transformation. The latter could not but exert negative repercussions on other reforms, notably in the political and strategic arenas. Indeed, comprehensive, well-targeted assistance might even be warranted to ensure that the lukewarm transformations that have kept these countries on a path of socioeconomic decline for all too long now will not further deteriorate. It should certainly not be allowed to hollow out whatever penchant for pluralistic democracy and market-based resource allocation might still be rescued and strengthened, if only to overcome the prevailing state of vacillating indecisiveness. Once such a recovery path will be within reach, the scenario of moving toward the kinds of support programs just outlined for the Balkan countries, suitably interpreted, could again be seriously contemplated.

In one way or another, then, all of these arrangements will involve working out to mutual satisfaction some degree of preferential access to the EU's market and to its financial resources, possibly at the explicit expense of other beneficiaries of preferential arrangements with the EU. Their impacts on EU members and present beneficiaries of the various preferential arrangements will need to be reconciled with the EU's economic and other interests in formalizing relations with both groups of transition economies. For countries remaining outside the EU framework altogether or that will conceivably enter into it only in a very remote future, the consequences for the present EU arrangements will naturally be less severe and daunting than those that may arise in fusing the other economies in transition into the EU framework as full members. Just the same, the EU can hardly afford to ignore them, if only for its own interests.

Conclusions

Relying on logic as well as experience since 1989, I have made a case for redirecting assistance efforts from the global community. The repercussions would not solely be in terms of the volume of earmarked funds. Certainly their quality would undergo considerable change. Also the institutional arrangement for delivery of such assistance would have to be redesigned to ensure a much more intrusive kind of participation in the deliberations about and the implementation of transformation agendas. These observations apply perhaps even more in evaluating the assistance that the EU has been orchestrating since 1989, especially in view of the fact that some transition economies will in the future become members, even though they are not particularly well prepared; others are likely to seek a similar status, although their ability to function constructively within the single market is even less assured; and the relationship with the remaining transition economies further east should also be forged into a strategic approach to remaking Europe as a whole.

The point of all this, of course, should be in part enabling most of the transition economies to regain growth and to engage in catch-up with levels of living, productivity, wealth, incomes, and so on that are thought to be "normal" for reasonably mature market economies. Whereas international assistance can be instrumental in identifying such a catch-up trajectory, and indeed in jumping onto it and walking along it for some time, the prime responsibility for doing so rests with those managing the transformation agendas. The core questions at stake I take up in the final chapter.

12

SUSTAINABILITY OF THE TRANSFORMATION

The *annus mirabilis* was inaugurated with fairly well-defined goals: pluralistic democracy and market-based resource allocation as basic frameworks permitting sustained catch-up with average levels of development in western Europe over time. This certainly applied to the eastern European countries, including the Baltic States. In light of the way in which the breakup of the Soviet Union occurred, the at times half-hearted efforts to elicit meaningful changes in the CIS States, and the contradictions in the courses pursued in all too many, one should be careful in proclaiming the above twin goals as applicable to *all* transition economies. One must furthermore reckon with varying degrees of backtracking and vacillation in several countries. But there is little doubt that managers of nearly all transition economies are motivated by concerns about, in the first instance economic, modernization. True, egregious corruption, graft, extortion, theft of state assets, nepotism, power hunger, and other negative, some outrightly criminal, attributes of the behavior of the managers of the transition and their immediate subordinates in all too many transition economies cast a pall on that purported motivation. Yet I stand by it. In the more western of these countries the model is well *on its way* to reaching the level of maturity achieved by the average western European country, but still removed from that coveted state; for the truly less developed of the successor States, and some others (Albania, Cambodia, China, Laos, Mongolia, and Vietnam), however, the prime policy issue revolves more around how best to engineer a takeoff that may eventually pave the way for steady modernization than concerns about how best to catch up in record time with, say, levels of living in western Europe.

This chapter elaborates on the notion of modernization in the context of the wholesale transformation, and in some cases only less-focused transitions, under way in the eastern part of Europe with some marginal comments on the other erstwhile state-socialist countries. I deal in particular with its economic support base. I first sketch the state of economic, political, and social affairs around the more common evaluation of successful transformation as a first stab at evaluating whether progress is being recorded. Next I consider some of the putative policy errors committed since 1989 with or without the support of outside assistance. Thereafter I clarify what I mean by modernization as applicable to the various groups of transition economies, but especially the more advanced ones. Then I sketch what is required by way of solid foundations for pursuing successfully a sustainable growth trajectory. The distinction between catch-up modernization and basic development is drawn as a prelude to discussing in the ensuing two sections the historical experience with modernization of the developed countries and the catch-up successful transformation of the east and southeast Asian NIEs in particular. Before concluding, I identify some of the policy options within the ambit of transition managers with a view to moving onto a "good" growth trajectory, one that once achieved is sustainable.

Section 1: Successful transformation – its meanings

Many claims have been made for the "success" of transformation policies. Most refer to the results of stabilization, liberalization, and privatization, and in some cases of institution building and the social safety net. It is a paradox of sorts, though, that the prime motivation of the seismic shocks of "1989" – regaining sustainable growth – has been all but removed from the debating table on success and its criteria. In this, crucial aspects of maintaining sociopolitical consensus throughout the unavoidable hardships and of constructing the institutions of the market necessary to reap the benefits of the "holy trinity" have not received their full due (see Chapter 8). This is doubly surprising for the two mentioned transformation building blocks are vital to maintaining policy credibility, not only *vis-à-vis* the domestic electorate, and to forging ahead with rounding off the framework to reap the holy trinity's benefits.

One cannot but be bewildered by the varying assessments of success, many couched in rather odd terms, that observers have been issuing. Consider stabilization: A marked reduction in inflation but still well at double-digit level, the elimination of the shortage economy (on the supply side) but with many goods disappearing from markets, a movement toward more general access to foreign exchange, the reduction in budget and current-account imbalances, a rise in exports, and other features in some combinations have been viewed as marking successful transition. All too often, these are seen in a highly partial perspective citing one or a few of these elements and treated with a terminology whose meaning is kept deliberately obscure, perhaps because of the perceived need for a positive appraisal (Willett and Al-Marhubi 1994). Neither is helpful in a dispassionate discourse as distinct from imparting in the short run positive psychological incentives. Even so, output growth in and of itself cannot be a good success indicator, if only in view of the huge production and income losses sustained since 1989, and in some even well before that. The pace has to be strong, bolstered by capital formation in activities that signal decisive structural change and shore up prospects for sustained expansion in the years ahead. In that light, one should not deviate from defining successful economic transformation over the medium run – gradually, but steadily, catching up with the more advanced countries – in terms of indicators of positive growth, its sustainability over the longer haul, and the ability of a country to bolster levels of living over a protracted period of time.

Important improvements, veritable strides indeed, have recently been booked in some transition economies. This cannot be denied. These gains deserve to be stressed but realistically. Indeed, the fundamentals for most economies remain woefully inadequate, rather depressing realities, and the outlook for any quick improvement, whence an impulse for sustainable growth may be imparted, is not particularly encouraging. For one thing, inflation is still double-digit, in all too many cases running at several percentage points per month. This stems in part from budget imbalances that are still sizable in too many transition economies, largely for lack of an adequate tax base and effective collection policies, while entitlement expenditures and debt-service obligations are generally rising. In several transition economies, these imbalances continue to be financed by other means than recourse to capital markets, either because they do not exist or they are still primitive and incomplete. Also, current-account imbalances in several countries are large and the prospects of closing the external gap on a predictable basis via sustainable long-term capital inflows, preferably in the form of FDI, are not particularly comforting. In addition, export gains continue to be booked overwhelmingly by firms in flux – really under threat of survival and divestment – for products with which these economies cannot realistically hope to merge themselves into the virtuous network of rapidly expanding intra-industry trade.

Furthermore, measured as well as real levels of unemployment are substantial in most countries, leading to very large economic, political, psychological, and social costs. Indeed, gains in income, wealth, and welfare for broad layers of the population are meager at best. For all too many the transformation has entailed a marked deterioration in real incomes and levels of living, material as well as otherwise, pushing many marginally below the poverty line. For all the dynamism of the new private sector, in most economies there continues to be substantial room for raising saving and channeling most of it into productive investment. The insufficiencies derive in part from limping financial intermediation. It also stems from the substantial uncertainty, thus justifying high risk premia, which deter long-term productive investment. Many other less bright features of the transition could be cited, even without delving into the noneconomic, especially the political and social, aspects of transformation policies. Sharply reduced social security, marked income and wealth dispersion, pauperization, deterioration in education and science, exodus of artists and scientists, falling health standards, and rising organized crime all offer food for thought about how best to qualify "successful transformation."

That said, I certainly do not want to denigrate the unquestionable achievements of many transition economies, including growth in the 3 to 7 percent range since about 1994 (but much higher and for a longer time in the Asian countries). But one must harbor misgivings about the widespread positive appraisals when the fundamentals for sustainable recovery and catch-up modernization are still quite shaky. Constraints on external payments in a number of transition

461

economies for reasons of both supply and demand, large capital inflows in some countries that may or may not be sustainable but are complicating monetary control in some, and continuing difficulties with lowering inflation while restoring balanced budgets in most suggest that policy makers of these countries are well advised to persist in their transformation efforts; but they may have to fine-tune in depth and breadth the relevant agenda for action. Unless domestic absorption can be shored up by modernizing capital expenditures financed largely from domestic savings, retained earning in the first place, it is difficult to see how these economies could jump onto the virtuous bandwagon of intra-industry trade.

Elsewhere, including most of the CIS and several Balkan States, the problems ahead are far more daunting; this applies *mutatis mutandis* too to the Baltic States that have recently exhibited some measure of control over inflation and proper exchange-rate management, so that these parameters can play a more appropriate role in resource allocation by independent economic agents. Most of the CIS countries may see their recession coming to an end and reach some positive growth by 1998. Until uncertainty about crucial markers of the wide-ranging societal reform programs will have been removed, credible economic stabilization can be enforced, and decisive measures activated to begin with the restructuring of these, in some respects footloose, economies, a sharp improvement in their economic fortunes is unlikely to materialize soon.

The transitions to date exhibit major differences in scope, depth, and range. Even so, the time frame of even the most modest blueprint on desirable transition policies, including institutional modifications, is now widely recognized to stretch far into the future, its duration ranging from one to several decades. Even in the most optimistic case, attaining a functioning polity around a reasonably behaved market economy is far off. It is more distant yet than the advocates of the spontaneous emergence of the market framework, and all necessary adjustments taking their cue from there, had erroneously assumed to be "within reach" at the transition's inception. In the process, it was fundamentally forgotten that what we call a "market" is not in fact a ready-made institution. Rather, it is no more than a reification of a set of behavioral and cultural relations existing at a given point in time, as a rule after having crystallized from protracted interactions, among economic agents in tne course of which durable ties become knit. Furthermore, the transitions are likely to last far longer for most of the CIS States than, say, for the central European countries. While many arduous tasks still lie ahead, the latter countries have already set important steps in the direction of macroeconomic stabilization and of enacting policy measures that will in time result in significant structural change.

Much remains to be done, however, before any of these economies will be able to embark on a solid path of self-sustainable growth. *A fortiori* the tasks ahead in countries such as in many of the CIS and Balkan States, where transition policies remain the subject of acute sociopolitical debate, are even more daunting. It would be unrealistic to expect that these complicated matters will be resolved quickly or that the transition processes of these countries can be completed any time sooner than now appears to be the case for, say, most central European countries and Slovenia.

How can one analytically and empirically come to grips with this conundrum? This is a matter for which I can at best hope to scratch the surface here. The contrasting positions that I have briefly depicted should ideally be combined into one coherent aggregate appraisal of the transformation policies in any one or a group of transition economies. The problem is familiar: How can one appropriately aggregate qualitative or quantitative measures that lack a common denominator? Among the many success indicators, a resumption of strong growth at moderate levels of inflation based largely on solid investment financed primarily from domestic savings in "modernizing activities," while far from perfect, is one criterion on which I place a premium. Everything else can then be discussed on their own merits. This offers a compromise on transformation programs whose appraisal is "caught between the faith of those who foresee their ultimate effects and the skepticism of those who experience only their immediate consequences" (Bresser Pereira, Maravall, and Przeworski 1993, p. 3).

Incidentally, I would also ascribe considerable importance to two other variables in evaluating the success of a transformation program. One is the progress achieved with the movement toward a stable, functioning democracy. That is a political system in which protection of material welfare against the transformation's burden – in terms of level, speed, as well as distribution over social groups – is accommodated in a consensual manner (see Chapter 8). It is also one that makes full use of democratic institutions in the formulation and implementation of transformation policies with a view to bolstering societal well-being, materially and otherwise. Hence progress toward the construction of these institutions as part of building civil society is of the utmost importance. A civil society is one in which the state can act with authority on the strength of the electorate's confidence. Powers to control corruption, crime, nepotism, insider trading, and many other odious aspects of the transition (see Chapter 8) must be available or built up. A lawless society, even with successful material growth being shared, cannot embody the success that the transitions set out to achieve. Also, a fair division of the benefits of growth, so that egregious income and wealth dispersions will not in due course tarnish the other characteristics of success, figures among my preferences in ascribing success to transformation policies. However, for lack of space I shall not venture into those contentious territories here.

I advocate the above more comprehensive approach to assessing success in transition economies in particular because the holy trinity of the "Washington consensus" is unlikely to lead to the kind of success coveted at the transition's inception. Its policy relevance is entirely predicated on the assumption that policy makers must quickly put in place the framework that unfetters economic agents, thus enabling them to exploit prevailing comparative advantages (chiefly low labor costs but in some countries also cheap raw materials). This is presumed to lead to "high-quality growth" (Camdessus 1995a, b) in purely hortatory fashion (Bresser Pereira, Maravall, and Przeworski 1993, pp. 203ff.). Unfortunately, neoclassical economics has next to nothing to say about how to resume growth or about the characteristics of a desirable growth trajectory. Neither has the libertarian approach, as demonstrated in many countries since the 1970s, though it may have contributed to stabilizing economies, empowering economic agents, and freeing up the environment from excessive regulation. Liberalization has certainly not imparted a major new impetus to productivity, enabled developing countries as a whole to catch up with the industrialized countries, or facilitated the expeditious restoration of sustainable growth in transition economies, if only because of the apparently sizable opportunities for catching up with developed market economies. If anything, the income gap between groupings of and within countries has further widened, at times exceeding the socially tolerable. The evidence that pursuing the holy trinity generates growth is in any case weak: Many developing countries have had to wait many years before gains in average per capita income became tangible, and then only in some countries; the other success indicators mentioned do not crop up at all.

A wholly different spin on the transformation agenda has been wrought by those who contend that liberalization (and implicitly libertarianism) is needed not only for its own sake, but also to whittle the overbearing role of the inherited state essentially to that of night watchman, with perhaps some modification for the social safety net. By utilizing the opportunities provided by the "extraordinary politics" offered as a result of the transition's eruption to destroy explicitly the venal elements of the state, the better-motivated policy makers can embark on the construction of democracy and a market economy (for an extreme view, see Åslund 1992, 1993; 1995a, b; Åslund, Boone, and Johnson 1996). Note that this tacitly *assumes* that governance capabilities in the transition economies are presently absent and that there is no point in seeking to acquire such capabilities. Likewise it subsumes that good governance capabilities emerge spontaneously from the transformation processes instigated through "shock therapy" or "pre-emptive strikes." Needless to say, all this is rather implausible. Even a cursory acquaintance with the outcome of the policies pursued by developed and developing market economies since the early 1970s should have imparted knowledge thereof. Also the core errors of the transition policies pursued to date should have elicited a different stance.

Section 2: Putative transition fallacies

Transition managers and their advisers have been blamed for many errors. Several can be dismissed on the ground that the options chosen were not compared with those available when choices had to be made (Balcerowicz 1993, 1994). Charging those in power who have failed to move ahead with a solid transformation agenda with dereliction is fine in my book, but that is not really critiquing the transition or transformation agenda. However, holding those in charge of transforming countries responsible for not having temporized in areas where going slow was not an option, as in taming runaway inflation, is logically incorrect. A careful dissection is therefore recommended.

2.1 – Policy advisory services, misjudgments, prejudices, and responsibility

Among the options that can logically be challenged two stand out (see Chapter 3). One category comprises policy matters where moving rapidly was simply not a realistic option (such as institution building). Charges that this may not have been the most desirable path to pursue must be phrased in terms of delaying moving ahead, or attempts at great leaps forward, while disregarding inter-dependence with policy actions that take time. The other group refers to options that permitted moving more rapidly as a rational policy choice (such as full external liberalization). Charges in this case can be levied, if at all, only in terms of what the sociopolitical consensus could have tolerated and the economy, and society as a whole, constructively digested, as well as in terms of ignoring interdependence with other components of the transformation agenda. Only a thorough acquaintance with conditions prevailing in the country about to embark on transformation can lead to realistic appraisals of policy choices with their varying advantages and drawbacks spelled out.

The unprecedented "1989 events" and their aftermath encouraged a vast number of academic economists and national, regional, and international organ-izations into taking some activist stance. Some did so largely as an intellectual exercise, using rigorous modeling that may or may not be relevant to the transi-tion's circumstances. If properly understood, such experiments are innocuous for policy making. Others, however, engaged themselves actively, at times with the missionary zeal of a convinced *agitprop* operator, in shaping the agenda for incisive transformation – Boycko, Shleifer, and Vishny (1995, p. 143) even advocate that to "be effective, aid simply has to be political"! Many came from mainstream economics or institutions imbued with orthodox demand-management doctrines and highly limited capacities for addressing the peculiar circumstances in which the eastern part of Europe found itself (see Chapter 11). Few of those embarking on "transition work" had any prior experience with or knowledge about these countries. Most were not prepared to invest time and effort to acquaint themselves with the "initial conditions" in these countries, forgetting that in real life there cannot be new beginnings without continuity. Not a few came to the issue with preconceived notions, oftentimes steeped in ivory-tower neoclassical economics or the virulent neoliberalism of the 1980s. Few of this clerisy had real-life experience in policy making or advisory services in situations that compared with those prevailing in the eastern part of Europe. Reductivism made them pontificate on all but irrelevant "best practice" policies. Only a few had ever thought in earnest about the more philosophical and historical preconditions for some of the foundations of their analyses. None of this was particularly helpful.

Finally, it is one of the great ironies of our age that the liberal theocracy counseling transition managers into proceeding rapidly and holistically for the sake of democracy and free markets, as well as some managers embracing such precepts themselves, have presented their arguments in a thoroughly autocratic, often arrogant fashion, suggesting demagogically the need for a "bold preemptive strike" for "there is no alternative" (Åslund, Boone, and Johnson 1996). This is odd: Even a cursory picture of a coherent transformation agenda shows otherwise (see Chapter 3). Any acquaintance with democracy or real markets would have readily demonstrated that, perhaps barring war and revolution, options are as a rule always available; very often the more temperate course through consensual politics is followed. There is hence truly "no other way" to well-punctuated and modulated gradualism.

Being critical of some policy measures properly conceived within those two areas for choice is one thing. Cogently blaming the responsible party is something else (compare, for example, Camdessus 1995a, b with his 1997). It is almost impossible to identify precisely what kind of policy advice or view was issued with some determination at which point of time on behalf of one institution or another, including domestic policy making. Particularly in the case of outside advisers, such an imputation presumes that their argument emanated from an "institutional" culture as distinct from "an institutional view" based on the culture, ideas, precepts, and values of top management of the assisting organ (Williams 1996). One must also identify the extent to which especially domestic decision makers understood the advice. This is difficult. It might be easier to ascertain whether the counseled policy was taken to heart and whether subsequent modifications were introduced that, in fact, broke with one or more of the premises on which the original advice had been predicated. That approach must overcome the obstacles of "learning" on the part of advisers and those being advised, as well as of changing circumstances. Perhaps a thorough exegesis of the policy advice to individual economies throughout the transition might be revealing. But such is beyond the scope of this monograph. I therefore focus on generic policies with a few illustrations.

2.2 – Dubious domestic policy stances

The shortcomings in the design, implementation, monitoring, assessment, and fine-tuning of the transformation agendas that I prefer to underline follow essentially from the fundamental precepts elaborated upon in Part II. I single out eight areas where "better" options could have been embraced in countries possessing minimally credible capacities for governance, or where such human capital could have been readily acquired, if sought, in spite of the convoluted sociopolitical situation. Closer attention to the initial conditions and resources at hand, to the prior experiences in managing major economic change in general, and to the ambitions of moving toward reasonably functioning market systems would have been instructive.

Arguably the most serious managerial problem arose from the assumption that the institutions required for the market to function properly could be established quickly, almost in a simple technocratic mode, hence that the role of the state even *during* the transition process itself should be compressed to an irreducible minimum. This argument is fallacious. It lacks an historical as well as a logical rationale. Its foundations rest on the religious belief in unbridled neoliberalism propped up by axiomatic neoclassical economics (Soros 1997). Not only was this "vision" wrong; adhering to it weakened the very platform for pursuing best-practice transition policies. The critical role of good governance, even in economic affairs, and of steering the transition to a pluralistic market-based economy was not sufficiently appreciated even in economies invested with the political authority to reasonably oversee these convoluted processes.

Second, although one can sympathize with the massive reaction against the thoroughly overbearing role formerly played by the Party (Kornai 1990a, 1992), assuming that all those who had collaborated with the pretransition rulers were tainted, hence unable to constructively participate in the creation of the new society, was a sweeping, if convenient excuse. This had important repercussions, such as for divestment of state assets, transforming SOEs, and protecting assets for objects that could not be divested quickly. It also diverted attention from the need to build up new public-sector capacities to discharge minimal tasks, let alone to engage professionally in the "destruction" of state assets and the subsequent "creation" of new assets. Hoping that this could be greased through massive inflows of FDI was a serious myth as FDI does not lead reforms (see Chapter 10). Likewise flourishing SMEs need an enabling environment. In other words, liberalism simply dismissed governance and state intervention as fundamentally misguided collectivism as an act of faith, not of fact. As a result, the state deserted society. It failed to address crucial issues pertaining to the technical failures of markets, particularly while they are being erected, and of how best to meet the evolving sociopolitical concerns, not as a reaction but as a proactive policy.

Third, privatization of state assets has been pursued as a *de facto* industrial policy in a passive mode, even though in virtually all transition economies the adoption of any type of industrial policy (or "central planning") was overtly spurned. It would have been pivotal to determine which existing SOEs should survive, in whole or in part, and which should not. The leadership's passivity has been very pronounced in terms of governance requirements for managing the divestment process and protecting state-owned assets while fostering their best-practice use, either on a temporary basis or as a lasting public-sector reform. Even in terms of building up capacity for dealing effectively with assistance providers – formulating appropriate requests for assistance and seeing to their swift implementation – acting on the go took precedence over building up a coherent framework via a more activist role of the state. There was initially too much emphasis on getting rid of "old style" management and turning assets over to "the people" in a quixotic quest for popular capitalism. The need for overcoming intricate principal–agent problems was simply not appreciated. This weak control over assets that the state ultimately owns has enabled many SOEs to protect themselves by adopting a thoroughly short-term horizon, resulting in decapitalization of the SOE particularly for assets that are viable in a longer perspective. It has also contributed to the government's deferral of explicit decisions regarding the fate of many SOEs, if only to stave off massive unemployment or contain significant regional imbalances.

Fourth, perhaps the most paradoxical state of affairs emerged from the presumed need to free up the nonstate sector as much as possible from adversities, and to turn these responsibilities over to the state. Claims, usually lodged one at a time, that the state should now be made responsible, among others, for bad bank and SOE debts, for cleaning up the environment, for retraining the labor force, for instituting a comprehensive social-safety net, for compensating former owners, and so on are simply not credible, if only because the required financial means are not available. Such a policy stance ignores the fundamental incompatibility between allotting to the state only a minimal role in economic affairs and, at the same time, offloading onto it liabilities that, by necessity, will force the state either to violate budgetary discipline or to compromise the social consensus (see Chapter 9).

Fifth, the need to rectify fiscal policies at the earliest opportunity was not sufficiently appreciated in the design of the transformation agendas, in part because budgets turned paradoxically to a surplus during the first months of the transition. The special reasons for this one-off situation were not well understood. Policy makers and their advisers appeared not to realize that it would be very hard to finance even a scaled-down role for government in socioeconomic affairs over the longer haul at a time of severe economic recession. Budget deficits have quickly become the hallmark of most transition economies, although at times masked through creative accounting. Continued government deficit while the financial infrastructure to mobilize resources in a noninflationary manner remains inadequate, has kept the pace of inflation abnormally high. It has also crowded out private investment, thereby impeding recovery.

Sixth, the full range of options for liberalizing domestic and external markets was never entertained. Radical price and foreign-exchange reforms by themselves do not set the stage for the market to take off, if only because so many of the institutions for it to function properly are at best *in statu nascendi*; likewise for temporizing with such changes. In the process, the domestic slump and even premature foreign competition may destroy valuable domestic assets. There are tradeoffs here that policy makers should carefully scrutinize.

Seventh, initially one of the least appreciated features of transition was the essential role of a functioning financial infrastructure, and the need to mobilize resources even under the prevailing economic depression. The latter must be integral to domestic liberalization to pave the way for new small private firms. This can be established only in an evolutionary mode. It requires first and foremost basic commercial-banking services (see Chapter 7). Far too much emphasis has been placed on the need to develop more sophisticated aspects of the financial infrastructure, such as stock markets. Also too much faith has been placed on foreign banking as a substitute for the limping domestic financial sector.

Finally, economic, political, and social uncertainty during the transformation has been very pronounced. There are all kinds of reasons, domestic as well as foreign, for this state of affairs. Many could probably not have been avoided given the context of the transformations. But the depth and breadth of others could have been contained if policy makers had proceeded with greater circumspection – not necessarily gradualism – in introducing societal experiments of questionable validity in logic, in intrinsic merit, or when seen against the backdrop of pertinent policy experience (see Chapter 3).

2.3 – Questionable external policy stances

Aside from the beneficial economic effects of external liberalization, other considerations have informed the transformation of trade and payment systems. These include ideology, politics, security concerns, and misperceptions of the country's genuine interests in "merging into the global economy." Only with those elements can one attempt to grasp the determined destruction of CMEA; the desire to move closer to the EC/EU soonest and to the IEOs without negotiating any transition regime; and the expectation that massive FDI would reignite economic expansion for the reasons cited in Chapter 10.

First, regarding management of the exchange rate and the exchange regime, the initial devaluation, possibly through free floating, has invariably been too large, hence more destructive than warranted. Treating the exchange rate as a nominal anchor (perhaps in conjunction with nominal wages or targets for monetary aggregates) of domestic transformation turned out to be self-defeating in all too many instances. Such an anchor may have been useful for a brief period of time, if only because it created temporary protection! When the nominal exchange rate became a fetish, policy makers lost the anchor's usefulness both for policy purposes and as a psychological prop. In many economies, the marked disparity between relative pretransition and world prices should have signaled the need for substantial adjustments in demand and supply, hence that it would be quite difficult to identify an equilibrium exchange rate. In any case, a fixed nominal rate can only be confidently set when the degree of uncertainty is comparatively small – by the transition's very nature unattainable for some time. Under the circumstances, it was not very wise to rely so heavily on exchange-rate depreciation. Undervaluation has debilitated economic activities that under more normal market conditions – namely those the transition is expected to lead up to – would have been able to survive on their own. Because it offers temporary protection, devaluation may for a while bolster exports, thus imparting the illusion of a successful emergence from recession. It would have been more adroit to establish a modulated *ad valorem* tariff and to manage the nominal and real exchange rates in tandem without necessarily tying one strictly to the other.

A managed nominal rate can impart as much credibility as a fixed commitment to a heavily undervalued one.

Also, most countries have stressed the need to move toward transparent and nearly automatic access to foreign exchange, at least for current commercial transactions by registered businesses, via the exchange-rate mechanism. Those that tried to do so through free floating have found out, like market economies earlier, that the benefits in terms of catalyzing economic confidence are elusive, and that some management must be embraced, perhaps in the context of auctioning off a considerable and growing part of the available foreign exchange. But auctions are useful only if they disclose information otherwise difficult to assemble, whence decision makers may derive an approximate equilibrium rate, which can later be utilized in fashioning the central bank's foreign-exchange policy, for example. This can materialize only when the auction is transparent, involves a sizable portion of foreign-exchange earnings, is not subject to a bewildering variety of confining rules on participation, and is conducted with increasing frequency only during a fairly short period of time (months at most).

Second, relatively low protection, transforming most quotas and related restraints into at most moderate *ad valorem* tariffs, and an exchange rate that helps to maintain equilibrium in the current account over the medium run would have been useful if the economy had flexibly adjusted to new demand and supply schedules. In the absence of an ambient market environment, foreign competition eliminated domestic production without the freed-up resources being mobilized for growth-promoting activities, thereby depressing aggregate economic performance. A more judicious choice of replacing the myriad of protective instruments under planning with *ad valorem* tariffs to be compressed over time in range and incidence might have been more desirable, provided effective temporary income transfers could have been arranged.

Third, in the process of pursuing external liberalization, CMEA ties and interrepublic links within the context of defunct federations were not suitably supported and reformed. Instead they were willfully destroyed or otherwise deliberately undermined for lack of a vision on where these economies ultimately belong and an appreciation of the importance of sustaining such demand and supply links, even if only temporarily. There was never any justification for the outright spurning of such ties, even if international markets for goods and capital had been more buoyant than they have proved to be. Technical alternatives for replacing the CMEA pricing, settlement, and trading regimes were available. Each such suggestion was dismissed with considerable derision (Brabant 1990, 1991a; Köves and Oblath 1994; Terry 1994), largely on political and security grounds. That intragroup ties should not be restored in such a market-driven setting was propounded relying on highly questionable arguments backed up with even worse-founded empiricism purporting to show these countries' near-term destinies in trade and global economic relations. The "support" these stances elicited in the international community, particularly the core assistance providers, can be comprehended only by invoking the kind of ignorance referred to above.

Fourth, to the extent that the destruction of existing ties was motivated by expectations of merging quickly into the global economy with ample access to all markets for goods and capital, this clearly was a mistake. International capital markets are far from integrated, certainly for segments of the world economy that are characterized by considerable economic, political, and social uncertainty. Markets for goods are better integrated. But not everyone can accomplish such integration except for natural resources or goods produced with low-cost labor. Relying on such comparative advantages, however, also tends to lower the chances of catching up with productivity in advanced countries and joining the virtuous circle of intra-industry trade. Few policy makers appear to have cared more than perfunctorily to date about shaping the export offer of their economy in the context of actual or potential competition abroad.

Fifth, many transition leaders, certainly in the more "western" countries, hoped to fuse their economies with the EU's in record time. This was never a promising proposition because the EU is a club with rules and regulations that a would-be member has to abide by to obtain its advantages. These rules and regulations were, and in many respects, continue to be, unsuitable for transition economies. The latter have obtained extraordinary benefits from the club, but undoubtedly far fewer than they had hoped for. Sixth, from the transition's start the promise of liberalization and privatization with basic stabilization focused policy makers' attention on massive inflows of FDI in particular. This demonstrated a very myopic perception of what motivates global capital mobility (see Chapter 5).

Finally, none of the policy makers and their advisers showed much interest for "transitory" regimes in joining the IEOs. This is regrettable. Even well-placed former advisers as well as key negotiators of accession to these regimes are now arguing that there should have been, and still is, room for such arrangements; the case in WTO is argued in Drábek 1996.

2.4 – Policy advisers and questionable rationalizations

Entrusting the task of transferring sizable western assistance for transition economies to the existing IEOs and their consultants has ignored three factors. One has been the vocation of these organs, hence their own financial, organizational, as well as intellectual limits, for engaging in a "new" venture on a massive scale at a record tempo for a highly limited actual or potential membership. Another is that these organs have inadequately heeded legacies of over four decades of state socialism. The *modi operandi* of these organizations were not particularly well suited to designing an appropriate transformation regimen, as distinct from their unquestionable ability to deliver on some ingredients of such a wholesome, balanced menu.

While intellectual debates on the virtues of the market may be useful, when it comes to advising policy makers much too much faith has been placed in the quick emergence of functioning markets and their guidance in modifying economic structures. There never was such flexibility on the supply side. Furthermore, the

471

assistance programs have not sought to establish a consensus in donor countries on what they might be willing to earmark for such aid, in which form, for which recipients, and at what point in time. Neither have they fully respected the "popular mood" on, hence sociopolitical consensus for, feasible transition strategies. Imposing some adviser's heavily front-loaded time preference was arrogant, and far from democratic, at the very least. Finally, the effort has failed, spectacularly in some cases, to deliver this assistance for particular purposes with the degree of efficiency that a more structured assistance strategy ought in principle to have afforded.

Putting it in brief, at least the following lessons could be derived from the stances taken by these outside advisers. First, they have obfuscated the tasks of the transformation by concentrating all too much on pitting the potential virtues of haste against the potential drawbacks of deliberateness, not realizing that a suitable combination of the two in due course becomes unavoidable. But path dependence may then bias the combination stumbled onto by sheer dint of circumstance. Second, some of this opaqueness in the debate has stemmed from the presumption that the essential core of the transformation agenda could be built rapidly or that the foundations could be laid for the subsequent, almost automatic, progression toward a robust, vibrant market economy over a comparatively brief period of time. Much emphasis has been placed on the virtuous growth impetus obtainable from opening up to international competition without assessing when these gains can become available, given prevailing market conditions. There can be no easy solution once the initial conditions for conceptualizing a coherent transformation agenda are duly reflected. Third, this short-termism has also emanated from the institutional thinking in, and the limited capabilities of, IEOs (see Chapter 11) as regards conceptualizing the legacies of state socialism. Of course, in some institutions, the Fund in particular, operations are by their nature designed to be wound down over a comparatively short period of time, perhaps up to three years. That may suffice for correcting external imbalances. But it is woefully short for comprehensive transformation (Berthélemy and Varoudakis 1996) while maintaining high capacity utilization.

Finally, no coherent assistance package as regards the disposition of donors, the real needs of the recipients, and the most efficient delivery of the appropriated funds for the most urgent transformation tasks was ever attempted. It basically remained uncertain when and in which form the committed funds would become available. Often its format was too rigid to be of much practical use. Likewise, the haphazard assessment of the recipients' needs allowed donors to indulge in duplication (such as on privatization), set an agenda for assistance that did not at all blend well with the country's needs (such as the creation of sophisticated stock exchanges), or ignore key matters (such as corporate governance and public-sector behavior) that should have merited priority if only because the transformation agenda must eventually be implemented with some order. Also, the delivery of assistance itself has been a preserve of divided loyalties and bureaucratic fiefdoms in the various agencies.

2.5 – A personal note on errors of omission and commission

This book is not the most suitable outlet for a public confession in the hope of being somehow absolved for my errors of judgment, but I have been a committed observer of the transformation with firm convictions on the broad framework of what needs to be done and on core components of what can realistically be undertaken in the countries for which I claim to possess some expertise. And I have been, albeit on a very modest scale, a sometime adviser – more in the mode of the devil's advocate than someone dispensing persuasive wisdom – in some transition economies under rather peculiar circumstances. Thus after all the above criticism it is only fair that I set out the five basic fallacies of judgment I committed, particularly in the early phases of the transitions.

First, I never imagined that the eastern European societies would be so resilient to massive shocks over a short period of time. Perhaps I did not realize the narcotic effect of a public relations' campaign adroitly stage-managed for a gullible public. By definition, advertising is the art "of selling illusions, the persuasions of the witches' craft" (Bell 1996, p. 38). Proselytizing for the virtues of this or that kind of policy, instrument, or institution stumbled upon the soothing promise of a short, bearable pain soon to be rewarded by the advantages of market-based pluralistic democracy. I failed to realize that this kind of snake oil could hold the masses in thrall or acquiesce them, even with such a profound disruption of existing social institutions, such as trade unions. It is perhaps the stunning effect of a well-swung sledge hammer that made the outcry from a tap on the fingers impossible.

Second, I thought it inconceivable that the massive destruction of liquid wealth in local currency would be taken by the population at large and that it would be willing to have its other wealth redistributed in such an inequitable fashion. Given the long-standing concerns about the omnivalidity of "societal property" and the languor of many citizens for the acquisitive spirit, including the building up of a self-directed wealth portfolio, I thought the citizenry at large would not acquiesce in the massive theft of state property, regardless of subterfuge. At the very least I had anticipated a determined outcry at the polls. Instead, what we have seen is a polite expression of dissatisfaction with yet another batch of public relations' promises taken supinely.

Third, at the outset I was much more skeptical than most observers about the privileged market access that the transition economies would soon obtain, notably in western Europe. Perhaps I had been too optimistic on the economic interlacing of these economies in the CMEA context. I certainly have been taken aback by the irrationality of policy stances regarding regional cooperation. The timidity with which policy makers have subjected themselves to the virus of assistance providers has also surprised me.

Fourth, although I have never carved my faith in politicians in oak, I took the emergence of a new political class in many transition economies to mean that these new brooms would not only sweep the dust of the past from the political corridors, but would also inspire the parliamentary debates with something akin to what Plato's benevolent philosopher king would have cherished. In this I have been sorely disappointed, in spite of my political skepticism.

Finally, for a long time I cherished hopes that the international community in general, and the western European one in particular, would come to the rescue of these economies in at least as magnanimous and imaginative a fashion as the United States did for western Europe after World War II; alas, in vain.

For the rest, if anything, I believe I have been too optimistic even in my skeptical treatment of the transition practices and concertations by the international community. But readers will undoubtedly be able to distill their own views on my culpability.

Section 3: Modernization and transition aspirations

One can be fairly certain about the aspirations of the more western of the transition economies: Emulating the average level of economic, political, and social development of western Europe. Less clear is where the other countries eventually wish to "belong" in the concert of nations. I venture to guess, though, that eventually these modernization aspirations will come to play a role also in adjudicating the success or failure of transformations in the group of countries that, for all practical purposes, may be considered as ranking among the traditional less-developed economies. Here I focus on what such catch-up end point might entail, if not for all transition economies, then at least for a subgroup detailed in Section 8.

As a theoretical frame of reference and a basis for comparison, modernization does not primarily stand for technological sophistication, industrialization, or average income levels attained. In the broader sense in which it applies to most transition economies, the notion encompasses too "democratization" of society. That can perhaps best be captured by broad-based social participation within the context of some variant of pluralistic democracy rather than an authoritarian or dictatorial regime (Sassoon 1996). An important ingredient of modernization in that sense is the spreading of what sociologists refer to as "modern culture," "modern values and norms," and a "modern mentality." I would rather not speculate on sociological matters. Suffice it to note that a "modern society" in the cited context (but for variants see Buzan and Segal 1996) can be sketched around five dimensions (Andorka 1996).

First, it is one based on an efficient market economy, the latter being viewed as a fairly comprehensive market-based system of resource allocation with minimal distortions. This implies a society in which in particular the "institutions" of the market are functioning appropriately, not necessarily better than in mature market economies but also not measurably worse. It also requires that the "second" economy is not encouraged through onerous taxes or corrupt fiscal enforcement. A modern market economy cannot function well when there exists a large layer of society engaged in criminal activities inhibiting other agents from deploying their participatory talents to best knowledge and aspirations. Note that a functioning market economy cannot be a precondition for reaching a stable social and political environment within which modernization can be pursued. Nor does the reverse hold in general. Congenital simplicity in recurring tendencies, particularly in American thought, that "capitalism" is good for modernization is not particularly persuasive (Greider 1997).

Second, the wealth-generating capacity of a modern society must play a role. That is to say, the economy, and all the political and social forces impacting on productive effort, must be able to generate comparatively high average incomes. A modern society must also ensure that disparities in income and wealth do not transgress on the socially tolerable. The amassing of the greatest concentration of wealth by the fewest individuals from the majority of society in record tempo, as in some transition economies, does not augur well for stability or for mobilizing these resources for modernization prior to passing through another transformatory phase. An increasingly rich minority facing an ever-more impoverished majority, even if only on a transitory basis, cannot constitute a modern society. More than a feeble attempt to integrate all layers must be launched. A modern society cannot tolerate a chronic underclass. It must provide for a welfare system that compensates for one part of society to be abandoned by the majority, let alone the richest layers.

Third, the political system must be pluralistic and democratic in some recognizable sense. Note that a modern society does not necessarily require a pluralistic democracy patterned after, say, the western European parliamentary regimes. But it cannot be situated far beyond the arena for political democracy that characterizes these societies. This leaves room for molding the polity in accordance with the traditions, sentiments, and preferences of the eastern society. Key here is stability and predictability of the political system and the ability of the polity to resolve conflicts in a reasonably expeditious manner. I do not quite subscribe to the notion that "modern" in this sense requires "only" that "the opposition succeeds in winning an election and taking over power for the second time" (Andorka 1996, p. 92), when there are as yet no stable political parties. Without the latter, the condition allows *ad hoc* parties to emerge as protest movements, for example. This may be adequate for "procedural democracy" but does not contribute much to verifying "substantive" democracy (Comisso 1997).

A stable pluralistic polity requires that societal issues be resolved according to precepts that the electorate at large can in principle be made aware of and share. That requires stable political parties in which the majority of the electorate can "vest" trust. Parties must also assimilate the art of compromise (Sztompka 1996b), preferably in a parliamentary setting. It would be a great source of danger if those disgruntled and, at present, passive masses could be mobilized by some extremist party. To date there are few comforting signs of a modern party structure emerging in any of the transition economies. Many of the elections held to date were dominated by protest voters, hence a political preference dependent on the course pursued by the party in power and its impacts on the sociopolitical fabric. Most parties lack clear and consistent programs. Many are *ad hoc* groupings formed purely as electoral vehicles bent primarily on benefiting from the populist appeal of a charismatic figure.

A polity can hope to resolve its core conflicts, and thus crystallize as a "modern" one, only when there exists a powerful "modern" middle class. That is indispensable. "Modern" in the latter sense suggests that society should have not only a dense layer of small shop keepers and merchants whose role is strengthened as modernization proceeds. But the middle class comprises also others, including those keen on ensuring the resolution of societal conflicts through the agencies of civil society. These encompass, among others, managers, the intelligentsia, professional people, some skilled workers, and the self-employed. That is to say, a sizable middle class in society itself must be democratically oriented and imbued with some modern mentality (Avineri 1995; Hobsbawm 1996; Sztompa 1996a).

Fourth, a modern society must be encompassing, enabling all those who wish to be members of it to be integrated into its framework and respecting its parameters until they can be modified or altered in a consensual manner. Society must be an integrated community, no member of which should feel excluded from the welfare and opportunities granted to the majority, or be compelled to join society's selvedge through enforced marginalization. Though no layer can be explicitly excluded from participation in a modern society, not all layers can be compelled to conform, of course; the state's coercive powers should be wielded sparingly but with determination. Those willing to participate should be enabled to take advantage of an extensive range of opportunities open to the individual as a result of modernization. A society that deliberately imparts to the individual the feeling of being at the mercy of authority cannot be deemed "modern." The same holds for a society that destroys, intentionally or not, traditional values and norms as well as the communities that might have offered some sort of protection against authority. That cannot be deemed "modern," regardless of its ability to generate physical wealth and material prosperity. At the same time, a modern society must embrace a social policy that protects the losers.

Finally, a modern society is one in which "modern" ways of thinking, norms, values, rules of behavior, and so on are prevalent and accepted as the "norm" by the majority. That is to say, a modern society cannot tolerate more than a certain degree of dissatisfaction, anomie, and alienation. It requires that members of society not only can but actually do take part in shaping their environment, that they should not feel at the mercy of authority but carve out their own destiny, and that they accept certain moral rules of behavior in business, political, and social intercourse as binding; the extension thereof beyond the nation state's borders is natural (Rodrik 1997), but I cannot detail these dimensions here. Without a modern culture, encompassing attitudes and mentality on the part of the individual, it seems hopeless to ensure the proper functioning of a market economy within a democratic setting. In this context, one should stress the importance of "trust" among members of society (Sztompa 1996a, b) as a key ingredient in seeing to it that the rougher edges of societal disagreements are expeditiously filed away in a peaceful manner.

When can such a modernization stage be attained? One can quip, as did Ralf Dahrendorf (1990, pp. 99–100) at the time of the "1989 events," that constitutional transformation could be achieved in six months; that it would take six years to improve the economic conditions to make themselves felt; but that it would take sixty years for the civic culture and society to evolve and bring about stabilization and the proper functioning of democracy and of a market economy. With the hindsight of nearly a decade of experience with transition, it is clear that the constitutional transformation has taken more than six months. Many do not yet possess a "modern" constitution but continue with the one inherited from state socialism with a patchwork of amendments to remove the most egregious abuses then tolerated. In all too many countries six years for reaching tangible economic improvements, certainly for the majority of the population, has been far too optimistic. I do not, of course, know whether it will take two generations for modernization to crystallize. In the final analysis, there can be no doubt that the time required to move onto the modernization trajectory and hold on to it has been far longer and the difficulties much more daunting than most policy makers, the transition managers, the assistance providers, and many outside observers had anticipated in the early years of the remaking of Europe. It is clear, however, that in all transition economies "the greatest sources of danger threatening a modern market economy and democracy are found in the political area, and derive from the fact that the culture of modern democracy has not yet spread and become stabilized" (Andorka 1996, p. 97). That tends to suggest that the priority indicator in adjudicating modernization must reside in cultural factors that play a part in the economic behavior of the members of a society, as underlined by Peter Gray (1996).

Section 4: The foundations and environment for sustainable growth

The minimal foundations for sustainable growth, and what could conceivably be done about them, are best understood by recalling three transition realities (see Chapter 3). First, functioning markets are not yet present. Claims that they urgently need to be unfettered through liberalization are an oxymoron. Proceeding in this manner cannot secure good governance – cooperation, competition, and coordination among disparate economic agents. All too many administrative, political, ideological, and fiscal realities explain this state of affairs, but they need not concern us here. The key point is that such markets have to be created almost from scratch. The task ranges from the assignment of property rights, over building banking and capital-market systems, to fostering labor markets and the organs of civil society, to specifying and adapting the economic role of the state, disseminating accurate and reliable information in a timely manner, all the way to jurisprudence and constitutional provisions. Who will see to their emergence as soon as feasible to steer endogenous growth?

Second, even when present some markets exhibit considerable failures that can potentially be contained. Especially factor markets (see Chapter 7) do not function well for reasons other than government-imposed restrictions or the failure of government to help remove obstacles to the free-roaming entrepreneurial spirit. Surely, as experience has demonstrated, many market failures cannot be eliminated without risking worse government failures. Even so, there are conditions under which some market failures can be corrected or contained through government action (see Chapter 9).

Finally, the transition economies are confronted with a dual task. On the one hand, a large share of the capital stock, both material and human, cannot survive in a functioning market environment. In a chaotic one, the risk of destroying the wrong capital or of writing off far more than need be is palpable. Furthermore, even if consonant with functioning markets such abrupt destruction is not necessarily reconcilable with any realistic societal consensus. In other words, such destruction must be enacted orderly. Markets such as they are in transition economies cannot accommodate most of these requirements, as recent experience has amply shown. On the other hand, creative change in the direction of modernization may be associated with substantial risk. Even if markets are extant, such risks may exceed what can be accommodated (see Chapter 7); it is hardly likely that it will be consonant with the social interest. That is to say, constructive creation viewed from what is needed to sustain modernization must also be pursued in some orderly fashion. Part and parcel thereof, but transcending the dual paradigm, is the improvement of cooperation, competition, and coordination in society, thus fostering good governance. Part of this agenda can be delivered by the forces required to manage downsizing and spur creative construction. But also instruments and institutions to improve markets, to supplement markets in a manner that is most consonant with market signals where they work, and to integrate markets, thus gaining scale effects, are urgently needed (see Chapter 3).

Delivering on the core of the transformation, then, requires a strategic approach (Solow 1993) with a dual target. One is to recognize that a substantial part of the inherited economic structure is unlikely to be competitive, yet many of its components cannot be abandoned overnight without provoking chaotic, dysfunctional social and political upheavals. Rather than allowing these sores to fester on their own, usually supported by some subsidy, there is a need to disengage those obsolete structures in an orderly fashion. The other task is to bolster creative activity to identify a new growth trajectory and indeed to move along it for a protracted period of time. That too requires management. With incipient markets at best, both policies depend on the full use and deliberate shaping of market competition, cooperation, and coordination to the degree feasible under the disequilibrium conditions typical of transition economies.

Creative-modernization leaps are ineluctably associated with transformation risks. The economic, political, and social conditions in transition economies are changing so much that uncertainty is rampant (see Chapter 3), thus discouraging productive investment and encouraging capital flight, simple intermediation, the underground economy, and so on. I have profound doubts that this is crystalliz-ing into the foundations for a sustainable growth dynamic. Instead, gaps left by state socialism or created by the insufficiencies of transformation policies are being exploited, thus giving rise to gyrations in economic activity, once overall economic performance is disaggregated into its meaningful components and the determinants of change are looked at more closely.

To be sure, the creative process cannot be produced by policy, whether tending toward extreme liberalism or not (Sachs and Warner 1996). It must necessarily be carried by organizations whose internal dynamism sets the pace of change and the nature and size of the risks to be assumed. One can decompose these elements according to the major determinants of how organizations function. For one thing, human and financial capital is assembled into the stock of a "firm," an entity that needs its own internal and external corporate-governance structures, certainly once the owner–manager relationship weakens and the dimensions of the firm transcend the capacities of one manager to formulate efficient decisions based on accessible information (see Chapter 7). Such a firm acquires domestic or foreign inputs, produces products or services whose range and design may constantly have to be upgraded with a production technology that depends in part on the firm's internal organization but also on process technology, and it must find markets for its products. In all these endeavors the firm is exposed to competition, which motivates it to reach best-practice performance seen in a longer-term perspective, such as expected returns on assets or asset values.

In transition economies, for some time external competition is waged largely by more mature economic actors located in economies that have been progress-ing along a well-established technological frontier or catch-up path for decades. For most actors in transition economies a trajectory for moving eventually toward a realistic technological frontier has yet to be identified. Decisions are also due on how best to walk along it, once selected. I contend that suitable policy and institutions *in addition* to whatever benefits the prevailing market conditions generate, or near-term improvements in market conditions guarantee, can and should be pursued by those in charge of critical elements of the transition agenda. Conversely, when markets germinate policies and institutions immanent in the marketplace and private-sector actors must take the relay. Such a purposeful and evolving industrial strategy can be fashioned by incorporating some of the lessons offered by the experience of the Asian NIEs in particular (see Section 7).

As depicted throughout Part II, the transitions need not only solid micro-economic foundations, but also a dependable macroeconomic framework. The development experience of virtually all successful countries amply underlines the importance of a stable and predictable macroeconomic framework supportive of generating growth. Without seeing to low inflation, a solid domestic currency, adequate access to credit, the efficient collection of savings for investment purposes (notably schemes that encourage corporate savings and self-financing), regularized competition in a fairly open environment, and other features of "normality," no sustainable growth path is likely to be identified, jumped onto, and sustained.

This is a useful juncture to reflect again on the holy trinity. Its essential tenets, especially when suitably interpreted and matched with other policies, are undeniable, but its virtues should not be exaggerated; and it is insufficient to accomplish the transformation tasks. Stabilization for its own sake leads nowhere: It is a necessary but by no means a sufficient condition for regaining growth and sustaining catch-up. Moreover, stabilization *can* be enhanced by suitable government intervention, for example, in the way balance-of-payments constraints are relieved (Singh 1995) and uncertainty, hence the risk premium of capital investment, is reduced. Liberalization without distinguishing between desirable activities for which increasing returns hold or enduring obstacles need to be overcome, on the one hand, and more normal competitive markets, on the other, becomes an end in itself. A closer reading of the west's development history fails to buttress the proposition that "modern man" is waiting to be set free (Williams 1996). Rather, modernization is associated with the institution of disciplinary techniques (such as time keeping, accounting, proceduralism, formal legalization, surveying, and a work culture). The attitudes, ways of thinking, and acting characterizing modernity must be constructed. Finally, divestment as a means of bolstering economic efficiency has been overblown (see Chapter 6). It is far more important to ensure reasonable corporate-governance structures and to support with great determination new SMEs. Critical in all this is fostering the institutional diversity required to coordinate economic activity, the complementarities embodied in economic change, and the complex incentives to ensure global integration (see Chapter 7).

Certainly, the strong complementary nature of technological development, investment, and training emphasizes the need to coordinate policy on broad fronts rather than to allow each to proceed in isolation. The main reason is that technologies are not identical or characterized by relatively stable production functions across industry and countries, and thus can neither be procured through markets nor rapidly assimilated and diffused throughout industry. Rather considerable time and effort are required to obtain, assimilate, use, and improve technological knowledge with a view toward enhancing productivity and upgrading industrial activity (Pack and Westphal 1986). Moreover, much technological dynamism derives from gradual and incremental improvements to existing products and processes, rather than from radical breakthroughs. Together these features draw attention to the need to gradually acquire and build upon appropriate capabilities. They also underline the importance of a learning culture for generating continual technological development through a two-pronged strategy. One part consists of formal education and R&D organized at an industry or national level. But that needs to be supplemented with experience-based learning, disciplined search and experimentation routines, and creative partnerships among designers, engineers, entrepreneurs, and managers in firms. Ensuring an appropriately skilled and adaptable labor force (Landes 1990), given particular demands of technological development (Barro 1991), through ALMPs is therefore critical. This has been even more the case with foreign capital: Although it provides an essential conduit of technology in the global economy, often in combination with a package of skills and opportunities, there are no automatic benefits from having companies whose global strategies can readily diverge from perceived national requirements. One can in fact argue that a capacity to benefit from spillovers from the technological frontier is required. That largely depends on internal factors, which tend to be country-specific (Targetti and Foti 1997). Without upgrading the capacity to assimilate technology a convergence path cannot be ensured, not even through FDI.

Finally, more than any other issue, the relation between trade and economic growth, hence the integration of countries into the global framework, has provided food for thought and controversy. Undoubtedly, the size and natural-resource profile of an economy influence competitive prospects in world markets. But reliance on factor endowments and export-led growth seems *a priori* no more certain to generate sustainable industrial expansion than more inward-oriented strategies. Yet, reform of trade regimes has become a decisive feature of development policies since the early 1980s. Multilateral agencies have turned it into a litmus test of the wider credibility of economic reforms (Ball and Rausser 1995; Greider 1997). The potential gains from trade liberalization have been carefully restated and managed trade reform, rather than rapid opening with export-led growth for its own sake, has been a critical determinant of rapid growth in NIEs (Berthélemy and Varoudakis 1996; Hirst and Thompson 1996; C. Johnson 1995; Rodrik 1995a, b; Root 1996; Sarel 1996; Singh 1995). The purpose of liberalization must be the stimulus that external competition can provide to both domestic and foreign investment. Such a response is not necessarily automatic. The benefits of export-led growth through liberalization may fail to materialize for many reasons; they cannot be assumed to crystallize automatically under imperfect competition or in thin capital markets. The effectiveness of trade liberalization very much depends on the credibility of the government that introduces the measures, and the latter's durability, consistency, and compatibility with other policy measures, as well as protectionism faced in major markets, which is particularly inimical to smaller economies (Singh 1990).

The convergence of theoretical research and country experiences yields a new context for discussing strategic policy. Successful industrialization must mean more than expanding physical capacity and labor inputs or orchestrating a temporary rise in output. It implies sustained gains in productivity and competitiveness by steadily lowering costs, improving product quality, upgrading productive capacity toward better-practice techniques and higher value-added activities, diversifying markets and products on a routine basis, and improving skills as part and parcel of normal work assignments. In all these respects, success remains premised on reaching efficiency at the firm level. For these reasons, industrial dynamism requires the formation of extensive linkages among firms within a particular industry, across industrial boundaries, and between industrial and other activities (Dunning 1992a; Porter 1990). Although many of the required linkages evolve from interactions of private agents, there is no reason to expect that this will always be so. Globalization of industrial activity reinforces this conclusion (Ostry 1992a, b; Rodrik 1997).

In this context I want to highlight briefly industrial policy as an ingredient of good economic governance and how it could possibly fit into the modernization drive (for details, see Brabant 1993a). I view it as a strategy formulated, and possibly initiated, by the state (or on its behalf) that encompasses mechanisms by which the actions of various layers of decision making about resource allocation in an economy can be coordinated, monitored, evaluated, and fine-tuned. Clearly, suitable governance capabilities must be in place or quickly acquired (Chang 1994), including perhaps through foreign assistance, if only to avert egregious rent seeking. But measures are also needed to recognize that sharing in the benefits of economic expansion can be a critical factor, both as an incentive to seek better and a reward for having done well, in sustaining the modernization process. These actions are designed to influence, by direct or indirect means, static resource allocation in and among economic sectors, and especially the pace and composition of dynamic economic expansion. The means used to reach this goal are selective commitments of resources to particular activities with a view to facilitating, accelerating, or retrenching their, or the broader-context, growth path, in the end yielding accelerated modernization for society as a whole. I am manifestly *not* advocating picking winners and losers largely on political grounds. I advocate contemplating industrial policy for a simple reason: If the principal economic purpose of the transformation is to catch up with the more advanced countries and to strengthen the underlying foundations of political democracy, it is difficult to envisage how such a new growth path can be discovered, walked along, and sustained over the long haul by relying principally on the "holy trinity." Industrial policy might be a critical component of a strategy designed to regain and sustain growth by fostering market-conforming, -correcting, and -integrating measures (see Chapter 3). It could also help to solidify the socio-political consensus, including through direct action to loosen up labor markets.

Market-correcting industrial policies imply selective support through integrated policy measures targeted at upgrading industrial activity in terms of higher productivity and improved capabilities. They need not require large public funds. But the nature of selective support is predicated on careful monitoring and effective sanctions, beginning with the very formulation of an industrial policy. The potential for these measures cannot be assessed in isolation from particular circumstances. Moreover, because the effectiveness of policies wanes with time as other agents adapt and because those directly benefiting from the policy also change, timely withdrawal of support must be built into these measures.

An emphasis on coordination failure requires the recognition that the governance framework more generally must be a central component of industrial policy. In the first place, it assumes a clear notion of industry, comprising a well-defined set of activities situated within clearly drawn boundaries. This makes targeting relatively manageable, particularly at the earlier stages of modernization. In addition, it assumes that the benefits from correcting market failure can be captured largely within national borders. Note that the benefits should be seen in terms of generating wealth to residents, not necessarily to "domestic" firms. The establishment of firms whose owners and managers are committed to invest further domestically is likely to require the flexible use of a variety of sanction mechanisms and incentives. Finally, it assumes a degree of collective responsibility and sophistication on the part of both the state and private-sector interests. Coordination, cooperation, and competition, thus, enter once again into the picture as central components of governing industrial policy.

Finally, industrial activity is largely organized inside firms rather than in markets. Uncertainty surrounding even the simplest of transformative activities in a world of continuous technological and product development carries the threat of falling behind competitors. For these reasons, firms must establish longer-term relations to ensure adequate supply conditions, friendly consumer relations, and access to capital to carry out required investments (Dunning 1992b; Porter 1990). These are essential to facilitate the transactions required to produce and distribute goods and resources and to upgrade industrial activity.

But economic governance transcends the role of the state and extends to various institutional linkages among firms and between firms and other economic agents in order to ensure the successful development, production, and marketing of goods and services (see Chapter 9). In particular, a decisive feature of governance must be anticipating and managing new types of industrial activities and encouraging the formation of new nonmarket organizations that can enhance coordination, cooperation, and competition. This is perhaps the greatest problem facing any competitive economy over the longer haul. While incremental changes are routinized in the transactions of successful economies, certain types of changes (such as the introduction of new technologies) are considerably more disruptive. They present new opportunities to industry but also adaptation problems. Overcoming them may require the fundamental restructuring of existing relations.

Organizational changes can be equally dramatic. In recent years, new types of relations within industry have become increasingly common as firms shift away from the production of standardized goods and establish niche markets and compete through quality and design. It is particularly important to establish subcontracting relations and networks or clusters for SMEs. However, these new relations increasingly transcend national boundaries and barriers through the growing presence of TNCs. These simultaneously offer rapid development through established financial, technological, and marketing facilities; but they also have the power to circumvent national policies or withdraw altogether.

Perhaps even more significant for the industrial-policy agenda, these technological and organizational changes have radically altered the relationship between industry and services as knowledge-based human capital as a source of economic growth has risen markedly.

Seen against this backdrop, industrial policy is essentially a response to perceived and actual fractures in these linkages either through neglect or because new linkages have not been built when required. This cannot simply be a state-administered repair exercise. The political dimension of modernization, as a rule via industrialization, is rich and complex; but beyond the remit of the present investigation. As argued in Chapter 8, governance must form an integral part of the process of successful industrialization and by implication, its supporting policies. It necessarily encompasses a matrix of exchange relationships among interdependent actors, including consumers and bureaucrats. This simply recognizes that a variety of links in finance, trade, and technology require governance mechanisms to be in place, other than the state or market (Best 1990; Richardson 1972) to produce and distribute economic wealth in general and facilitate, accelerate, or retrench the growth of particular economic activities in response to technological and commercial pressures. Developing this diversity must be a central component of industrial policy. In that perspective one should also regard the tensions between liberalization and the continual upgrading of industrial activity during modernization. This requires careful management, provided basic capabilities are in place. If some time is required to build up production and exporting capacities and capabilities, the trade regime and corresponding incentives must be appropriately tailored to the longer term.

The globalization of industrial activity has both heightened the importance of these exporting capabilities and highlighted the difficulties national governments face in finding appropriate responses. Unlike the traditional infant-industry argument, which assumed one-off protection, the evolving nature of industrial activity suggests that the timely reduction and withdrawal of different supports as much as granting supports *per se* constitute the most critical issue. As depicted in Section 7, the east and southeast Asian NIEs have demonstrated that import-substitution strategies through reverse engineering in the early stages of development combined with a variety of selective trade barriers in support of infant industry can be a precondition of subsequent growth. Moreover, liberalization, when adopted, has been neither rapid nor uncontrolled, but tailored to the needs and potential of particular industries. Equally, targeted support to industries has not only had a strong export-bias; it has also been designed with a finite life span and withdrawn appropriately. Again, this adjustment has not been a *deus ex machina* – occurring exactly when, with hindsight, it was required. Governance has been very much a trial-and-error process based on monitoring, assessing, and correcting mistakes, sometimes after substantial losses.

Structuring incentives according to specific needs of time and place is a key feature of the experiences with rapid industrialization. Consequently, the appropriate policy axis on which to discuss integration shifts from a universal demand for more or less protection for industry in general to a more strategic call for efficient import-substitution and export-promotion measures whenever desirable, given the industrial strategy and the progress already achieved through it. Several NIEs have pursued such a course with considerable success, which is not to say that this policy will remain valid for all times or that it would be entirely suitable elsewhere.

Section 5: Basic development and catch-up modernization

Real success with transformation appears to be predicated on the identification and application of a carefully structured and managed growth strategy, one that will be sustainable over the long haul through productivity gains and yield equitable growth at a level permitting catch-up with the more advanced countries financed primarily from domestically raised resources. There are good reasons to argue that, with some exceptions, the economies in transition do not yet possess the capabilities of inserting themselves smoothly into the dynamic process of intra-industry trade, notably in manufactures, that constitutes the backbone of the EU's single market. Such insertion capabilities crystallize only after a country has identified and walked along a self-sustainable growth trajectory for some time.

Engineering this endogenous growth strategy, relying on the experience of western European latecomers and selected NIEs, is something that I cannot detail in just a few paragraphs (see Brabant 1993a, pp. 171ff.). Contrasting these perceptions with the broad agendas set by alternative theories is even more difficult. I can at best hope to elicit more cogent reflections on transformation tasks by pondering the fundamental questions of economic development set forth in Section 6. Alternative visions of how economies in equilibrium function, such as the neoclassical agenda, or how the entrepreneurial spirit can be mustered to roam freely, as in the Austrian agenda (Brabant 1993a, pp. 172–81; Sawyer 1992), have not really contributed to understanding the dynamic processes at work in successful modernization. These present coherent visions only within narrow perceptions of the real world, one free of social and other conflicts. More illuminating approaches to economic development can be identified from the way in which countries have succeeded in their modernization or failed to impart a positive impetus to emerging from their backwardness. Each involves a particular view of how markets work, of the relevant objectives of economic policy, of the nature of economic interdependence, and of pragmatically molding governance capabilities. The salient stylized facts can usefully be posited around such concepts as learning, uncertainty, integration, and globalization. These and other features call for greater harmonization of forces in society that exhibit central features of what is largely immanent, hence endogenous, in the development process.

After the many mistakes made with development policies in the postwar period in particular, imperfections of markets and the danger of gross government errors should be beyond dispute. In the face of the recent growth experience of countries with public-sector activism, with few exceptions striving for pure markets fails to lead to an ambient environment for guiding rapid structural change. Sustainable development requires broader guidance mechanisms and incentives than either the market or the state can impel upon individual agents. At the same time, market institutions need to be created, maintained, and upgraded, including through proper governance. Spontaneous market forces, even under favorable environmental conditions, are not likely to deliver on these tasks. Instead they tend to accentuate imperfections, as between goods and factor markets, if no other caretaker redresses the situation. Under certain conditions, this may be the government or nonstate governance structures whose results are neither adjudicated in the marketplace according to profit realized nor validated through the coercive powers vested in the state.

A crucial role may accrue to government also in helping to identify, and at times foster, the foundations of a sustainable growth path precisely because catching up with more advanced countries requires jumping hurdles that, given the uncertainty and scale of the required commitment, private initiative is likely to eschew. That is to say, the essence of the approach toward economic modernization revolves around policy intentions on how best to nurse along other than steady-state growth, or dynamic economic efficiency, through an "industrial strategy" targeted at the production process itself, that is, in the microeconomic sphere, rather than solely by modulating macroeconomic policy. Forging the actual production process over time by acting upon "investment" in the broad sense – that is building capabilities in structures, machinery, people, organizations, and so on – is at the heart of endogenizing growth. But it can only be a means toward strengthening other critical determinants of generating steady gains in factor productivity.

The key recognition is that firms are not simple production functions, as in neoclassical economics. Neither are they simple exploiters of opportunities stemming from asymmetric information, as in the Austrian approach. Rather, they pursue organizational cohesion and profit through commitment, worker participation, and cooperation. They do so because considerable information and knowledge reside with individual or groups of workers as nonowners. That resource can be mobilized, thereby enhancing efficiency, only within the right institutional setting. For this an appropriate macroeconomic framework is essential; indeed, it may be a prerequisite for success. But the full array of microeconomic considerations deserves to be heeded as well (see Section 4). This can be extended to just about all corporate actors in society.

In short, the functioning of organizations depends on internal processes (Swaan and Lissowska 1996). They codetermine political, social, and cultural aspects of resource allocation under strategic management. Furthermore, such behavior at the firm level brings economic agents into conflict through rivalry, which may threaten profit and survival. At that point, firms seek to merge or foster agreements for networking – the equivalent of developing trust, which is vital to intrafirm management – and blending it with market incentives (A. D. Chandler 1977; Kay 1992; Porter 1990). Indeed, endogenous growth does not obviate the need for competition and rivalry. Quite the contrary: They are essential to its success. But more is needed to mitigate the resources "wasted" such as through excessive advertising, product differentiation, change generated by the competitive process, idling workers and production capacity, or regional disparities. There is hence a built-in tendency pushing toward monopoly and concentration of activities because of cumulative causation.

An integral component of this approach is the realization that substantial parts of coordination, competition, and cooperation as the essence of good economic governance (see Chapter 8) are achieved *within* firms and households or groups whose decisions are not directly validated in the marketplace. When appropriate, "planning" is undertaken to mold market relations and the development process more generally. This occurs through a complementary relationship among market (and plan), firms, and government, but this time with the government essentially responding to the private sector's expressed need for more encompassing and better-quality governance. In addition to assuming antitrust stances, the state must play a proactive, developmental role. The latter involves the positive promotion of industrial expansion through targeting or strategic industrial policy (Dietrich 1992), possibly with state agencies taking on an entrepreneurial role directly or indirectly. This creates opportunities for private firms otherwise not available, but it also calls for exercising caution in creating SOEs and in ensuring that these firms be subject as much as possible to market discipline, at least for factor inputs. Also, managerial criteria should be devised by which this outcome can be ensured, especially in emerging democracies bent on quickly eradicating the vested interests of the old regimes.

Section 6: Historical experience and modernization

Why some nations are richer than others, why growth rates differ, and why integration benefits some countries and hurts others, why countries at a certain level of development appear on the whole to sustain the convergence process characteristic of their historical emancipation, and whether anything could be undertaken to reverse recent trends indicating a lack of broad convergence in levels of wealth between most developing and developed countries (Berthélemy and Varoudakis 1996) have been among the bread-and-butter questions of development economics for over two centuries. They continue to pose perplexing problems. Whatever the paradigms advocated or the policies tried out, there can be little doubt that "learning" in all of its dimensions – learning to learn, to choose, to import, to do, and so on – remains *the* most critical variable in inducing and conveying sustainable structural transformation. "Learning capabilities" cannot be delivered flexibly, that is, in an adaptive mode as experience is gained, through either *laissez-faire* or a highly centralized economic policy. Rather, the features of a well-functioning economy geared toward exploiting comparative advantages in a competitive setting (not necessarily deriving from an extremely open trade regime) should be exploited to the full so that markets are more and more integrated, created where absent, and complemented when feasible and justifiable through measures that seek to emulate as closely as possible market-based incentives.

The benefits of decentralized, almost-instantaneously adapting processes within the market framework, if available, may be palpable. But they are unlikely to be sustainable, especially in economies bent on making a great leap forward by way of catching up with mature economies. A modernization strategy in all but "starter industrializers" aims at removing inherited economic differences. It does so through the mastery, and frequently the adaptation, of unfamiliar, often complicated technologies and the complementary development of diverse individual and collective skills. In all this, economic actors need to seek out dynamic comparative advantages by deliberately interfering with the established, largely short-termist criteria for decision making. This agenda includes positive action on the part of the state. But it also presumes a degree of economic governance that transcends what the state itself can conceivably engineer by way of bolstering the pace of economic development.

There are good reasons to argue that latecomers, precisely because they are latecomers, confront opportunities, such as from available technology, that should facilitate their catching up with best-practice economies. At the same time, they must face up to challenges that differ distinctly from those that the pioneers (except economies that benefited from unusual natural resources and/or a huge internal market, as in the United States) had to tackle. One evident opportunity is the availability of a stock of commercially viable technology of various vintages. Catching up is, however, a far more complex assignment than simply acquiring the technology of successful economies. Such borrowing requires, what Moses Abramovitz (1986) calls, "social capability," or an aptitude for technical competence through education and training, historical conditioning, and the existence of the appropriate political, commercial, industrial, and financial institutions (Targetti and Foti 1997). In other words, lagging behind may be an advantage when a country possesses in a nontrivial way the rudimentary capability to assimilate, modify, adapt, maintain, and repair such technology (Rosenberg 1988). This can be ensured only once certain conditions are met (Berthélemy and Varoudakis 1996; Hirst and Thompson 1996; R. R. Nelson 1995). Of vital importance is an adequate infrastructure of competent skills partly acquired through education, but also organizational capabilities must be available, such as "the institutions of the market," including foreign competition and flexible exit and entry of firms. The economy must furthermore possess certain facilities, such as infrastructure, or the institutions that permit firms to function in all but the most elementary, slowly and autonomously maturing, environment in which industrial modernization first got under way.

Aside from the challenge to acquire such a social capability, as noted, latecomers as a rule face a degree of uncertainty that differs from the risks that the pioneers earlier successfully tackled; and the pioneer capitalist was quite vulnerable in his social role as the carrier of technological change. Not only is the degree of uncertainty larger, but also the kind of uncertainty differs. For one thing, imitating early starters places latecomers at the mercy of the former's competitive prowess and organization. Furthermore, judging from the development gap relative to more mature economies, imitating and adapting may have to be started at a scale – hence a demand for risk capital – that well exceeds the risk and lumpiness of investments earlier confronted by the "leading" as opposed to the "follower" developers. Successful performance with such risk capital is by no means guaranteed. In any case, setbacks and errors should preferably be converted into useful lessons rather than allowed to inhibit progress along a dynamic development trajectory. Indeed, the history of capitalism is replete with examples that demonstrate the progressive introduction of a large number of institutional provisions to facilitate the commitment of resources to the innovation process by reducing or replacing limitations on risk. An activist state can socialize part of that risk through its progrowth stance. Experience has demonstrated its usefulness even under more stable conditions than those typical of transition economies. Indeed harnessing an industrial strategy for sustained economic development has never been easy. Setbacks and errors are bound to occur. Key is recovering and learning from them.

When all is said and done, closing the development gap was anything but a natural process in nearly all successful economies. It certainly was not accomplished by producing and exporting only low-wage goods with the simplest technologies in an open economic environment. Nearly all successful industrializers (excepting the United Kingdom as pioneer and the resource-rich countries with large, almost self-sufficient markets, such as the United States) relied on considerable protection against competition from abroad, notably the pioneers, for the implementation of their industrial ambitions. But core industrialization encompassed a far richer palette of innovation, imitation, and learning mechanisms to enhance industrial capabilities. It also forged considerable institutional innovation. Most striking was the enhanced role for the state to coerce, cajole, and coordinate the technological, human, and financial efforts required, notably in molding the structure and scope of private capital formation. Furthermore, with the rise of sophistication and scale of technologies, the pressures to ensure profitable exploitation led to more hierarchical firms in which these production decisions could be coordinated. Furthermore, closer links were forged with independent sources of finance, both private and public, and large distribution networks were organized. These firms often sought to create and protect a technological edge through their own R&D, including design capacities. Moreover, they were quick to use their lead in all these areas to expand production abroad. Subsequent development suggests an ongoing process of convergence in the economic performance of these core economies with increasing industrial sophistication buttressed by rapidly expanding intra-industry trade. The latter has constituted the cornerstone of the fast postwar expansion of trade among developed countries; indeed it was one crucial precondition for the "golden age" of capitalism (Marglin and Schor 1990).

The development experience of industrially mature countries suggests that, while inherent scale and resource advantages can in part account for differences in performance, explicit policy choices have been equally important in establishing and maintaining a certain industrial structure, depending on prevailing realities such as available primary factor resources, access to foreign capital, the risk of making large and lumpy investment decisions, the transformation of inherited external ties, and the shortage of domestic entrepreneurs. Latecomers were aware that this could hardly be accomplished by exploiting given comparative advantages. Virtually all sought deliberate import substitution, domestic resource mobilization, and investment guidance. These unbalanced growth strategies introduced their own innovative features in response to the pressures for sustaining change under prevailing realities such as primary-factor resources, access to foreign capital, the risk of making large and lumpy investment, the transformation of inherited external ties, and the shortage of domestic entrepreneurs.

Section 7: Catch-up in east and southeast Asia and its lessons

The above-cited experience with its lessons can be enhanced by looking at the more recent successful modernization in Asian NIEs. In doing so, one should be aware of the schizophrenia that prevails in the profession as regards the main mechanism of their successful catch-up (Sarel 1996), sometimes even in one publication (Berthélemy and Varoudakis 1996). One side emphasizes the liberal foreign regimes and domestic market-based decisions. The other draws its conclusions primarily from the more institutional aspects of successful modernization policies. I have found the latter's suggestions (for a selection of the main indicators and conclusions, see Akyüz 1993a; Amsden 1989, 1992, 1993b; Bruton 1992; Castells 1992; Chang 1994; C. Johnson 1987, 1995; Lall 1990, 1994; Noble 1989; Rodrik 1995a, b; Root 1996; Samuels 1990; Singh 1994, 1995; Wade 1988, 1990, 1995) to be more convincing. But I cannot here delve into the details of this controversy (Brabant 1993a, pp. 207ff.). Suffice it to cite seven of the more illuminating features in a condensed form that may be relevant for transition economies.

First, these NIEs have had strong involvement of the nonmarket sector in managing economic change. In some cases, this included intrusive centralized administrative, business, financial, and political powers. In others, it called for temporarily decentralizing the responsibility of governing economic change in favor of nonmarket actors that are not formally part of government. Many such nonmarket actors have had to be nurtured along in the process of governing the developmental state.

Second, successful government involvement in economic affairs has been monitored largely by criteria that, in one way or another, validate the favored activities relative to world markets and indeed through active international competition; but not necessarily through free trade. The favored activities were as a rule selected on the basis of some variant of revealed comparative *dis*advantage (such as underrepresentation of the product relative to some comparator country or the world as a whole) for products with an apparently high income elasticity, potentially substantial gains in factor productivity, and with promising forward and backward technological linkages. Also, these benefits were in general granted for a fixed period of time at the end of which the activity was expected to become sufficiently profitable to withstand international competition on its own. If not, the benefits could be withdrawn in a credible manner.

Third, a comparatively small amount of public money has been earmarked to leverage industrial policy, if only because government has influenced economic affairs principally through other channels. As much as possible, targeted assistance has been designed to gear up symbiotic progrowth decisions of the private sector. Targeted assistance may therefore be appropriate within the context of comparatively good economic governance, as defined earlier, for the activities of diverse economic actors. In fostering this coordination, cooperation, and competition, full use has been made of all kinds of nonmarket institutions. Some had to be created and indeed divested once circumstances permitted the private sector to take the relief. The switch is invariably accompanied by tensions and conflicts that need to be managed through good governance.

Fourth, government's involvement in industrial policy has been delivered through, on the whole, a competent, devoted, rewarded, and respected civil service. But it has not been omniscient. Neither has it been free of corruption. Nonetheless, it has achieved a high degree of cooperation in the civil service in particular. Its robustness derives also from explicit policies to cultivate highly trained professionals and attract them to the public sector. Moreover, the core task of managing the development strategy has by and large been entrusted to a small group of competent civil servants enjoying considerable discretion in designing, implementing, monitoring, assessing, and fine-tuning the development strategy and in orchestrating the coordination, cooperation, and competition characteristic of good governance.

Fifth, the role of government in managing structural change has been patterned so that actions do not backfire. It is much more difficult to marshal commercial, financial, fiscal, technology, and education policies for fostering modernization in a fully open environment, including capital markets. The developmental state therefore embraces commercial, financial, and technology policies enabling the implementation and refinement of the core industrial policy. Most NIEs have maintained anything but free capital markets or free trade and exchange regimes. Rather they have selectively liberated external activities with considerable management over a fairly protracted period of time. Nor has this shift occurred smoothly in the sense that its actions and existence could be justified at all times until discontinued even when strategic-trade decisions in retrospect seem sensible. This is not necessarily misguided when time is required to build up export capabilities and break into the system of economic exchange at a point other than comparative advantage in low-cost labor or in natural resources, given imperfect competition, externalities, economies of scale, and the economics of learning (Amsden 1993b; Boltho and Holtham 1992; Chang 1994; Lall 1994).

Sixth, government tends to get involved in comanaging industrial change by socializing part of the risk that would otherwise discourage private enterprise from starting up, or from transforming its inherited facilities into, such a new and risky endeavor. If so, it is foolhardy to hold government's involvement in economic affairs under all circumstances to much more demanding success criteria than those applicable to the private sector. Rather, capabilities are needed to evaluate success and disengage from losing activities while building further upon successes attained.

Finally, a modernization policy should preferably be grafted onto the targeted supply of public goods, notably education and basic infrastructure; onto the consensus on socioeconomic change; and onto its largely economic rewards, sociopolitical stability, and security. In this context education in all of its formal and informal dimensions deserves special emphasis primarily because generating human capital to manage the process of technological change is a much more complex task than, say, putting in place physical infrastructure.

Successful modernization coordinates dynamic competition. It thus implies more than augmenting the physical capacity of industry or orchestrating a temporary rise in output. Its critical determinants are continual improvement of productivity and competitiveness through a variety of mechanisms affecting costs, product choice and quality, productive capacity, skill diversification, and other components. But this array cannot usefully be reduced to the ability to discipline the private sector by judicious use of carrot-and-stick mechanisms, particularly when the latter are by and large equated with pecuniary rewards and punishments. To diminish the successes achieved by recalling the failures of some of the industrial-policy measures without being quite selective is not very helpful. Certainly, success is premised on the efficiency of the individual firm. But industrial dynamism is also predicated on the formation of extensive linkages among firms within a particular industry, across industrial boundaries, and between industrial and other activities that are not generally accommodated through "market price" channels, as noted. Coordinating all this means that institutional innovation forms an integral part of successful modernization.

Section 8: On the sustainability of the gains booked and policy options

Of course, the above experiences cannot be transferred in their entirety to the transition economies, if only because the latter's "destruction" and "creation" are far more complex. Nonetheless, some features, notably those that are not

492

uniquely Asian or time bound, can usefully be assessed for their potential relevance and transferability. Seen against the backdrop of the Asian NIEs, the historical experience of eastern Europe, and the failed experiments with state socialism when contrasted with modernization, one may well ask whether it is possible for the transition economies individually or as a group to be successful and attain acceptable rates of growth if current managerial precepts on trans- formation are adhered to. Unlike the neoliberal drum beat, I feel that current signs of an economic upturn, however welcome, should not be confounded with the success criterion specified in Section 4. Achieving sustainable growth on present policy stances is unlikely. For one thing, export markets for traditional products will not remain buoyant. Also, exporters cannot withstand pressure for price and wage adjustments that erode their static comparative advantage. Furthermore, the conditions for bolstering factor productivity and for moderniz- ing economic structures, on which ultimately the pace and sustainability of growth depend, are not (yet) realized. Moreover, there is at best limited evidence of substantial investment financed principally from domestic sources. Finally, foreign capital with its geographical and sectoral specificities is not well integrated in the growth trajectory and may wreak more harm than good in the longer run if based largely on cheap labor.

One may, of course, be quite skeptical about the ability of the transition economies to emerge from their historical confinement (Hobsbawm 1993). True, eastern Europe in particular has been disillusioned about its past and is dis- appointed about its present situation and uncertainty about the future. Yet, the unique fallout of the *annus mirabilis* may inspire at least some leaders to forge ahead in a different, hopefully a more promising, direction. Looking carefully at the modernization approach pursued by successful latecomers as an alternative or complement to relying primarily on export-led growth strategies placed within the simplistic neoclassical framework can at least offer suggestions. Automatic resource mobilization for growth is unlikely to occur. I find it inherently difficult to envisage how these countries could catch up to levels of living, income, productivity, and technology in western Europe when the growth strategy is focused on conquering external markets or attracting FDI essentially on the basis of cheap labor or through preferences that are not securely tied to technology or training commitments (Flemming 1993, p. 198) as anchors for further economic expansion paced by productivity gains. There can be no costless and easy road to modernization. Experiences of latecomers suggest that they have succeeded *in spite of* a global emphasis on speedy liberalization and of the homilies to unfettered market-based decision making, thus providing a welcome foil to those mesmerized by the beauty and ease of tacking on to the virtuous circle inspired by the Washington consensus. At most, their experiences support arguments for a *qualified opening* rather than liberalization for its own sake. If some time is required to build up production and exporting capabilities, which is a reasonable working hypothesis for transition economies, the trade regime and corresponding incentives must be tailored to the longer term.

Successful development cannot realistically be envisioned without effective resource mobilization, notably of capital and labor in their various gradations (Solow 1993). But it must entail more than expanding physical capacity and labor inputs or orchestrating a temporary rise in output. It is predicated on sustained gains in productivity and competitiveness through continual lowering of costs, improving product quality and skills, bettering production techniques particularly for higher value-added activities, and diversifying markets and products. For that capabilities must be acquired to augment the quality of inputs but also the ambiance of the environment within which modernization in production and in distribution is to be cast. Success ultimately depends on reaching efficiency at the firm level, which requires the formation of extensive linkages in production, finance, research, trade, and other sectors at home and abroad. Many will arise from the interactions of private agents. When links have fractured as a result of neglect or have not been established when required, good economic governance and some form of industrial policy will be needed to activate them to alleviate uncertainty, risk, and asymmetric information particularly in capital markets. Such efforts to tackle these and related hindrances revolve around policies explicitly designed to promote steady-state growth through temporary incentives that do not strictly conform with markets. These need to be linked to selected indicators of how to compete in international markets after some adjustment phase. This ability to adapt to better-practice technology provides the source for dynamic economic efficiency, hence the support base for further growth.

In any case, the unquestionable benefits of trade liberalization with functioning markets can no longer be assumed to hold in situations with imperfect competition, externalities, economies of scale, and the economics of learning in all of its dimensions (Boltho and Holtham 1992). Under those circumstances time is required to build up capacities that fuel strategic exports supportive of modernization. As noted, modernizing economies must break into global economic exchange at a point other than comparative advantage in low-cost labor or in natural resources. They need capabilities to improve marketing, to access better technology, or to streamline organization singly or in combination. Entry into western markets on favorable, discriminatory terms, allowing the fledgling private and badly supervised SOEs to exploit their short-term advantages, and building up alliances with foreign capital may all provide temporary relief. But are they likely to become sustainable sources of support for longer-term growth? I advance the proposition that the latter cannot be found chiefly by letting the transition economies compete on prevailing terms.

The purpose of liberalization in countries such as the transition economies, then, must be to exploit scale economies and build up new, dynamic comparative advantages through the stimulus that competing in global markets can provide to domestic investment financed largely from domestic savings. However, the benefits of liberalization cannot be assumed where imperfect competition prevails or capital markets are thin. The effectiveness of trade liberalization very much depends on the credibility of the government that introduces the measures, as well as on the latter's durability and consistency with other policies. If liberalization coincides with macroeconomic instability or with an unstable political climate, as has been the case throughout the transition economies, the proclivity toward underinvestment and short-termism in resource allocation tends to be reinforced. Calling for massive capital inflows in a climate where domestic savers prefer to park their stake abroad seems at least disingenuous. Attracting foreign investment by granting foreigners all kinds of favors cannot provide a durable basis for sustained growth; it encourages rent seeking. In any case, sustainable development requires broader guidance mechanisms and incentives for individual agents than either the market or pervasive central intervention can provide. At the same time, market institutions must be maintained and upgraded, including through proper governance. But also the critical instrumental value of private initiative must be recognized and allowed to mold market institutions within the overall macroeconomic framework governed by central policy makers.

Likewise, government may play a crucial role by identifying and supporting a strategy for sustainable growth. This requires appropriate institutions and policies, including notably efforts to mobilize primarily domestic savings for capital formation. However, there is no guarantee that the market by itself can fulfill this function, particularly when it is not well developed and its components exhibit asymmetries. Of course, endogenous growth does not obviate the need for competition and rivalry. However, if the goal is to deliberately shape and make creative use of market competition, cooperation, and coordination with a view to channeling resources into development, thereby generating new opportunities for private firms (Brabant 1993a), more is needed.

I have argued earlier for considering an endogenous growth strategy as the best means for most transition economies, particularly those possessing governance capabilities, to catch up with the more advanced countries in western Europe. The chief argument starts from dissatisfaction with the once popular interpretation that the successful NIEs were sucked into unimpeded trade channels largely through the exclusive production of labor-intensive goods embodying low value added. Any credible modernization policy must address the complicated issues arising from the strong complementary nature of technological development, investment, and training; hence the need to coordinate policy on broad fronts (Abramovitz 1986), rather than to allow each to proceed in isolation. The main reason is that technologies are not identical or characterized by relatively stable production functions across industry and countries. Indeed, they are not off-the-shelf, procurable at comparatively low cost through capital imports or FDI. Neither can they be rapidly assimilated and diffused throughout the economy. There is at least a need for complementary investments and institutional change to ensure an appropriately skilled and adaptable labor force (Landes 1990), given particular demands of technological development (Barro 1991). Active education and training through public and private initiatives have been required to import, to adapt, to identify, and to overcome design and development problems in harnessing available technologies for particular socioeconomic conditions. This has involved formal and firm-specific training, inhouse R&D, and purposeful accumulation of tacit industrial knowledge in such areas as production, quality control, and marketing. All have been decisive in ensuring competitiveness. These considerations apply at least equally when the expanding role of TNCs is incorporated into the analysis. As noted, the benefits of FDI by firms whose global strategies diverge measurably from perceived national requirements are not automatic.

Unbridled entry of capital or offshore facilitation cannot be a panacea. Either may inhibit sustaining the modernization path and even entail problems, such as when pressures for real-wage increases in the modernizing economy can no longer be held off. Without imposing guidelines on capital inflows, congruence of domestic and foreign interests is fortuitous as foreign investment enters for its own reasons, motivated largely by cheap labor. Without denigrating especially FDI, the primary emphasis in modernization is the purposeful mobilization of resources primarily in the domestic economy to reach a "good modernization path," one based on steady productivity gains. Swift and efficient financial intermediation, at least through functioning commercial banks, therefore plays a critical role in encouraging domestic investment and repatriation of flight capital once other stability conditions reduce the prevailing degree of uncertainty.

Something more is needed to identify an outward-oriented, self-sustainable growth path. That is unlikely to be based on the current dominance in exports of "traditional" goods. The current comparative advantages are transitory. In any case, these are goods for which demand in developed countries is not very dynamic and that tend to be excluded through managed trade. Recent FDI inflows, where earmarked for material production, appear to be largely motivated by cheap labor and/or inexpensive raw materials. Other capital inflows have taken on a speculative character, which has complicated macroeconomic management, notably monetary control. The development record of west European latecomers and of the successful NIEs suggests that foreign investment, even in the form of FDI, by itself cannot carry a country's modernization efforts; it can only provide synergy, particularly in the smaller countries whose future must inextricably be found in far-reaching merger into the global economy.

As argued in Chapter 5, newer small firms play a critical role in modernization and indeed in conveying the structural transformation envisaged when the real opportunities for change are heeded. These include the state of markets, of property rights, of technical change, of entrepreneurship, and of efficient managerial operations. In that respect, sustainable development is likely to spring primarily from the vibrancy of new firms and their ability to amass retained profits for expansion in breadth and in depth. Their importance in all likelihood will outweigh the role of core privatized, restructured, or commercialized SOEs in bolstering the momentum for structural adjustment in the short to medium run.

Recent research in the area of technical change offers support for such measures by recognizing that technological knowledge is not a readily transferable public good fully embodied in mobile physical capital. Rather, considerable time and effort are required to obtain, assimilate, use, and improve technological knowledge with a view toward enhancing productivity and upgrading industrial activity (Pack and Westphal 1986). Moreover, much technological dynamism derives from gradual and incremental improvements to existing products and processes, rather than from radical breakthroughs that dramatically enhance performance. Together these two features draw attention to the need to gradually acquire and build upon appropriate capabilities and the importance of a learning culture to the process of continual technological development. The latter comes to pass through formal educational channels and R&D activity organized at an industry or national level, and through hands-on learning, disciplined search and experimentation routines, and creative partnerships among designers, engineers, entrepreneurs, and managers in firms.

Conclusions

Recent modernization experiences challenge the simple dichotomy between state and market coordination, particularly when the former is taken as the failure of state socialism and the latter as the triumph of capitalism. There is no single reasonably modern society extant in which either the pure market or the pure plan explain why modernization policies succeed or fail. There is a role for government in a market setting, just as a functioning market economy cannot be imagined without allocating space for a vast array of NPOs. The willingness to target and support selected industries if only by improving infrastructure, institutions, and education, has strengthened the technological and export potential of (particularly large-scale) private-sector firms with strong disciplinary action against recalcitrant firms failing, or reluctant, to conform to the perceived needs of economic development as captured in the prevailing sociopolitical consensus (Wade 1988, 1990). Consequently, the linkages and incentives established to ensure coordination among the actions of a powerful developmental state committed to sustainable modernization by upgrading its industrial activity, large public and private-sector firms subject to competitive pressures on world markets, and financial institutions committed to longer-term investment goals have appeared to be singularly diverse and complex. Without a properly anchored growth strategy and the requisite management of the catch-up process by other than for-profit agencies, private initiative is unlikely to be sufficiently well placed to reap the benefits of its own stances. On the other hand, given the large differences between private and social benefits and costs, government intervention of the right kind, at the right time, and to the right beneficiaries deserves at least to be contemplated. This has implications for crowding-in financing by government, for its education and health policies, for its own stances on mobilizing savings for investment purposes, and so on.

In short, there is room for redirecting the focus of attention in transformation agendas and economic performance of transition economies to the goals that were at the origin of the "1989 events." The contours of a modernization strategy depend critically on resource mobilization to jump catch-up hurdles. That is unlikely to be forthcoming by adhering to present policy stances. Though the preferred phasing depends on concrete circumstances of time and place, as a rule external financial liberalization will be appropriate toward the later phases of the sequenced transformation. True, complementing this through good economic governance, the erection of the still missing or limping institutions of the market, and establishing and maintaining the sociopolitical consensus may require capabilities at the level of central government that, at least for now, are lacking. But every effort should be made to acquire them soonest, including through foreign assistance. But transition economies will modernize largely on the strength of their domestic resources. Hence, efforts to encourage and appropriately allocate domestic savings are in order. Finally, if carefully nurtured and blended with the modernization strategy, particularly the kind that derives from longer-term commitments to production, technology transfer, and human training, capital inflows could play a complementary role, certainly once the catch-up strategy takes hold and expectations that economic agents are progressing along a new, sustainable growth path carried by new small firms solidify.

CONCLUSIONS

Rather than recapitulating the main points made in each chapter, I conclude this monograph with a few observations on broad aspects of the topics dealt with.

On the relationship between transition and transformation

In the distinction introduced transformation refers to incisive changes in economic affairs in particular whereas transition signals a break with the state-socialist past *and* moving ahead with the transformatory tasks at hand but in a much less structured and bold manner. Neither should be identified with "shock therapy" or "gradualism" (see Chapter 3). Clearly, not all transition economies as commonly defined can comfortably be grouped into either category. Some are moving ahead in a precarious balance between transition and transformation approaches. Others do not belong to either. Indeed, several have ruptured with state socialism only perfunctorily, replacing the authoritarianism and all-embracing arrogance of communist ideology mutated into the deadweight losses of state socialism with something equally superficial and repugnant. This new regimentation and vacillation around fixed points of a moribund eschatology cannot improve society's health and wealth and well-being, let alone in a sustainable manner and on a widely shared basis.

This third group of "transition economies," such as Belarus and Turkmenistan, complicate analysis for the lack of progress even toward market construction, let alone political democracy, has been varying among the diverse societal processes previously encompassed under the label of state socialism. Very little of what I have elaborated upon throughout this volume applies to the experience of these countries, as distinct from the lessons that can be learned from their failures, and from the experiences of the two main groups of transition economies for their future transformation. The reason is simple: They have chosen, if only by default, to eschew undertaking transformations of various dimensions, limiting their variations on state socialism to further tinkering with a defunct system. This applies also to several countries that, after early enthusiasm for genuine restructuring of society and polity, have markedly backtracked on incipient transformations, thereby exacerbating the situation inherited at the transition's inception.

Useful lessons could be extracted and heeded from those failures as well. They could measurably benefit those in charge of these countries, but also their inside and outside advisers. Also those who in due course will head the effort to foster transitions in laggard countries could profit from the experience. In fact, managers of transitions in all countries involved in the unprecedented determination to foster market-based resource allocation and a pluralistic democracy can gain from the experiences gathered throughout the group of countries, those that succeeded as well as those that failed or backtracked. Building up a human capital stock versed in transitology is one thing. Being prepared to intervene in a constructive manner is something else. In that sense virtually all of the experiences gathered should be relevant to all actors involved once the leaders of one or more of these countries decide, perhaps for the second or third time, to embark on genuine, structured transformation as a prerequisite for modernizing their society. The painful restart through which Bulgaria and Romania, and indeed Albania albeit on a different plane, to cite only the most glaring instances of failed transitions, are passing in early 1997 provides vivid illustrations of the more generally applicable case stated. Of course, that human capital stock suitably remolded should come in very handy as well in tackling the tasks of transformation in other countries, on which more below.

The coherence of the transformation agenda and sequencing

Throughout this volume I have stressed the importance of ensuring coherence in the transformation agenda. This not only means consistency across the various components, but also requires dovetailing as much as possible the various policy steps over time, given that some tasks should not be postponed, some must be deferred till later, and others can be accelerated or delayed depending on concrete circumstances. This mix varies according to the broad tasks of the transition – stock and flow stabilization, internal and external liberalization, privatization in all of its formats, institution building so that markets can jell, and reaching and sustaining a minimal sociopolitical consensus. As noted, they vary also over the concrete elements of each component and, of course, the focal points shift over time and perhaps over kinds of economic activities as experience mounts. Harmonizing all this is a daunting assignment. One should harbor no illusion that ideal solutions are there for the taking. Even so, it is crucial that such coherence be maintained and that efforts to improve upon the perhaps precarious harmony reached are mobilized on a nearly continuous basis. I emphasize this even though weighty adverse developments rank among the near-certain risks of societal transformation and repositioning these countries in the broader global and regional contexts with some outside assistance. I have furthermore argued how imperative it is to streamline and fine-tune the transformation program as experience is gained, without falling into a possibly deadening stop-go routine.

Notions intimating that any government of a transition economy could conceivably draft an "optimal" blueprint, then embark on its seamless implementation, and finally enact smooth fine-tuning deserve prominence only in textbook simplifications. Nonetheless, when there is a rare opportunity to deliberate on what could and should be done, transition managers may well profit from being able to refer to a road map on the main components of genuine transformation. Its principal purpose should be isolating the measures that need to be taken fast from those that cannot be taken as speedily and from others for which policy choice is available. In this manner, policy makers and their advisers could ensure that all measures embraced exhibit as much as possible internal compatibility. Such an approach to complex problems would also help in formulating, and expeditiously implementing, the decisions on what to do next without compromising what has already been achieved or what will have to be prospectively tackled.

In this context, allow me one comment on the widespread advice, largely issued as a mantra, emanating in particular from the multilateral assistance providers: Speed is of the utmost importance in holding the cost of transformation within manageable bounds, indeed in minimizing them, and moving soonest onto a "quality growth path." This is, of course, wonderful rhetoric, useful for public-relation purposes, and a *pro domo*, but certainly not *pro Deo*, plea. Such a bromide may exhort transition managers into action. It also exemplifies Bergson's "illusion of retrospective determinism" for it purports to confirm what these advisers had been promoting all along, sometimes by arrogantly imposing their very own time preference.

It is self-evident, almost sheer tautology, to argue that delaying transformation tasks in need of being introduced quickly and in a comprehensive manner, such as price liberalization for most goods and services and mopping up any dysfunctional "monetary overhang," is crucial. If delaying were to exacerbate costs it would only reinforce the argument for speed. But its pedestal is its intrinsic merit for advancing at all with structural transformation. Essential restructuring and establishment of "institutions of the market" can be speeded up only in a relative sense. That applies too to the acquisition of the skills required to function in an emerging market environment. Those heading the design and managing the transformation must be aware that headway must be carved out largely with the resources at hand, including on managing state assets.

Attempts to rush into transformation on the presumption that these and other market institutions do not matter, or are already available, with almost Bolshevik zeal cannot but escalate costs beyond moving resolutely but in a deliberate manner toward erecting them. This is not a facetious counterargument. Policy stances aimed at constructing safety nets that cannot be financed are not useful. Neither is transferring all "market ills" to the government for which it does not even possess coping facilities. Suddenly opening up the real and financial economy to full international competition may create havoc. Likewise for liberalizing entry into the financial sectors without having in place adequate prudential regulations and surveillance mechanisms that can actually be applied

501

as designed. In short, there can be no omnivalent tradeoff between speed and deliberateness. It all depends on what one is considering for speeding up or for innovating otherwise in the concrete context of the transition. Where there is room for choice, not just in the technical sense but also from the perspective of sustaining sociopolitical support, moving fast obviously leads to an early return to positive growth, if only by way of making up for the lost output during the early stages of the transition, or even the state-socialist depression in some cases. The litmus test of success derives, however, from extending this upturn and transforming it into sustainable catch-up growth.

Two related implications need to be pointed out. One is that the forceful destruction of the CMEA, just like the precipitate plummeting of commercial relations among the successor States of the Soviet Union and Yugoslavia, and to a lesser extent of Czechoslovakia, cannot be regarded as an exogenous phenomenon, except for the three developing-country members (Cuba, Mongolia, and Vietnam). True, the CMEA had been on a corrosive path for some time prior to the "1989 events" and integration among the seven European members was by far not as advanced as, say, within the now defunct federations. But the politically and strategically motivated decision to impose "world market conditions" on CMEA relations in a great hurry while reorienting commercial ties toward the west contributed more than marginally to the downward spiral in CMEA relations. It was also directly affected by the sharp economic recession resulting from the adoption of transformation policies in crucial partners – Czechoslovakia, the GDR, and Poland in particular – and, of course, the worsening crisis engendered by reform vacillation in the Soviet Union.

Another implication is that the choice of pursuing incisive transformation policies is not a random event. It cannot be if the transforming country maintains any sizable ties with other transition economies. That poses identification problems in specifying correctly the logical relationships one wishes to test for. Of course, there are other problems such as the assumption that "liberalization" is an independent decision randomly distributed across transition economies and uncorrelated with other variables and indeed the success of stabilization. Econometric exercises that purport to demonstrate the rapid-mover advantages when palpable variables are missing and the relationship is misspecified offer at best pseudo evidence for the maintained hypothesis. Initial conditions do matter. They affect not only the "best" choice of the transformation agenda, and when to commence with its implementation, but also the likelihood of success and how it should properly be specified. If initial conditions are correlated with both the choice of transformation policies and the probability of successful stabilization, intertemporal comparisons become much more difficult to interpret than the econometric exercises conducted to date are able to disclose. Similarly, if initial conditions are not identical across the various transition economies, as seems likely, econometric cross-country comparisons may or may not be disclosing hard information as regards the desirability of moving fast. It may all depend on the missing variables or the wrong specification!

The upshot of this debate in the literature and the advisory stances should be that, if the environment for formulating and implementing the transformation agenda can be improved upon by reducing the pervasive uncertainty, restructuring can be accelerated. This in turn engenders a faster rebound in fiscal and export revenues, support for reform, a decline in unemployment and poverty, new investment and business activity, and so on. Setting the rules of the new game, that is, putting in place the vestiges of the institutions that eventually settle the character of the market, facilitates adhering to a reasonably coherent transformation agenda. Again the gut feeling may be that moving "fast" offers its own rewards. But I would counsel caution in simply repeating this mantra to policy makers confronted with quite different situations.

Assisting the transition economies and governance

I have argued the case for assisting the transition economies as a compelling obligation for the international community and western Europe in particular. It is just that because it is in the self-interest of the international community, again with special reference to western Europe, to forge ahead with establishing stable, predictable, prosperous, and open-minded societies in the countries emerging from under the knout of state socialism. These interests reach from the banal economic benefits accruing from commerce and finance, all the way to the less quantifiable and tangible advantages of securing a transparent, reliable, and predictable political environment. Other motivations for claiming assistance entitlement, be they political, security, cultural, historical, or moral, should not be ignored, of course. In the end, however, they play a decidedly lesser role in effectively mobilizing resources in favor of an agreed-upon transformation agenda. Working out the latter's technical planks should come first unless complete economic, political, and social chaos happens to be the unenviable reality. As a rule, however, the state of affairs in transition economies does not warrant war-like approaches to rooting out evil and combating entrenched opponents of change.

In advocating the need for international assistance I have also emphasized the ensuing obligations for the citizens of countries extending the assistance, directly or indirectly; for those called upon to deliver the assistance according to some criteria of efficiency and interests; as well as for the recipient countries. Given the unprecedented magnitude and peculiar characteristics of the transformation, a valid case can be made, logically as well as instrumentally, for viewing assistance as an objective with three dimensions. One is mobilizing the resources that donors are willing to appropriate in some effective manner, for which the determination of volume, composition, and timing are crucial. The second is to be clear about the nature of the transitions, the sociopolitical and economic constraints under which these mutations must necessarily be sought, and what could realistically be devised to ensure that the programs become domestically "owned," hence supported, while aiming at arousing the desired changes. This is not a routine matter. It is not something that can be placed within the context of universal organizations with specific mandates and rigid ways of approaching restructuring within an agreed-upon discipline rather than working toward a stage where such commitments can reasonably be adhered to and delivered upon.

From this it follows that broad execution of assistance should preferably be entrusted to a special task force consisting of competent professionals who can afford, with the consent of the transition leadership, to immerse themselves hands-on, during the early phases on a day-to-day basis, in modulating the assistance programs and, where invited, the transformation agenda as well. Their coordinating role should, of course, come first so that the specific advantages of the various bi- and multilateral assistance organs can be utilized as well as circumstances afford. There certainly is no need for launching yet another stab at highly centralized hierarchical planning.

Success with transition and moving onto a catch-up modernization path

It is instructive to remind ourselves once in a while of the original objectives of the *annus mirabilis* and thus to compare achievements and the directions in which the transition economies appear to be heading with the aspirations spawned by the "1989 events," or the other way around. Of course, some were far too ambitious or even unrealistic, and should therefore not be invoked at this stage. Joining the EU soonest was one of those naïve, misguided objectives. I have proposed that the alpha and omega of the economic ambitions and hopes should be working toward sustainable catch-up growth and modernization over the long haul. In that perspective, in spite of the welcome improvements in economic affairs in recent years, the foundations for a modernization trajectory with sustainable catch-up growth do not yet seem to be in place in any transition economy. But conditions in some countries are more promising than in others. Nevertheless, those in charge of orchestrating structural transformations should work assiduously toward removing the fragility of the progress made. One must admittedly recognize that there are other criteria according to which the successes and failures of transition and transformation can be adjudicated. Some are subordinate to economic priorities. Several others stand separate from economic affairs. Entering into a discussion of those cultural, political, and social dimensions of transformation would have carried me too far afield. They not only constitute plausible areas for fruitful investigation, but also are desirable extensions of this inquiry toward the more holistic appreciation of unprecedented societal mutations.

Governing the new European framework

Transformation cannot be confined to the transition economies. I have stressed already the need of fostering cooperation among these countries, not just to revive trade and economic cooperation. I affirm this well realizing that these countries fervently desire to merge themselves more completely into the global economic and political frameworks. Some do indeed aspire toward full membership in or a very close association with the EU. On present policy stances and the evidence at hand as regards the suitability of the candidates for EU membership, arguments that these privileged partners will soon be in a position to comply with all requirements for full membership sound hollow. They are not especially helpful in advancing the cause of these countries or, for that matter, in the constructive remaking of Europe. Areas in which the privileged transition economies fall short include their as yet limited ability to withstand buoyant competition for intra-industry trade and to carve out such a niche in the EU's single market. The situation in other transition economies, both those that may eventually aspire in a credible manner to membership and others that covet a looser form of association for whatever reason, is even less in line with "normal" international economic relations. In consequence, a persuasive case can be made for facilitating appropriate transformations in the international and regional organs as well.

Addressing core issues of managing the global economy

Membership in the IEOs can now be universal, given that most of the world is prepared to subscribe to the broad contours of the prevailing international economic regimes. Not only does this offer the possibility of rethinking the regimes so as to modify them for countries that cannot in reality fully abide by the associated disciplines, yet could benefit from being "in" the regimes without the latter status unduly harming the present membership, but also it leaves an opportunity to reassess the many issues of global economic management in the light of the core development problems of the day and those likely to be around the horizon in the years ahead. The problems addressed when the regimes were first innovated – securing sustainable growth, stability, predictability, transparency, and reliability with a fair sharing of the gains thus made possible – remain at least as acute as they were during the four decades or so when the Cold War inhibited "universality" of those regimes and institutions. It should now be possible for the international community to work out a new *modus vivendi* with the full participation of the countries that heretofore "preferred" their own arrangements.

One of the important issues yet to be addressed is the future of ODA, especially at the multilateral level, in a globalizing world that, without activism, seems inherently to marginalize certain groups of countries, such as those of sub-Saharan Africa. The danger that the tendency to be excluded from the global framework may be perpetrated also for the lesser developed transition economies deserves to be nipped in the bud. The same applies to the evaluation of whether it might be desirable to script a transition phase for countries desirous of joining a given regime for which they are not yet adequately prepared. Ushering China or Russia into the WTO any time soon should provide an opportunity to rethink the merits of associating membership immediately with the existing disciplines. Pragmatic solutions could usefully be placed within the context of the conditions for generating "convergence" in economic performances with the lesser developed countries being able to catch up with the mature members of the global community.

Such revamping could take the form of a permanent rearrangement of the regimes in place with their custodial institutions in recognition of three facts. One is that the IEOs in place were established for fairly mature market economies for whom a set discipline could rationally be decreed and applied. Second, their *modi operandi* have not always been suitable to the needs of, say, the lesser developed countries (more generally countries where markets are not well integrated) or the tasks of policy making cannot be confined in a reductive fashion to demand management driven from the current-account side. That is to say, the regimes are intended primarily to enforce the disciplines and ensure that deviants are coaxed back into the agreed fold. How to do so constructively for countries that do not fit the mold has by and large remained an unresolved question. Finally, the environment of the 1940s in which these regimes were conceived is hardly appropriate to the present tasks of managing the global economy with a view to generating transparency, stability, reliability, predictability, and equity in global economic, and broader, relations. However, some elements of the desirable revamping can usefully be cast in a transitory format simply in recognition of "extraordinary" conditions in part of the membership, in which case a strategy for transition to full participation should be drawn up in a credible manner between the individual organ and the countries at issue.

The limits of multilateral governance and lessons from eastern Europe's transformations

The uniqueness of the transition and transformation experiments should offer ample food for thought, and humility, on what can realistically be undertaken within the national, regional, and global contexts. The lessons to be derived would be particularly useful when extending in time or to other countries similar exercises in promoting views on desirable societal transformations. I include here the transition economies that for one reason or another have so far eschewed meaningful transformation.

I shall not repeat all of the lessons that I have touched upon in this book. Just the same, it may be useful to point again to the crucial importance of establishing a coherent transformation agenda; of being fully aware of the initial conditions and the circumstances within which the transformation must unfold;

of flexibility and imagination as well as a good dose of pragmatism in formulating, implementing, assessing, and fine-tuning policies; of heeding the limits to institutional renaissance; and indeed of the overriding goal of the transformation to improve the quality of the life for citizens in several dimensions of freedom from want but also from political oppression. If established multilateral institutions are, then, assigned to assist in fostering good governance of the transformation agenda, there should be broad recognition of the need for transition regimes in their own behavior as well. That might perhaps pave the way to reconsidering in a pragmatic manner how best to manage the global economy with the above-cited goals without forcing countries into an ill-fitting straitjacket.

BIBLIOGRAPHY

Abouchar, Alan (1991), "The Soviet economy: whence. Where. Whither? Why?" *Comparative Economic Studies*, vol. 33, no. 3, 67–93.

Abramovitz, Moses (1986), "Catching up, forging ahead, and falling behind," *Journal of Economic History*, vol. 46, no. 2, 385–406.

Adaman, Fikret and Pat Devine (1996), "The economic calculation debate: lessons for socialists," *Cambridge Journal of Economics*, vol. 20, no. 5, 523–37.

Aglietta, Michel and Philippe Moutot (1993), "Redéployer les réformes," *Economie Internationale*, no. 54, 67–103.

Akyüz, Yilmaz (1993a), "Financial liberalization: the key issues," in *Finance and the real economy – issues and case studies in developing countries*, edited by Yilmaz Akyüz and Günther Held (Santiago: ESCAP, UNCTAD, and WIDER), pp. 19–68.

—— (1993b), "Does financial liberalization improve trade performance?" in *Trade and growth – new dilemmas in trade policy*, edited by Manuel R. Agosin and Diana Tussie (New York: St. Martin's Press), pp. 142–64.

Alchian, Armen A. (1987), "Property rights," *The new Palgrave – a dictionary of economics, vol. 3* (London: Macmillan), pp. 1031–4.

Alexander, William E., Tomás J.T. Baliño, and Charles Enoch (1996), "Adopting indirect instruments of monetary policy," *Finance & Development*, vol. 33, no. 1, 14–17.

Altmann, Franz-Lothar, Wladimir Andreff, and Gerhard Fink (1995), "Die zukünftige Erweiterung der EU in Mittelosteuropa," *Südosteuropa*, vol. 44, no. 5, 235–58.

—— and Cornelius Ochmann (1995), "Central and eastern Europe on its way into the European Union – a report on the state of readiness for integration," in *Central and eastern Europe on the way into the European Union – problems and prospects of integration*, edited by Werner Weidenfeld (Gütersloh: Bertelsmann Foundation Publishers), pp. 9–20.

Amsden, Alice H. (1989), *Asia's next giant: south Korea and late industrialization* (New York and Oxford: Oxford University Press).

—— (1992), "A theory of government intervention in late industrialization," in *State and market in development – synergy or rivalry?* edited by Louis Putterman and Dietrich Rueschemeyer (Boulder, CO and London: Lynne Rienner), pp. 53–84.

—— (1993a), "From P.C. to E.C.," *The New York Times*, 12 January, A21.

—— (1993b), "East Asian financial markets: why so much (and fairly effective) government intervention?" in *Finance and the real economy – issues and case studies in developing countries*, edited by Yilmaz Akyüz and Günther Held (Santiago: ESCAP, UNCTAD, and WIDER), pp. 69–101.

Andorka, Rudolf (1996), "Heading toward modernization?" *The Hungarian Quarterly*, vol. 37, Autumn, 90–8.

Åslund, Anders (1992), "Go faster on Russian reform," *The New York Times*, 7 December, A19.

—— (1993), "The nature of the transformation crisis in the former Soviet countries," in *Overcoming the transformation crisis – lessons for the successor States of the Soviet Union*, edited by Horst Siebert (Tübingen: JCB Mohr [Paul L. Siebeck]), pp. 39–56.

—— (1995a), *How Russia became a market economy* (Washington, DC: Brookings Institution).

—— (1995b), "The Russian road to the market," *Current History*, vol. 94, October, 311–16.

——, Peter Boone, and Simon Johnson (1996), "How to stabilize: lessons from post-communist countries," *Brookings Papers on Economic Activity*, no. 1, 217–91 and 309–13.

—— and Richard Layard, eds. (1993), *Changing the economic system in Russia* (London: Pinter and New York: St. Martin's).

Atje, R. and B. Jovanovic (1993), "Stock markets and development," *European Economic Review*, vol. 37, no. 4, 632–40.

Avineri, Shlomo (1995), "Chancen und Hindernisse auf dem Weg zu einer bürgerlichen Gesellschaft in Mittel- und Osteuropa," in *Demokratie und Marktwirtschaft in Osteuropa*, edited by Werner Weidenfeld (Gütersloh: Bertelsmann Stiftung), pp. 57–66.

Backhaus, Jürgen G. (1989), "Privatization and nationalization – a suggested approach," *Annals of Public and Cooperative Economics*, vol. 60, no. 3, 307–28.

Balázs, Péter (1996), "The 'globalisation' of the eastern enlargement of the European Union: symptoms and consequences" (paper prepared for the "Third Ghent Colloquium on The Relations Between the European Union and Central and Eastern Europe: The Political, Economic and Legal Dimension," Ghent [Belgium], 7–8 March).

Balcerowicz, Leszek (1993), "Common fallacies in the debate on the economic transition in central and eastern Europe" (London: European Bank for Reconstruction and Development, Working Paper no. 11, October).

—— (1994), "Poland," in *The political economy of policy reform*, edited by John Williamson (Washington, DC: Institute for International Economics), pp. 153–77.

——, ed. (1995a), *Socialism, capitalism, transformation* (Budapest, London, and New York: Central European University Press).

—— (1995b), "Understanding post-communist transitions," in *Socialism, capitalism, transformation*, edited by Leszek Balcerowicz (Budapest, London, and New York: Central European University Press), pp. 145–65.

—— and Alan Gelb (1994), "Macropolicies in transition to a market economy: a three-year perspective" (Washington, DC: The World Bank, Annual Bank Conference on Development Economics, 28–29 April, mimeo).

Baldwin, Richard E. (1994), *Towards an integrated Europe* (London: CEPR).

—— (1996), "Progressive economic integration: making the magic work again," *Economics of Transition*, vol. 4, no. 2, 512–14.

Ball, Richard and Gordon Rausser (1995), "Governance structures and the durability of economic reforms: evidence from inflation stabilizations," *World Development*, vol. 23, no. 6, 897–912.

Bardhan, Pranab (1990), "Symposium on the state and economic development," *Journal of Economic Perspectives*, vol. 4, no. 3, 3–7.

—— (1991), "Risktaking, capital markets, and market socialism" (paper presented to the conference "Perspectives on Market Socialism," Berkeley, CA, 16–19 May).

509

Barro, Robert J. (1991), "Economic growth in a cross-section of countries," *The Quarterly Journal of Economics*, vol. 106, no. 2, 407–43.

Barzel, Yoram (1989), *Economic analysis of property rights* (Cambridge: Cambridge University Press).

Beckerman, Wilfred (1986), "How large a public sector?" *Oxford Review of Economic Policy*, vol. 2, no. 2, 7–24.

Begg, David K. H. (1996), "Monetary policy in central and eastern Europe: lessons after half a decade of transition" (Washington, DC: International Monetary Fund, WP/96/108, September).

—— and Richard Portes (1992), "Enterprise debt and economic transformation: financial restructuring of the state sector in central and eastern Europe" (London: CEPR, Discussion Paper Series no. 695, June).

Beleva, Iskra (1993), "Transformatsiyata na trudoviya model v Bŭlgariya i izpolzvaneto na trudovite resursi," *Ikonomicheska misŭl*, vol. 38, no. 9/10, 62–73.

Belka, Marek (1994), "Financial restructuring of banks and enterprises in Poland," *MOCT-MOST*, vol. 4, no. 3, 71–84.

Bell, Daniel (1996), "The protestant ethic," *World Policy Journal*, vol. 13, no. 3, 35–9.

Bennett, Adam G.G. (1993), "The operation of the Estonian currency board," *IMF Staff Papers*, vol. 41, no. 2, 451–70.

Bergsten, C. Fred and C. Randall Henning (1996), *Global economic leadership and the Group of Seven* (Washington, DC: Institute for International Economics).

Bergstrom, Theodore C. and Oded Stark (1993), "How altruism can prevail in an evolutionary environment," *American Economic Review*, vol. 83, no. 2, 149–55.

Bernhard, Michael (1996), "Civil society after the first transition: dilemmas of post-communist democratization in Poland and beyond," *Communist and Post-Communist Studies*, vol. 29, no. 3, 309–30.

Berthélemy, Jean-Claude and Aristomène Varoudakis (1996), *Policies for economic take-off* (Paris: Organisation for Economic Co-operation and Development).

Best, Michael H. (1990), *The new competition – institutions of industrial restructuring* (Cambridge: Polity Press).

Biersteker, Thomas J. (1990), "Reducing the role of the state in the economy: a conceptual exploration of IMF and World Bank prescriptions," *International Studies Quarterly*, vol. 34, no. 4, 477–92.

Bihr, Alain (1992), "Malaise dans l'état-nation," *Le Monde Diplomatique*, no. 2, 7.

Birnbaum, Norman (1996), "Socialism reconsidered – yet again," *World Policy Journal*, vol. 13, no. 3, 40–51.

Blaha, Jaroslav (1993), "Les tsiganes en République tchèque, Slovaquie et Hongrie," *Le Courrier des Pays de l'Est*, no. 383, 86–94.

Blanchard, Olivier, Rudiger Dornbusch, Paul Krugman, Richard Layard, and Lawrence Summers (1991), *Reform in eastern Europe* (Cambridge, MA and London: MIT Press).

——, Simon Commander, and Fabrizio Coricelli (1995), "Unemployment and restructuring in eastern Europe and Russia," in *Unemployment, restructuring, and the labor market in eastern Europe and Russia*, edited by Simon Commander and Fabrizio Coricelli (Washington, DC: The World Bank), pp. 289–329.

Blankart, C. (1985), "Market and non-market alternatives in the supply of public goods: general issues," in *Public expenditure and government growth*, edited by F. Forte and Alan Peacock (Oxford and New York: Basil Blackwell), pp. 192–203.

Blommestein, Hans J. (1993), "Financial sector reform and monetary policy in central and eastern Europe," in *The new Europe: evolving economic and financial systems in east and west*, edited by Donald E. Fair and Robert J. Raymond (Dordrecht, Boston, MA, and London: Kluwer Academic Publishers), pp. 145–67.

—— and Michael Marrese (1991), "Creating conditions for the development of competitive markets in economies in transition" (revised draft of the paper prepared for the conference "The Transition to a Market Economy in Central and Eastern Europe," organized by the OECD's Centre for Co-operation with the European Economies in Transition and the World Bank, Paris, 28–30 November 1990).

——, ——, and Salvatore Zecchini (1991), "Centrally planned economies in transition: an introductory overview of selected issues and strategies," in *Transformation of planned economies: property rights reform and macroeconomic stability*, edited by Hans Blommestein and Michael Marrese (Paris: Organisation for Economic Co-operation and Development), pp. 11–28.

Boeninger, Edgardo (1992), "Governance and development: issues and constraints," *Proceedings of the World Bank Annual Conference on Development Economics, 1991* (Washington, DC: The World Bank), pp. 267–87.

Boeri, Tito (1994), "'Transitional' unemployment," *Economics of Transition*, vol. 2, no. 1, 1–25.

—— (1995), "Unemployment dynamics and labor market policies," in *Unemployment, restructuring, and the labor market in eastern Europe and Russia*, edited by Simon Commander and Fabrizio Coricelli (Washington, DC: The World Bank), pp. 361–83.

—— and Gyorgy Sziraczki (1993), "Labor market developments and policies in central and eastern Europe; a comparative analysis," in *Structural change in central and eastern Europe: labor market and social policy implications*, edited by Georg Fischer and Guy Standing (Paris: Organisation for Economic Co-operation and Development), pp. 241–61.

Böhm, Andreja (1990), "The state holding corporation: an incomplete divisional form of organization," *Public Enterprise*, vol. 10, no. 1, 44–53.

Bohn, John A., Jr., and David H. Levey (1991), "Models of capital market development," in *The emerging Russian bear – integrating the Soviet Union into the world economy*, edited by Josef C. Brada and Michael P. Claudon (New York and London: New York University Press), pp. 87–113.

Boltho, Andrea and Gerald Holtham (1992), "The assessment: new approaches to economic growth," *Oxford Review of Economic Policy*, vol. 8, no. 4, 1–14.

Bonin, John P. and István P. Székely, eds (1994), *The development and reform of financial systems in central and eastern Europe* (Aldershot and Brookfield, VT: Edward Elgar).

Bonnell, Victoria E. (1996), "Winners and losers in Russia's economic transition," in *Identities in transitions – eastern Europe after the collapse of communism*, edited by Victoria E. Bonnell (Berkeley, CA: University of California at Berkeley), pp. 13–28.

Borensztein, Eduardo and Manmohan S. Kumar (1991), "Proposals for privatization in eastern Europe," *IMF Staff Papers*, vol. 38, no. 2, 300–26.

Borish, Michael S. and Michel Noël (1996), "Private sector development in the Visegrad countries," *Finance & Development*, vol. 33, no. 4, 45–8.

Borko, Y. (1996), "Intra-European relations and Russia" (paper prepared for the "Third Ghent Colloquium on The Relations Between the European Union and Central and Eastern Europe: The Political, Economic and Legal Dimension," Ghent [Belgium], 7–8 March).

Bouin, Olivier and Charles-Albert Michalet (1991), *Rebalancing the public and private sectors: developing country experience* (Paris: Development Centre of the Organisation for Economic Co-operation and Development).

—— and Christian Morrison, eds (1996), *Les Privatisations – un état des lieux* (Paris: Presses des Sciences Po, special issue no. 6 of *Revue Économique*).

Bowles, Samuel and Herbert Gintis (1986), *Democracy and capitalism – property, community, and the contradictions of modern social thought* (New York: Basic Books).

Boycko, Maxim, Andrei Shleifer, and Robert Vishny (1995), *Privatizing Russia* (Cambridge, MA and London: MIT Press).

——, ——, and —— (1996a), "A theory of privatisation," *The Economic Journal*, vol. 106, no. 435, 309–19.

——, ——, and —— (1996b), "Second-best economic policy for a divided government," *European Economic Review*, vol. 40, nos. 3–5, 767–74.

Brabant, Jozef M. van (1973), *Bilateralism and structural bilateralism in intra-CMEA trade* (Rotterdam: Rotterdam University Press).

—— (1980), *Socialist economic integration – aspects of contemporary economic problems in eastern Europe* (Cambridge and New York: Cambridge University Press).

——(1987a), *Adjustment, structural change, and economic efficiency – aspects of monetary cooperation in eastern Europe* (Cambridge and New York: Cambridge University Press).

—— (1987b), *Regional price formation in eastern Europe – on the theory and practice of trade pricing* (Dordrecht, Boston, MA, and Lancaster: Kluwer Academic Publishers).

—— (1989), *Economic integration in eastern Europe – a handbook* (Hemel Hempstead: Harvester Wheatsheaf and New York: Routledge).

—— (1990), *Remaking eastern Europe – on the political economy of transition* (Dordrecht, Boston, MA, and London: Kluwer Academic Publishers).

—— (1991a), *Integrating eastern Europe into the global economy – convertibility through a payments union* (Dordrecht, Boston, MA, and London: Kluwer Academic Publishers).

—— (1991b), *Centrally planned economies and international economic organizations* (Cambridge and New York: Cambridge University Press).

—— (1992a), *Privatizing eastern Europe – the role of markets and ownership in the transition* (Dordrecht, Boston, MA, and London: Kluwer Academic Publishers).

—— (1992b), *Unravelling the ruble regime* (London: European Policy Forum).

—— (1993a), *Industrial policy in eastern Europe – governing the transition* (Dordrecht, Boston, MA, and London: Kluwer Academic Publishers).

—— (1993b), "The new east in multilateral economic organizations," in *The new eastern Europe in the global economy*, edited by Jozef M. van Brabant (Boulder, CO: Westview Press), pp. 79–109.

—— (1993c), "Lessons from the wholesale transformations in the east," *Comparative Economic Studies*, vol. 35, no. 3, 73–102.

—— (1994a), "Transforming bank and enterprise balance sheets in eastern Europe," *MOCT-MOST*, vol. 4, no. 3, 7–36.

—— (1994b), "Bad debts and balance sheets in transforming eastern Europe," *Russian & East European Finance and Trade*, vol. 30, no. 2, 5–33.

—— (1994c), "Towards rational banking in transition economies" (paper presented at the Third Freiberg Symposium on Economics "The Emergence and Evolution of Markets," Freiberg [Germany], 1–3 September).

—— (1994d), "Money as an essential vehicle for rational financial intermediation" (paper presented to the conference on "Social and Economic Problems of Ukraine as

Transitional Society at the Break of Millennium," organized by the University of Kiev, Kiev [Ukraine], 1–4 December).

—— (1995a), *The transformation of eastern Europe – joining the European integration movement* (Commack, NY: Nova Science Publishers).

—— (1995b), "Western assistance to PETs, the monetary system, and global integration," in *The global monetary system after the fall of the Soviet empire – in memoriam Robert Triffin 1911–1993*, edited by Miklós Szabó-Pelsőczi (Aldershot: Avebury), pp. 11–33.

—— (1996), *Integrating Europe – the transition economies at stake* (Dordrecht, Boston, MA, and London: Kluwer Academic Publishers).

—— (1997a), "Transformation, endogenous growth, and the new east's global integration," in *Trade and payments in transforming economies of central and eastern Europe*, edited by Lucjan Orlowski and Dominick Salvatore (New York, Westport, CT, and London: Greenwood Press).

—— (1997b), "The World Trade Organization and the transition economies," in *Eastern Europe and the world economy – challenges of transition*, edited by Iliana Zloch-Christy (Aldershot and Brookfield, VT: Edward Elgar).

—— (1997c), "The morning after: regional cooperation – challenges and possibilities" (paper presented at the conference on "Eastern Europe's Foreign Insertion," organized by the Universidad Complutense de Madrid, Madrid [Spain], 25–26 May).

Brainard, Lawrence (1991), "Strategies for economic transformation in central and eastern Europe: role of financial market reform," in *Transformation of planned economies: property rights reform and macroeconomic stability*, edited by Hans Blommestein and Michael Marrese (Paris: Organisation for Economic Co-operation and Development), pp. 95–108.

Brautigam, Deborah (1991), *Governance and economy – a review* (Washington, DC: The World Bank, Working Paper 815, December).

Bresser Pereira, Luiz Carlos, José Maria Maravall, and Adam Przeworski (1993), *Economic reforms in new democracies – a social-democratic approach* (Cambridge and New York: Cambridge University Press, 1993).

Breton, Albert and Ronald Wintrobe (1986), "The bureaucracy of murder revisited," *Journal of Political Economy*, vol. 94, no. 5, 905–26.

Brett, E.A. (1988), "States, markets and private power: problems and possibilities," in *Privatisation in less developed countries*, edited by Paul Cook and Colin Kirkpatrick (New York and London: Harvester Wheatsheaf), pp. 47–67.

Breyer, Stephen and Paul W. MacAvoy (1987), "Regulation and deregulation," *The new Palgrave – a dictionary of economics*, vol. 4 (London: Macmillan), pp. 128–33.

Bruno, Michael (1992), "Stabilization and reform in eastern Europe – a preliminary evaluation," *IMF Staff Papers*, vol. 39, no. 4, 741–77.

Brus, Włodzimierz (1990), "The compatibility of planning and market reconsidered," *Studies in Comparative Communism*, vol. 23, no. 3/4, 341–8.

Bruton, Henry J. (1992), "International aspects of the role of government in economic development," in *State and market in development – synergy or rivalry?* edited by Louis Putterman and Dietrich Rueschemeyer (Boulder, CO and London: Lynne Rienner), pp. 101–30.

Buch, Claudia M. (1993a), "Das erste Jahr der Krone – Estlands Erfahrungen mit der Währungsreform," *Die Weltwirtschaft*, no. 4, 441–65.

—— (1993b), "Banking reform in eastern Europe: an institutional approach," *MOCT-MOST*, vol. 3, no. 3, 73–94.

Buchanan, James M. (1987), "Man and the state," in *Socialism: institutional, philosophical and economic issues*, edited by Svetozar Pejovich (Dordrecht, Boston, MA, and Lancaster: Kluwer Academic Publishers), pp. 3–9.

Buck, Trevor, Steve Thompson, and Mike Wright (1991), "Post-communist privatisation and the British experience," *Public Enterprise*, vol. 11, no. 2/3, 185–200.

Buiter, Willem H., Ricardo Lago, and Nicholas Stern (1996), "Promoting an effective market economy in a changing world" (London: CEPR, Discussion Paper Series no. 1468, October).

Burda, Michael C. (1995), "Labor market institutions and the economic transformation of central and eastern Europe," in *Unemployment, restructuring, and the labor market in eastern Europe and Russia*, edited by Simon Commander and Fabrizio Coricelli (Washington, DC: The World Bank), pp. 331–60.

—— and Martina Lubyova (1995), "The impact of active labour market policies: a closer look at the Czech and Slovak Republics" (London: CEPR, Discussion Paper Series no. 1102, February).

Butenko, Anatoliy (1992), "Von 'samtenen' und anderen Revolutionen in Osteuropa," *Osteuropa*, vol. 42, no. 12, 1068–77.

Buzan, Barry and Gerald Segal (1996), "The rise of 'lite' powers – a strategy for the post-modern state," *World Policy Journal*, vol. 13, no. 3, 1–10.

Cairncross, Alec (1985), "Economics in theory and practice," *American Economic Review*, vol. 75, no. 2, 1–14.

Calvo, Guillermo (1992), "Financial aspects of currency boards," in *Proceedings of a conference on currency substitution and currency boards*, edited by Nissan Liviatan (Washington, DC: The World Bank), pp. 22–4.

—— and Jacob A. Frenkel (1991a), "From centrally planned to market economy: the road from CPE to PCPE," *IMF Staff Papers*, vol. 38, no. 2, 268–99.

—— and —— (1991b), *Obstacles to transforming centrally-planned economies: the role of capital markets* (Washington, DC: International Monetary Fund, WP/91/66).

—— and Manmohan S. Kumar (1993), "Financial markets and intermediation," in *Financial sector reforms and exchange arrangements in eastern Europe* (Washington, DC: The International Monetary Fund), pp. 1–33.

Camdessus, Michel (1995a), "Poland's economic transition: lessons learned and challenges remaining," *IMF Survey*, vol. 24, no. 1, 9–11.

—— (1995b), "Camdessus discusses progress in transition economies in central and eastern Europe," *IMF Survey*, vol. 24, no. 2, 21–4.

—— (1997), "Address at the Moscow Institute of International Affairs, Moscow, 2 April 1997" (Washington, DC: International Monetary Fund, Internet posting).

Campbell, John L. and Leon N. Lindberg (1991), "The evolution of governance regimes," in *Governance of the American economy*, edited by John L. Campbell, J. Rogers Hollingsworth, and Leon N. Lindberg (Cambridge and New York: Cambridge University Press), pp. 319–55.

Campos, Jose Edgardo and Hadi Salehi Esfahani (1996), "Why and when do governments initiate public enterprise reform?" *The World Bank Economic Review*, vol. 10. no. 3, 451–85.

Carlin, Wendy and Colin Mayer (1992), "Enterprise restructuring," *Economic Policy*, no. 15, 311–52.

Castells, Manuel (1992), "Four Asian tigers with a dragon head – a comparative analysis of the state, economy, and society in the Asian Pacific rim," in *States and development in the Asian Pacific rim*, edited by Richard P. Appelbaum and Jeffrey Henderson (Newbury Park, CA, London and New Delhi: SAGE Publications), pp. 33–70.

Chandler, Alfred D. (1977), *The visible hand: the managerial revolution in American business* (Cambridge, MA: Harvard University Press).

Chandler, J. A. (1991), "Public administration and private management. Is there a difference?" *Public Administration*, vol. 69, no. 3, 385–92.

Chang, Ha-Joon (1994), *The political economy of industrial policy* (New York: St. Martin's Press).

—— and Peter Nolan, eds. (1995), *The transformation of the communist countries – against the mainstream* (New York: St. Martin's Press).

—— and Ajit Singh (1991), "Public enterprises in developing countries and economic efficiency – a critical examination of analytical, empirical, and policy issues (Cambridge: University of Cambridge, mimeo).

Cheung, Steven N.S. (1987a), "Economic organization and transaction costs," *The new Palgrave – a dictionary of economics, vol. 2* (London: Macmillan), pp. 55–7.

—— (1987b), "Common property rights," *The new Palgrave – a dictionary of economics, vol. 1* (London: Macmillan), pp. 504–6.

Chhibber, Ajay (1997), "Institutions, the state, and development outcomes" (Washington, DC: The World Bank, mimeo, 7 February).

Chick, Martin (1990) "Politics, information and the defence of market power," in *Governments, industries and markets – aspects of government–industry relations in the UK, Japan, west Germany and the USA since 1945*, edited by Martin Chick (Aldershot and Brookfield, VT: Edward Elgar), pp. 1–9.

Coase, Ronald (1960), "The problem of social cost," *Journal of Law and Economics*, vol. 3, no. 1, 1–44.

Cochrane, John H. and Barry W. Ickes (1991), "Inflation stabilization in reforming socialist economies: the myth of the monetary overhang," *Comparative Economic Studies*, vol. 33, no. 2, 97–122.

Collins, Paul and Malcolm Wallis (1990), "Privatization, regulation and development: some questions of training strategy," *Public Administration and Development*, vol. 10, no. 4, 375–88.

Comisso, Ellen (1991), "Property rights, liberalism, and the transition from 'actually existing' socialism," *East European Politics and Societies*, vol. 5, no. 1, 162–88.

—— (1992), "The political conditions of economic reform in socialism," in *Reform and transformation in eastern Europe – Soviet-type economics on the threshold of change*, edited by János M. Kovács and Márton Tardos (London and New York: Routledge), pp. 225–46.

—— (1997), "Is the glass half full or half empty? – reflections on five years of competitive politics in eastern Europe," *Communist and Post-Communist Studies*, vol. 30, no. 1, 1–21.

Commander, Simon and Tony Killick (1988), "Privatisation in developing countries: a survey of the issues," in *Privatisation in less developed countries*, edited by Paul Cook and Colin Kirkpatrick (New York and London: Harvester Wheatsheaf), pp. 91–124.

Cook, Paul and Colin Kirkpatrick, eds (1988a), *Privatisation in less developed countries* (New York and London: Harvester Wheatsheaf).

—— and —— (1988b), "Privatisation in less developed countries: an overview," in *Privatisation in less developed countries*, edited by Paul Cook and Colin Kirkpatrick (New York and London: Harvester Wheatsheaf), pp. 3–44.

—— and ——, eds (1995), *Privatisation policy and performance – international perspective* (New York and London: Prentice Hall – Harvester Wheatsheaf).

—— and Martin Minogue (1990), "Waiting for privatization in developing countries: towards the integration of economic and non-economic explanations," *Public Administration and Development*, vol. 10, no. 4, 389–403.

Cooter, Robert D. (1987), "Coase theorem," *The new Palgrave – a dictionary of economics, vol. 1* (London: Macmillan), pp. 457–60.

Corbett, Jenny and Colin P. Mayer (1991), "Financial reform in eastern Europe: progress with the wrong model," *Oxford Review of Economic Policy*, vol. 8, no. 4, 57–75.

Csontos, László, János Kornai, and István György Tóth (1997), "Tax-awareness and the reform of the welfare state – results of a Hungarian survey" (Cambridge, MA: Harvard Institute of Economic Research, Discussion Paper no. 1790, January).

Cullis, John G. and Philip R. Jones (1987), *Microeconomics & the public economy – a defence of Leviathan* (Oxford and New York: Basil Blackwell).

Dąbrowski, Marek (1996), "Different strategies of transition to a market economy – how do they work in practice?" (Washington, DC: The World Bank, Policy Research Working Paper no. 1579, March).

Dahl, Robert A. and Charles E. Lindblom (1953), *Politics, economics, and welfare – planning and politico-economic systems resolved into basic social processes* (New York, Evanston, IL, and London: Harper & Row).

Dahrendorf, Ralf (1990), *Reflections on the revolution in Europe – in a letter intended to have been sent to a gentleman in Warsaw* (New York: Times Books).

Dasgupta, Partha (1986), "Positive freedom, markets and the welfare state," *Oxford Review of Economic Policy*, vol. 2, no. 2, 25–36.

Datta-Chaudhuri, Mrinal (1990), "Market failure and government failure," *Journal of Economic Perspectives*, vol. 4, no. 3, 25–39.

David, Paul A. (1992), "Knowledge, property, and the system dynamics of technological change" (paper prepared for the World Bank's "Annual Conference on Development Economics," Washington, 30 April–1 May).

Dawid, Herbert and Gustav Feichtinger (1996), "On the persistence of corruption," *Journal of Economics – Zeitschrift für Nationalökonomie*, vol. 64, no. 2, 177–93.

Dehejia, Vivek H. (1997), "Will gradualism work when shock therapy doesn't?" (London: CEPR, Discussion Paper Series no. 1552, February).

Delorme, Robert and Christine André (1983), *L'État et l'économie* (Paris: Le Seuil).

Demsetz, Harold (1967), "Toward a theory of property rights," *The American Economic Review – Papers and Proceedings*, vol. 57, no. 2, 347–59.

Deyo, Frederic C. (1987), "Introduction," in *The political economy of the new Asian industrialism*, edited by Frederic C. Deyo (Ithaca, NY: Cornell University Press), pp. 11–22.

Dietrich, Michael (1992), "The foundations of industrial policy," in *Current issues in industrial economic strategy*, edited by Keith Cowling and Roger Snugden (Manchester and New York: Manchester University Press), pp. 16–32.

Dimitrova, Elka (1993), "Ima li 'zhenski pazar', no na truda?" *Ikonomika*, vol. 9, No 11, 28–39.

Dobrinsky, Rumen (1994), "The problem of bad loans and enterprise indebtedness in Bulgaria," *MOCT-MOST*, vol. 4, no. 3, 37–58.

Don, Henk and Paul Besseling (1996), "Social security reforms: why and how?" *CPB Report*, [vol. 1], no. 4, 13–17.

Dornbusch, Rudiger (1991a), "Comments and discussion," *Brookings Papers on Economic Activity*, no. 1, 88–92.

—— (1991b), "Strategies and priorities for reform," in *The transition to a market economy –*

the broad issues, vol. I, edited by Paul Marer and Salvatore Zecchini (Paris: Organisation for Economic Co-operation and Development), pp. 169–83.

—— (1992), "The case for trade liberalization in developing countries," *Journal of Economic Perspectives*, vol. 6, no. 1, 69–85.

Drábek, Zdeněk (1996), "The stability of trade policy in the countries in transition and their integration into the multilateral trading system," *The World Economy*, vol. 19, no. 6, 721–45.

Dunning, John H. (1992a), "The global economy, domestic governance, strategies and transnational corporations: interactions and policy implications," *Transnational Corporations*, vol. 1, no. 3, 7–45.

—— (1992b), "The competitive advantage of countries and the activities of transnational corporations," *Transnational Corporations*, vol. 1, no. 1, 135–68.

Eatwell, John, Michael Ellman, Mats Karlsson, D. Mario Nuti, and Judith Shapiro (1995), *Transformation and integration – shaping the future of central and eastern Europe* (London: Institute for Public Policy Research).

EBRD (1993), "Banking reform in central and eastern Europe," *EBRD Economic Review – Current Economic Issues*, (July), 8–16.

—— (1995), *Transition report 1995 – investment and enterprise development* (London: European Bank for Reconstruction and Development).

—— (1996), *Transition report 1996 – infrastructure and savings* (London: European Bank for Reconstruction and Development).

Economist (1993), "Capitulating to capitalism," *The Economist*, 8 May, 95–6.

Elster, John and Aanund Hylland, eds (1989), *Foundations of social choice theory* (Cambridge and New York: Cambridge University Press).

Estrin, Saul (1991a), "Some reflections on self-management, social choice, and reform in eastern Europe," *Journal of Comparative Economics*, vol. 18, no. 2, 349–66.

—— (1991b), "Privatisation, self-management and social ownership," *Communist Economies & Economic Transformation*, vol. 3, no. 3, 355–65.

European Commission (1995a), "Annual report concerning the financial year 1994 together with the institutions' replies," *Official Journal of the European Communities*, C303, 14 November.

—— (1995b), "Conclusions of the European Council, Madrid, 15–16 December 1995" (Brussels: European Commission [undated document; probably late December]).

—— (1995c), *Towards greater economic integration – the European Union's financial assistance and trade policy for central and eastern Europe and the New Independent States* (Brussels: European Commission, October).

—— (1996), "Relations between the European Union and central and eastern European countries (CEEC)" (Brussels: European Commission [undated communication; probably February]).

—— (1997a), "Together in Europe," no. 106 (Brussels: European Commission, 1 April).

—— (1997b), *European Dialogue*, no. 2 (Brussels: European Communities, Internet posting, 16 April).

Fershtman, Chaim (1990), "The interdependence between ownership and market structure: the case of privatization," *Economica*, vol. 57, no. 3, 319–28.

Fine, Ben (1991), "Scaling the commanding heights of public enterprise economics," *Cambridge Journal of Economics*, vol. 15, no. 2, 127–42.

Fischer, Stanley (1991), *Privatization in east European transformation* (Cambridge, MA: NBER Working Paper no. 3703, May).

517

—— (1992) "Stabilization and economic reform in Russia" (paper prepared for the conference "Eastern European Trade Policy Issues," organized by the European Bank for Reconstruction and Development, London, 25–27 March).

—— (1996), "Maintaining price stability," *Finance & Development*, vol. 33, no. 4, 34–7.

—— (1997), "Financial system soundness," *Finance & Development*, vol. 34, no. 1, 14–16.

Flemming, John S. (1993), "The role of external assistance in overcoming the transformation crisis," in *Overcoming the transformation crisis – lessons for the successor States of the Soviet Union*, edited by Horst Siebert (Tübingen: JCB Mohr [Paul L. Siebeck]), pp. 197–204.

Fougerolles, Jean de (1995), "The Latin American experience with private pension funds: lessons for eastern Europe," *Transition*, vol. 6, no. 7/8, 4–7.

Fox, Louise (1994), "What to do about pensions in transition economies?" *Transition*, vol. 5, no. 2/3, 3–6.

—— (1995), "Can eastern Europe's old-age crisis be fixed?" *Finance & Development*, vol. 32, no. 4, 34–7.

Franz, Wolfgang (1995), "Central and east European labour markets in transition: developments, causes, and cures" (London: CEPR, Discussion Paper Series no. 1132, February).

Freinkman, Lev M. and Irina Starodubrovskaya (1996), "Restructuring of enterprise social assets in Russia – trends, problems, possible solutions" (Washington, DC: The World Bank, Policy Research Working Paper no. 1635, August).

Frischtak, Leila (1996), "Overview: from policy reform to institutional change," in *Governance, leadership, and communication – building constituencies for economic reform*, edited by Leila Frischtak and Izak Atiyas (Washington, DC: The World Bank, 1996), pp. 1–32.

—— and Izak Atiyas, eds (1996), *Governance, leadership, and communication – building constituencies for economic reform* (Washington, DC: The World Bank, 1996).

Fry, Maxwell J. and D. Mario Nuti (1992), "Monetary and exchange-rate policies during eastern Europe's transition: some lessons from further east," *Oxford Review of Economic Policy*, vol. 8, no. 1, 27–43.

Frydman, Roman and Andrzej Rapaczyński (1991), "Markets and institutions in large-scale privatization: an approach to economic and social transformation in eastern Europe," in *Reforming central and eastern European economies – initial results and challenges*, edited by Vittorio Corbo, Fabrizio Coricelli, and Jan Bossak (Washington, DC: The World Bank), pp. 253–74.

—— and —— (1993), "Insiders and the state: overview of responses to agency problems in east European privatizations," *Economics of Transition*, vol. 1, no. 1, 39–59.

—— and Stanislaw Wellisz (1991), "The ownership-control structure and the behavior of Polish enterprises during the 1990 reforms: macroeconomic measures and microeconomic responses," in *Reforming central and eastern European economies – initial results and challenges*, edited by Vittorio Corbo, Fabrizio Coricelli, and Jan Bossak (Washington, DC: The World Bank), pp. 141–56.

FT (1993), "Last chance in Russia," *Financial Times*, 4 March, 13.

Funke, Norbert (1993), "Timing and sequencing of reforms: competing views and the role of credibility," *Kyklos*, vol. 46, no. 3, 337–62.

Furubotn, Eirik G. and Svetozar Pejovich (1972), "Property rights and economic theory: a survey of recent literature," *The Journal of Economic Literature*, vol. 10, no. 2, 1137–62.

Gabanyi, Anneli Ute (1997), "Revolutionen in Ostmitteleuropa – Ursachen, Gemeinsamkeiten, Perspektiven," *Osteuropa*, vol. 47, no. 1, 3–25.

Galal, Ahmed (1989), "Institutional framework for efficient and sustainable restructuring of state-owned enterprises," *Public Enterprise*, vol. 9, no. 2, 111–22.

Galbraith, John K. (1990), "The rush to capitalism," *The New York Review of Books*, vol. 37, no. 16, 51–2.

—— (1996), *The good society – the humane agenda* (Boston, MA and New York: Houghton Mifflin).

Garton Ash, Timothy (1996), "Hungary's revolution: forty years on," *The New York Review of Books*, vol. 43, no. 18, 18–22.

Gathon, Henry-Jean and Pierre Pestieau (1996), "La performance des entreprises publiques. Une question de propriété ou de concurrence?" *Revue Économique*, vol. 47, no. 6, 1225–38.

Gellner, Ernest (1994), *Conditions of liberty: civil society and its rivals* (London: Penguin).

Ghai, Yash P. (1990), "The management of public enterprises through holding corporations," *Public Enterprise*, vol. 10, no. 1, 18–26.

Ghosh, Atish R., Ann-Marie Gulde, Jonathan D. Ostry, and Holger Wolf (1996), *Does the exchange rate regime matter for inflation and growth?* (Washington, DC: International Monetary Fund, September).

Gilpin, Robert, with the assistance of Jean M. Gilpin (1987), *The political economy of international relations* (Princeton, NJ: Princeton University Press).

GRADE (1992), "Governance and development: a program of studies and dissemination" (Lima: Grupo de Análisis para el Desarrollo, July, mimeo).

Gray, Boyden (1993), "When currencies collapse – the smart way to help the old Soviet bloc," *The New York Times*, 29 December, A11.

Gray, Cheryl W. (1991), "Tax systems in the reforming socialist economies of Europe," *Communist Economies & Economic Transformation*, vol. 3, no. 1, 63–79.

—— (1996), "In search of owners – lessons of experience with privatization and corporate governance in transition economies" (Washington, DC: The World Bank, Policy Research Working Paper no. 1595, April).

—— and Arnold Holle (1996a), "Bank-led restructuring in Poland – an empirical look at the bank conciliation process" (Washington, DC: The World Bank, Policy Research Working Paper no. 1650, September).

—— and —— (1996b), "Bank-led restructuring in Poland – bankruptcy and its alternatives" (Washington, DC: The World Bank, Policy Research Working Paper no. 1651, September).

Gray, H. Peter (1996), "Culture and economic performance: policy as an intervening variable," *Journal of Comparative Economics*, vol. 23, no. 3, 278–91.

Gray, John (1989), *Limited government: a positive agenda* (London: Institute of Economic Affairs).

—— (1992), *The moral foundations of market institutions*, with commentaries by Chandran Kukathas, Patrick Minford, and Raymond Plant (London: Institute of Economic Affairs Health and Welfare Unit).

Greenwald, Bruce C. and Joseph E. Stiglitz (1986), "Externalities in economies with imperfect information and incomplete markets," *The Quarterly Journal of Economics*, vol. 101, no. 2, 229–64.

Greider, William (1997), *One world, ready or not: the manic logic of global capitalism* (New York: Simon & Schuster).

Grosfeld, Irena and Claudia Senik-Leygonie (1996), "Trois enjeux des privatisations à l'Est," *Revue Économique*, vol. 47, no. 6, 1351–71.

Grossman, Gene M. (1990), "Promoting new industrial activities: a survey of recent arguments and evidence," *OECD Economic Studies*, no. 14, 87–125.

Guitián, Manuel (1991), "Comments and discussion," *Brookings Papers on Economic Activity*, no. 1, 92–8.

—— (1993), "From the plan to the market: banking and financial reform aspects," in *The new Europe: evolving economic and financial systems in east and west*, edited by D. E. Fair and Robert Raymond (Dordrecht, Boston, MA, and London: Kluwer Academic Publishers), pp. 113–29.

Haggard, Stephan, John McMillan, and Christopher Woodruff (1996), "Trust and search in Vietnam's emerging private sector" (London: CEPR, Discussion Paper Series no. 1506, November).

Halpern, László and Charles Wyplosz (1996), "Equilibrium exchange rates in transition economies" (Washington, DC: International Monetary Fund, WP/96/125, November).

Ham, John, Jan Švejnar, and Katharine Terrell (1995), "Czech Republic and Slovakia," in *Unemployment, restructuring, and the labor market in eastern Europe and Russia*, edited by Simon Commander and Fabrizio Coricelli (Washington, DC: The World Bank), pp. 91–146.

Hanke, Steve H. (1994), "Dangers posed by a larger rouble zone," *The Financial Times*, 19 January, 10.

—— (1997), " New currency boards come to the Balkans," *Transition*, vol. 8, no. 1, 8–9.

——, Lars Jonung, and Kurt Schuler (1993), *Russian currency and finance: a currency board approach to reform* (London and New York: Routledge).

—— and Kurt Schuler (1992), "Currency boards for Latin America," in *Proceedings of a conference on currency substitution and currency boards*, edited by Nissan Liviatan (Washington, DC: The World Bank), pp. 13–21.

—— and —— (1994a), "Currency board-like systems are not currency boards," *Transition*, vol. 5, no. 6, 13.

—— and —— (1994b), "Currency board to eliminate inflation in Russia?" *Transition*, vol. 5, no. 4, 4–5.

Hankiss, Elemér (1990), *East European alternatives* (Oxford: Clarendon Press).

Hannig, Alfred (1994), "Die Rolle von Sparkassen im Finanzsystem der Transformationsländer," *Konjunkturpolitik*, vol. 40, no. 1, 67–99.

Hansen, John and Piritta Sorsa (1994), "Estonia: a shining star from the Baltics," in *Trade in the new independent States*, edited by Constantine Michalopoulos and David G. Tarr (Washington, DC: The World Bank), pp. 115–32.

Hansson, Ardo H. (1993), "The Estonian kroon: experiences of the first year," in *The economics of new currencies* (London: CEPR), pp. 85–107.

—— (1994), "The political-economy of macroeconomic and foreign trade policy in Estonia," in *Trade in the new independent States*, edited by Constantine Michalopoulos and David G. Tarr (Washington, DC: The World Bank), pp. 133–40.

Hardtkamp, Jannes (1997), "Central Statistics Office tries to change with the times," *Hungary Report*, 3 February (Budapest: KSH, Internet posting).

Harris, Richard D.F. (1997), "Stock markets and development: a re-assessment," *European Economic Review*, vol. 41, no. 1, 139–46.

Hausner, Jerzy, Bob Jessop, and Klaus Nielsen, eds. (1995), *Strategic choice and path-dependency in post-socialism – institutional dynamics in the transformation process* (Aldershot: Edward Elgar).

Havel, Václav (1996), "The hope for Europe," *New York Review of Books*, vol. 43, no. 8 [*sic*: probably 11], 38–41.

Hay, Donald (1993), "The assessment: competition policy," *Oxford Review of Economic Policy*, vol. 9, no. 2, 1–26.

Heath, John (1990), "The role of holding companies in the organisation and management of public enterprises: some comparisons," *Public Enterprise*, vol. 10, no. 1, 34–43.

Heertje, Arnold (1989), "Introduction," in Stiglitz, Joseph E. *et al.*, *The economic role of the state* (Oxford: Basil Blackwell in association with Bank Insinger de Beaufort), pp. 1–8.

Helliwell, John F. (1994), "Empirical linkages between democracy and economic growth," *British Journal of Political Science*, vol. 24, no. 2, 225–48.

Helm, Dieter (1986), "The assessment: the economic borders of the state," *Oxford Review of Economic Policy*, vol. 2, no. 2, i–xxiv.

—— and George Yarrow (1988), "The assessment: the regulation of utilities," *Oxford Review of Economic Policy*, vol. 4, no. 2, i–xxxi.

Hemming, Richard and Ali M. Mansoor (1988), *Privatization and public enterprises* (Washington, DC: International Monetary Fund, Occasional Paper no. 56).

Henley, Andrew and Euclid Tsakalotos (1991), "Corporatism, profit squeeze and investment," *Cambridge Journal of Economics*, vol. 15, no. 4, 425–50.

Hicks, John R. (1983), "The Austrian theory of capital and its re-birth in modern economics," in *Classics and moderns – collected essays on economic theory, vol. III* (Cambridge, MA: Harvard University Press), pp. 96–112.

Hirst, Paul and Grahame Thompson (1996), *Globalization in question – the international economy and the possibilities of governance* (Cambridge: Polity Press, 1996).

Hobsbawm, Eric J. (1993), "The new threat to history," *The New York Review of Books*, vol. 40, no. 21, pp. 62–4.

—— (1996), "The future of the state," *Development and Change*, vol. 27, no. 2, 267–78.

Hoekman, Bernard and Simon Djankov (1996), "Intra-industry trade, foreign direct investment, and the reorientation of eastern European exports" (Washington, DC: The World Bank, Policy Research Paper no. 1652, September).

Honohan, Patrick (1997), "Currency board or central bank? Lessons from the Irish Pound's link with sterling, 1928–79," *Banca Nazionale del Lavoro Quarterly Review*, vol. 50, no. 1, 39–67.

Horton, Mark A. (1996), "Health and education expenditures in Russia, the Baltic States and the other countries of the former Soviet Union" (Washington, DC: International Monetary Fund, WP/96/126, November).

Horvat, Branko (1991), "Reprivatisation or something else?" *Communist Economies & Economic Transformation*, vol. 3, no. 3, 367–73.

Hussain, Athar and Nicholas Stern (1993), "The role of the state, ownership and taxation in transitional economies," *Economics of Transition*, vol. 1, no. 1, 61–87.

Hutchings, Robert L. (1994), "Five years after – reflections on the post-communist transitions and western assistance strategies," in *East-central European economies in transition*, edited by the Joint Economic Committee, Congress of the United States (Washington, DC: US Government Printing Office, 1994), pp. 176–90.

Hyden, Goran (1992), "Governance and the study of politics," in *Governance and politics in Africa*, edited by Goran Hyden and Michael Bratton (Boulder, CO and London: Lynne Rienner), pp. 1–26.

Ibrahim, Saad Eddin and Hans Lofgren (1996), "Successful adjustment and declining governance? The case of Egypt," in *Governance, leadership, and communication – building constituencies for economic reform*, edited by Leila Frischtak and Izak Atiyas (Washington, DC: The World Bank, 1996), pp. 159–204.

Ickes, Barry W. (1990), "Obstacles to economic reform of socialism: an institutional-choice approach," *Annals of the American Academy of Political and Social Sciences*, vol. 507, no. 1, 53–64.

—— (1996), "Comments and discussion," *Brookings Papers on Economic Activity*, no. 1, 298–305.

Ignatieff, Michael (1995), "On civil society – why eastern Europe's revolutions could succeed," *Foreign Affairs*, vol. 74, no. 2, 128–36.

Ikenberry, G. John (1992), "A world from scratch," *The New York Times*, 26 December, 21.

IMF (1993), "Reforming centrally planned economies: what have we learned?" *IMF Survey*, vol. 22, no. 16, 241, 247–51.

—— (1997a), "Currency board arrangements more widely used," *IMF Survey*, vol. 26, no. 4, 54–7.

—— (1997b), "Bank restructuring strategy should be linked to macroeconomic policy," *IMF Survey*, vol. 26, no. 5, 70–1.

—— (1997c), "Transition economies need health and educational reforms," *IMF Survey*, vol. 26, no. 5, 72–4.

Islam, Shafiqul (1993), "Conclusion: problems of planning a market economy," in *Making markets – economic transformation in eastern Europe and the post-Soviet states*, edited by Shafiqul Islam and Michael Mandelbaum (New York: Council on Foreign Relations Press), pp. 182–215.

Janos, Andrew C. (1996), "What was communism: a retrospective in comparative analysis," *Communist and Post-Communist Studies*, vol. 29, no. 1, 1–24.

Jenkinson, Tim and Colin Mayer (1996), "The assessment: contracts and competition," *Oxford Review of Economic Policy*, vol. 12, no. 4, 1–10.

Johnson, Björn and Bengt-Åke Lundvall (1989), "The limits of the pure market economy," in *Samhällsvetenskap, ekonomi och historia – festskrift till Lars Herlitz*, edited by Jan Bohlin *et al.* (Göteborg: Daidalos), pp. 85–106.

Johnson, Chalmers (1987), "Political institutions and economic performance: the government–business relationship in Japan, south Korea, and Taiwan," in *The political economy of the new Asian industrialism*, edited by Frederic C. Deyo (Ithaca, NY: Cornell University Press), pp. 136–64.

—— (1995), *Japan: who governs? The rise of the developmental state* (New York and London: W.W. Norton).

Kallas, Siim (1993), "Estonia's currency board anchors its economy as adjustment proceeds – summary," *IMF Survey*, vol. 22, 29 November, 366–8.

Kamiński, Bartlomiej, Zhen Kun Wang, and L. Alan Winters (1996), "Export performance in transition economies," *Economic Policy*, no. 23, 421–36.

Kaminski, Matthew (1996), "Consultancy blooms in Ukraine's sunnier climate," *Financial Times*, 18 April, 2.

Kanel, Don (1974), "Property and economic power as issues in institutional economics," *Journal of Economic Issues*, vol. 8, no. 4, 827–40.

Kaufmann, Daniel and Aleksander Kaliberda (1996), "Integrating the unofficial economy into the dynamics of post-socialist economies – a framework of analysis and evidence" (Washington, DC: The World Bank, Policy Research Working Paper no. 1691, December).

Kay, John A. (1986), "The rationale of taxation," *Oxford Review of Economic Policy*, vol. 2, no. 2, 1–6.

—— (1992), *Foundations of corporate success: how business strategies add value* (Oxford: Oxford University Press).

—— and John S. Vickers (1988), "Regulatory reform in Britain," *Economic Policy*, no. 7, 288–351.

Kennedy, Paul (1993), "True leadership for the next millennium," *The New York Times*, 3 January, E11.

Kent, Calvin A., ed. (1987a), *Entrepreneurship and the privatizing of government* (New York and Westport, CT: Quorum Books).

—— (1987b), "Privatization of public functions: promises and problems," in *Entrepreneurship and the privatizing of government*, edited by Calvin A. Kent (New York and Westport, CT: Quorum Books), pp. 3–22.

Keohane, Robert O. (1984), *After hegemony – cooperation and discord in the world political economy* (Princeton, NJ: Princeton University Press).

—— (1986), "Reciprocity in international relations," *International Organization*, vol. 40, no. 1, 1–27.

Kester, W. Carl (1992), "Industrial groups as systems of contractual governance," *Oxford Review of Economic Policy*, vol. 8, no. 3, 24–44.

Killick, Tony (1990), *A reaction too far – economic theory and the role of the state in developing countries* (London: Overseas Development Institute).

Kirova, Krasimira (1993), "Bezrabotitsata i razkrivane na novi rabotni mesta," *Ikonomicheska misŭl*, vol. 38, no. 7/8, 40– 51.

Klaus, Václav (1991a), "I get angry, I will explain," translated from *Respekt*, 1991:29, pp. 5–6 in *Foreign Broadcasting Information Service – Daily Report: Eastern Europe*, 12 August (FBIS-EEU-91-155), pp. 9–12.

—— (1991b), "Price liberalization and currency convertibility: twenty days after," in *Currency convertibility in eastern Europe*, edited by John Williamson (Washington, DC: Institute for International Economics), pp. 9–13.

Kornai, János (1990a), *The road to a free economy – shifting from a socialist system: the example of Hungary* (New York: W. W. Norton).

—— (1990b), *The affinity between ownership and coordination mechanisms – the common experience of reform in socialist countries* (Helsinki: World Institute for Development Economics Research).

—— (1992), "The postsocialist transition and the state: reflections in the light of Hungarian fiscal problems," *American Economic Review*, vol. 82, no. 2, 1–21.

—— (1996a), "The social issue in the era of transition – in conversation with Mihály Laki," *The Hungarian Quarterly*, vol. 37, Spring, 58–71.

—— (1996b), "Paying the bill for goulash-communism – Hungarian development and macro stabilization in a political-economy perspective" (Cambridge, MA: Harvard Institute of Economic Research, Discussion Paper Series no. 1748, February).

Köves, András (1994), "From 'great leaps forward' to normalcy: some issues in transitional policies in eastern Europe," *UNCTAD Review 1994* (New York: United Nations Publication, sales no. E.94.II.D.19), pp. 155–67.

—— and Gábor Oblath (1994), "The regional role of the former Soviet Union and the CMEA: a net assessment," in *East-central European economies in transition*, edited by the Joint Economic Committee, Congress of the United States (Washington, DC: US Government Printing Office, 1994), pp. 355–66.

Kramer, Heinz (1993), "The European Community's response to the 'new eastern Europe'," *Journal of Common Market Studies*, vol. 31, no. 2, 213–44.

Krasner, Stephen D. (1982), "Structural causes and regime consequences: regimes as intervening variables," *International Organization*, vol. 36, no. 2, 185–205.

—— (1983), *International regimes* (Ithaca, NY: Cornell University Press).

Kregel, Jan A. (1990), "Market design and competition as constraint to self-interested behaviour," in *Economic policy and the market process – Austrian and mainstream economics*, edited by K. Groenveld, J. A. H. Maks, and J. Muyskens (Amsterdam: North-Holland), pp. 45–57.

—— (1994), "Capital flows: globalization of production and financing development," *UNCTAD Review, 1994* (New York: United Nations Publication, sales no. E.94.II.D.19), pp. 23–38.

Krueger, Anne O. (1990), "Government failure in development," *Journal of Economic Perspectives*, vol. 4, no. 3, 9–23.

—— (1993), "Virtuous and vicious circles in economic development," *American Economic Review*, vol. 83, no. 2, 351–5.

—— (1997), "Trade policy and economic development: how we learn?" *American Economic Review*, vol. 87, no. 1, 1–22.

Krugman, Paul (1995) "Dutch tulips and emerging markets," *Foreign Affairs*, vol. 74, no. 4, 28–46.

Krumm, Kathie, Branko Milanović, and Michael Walton (1995), "Transfers and the transition from central planning," *Finance & Development*, vol. 33, no. 3, 27–30.

Kuttner, Robert (1997), *Everything for sale – the virtues and limits of markets* (New York: A Twentieth Century Fund Book/Alfred A. Knopf, 1997).

Laffont, Jean-Jacques (1996), "Privatisation et incitations," *Revue Économique*, vol. 47, no. 6, 1239–51.

—— and Jean Tirole (1991), "The politics of government decision-making: a theory of regulatory capture," *The Quarterly Journal of Economics*, vol. 106, no. 4, 1089–127.

Lainela, Seija and Pekka Sutela (1994), *The Baltic economies in transition* (Helsinki: Bank of Finland).

Lall, Sanjaya (1990), *Building industrial competitiveness in developing countries* (Paris: Organisation for Economic Co-operation and Development).

—— (1994), "Industrial policy: the role of government in promoting industrial and technological development," *UNCTAD Review 1994* (New York: United Nations Publication, sales no. E.94.II.D.19), pp. 65–89.

—— and Georg Kell (1991), "Industrial development in developing countries and the role of government interventions," *Banca Nazionale del Lavoro Quarterly Review*, vol. 44, no. 3, 271–92.

Lampert, Heinz (1990), "Die Bedeutung der Gerechtigkeit im Konzept der sozialen Marktwirtschaft," *Hamburger Jahrbuch für Wirtschafts- und Gesellschaftspolitik*, vol. 35, 75–91.

Landell-Mills, Pierre and Ismail Serageldin (1991), "Governance and the development process," *Finance & Development*, vol. 28, no. 3, 14–17.

—— and —— (1992), "Governance and the external sector," in *Proceedings of the World Bank Annual Conference on Development Economics, 1991* (Washington, DC: The World Bank), pp. 303–20.

Landes, David (1990), "Why are we so rich and they so poor?" *American Economic Review*, vol. 80, no. 2, 1–13.

Landesmann, Michael A. and István P. Székely, eds (1995), *Industrial restructuring and trade reorientation in eastern Europe* (Cambridge and New York: Cambridge University Press).

Lankes, Hans-Peter and A.J. Venables (1996), "Foreign direct investment in economic transition: the changing pattern of investments," *Economics of Transition*, vol. 4, no. 2, 331–47.

Laski, Kazimierz (1992), "Der aktuelle Stand der Diskussion über die Transformationsprobleme," *Europäische Rundschau*, vol. 20, no. 4, 35–43.

—— (1996), "An alternative economic policy for central and eastern Europe," in *Economics of transition – structural adjustments and growth prospects in eastern Europe*, edited by Mark Knell (Cheltenham and Brookfield, VT: Edward Elgar, 1996), pp. 87–115.

Lateef, K. Sarwar (1992), "Comment on 'Governance and development,' by Boeninger," *Proceedings of the World Bank Annual Conference on Development Economics, 1991* (Washington, DC: The World Bank), pp. 295–7.

Lavigne, Marie (1995), *The economics of transition – from socialist economy to market economy* (London: Macmillan).

Ledyard, John O. (1987), "Market failure," in *The new Palgrave – a dictionary of economics, vol. 3* (London: Macmillan), pp. 326–8.

Lee, Barbara and John Nellis (1990), "Enterprise reform and privatization in market economies" (Washington, DC: The World Bank, April, mimeo).

Leman, Cristopher K. (1989), "The forgotten fundamental: successes and excesses of direct government," in *Beyond privatization – the tools of government action*, edited by Lester M. Salamon (Washington, DC: Urban Institute Press), pp. 53–87.

Leven, Bożena (1993), "Unemployment among Polish women," *Comparative Economic Studies*, vol. 35, no. 4, 135–45.

—— (1997), "Distributional effects of Poland's transition – the status of pensioners" (paper prepared for the 1997 ASSA meetings in New Orleans, LA, manuscript).

Levine, Ross and David Scott (1993), "Old debts and new beginnings: a policy choice in transitional socialist economies," *World Development*, vol. 21, no. 3, 319–30.

Levitas, Anthony (1990), "Solidarity banks: infrastructure from the bottom up," *Communist Economies*, vol. 2, no. 1, 95–9.

Liebich, André (1991), *Whither eastern Europe* (Toronto, ONT: Canadian Institute of International Affairs).

Lindbeck, Assar (1993), *Unemployment and macroeconomics* (Cambridge, MA and London: MIT Press).

Lindberg, Leon N., John L. Campbell, and J. Rogers Hollingsworth (1991), "Economic governance and the analysis of structural change in the American economy," in *Governance of the American economy*, edited by John L. Campbell, J. Rogers Hollingsworth, and Leon N. Lindberg (Cambridge and New York: Cambridge University Press, 1991), pp. 3–32.

Lindblom, Charles E. (1977), *Politics and markets – the world's political-economic systems* (New York: Basic Books).

—— (1990), *Inquiry and change – the troubled attempt to understand and shape society* (New Haven, CT and London: Yale University Press).

Lipton, David and Jeffrey D. Sachs (1990a), "Creating a market economy in eastern Europe: the case of Poland," *Brookings Papers on Economic Activity*, no. 1, 75–133.

—— and —— (1990b), "Privatization in eastern Europe: the case of Poland," *Brookings Papers on Economic Activity*, no. 2, 293–341.

Liviatan, Nissan, ed. (1992), *Proceedings of a conference on currency substitution and currency boards* (Washington, DC: The World Bank).

Loayza, Norman A. (1997), "The economics of the informal sector – a simple model and some empirical evidence from Latin America" (Washington, DC: The World Bank, Policy Research Working Paper 1727, February).

Long, Millard (1993), "Financial aspects of enterprise restructuring," in *The new Europe: evolving economic and financial systems in east and west*, edited by Donald E. Fair and Robert J. Raymond (Dordrecht, Boston, MA, and London: Kluwer Academic Publishers), pp. 131–44.

Ludlow, Peter and Niels Ersbøll (1996), "Towards 1996: the agenda of the Inter-governmental Conference," in *Preparing for 1996 and a larger European Union: principles and priorities* (Brussels: Centre for European Policy Studies), pp. 1–61.

Lyon, James (1996), "Yugoslavia's hyperinflation, 1993–1994: a social history," *East European Politics and Societies*, vol. 10, no. 2, 293–327.

MacAvoy, Paul W., W.T. Stanbury, George Yarrow, and Richard J. Zeckhauser, eds (1989), *Privatization and state-owned enterprises – lessons from the United States, Great Britain and Canada* (Boston, MA, Dordrecht, and London: Kluwer Academic Publishers).

Marglin, Stephen A. (1990), "Lessons of the golden age: an overview," in *The golden age of capitalism: reinterpreting the postwar experience*, edited by Stephen A. Marglin and Juliet B. Schor (Oxford: Clarendon Press, 1990), pp. 1–38.

—— and Juliet B. Schor, eds (1990), *The golden age of capitalism: reinterpreting the postwar experience* (Oxford: Clarendon Press).

Markowski, Stefan and Sharon Jackson (1994), "The attractiveness of Poland to direct foreign investors," *Communist Economies & Economic Transformation*, vol. 6, no. 4, 515–35.

Mates, Neven (1992), "Does the government have to clean bank balance sheets in transitional economies?" *Communist Economies & Economic Transformation*, vol. 4, no. 3, 395–409.

Mauro, Paolo (1995), "Corruption and growth," *The Quarterly Journal of Economics*, vol. 110, no. 3, 681–712.

—— (1996), "The effects of corruption on growth, investment, and government expenditure" (Washington, DC: International Monetary Fund, WP/96/98, September).

Mayer, Colin (1993), "In the image of the west: creating financial systems in eastern Europe," in *The new Europe: evolving economic and financial systems in east and west*, edited by Donald E. Fair and Robert J. Raymond (Dordrecht, Boston, MA, and London: Kluwer Academic Publishers), pp. 61–8.

McDermott, C. John and Robert F. Wescott (1996), *Fiscal reforms that work* (Washington, DC: International Monetary Fund).

McKinnon, Ronald I. (1991a), "Liberalizing foreign trade in a socialist economy: the problem of negative value-added," in *Currency convertibility in eastern Europe*, edited by John Williamson (Washington, DC: Institute for International Economics), pp. 96–115.

—— (1991b), *The order of economic liberalization – financial control in the transition to a market economy* (Baltimore, MD and London: Johns Hopkins University Press).

Melich, Jiří S. (1997) "The post-communist mind – how real a phenomenon? (socio-psychological legacies of communist rule)" (Ottawa, ONT: Carleton University, Discussion Paper, Internet posting, 27 January).

Melo, Martha de and Cevdet Denizer (1997), "Monetary policy during transition – an overview" (Washington, DC: The World Bank, Policy Research Working Paper no. 1706, January).

——, ——, and Alan Gelb (1996), "Patterns of transition from plan to market," *The World Bank Economic Review*, vol. 10, no. 3, 397–424.

Messerlin, Patrick (1996), "The MFN and preferential trade policies of the CECs: Singapore and Geneva are on the shortest road to Brussels" (Paris: Institut d'Études Politiques, mimeo, August).

Michnik, Adam (1993), "An embarrassing anniversary," *The New York Review of Books*, vol. 40, no. 11, 19–21.

Mickiewicz, Tomasz (1996a), "The spatial dimension of transformation: time pattern and ownership factors on the micro level," *Europe-Asia Studies*, vol. 48, no. 7, 1187–202.

—— (1996b), "The state sector during economic transformation: employment, wages and investment," *Communist Economies & Economic Transformation*, vol. 8, no. 3, 393–410.

Milanović, Branko (1994), "A cost of transition: 50 million new poor and growing inequality," *Transition*, vol. 5, no. 4, 1–4.

Mizsei, Kálmán, ed. (1994), *Developing public finance in emerging market economies* (New York: Institute for EastWest Studies).

—— and Jacek Rostowski (1994), "Fiscal crises during economic transition in east central Europe: an overview," in *Developing public finance in emerging market economies*, edited by Kálmán Mizsei (New York: Institute for EastWest Studies), pp. 1–17.

Moene, Karl Ove and Michael Wallerstein (1993), "What's wrong with social democracy?" in *Market socialism – the current debate* (New York and Oxford: Oxford University Press), pp. 219–35.

Mokrzycki, Edmund (1991), "The legacy of real socialism and western democracy," *Studies in Comparative Communism*, vol. 24, no. 2, 211–17.

Morin, François (1996), "Privatisation et dévolution des pouvoirs – le modèle français du gouvernement d'entreprise," *Revue Économique*, vol. 47, no. 6, 1253–68.

Mueller, Dennis C. (1989), *Public choice II* (Cambridge and New York: Cambridge University Press, rev. edn).

Munzer, Stephen R. (1990), *A theory of property* (Cambridge and New York: Cambridge University Press).

Murphy, Kevin J. (1989), "The control and performance of state-owned enterprises: comment," in *Privatization and state-owned enterprises – lessons from the United States, Great Britain and Canada*, edited by Paul W. MacAvoy, W.T. Stanbury, George Yarrow, and Richard J. Zeckhauser (Boston, MA, Dordrecht, and London: Kluwer Academic Publishers), pp. 59–68.

Murrell, Peter (1992), "Evolutionary and radical approaches to economic reform," *Economics of Planning*, vol. 25, 79–95.

—— (1995), "The transition according to Cambridge, Mass.," *Journal of Economic Literature*, vol. 33, no. 1, 164–78.

Mussa, Michael (1986), "The adjustment process and the timing of trade liberalization," in *Economic reform in developing countries*, edited by Armeane M. Choksi and Demetris Papageorgiou (Oxford: Blackwell), pp. 68–124.

Nagy, András (1991), "'Social choice' in eastern Europe," *Journal of Comparative Economics*, vol. 18, no. 2, 266–83.

Nankani, Helen B. (1988), *Techniques of privatization of state-owned enterprises – vol. II: selected country case studies* (Washington, DC: World Bank).

Nash, Nathaniel C. (1995), "A strong leash for currencies on a rampage," *The New York Times*, 5 February, F3.

Nelson, Joan M. (1992), "Comment on 'Governance and development,' by Boeninger," *Proceedings of the World Bank Annual Conference on Development Economics, 1991* (Washington, DC: The World Bank), pp. 289–93.

Nelson, Richard R. (1986), "Incentives for entrepreneurship and supporting innovations," in *Economic incentives*, edited by Bela Balassa (London: Macmillan), pp. 173–87.

—— (1995), "Recent evolutionary theorizing about economic change," *Journal of Economic Literature*, vol. 33, no. 1, 40–90.

Newbery, David M. (1991), "Sequencing the transition" (London: CEPR, Discussion Paper Series no. 575, August).

Niehans, Jürg (1987), "Transaction costs," *The new Palgrave – a dictionary of economics, vol. 4* (London: Macmillan), pp. 676–9.

Noble, Gregory W. (1989), "The Japanese industrial policy debate," in *Pacific dynamics: the international politics of industrial change*, edited by Stephan Haggard and Chung-in Moon (Boulder, CO: Westview Press and Inchon: Center for International Studies, Inha University), pp. 53–95.

Nolan, Peter (1992), "Transforming Stalinist systems: China's reforms in the light of Russian and east European experience" (Cambridge: Department of Applied Economics, University of Cambridge, Discussion Papers on Economic Transition DPET 9203, August).

North, Douglas C. (1989), "Comments 2," in Stiglitz, Joseph E. *et al.*, *The economic role of the state* (Oxford: Basil Blackwell in association with Bank Insinger de Beaufort), pp. 107–15.

—— (1990), *Institutions, institutional change and economic performance* (Cambridge and New York: Cambridge University Press).

—— (1991), "Institutions," *Journal of Economic Perspectives*, vol. 5, no.1, 97–112.

Nuti, D. Mario (1987), *Financial innovation under socialism* (Florence: Istituto Universitario Europeo).

—— (1988), "Competitive valuation and efficiency of capital investment in the socialist economy," *European Economic Review*, vol. 32, no. 1, 2–6.

—— (1989), "Feasible financial innovation under market socialism," in *Financial reform in socialist economies*, edited by Christine Kessides, Timothy King, Mario Nuti, and Catherine Sokil (Washington, DC: The World Bank), pp. 85–105.

—— (1991), "Privatisation of socialist economies: general issues and the Polish case," in *Transformation of planned economies: property rights reform and macroeconomic stability*, edited by Hans Blommestein and Michael Marrese (Paris: Organisation for Economic Co-operation and Development), pp. 51–68.

—— (1992a), "Market socialism: the model that might have been but never was," in *Market socialism or the restoration of capitalism?* edited by Anders Åslund (Cambridge and New York: Cambridge University Press), pp. 17–31.

—— (1992b), "Economic inertia in the transitional economies of eastern Europe" (Brussels: Commission of the European Communities, mimeo).

—— (1996), "Inflation, interest rates and exchange rates in the transition," *Economics of Transition*, vol. 4, no. 1, 137–58.

—— and Richard Portes (1993), "Central Europe: the way forward," in *Economic transformation in central Europe – a progress report*, edited by Richard Portes (London: CEPR and Brussels: Commission of the European Communities), pp. 1–20.

OECD (1992), *Reforming the economies of central and eastern Europe* (Paris: Organisation for Economic Co-operation and Development).

—— (1996a), *Lessons from labour market policies in the transition economies* (Paris: Organisation for Economic Co-operation and Development).

—— (1996b), *Assistance programmes for central and eastern Europe and the former Soviet Union* (Paris: Organisation for Economic Co-operation and Development).

Olson, Mancur (1984), *The rise and decline of nations – economic growth, stagflation, and social rigidities* (New Haven, CT and London: Yale University Press).

—— (1993), "Dictatorship, democracy, and development," *American Political Science Review*, vol. 87, no. 3, 567–76.

Osband, Kent and Delano Villanueva (1993), "Independent currency authorities: an analytic primer," *IMF Staff Papers*, vol. 40, no. 1, 202–16.

Osborne, David and Ted Gaebler (1992), *Reinventing government – how the entrepreneurial spirit is transforming the public sector* (Reading, MA: Addison-Wesley).

Ostry, Sylvia (1992a), "Beyond the border: the new international policy arena," in *Strategic industries in a global economy: policy issues for the 1990s* (Paris: Organisation for Economic Co-operation and Development), pp. 81–95.

—— (1992b), "The domestic domain: the new international policy arena," *Transnational Corporations*, vol. 1. no. 1, 7–26.

Pack, Howard and Larry E. Westphal (1986), "Industrial strategy and technological change – theory versus reality," *Journal of Development Economics*, vol. 22, no. 1, 87–128.

Panić, Mića (1992), "The future role of the state in eastern Europe" (Cambridge, mimeo).

Pannier, Dominique, ed. (1996), *Corporate governance of public enterprises in transition economies* (Washington, DC: The World Bank, 1996).

—— and Salvatore Schiavo-Campo (1996), "Corporate governance reform: the context of corporate governance," in *Corporate governance of public enterprises in transition economies*, edited by Dominique Pannier (Washington, DC: The World Bank, 1996), pp. 3–25.

Pareto, Vilfredo (1935), *Treatise on general sociology* (New York: Harcourt, Brace, Jovanovitch).

Peebles, Gavin (1994), "Review of Hanke, Jonung, and Schuler 1993," *Europe-Asia Studies*, vol. 46, no. 6, 1059–61.

Pejovich, Svetozar (1983), "Innovation and alternative property rights," in *Innovationsprobleme in Ost und West*, edited by Alfred Schüller, Helmut Leipold, and Hannelore Hamel (Stuttgart: Gustav Fischer Verlag), pp. 41–9.

—— (1990), *The economics of property rights: towards a theory of comparative systems* (Dordrecht, Boston, MA, and London: Kluwer Academic Publishers).

Peltzman, Sam (1989), "The control and performance of state-owned enterprises: comment," in *Privatization and state-owned enterprises – lessons from the United States, Great Britain and Canada*, edited by Paul W. MacAvoy, W.T. Stanbury, George Yarrow, and Richard J. Zeckhauser (Dordrecht, Boston, MA, and London: Kluwer Academic Publishers), pp. 69–75.

Pestieau, Pierre (1989), "Measuring the performance of public enterprises – a must in times of privatization," *Annals of Public and Cooperative Economics*, vol. 60, no. 3, 293–305.

Pettis, Michael (1996), "The liquidity trap – Latin America's free-market past," *Foreign Affairs*, vol. 75, no. 6, 2–7.

Phelps, Edmund S., Roman Frydman, Andrzej Rapaczyński, and Andrei Shleifer (1993), "Needed mechanisms of corporate governance and finance in eastern Europe" (London: EBRD, Working paper no. 1, March).

529

Pickel, Andreas (1992), "Jump-starting a market economy: a critique of a radical strategy for economic reform in light of the east German experience," *Studies in Comparative Communism*, vol. 25, no. 2, 177–91.

Pitiot, Hélène and Laurence Scialom (1993), "Système bancaire et dérapage monétaire," *Economie Internationale*, no. 54, 137–56.

Polányi, Karl (1944), *The great transformation* (New York: Rhineholt; reprint edition, New York: Farrar, Straus and Giroux, 1975).

Porter, Michael E. (1990), *The competitive advantage of nations* (New York: The Free Press).

Portes, Richard (1991), "Introduction," *European Economy*, special edition no. 2, 1–15.

Przeworski, Adam (1993), "Economic reforms, public opinion, and political institutions: Poland in the eastern European perspective," in *Economic reforms in new democracies – a social-democratic approach*, edited by Luiz Carlos Bresser Pereira, José Maria Maravall, and Adam Przeworski (Cambridge and New York: Cambridge University Press, 1993), pp. 132–98.

Public Enterprise (1990), "Editorial introduction," *Public Enterprise*, vol. 10, no. 1, 9–17.

Ramanadham, V.V., ed. (1988), *Privatisation in the UK* (London and New York: Routledge).

Rapp, L. (1986), *Techniques de privatisation des entreprises publiques* (Paris: Librairies Techniques).

Rausser, Gordon C. and S. R. Johnson (1993), "State-market-civil institutions: the case of eastern Europe and the Soviet republics," *World Development*, vol. 21, no. 4, 675–89.

Rawls, John (1972), *A theory of justice* (Oxford: Oxford University Press).

Reinicke, Wolfgang H. (1992), *Building a new Europe – the challenge of system transformation and systemic reform* (Washington, DC: Brookings Institution).

Rice, Eric (1991), *Managing the transition – enhancing the efficiency of eastern European governments* (Washington, DC: The World Bank, Working Paper 757).

Richardson, G. B. (1972), "The organisation of industry," *The Economic Journal*, no. 327, 883–96.

Richter, Andrea and Mark E. Schaffer (1996), "The performance of *de novo* private firms in Russian manufacturing," in *Enterprise restructuring and economic policy in Russia*, edited by Simon Commander, Qimiao Fan, and Mark E. Schaffer (Washington, DC: The World Bank), pp. 253–73.

Richter, Sándor (1996), " The Visegrád group countries' expectations *vis-à-vis* western Europe," *Russian & East European Finance and Trade*, no. 1, 6–41.

Robbins, Lionel (1952), *The theory of economic policy* (London: Macmillan).

Rodrik, Dani (1992a), "Foreign trade in eastern Europe's transition: early results" (London: CEPR, Discussion Paper Series no. 676, June).

—— (1992b), "Making sense of the Soviet trade shock in eastern Europe: a framework and some estimates" (London: CEPR, Discussion Paper Series no. 705, July).

—— (1995a), "Trade liberalization in disinflation," in *Understanding interdependence – the macroeconomics of the open economy*, edited by Peter B. Kenen (Princeton, NJ: Princeton University Press, 1995), pp. 291–312.

—— (1995b), "Getting interventions right: how south Korea and Taiwan grew rich," *Economic Policy*, no. 20, 69–111.

—— (1997), "Sense and nonsense in the globalization debate," *Foreign Policy*, no. 107, 19–35.

Róna-Tas, Ákos, (1994) "The first shall be the last? – entrepreneurship and communist cadres in the transition from socialism," *American Journal of Sociology*, vol. 100, no. 1, 40–69.

—— (1996), "Post-communist transition and the absent middle class in east-central Europe," in *Identities in transitions – eastern Europe after the collapse of communism*, edited by Victoria E. Bonnell (Berkeley, CA: University of California at Berkeley), pp. 29–44.

Root, Hilton L. (1996), *Small countries, big lessons – governance and the rise of east Asia* (Hong Kong, New York, and Oxford: Oxford University Press, 1996).

Rose-Ackerman, Susan (1997), "Corruption and development" (Washington, DC: The World Bank, paper prepared for the "Annual Bank Conference on Development Economics," Washington, DC, 30 April–1 May 1997).

Rosenberg, Nathan (1988), "Technical change under capitalism and socialism" (Stanford, CA: Stanford University, January, mimeo).

Ross, S. (1973), "The economic theory of agency: the principal's problem," *American Economic Review*, vol. 63, no. 2, 134–9.

Rostowski, Jacek (1994a), "Systemic requirements for monetary stability in eastern Europe and the former Soviet Union" (Washington, DC: International Monetary Fund, WP/94/24, February).

—— (1994b), "The banking system, credit and the real economy in economies in transition" (paper prepared for the conference "Banking Reform in FSU and Eastern Europe: Lessons from Central Europe," Budapest, 14–15 January, mimeo).

Ryan, Alan (1987), "Property," *The new Palgrave – a dictionary of economics, vol. 3* (London: Macmillan), pp. 1029–31.

Rybczyński, Tadeusz M. (1991a), "The role of finance in restructuring eastern Europe," *ECU Newsletter*, no. 3, 8–12.

—— (1991b), "The sequencing of reform," *Oxford Review of Economic Policy*, vol. 7, no. 4, 26–34.

Sachs, Jeffrey D. (1991a), "Accelerating privatization in eastern Europe" (paper prepared for "World Bank Annual Conference on Development Economics, 1991," organized by The World Bank, Washington, DC, 25–26 April).

—— (1991b), "Privatization is top priority in eastern Europe, says Sachs," *IMF Survey*, vol. 20, 27 May, 170–1.

—— (1991c), "Crossing the valley of tears in east European reform," *Challenge*, vol. 34, no. 5, 26–34.

—— (1992), "Privatization in Russia: some lessons from eastern Europe," *The American Economic Review*, vol. 82, no. 2, 43–8.

—— (1993), "Russian Sachs Appeal – the G7 has one last chance," *The International Economy*, vol. 7, no. 1, 50–3.

—— and Andrew M. Warner (1996), "Achieving rapid growth in the transition economies of central Europe" (Cambridge, MA: Harvard Institute for International Development, Development Discussion Paper no. 544, July).

Sacks, Stephen R. (1983), *Self-management and efficiency – large corporations in Yugoslavia* (London: George Allen & Unwin).

Sah, Raaj K. and Martin L. Weitzman (1991), "A proposal for using incentive pre-commitments in public enterprise funding," *World Development*, vol. 19, no. 6, 595–605.

Salamon, Lester M., ed. (1989), *Beyond privatization – the tools of government action* (Washington, DC: The Urban Institute Press).

Samuels, Richard J. (1990), "The business of the Japanese state," in *Governments, industries and markets – aspects of government–industry relations in the UK, Japan, west Germany and the USA since 1945*, edited by Martin Chick (Aldershot and Brookfield, VT: Edward Elgar), pp. 36–60.

Samuelson, Paul A. (1993), "Altruism as a problem involving group versus individual selection in economics and biology," *American Economic Review*, vol. 83, no. 2, 143–8.

Sapir, Jacques (1993), "Formes et nature de l'inflation," *Economie Internationale*, no. 54, 25–65.

Sappington, David E.M. (1991), "Incentives in principal–agent relationships," *Journal of Economic Perspectives*, vol. 5, no. 2, 45–66.

—— and Joseph E. Stiglitz (1987), "Privatization, information and incentives," *Journal of Policy Analysis and Management*, vol. 7, no. 3, 567–82.

Sarel, Michael (1996), *Growth in east Asia – what we can and what we cannot infer* (Washington, DC: International Monetary Fund).

Sassoon, Donald (1996), *Social democracy at the heart of Europe* (London: Institute for Public Policy Research).

Sawyer, Malcolm (1992), "On the theory of industrial policy," in *Current issues in industrial economic strategy*, edited by Keith Cowling and Roger Snugden (Manchester and New York: Manchester University Press), pp. 3–15.

Schweikert, Rainer (1994), "Stabilization and real adjustment in emerging market economies – lessons from macroeconomic reforms in the southern cone," *Intereconomics*, vol. 29, no. 5, 244–52.

—— (1995), "Searching for credible exchange rate regimes in the former Soviet Union," *Intereconomics*, vol. 30, no. 3, 126–32.

—— and Manfred Wiebelt (1996), "Finanzpolitik im Aufholprozeß – Lehren aus Europa, Lateinamerika und Asien," *Die Weltwirtschaft*, no. 3, 318–44.

Sen, Amartya (1991), "Development strategies: the roles of the state and the private sector," *Proceedings of the World Bank Annual Conference on Development Economics, 1990* (Washington, DC: The World Bank), pp. 421–5.

Shapiro, Carl and Robert D. Willig (1990), "Economic rationales for the scope of privatization," in *The political economy of public sector reform and privatization*, edited by Ezra N. Suleiman and John Waterbury (Boulder, CO: Westview Press), pp. 55–87.

Shelley, Louise I. (1997), "The price tag of Russia's organized crime," *Transition*, vol. 8, no. 1, 7–8.

Shleifer, Andrei and Robert W. Vishny (1993), "Corruption," *The Quarterly Journal of Economics*, vol. 108, no. 3, 599–617.

Silk, Leonard, Mark Silk, *et al.* (1996), *Making capitalism work* (New York: New York University Press).

Simon, Herbert A. (1991), "Organizations and markets," *Journal of Economic Perspectives*, vol. 5, no. 2, 25–44.

Singh, Ajit (1990), "The stock market in a socialist economy," in *Economic reform in post-Mao China*, edited by Peter Nolan and Dong Furen (Cambridge: Polity Press), pp. 161–78.

—— (1992a), "'Close' vs. 'strategic' integration with the world economy and the 'market-friendly approach to development' vs. an 'industrial policy' – a critique of the World Development Report 1991 and an alternative policy perspective" (Cambridge: University of Cambridge, Faculty of Economics, mimeo, April).

—— (1992b), "Industrial policy in the third world in the 1990s: alternative perspectives," in *Current issues in industrial economic strategy*, edited by Keith Cowling and Roger Snugden (Manchester and New York: Manchester University Press), pp. 123–43.

—— (1994), "Growing independently of the world economy: Asian economic development since 1980," *UNCTAD Review 1994* (New York: United Nations Publication, sales no. E.94.II.D.19), pp. 91–105.

—— (1995), "How did east Asia grow so fast? Slow progress towards an analytical consensus" (Geneva: UNCTAD, Discussion Papers, no. 97, February).

Slay, Ben (1992), "The banking crisis and economic reform in Poland," *RFE/RL Research Report*, vol. 1, no. 23, 33–40.

—— and Luisa Vinton (1994), "Bad debts and the Polish restructuring program," *MOCT-MOST*, vol. 4, no. 3, 85–108.

Smith, Roy C. and Ingo Walter (1993), "Bank–industry linkages: models for eastern European economic restructuring," in *The new Europe: evolving economic and financial systems in east and west*, edited by Donald E. Fair and Robert J. Raymond (Dordrecht, Boston, MA, and London: Kluwer Academic Publishers), pp. 41–60.

Solow, Robert M. (1993), "Policies for economic growth," in *Tinbergen lectures on economic policy*, edited by A. Knoester and A.H.E.M. Wellink (Amsterdam, London, New York, and Tokyo: North-Holland), pp. 127–40.

Sood, Anil (1990), "Enterprise reform and restructuring in central and eastern Europe" (paper prepared for the conference "The Transition to a Market Economy in Central and Eastern Europe," organized by Centre for Co-operation with the European Economies in Transition and the World Bank, Paris, 28–30 November).

Soros, George (1997), "The capitalist threat," *The Atlantic Monthly*, February, 45–58.

Standing, Guy (1994), "The changing position of women in Russian industry: prospects of marginalization," *World Development*, vol. 22, no. 2, 271–83.

Staniszkis, Jadwiga (1991), "'Political capitalism' in Poland," *East European Politics and Societies*, vol. 5, no. 1, 127–41.

—— (1992), "Main paradoxes of the democratic change in eastern Europe and the Soviet Union," in *Constructing capitalism – the reemergence of civil society and liberal economy in eastern Europe and the Soviet Union*, edited by Kazimierz Poznański (Boulder, CO: Westview Press), pp. 179–97.

Stanners, W. (1993), "Is low inflation an important condition for high growth?" *Cambridge Journal of Economics*, vol. 17, no. 1, 79–107.

—— (1996), "Inflation and growth," *Cambridge Journal of Economics*, vol. 20, no. 4, 509–12.

Starbatty, Joachim (1996), "Anmerkungen zur Interdependenz politischer und wirtschaftlicher Ordnungen im Transformationsprozeß," *Ordo*, vol. 47, 33–50.

Stark, David (1992), "Path dependence and privatization strategies in east central Europe," *East European Politics and Societies*, vol. 6, no. 1, 15–51.

—— (1996), "Recombinant property in east European capitalism," *American Journal of Sociology*, vol. 101, no. 4, 993–1027.

Stelzer, Irwin (1988), "Britain's newest import: America's regulatory experience," *Oxford Review of Economic Policy*, vol. 4, no. 2, 69–79.

—— (1989), "Privatisation and regulation: oft-necessary," in *Privatisation & competition – a market prospectus*, edited by Čento Veljanovski (London: Institute of Economic Affairs), pp. 70–7.

Stern, Nicholas (1989), "The economics of development: a survey," *The Economic Journal*, vol. 99, no. 3, 597–685.

—— (1991), "Development strategies: the roles of the state and the private sector," *Proceedings of the World Bank Annual Conference on Development Economics, 1990* (Washington, DC: The World Bank), pp. 425–9.

Stevenson, Andrew, Vitantonio Muscatelli, and Mary Gregory (1988), *Macroeconomic theory and stabilisation policy* (London and New York: Philip Allan).

Stiglitz, Joseph E. (1986), *Economics of the public sector* (New York and London: Norton).

—— (1987), "Principal and agent," *The new Palgrave – a dictionary of economics*, vol. 3 (London: Macmillan), pp. 966–72.

—— (1989a), "On the economic role of the state," in Joseph E. Stiglitz *et al.*, *The economic role of the state* (Oxford: Basil Blackwell in association with Bank Insinger de Beaufort), pp. 11–85.

—— (1989b), "Markets, market failures, and development," *American Economic Review*, vol. 79, no. 2, 197–203.

—— (1991a), "Development strategies: the roles of the state and the private sector," *Proceedings of the World Bank Annual Conference on Development Economics, 1990* (Washington, DC: The World Bank), pp. 430–3.

—— (1991b), *Government, financial markets, and economic development* (Cambridge, MA: NBER Working Paper no. 3669, April).

—— (1991c), "Capital markets and economic fluctuations in capitalist economies" (paper presented to the Sixth Annual Congress of the European Economic Association, Cambridge, 30 August – 2 September).

—— (1993), "The role of the state in financial markets" (Washington, DC: The World Bank, paper presented to "Annual Bank Conference on Development Economics," 3–4 May, mimeo).

—— (1994), *Whither socialism?* (Cambridge, MA and London: MIT Press).

—— (1997a), "The role of government in economic development," in *Annual Bank Conference Development Economics, 1996*, edited by Michael Bruno and Boris Pleskovic (Washington, DC: World Bank), pp. 11–23.

—— (1997b), "The role of government in the economies of developing countries," in *Development strategy and management of the market economy* – vol. I, edited by Edmond Malinvaud *et al.* (Oxford and New York: Oxford University Press), pp. 61–109.

Suleiman, Ezra N. and John Waterbury, eds (1990), *The political economy of public sector reform and privatization* (Boulder, CO: Westview Press).

Sundararajan, V. (1996), "The role of prudential supervision and financial restructuring of banks during transition to indirect instruments of monetary control" (Washington, DC: International Monetary Fund, November).

Švejnar, Jan (1995), "Economic transformation in central and eastern Europe: the tasks still ahead," in *Economic transformation – the tasks still ahead*, edited by Thomas Walter (Washington, DC: Per Jacobsson Foundation), pp. 3–15.

Swaan, Wim and Maria Lissowska (1996), "Capabilities, routines, and east European economic reform: Hungary and Poland before and after the 1989 revolutions," *Journal of Economic Issues*, vol. 30, no. 4, 1031–56.

Swann, Dennis (1988), *The retreat of the state – deregulation and privatization in the UK and US* (Ann Arbor, MI: University of Michigan Press).

Szálai, Erzsébet (1991), "Integration of special interests in the Hungarian economy: the struggle between large companies and the Party and state bureaucracy," *Journal of Comparative Economics*, vol. 18, no. 2, 284–303.

Sziraczki, Gyorgy and Jim Windell (1993), *The impact of employment restructuring on disadvantaged groups in Bulgaria and Hungary* (Geneva: International Labor Office, Working Paper no. 62).

Sztompa, Piotr (1996a), "Looking back: the year 1989 as a cultural and civilizational break," *Communist and Post-Communist Studies*, vol. 29, no. 2, 115–29.

—— (1996b), "Trust and emerging democracy: lessons from Poland," *International Sociology*, vol. 11, no. 1, 37–62.

Tangermann, Stefan (1993), "Some economic effects of EC agricultural trade preferences for central Europe," *Journal of Economic Integration*, vol. 8, no. 2, 152–74.

Tanzi, Vito (1991), "Eastern Europe: the state's role in mobilizing savings," *IMF Survey*, vol. 20, 27 May, 166–70.

Targetti, Ferdinando and Alessandro Foti (1997), "Growth and productivity: a model of cumulative growth and catching up," *Cambridge Journal of Economics*, vol. 21, no. 1, 27–43.

Temkin, Gabriel (1996a), "Information and motivation: reflections on the failure of the socialist economic system," *Communist and Post-Communist Studies*, vol. 29, no. 1, 25–41.

—— (1996b), "The new market socialism – a critical review," *Communist and Post-Communist Studies*, vol. 29, no. 4, 467–78.

Terry, Sarah M. (1994), "Intraregional political and economic relations," in *East-central European economies in transition*, edited by the Joint Economic Committee, Congress of the United States (Washington, DC: US Government Printing Office, 1994), pp. 367–92.

Thompson, David J. (1988), "Privatisation: introducing competition, opportunities and constraints," in *Privatisation in the UK*, edited by V.V. Ramanadham (London and New York: Routledge), pp. 39–58.

Tirole, Jean (1991), "Privatization in eastern Europe: incentives and the economics of transition" (Cambridge, MA: MIT, mimeo, July).

Tobin, James (1987), "Financial intermediaries," *The New Palgrave – a dictionary of economics*, vol. 2 (London: Macmillan), pp. 340–8.

—— (1993), "On the theory of macroeconomic policy," in *Tinbergen lectures on economic policy*, edited by A. Knoester and A.H.E.M. Wellink (Amsterdam, London, New York, and Tokyo: North-Holland), pp. 89–102.

UNCTAD (1993), *Explaining and forecasting regional flows of foreign direct investment* (New York: United Nations Publication, sales no. ST/CTC/SER.A/26).

UNDP (1997), *Human development report, 1997* (New York: United Nations Development Programme).

UNECE (1990), *Economic survey of Europe in 1989–1990* (New York: United Nations Publication, sales no. E.90.II.E.1).

—— (1991a), *Economic survey of Europe 1990–1991* (New York: United Nations Publication, sales no. E.91.II.E.1).

—— (1991b), *Economic bulletin for Europe – vol. 43* (New York: United Nations Publication, sales no. E.91.II.E.39).

—— (1992), *Economic survey of Europe 1991–1992* (New York: United Nations Publication, sales no. E.92.II.E.1).

—— (1993), *Economic survey of Europe in 1992–1993* (New York: United Nations Publication, sales no. E.93.II.E.1).

—— (1994), *Economic survey of Europe in 1993–1994* (New York: United Nations Publication, sales no. E.94.II.E.1).

—— (1995), *Economic survey of Europe in 1994–1995* (New York: United Nations Publication, sales no. E.95.II.E.1).

—— (1996a), *Economic survey of Europe in 1995–1996* (New York: United Nations Publication, sales no. E.96.II.E.1

—— (1996b), "The re-emergence of trade among the east European and Baltic countries: commercial and other policy issues," *Economic Bulletin for Europe*, vol. 48, 75–91.

—— (1997), *Economic survey of Europe in 1996–1997* (New York: United Nations Publication, sales no. E.97.II.E.1).

UNWES (1992), *World economic survey, 1992* (New York: United Nations Publication, sales no. E.92.II.C.1).

—— (1994), *World economic survey, 1994* (New York: United Nations Publication, sales no. E.94.II.C.1).

Vandenbussche, Hylke (1996), "Is European antidumping protection against central Europe too high?" *Weltwirtschaftliches Archiv – Review of World Economics*, vol. 132, no. 1, 116–38.

Veljanovski, Čento, ed. (1989), "Privatisation: monopoly money or competition?" in *Privatisation & competition – a market prospectus*, edited by Čento Veljanovski (London: Institute of Economic Affairs), pp. 26–51.

Verheijen, Tony (1996), "The relevance of 'western' public management reforms for central and eastern European Countries," *Public Management Forum*, vol. 2, no. 1, 8–9.

Vickers, John S. (1991) "Government regulatory policy," *Oxford Review of Economic Policy*, vol. 7, no. 3, 13–30.

—— (1996), "Market power and inefficiency: a contracts perspective," *Oxford Review of Economic Policy*, vol. 12, no. 4, 11–26.

—— and Vincent Wright (1988), "The politics of industrial privatisation in western Europe: an overview," *West European Politics*, vol. 11, no. 4, 1–30.

—— and George Yarrow (1988), *Privatization: an economic analysis* (Cambridge, MA: MIT Press).

Villanueva, Delano (1993), "Options for monetary and exchange arrangements in transition economies" (Washington, DC: International Monetary Fund, PPAA/93/12, September).

Viner, Jacob (1960), "The intellectual history of laissez faire," *Journal of Law and Economics*, vol. 3, no. 4, 45–69.

Vittas, Dimitri and Roland Michelitsch (1995), "Pension funds in central Europe and Russia – their prospects and potential role in corporate governance" (Washington, DC: The World Bank, Policy Research Working Paper no. 1459, May).

Vrbetić, Marta (1995), "European Union and its neighbors in the east and south," *Euroscope Reports*, December, 3–7.

Vuylsteke, Charles (1988), *Techniques of privatization of state-owned enterprises – vol. I: methods and implementation* (Washington, DC: World Bank).

—— (1990), "Privatization in emerging economies – constraints and practical responses" (paper prepared for the conference "Privatization and Ownership Changes in East and Central Europe," organized by the World Bank, Washington, DC, 13–14 June).

Wade, Robert (1986), *Village republics: economic conditions for collective action in south Asia* (Cambridge and New York: Cambridge University Press).

—— (1987), "The management of common property resources: finding a cooperative solution," *The World Bank Research Observer*, vol. 2, no. 2, 219–34.

—— (1988), "The role of government in overcoming market failure: Taiwan, Republic of Korea and Japan," in *Achieving industrialization in east Asia*, edited by Helen Hughes (Cambridge and New York: Cambridge University Press), pp. 129–62.

—— (1990), *Governing the market – economic theory and the role of government in east Asian industrialization* (Princeton, NJ: Princeton University Press).

—— (1995), "The east Asian miracle: why the controversy continues," in *International monetary and financial issues for the 1990s*, vol. V (New York: United Nations Publication, sales no. E.95.II.D.3), pp. 65–79.

Walters, Alan (1987), "Currency boards," *The new Palgrave – a dictionary of economics*, vol. 1 (London: Macmillan), pp. 740–2.

—— (1992), "Currency boards and their history," in *Proceedings of a conference on currency substitution and currency boards*, edited by Nissan Liviatan (Washington, DC: The World Bank), pp. 4–6.

Walters, Alan Rufus (1987), "Privatization: a viable policy option?" in *Entrepreneurship and the privatizing of government*, edited by Calvin A. Kent (New York and Westport, CT: Quorum Books), pp. 35–64.

Weber, Max (1946), "Bureaucracy," in *From Max Weber: essays in sociology*, edited by Hans H. Gerth and C. Wright Mills (New York: Oxford University Press), pp. 196–244.

Weidenfeld, Werner, ed. (1995a), *Central and eastern Europe on the way into the European Union – problems and prospects of integration* (Gütersloh: Bertelsmann Foundation Publishers).

—— (1995b) *Demokratie und Marktwirtschaft in Osteuropa* (Gütersloh: Bertelsmann Stiftung).

—— (1995c), "Die Verantwortung des Westens für den Wandel in Mittel- und Osteuropa," in *Demokratie und Marktwirtschaft in Osteuropa*, edited by Werner Weidenfeld (Gütersloh: Bertelsmann Stiftung), pp. 17–33.

—— (1996a), *Central and eastern Europe on the way into the European Union* (Gütersloh: Bertelsmann Foundation).

—— (1996b), *A new Ostpolitik – strategies for a United Europe* (Gütersloh: Bertelsmann Foundation).

Weisberg, Jacob (1996), *In defense of government – the fall and rise of public trust* (New York: Scribner).

Weisbrod, Burton A. (1988), *The nonprofit economy* (Cambridge, MA: Harvard University Press).

—— (1989), "Rewarding performance that is hard to measure: the private nonprofit sector," *Science*, no. 244 (5 May), 541–6.

Weiss, Charles Jr. (1997), "Eurasia letter: a Marshall Plan we can afford," *Foreign Policy*, no. 106, 94–109.

Weitzman, Martin L. (1993), "Economic transition – can theory help?" *European Economic Review*, vol. 37, no. 2/3, 549–55.

WERI (1995), *Poland – international economic report, 1994/95* (Warsaw: Warsaw School of Economics).

Willett, Thomas D. and Fahim Al-Marhubi (1994), "Currency policies for inflation control in the formerly centrally planned economies," *The World Economy*, vol. 17, no. 6, 795–815.

Williams, David G. (1996), "Governance and the discipline of development," *Journal of Development Research*, vol. 8, no. 2, 157–77.

Williamson, John (1985), "On the system of Bretton Woods," *American Economic Review*, vol. 75, no. 2, 74–9.

—— (1990), "Convertibility, trade policy and the payments constraint" (paper prepared for the conference "The Transition to a Market Economy in Central and Eastern Europe," organized by Centre for Co-operation with the European Economies in Transition and the World Bank, Paris, 28–30 November).

—— (1991), *The economic opening of eastern Europe* (Washington, DC: Institute for International Economics).

—— (1993), "Democracy and the 'Washington consensus'," *World Development*, vol. 21, no. 8, 1329–36.

——, ed. (1994a), *The political economy of policy reform* (Washington, DC: Institute for International Economics).

—— (1994b), "In search of a manual for technopols," in *The political economy of policy reform*, edited by John Williamson (Washington, DC: Institute for International Economics), pp. 11–28.

—— and Stephan Haggard (1994), "The political conditions for economic reform," in *The political economy of policy reform*, edited by John Williamson (Washington, DC: Institute for International Economics), pp. 527–96.

Williamson, Oliver E. (1963), "Managerial discretion and business behaviour," *American Economic Review*, vol. 53, no. 5, 1032–57, reproduced in *Economic organization – firms, markets and policy control*, edited by Oliver E. Williamson (New York and London: Harvester Wheatsheaf, 1986), pp. 6–31.

—— (1967), "Hierarchical control and optimum firm size," *Journal of Political Economy*, vol. 75, no. 2, 123–38, reproduced in *Economic organization – firms, markets and policy control*, edited by Oliver E. Williamson (New York and London: Harvester Wheatsheaf, 1986), pp. 32–53.

—— (1979), "Transaction cost economics: the governance of contractual relations," *Journal of Law and Economics*, vol. 22, no. 2, 233–61, reproduced in *Economic organization – firms, markets and policy control*, edited by Oliver E. Williamson (New York and London: Harvester Wheatsheaf, 1986), pp. 101–30.

—— (1981), "The modern corporation: origins, evolution, attributes," *Journal of Economic Literature*, vol. 19, no. 4, 1537–68, reproduced in *Economic organization – firms, markets and policy control*, edited by Oliver E. Williamson (New York and London: Harvester Wheatsheaf, 1986), pp. 131–73.

Willig, Robert D. (1993), "Public versus regulated private enterprise" (Washington, DC: The World Bank, paper presented to "Annual Bank Conference on Development Economics," 3–4 May, mimeo).

Winiecki, Jan (1991), *Resistance to change in the Soviet economic system – a property rights approach* (London and New York: Routledge).

—— (1996), "The superiority of eliminating barriers to entrepreneurship over privatization activism of the state," *Banca Nazionale del Lavoro Quarterly Review*, vol. 49, no. 3, 313–31.

Winters, L. Alan (1994), "Who should run trade policy in eastern Europe and how?" (London: CEPR, Discussion Paper Series no. 1043, October).

——, ed. (1995), *Foundations of an open economy – trade laws and institutions for eastern Europe* (London: CEPR).

Wolf, Charles, Jr. (1990), *Markets and governments – choosing between imperfect alternatives* (Cambridge, MA and London: MIT Press).

Wong, Chorng-Huey (1992), "Reform of monetary policy instruments – what are some of the issues in the development of a market-based system of monetary control?" *Finance & Development*, vol. 29, no. 1, 16–18.

World Bank (1983a), "The role of the state," *World Development Report 1983* (Washington, DC: The World Bank), pp. 47–56.

—— (1983b), "Managing state-owned enterprises," *World Development Report 1983* (Washington, DC: The World Bank), pp. 74–87.

—— (1987), "The role of government," *World Development Report 1987* (Washington, DC: The World Bank), pp. 58–77.

—— (1988), "Strengthening public finance through reform of state-owned enterprises," *World Development Report 1988* (Washington, DC: The World Bank), pp. 168–81.

—— (1991), "Rethinking the state," *World Development Report 1991* (Washington, DC: The World Bank), pp. 128–47.

—— (1992), *Governance and development* (Washington, DC: The World Bank).

—— (1996), *From plan to market* (Washington, DC: The World Bank, World Development Report 1996).

—— (1997), *The state in a changing world* (Washington, DC: The World Bank, World Development Report 1997).

WTO (1996), "Membership of the World Trade Organization" (Geneva: WTO, Internet posting, 13 December).

Wünsche, Horst Friedrich (1991), "Die Komplexität der sozialen Marktwirtschaft – dauernde ordnungspolitische Anstrengungen nötig," *Neue Zürcher Zeitung*, 10 October, 17.

Yarrow, George (1986), "Privatization in theory and practice," *Economic Policy*, no. 2, 324–77.

—— (1989), "Does ownership matter?" in *Privatisation & competition – a market prospectus*, edited by Čento Veljanovski (London: Institute of Economic Affairs), pp. 52–69.

Zeckhauser, Richard J. and Murray Horn (1989), "The control and performance of state-owned enterprises," in *Privatization and state-owned enterprises – lessons from the United States, Great Britain and Canada*, edited by Paul W. MacAvoy, W.T. Stanbury, George Yarrow, and Richard J. Zeckhauser (Boston, MA, Dordrecht, and London: Kluwer Academic Publishers), pp. 7–57.

INDEX

Note: page number in italics refer to tables.

commercial banking: bad debt 268–72, 273–4; capital market 116; confidence 275; devolution 152; funding 266; liberalization 468–9; market economies 264; recapitalization 273–5; regulation 172, 276; SOEs 188–9, 272, 274; transition economies 264–8; washout solution 272
commercial borrowing 389
commercialization 213, 216, 291, 326, 357–8, 452
commodity prices 182
communality 254
communism 10; agrarian countries 26; and capitalism 21; diversity 24; ideology 20, 21–5, 89, 261; imposed 20, 26; industrial development 25–31; modernization 20, 21; rank 23; welfare state 21, 27–8
Communist Party: administration 36, 232; regional/local cells 45; *see also* *nomenklatura*
comparative advantages 366, 446, 463–4, 487–8
competition: capitalism 255; CMEA 81; environment 278; in European Union 420, 444; external 479; foreign 192–3, 195–6; fostering of 184–91; institutions 109, 117; liberalization 180, 188–9, 480; markets 255; privatization 215; SMEs 117
compromise 475–6
confidence: commercial banking 275; currency 153–4; transition economies 419, 454
confiscation 147, 217, 258, 259–60, 262
conglomerates, disaggregated 184
consensus: *see* social consensus
consumer price index 136
consumer prices 39–40, 47–8
consumers 50–1, 58–9, 134, 301
consumption 34, 145
contracting out 225–6
contracts 190; direct enterprise 80; enforcement 177; financial 116; insecurity 190, 341; legislation 186, 262, 360; management 219, 235, 239
convertibility: capital account 199–200; currency 155, 198, 402; currency board 159; rubles 183–4
Cook, Paul 219, 354, 355, 356, 362
cooperation: CMEA 81; foreign 30–1, 66, 80; regional 473

cooperative ownership 55–6
coordination 46–8, 123–6, 154; central planning 45, 178; civil society 295; development and training 480; devolution 67, 74–7; firms 486–7; government failure 121–3; inflexibility 34; institutions 289–92; liberalization 125; market 178–80, 370, 497; market failure 120–1; modernization 126, 497; prices 47–8; transformation 118–19; transition 3–4
coordination failure 120–6, 483
Cooter, Robert D. 259, 353
Copenhagen commitment 422
Corbett, Jenny 212, 266, 279, 281
Coricelli, Fabrizio 317
corporate governance 293–5
corporatism 287
corporatization 212–13, 216, 233, 291, 357–8, 452
corruption 339–40; bribes 190; government failure 123; inflation 146; leadership 25; privatization 242, 247–8; stability 143; state agency officials 191
cost uncertainty 128
credibility: currency 128–9, 153; currency board 160; exchange rate policies 183–4; losses 165; policies 108, 113, 119; transformation 127, 418
credit policy 38–9
creditworthiness 265
crime, control of 463
criminal activity 57, 97–8, 340, 475
Croatia 90
cross-firm acquisition 236
Csontos, László 8
Cullis, John G. 354
Cultural Revolution, China 88
culture 81, 301, 337–8
currency: colonial 157–9; convertibility 155, 159, 198, 402; credibility 128–9, 153; destruction of 473; monetary uncertainty 128–9; pseudo 198; reforms 148–9; reserve 170; stability 150, 153–4; national 154–5; *see also* currency devaluation
currency board 157–9; advantages 155, 160, 198; conditions 159; disadvantages 161–2, 415; IMF 157, 163; timing 163–6
currency corridor 198
currency devaluation 112–13, 161, 196
Czech Republic: FDI 391–2; housing 327;

494–5; trade and exchange 183, 208–9;
transformation 177–8
libertarianism 464, 466
Liebich, André 366
lifetime employment 118, 298, 299, 302
Lindbeck, Assar 285
Lindberg, Leon N. 308, 313
Lindblom, Charles E. 7, 308, 344, 347, 373
Lipton, David 126, 217
Lissowska, Maria 486
litas 161
Lithuania 158, 161, 164, 165, 332
Liviatan, Nissan 163
living standards 454
loans 84, 270, 390
Loayza, Norman A. 190
Lofgren, Hans 309
London Club, transition economies 389
Long, Millard 268
Lubyova, Martina 324
Ludlow, Peter 424
Lundvall, Bengt-Åke 348, 360
Lyon, James 146, 346

MacAvoy, Paul W. 224, 354, 360
McDermott, C. John 176
McKinnon, Ronald I. 195, 264
McMillan, John 186, 249
macroeconomics: adjustment programs
167–8; banking 143; demand
uncertainty 128; divestment 227;
economic growth 479–80; evaluated
133–4; labor market 284; reform 66,
81–2, 127; stabilization 141–5, 152–3;
statistics 288–9; transition 108;
unemployment 325
Madrid Council 422
mafia 341
management: as human capital 261–2,
479; and institutions 467; *nomenklatura*
appointed 217; post-transition 91–2,
95, 118–19, 263; and privatization
228–30, 356; state socialism 228–9
management buyouts 236, 242
management contracts 219, 235, 239
managers: banking 267; controlled 31, 33;
education of 407–8; monitored 355;
and owners 294; skills 244; SOEs 63,
217, 222, 226, 292, 355; transformation
118–19
Mansoor, Ali M. 354
Maravall, José Maria 285, 463, 464

Marglin, Stephen A. 400, 490
market: adaptation 263; competition 255;
coordination 178–80, 370, 497;
creation 477–8; divestment 223; free
348, 359; governance 311–12;
government intervention 346–50, 351,
363; information 184; legality 262–4;
neoclassical 109, 120; NPOs 349, 497;
property rights 251–3; as social
institution 108–10; SOEs 487;
theory/practice 471–2; uncertainty
311; *see also* capital markets; labor
markets
market-augmenting policies 125
market-based decisions 345, 359–60, 401
market-based monetary instruments
171–2
market-conforming policies 124
market-correcting policies 125–6
market economy 119–20, 131–3;
adjustment policy 42; commercial
banking 264; coordination 178–80,
370, 497; democracy 252, 305–6, 345,
464, 466; divestment 223; fiscal policy
37; governance 311–12; human capital
478; IEOs 506; mediation 252;
monetary policy 36; state role 347, 348;
transition 2–3
market entry/exit 189, 190, 231
market failure 120–1, 478; capital markets
278–9; correcting 119, 483;
externalities 258; government
intervention 345, 378; labor market
118; state 346–7, 348, 349–50, 361
market imperfections 349
market institutions 5, 249, 250–1, 278,
386, 467, 474, 486, 488
Markowski, Stefan 410
Marrese, Michael 211
Marx, Karl 21, 29, 39
Marxism 21–2, 27
Marxism-Leninism 27
material balance 44, 53, 66
Mates, Neven 269
Mauro, Paolo 341
Mayer, Colin 126, 212, 224, 266, 268,
279, 281, 349, 355, 359, 363
Mayer, John 266
Melich, Jiří* 91
Melo, Martha de 14, 148, 150, 169, 171,
310
Mensheviks 21
merit claims 241

as infrastructure for industry 95–6;
limited range 37, 244; nonproductive
95–6; privatized 258; public/
semi-public 347, 351; state socialism
315, 316–17
Shapiro, Carl 355, 356, 357
shares: distribution 216, 234, 235, 238,
239–40; ESOPs 236, 240, 283; floated
abroad 235
Shelley, Louise I. 339, 341
Shleifer, Andrei 106, 341, 465
shock therapy 4–5, 6, 7; development
375–6; examples 105; Poland 17,
136–7; prices 180; property rights 106;
retirement ages 332; transformation
102–4, 105–6
short-termism 472, 495
Silk, Leonard and Mark 300
Simon, Herbert A. 293
Singh, Ajit 279, 281, 356, 364, 480, 481,
490
skill levels 231, 284, 319–20, 362
Slay, Ben 264, 270, 274
Slovakia 392
Slovenia 90, 392
SMEs (small and medium-sized
enterprises) 114, 184, 467, 483–4;
competition 117; entrepreneurial spirit
187–8; environment 114, 187, 467;
loans 184–5; and market formation
184; modernization 496; networks
483–4; obstacles 185–6; start-up costs
186
Smith, Roy C. 268
SNA (system of national accounts) 82
social capability 488
social consensus 84–6, 99–100, 174, 218,
220, 302, 303–7, 497
social contract 218, 299, 329
social safety net 181, 284, 302–3, 327–8,
335–6, 460
social security: early-retirement 318; as
nonwage benefit 92, 298–303; pensions
328–9; policy making 300; state role
89, 361; vulnerable people 306, 307,
327
social services 299, 326–8, 336–7
social welfare 42, 54–5, 92, 134, 175, 241,
316
socialism 10, 21, 27
society 1–2, 117, 476–7
SOEs (state-owned enterprises): assets 219,
231–2; bankruptcy 73, 174;

commercial banking 188–9, 272, 274;
commercialism 316; control over
356–7; corporatization 233; debts 267;
decapitalized 468; decentralization 65,
66–7; economic function 117;
entrepreneurialism 45–6, 244;
exchange rates 71; financing 188–9;
foreign trade 71; future of 353–8;
government revenue 237; horizontal
relations 76; independence 18, 75–6;
inefficiency 354; investment 69; legal
status 261; local administration 235;
managers 63, 217, 222, 226, 292, 355;
market discipline 487; objectives 350,
353–4, 355–6; Poland 49, 238; political
254; privatization 211, 214; profitability
67, 69, 72–3, 173, 247, 365; as public
bureaucracies 219–20; public domain
371–2; restructuring 174, 221–2,
357–8, 372; social welfare 54–5, 134,
175; and state 36–7, 49; subdivided
222
Solow, Robert M. 478, 494
Sood, Anil 188
Soros, George 366, 374, 375, 467
Sorsa, Piritta 158, 163
sovereignty 252
Soviet Union (former) 10; budgetary
control 82, 97; and CMEA 53, 84;
communism 21; debt 84; FDI 391, 392;
industrial sector 94; influence 20;
TACIS 439, 456; trade flows 383, *384*
specialization 264, 265, 277
stability, as public good 143, 152–3,
476–7
stabilization 5, 480; capital inflows
149–52; economic 451; inflation 146,
460–1; macroeconomics 141–5, 152–3;
monetary 111–12, 142, 145, 149–52,
460–1; political 410; privatization 216;
as public good 152–3, 176; shock
therapy 103, 106–7; stocks 141, 147,
148
stabilization programs 166–8, 451–2
stakeholders 226–7
Stalin, Josef 22, 23
Stalinism 25
standards 82, 362–3
Standing, Guy 319
Staniszkis, Jadwiga 106
Stanners, W. 146, 451
Starbatty, Joachim 369
Stark, David 254